AF005301

needlesports.com

Peter Winterbottom on FA of Stalingrad, Pillar Rock, Photo Stephen Reid

LAKE DISTRICT ROCK

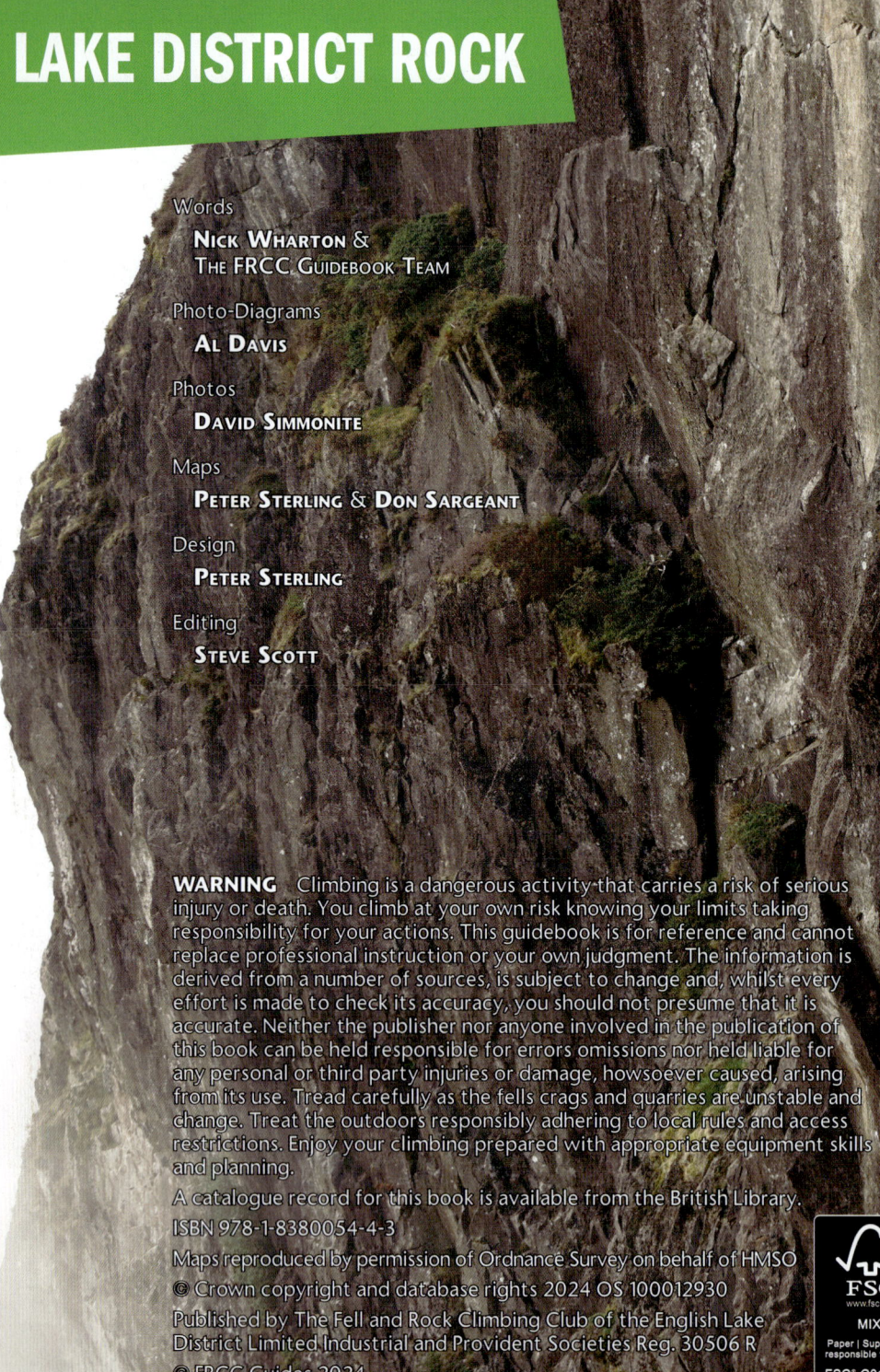

Words
Nick Wharton &
The FRCC Guidebook Team

Photo-Diagrams
Al Davis

Photos
David Simmonite

Maps
Peter Sterling & **Don Sargeant**

Design
Peter Sterling

Editing
Steve Scott

WARNING Climbing is a dangerous activity that carries a risk of serious injury or death. You climb at your own risk knowing your limits taking responsibility for your actions. This guidebook is for reference and cannot replace professional instruction or your own judgment. The information is derived from a number of sources, is subject to change and, whilst every effort is made to check its accuracy, you should not presume that it is accurate. Neither the publisher nor anyone involved in the publication of this book can be held responsible for errors omissions nor held liable for any personal or third party injuries or damage, howsoever caused, arising from its use. Tread carefully as the fells crags and quarries are unstable and change. Treat the outdoors responsibly adhering to local rules and access restrictions. Enjoy your climbing prepared with appropriate equipment skills and planning.

A catalogue record for this book is available from the British Library.
ISBN 978-1-8380054-4-3

Maps reproduced by permission of Ordnance Survey on behalf of HMSO
© Crown copyright and database rights 2024 OS 100012930

Published by The Fell and Rock Climbing Club of the English Lake District Limited Industrial and Provident Societies Reg. 30506 R

© FRCC Guides 2024

Aquarius, Pavey Ark HVS (page 57) Steve Scott — David Simmonite

CONTENTS

LAKE DISTRICT ROCK	2
WE ARE WIRED	6
FRCC	7
INTRODUCTION	8
Introduzione, Italiano	10
Introduction, Français	10
Einleitung, Deutsche	11
Introducción, Español	11
GRADES	12
USING THIS GUIDEBOOK	14
Character	14
When to Come	14
Equipment	14
Access & Conservation	14
Getting Here & Maps	14
Accommodation	15
Climbing Walls	15
New Routes etc.	15
CRAG GUIDE	16
LANGDALE	20
Raven Crag Walthwaite	22
Scout Crags	26
White Ghyll	32
Stickle Barn Crag	44
Pavey Ark	46
Raven Crags	58
Middlefell Buttress	60
Raven Crag	66
East Raven Crag	74
Gimmer Crag	76
Neckband Crag	90
Bowfell Area	94
Flat Crags	96
Cambridge Crag & North Buttress	98
Bowfell Buttress	100
Shelter Crag	106
Kettle Crag	112
CONISTON	116
Blind Tarn Crag	118
Dow Crag	120
Grey Crag	138
Little How Crag	141
DUDDON	144
Lickle Crag	146
Stonestar Crag	148
Wallowbarrow Crag	150
Sunny Pike	156
Brandy Crag	160
Brandy Crag West	162
Burnt Crag	164
Great Blake Rigg	168
Far Hill Crag	172
Castle How	174
WRYNOSE	178
Little Stand	180
Gaitscale Buttress	186
Gaitkins	188
Black Crag	192
Long Scar	198
ESKDALE	202
Brantrake	204
Bell Stand	208
Gate Crag	210
Hare Crags	212
Heron Crag	218
Esk Buttress	222
Hardknott Crag	232
Bursting Crag	234
SCAFELL	236
Scafell Crag	238
East Buttress	258
Pikes Crag	260
WASDALE	264
Buckbarrow	264

Pillar Rock — 📷 Tony Stephenson

GABLE ... 270
- Kern Knotts ... 272
- The Napes ... 276
- Gable Crag ... 288

ENNERDALE ... 294
- Boat How Crags ... 296
- Pillar Rock ... 300
- Steeple - East Face ... 319

BUTTERMERE ... 320
- High Crag ... 322
- Raven Crag High Stile ... 330
- Grey Crag ... 335
- Eagle Crag ... 341
- Buckstone How ... 345
- Yew Crag Knotts ... 348

NEWLANDS ... 350
- Miners' Crag ... 352
- Grey Buttress ... 354

BORROWDALE ... 356
- Falcon Crags ... 358
- Reecastle Crag ... 362
- Goats Crag ... 364
- Gowder Crag ... 366
- Shepherd's Crags ... 369
- Black Crag ... 382
- Quayfoot Buttress ... 388
- Bowderstone Crags ... 391
  - Woden's Face ... 392
  - Woden's Needle ... 395
  - Bowderstone Pinnacle ... 395
  - Hell's Wall ... 396
- Steel Knotts ... 398
- Steel Knotts Bluff ... 401
- Goat Crag ... 402
- Bleak How Buttress ... 406
- Upper Heron Crag ... 408
- Fat Charlie's Buttress ... 410
- Sergeant's Crag Slab ... 412
- Cam Crag ... 416
- Combe Gill ... 418
  - Glaciated Slab ... 420
  - Dove's Nest ... 421
  - Raven Crag ... 423
- Gillercomb ... 426

THIRLMERE ... 428
- Castle Rock of Triermain ... 430
- Raven Crag ... 438
- Iron Crag ... 442

ULLSWATER ... 446
- Eagle Crag ... 448
- Dove Crag ... 452
- Raven Crag Threshthwaite Cove ... 458

OUTLYING ... 462
- Armathwaite ... 464
- Gouther Crag ... 474
- Buckbarrow Crag ... 480
- White Stone ... 484

SPORT ... 486
- Scawgill Bridge Quarry ... 488
- Coudy Rocks ... 492
- Bramcrag Quarry ... 494
- Scout Scar ... 498
- Chapel Head Scar ... 503
- Millside ... 509
- St Bees ... 511

SLATE ... 516
- Hodge Close Quarry ... 518
- Runestone Quarry ... 524
- Moss Rigg Quarry ... 529

BOULDERING ... 534
TICK LISTS ... 538
INDEX ... 539

ROUTE COMBINATIONS ... 15
THE GREAT GIFT ... 293
SUPPORTERS
- Needle Sports ... 1
- Eden Rock ... 9
- Rinaldo's ... 13
- Kong Adventures ... 13
- Rock + Run ... back page
- Lakeland Climbing Centres ... inside rear
- Petzl ... rear flap
- The Climbers Shop ... rear cover

WE ARE WIRED

Britain is endowed with a rich legacy of rock climbing guidebooks. From the outset climbers noted their efforts, recording their pioneering ascents so others could follow in their footsteps and marvel at their achievements. In 1909 the first complete guide was published by The Climbers' Club to the mountain crag of Lliwedd in Eryri, North Wales. Since then clubs have maintained and updated this incredible record giving climbers the most up-to-date and accurate account of climbing in Britain.

FRCC GUIDES published the first guide to a Lake District crag, Doe Crag, in 1923 as part of a series covering the whole District. This work is undertaken by volunteers, climbers committed to contributing something invaluable for the rest of us.

Wired brings these clubs together. Under this banner, the voluntary guidebook producers combine their collective knowledge, skill and enthusiasm to share this information in new and creative ways.

www.wired-guides.com

Thank you for buying this guidebook. If you are enjoying the fabulous selection of routes in this book you will be delighted to hear there are thousands more for you to explore. Rock climbs in the Lake District have been painstakingly recorded and collated by volunteers within the Club for over 100 years. Information is published in definitive guidebooks by FRCC GUIDES covering the whole of Cumbria. These detailed books have distinct corresponding colours used throughout and in the **Crag Guide**. For example, this selective guide describes 200+ routes on 15 crags in **Langdale**. The current definitive guide to Langdale describes over 900 routes on over 57 crags. Similarly the current **Borrowdale** guidebook covers over 800 routes on over 50 crags in the valley, compared to the 200+ routes on 19 crags described in the Borrowdale section here. You can buy these books

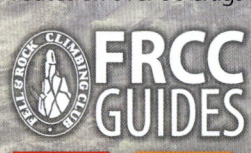

Wired Guides are published by a co-operative of UK definitive guidebook publishers: the **British Mountaineering Council**, **The Climbers' Club**, the **Fell & Rock Climbing Club** of the English Lake District, the **Scottish Mountaineering Club**, the **Yorkshire Mountaineering Club**, the **Northumbrian Mountaineering Club**, **Red Rose Rock**, and the **Cleveland Mountaineering Club**. Wired guidebooks aim to document the whole of the UK describing the very best — world-class — rock climbing these beautiful green islands have to offer.

Wired collaborators:

 The **Fell & Rock Climbing Club** of the English Lake District
www.frcc.co.uk

 The **BMC**
www.thebmc.co.uk

 The Climbers' Club
www.climbers-club.co.uk

 The **Yorkshire Mountaineering Club**
www.theymc.org.uk

 The **Northumbrian Mountaineering Club**
www.thenmc.org.uk

 The **Scottish Mountaineering Club**
www.smc.org.uk

 Red Rose Rock

 The **Cleveland Mountaineering Club**
www.clevelandmc.com

The **Fell & Rock Climbing Club** was founded in 1906 to "Encourage the pursuits of fell walking and rock climbing, particularly in the English Lake District."

With over 1,000 members the Club:

- Offers an extensive list of meets in the UK and abroad.
- Owns seven huts: five in the Lake District, shown on the climbing area maps in this book ⌂; and two in Scotland.

Membership has always been open to all experienced fell walkers and climbers.

Joining FRCC

www.frcc.co.uk/joining/

FRCC Mini Guides

www.frcc.co.uk/mini-guides/

FRCC Guidebooks

www.frcc.co.uk/shop/

from climbing shops or online from the FRCC website. The FRCC also provides a number of free-to-download mini-guides for you to enjoy.

We would like to extend massive thanks to all the people who have been involved in the creation of this book, all those that came before us and to the advertisers; who we urge you to support. There is a huge amount of work involved in producing what you have in your hands: route descriptions and crag approaches need writing and checking; photo-diagrams need to be prepared; action photos need taking, with volunteers acting as models. Finally, this mass of information is brought together to create an inspirational, practical and usable guidebook.

NICK, AL, PETE & STEVE

     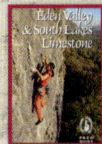  

Langstrath — 📷 PETER STERLING

Scafell Crag, Central Buttress — 📷 TOM MCNALLY

INTRODUCTION

Welcome to the Lake District, we hope you enjoy your visit. This beautiful region offers a tremendous variety of climbing with roadside to high-mountain venues. Most of the climbing described here is 'trad', requiring a full rack of leader-placed protection. There are a number of 'sport' venues and a wide range of bouldering opportunities (www.lakesbloc.com).

The Lake District is designated as a UNESCO World Heritage Site. Its narrow, glaciated valleys radiate from the central Scafell massif with high fells and slender lakes exhibiting extraordinary natural beauty and harmony. This romance attracts poets, artists, writers, and adventurers. Widely regarded as the home of English rock climbing, the first recorded climb in England, on Pillar Rock, dates from 1826. Lakeland crags have been, and continue to be, at the forefront of trad climbing development.

Each valley/area has its own characteristics. This guide provides an overview of the best routes across the whole district. The selection offers something for climbers of all abilities, sufficient for one or two visits to each crag. Beyond that, each valley/area is served by its own definitive guidebook published by local volunteers from the FRCC www.frcc.co.uk/shop.

The rock is predominantly volcanic rhyolite; you may also encounter granite (Eskdale), sandstone (St Bees, Armathwaite and Coudy Rocks), micro-granite (Bramcrag Quarry), limestone (Chapel Head, Scout Scar, Millside) and slate (Hodge Close, Runestone).

Bolts on the crags in the Sport section are generally in good condition. Most have been placed by the Cumbria Bolt Fund. Donations can be made here: www.cumbriaboltfund.com. Other fixed gear - pegs, *in-situ* wires and abseil anchors - should be assessed and used with caution.

There are many options for accommodation from camping and hostels to luxury hotels. Getting around is easily done by car, using the bus or a bike is an option for some crags. Parking can sometimes be a challenge. Climbing equipment can be bought from the wide range of outdoor shops in many of the towns and villages.

Paul II, Gaitkins VS (page 190) Tim Whiteley — David Simmonite

www.edenrockclimbing.com

INTRODUZIONE

Benvenuti nel Lake District, vi auguriamo una piacevole visita. La regione offre una grossa varietà di arrampicate, con opzioni che spaziano da falesie a bordo strada fino a quelle in ambiente di montagna. La maggior parte dell'arrampicata descritta è tradizionale ('trad') e quindi richiede un set completo di protezioni mobili ma ci sono anche siti per l'arrampicata sportiva e il bouldering (www.lakesbloc.com).

Il Lake District è Patrimonio Mondiale dell'Unesco. Le sue strette valli glaciali che si irradiano dal massiccio centrale di Scafell, con i loro ripidi pendii e numerosi piccoli laghi, vantano una straordinaria bellezza e armonia. Si tratta di un luogo di profonda tradizione e, non a caso, è stato soggetto di molti poeti, artisti e scrittori. È stato inoltre teatro di una lunga storia di arrampicata a partire dalla prima salita di Pillar Rock avvenuta nel 1826. Fino ai nostri giorni, le falesie del Lake District sono state e continuano ad essere palestra per l'evoluzione dell'arrampicata trad di alto livello. Ciascuna valle he le sue distinte caratteristiche. Questa guida offre una sintesi delle migliori vie di arrampicata dell'intera ragione. La selezione fatta comprende opzioni per tutti i livelli di abilità, con almeno una o due vie per ciascun grado in tutte le falesie. Per chi volesse approfondire ciascuna valle/area e' descritta in dettaglio da guide specifiche pubblicate da FRCC (www.frcc.co.uk/shop).

La maggior parte della roccia è riolite vulcanica ma si trovano anche granito (Eskdale), arenaria (St Bees, Armathwaite and Coudy Rocks), granito a grana fine (Bramcrag Quarry), calcare(Chapel Head, Scout Scar, Humphrey Head, Millside Scar) e ardesia (Hodge Close, Runestone). L'equipaggiamento delle falesie sportive e' generalmente in buone condizioni ed è stato per lo più realizzato dal Cumbria Bolt Fund (donazioni possono essre fatte qui: www.cumbriaboltfund.com. Le altre protezioni presenti (ad esempio chiodi o cordoni di calata) vedono essere esaminati attentamente e usati con cautela.

Ci sono molte possibilità per il pernottamento, da campeggi e ostelli della gioventù fino ad hotel di lusso. Muoversi richiede un veicolo perché il trasporto pubblico è piuttosto limitato. Parcheggiare presso alcune falesie può essere difficile. Attrezzatura d'arrampicata può essere acquistata facilmente presso i numerosi negozi di articoli sportivi locali.

Bienvenues au Lake District, nous vous souhaitons une excellente visite. La région offre une grande variété d'escalades, avec un choix de sites au bord de route à ceux de haute montagne. La plupart des escalades décrites ici sont « traditionnelles », nécessitant des protections amovibles placées par le leader, mais il y a aussi de nombreux sites pour l'escalade sportive et un large éventail de possibilités de bloc (www.lakesbloc.com).

Le Lake District est classée au patrimoine mondial de l'UNESCO. Ses vallées étroites et glaciers rayonnant à partir du massif central du Scafell, avec leurs pentes abruptes et leurs lacs élancés, présentent une beauté et une harmonie extraordinaires. C'est un lieu plein de tradition et, sans surprise, associé à de nombreux poètes, artistes et auteurs. Il y a une longue histoire d'escalade depuis la première ascension enregistrée sur Pillar Rock en 1826. Jusqu'à nos jours, les rochers de Lakeland ont été et continuent d'être à l'avant-garde du développement de l'escalade traditionnelle. Chaque vallée/zone a ses propres caractéristiques. Ce livre donne un aperçu des meilleurs itinéraires à travers toute la région. La sélection couvre toute la gamme de niveaux avec suffisamment pour une ou deux visites de chaque falaise à tous les niveaux. Au-delà de cela, chaque vallée/zone est décrite par son propre guide complet publié par des bénévoles locaux du FRCC (www.frcc.co.uk/shop).

La majeure partie du rocher est constituée de rhyolite volcanique, mais vous pouvez également rencontrer du granit (Eskdale), du grès (St Bees, Armathwaite et Coudy Rocks), du microgranite (Bramcrag Quarry), du calcaire (Chapel Head, Scout Scar, Humphrey Head, Millside Scar) et ardoise (Hodge Close, Runestone). Les spit qui se trovent dans les falaises sportives sont généralement en bon état. La plupart ont été placés par le Cumbria Bolt Fund. Des donations peuvent être faits ici : www.cumbriaboltfund.com. Les autres protections fixes – pitons, câbles in situ et ancrages de rappel doivent être évaluées et utilisées avec prudence.

Il existe de nombreuses options d'hébergement, du camping et des auberges aux hôtels de luxe. Pour se déplacer, il faut vraiment un véhicule car les transports en commun sont un peu limités. Le parking peut parfois être un défi. Le matériel d'escalade peut être acheté dans les magasins de plein air présents dans de nombreuses villes et villages.

INTRODUCTION

EINLEITUNG

Willkommen im Lake District, eine der schönsten Klettergegenden im Norden Englands. Die Region bietet eine große Vielfalt an Klettermöglichkeiten, die sowohl direkt vom Straßenrand zugänglich sind oder bis ins die höheren Berge reichen. Die meisten der hier beschriebenen Kletterrouten sind "trad", also alpin abzusichernde Kletterrouten, d. h. sie erfordern eine vollständige Absicherung durch einen Vorsteiger, aber es gibt auch zahlreiche "sportliche" Routen und eine große Auswahl an tollen Bouldermöglichkeiten. (www.lakesbloc.com).

Der Lake District zählt zum UNESCO-Welterbe. Seine engen, vergletscherten Täler, die sich vom zentralen Scafell-Massiv ausbreiten, mit ihren steilen Hängen und schlanken Seen sind von außergewöhnlicher Schönheit und Harmonie. Es ist ein traditionsreicher Ort, der nicht umsonst mit vielen Dichtern, Künstlern und Schriftstellern in Verbindung gebracht wird. Das Klettern hat hier Tradition: 1826 wurde die erste Besteigung des Pillar Rocks dokumentiert. Bis heute spielen die Felsen von Lakeland eine Vorreiterrolle in der Entwicklung des Trad-Kletterns. Jedes Tal/Gebiet hat seine eigenen Besonderheiten. Dieses Buch bietet einen Überblick über die schönsten Routen in der gesamten Region. Bei der Auswahl der Routen wurde darauf geachtet, dass alle Schwierigkeitsgrade abgedeckt sind und jedes Klettergebiet ein bis zwei Mal besucht werden kann. Darüber hinaus gibt es für jedes Tal/Gebiet einen eigenen umfassenden Führer, der von lokalen Freiwilligen des FRCC herausgegeben wird (www.frcc.co.uk/shop).

Der größte Teil des Gesteins ist vulkanischer Rhyolith, aber man kann auch Granit (Eskdale), Sandstein (St Bees, Armathwaite und Coudy Rocks), Mikrogranit (Bramcrag Quarry), Kalkstein (Chapel Head, Scout Scar, Humphrey Head, Millside Scar) und Schiefer (Hodge Close, Runestone) finden. Alle Bohrhaken, die an den Sportkletterfelsen zu finden sind, befinden sich im allgemeinen in gutem Zustand. Die meisten wurden vom Cumbria Bolt Fund angebracht. Spenden können hier getätigt werden: www.cumbriaboltfund.com. Andere feste Sicherungen - Schlaghaken, Drahtseile und Abseilstellen - sollten mit Bedacht eingesetzt werden.

Es gibt viele Unterkunftsmöglichkeiten, vom Camping über Herbergen bis hin zu Luxushotels. Um die Gegend zu erkunden, braucht man ein Fahrzeug, da öffentliche Verkehrsmittel nur begrenzt verfügbar sind. Das Parken kann manchmal eine Herausforderung sein. Kletterausrüstungen können in den zahlreichen Outdoor-Läden in vielen der lokalen Orte und Dörfer gekauft werden.

Keswick im Norden und Ambleside im Süden bieten zum Beispiel eine Anzahl an gut ausgestatteten Kletter-Läden, Supermärkten, Tankstellen, Cafés, Pubs und Restaurants. Die meisten Dörfer haben einen netten Pub und einen kleinen Einkaufsladen.

Bienvenido al Distrito de los Lagos, esperamos que se divierta en su visita. La región ofrece una gran variedad de escalada con opciones tanto al lado de la carretera como en lugares de alta montaña. La mayoría de las escaladas que se describen aquí son "Trad" y requieren un equipo completo de protección de alta gama, pero hay también muchos lugares de deporte y una gran variedad de oportunidades de tipo Boulder (www.lakesbloc.com).

El Distrito de los Lagos es un lugar considerado Patrimonio de la Humanidad por la UNESCO. Sus angostos valles glaciares que emanan desde el macizo central de Scafell con sus empinadas laderas y estrechos lagos muestran una belleza y una armonía extraordinarias. Es un lugar lleno de tradición y como era de esperar, es asociado con muchos poetas, artistas y escritores. Hay una historia larga de escalada en roca desde la primera escalada de roca registrada en Pillar Rock en 1826. Hasta el día de hoy los riscos de la región de los lagos han sido y siguen siendo vanguardia en el desarrollo de la escalada trad. Cada valle / área tiene su propias características. Este libro provee una visión de conjunto de las mejores rutas en todo el distrito. La selección cubre toda la gama de habilidades, proporcionando una o dos visitas a cada risco para todos los grados de dificultad. Más allá de eso, cada valle / área está descrito en su propia Guía explicativa publicada por los voluntarios locales del FRCC (www.frcc.co.uk/shop).

La mayor parte de la roca es volcánica riolita, pero quizá también encuentre el granito (Eskdale), la arenisca (St Bees, Armathwiate y Coudy Rocks), el micro-granito (Bramcrag Quarry) La caliza (Chapel Head, Scout Scar, Humphrey Head, Millside Scar) y La pizarra (Hodge Close y Runstone). Todos los pernos instalados en los riscos en la zona de deportes están en general en buenas condiciones. La mayoría han sido colocados por el Cumbria Bolt Fund. Una donación se puede hacer aquí: www.cumbriaboltfund.com . Otras protecciones fijas- piquetas, cables in situ y anclajes de rappel deben evaluarse y usarse con precaución.

Hay muchas opciones de alojamiento, desde campings y hostales a hoteles de lujo. Para moverse realmente se necesita un vehículo privado ya que el transporte público es limitado. El estacionamiento a veces puede ser un desafío. Se puede comprar equipo de escalada en la amplia gama de tiendas al aire libre en muchos de los pueblos.

INTRODUCCIÓN

GRADES

Trad routes are graded using English grades for a ground-up on-sight ascent with leader-placed protection. Adjectives describe overall difficulty; **Difficult, Severe**, ... combined with numbers to indicate the technical difficulty of the hardest sequence of moves; 4c, 5a, 5b, ...

Sport climbs use French grades. To provide additional insight into the technical difficulty, on some crags, combined English and French grades are used for the very hardest trad climbs, generally above E5. These are not Sport climbs - they are serious trad climbs of the highest order of difficulty.

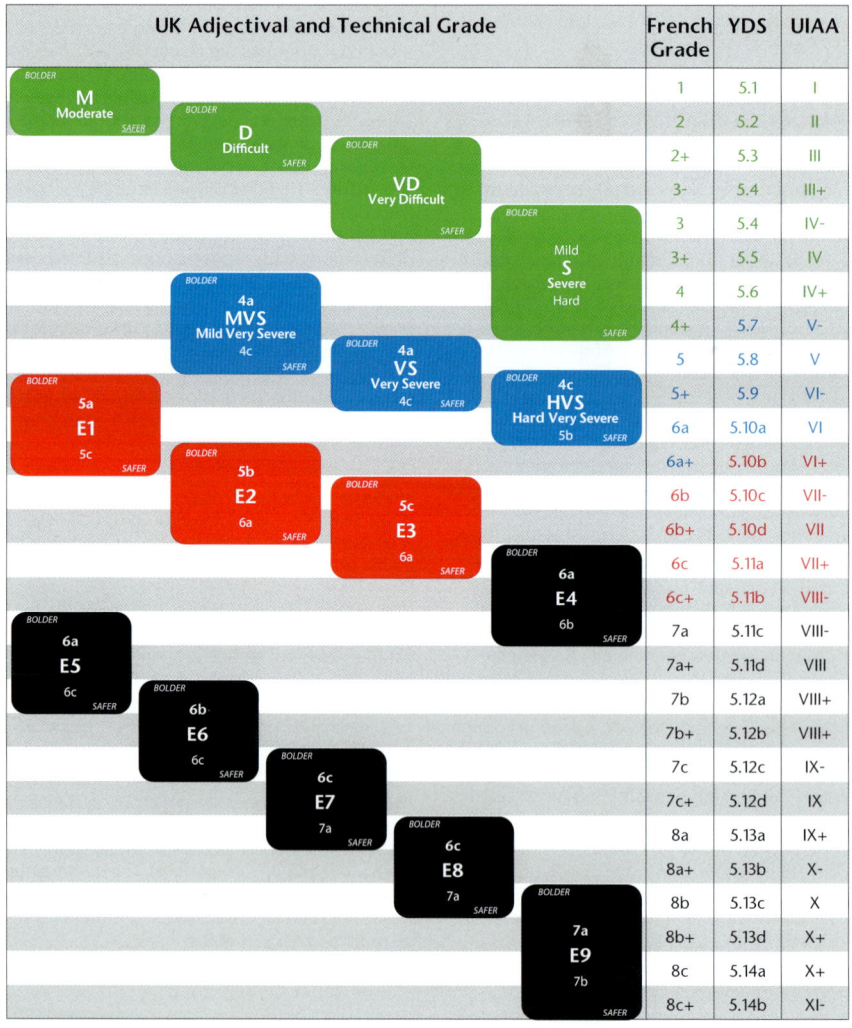

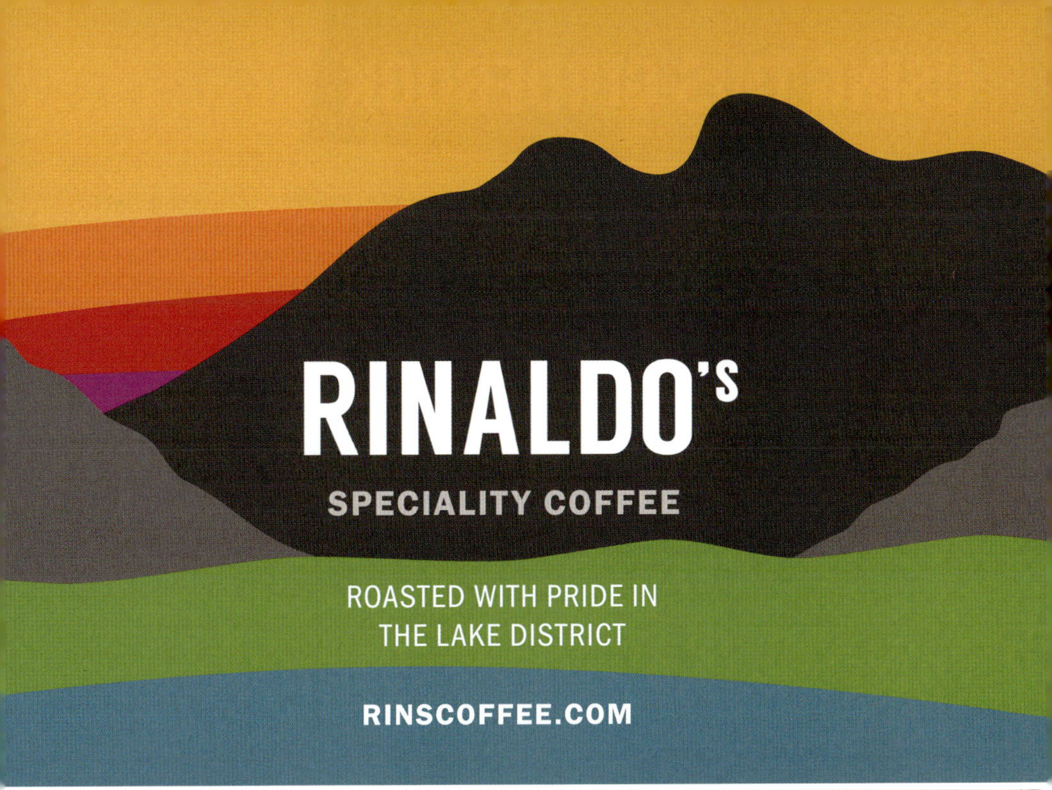

RINALDO's
SPECIALITY COFFEE

ROASTED WITH PRIDE IN
THE LAKE DISTRICT

RINSCOFFEE.COM

KONG ADVENTURE

USING THIS GUIDEBOOK

Character
The crags described offer a superb variety of climbing with something for everyone, almost always in a lovely setting. The complex geology has created huge diversity in rock type, elevation and aspect with highly featured rock at every angle. This is reflected in climbing style and outlook which all contribute to the ambience. For visiting and local climbers this offers tremendously interesting outings, as no two crags are likely to feel the same.

Let's be honest about the elephant in the room – the Lake District is prone to rain from time to time. But then, if it didn't rain, we wouldn't have Lakes and then it would just be … The District, which isn't such an evocative name! Seathwaite, at the top of Borrowdale, is the wettest place in England. But when it isn't raining it is magnificent. The simple rule is to check the forecast and plan and equip yourself accordingly. As they say here "if you don't like the weather … wait a minute!" The nature of the geography means that warm, moist air coming off the Irish Sea rises when it hits the high ground of the Lakeland fells creating clouds, which often sit over the tops.

Partly due to the weather, partly the reduced footfall over recent years and possibly also as a result of an improved, cleaner atmosphere, some of the crags are prone to vegetation. The most popular routes stay clean and rarely is it bad enough to truly detract from the enjoyment. Some crags have been left out of this edition because the routes are no longer clean enough.

When to Come
There is no guarantee of a time when the weather will be really good, particularly in light of the changing climate of recent years. From Easter to Autumn gives the best chance. Some of the crags dry quite quickly. In July and August, when the sun is out, it can be quite warm and the UV strong. An idea of average monthly tempatures and daily rainfall are shown opposite.

Equipment
A full rack of gear is required for the majority of the trad climbs described here: cams, nuts and slings. A larger than usual selection of thin slings is often useful for threads and placing over flakes and spikes. A pair of 60m half-ropes is recommended, particularly if looking to abseil although 50m ropes will often suffice.

Many routes have pre-placed pegs, which are in variable condition, although some are absolute shockers! You should make your own assessment and always try to find a back-up of your own. Similarly with any fixed abseil points around the area; the fact that they are shown on topos is no guarantee of their presence or condition on the day of your visit. Many of the sport routes have been equipped by the Cumbria Bolt Fund – all donations towards the continuation of this work are welcome (www.cumbriaboltfund.com). There is a strict ethic of not placing bolts for protection in the mountain crags. There are some excellent shops selling climbing equipment in the area – most notably in Keswick and Ambleside.

Access & Conservation
Most crags listed here have well-established access and recommended approaches are provided. Some crags do have seasonal restrictions to protect nesting birds – Ravens and Peregrine Falcons. Please respect these. Details are provided in the text and often signs will be erected on the approaches to crags. Check BMC Regional Access Database (RAD) for updates.

Getting Here
Fly: The closest airports are Manchester, Liverpool and Newcastle; all about two hours' drive. Manchester in particular is well connected by train to the area.

Train: Oxenholme, The Lake District is a mainline station just outside Kendal with good access from London and the South as well as Scotland. A smaller branch line links to Kendal itself and Windermere. Penrith is the next stop north after Oxenholme on the main line.

Bus: There are bus routes all around the district, which can be useful for reaching Langdale, Coniston, Borrowdale, some of the Ullswater venues and the crags around Thirlmere. Other destinations will be a lot more limited and require a great deal of planning.

Car: Is the simplest and most flexible. Traffic on narrow roads can be busy please be patient and use passing places sensibly. Or, leave early in the morning. Car parking options are listed; some are limited. Please park with consideration.

Maps
OS Explorer 1:25k – OL 4,5,6,7
Harveys Lake District 1:25k – N, E, W, SE
Harveys 1:40k – British Mountain Map Lake District

Accommodation
Hugely popular with visitors, the choice of accommodation is vast: campsites, hostels and camping barns in most valleys plus plenty of B&Bs, hotels and self-catering options. Information is available from Tourist Information Centres www.lakedistrict.gov.uk/visiting/where-to-stay

Vanlife: With consideration you'll find spots to park a campervan.

Wild camping: Strictly speaking this is not allowed but is tolerated high up in the fells, particularly in more remote areas. Remove **all** trace and carry out everything; don't light fires; the becks and streams are probably somebody's water supply, so treat them with respect.

Climbing Walls
If driven indoors by the weather, there are a number of options to choose from: Kendal, Keswick, Penrith, Carlisle, Ulverston, and Ambleside.

New Routes, Corrections, Comments etc.
Go to FRCC website:
www.frcc.co.uk/rock-climbing/

Free downloads of topos for some smaller or new venues are also available.

Monthly °C & Rain	Jan	Feb	Mar	Apr	May	Jun	Jul	Aug	Sep	Oct	Nov	Dec
Avg. Max. °C	7	8	10	12	16	18	20	19	17	13	10	8
Avg. Min. °C	2	2	3	4	7	10	12	11	9	7	4	2
Avg. Rain Days/Month	20	17	16	15	14	16	17	16	18	19	20

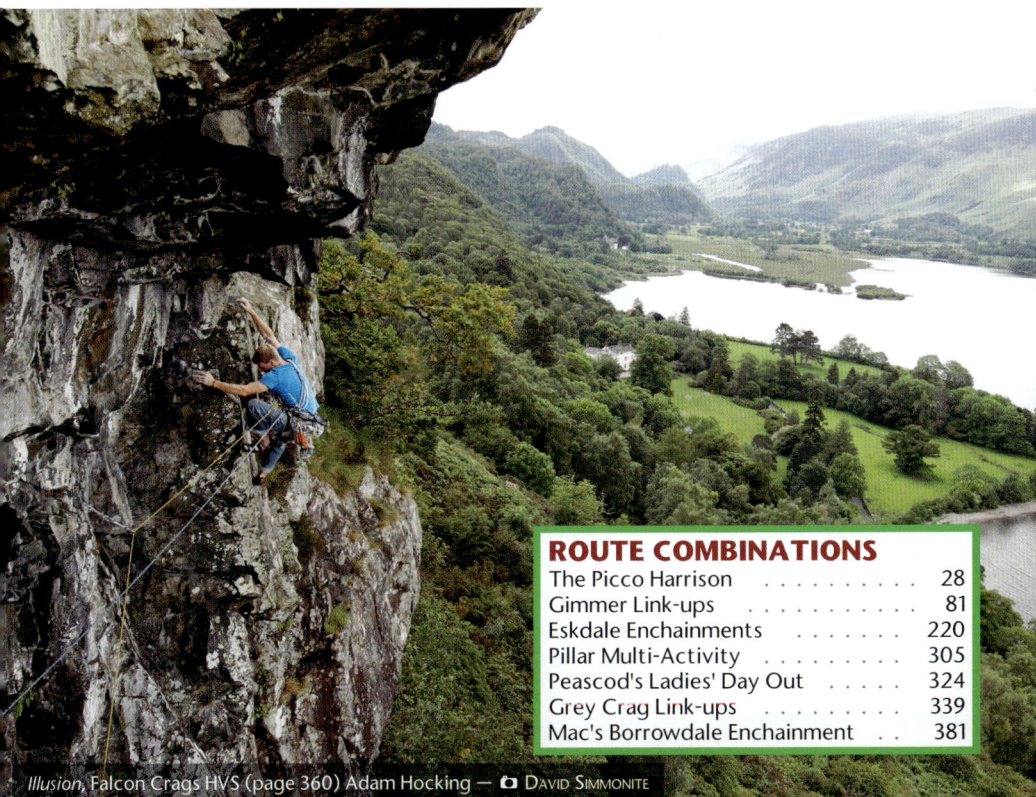

ROUTE COMBINATIONS
The Picco Harrison	28
Gimmer Link-ups	81
Eskdale Enchainments	220
Pillar Multi-Activity	305
Peascod's Ladies' Day Out	324
Grey Crag Link-ups	339
Mac's Borrowdale Enchainment	381

Illusion, Falcon Crags HVS (page 360) Adam Hocking — David Simmonite

CRAG GUIDE

Region	Crag	Routes	← VD	S	VS	HVS	E1	E2	E3	E4	E5
Langdale	Raven Crag Walthwaite	15		2	3	5	2		1		2
Langdale	Scout Crags	14	7	2	2		1				2
Langdale	White Ghyll	23		4	5	4	5	2	2		1
Langdale	Stickle Barn Crag	7	1	1	3	1	1				
Langdale	Pavey Ark	30	4	2	4	5	4	3	2	4	2
Langdale	Middlefell & Raven Crags	34	3	8	5	8	1	4		1	4
Langdale	Gimmer Crag	34	4	6	9	4	7	2	1	1	
Langdale	Neckband Crag	8			1	2	1	3		1	
Langdale	Flat, Cambridge & Bowfell	20	3	2	2		4	2	1	3	
Langdale	Shelter Crag	10	1		3	1	4	1			
Langdale	Kettle Crag	12	1	3	8						
Coniston	Blind Tarn Crag	7			1	1			4		1
Coniston	Dow Crag	34	2	7	5	4	2	6		4	4
Coniston	Grey Crag	4			4						
Coniston	Little How Crag	7	1	3	2	1					
Duddon & Wrynose	Lickle Crag	8			4	2	2				
Duddon & Wrynose	Stonestar Crag	6			1	1	1	2	1		
Duddon & Wrynose	Wallowbarrow Crag	10	1	3	6						
Duddon & Wrynose	Sunny Pike	17	4	3	4	3	3				
Duddon & Wrynose	Brandy Crags	17		3	4	3	2	2	3		
Duddon & Wrynose	Burnt Crag	9						1	4	2	2
Duddon & Wrynose	Great Blake Rigg	12			2	1		4	1	2	2
Duddon & Wrynose	Far Hill Crag	8					1	1	2	3	1
Duddon & Wrynose	Castle How	10				3	2		2	1	2
Duddon & Wrynose	Little Stand	19		3	3	1	3	5	2	1	
Duddon & Wrynose	Gaitscale & Gaitkins	34	4	5	6	5	4	4	2		
Duddon & Wrynose	Black Crag & Long Scar	38	6	8	8	5	2	2	3	2	2
Eskdale	Brantrake	13	3	1	3	2	1	1	1		
Eskdale	Bell Stand	12		1	2	3		3	1		2
Eskdale	Gate Crag	7					3	1	1	2	
Eskdale	Hare Crags	21	2	3	3	2	3	3	1	1	3
Eskdale	Heron Crag	4			2		1		1		
Eskdale	Esk Buttress	18		2	2	3	2	2	3	2	2
Eskdale	Hardknott Crag	5				1		2		2	
Eskdale	Bursting Crag	16	5	7	4						
Scafell & Wasdale	Scafell Crag	48	1	4	9	7	5	5	8	4	5
Scafell & Wasdale	Pikes Crag	6	2	1	2	1					
Scafell & Wasdale	Buckbarrow	16		1	5	2	4	2		1	1
Gable & Ennerdale	Kern Knotts	14	1	1	4		3	1	2	2	
Gable & Ennerdale	The Napes	25	5	5	4	2	3	1	1	2	2
Gable & Ennerdale	Gable Crag	10		1	1	3	1	1	3		
Gable & Ennerdale	Boat How Crags	13		1	1	1	1	2	4	1	2
Gable & Ennerdale	Pillar Rock	27	3	5	8	3	3	3	1	1	
Gable & Ennerdale	Steeple - East Face	1	1								
			← VD	S	VS	HVS	E1	E2	E3	E4	E5

Approach	Aspect	Notes	Page	
5 mn	S	A decent short crag, close to the road.	22	
10..20 mn	S	A range of different crags. Lower is popular with groups.	26	
45 mn	W	Imposing crag with some steep lines and a good range of grades.	32	
15 mn	S	Clean, sunny and easy access short climbs.	44	Langdale
1 hr	SE	Big crag with lots of options. Some classic lines.	46	
15..20 mn	SW	Easy access, sunny climbing. Very popular.	60	
1 hr	S	One of the best high crags that catches the sun. Lots to go at.	76	
1¼ hr	N	Some great lines, good on a hot day.	90	
1½ hr	N	Big, classic high mountain crags.	94	
1½ hr	E	Quiet crag with good, rough rock.	106	
30 mn	W	Quick drying with plenty of easy options.	112	
1 hr	E	Good crag in a delightful setting with morning sun.	118	Coniston
1 hr	E	One the best big crags with a wide range of excellent routes.	120	
40 mn	E	Some worthwhile routes; needs a dry spell.	138	
1 hr	SE	Nice, quiet location tucked away at the top of Coppermines valley.	141	
30 mn	E	Lovely, isolated crag in a delightful setting.	146	
5 mn	SW	Good clean rock, handy for the road.	148	
15..20 mn	SW	Great climbing at the lower end of grades.	150	
30 mn	S	Easy climbing in a sunny location.	156	
45..50 mn	S	Brandy West is ideal for easier routes.	160	
20 mn	S	Best crag in the valley for the harder climber.	164	Duddon & Wrynose
1 hr	S	Good range of routes on great rock.	168	
1 hr	NW	Good collection of steep, harder lines.	172	
15..20 mn	SE & SW	Very easy access, pleasant short routes.	174	
45..55 mn	SW	Incredibly rough rock. Steep pull up the hill to get there.	180	
40, 55 mn	S	Numerous short outcrops. Good rock, nice surroundings.	186, 188	
25, 20 mn	SW	Lots of short routes on brilliant rock and with easy access.	192, 198	
10 mn	NW	Good granite next to the road.	204	
15 mn	S	Quick drying, rough granite.	208	
20 mn	NW	Slightly esoteric crag with some good lines.	210	
15 mn	SW	Good collection of short buttresses of clean granite.	212	Eskdale
30 mn	SE	Home to one of the best E1 climbs in the Lakes.	218	
1½ hr	SE	Magnificent large crag with a sunny aspect in great location.	222	
5 mn	W	Steep and hard, next to the road.	232	
15 mn	W	Delightful venue, easy routes on perfect rock plus an amazing view.	234	
1½ hr	N	Biggest crag in the Lakes with a long history. A must for everyone.	238	Scafell & Wasdale
1¾ hr	W	Large crag giving a true mountaineering experience.	260	
35 mn	S	Good low-level option, easily accessible.	264	
1¼ hr	S	Fabulous, short clean routes with an amazing view.	272	
1½ hr	SE..SW	Magnificent area steeped in history with great selection of routes.	276	
1½ hr	N	Superb routes but needs some good weather.	288	Gable & Ennerdale
2 hr	NE	Remote crag, well worth the effort.	296	
2½ hr	N, E, W	Huge, rambling crag with many facets. Lots of history.	300	
3 hr	W	Very remote, beautiful location. Fine mountaineering route.	319	

CRAG GUIDE

Region	Crag	Routes	VD	S	VS	HVS	E1	E2	E3	E4	E5
Buttermere & Newlands	High Crag	18		1	3	3	7		4		
	Raven Crag High Stile	12	1	2	2		3	1	2	1	
	Grey Crag	21	7	6	8						
	Eagle Crag	5			2		1		2		
	Buckstone How	9		1	1	4	1	2			
	Yew Crag Knotts	7			2	1	2	2			
	Newlands	7		1	2	2	2				
Borrowdale	Falcon Crags	13			2	2	3	4	1	1	
	Reecastle Crag	15				2	1	3	3	2	4
	Goats Crag	13		2	1	2	2	3	1	2	
	Gowder Crag	2			1	1					
	Shepherd's Crags	48	12	3	12	5	6	5	3		2
	Black Crag	12		1	3	3	2		2	1	
	Quayfoot Buttress	7	1		1	3	1	1			
	Bowderstone Crags	19	3	4	3		1	1	1	1	5
	Steel Knotts & Bluff	15	2	3	2	2	1	2	2	1	
	Goat Crag	9					2	1	2	1	3
	Bleak How Buttress	4				2	1	1			
	Upper Heron Crag	6					1	4		1	
	Fat Charlie's Buttress	7			2	1	2	2			
	Sergeant's Crag Slab	8			1	3	2	2			
	Cam Crag	8							2	2	4
	Combe Gill	25	7	7	9	2					
	Gillercomb	2	1	1							
Thirlmere & Ullswater	Castle Rock of Triermain	23	2	3	3	3	4	5	2	1	
	Raven Crag Thirlmere	9			1		1		3	2	2
	Iron Crag	12					2	2		2	6
	Eagle Crag	8		1	3	2		2			
	Dove Crag	15		1		1	1	3		1	8
	Raven Crag Threshthwaite	10						1	2	3	4
Outlying	Armathwaite	25		4	3	2	4	4	5	1	2
	Gouther Crag	18	1	4	3	2	2		4	1	1
	Buckbarrow Crag	7		2		3	2				
	White Stone	9	1	2	3	3					
Sport & Slate	Scawgill Bridge Quarry	20			13			7			
	Coudy Rocks	8			2			4		2	
	Bramcrag Quarry	13			9			4			
	Scout Scar	17			6			5		6	
	Chapel Head Scar	16			1			5		10	
	Millside	7			1			1		5	
	St Bees	21	1		6			11		3	
	Hodge Close Quarry	16			1			7		8	
	Runestone Quarry	21	1		13			5		2	
	Moss Rigg Quarry	11			2			7		2	
			← F3 .. F4+		F5 .. F6a+		F6b .. F6c+			F7a .. F7b →	

Approach	Aspect	Notes	Page	
45 mn	NE	Closer than you think, great routes.	322	Buttermere & Newlands
2 hr	SW	Lovely location overlooking Ennerdale and some good climbing.	330	
1½ hr	SE	Long, easy, mountain routes on immaculate rough rock.	335	
1¼ hr	NE	Needs a good spell of dry weather but grab it when you can.	341	
15 mn	SW	Accessible, steep and exposed.	345	
20 mn	SW	Clean rock, reasonable access.	348	
1¼ hr	W	A quiet backwater with varied climbing.	350	
10 mn	W	Steep and strenuous with sloping holds. Very good climbing.	358	Borrowdale
5 mn	NW	Short and steep requiring strong fingers.	362	
20 mn	SW	Quick drying, lovely setting and nice range of routes.	364	
10 mn	W	A couple of classic routes. Beware of the giant ants.	366	
15 mn	W	Very popular, roadside crag with something for everyone.	369	
25 mn	W	Superb climbing in an idyllic location. One of Borrowdale's finest.	382	
5 mn	W	Easy access, compact rock.	388	
5..20 mn	W	A mix of the easiest and the hardest - all are good.	391	
20 mn	SE	Great in the morning while the rest of the crags are still in the shade.	398	
50 mn	NE	Some brilliant, steep lines offering a great challenge.	402	
40 mn	W	Good rock, prone to be a bit dirty.	406	
1 hr	W	Great location, clean rock. Well worth the hike up.	408	
20 mn	W	Very easy access. Start or finish your day here.	410	
1 hr	W	Superb, rough slabs. Justifiably very popular.	412	
45 mn	E	Hard climbs on amazing rock.	416	
30..50 mn	NE, NW, S	A good mix of easier routes.	418	
1 hr	SE	Classic, mountaineering feel on a big crag.	426	
10 mn	NW & S	Easy access with a wide range of excellent routes.	430	Thirlmere & Ullswater
25 mn	E	Big, imposing crag with impressive lines.	438	
40 mn	E	Lovely, quiet location. Lower crag is even steeper than it looks.	442	
1½ hr	SE	Sunny, open climbing. A good choice for the mid-grades.	448	
1¼ hr	NE	Steep and imposing. A very impressive crag.	452	
45 mn	SE	Fabulous crag above E3 - more stars than a night at the Oscars.	458	
15 mn	SW	Sandstone climbing in the woods above the river. Delightful.	464	Outlying
30 mn	NW	A good range of routes, something for everyone.	474	
35 mn	SW	A big feel with easy access.	480	
10 mn	W	Nice crag close to the road. Useful on the way to or from elsewhere.	484	
5 mn	S	Roadside sport climbing with a handy grade spread.	488	Sport & Slate
5 mn	SW	Steep, clean, well-bolted lines on perfect sandstone.	492	
10 mn	W	Very popular, due to easy access but beware of loose blocks.	494	
15 mn	W	Lovely location overlooking the Lyth Valley. More easy options.	498	
15 mn	W	Some of the best limestone around. A great selection of hard lines.	503	
10 mn	SE	Short but interesting lines in the trees.	509	
20 mn	W	Clean, vertical sandstone next to the sea - idyllic.	511	
5 mn	W	A big hole in the ground. Classic, airy slate climbing.	518	
30 mn	NW	Pleasant, slabby slate routes with friendly bolting.	524	
25 mn	W & E	Atmospheric and brilliant slate climbing in a huge hidden hole.	529	

LANGDALE

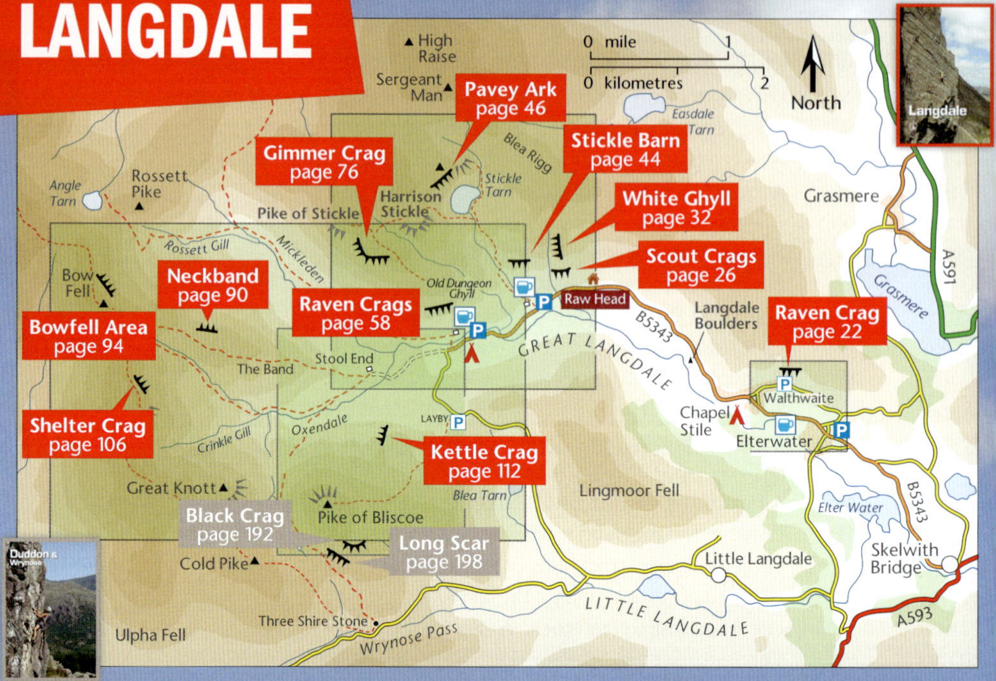

Map locations:
- **Pavey Ark** page 46
- **Gimmer Crag** page 76
- **Stickle Barn** page 44
- **White Ghyll** page 32
- **Scout Crags** page 26
- **Neckband** page 90
- **Raven Crags** page 58
- **Raven Crag** page 22
- **Bowfell Area** page 94
- **Shelter Crag** page 106
- **Kettle Crag** page 112
- **Black Crag** page 192
- **Long Scar** page 198

Langdale has everything, a wide range of fantastic climbing from easy access valley venues to high mountain crags, many of them with a predominantly sunny aspect. Add to that, the nearby pubs, camping and other accommodation making this the most popular valley for climbers. The stunning scenery and proximity to the high fells is also attractive to everyone else - it gets really busy on fine days. There is a regular bus service up and down the valley from Ambleside.

Prometheus, Middlefell Buttress HVS (page 64) Keith Sanders — David Simmonite

RAVEN CRAG WALTHWAITE

OS Grid Ref: NY 325 057
Altitude: 180m

Enterprize VS (opposite) Steve Scott — Keith Sanders

Popular, quick-drying mid-grade routes a short walk from the road. This small crag makes an ideal spot for a short day or evening. Belays can be difficult to arrange at the top and a large boulder 20m back is a convenient bollard. The rock is generally sound but can shear - be careful.

Seasonal restriction: 15th Feb to 31st May.

Approach: Limited off-road parking below the crag. Go through the gate and follow the well-marked rising path. Alternatively, park in the layby on the road near the Wainwright Inn.

Descent: Either side.

① Route 1   22m   S   ★
Pleasant climbing yet with sparse protection. From the large holly tree, move up to a ledge and follow the well-marked slab left then right.
Pre-1950

② Enterprize   22m   VS 4b   ★★
Excellent climbing on the bold arête. From the tree, climb right of the arête in a groove. A foot ledge up and left leads onto the arête then continue in fine style to the top.
Photo opposite.
N Gough 17.09.1963

③ Hardup Wall   22m   VS 4b   ★
A poorly-protected groove leads to a ledge, then an awkward move gains easier ground.
1950s

④ For Whom the Bell Tolls   25m   E3 5b   ★
Follow *Hardup Wall* to its ledge and arrange as many runners as possible. Now traverse delicately right across the wall. Disengage the brain to gain and climb the lonely rib until a long reach gains a jug. Finish more easily up the arête.
M Dale, D Wood 12.06.2011

⑤ Route 2   37m   HS 4b   ★★★
Interest and variety make this a popular gem. Start at the toe of the buttress by a short arête.
1 10m Climb the groove moving left onto the rib to reach a spacious ledge.
2 27m 4b Climb the shallow square-cut groove to reach pockets. Traverse right for 3m (crux) then head up into a corner. Climb this and swing left to a groove which provides a fittingly tricky finish.
Pre-1950

⑥ Tritus   27m   HVS 5a   ★★★
An excellent steep and very direct pitch on superb rock. Start behind the upper of two large trees. Climb the bulging wall on juggy holds to a resting place beneath twin grooves. Climb the tapering right-hand groove until it morphs into a rib. Follow the left-hand side of this rib.
Photo page 25.
RM Biden, K Forsythe 1977

Langdale

7. Tritus-Protus Combination 27m HVS 5a ★★★
Steep with an exposed finish, it is the best route on the crag. Start behind the upper of two holly trees. Climb straight up the wall on juggy holds to a resting place beneath twin grooves. Step left and climb the larger left-hand groove and wall to the final slanting roof. A small clean groove cuts through the left side of this to provide a direct and spectacular finish - easier than it looks.

8. Into the Light 25m E5 6a ★
A very committing route, the original way and a natural line up the blank wall. Start at a crack 2m left of *Walthwaite Gully*.
1 10m 4a Climb the crack to the large ledge.
2 15m 6a Climb left of a short groove above and just left of the angle of the gully to a pocket (cam). Follow the line of flakes leftwards with difficulty then make a very hard move to gain better holds on the wall above, which is followed to the top. The cam in the small pocket provides the only glimmer of light on this serious pitch.
D Birkett, P Ramsden, B Rogers 10.09.1988

9. Light Fandango 15m E5 6b ★
A very direct technical problem squeezed in, starting up *Into the Light*. From the pocket (cam), move up slightly right and climb directly up the wall.
S Wood, N Wharton, W Walker 13.06.2011

10. Walthwaite Gully 27m VS 4c ★
Not a gully at all! This fine corner gives exciting climbing in a sheltered setting. Start by a small hawthorn tree at the bottom of the main angle.
1 10m 4c Climb the corner to the large ledge. Easy for gritstoners!
2 17m 4c Follow the fierce-looking crack up the corner and rightwards round the roof to finish through the holly tree, fortunately of the not-too-prickly variety.
JA Austin, JM Ruffe 18.05.1957

11. Persephone 23m HVS 5a ★★
A good climb, sustained at the top, with sparse protection. Climb a shallow groove left of the overhangs, then up and right, across a tricky overhang (gear), to the top of a small slab. Continue up with interest to comfortable exit holds.
M Scrowston, D Till 13.06.2008

| 5 | Route 2 | HS 4b | ★★★ |
| 6 | Tritus | HVS 5a | ★★★ |

Raven Crag Walthwaite | 25

12 Swing to the Right 22m E1 5b ★★
Interesting and varied. From a ledge at 2m, climb right into a stepped corner below a roof. Swing to the right across the rib and up the wall on better holds.
I Williamson, J Billingham 14.06.1987

13 Party Animal 22m E2 5b ★★
Spicy with a bold start; less precarious if you spot the nut slot just below and left of a tiny triangular niche. Protected by a flake, teeter uncertainly leftwards on sloping holds (nut). Make a tricky move then better holds ease the tension to reach the roof. Step right then make difficult moves to gain a ledge. Finish easily up the groove.
I Williamson, J White 11.06.1987

14 Proportional Representation 20m HVS 5a ★
A fair pitch starting on top of the higher block behind the ash tree. Move up and left to enter a short groove. Exit left and finish up another groove.
J White, G Hussey 19.06.1987

15 Militant Tendency 20m HVS 5a ★
A steady route with a bold finish. Climb a groove rightwards to knobbly black rock. Follow another short groove then enter a left-facing niche in the final bulging wall (runners). Finish through the bulges (sling) on the right-hand side of the niche.
J White, I Williamson 19.06.1987

Tritus HVS (page 23) Peter Sterling — 📷 Keith Sanders

SCOUT CRAGS
OS Grid Ref: NY 298 069
Altitude: 240m

Route 1 VD (page 31) Steve Scott — David Simmonite

Three very different crags range up the hillside. **Lower Scout** is very convenient, popular with groups and polished. **Middle Scout** is steep, fierce and scary. **Upper Scout** is longer, more laid back and provides some lovely, easier-grade routes.

Approach: The crags are all usually approached via a path from the main road, to the right of a roadside barn 200m east of the car parks by the New Dungeon Ghyll. They can also be approached from the path to White Ghyll by continuing along the hillside where the path to White Ghyll heads up the gill.

See overview page 28.

Lower Scout

A victim of easy access and modest height, the crag is popular for novices. Burnished to a high gloss and worn at top and bottom. The routes are worth climbing.

Approach: Follow the track from the road and through a field uphill past the right side of a barn, some 200m east of the New Dungeon Ghyll car parks. This leads very simply to the lower crag.

Descent: To the left.

1 Cub's Arête 11m S ★
Start below a prominent roof and immediately right of a drainage dirt streak. Climb the groove and small overlap just left of the arête to the overhang. Make an airy little traverse right to escape.

2 Cub's Groove 13m VD ★
An excellent short introduction to climbing. Start a couple of metres left of the steep crack. A right-slanting line of polished holds leads to ledges. Now, either traverse ledges back left to finish, or finish direct past the holly stump.

3 Cub's Crack 13m HS 4b ★
The steep crack leading to the tree gives a good but slippery introduction to jamming (though it seems to get harder with the passing years), with an awkward section by the prominent nose at 5m.
J Summermatter Oct 1927

4 Cub's Wall 13m VD ★
Starting just right of the steep crack at a shallow left-facing groove, climb up with minimal protection until forced left onto a ledge system. Climb direct past the holly stump on magnificent holds.

5 The New Partnership 15m E1 5b
A direct eliminate which takes the triangular overhanging nose at the top of the crag. Start 2m left of the big corner. Don blinkers and climb the vague rib. Finish strenuously on good but spaced holds up the thin crack running just left of the pointed tip of the nose.
R Davis, M Hicks 5.05.1984

6 Oh Heck Direct 14m MVS 4b
A good line spoilt by the layer of dirt washing down from the top. Climb the big right-angled corner direct, stepping out right towards the top for a precarious finish.
D Briggs, A Kelly 8.08.1968

7 The Slab 12m MVS 4b ★
An especially polished climb, this takes the attractive slab forming the right-hand side of the corner. Starting on the left, work up rightwards to the arête. Climb this until a move left leads to a triangular niche and an insecure, tricky move to gain easier ground.
J Summermatter Oct 1927

Middle Scout

This steep outcrop hosts short fiercely steep problems to test fingers and nerves. Rock and protection are worrying. The crag stays dry in summer.

Approach: Walk up the left-hand side of **Lower Scout** and over the stile.
Descent: To the right.

8 The Beatles 18m E6 6b ★★
Serious. This tenuous line offers small holds of brittle rock with minimal protection. Trend rightwards to a flake. Move left (crucial micro-wires) then tackle the impending wall. Micro wires, 2 skyhooks and not much else.
T Walkington 8.09.1981

9 Elvis 18m E5 6a ★★
Starts hard and just gets harder. Immediately steep moves right of the tree gain an undercut. Span left to a thin crack which is climbed to a stretchy finish.
Photo below.
T Walkington, A Trull 2.04.1981

Elvis E5 (above) Ramon Marin — Ron Kenyon

Upper Scout Crag **Scout Crags**

Upper Scout Crag

⏱ 20 min

The angle is more laid-back and the rock is rough, providing some lovely easier routes

Approach: Follow the path past **Lower** and **Middle Scout**.

Descent: From the highest point of the crag, an exposed well-worn path scrambles down and left, ending in a short crack down glaciated slabs into an easy descent gully.

⑩ The Glaciated Rib 50m D ★★

An excellent pitch. Start some 50m up the descent gully at a clean rib, to the left of the descent route. Protection is initially sparse. Climb the delightful slab passing between a tree at 10m and a large flake on the left. Continue up the rib. Diagram page 28.

Descent: across to the left, or right and down the regular descent.

⑪ Route 2 55m VD ★★

Start at a detached spur of rock.
1 10m A stepped groove is best entered from the right and leads to a terrace. Nut belay at the back.
2 13m A polished crack leads to a short corner from which an awkward move up rightwards gains a ledge. Tree belay.
3 13m Traverse 3m right and make some interesting moves up and just left of the overhangs to belay in the groove above.
4 19m Step back left and climb the easy-angled rib to the top.
F Graham Oct 1922

⑫ Route 1 50m VD ★★★

An excellent route following the line of the central rib. The second pitch in particular is one of the best of its grade in the valley.
1 14m Climb the short left-slanting ramp and pocketed slabby grooves above to a block belay at the base of the arête.
2 36m Climb onto the block and traverse right onto the arête which leads on wonderful pocketed rock in a delightfully exposed position to a ledge. Continue past flakes and easier slabs to nut and chipped flake belays at the end of the difficulties. Adequate protection - carry a good range of nuts.
Photo page 26.
F Graham Oct 1922

⑬ Route 1.75 D ★★

The easiest way up the centre of the crag, with pleasant open climbing.
2 32m From the belay block, climb into the bottom of the main corner and follow good holds diagonally leftwards above the overhangs. Alternatively, ignore the stance and continue wandering up slabs to the top.

⑭ The Ramsbottom Variation 32m VD ★★

An excellent variation taking the prominent central corner in the upper half of the crag.
2 32m Climb above the block into the main corner climb its right-hand side until the corner bulges. Surmount this with a step up left and continue up slabs.

WHITE GHYLL

OS Grid Ref: NY 298 072
Altitude: 400m

The Slabs, Route 2 S (page 34) Richard Greaves — David Simmonite

Langdale

White Ghyll is the impressive crag towering over the true left bank of the gill approximately 500m south of Stickle Gill. It is an imposing sight from the road with soaring grooves and arêtes in its lower half and impressive overhangs further up the gill. It is best suited to those climbing at **VS** and above with these routes often tackling ground that looks much harder.

Approach: The crag has an easy approach, albeit a bit of a stiff pull in the steeper parts of the gill. From the New Dungeon Ghyll Hotel, a gated track leads out towards the fell. Go over the wooden bridge and the next slate bridge. Follow the track for 50m then turn right and follow a path along a wall across the fellside into the gill itself. Huff and puff your way up this until respite at a large sycamore tree beneath the **Lower Crag**. This can be used as a base for all routes. Beware of loose rock even when at the relative safety of the tree.

Overview page 44.

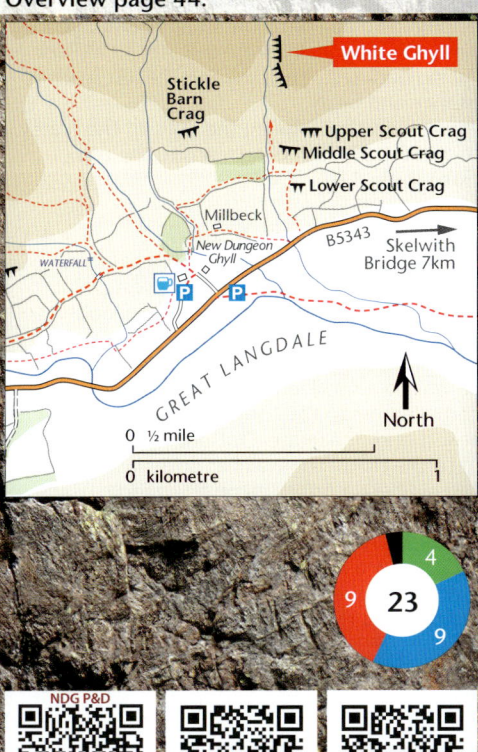

 GPS 54.447244
-3.089625

 BMC
White Ghyll

 OS Grid Ref
NY 298 072

NY 293 063

Upper Crag

An imposing cliff with an array of steep walls and overhangs. The harder routes tackle these features head-on; the easier ones find sneaky ways around the obstacles through very impressive ground. At the left-hand end, before the meat of the buttress, is a very pleasant-angled slab with a couple of fine routes.

Descent: For all routes except the Slabs descend grassy ground above the crag to pick up the top of Easy Rake; cairns.

Be careful not to dislodge rocks on climbers below.

❶ The Slabs, Route 2   43m   S   ★★
Start at the left side of the slabs by a large flake.
1 11m Climb a steep crack, using a flake where it steepens, to a stance on a small ledge and flake belay.
2 21m Traverse left to the edge and use a good hold to pull onto the small slab above. Climb this diagonally right and ascend a crack running back left. The ridge on the left leads to a stance and belay.
3 11m Follow the ridge on the right of the grassy scoop. 25m of scrambling leads to the top.
Photo page 32.
S Cross, E Fallowfield, C Tatham 1933

❷ The Slabs, Route 1   66m   S   ★★★
A really enjoyable excursion which has some interesting moves. Start at the lowest point.
1 13m A steady pitch straight up to a ledge. Belay at its left end.
2 29m Make a fine rising traverse left across the wall to a small ledge. Climb the steep groove above to the foot of a smooth wall at the left end of a ledge. Optional spike belay 3m to the right. The wall has an awkward start then, on better holds, climb the middle of the three grooves to a ledge. A further groove slanting up rightwards leads to the terrace; belay below a fine-looking rib.
3 24m Start the rib on its right and follow it pleasantly to the top.
G Barker, AT Hargreaves 15.09.1930

❸ Forget-Me-Not   62m   E1 5b   ★★
A harder option, start below the twin cracks, 5m right of the lowest point of the slab.
1 23m 5a Gain the twin cracks and climb them. Stand on the flake, pull over a slight bulge via a small spike and continue diagonally left to a spike belay.
2 15m 5a Climb the groove and slightly dirty wall to the ledge.
2a 15m 5b Best when combined with P1; follow a faint right-leaning flake crack at first and then precariously up to finish at a ledge.
3 24m Scramble off leftwards or follow the pleasant, steep rib above as for *The Slabs, Route 1*.
P1 M Sinker, R Isherwood 1963
P2 RW Graham, A Hyslop, TW Birkett 1980

❹ White Ghyll Chimney   57m   S 4a   ★★
A classic 'must' for aficionados of this traditional genre. It climbs the impressive cleft formed by the junction of the central overhanging section and the slabs on its left. Start at the foot of the cleft where a ramp runs up into the initial groove.
1 15m Easily up the groove to the large ledge and upstanding flake.
2 30m 4a Walk up 6m to a sentry box (thread), above which the chimney narrows to a crack. Climb the cave for 3m and then make a difficult move to gain a sloping hold on the left. Delicately reach some small handholds and continue more easily up a steep leftward diagonal groove to a ledge 6m higher. If the chimney is damp, a harder (MVS) but drier detour can be made by stepping down at the sentry box and traversing left for 5m before climbing directly on small holds to the diagonal groove of the original pitch.
3 12m Return 3m from the belay and climb the wall above for 5m. A delicate traverse then leads back into the chimney which provides a fitting finish.
HB Lyon, J Herbert, HP Cain 11.08.1923

❺ Chimney Variant   52m   E1 5b   ★★
Justifiably popular with interesting unusual climbing and superb positions. Its essence lies along the undercut gangway leading rightwards from the chimney and up the short but handsome square-cut hanging groove.
1 15m *White Ghyll Chimney* P1.
2 28m 5b Continue up the chimney to the overhang. Pull over this and move right onto the gangway and shimmy rightwards to the base of the groove. Tricky moves up this lead to a step out right onto the rib. Belay just above.
3 9m Finish up the easier groove.
JA Austin, I Roper, D Miller 30.04.1966

6 Warrior 49m E5 6a ★★
A fierce climb of sustained and technical interest.
1 15m *White Ghyll Chimney* P1.
2 34m 6a Climb the steep wall of *Paladin* for a few moves then step left onto a short slanting slab. Cross this and pull out leftwards to gain the gangway of *Chimney Variant*, move left and climb through bulges to a groove. Climb the steep wall on the right and move slightly left to yet more overhangs. Move right to finish at the top of *Paladin*.
E Cleasby, R Matheson 4.06.1977

7 Paladin 49m E3 5c ★★★
Climbs the biggest hanging groove in the overhangs. Sustained, strenuous and exposed climbing. Definitely 'out there'.
1 15m *White Ghyll Chimney* P1 to the upstanding flake.
2 34m 5c Climb the deceptively steep and fingery wall, trending rightwards into a corner. Step left and climb a slab and bulging wall to move into the corner below the roof. Follow an ominous-looking block rightwards to get established in the main groove. Move up with difficulty and exit left into comparative calm below a subsidiary groove. Climb the left wall of this, passing another awkward move to easy ground.
R Matheson 26.03.1970

8 Haste Not 59m VS 4c ★★★★
This impertinent excursion probes the monumental barrier of overhangs. Excellent climbing, featuring an exposed and enthralling traverse. Start in the right-facing corner, just right of a broad hanging rib.
1 22m 4b Climb the slab to the roof. Cross the left wall with difficulty to gain a groove in the slab on the front. This leads via an awkward bulge to a large ledge and upstanding flake.
2 15m 4c Traverse easily rightwards for 5m to where a steep wall leads to the big roofs. A delicate step right gains a cramped gangway system running rightwards under the overhangs. Follow this and descend a bottomless coffin-like groove to a resting place in a short left-facing corner. Step up the corner, swing right onto the rib and traverse right to belay in the next corner.
3 22m 4b Step back left and climb awkwardly into a short groove at the right-hand end of the overlap. Pull out left and up the narrow rib just right of the bilberry ramp, or finish up the thin crack in the immaculate white wall.
RJ Birkett, L Muscroft 9.05.1948

9 Haste Not Direct 56m E3 5c ★★
Another direct line with varied climbing and a sensationally placed crux. Start in the deep left-facing corner.
1 21m 4c Climb the corner to the roof and exit right onto the rib. Move right again to belay in the cave.
2 23m 5c Move up left through the overhangs to enter a slim groove (old peg) and, after a few feet, pull out left to a resting place. Continue steeply to reach the *Haste Not* traverse. The notorious bulging flake crack above is tricky to start, wildly spectacular to continue and strenuous throughout, yet thoroughly worth the effort. Belay on the bilberry ledge.
3 12m 4b Amble up the pleasant rough white slabby wall to the top.
J A Austin, R Valentine 2.05.1971

10 White Ghyll Eliminate 62m E2 5c ★★
An exhilarating climb up the compellingly steep crack springing from the right-hand side of the recess. Start at the foot of the slab.
1 20m 4b Climb the slab trending slightly rightwards until a steepening at 16m suggests a short traverse left, then up to a recess.
2 15m 5c Step right and survey the crack above. With a positive mindset of "How Hard Can it Be?", pull steeply into the crack and follow it to a stance in the 'coffin' groove on the *Haste Not* traverse (good for keeping an eye on one's second). Debilitatingly well-protected, harder for the short E3 6a.
3 27m 5b An awkward short straight crack in the same line splits the roof above. Climb it to the base of a bilberry ramp and continue up the thin crack in the pleasant rough white slabby wall above.
A Evans, D Parker, G Miller 9.05.1971

The Gordian Knot VS (page 38) — 📷 Dick Allen

11 The Gordian Knot 56m VS 4c ★★★ 💎

A climb of great character following a natural line. Sustained and not well-protected on the crux corner. Start at the foot of the slab which forms the right-hand side of a prominent rib running up to the overhangs.
1 20m 4b A pleasant pitch. Climb the slab trending slightly rightwards until a steepening at 16m suggests a short traverse left, then up to a recess with an anvil-like flake; belay.
2 14m 4c A teasing pitch on first acquaintance. Traverse easily right for 4m to an exposed ledge below the corner. Bridge through the bulge via a small ledge on the right wall (crux) and move back leftwards into a recess. Continue up to a belay on ledges just below the top of the corner.
3 22m 4b Climb the wide corner and exit right onto a ledge. Climb the steep wall above the left side of the ledge to finish.
Photo page 42 & 36.
JW Haggas, E Bull 15.09.1940

12 What Not 65m HVS 4c ★★

An amazing trip; serious, sustained, some suspect rock and a hanging belay build the suspense.
1 & 2 33m 4b P1 and 2 of *Perhaps Not*.
3 32m 4c Traverse left into *The Gordian Knot* then make a few moves up the corner to a tiny ledge on the right. Continue to a ledge on the arête then climb a crack and rib to the left end of a long ledge. Finish up the wall.
AC Cain, V Stevens 15.08.1955

13 Perhaps Not 63m HVS 5a ★★

Audaciously finding a way through the main barrier of overhangs, the climbing is bold, serious and exposed with some suspect rock. Start at the foot of a prominent rib.
1 17m Follow the rib and short wide crack to a ledge beneath the overhangs.
2 16m 4b Climb delicately leftwards up the slab to the roof where a line of large holds allows you to gambol out into space to a hanging belay (with a variety of cams and other attachments) beneath a short, capped chimney groove.
3 9m 5a Technical climbing into the chimney and rightwards out of it at the overhang leads to a stance and belay. Faith in what may be above is required when the holds disappear.
4 21m 4b Step left and climb a vague crack in the wall to a ledge; finish directly up the wall.
RJ Birkett, L Muscroft 15.05.1949

14 White Ghyll Wall 68m VS 4c ★★★

A magnificent outing, weaving around the right-hand side of the mighty array of overhangs. An excellent introduction to the buttress and 'VS work'. Start at the foot of the prominent rib right of the ash tree.
1 25m Follow the rib and short wide crack to a ledge beneath the overhangs and traverse right for 8m to a stance beneath an undercut left-facing scoop.
2 15m 4c Ascend the scoop and climb a problematic overlap (by either side) to a small ledge at the foot of a large open corner. Move leftwards onto the steep wall and climb for 6m to an overhung ledge. Belay 2m down to the left in a slanting groove.
3 28m 4b From below the belay, traverse delicately left for 2m out onto the slabs then climb diagonally up left, passing two prominent ledges. Finish up the wall above the right side of the second ledge.
Photo opposite.
RJ Birkett, L Muscroft, T Hill 9.05.1946

15 The Veil 63m HVS 5a ★★

Pleasant climbing taking a reasonably direct line. Beware of loose rock on P1. Start 6m up Easy Rake, beneath a prominent metre-wide overhang at 7m, split by a slanting crack.
1 24m 5a Climb to the overhang and pull through its central break with difficulty onto the slab above. Climb right, then a short leftward-slanting ramp moving back right at its top, across a ledge, to a detached block under the overlap.
2 23m 5a Left of the block a small left-facing fault on the lip of the overhang is the key to a poorly protected pull onto the slab above, reaching sharp holds. Step left and climb a short flake to a steep wall. Traverse rightwards to spikes at the foot of the main corner. Climb the corner to the overhang then traverse left to a ledge. Pull up to gain a larger ledge above the overhangs.
3 16m 4c From the left end of the ledge, move up the wall and step right. Continue directly to the top.
GL Swainbank, C Read 28.06.1998

White Ghyll Wall VS (opposite) — 📷 David Simmonite

Lower Crag

Encountered first on the approach, the **Lower Crag** is open and far less intimidating than its fearsome neighbour. The clearly defined corners, arêtes and walls provide excellent climbing.

Descent: Abseil or scramble up to join Easy Rake, the descent from the **Upper Crag**.

16 Hollin Groove 82m HS 4b ★★

A pleasant varied route taking in the fine corner at mid-height. Start at a crooked crack in a short corner with a small slabby ledge at head-height in its left rib. This is some 20m above the large sycamore tree and just right of the main groove above.

1 23m 4b Climb the stubborn crack to a ledge. Step left and climb the rib via a groove to a battered tree beneath the main corner.
2 24m Climb the fine right-angled corner above and walk 13m back to belay at the rib ahead.
3 35m The steep rib leads to a spike. Continue pleasantly up the rib to the top.
RJ Birkett, L Muscroft 1.08.1945

17 Slip Knot 41m VS 4b ★★★★

The most popular route at **White Ghyll** with absorbing climbing in superb positions. Scramble up to a ledge below the corner.
1 21m 4a Climb the corner before traversing onto the right wall where excellent holds lead to a spacious ledge and belay under the roofs.
2 20m 4b Traverse left into the corner and make a thought-provoking move across the left wall to gain the rib. Climb this with an exhilarating move over a bulge to a niche on the left. Continue up the steep wall on the right. Belay well back.

Can be climbed in one 40m pitch by moving left across the corner 3m below the ledge then following a foot ledge onto the rib, or by using very long slings at the belay.

Photo opposite.
RJ Birkett, L Muscroft 25.05.1947

Slip Knot VS (opposite) Neil Colquhoun — David Simmonite

18 Do Not Direct   46m   E1 5b   ★★
A first-class route with varied climbing and a superbly positioned second pitch. Start by scrambling up the grassy ramp.
1 25m 5b Climb the groove to a ledge and large spike on the right below a fine crack. The wall is slightly undercut, which impedes access to the crack, but once started it is easier than it looks and gobbles protection. Belay on the spacious ledge above.
2 21m 5a Climb the square-cut groove above the right edge of the belay ledge to an overhang. Traverse steeply up and left across the wall on large handholds, until a final awkward move round the nose leads to a ledge. Easier climbing provides a relaxing finish.
P1 L Brown, P Muscroft 1960
P2 RJ Birkett, L Muscroft 1949

19 Waste Not,   32m   E1 5b   ★★★
Want Not
An exceptional wall climb using an inverted stepped fault. Climb the corner of *Laugh Not* then make committing moves left to gain the fault. Follow this then pockets across the wall to the rib. Climb this past the roof to a groove which provides a steady finish.
W Lounds, P Sanson June 1977

20 Laugh Not   35m   HVS 5b   ★★★
A compelling clean-cut line with sustained, well-protected climbing; strenuous, despite decent resting places. The very smooth crux is testing. Climb the long corner, with a perplexing move to pass a small overlap, into the cave beneath the roof (runners, beware rope drag). Step down and traverse the thin wall rightwards to a ledge on the rib or, more spectacularly, reach up right to a prominent flat hold on the lip of the overhang and swing right on big jugs to the ledge. Go on, commit yourself - it's not as hard as you think!
J Brown, R Moseley, T Waghorn 17.10.1953

21 Sahara   30m   E2 6a   ★★
The crux is technical and well-protected. Start below the long corner of *Laugh Not*. Climb rightwards to enter a right-facing niche then up a small corner to a thin crack in the slab. Climb this with difficulty into the cave. Finish over the roof.
S Howe, C Dale, D Kay 23.08.1981

22 Man of Straw   28m   E1 5b   ★★
Delightful climbing, sustained but never desperate, requiring solid footwork. Start beneath a wide crack leading to a groove. Climb the crack to a small ledge at the foot of the groove. Teeter up this almost to the roof when a short traverse left round two small ribs gains a slab (runners in the thin diagonal crack above). From here, a delightful two-step move right above the roof leads to the arête and nut belays.
JA Austin, DG Roberts 3.04.1965

23 Ethics of Heather   25m   VS 4c   ★★
Lovely grippy rock make this a very good pitch. Gain and follow the right edge of the slab.

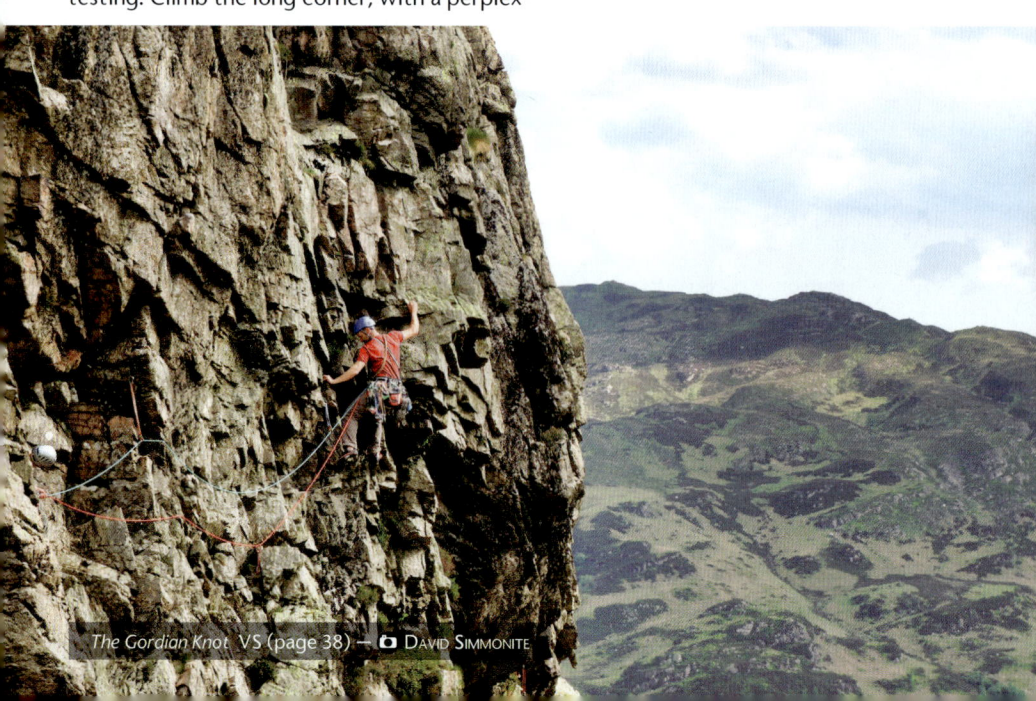

The Gordian Knot VS (page 38) — 📷 David Simmonite

STICKLE BARN CRAG

OS Grid Ref: NY 295 069
Altitude: 220m

Stickle Barn Crag

P Stickle Barn

Although only small, this easily accessed outcrop provides clean sunny routes on good rock.

Approach: From Stickle Barn CP, a gated track leads north across a wooden bridge then a slate bridge to a steep gated track. After 50m go right through a gate along a wall then head up to the crag.

Descent: Round to the right of the crag.

1 Left Wall Direct 10m VS 4b
Starting a metre left of *Left Wall*, climb directly to the top via a vague crack with marginal protection.
M Scrowston, J Loxham 28.12.2008

2 Left Wall 12m VD
Start 8m left of the deep flared chimney. Follow a rising traverse rightwards towards the ledge of *Heather Groove* then back diagonally up left to finish via a depression in the impending wall.

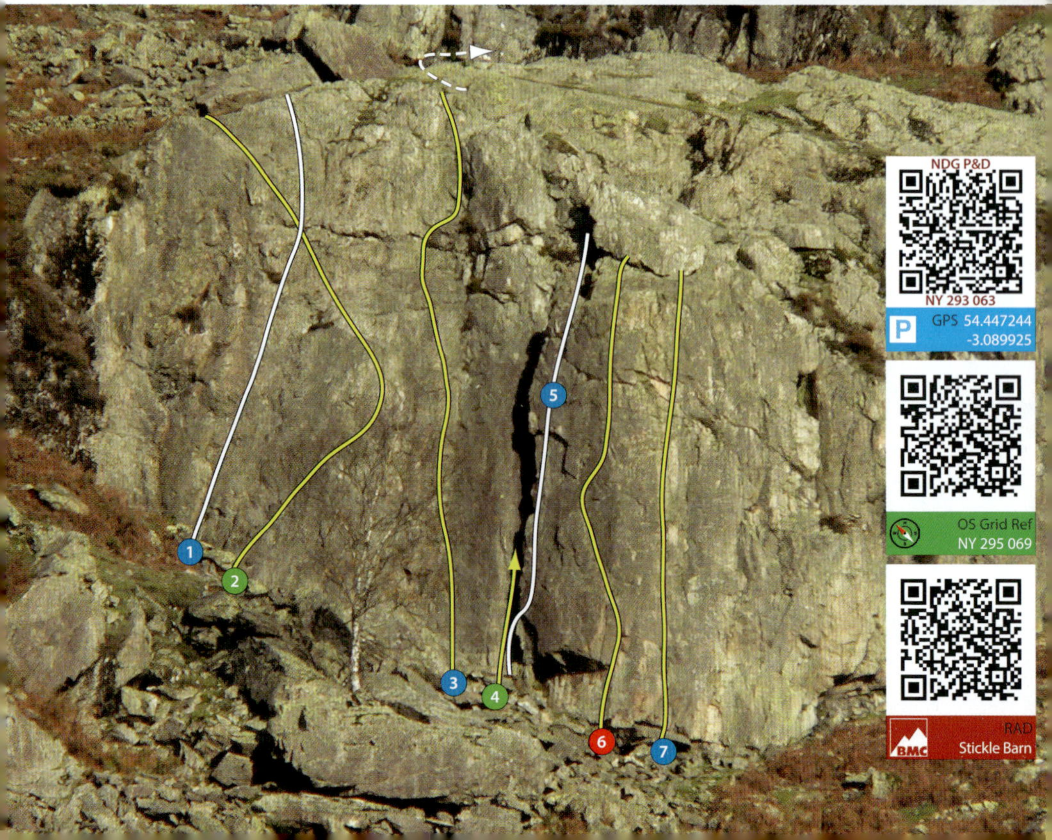

Langdale

Stickle Barn & White Ghyll — © MAX BIDEN

③ Heather Groove 12m MVS 4b ★
The pleasant groove is climbed mainly by its left wall to a ledge. The short finishing groove is best entered from the left.

④ Left Chimney 10m S
The deep flared chimney forming the left side of the huge flake.

⑤ Main Wall Left-Hand 12m HVS 5a
Climb the undercut wall, the crux being the overlap at two-thirds height.

⑥ Main Wall Rib 12m E1 5b ★
Neat climbing up the line of the slight rib bounding the left side of the front face - quite serious. Starting off a boulder, gain the ledge at 4m and trend left up a shallow groove to a ledge (runners), make a delicate step up (crux) and move right onto the front of the rib, above which the holds improve.

⑦ Main Wall Crack 12m VS 4c ★★
Good climbing with well-maintained interest and good protection for the diligent. A polished start gains the ledge at 4m. Now climb directly up the centre of the wall following the line of a thin crack and finish with a short step right to gain easier ground.

PAVEY ARK
OS Grid Ref: NY 286 079
Altitude: 540m

Rake End Wall VS (page 52) Nick Wharton — David Simmonite

A great crag set in a beautiful location overlooking Stickle Tarn with extensive views down to Windermere, across the South Lakes and beyond. There is a wide selection of routes available to suit all levels and tastes. **Pavey Ark** forms part of the iconic Langdale Pikes skyline. It faces south-east so enjoys sunshine for most of the day. Running diagonally up the large, rambling crag, from bottom right to top left is the popular scramble of Jack's Rake. The climbs below Jack's Rake can be readily linked with a route above creating brilliant multi-pitch excursions. The rock at the top is particularly rough and featured - a delight to climb on. In addition, the steeper wall to the right, known as the East Buttress is home to a fabulous set of, mostly, harder lines.

Approach: From the National Trust car park at the side of Stickle Barn. Follow the west side of the gill until a bridge is crossed and the east side is followed. This eventually re-crosses the gill just below the tarn. Once at the tarn, paths lead round either side to the crag opposite. The best option is to go clockwise.

Descent: Down Jack's Rake or East Gully.

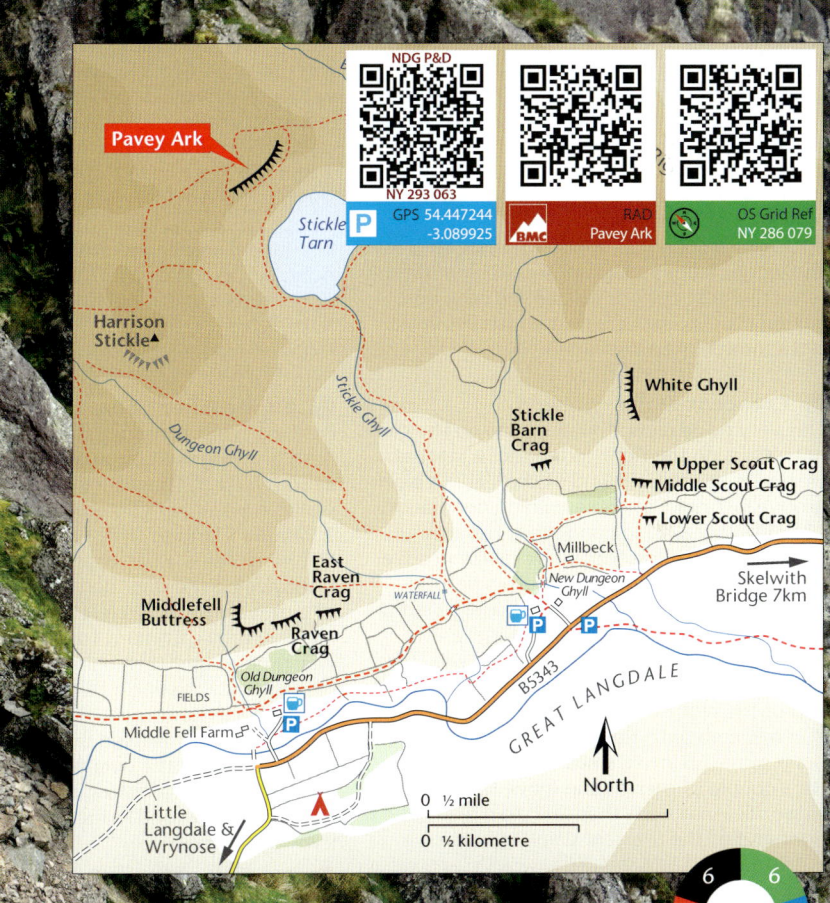

Climbs below Jack's Rake

A series of walls and slabs with occasional overlaps lie below the diagonal of Jack's Rake.

Approach: About 40m below the foot of Jack's Rake, a path branches left from the main track and runs beneath the lower tier. 60m along this, you arrive below the undercut arête of *Cruel Sister*.

Descent: Jack's Rake, or continue up a route above.

1 Crescent Climb 100m M ★★
An alpine style adventure up the broken arête with an exposed crescent-shaped traverse across the top of *Crescent Slabs*. There is a risk of stonefall from scramblers on Jack's Rake.
1 55m Follow the arête to the left end of the Crescent; ledge with flake belay above. Copious stances, picnic hampers, scientific observations and doubtful belays en route.
2 15m Traverse pleasantly right on large holds beneath the overhang.
3 30m Scrambling up slabby rock, steep grass and ledges leads to Jack's Rake. After a suitably reflective rest period, the summit may be gained via *Gwynne's Chimney* which lies enticingly some 12m to the right.
F Botterill, WE Palmer April 1907

2 Crescent Slabs 60m S ★★
This very good climb follows a line up the clean open slabs on the right of the moss. Start at a weakness at the right end of the slabs; a black groove just right of some bulging overhangs.
1 36m Follow a rising gangway leftwards (usually wet) to the foot of a shallow groove. Ascend this for a couple of metres before working left over easier slabs to a large ledge. The groove can be avoided by vegetated climbing further left. Continue up steep slabs to belay below a large block at the right-hand end of the highest central terrace of the slabs.
2 24m Climb onto the block and make a difficult move up into a small scoop. Climb this for a couple of metres and move left to a small ledge. Pleasant slabs then lead to a belay at the right end of the *Crescent Climb* traverse.
GS Bower, AW Wakefield 19.06.1920

Cook's Tour **VD**, a short walk right down Jack's Rake, makes a fine continuation.

3 Capella 70m E1 5b ★★★ ♦
An excellent route which takes a good natural line, finishing up a series of walls and corners. Well-protected, with good rock and interesting climbing. It dries faster than *Arcturus*. Start below a prominent birch tree growing out of the base of the initial overhang. The tree is not required for progress and is suffering from overuse - please treat it with respect.
1 32m 5b Climb to a niche-like overhung ledge on the right side of the tree. Using holds on the left, bridge up to gain the lip of the overhang. Follow the pocketed crackline trending rightwards up the wall for 4m then make a 2m traverse left. Go straight up past a flake and ledge then diagonally right to beneath a steepening wall. Move right, climb the right side of this and pull up left to a ledge. Move up to a ledge with a tree belay. It's easy to miss the traverse left and continue up with greater difficulty to rejoin the route below the belay.
2 38m 5b Starting left of the tree, climb the shallow groove on its left side and gain the steep wall above. Move rightwards into a short left-facing corner and climb to a ledge on the right. Go up left to another ledge. Move up rightwards and climb a fingery wall to a large flake. From its top, enter a shallow corner and follow it to the top. Step left to belay.
GL Swainbank, C Read 10.08.1997

4 Big Brother 66m E4 6a ★★★
Bold, committing and sustained. Start below a bush growing in a corner above the initial wall as for *Arcturus*. The difficulties on the upper wall can be circumvented; E3 5c.
1 50m 6a Climb to the overhang and over leftwards using a flat-topped brown boss. Continue up the slab then the grey wall, right of a mossy streak and left of a corner, to the halfway break. Commit to the thin crack in the wall on the right then unlock a very technical sequence passing a thin horizontal break to reach a large suspect flake, continue to a distinct break traversed by *Arcturus*.
2 16m 5a Climb the overlap, step left then climb the corner finishing up grass ledges. Belay on the second ledge (P3 *Cruel Sister*).
N Wharton, S Scott 4.06.2012

5 Arcturus 81m E2 5b ★★★
Offering fine open climbing in excellent situations, this tremendous route finds the easiest way up the impressive two-tier wall which dominates this part of the crag. The standard is well-maintained at HVS except for a short section on the first pitch which is both more serious and more

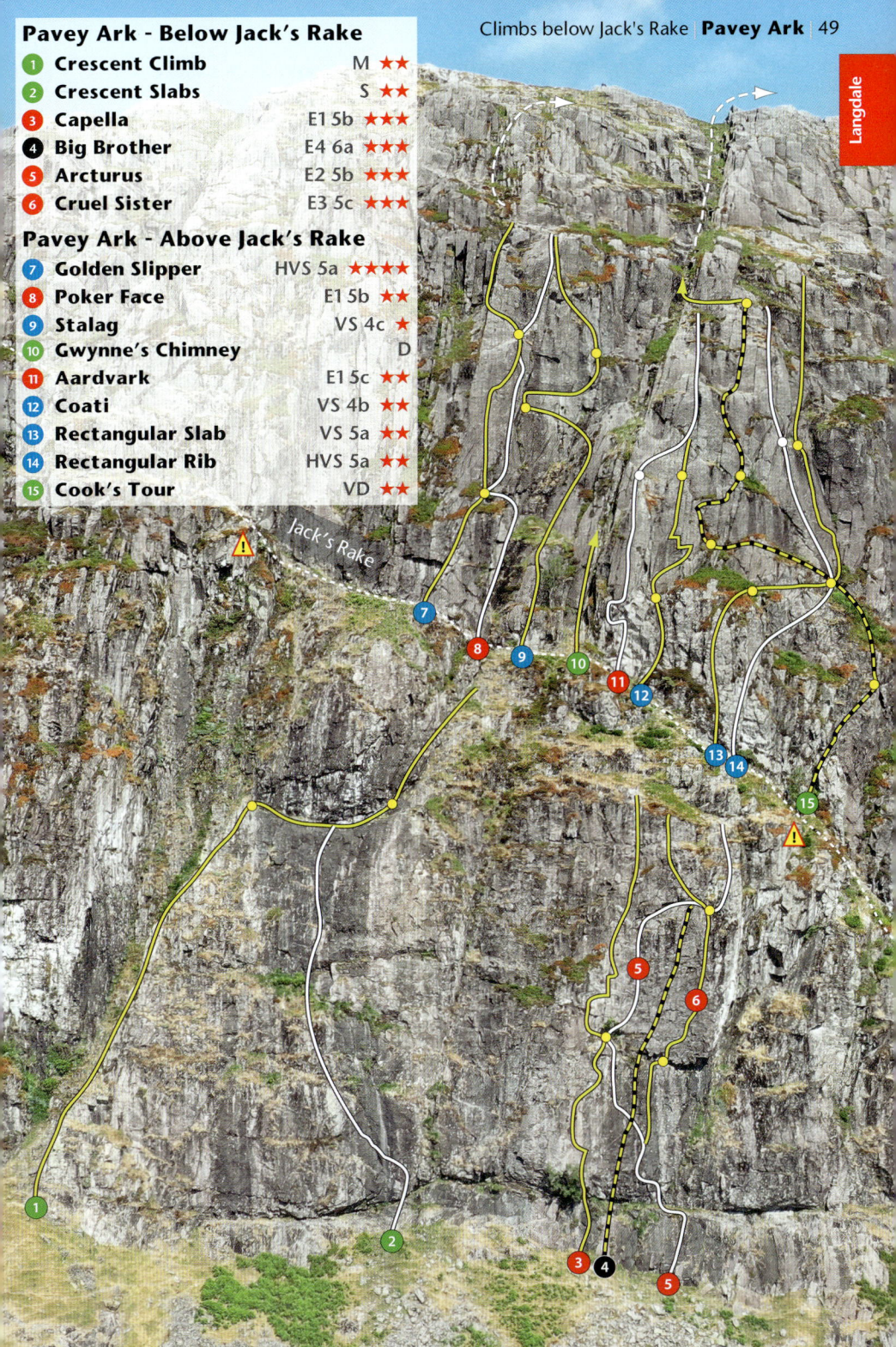

Pavey Ark – Below Jack's Rake

1. Crescent Climb — M ★★
2. Crescent Slabs — S ★★
3. Capella — E1 5b ★★★
4. Big Brother — E4 6a ★★★
5. Arcturus — E2 5b ★★★
6. Cruel Sister — E3 5c ★★★

Pavey Ark – Above Jack's Rake

7. Golden Slipper — HVS 5a ★★★★
8. Poker Face — E1 5b ★★
9. Stalag — VS 4c ★
10. Gwynne's Chimney — D
11. Aardvark — E1 5c ★★
12. Coati — VS 4b ★★
13. Rectangular Slab — VS 5a ★★
14. Rectangular Rib — HVS 5a ★★
15. Cook's Tour — VD ★★

Climbs below Jack's Rake | Pavey Ark | 49

Langdale

difficult; fortunately, it is also the least steep part. When combined with *Golden Slipper* this provides a superb and continuously interesting way up the full height of the crag. Start directly below a holly bush growing in the base of a corner above the initial wall, 12m right of a birch tree.
1 33m 5b Climb the initial wall to the base of the corner. Traverse left for 2m to an undercut rib. Climb the rib for 2m then move left to a jammed flake (thread). Move right and up onto a large foothold (peg). Delicate moves bring the reward of holds and runners. Avoid the smooth section above by working left to a thin crack which leads to a shallow niche; above is a stance at a tree.
2 32m 5a Pull over the small overlap on the right and climb a shallow groove to a small ledge. Step back into the line of the groove and climb the thin crack to a narrow ledge, with a large ledge a little higher. Traverse right beneath the overlap crossing a delicate and exposed little slab at the end. Step down to belay on the large ledge below.
3 16m 4c From the right end of the belay ledge, a tricky rib soon leads to easier ground and a belay. Jack's Rake is just off to the right.
JA Austin, E Metcalf 28.04.1962

❻ Cruel Sister   73m   E3 5c   ★★★
This brilliant climb follows the left-hand side of the superb undercut rib which forms the right edge of the upper wall. The crux, with its spaced protection, commands respect. The peg on P2 may not be in good condition. Start as for *Arcturus*.
1 30m 5b Follow *Arcturus* to the juggy foothold level with the peg and move rightwards to a ledge below the obvious shallow groove. Climb this to the ledge under the overhang and move right to belay.
2 25m 5c Pull onto the wall behind the belay and traverse airily right to gain the wall above the overhang (peg). Step up, traverse right (skyhook) to a block on the edge then go up to a good foothold. Climb the wall trending slightly left to a small overlap. Surmount this and gain a steep crackline which leads to a ledge. A magnificent pitch.
3 18m 5a Traverse left for 3m and pull over the overlap above on good, widely spaced holds. Step left and climb the obvious corner to grass ledges. Move right then back left onto the second ledge for belays.
R Matheson, S Colvin 20.04.1972

Climbs above Jack's Rake
The following routes are situated above and accessed from Jack's Rake.

❼ Golden Slipper   60m   HVS 5a   ★★★★
This thoroughly enjoyable climb ascends the centre of the elegant pillar of perfect rock. Protection is adequate for the diligent. Start at a gangway slanting right to a line of overhangs at 6m just left of the top of the tricky step in the level section of Jack's Rake.
1 18m 4c Follow the gangway easily to the overhang and step right onto a grassy ledge. Climb the steep wall above to another ledge at the foot of the steepening slab.
2 24m 5a Climb a shallow left-facing corner in the slab on superb bubbly rough rock. At its top, where the slab becomes a wall, traverse across to the rib on the right and ascend to a large ledge.
3 18m 4a Traverse left and climb the rib to the top.
JA Austin, RB Evans 19.07.1958

❽ Poker Face   67m   E1 5b   ★★
Excellent climbing up the slim wishbone-shaped groove splitting the arête right of *Golden Slipper*. The sense of exposure in the groove is offset by the superb protection. If the first pitch is damp, start up P1 of *Golden Slipper* instead. Start just right of the tricky step in Jack's Rake.
1 25m 4b Go up easily to a ledge on the left. Climb the slabby corner, past a tree, to another ledge with a large block on the left. Climb straight up from the block and after about 5m traverse left to a ledge.
2 24m 5b Slabby rock leads up right into the thin groove on the edge of the buttress. Climb the groove until it steepens considerably about 3m below the top. Make a difficult move left onto a slab and follow this up to a large ledge; or continue climbing the groove at a slightly higher standard.
3 18m 4c Climb the right-hand rib above the stance with an awkward move to start its upper part; or climb P3, *Golden Slipper*, the original and more pleasant way.
JA Austin, K Wood 16.07.1966

❾ Stalag   66m   VS 4c   ★
Start just left of the prominent *Gwynne's Chimney*.
1 35m 4c Move up past a small ledge with a large rowan tree to the big ledge above on the left. Continue up slabs to a steep wall; up this for 5m where an awkward move gains an obvi-

ous traverse line. Follow this left to a ledge in the corner.
2 15m 4b Traverse the sharp-edged flake across the steep right wall until a pull up can be made to a comfortable niche. Continue along the traverse to a small ledge then climb a short wall to a stance.
3 16m 4b Climb the steep little slab on the left to a small exposed ledge; continue over a small ledge to a pile of blocks. Swing round the rib on the left and follow it to the top.
JA Austin, RB Evans 29.06.1958

🔟 Gwynne's Chimney   30m   D
A pleasant little chimney. Start to the right of a large tree below the chimney. Climb the chimney for 17m. Continue directly or, more pleasantly, step right to the arête and climb it to a ledge. Continue by a choice of easier climbing and scrambling up the remaining fault and its slabby right-hand ridge.
HA Gwynne and party April 1892

1️⃣1️⃣ Aardvark   55m   E1 5c   ★★
An excellent exposed route with contrasting climbing up the steep arête above a small quartz-sprinkled sloping ledge. Start below the arête 6m down to the right of *Gwynne's Chimney*.
1 33m 5c Strenuous moves lead up to a poor rest under a small overhang (peg). Make a difficult sequence left to gain the haven of a sloping ledge. A delicate traverse up and rightwards across the wall leads to a small spike on the arête which is then followed to a ledge and spike belay.
2 22m 4a Climb a short wall on the right to gain the top of a long ramp-like groove. Cross this rightwards and follow a line of flakes to a left-facing corner and the top.
P Long, DJ Harding 30.09.1972

1️⃣2️⃣ Coati   61m   VS 4b   ★★
A delightful way up the crag; a satisfyingly direct line on superb rock. Start about 12m right of *Gwynne's Chimney* lower down Jack's Rake, where the steep wall above is split by a groove.
1 18m 4b Scramble over ledges then climb the groove moving right at its top to a rib and a small ledge on the left.
2 22m 4b Follow a slab rightwards to a ledge then climb the innocuous bulge into a right-facing corner. Step left into a narrow corner then left again to a groove fading to a crack in a slab. Climb the crack (spike) then swing down and right, round a rib and across to a large jammed flake.
3 21m 4b Step off the flake and pull onto the right wall of the right-facing corner. The angle eases quickly then steepens dramatically. Bridge up the corner to reach flakes that lead rightwards into the final left-facing corner. Nut belays in the slab behind. Easy scrambling leads to the summit.
RM Biden, C Harrod 29.08.2011

1️⃣3️⃣ Rectangular Slab   83m   VS 5a   ★★
An interesting route whose objective is the large right-facing slab offset high up the cliff. Start just left of a steep shallow rightward-facing corner with a bush at its base.
1 45m 4c Take the easiest way up the wall one metre left of the corner until it is possible to trend out rightwards (suspect flakes) to reach a projecting block at the foot of two grooves. Ascend the left-hand groove, moving out onto the steep left wall for the last couple of metres to reach the big terrace at 25m (belay). Walk 20m to the right to the foot of the main slab.
2 28m 4b Climb the corner on the right to a tree then make a delicate traverse across the slab to its left-hand arête. Follow the thin crack which slants up to the right, steepening towards the finish at a ledge.
3 10m 5a The sting in the tail (escape can be made off to the right if this does not appeal). Up an easy slab to a steep little crack in the right wall of the corner above. Climb this with difficulty stepping right at the top to a ledge.
JA Austin, E Metcalf 20.05.1960

1️⃣4️⃣ Rectangular Rib   78m   HVS 5a   ★★
Interesting climbing up the left-hand rib of *Rectangular Slab*, typical of the best bubbly Pavey rock, but not well-protected on the rib itself. Start at the steep shallow corner with a bush at its base.
1 40m 5a Climb the corner then the pleasant slabs rightwards.
2 24m 5a Avoid the steep initial section by climbing left of the rib until it is possible to move boldly right where the angle eases. Now follow the left edge to a ledge below a niche.
3 14m 4c Effect an entry into the niche, step left and follow short walls and slabs to the top.
MG Mortimer, MG Allen 13.10.1974

🟠 15 Cook's Tour   88m   VD   ★★

A good mountaineering route with some excellent pitches. Start at a leftward-facing short easy groove, opposite a large rowan tree at the top of the long steep section of Jack's Rake. Much harder if the rock is damp.
1 16m The open groove leads to a pinnacle platform; continue up the steep slabby corner, moving round to the right onto the top of a flake pinnacle.
2 12m From the corner on the left, easy climbing is followed by a short trek up steep vegetation to the foot of the imposing *Rectangular Slab*.
3 22m Move up to a large grass ledge 5m up on the left; walk along it for 14m to a flake belay below an easy-angled V-groove slanting up to the left.
4 11m Climb the groove for 6m to below a wedged flake and step out right onto a grass ledge, with a large flake at its far right-hand end. Traverse round the outside of this flake then up to a grassy ledge beneath a short right-facing corner.
5 27m Ascend the corner to the top of the flake then up left to another corner. Continue up the steep slab to a ledge. Finish up the wall above, first slightly right, then straight up.
J Cook, GB Elliott 14.03.1943

🟠 16 Rake End Chimney   70m   D   ★★★

An excellent climb which ascends the deep, often green, chimney located about 20m up Jack's Rake. A classic of its kind. Start at the foot of the chimney.
1 10m Go up easy steps to the chimney proper.
2 20m Climb the chimney past two ledges and over a chockstone.
3 20m Walk up the gully.
4 20m Climb up to and through the window and then go up the right wall to a small cave. Pass this on the left to finish easily.

🟠 17 Rake End Wall   58m   VS 4c   ★★★ ♦

A splendid route finding the easiest way up the right rib of *Rake End Chimney*. Enjoyable climbing on excellent rock with a well-maintained standard and thought-provoking crux. Start below a rib 5m right of the chimney.
1 21m 4b Starting on the right, climb up past a wedged flake and go up an ill-defined crack until its steepening necessitates a move round the corner to the right. Follow a diagonal crack to a huge block beneath the overhanging corner crack and belay on its right.
2 25m 4c The imposing corner crack above the block has some useful holds on the left wall and leads to a ledge. Step left from the left end of the ledge onto a fine slab. Climb up this into a small groove on the right of a slight overhang. Climb the groove for a couple of metres until an awkward move left gains the arête. Follow this to the large terrace in *Rake End Chimney*.
3 12m 4b From the top end of the terrace, climb the left edge of the right-bounding wall of the chimney with a detour right to avoid the steepest section.
Photo page 46.
HA Carsten, EH Phillips 9.08.1945

🟠 18 The Rib Pitch   36m   HVS 5a   ★★ ♦

Standing in splendid isolation, this superb pitch is steep bold and exposed; savour it. From the stance at the top of P2 of *Rake End Wall*, make an upward traverse left to climb the rib.
JA Austin, JM Ruffe 1.06.1958

🟠 19 The Bracken-clock   102m   E2 5c   ★★★

Excellent clean open climbing up the steep smooth wall. Start below a shallow groove 20m up Jack's Rake where its bed contains a smooth slab split by a quartz vein.
1 18m 5a Follow the shallow groove past a difficult bulge to the right end of a ledge. Belay at the left end.
2 14m 5c Climb the smooth slab to a jug (runner). Continue straight up with some difficulty to reach a traverse line and belay.
3 20m 5b Traverse right below the bulging wall for about 4m to a tiny platform on the edge of the smooth slabs. Climb directly up over an awkward bulge then go up to the right into an open groove overlooking *Stoat's Crack*. Climb this to a ledge below a smooth little scoop.
4 24m 4a Go up the scoop and walk to the right end of the ledge above. Follow slabs and ledges, trending right to a ledge below the final pitch of *Stoat's Crack*.
5 26m Finish up the pleasant rib about 6m to the left.
JA Austin, NJ Soper, A Faller 14.06.1970

Climbs above Jack's Rake **Pavey Ark** 53

Pavey Ark - Above Jack's Rake

16	Rake End Chimney	VS 4c ★★★
17	Rake End Wall	VS 4c ★★★
18	The Rib Pitch	HVS 5a ★★
19	The Braken Clock	E2 5c ★★★
20	Stoat's Crack	HS ★★

Langdale

Jack's Rake

East Gully

20 Stoat's Crack 112m HS ★★

This pleasant route finds the easiest way up a very big area of steep rock and provides enjoyment with a mountaineering air. Quite bold and exposed in places. Start just right of the foot of Jack's Rake, below a prominent left-slanting right-facing corner 16m up the crag.
1 16m Scramble up blocks and ledges rightwards to gain the grassy ledge below the corner.
2 20m Go up the crack for about 8m, break out left and ascend to a stance on the corner.
3 26m Traverse to the groove on the left and follow this and the open corner above to a capacious overhung ledge.
4 24m Step around to the left, along the grass terrace, and climb an open groove, finishing to the right. Traverse left along another ledge to a bilberry-filled groove. Climb this and grass above until it is possible to move right for 5m to belay below a sweep of slabs.
5 26m Climb pleasant slabs, delicately at first, then a short wall and slabs lead leftwards to a huge detached block. 30m of scrambling finishes the climb.
BR Record, JR Jenkins 28.06.1933

East Wall

The steep and impressive east-facing wall above East Gully offers some formidable pitches.

Approach: For *Mother Courage* scrabble up steep vegetated ground. *Astra* provides the way to routes 23, 24 and 25. Routes on the right-hand side can be reached by scrambling left along a break from the main gully.

Descent: Up and right then down East Gully.

21 Mother Courage 50m E4 6a ★★★

The steep mottled wall gives a memorable trip; excellent, sustained and strenuous climbing on reasonable holds. Not too well-protected. Start just left of a distinctive dirty groove gained by precarious scrambling from either left or right. Climb the narrow gully to reach a series of exposed sloping ledges (4a).
1 43m 6a Climb the wall to a narrow ledge just left of the tree. The wall above the short steep gangway on the left leads strenuously to a flat hold. Continue direct to a bulge, pull over rightwards then immediately back left to the foot of a steep groove (peg). Climb the groove and pull out right to a good hold. Climb towards a bush up on the right then boldly up a rib on the left to a bay.
2 7m 4c Step right onto the rib and climb this to the top. Belay well back.
E Cleasby, R Matheson 8.07.1976

22 Red Groove 42m E1 5b ★★

The shallow red groove above and right of the large holly tree is gained from the right and gives an enjoyable and interesting climb. The top pitch is a delightful technical exercise on superbly rough rock. Start about 15m left down the ramp, almost level with the tree and below easy rocks leading into a shallow right-facing groove.
1 28m 5b Climb easily up the wall for 5m. Semi-hand traverse left across the impending wall, pull up to a higher line and step left into a niche. Climb into the easier groove which leads to a juniper terrace.
2 14m 5a Climb the impending V-groove to the right.
JA Austin, E Metcalf 3.07.1960

23 Impact Day 33m E8 6c ★★★

An arrogant and tenuous route up the headwall. It provides sustained and strenuous climbing. Start left of the main corner where a mossy streak drops down from the half-way horizontal crack. Climb the vague rib left of the mossy streak to a hole then dynamically left then back right (peg). The left edge of the mossy streak leads to the horizontal break where the angle changes from merely vertical to impending. Protection can be arranged here and a 'shakeout'. Move left about one metre and make powerful moves on sloping holds and undercuts (crux) up and rightwards to gain good edges (peg). Climb straight up and make a desperate pull-up from a one-finger pocket to gain another sloping hold. This facilitates the final difficult moves necessary to enter the short shallow scoop overhead. Finish up this.
Photo page 56.
D Birkett 4.05.1999

24 Sixpence 33m E6 6b ★★★

A magnificently sustained and strenuous route up the impending wall and audacious hanging groove high in the wall. Start below the steep corner climbed by *Eclipse*. Climb the corner for 6m to a ledge on the right. Step up into the groove (runner) then traverse left onto the wall and climb direct to a jug on the horizontal break. Pull up and enter the groove. Initial progress is not easy; eventually a small ledge on the right can be reached, followed shortly by the top, strength permitting.
A Atkinson, KW Forsythe, RO Graham, TW Birkett 21.07.1981

Impact Day E8 (page 54) James Pearson — 📷 David Simmonite

25 Eclipse 45m E4 6a ★★

A superb pitch with a sketchy crux. Start below the corner at the top of P2 of *Astra*.
1 21m 6a Climb the corner, passing a ledge on the right, to a difficult and bold exit right onto a ledge.
2 24m 4c Follow the stepped corner above then pull out right into the base of the finishing groove.
P Whillance, P Botterill, S Clegg 26.04.1976

26 Astra 84m E2 5c ★★★★

Initially strenuous then delicate, this fabulous route gains the superb slim groove in the rib by way of some exposed wall climbing. Start mid-way up East Gully at a small gully between East Gully and the base of East Wall.
1 16m 4a Pull left onto a slab. Make a rising traverse left till a large flake enables a long stride into a grassy groove on the left.
2 8m 4b Climb a steep awkward little wall onto a narrow slab then move up to a stance below an impressive corner. Belay or continue up P3.
3 21m 5c Cross the slab to its right side make an exposed step round the rib and pull onto the steep undercut wall (hidden finger pocket out right) to gain the prominent flake on the right (protection). Climb up and left delicately to where the angle eases. Move up and right to a thin crack and make a long reach right round the rib for a hidden pocket; swing round onto a slab and small stance.
4 34m 5a Climb the narrowing slab right of the groove above on superb rock and continue in the same line to a ledge. The awkward blind V- groove ahead is climbed to another ledge and belay on the left.
5 5m Finish up the short crack then easy scrambling.
JA Austin, E Metcalf, DG Roberts 27.05.1960

27 Fallen Angel 46m E4 6a ★★★

A superb and technically demanding climb up the impressive impending right-slanting pea-pod groove. Start on a large ledge below the groove. Climb the wide crack leading into the pod. Up this, over a difficult bulge (crux) and continue until the groove opens out and the slab on the right can be gained. Climb this rightwards to a crack and good foothold. Follow the thin crack above for 6m and step right to another crack leading right to a bollard on the arête. Move left and into another groove which is climbed to the top.
E Grindley, I Roper 1972

28 Cascade 70m HVS 5a ★★★

The original route gives a flavour of the climbing. Start mid-way up East Gully in a small gully, at the same point as *Astra*.
1 21m 4c Step across the steep wall and pull round onto the belt of slabs. Go up the right-hand side of the slabs, almost overlooking the gully, to a grass ledge below a 3m corner.
2 21m 5a Climb the corner to a ledge below the main slab line. (This is somewhat out of keeping with the rest of the climb and, if unappealing, the slab can gained more easily by climbing round to the left and up into the corner.) The main corner is topped by a rock ledge. Continue up the corner almost to this ledge where steepening rock forces a few moves right and up onto a sloping ledge. Belay here, level with the rock ledge.
3 28m 5a Climb the short wall left of the crack-line above, moving rightwards toward the top to gain a grassy ledge. The bulging chimney above is filled with a huge cigar-shaped rock. Easier climbing up the cracks on either side of the cigar lead to the top.
JA Austin, RB Evans 26.05.1957

29 Cascade Direct 49m E3 5c ★★

A splendid pitch giving technical fingery climbing up the main vertical continuation grooveline. Start at the bottom of the 3m corner. Climb P2 of *Cascade* to its belay ledge and move left into the main corner again. The continuation corner groove is tantalisingly out of reach beyond a guarding wall. Some difficult climbing using the edge on its right gains the corner, all generally well-protected by small wires. Continue easily up the corner and exit left at the overhang to a ledge.
P Long, AD Barley 11.09.1971

30 Aquarius 49m HVS 5a ★★★

A fine pitch up the right-bounding rib of *Cascade*, with excellent climbing and good protection. It does, however, take a while to dry out. Approach by traversing in from the gully and belay at a flake crack below the 3m corner of *Cascade*. Climb a flake crack on the right arête to good holds that permit moves left onto the edge of the slab. Follow a thin grooveline up the right-hand edge of the slab with increasing difficulty near its top. Continue up the same line until it reaches the chimney and cigar on *Cascade*. Finish up this.
Photo page 3.
RM Biden, I Gray 1.08.2003

RAVEN CRAGS

Sunny, accessible and fun, with all-year climbing at every level. These enticing crags span the fell a short walk above the Old Dungeon Ghyll Hotel.

Langdale Pikes — Max Biden

MIDDLEFELL BUTTRESS

OS Grid Ref: NY 285 064
Altitude: 200m

Middlefell Buttress D (page 64) — David Simmonite

The clean sweep of rock marching up the fellside provides one of the most popular and accessible easy routes in the valley, regularly used for instruction, climbable in all conditions. To the left, the **Lower Gully Wall** has a couple of high-quality harder routes, while the steep **Mendes Wall** to the right has some very good mid-grade routes.

See overview page 58.

Approach: Walk round to the back of the ODG hotel then west through the gate. Cross the cobbled stream bed and bear right up towards trees and a defined track. At some fencing, go through the gate to continue along the engineered path diagonally rightwards to the foot of **Raven Crag**. **Middlefell Buttress** is to the left.

Descent: ⚠ From the top of **Middlefell Buttress**, traverse left, cross the gully to an exposed path down a broad shoulder, re-entering the gully near the bottom. For routes on the **Mendes Wall**, head left along the terrace then down Middlefell Gully. Or, abseil into the gully.

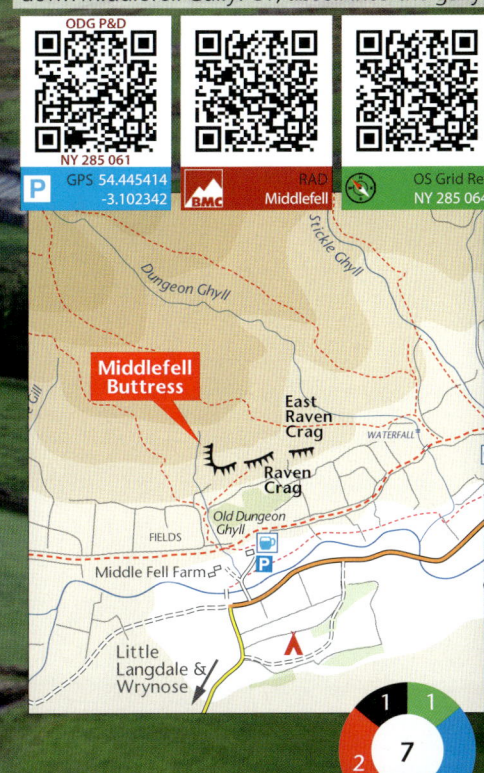

Lower Gully Wall

Approach: From the base of *Middlefell Buttress* walk left into the gully.

❶ **Armalite** 30m E4 6a ★★
An absorbing pitch up the middle of the dome, with protection that is easy to miss. The rock is a little suspect in places. Start from a sloping block beneath a vague crack in the centre of the wall. Climb the crack for 4m (peg), step down and move left and up to gain a long narrow foothold (hidden runner above). From the left end of the foothold, move up further leftwards on tiny incuts to a large hidden pocket (peg). Pull up onto the smooth slabby wall above (small wires) and climb this slightly leftwards into a shallow scoop which leads to easier ground.
E Cleasby, R Matheson 10.08.1979

❷ **Fear Control** 30m E2 5b ★★
A good direct on *Fear and Loafing*. Pull over the overlap then straight up to the overhang. Over the left side of this and up the wall above.
T Rogers, R Graham 11.05.2018

❸ **Fear and Loafing** 36m HVS 5a ★★★
The walls and groove at the right-hand side of *Armalite* give a very fine climb. Start from a pedestal ledge 4m right and lower than *Armalite*. Climb the steep wall above the ledge pulling through the overlap. A step right gives access to a shallow groove; follow this to a small overhang and move left to ascend the impending wall via excellent handholds. Finish up thin cracks on the left side of the arête.
Photo below.
M Scrowston, PC Bennett 2.11.2017

Fear and Loafing HVS (above) Steve Scott — 📷 David Simmonite

Middlefell Buttress

④ Middlefell Buttress 75m D ★★★★
The most popular climb in Langdale can be climbed in any season or conditions. No surprise then that the route is polished. Start below either side of a blocky chimney.
1 15m Climb either side of the chimney past a pinnacle to a ledge.
2 45m Climb a short slabby wall and follow the well-worn trail up the rounded rib to belay just below a large terrace. A particularly polished ramp at around 8m is awkwardly delicate but there are useful intermittent stances and belays.
3 15m Move up to the wall behind the terrace and re-belay. Start the wall by traversing in from either the right (original) or left (harder) to gain cracks and the final corner. Climb this, exiting right.
Photo page 60.
J Laycock, SW Herford, AR Thomson 24.09.1911

⑤ Prometheus 40m HVS 5a ★★
A high-quality route with a well-protected crux. Start one metre left of the large pinnacle.
1 30m 5a Climb the wall heading towards the foot of a groove. Strenuous moves lead to an exit right onto the rib. Delicate moves up lead to easier ground and a large terrace.
2 10m 4a Climb the juggy wall at the left end of the terrace and scramble upwards to belays.
Photo page 21.
M Scrowston, PC Bennett 6.11.2011

⑥ Mendes 48m VS 4c ★★
A terrific route with some excellent positions up the centre of the intimidating wall. Start on slabby rock below the overhang.
1 38m 4c Climb easily leftwards beneath and beyond the overhang until almost above the large pinnacle. Ascend a small slabby overlap and the wall above then traverse back right across to and up a shallow groove. Traverse right again for a couple of metres until good small holds lead straight up. A final pull up left gives access to easier-angled rock. Continue up to a grassy terrace beneath a short steep wall.
2 10m 4a Climb the steep wall via the obvious short crack.
P Woods, J Sutherland 2.02.1953

⑦ The Gamekeeper 42m E2 5c ★
A good steep pitch up the centre of the wall. Start at a vague crack about 2m right of the short hanging corner at the right end of the overhang.
1 33m 5c Climb the vague crackline until an awkward move right can be made into a shallow scoop at about 15m. Continue up leftwards to the right end of the grassy terrace.
2 9m Climb the groove behind to the top.
D Harding, E Grindley 22.07.1967

Pluto HVS (page 68) Catherine Plum — 📷 Keith Sanders

RAVEN CRAG
OS Grid Ref: NY 285 064
Altitude: 200m

Fine Time E5 (page 68) Stuart Wood & Dom Bush — David Simmonite

The large buttress directly above the Old Dungeon Ghyll Hotel provides a good range of routes across all the grades. The rock is clean, some part of the crag is in the sun pretty much all day and the approach takes minutes - what's not to like? It can be very popular.

Approach: Just through the gate behind the Old Dungeon Ghyll Hotel, a path heads off right from the Mickleden track through some trees and then onto a more distinct path up rightwards over screes.

Overview page 58.

Descent: Take care! For most routes head rightwards (facing in) to find an *in-situ* abseil point to reach ledges then scramble down. Do not descend leftwards into Raven Crag Gully. From the top of *Centipede,* contour rightwards across a stream then follow a path down steep terrain to the west of **East Raven Crag.**

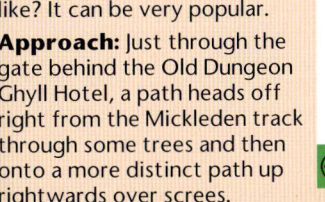

① **Evening Wall**   47m   S 4a   ★★
Interesting and varied climbing, best in the afternoon. Start in the gully bed 6m left of a pinnacle.
1 11m Climb for 4m until the wall steepens; make a traverse right into a shallow corner. Step right and move up to a small stance.
2 15m Climb to a ledge and traverse easily left to a short steep groove. Climb this over a bulge and traverse left again to a ledge.
3 21m 4a Strenuously delicate moves lead up and right onto the exposed arête which then leads to the top on good holds. It is possible to avoid the polished rock by making a bold semi-hand traverse on good holds round to the right and onto the rib, which soon rejoins the normal finish.
Photo page 70.
A Gregory, JW Tucker, J Woods 6.10.1947

② **Holly Tree Traverse**   49m   VD   ★★
An interesting left-to-right traverse across the easiest section of the buttress, with some fine positions. The first few metres of P2 are the crux. Alas, no longer possessing its holly tree but substitute 'Oak Tree' instead. Start at the foot of Raven Crag Gully, below a prominent 3m pinnacle.
1 6m Scramble up to belay behind the large pinnacle.
2 26m Climb the groove behind the pinnacle (or its left-hand rib) for 3m until it is possible to make an awkward traverse right to a sentry box on the *The Original Route.* Continue traversing up and right across a vegetated groove, heading for an obvious oak tree belay in the upper groove of *Holly Tree Direct.*
3 8m Climb the rib to the right of the groove and traverse right to a ledge below a small right-angled corner.
4 9m The corner is climbed on good holds to the top.
A Gregory, CH Peckett, J Woods 25.10.1949

③ **Oak Tree Wall**   45m   S 4a   ★★
Good interesting climbing needing careful protection. Start below a large oak tree, about 12m left of the toe of the buttress.
1 14m Not as overgrown as it looks. Climb a short corner crack to the tree, move right onto the wall and go up to a large ledge with a pinnacle at its left end.
2 31m 4a Move up the rib behind the pinnacle to a small ledge below a bulging wall. An awkward move gains an overhung gangway that leads up right to a small exposed stance at 17m. Step up left over the overlap then climb rightwards to below the final bulge, turned on its left by a shallow scoop.
A Gregory, J Woods 12.07.1947

④ **The Original Route**   61m   S 4a   ★★★ 💎
An excellent route taking a clean line of natural weakness. Start at the lowest point of the buttress, 5m right of a large tree.
1 12m 4a Follow well-worn rock up leftwards and either pull into an awkward crack which is followed to a ledge below a fine narrow pillar, or continue up left onto a ledge from where a quartzy wall leads to the same point.
2 15m 4a The pillar is initially awkward with small holds to a jug and mantleshelf. Move up to a long ledge (protection or belay). Continue easily left to a large pinnacle; belay.
3 34m Move back right then climb the wall trending slightly right to a group of ledges. Follow a conspicuous rising line to a groove. Move up then left under a bulge then across left to climb a steep section to reach easier ground.
S Watson, D Usher, R Holmes, W Cowen, N Middleton 10.08.1930

5 Holly Tree Direct 75m HVS 5a ★★★
A good route requiring an unexpectedly delicate touch on its sustained second pitch. It takes one of the best lines on the crag; the long groove in the centre of the buttress is obvious, despite the demise of the holly. Start as for The Original Route.
1 26m 4c Climb the wall and very shallow right-facing corner to a ledge below an obvious larger corner. Climb the corner to a large ledge and pinnacle just left of the steep upper section of the groove.
2 29m 5a Climb the left-hand groove for 3m and make a step right onto the bottom of a small slabby wall immediately above the initial overhang (runners higher up the groove). Extend out right onto a good foothold in the main groove, pull across and climb up to a resting place. Continue up the groove, steep and delicate at first, then easing where the groove opens out. Hanging belay.
3 20m 4c Step left and finish up the rib.
H Drasdo, E Mallinson 27.07.1952

6 Trilogy 31m E5 6a ★★★
A magnificent pitch up the great overhung corner that bounds the left side of the central wall. The old pegs are unreliable. Despite modern gear, especially small wires, it is still a bold proposition. Extra spice is added by some suspect rock. Climb the corner to a resting place below the large upper overhang. Pull through right of the corner to a tiny ledge on the left, step back right and continue directly to the top up a short steep groove to belay. Scrambling remains.
G West, J Hadfield, R Hughes (aid) 1957

7 Pluto 73m HVS 5a ★★★
A long sustained climb of increasing difficulty probing the central wall before being forced off right to finish up a delicate rib. A steep left-facing corner leads up to the left-hand end of the prominent long diagonal overlap.
1 20m 4c Climb the fine corner to a ledge and block belay.
2 27m 4c Traverse rightwards below the overlap (some suspect holds) until an awkward move across a groove leads to a commodious ledge.
3 36m 5a Step back left then climb the blunt rib on small holds trending rightwards. Above a small overlap traverse left on a prominent line, crossing a green groove, to gain easy ground. Belay well back.
Photo page 64.
AL Atkinson, JR Warner 1958

8 Dawes Rides a Shovelhead 31m E8 6c ★★★
A difficult, bold challenge, straight up the centre of the buttress. A sanguine approach is probably best, this not being a route for the nervous. Poor condition of the final two pegs will increase the grade for an on-sight lead. Pull through the roof at the shallow scoop and up the wall (2 pegs). Make hard moves first right of, then into, a small left-facing corner and reach up right to a good hold (2 poor sawn-off pegs). Make a long reach, or jump, to the lip of the roof then embrace fine holds for the powerful move to finish.
D Birkett 17.05.1991

9 R'n'S Special & Edge Finish 35m E5 6a ★★★★
A stimulating trip, with the minimum of protection, across the bottom of the wall; sustained, delicate climbing which has become harder with the loss of a couple of holds. Start below the corner of Trilogy. Traverse rightwards under the overlap, as for Pluto, until possible to climb across the roof into a shallow scoop. Climb a short way (nuts); make a very thin traverse right just above the roof (below an old bolt) to finally move right to a better hold and small pocket. Move up then right, all still very thin, to gain a good foothold on the rib. **Edge Finish:** Climb the exposed edge directly over bulges on positive sharp holds on the right to reach a fine jammed block. Swing up and left into a groove and pull over to easier ground.
G Summers, E Cleasby (1 pa) 1.05.1977;
R Matheson, K Phizacklea 24.09.2012

10 Fine Time 46m E5 6b ★★
Brutally strenuous and uncompromising. Scramble to the foot of a rib below and left of the overhanging crack and a mass of ivy. Climb the rib to a ledge below the roof. Step right to the crack, climbed with total determination (peg) to reach another slanting crack. Climb this then continue more easily to a second overhang, pass this on the left on good holds to reach the finishing slab.
Photo page 66.
P Livesey, J Hammond 1972

⑪ Bilberry Buttress Eliminate with the Green Groove Finish   65m   E2 5c ★★

A superb diverse and interesting way up the crag. Start immediately left of *Bilberry Buttress*.
1 20m 5b Climb a slabby rib to gain a triangular niche a few metres left of the wide crack. Pull over onto the slab above and climb this direct to the belay.
2 18m 5b Can be combined with P1 to create more continuous interest. Stay close to the rib with a short diversion to the left side of the crux bulge on P2 of *Bilberry Buttress*. The upper half is clean and delicate but with little protection.
3 27m 5c Step down left into the prominent groove. Climb this with a very precarious move to the left to avoid a bulge at 8m (long reach or flexibility useful, preferably both). Regain the groove and climb to a rising diagonal leftward traverse which leads to the top.
P1: M Bagness, J Kelly P3: R Matheson, M Matheson 2007/1972

⑫ Bilberry Buttress   73m   VS 4c ★★★

Classic VS climbing with two challenging cracks and a questing airy finish. Start at the lowest point of the right side of the crag below a curving hand-jam crack.
1 20m 4b Scramble up to the foot of the crack and follow it to a ledge.
2 18m 4c Climb the thin crack in the steep wall passing a bulge to a magnificent finishing hold. Follow the ridge to a large sloping ledge.
3 35m 4b Traverse the ledge rightwards to a shallow crack. Climb this for a couple of metres and make a short traverse left beneath a large detached block to a scoop. Continue traversing across a green groove to an easy finish.
CF Rolland, JF Renwick 27.06.1941

⑬ Savernake   59m   MS ★

A pleasant route weaving the easiest way up this part of the crag. Start at the lowest point of the crag just right of *Bilberry Buttress*.
1 20m Scramble up to a large V-crack which is followed to a ledge.
2 21m Walk down left, then go up broken rocks in the corner which gradually steepens to a fine exposed finish.
3 18m Traverse the sloping ledge to its upper right end and climb a broken corner for 2m until a step left can be made into a dirty scoop. Continue up over a detached block to reach a ledge. Escape right.
JEQ Barford, MP Ward 5.09.1943

⑭ Elevation   43m   HS 4a ★★

A good companion route to *Revelation*; more sustained and well-protected, but not quite as varied. Start at a small polished scoop at the foot of the buttress as for *Revelation*. Climb the scoop and after 5m, step left onto a rough slab and climb the thin crack in this to a steepening. Step either left or right to gain a flake. Move left beneath the overlap to gain the crack above and ascend the wall, trending eventually rightwards to the oak tree.
Photo page 72.
M Scrowston, F Scrowston 03.06.2012

⑮ Revelation   43m   HS 4a ★★★

A splendid gem on clean rock, especially attractive in the early morning sun. Start at a small polished scoop at the foot of the buttress.
1 12m Climb the scoop and, trending slightly rightwards, continue on small well-marked holds to a ledge below an overhanging wall.
2 31m 4a Exciting climbing on small incut holds up the short overhanging wall and strenuous crack (crux) leads to a small ledge on the left. Move up and traverse right round a projecting nose. Climb its right-hand side to a sloping ledge at 15m then up over bulging rocks to the oak tree.
A Gregory, B Black, J Woods 29.03.1948

Evening Wall S (page 67) Robin Smithurst
📷 Nick Wharton

(16) Kneewrecker Chimney   38m   HVS 5a   ★★

An interesting and aptly-named route with a strenuous well-protected top pitch. Start below the prominent hanging flake crack, and just left of a broken tree stump.
1 27m 4b Climb the wall on the left until an open scoop can be gained. Follow the scoop to a sloping ledge. Step back to the right and climb the strenuous flake crack.
2 11m 5a Attack the overhanging V-chimney behind the tree. Resorting to the use of at least one knee to gain a tiny ledge on the right is probably compulsory for all those who are not either double-jointed or of smaller build. Step up and move left round the corner on good holds. Climb more easily to the top.
AR Dolphin, J Bloor 7.06.1949

(17) Centipede Direct   31m   E2 6a   ★

Start at the thin hairline crack.
1 11m 6a Climb the desperate crack (peg) to belay on the right below the overhang.
2 20m 5c Climb to the overhang. Step right below it and pull up (peg) to a small ledge. Continue up the arête to a ledge.
P Freyburger, T Walkington Jul 1980

(18) Centipede   90m   S 4a   ★★

An excellent route taking the natural line of weakness up the triangular buttress. Start below and just right of a wide hanging crack which is just right of the base of a pinnacle flake on the lower section of the buttress.
1 18m Climb the steep rib on good holds until a short traverse left enables the upper part of the wide crack to be gained by a tricky move. Follow this to a ledge. Belay on the giant flake.
2 15m From the top of the flake, move rightwards and climb to a mantelshelf (poor protection). Continue until a traverse left under the overhang leads round to a stance in the corner below a diagonal crack.
3 15m Step down and traverse horizontally across the wall on the right to a small ledge at the base of the arête above the overhang. Follow the arête to a ledge. Belay well back at the foot of the next pitch.
4 42m Climb onto a rickety flake that may now have disappeared and continue up a series of slabs separated by steeper trickier steps.
A Gregory, C Peckett 10.07.1948

Elevation HS (page 70) Catherine Plum — KEITH SANDERS

EAST RAVEN CRAG

OS Grid Ref: NY 287 065
Altitude: 240m

A short valley outcrop with a variety of single pitch routes on compact rock.
Approach: Continue past **Raven Crag** across the scree and hillside.
Descent: Left of the crag.

1 Mamba 18m S 4a ★★
A steep and pleasant wall. Climb the tapering slabby rib. Step left at its top and make a tricky move onto a ledge.
Photo opposite.
AR Dolphin, J Bloor 28.05.1950

2 Ophidia 18m VS 4c ★★
Climb the capped V-groove and wall above, trending right.
RM Biden, I Gray 7.07.1994

3 By Jingo 18m E1 5a ★★
Fine wall climbing with just adequate protection. Climb a vague raggedy crack then boldly up the wall above to finish.
SJH Reid, C Read, C Jones, A MacDonald 16.04.2000

4 Jingo 18m VS 4b ★
Another pleasant wall climb but a little thin on protection. Climb up into the right-hand of two short grooves. From the top of this, pull up leftwards and continue to the top.

5 Speckled Band 20m VD ★
Good climbing up the obvious right-slanting gangway, passing a spike ledge, for some 14m then back left on shelving rock.
J Bloor, P Tuke, J Renwick 28.05.1950

6 Rowan Tree Groove 36m HVS 4c ★★
Not technically hard, but committing and poorly protected in places. Start up the shallow flaky groove in the wall to a blunt pinnacle; step up and then go left to gain the slab below the groove. Enter the groove with difficulty and climb it to the overhangs. Traverse right to the rib and follow it to the top.
JA Austin, JM Ruffe, R Jackson 19.05.1957

7 Ramrod 30m HVS 4c ★★
Good climbing up the slim groove system. Care required with rock at the start which is not well-protected. Start directly below the top groove. Climb up and left to a blunt pinnacle and continue up the left-hand rib of a short smooth V-groove to a ledge below the overhangs. Pull directly over and climb the slim groove above.
JA Austin, I Roper, T Parker 17.09.1966

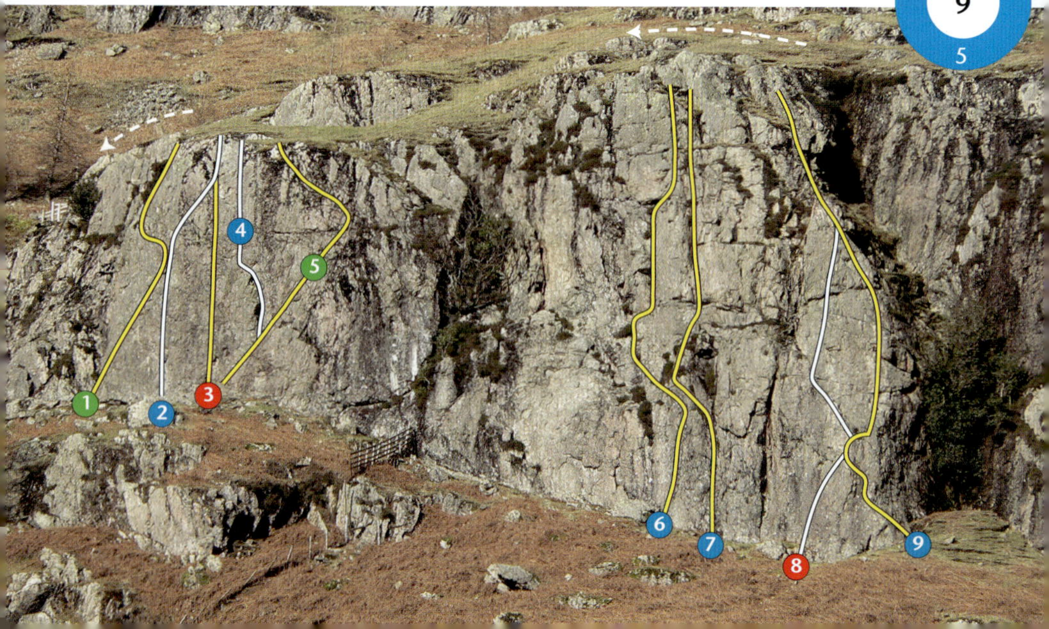

8 **The Chopper** 30m E1 5b ★★
The attractive steep clean wall. Start below the middle of the wall. Climb the wall rightwards to a ledge. Ascend the left-slanting crack; gain the cracks in the wall above. Follow these to a ledge then up the slim pillar above to the top.
I Williamson, P Cornforth 1983

9 **Baskerville** 30m VS 4c ★★
The steep rib gives a delightful, but fingery, pitch on lovely clean rock. Starting from the rib on the right, climb a shallow groove leftwards to a ledge at 5m. Step right and follow the left-hand side of the rib. Pulling over a short bulging wall gives food for thought (runner on the right), but leads to easier ground.
AR Dolphin, J Bloor 24.04.1949

Langdale

Coniston

Mamba S (opposite) Simon Willis — DAVID RANBY

GIMMER CRAG

OS Grid Ref: NY 277 070
Altitude: 525m

Springbank E2 (page 86) — 📷 David Simmonite

A wide range of tremendous routes and a rich history make **Gimmer** the Pride of Langdale. The rock is clean and solid with a stunning outlook commanding the valley floor. This and its southerly aspect make it one of the finest venues in the district. It is rightly popular. With a number of adjacent faces some truly impressive link-ups are possible. The crag catches the sun for most of the day although can be exposed to the wind. The **North-West Face** catches the afternoon and evening sun.

Approach: From Stickle Barn and the National Trust car park, take the main path for Dungeon Ghyll and the Langdale Pikes. After 500m, go over a stile, cross the gill and follow a path for approximately 1km until it flattens out onto an open plateau. Continue west heading for the crag which soon comes into view. At a large cairn where the main path starts to rise more steeply, take a faint track leftwards, descending slightly at the end to meet the crag at the main gearing-up point below the **South-East Face**.

Overview page 58.

Appraoch, ODG: Take the path towards **Raven Crag** to the gate in the fence. Turn left onto a track below the fence crossing a stile then climb scree. Continue in the same direction for 50m to a clearer path leading right then left across terraces. Follow this diagonally leftwards, crossing a ravine, then horizontally to reach the base of the crag. Alternatively, take the track along Mickleden to Grave Gill, then trudge arduously up to the crag.

Langdale

North-West Face (Upper Section)

Approach: Follow the path around the toe of the crag and up beneath the Lower Section of the **North-West Face**.

Descent: Make a 15m scramble up from behind the summit block, then pick your way across rock ledges into a gully. Exit by scrambling down this to finally gain the ridge.

① Carpetbagger 70m VS 4c ★★
Fine climbing on good rock. Some 20m up the gully above *The Crack* a large rock creates two dry waterfalls. Scramble up the right-hand fall then cross a vertical field to reach a grassy bay. Belay here, below a groove (rope advised).
1 22m 4c Climb diagonally right to reach a ledge right of the groove then up the overhung slab to gain a slim tapering groove on the right. Climb the groove then continue right of a rib for 10m to reach a ledge. Traverse right beneath a dubious flake. Belay below a large overhang.
2 27m 4c Make an ascending traverse left below small overhangs. Just before reaching the arête, move up onto a slab then continue up a tricky groove to a corner below a dirty-looking mossy line.
3 21m 4c Semi-hand-traverse right below the overlap then finish by climbing the arête.
N Allinson, NJ Soper 9.06.1968

② Grand Finale 68m E1 5b ★★★
A splendid route culminating in an exposed very well-protected perplexing crux.
1 26m 4c Climb the groove, 10m right of *Carpetbagger*, moving left to climb the left side of the arête.
2 12m 5a Climb the rib on the left side of a slab then step right and continue (spike) to a tiny stance.
3 30m 5b Climb to the overhang. Traverse left then up to an overhanging crack (gear). Reach right to a downward-pointing spike then use hidden holds to gain a ledge. Belay here to provide moral support; then continue up the groove trending left to finish.
C Read, GL Swainbank 25.10.1997

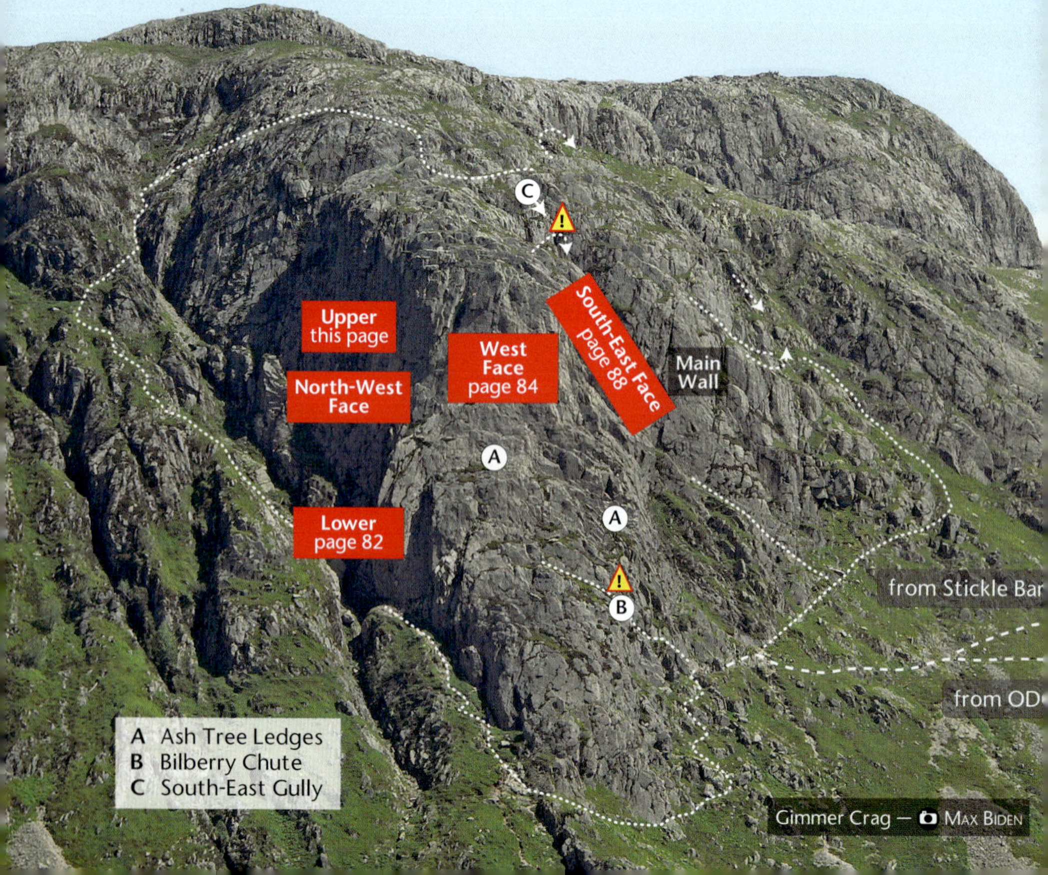

A Ash Tree Ledges
B Bilberry Chute
C South-East Gully

Gimmer Crag — Max Biden

❸ Inertia 93m HVS 5a ★★
Satisfying superbly exposed climbing, once above the indifferent start. Start 2m left of *The Crack*.
1 42m Climb the steep wall then easily up and left to a corner. Move across the scoop on the right then take the rib to a ledge. Step left then climb the slab to a vegetated corner; up this for 10m to a ledge at the foot of a prominent corner.
2 27m 5a Gain the top of a small pedestal then pull round the overhang into the groove on the right. Make a few moves up then exit right onto a rib. Move up this with difficulty then across right to a sentry box. Climb the crack on the left until stopped by a roof; step right then step right to a small stance.
3 24m 5a On the left, a long narrow slab slanting up to the left finishes against a line of small square-cut overhangs. Climb the slab then the corner crack where it steepens, to the end of these overhangs. Climb rightwards along a slanting groove to finish.

❹ Outside Tokyo/ Dight 68m E1 5b ★★★
An excellent historical hybrid taking the best line up the slabby wall immediately left of *The Crack*. Interesting and quite technical climbing. Good protection.
1 21m 5b Easily up the corner and left to the foot of a slim groove with a series of slanting steps leading to a pedestal belay.
2 31m 5b Mantelshelf as for *The Crack* and step right to a thin crack which leads to ledges below some overlaps. Pull over the first with difficulty, stepping right into the thin crack above. Follow this past a second and smaller overhang then climb more easily to a sentry box on the left. Ascend the crack on the left to some more small overhangs and go right beneath these to a small stance.
3 16m 5a Climb the corner above for a couple of metres before pulling up strenuously, round a small rib, into the groove on the right. Ascend this to easier ground.

❺ The Crack 74m VS 4c ★★★★
A combination of a fine natural line, exposed and sustained climbing and excellent rock make this one of Lakeland's grandest crack climbs, undoubtedly deserving its classic status. Start at the foot of an easy-angled corner which leads up to the foot of the crack.
1 26m 4c Scramble into the corner and climb the clean-cut crack until a delicate traverse across the left wall leads to the foot of a short groove. Climb this to a ledge and pedestal belay.
2 26m 4c Climb the thin cracks above the belay to gain the horizontal break (the Mantelshelf) which leads left to a large ledge at 8m. A hard pull up on the steep ridge leads to better holds and an easy traverse back right into the crack; The Sentry Box. A strenuous pull out of this leads to a ledge; The Bower.
3 22m 4c The deep corner crack provides a sustained pitch, with a problematic overhang en-route.
AB Reynolds, GG Macphee 5.05.1928

❻ Gimmer String 78m E1 5b ★★★★
A brilliant combination of pitches, strung together to provide varied and enjoyable climbing in exposed situations. Low in its grade but with difficulty increasing as height is gained.
1 26m 4c P1 of *The Crack*.
2 25m 4c Traverse right to the top of a pinnacle spike beneath a roof and step right to below the wide crack. Pull awkwardly into it and continue to a stance.
3 27m 5b Climb straight up for a short way to some dubious blocks, then traverse left to a small ledge on the rib which is both undercut and overhung. Climb a thin crack on the right of the rib for about 5m until a difficult pull leads round to the other side of the rib overlooking *The Crack*. Climb the arête trending left to a thin crack which leads up a short problematic wall until forced out right to an abrupt finish.
Photo opposite.
JA Austin, E Metcalf, D Miller 15.07.1963

❼ Midnight Movie 77m E4 6b ★★★
An excellent direct line providing a fine and varied way up the crag. Pitches 2 and 3 give a stunning piece of climbing when run together.
1 25m 5b Climb *The Crack* for 12m to a ledge. Climb up twin cracks in the impending wall above past a hanging niche to belay on a grass ledge.
2 16m 6b The thin crack in the slabby wall above is well-protected, apart from the final section, and gives some hard climbing on screamingly small holds leading to the *Kipling Groove* undercling. Take a belay down to the right, or continue:
3 36m 6a Pull through the middle of the roof as for *Equus* and follow this for 6m. Pull right into a crackline which proves technical and strenuous. This leads to the crux of *Kipling Groove*, up which it finishes.
R Graham, TW Birkett Spring 1982

GIMMER LINK-UPS

These great combinations marry classic routes on the lower and upper sections providing memorable and long adventures.

- ☐ **Ash Tree Slabs** & **'A' Route** — MS
- ☐ **Aterisk** & **'D' Route** — MVS
- ☐ **North-West Arête** & **'F' Route** — VS
- ☐ **Intern** & **Whit's End Direct** — E1
- ☐ **Crystal** & **Kipling Groove** — E1

Gimmer String E1 (opposite) Scott Quinn — 📷 Nadir Khan

North-West Face (Lower Section)

Approach: Follow the path around the toe of the crag and up to a platform area by *Ash Tree Slabs*.

Descent: An *in-situ* abseil point may be in place above the **North-West Face**. Alternatively scramble off rightwards (facing in) with care, down the Bilberry Chute.

8 Detour 36m VS 4c ★★
Delightful climbing which straightens out *Asterisk* and gives a well-protected route up the middle of the wall. Climb the wide crack direct to the crescent ledge. From its right-hand end follow the crack up left to a right-slanting scoop. Climb this to the small roof at the top which is then negotiated by an exhilarating move left on excellent holds. The thin crack above leads to the top.
SJH Reid, N Timmins 9.06.1995

9 Asterisk 38m MVS 4b ★★★
A splendid pitch, mostly on jugs. Modern protection has taken much of the '...risk' away. Start at a rock ledge slanting up right, opposite the top of the large jammed boulder in the gully bed. The crescent-shaped ledge 7m above is gained by traversing the rock ledge rightwards until good holds lead up a short groove to its right-hand end. Follow the series of steps diagonally up right for 6m to a small niche and vertical crack in the centre of the wall. Climb this until the crack fades. Move up to where the crack reappears and follow it to the top, initially on small holds. It is also possible to finish up the wall on the left of the crack.
HS Gross, G Basterfield, B Tyson 13.05.1928

10 North-West Arête 42m VS 4b ★★★★
A beautifully exposed route on good rock and generally excellent holds. Start at the left end of an obvious very thin quartz ledge in the gully wall by the large jammed boulder. Climb easily right to gain the wall. Ascend the wall to a small overlap. Traverse right and up a crack which leads to the foot of a groove cutting through the left side of the overhangs. Climb this groove on good holds and move right immediately above the overhang to gain the arête. Climb it more or less directly to a final thin flake crack in the crest which needs to be treated with care.
RJ Birkett, V Veevers 15.09.1940

11 Intern 48m E1 5b ★★★
Excellent and sustained, combined with *Whit's End Direct* makes a superb way up. Start at a level platform below a right-slanting crack.
1 18m 5b Climb the crack for a few metres until it is possible to step left to gain the narrowing left-slanting slab. Cross to its left edge, which overlooks the gully, using holds on the slab above. Pull up into a short groove and climb this to the foot of a left slanting gangway. A technical and sustained pitch.
2 30m 5a Climb the gangway for a short distance before moving back right to climb the wall above the belay. Crossing the bulge above necessitates some bold moves that lead into a steep groove. Follow this to a rib on the left which is climbed to finish up the thin crack in its crest.

12 Ash Tree Slabs 48m VD ★★★
This great and ever-popular little climb takes the handsome sweep of slabs 25m up the gully from the huge detached flake. Continuing up '*D*' *Route* makes an excellent combination. Start by scrambling up into a small bay at the foot of the slabs.
1 16m Climb 3m up the corner and traverse diagonally left on good holds to the edge of the slab and follow this to a ledge. Or climb the left edge of the slab directly to the end of the diagonal traverse at the same grade.
2 32m Climb 3m up to the left to a platform from which a groove leads up to the right. Follow this until it eases and continue up slabs to finish on Ash Tree Ledges.
GS Bower, AW Wakefield 20.06.1920

13 Ash Tree Corner 48m VS 4c ★★
The fine corner forming the right-hand side of *Ash Tree Slabs* is followed to the top starting in the bay at the foot of the slabs.
R Graham, J Graham 23.04.1981

14 Crystal 38m E1 5b ★★
An excellent sustained pitch up the steep wall overlooking *Ash Tree Slabs*. Climb the very steep crack in the wall and move left to below a vague grooveline. Stepping left and climbing up neatly negotiates each of the bulges, until a more direct line leads to easier ground
TW Birkett, A Atkinson, D Lyle 1.06.1981

15 Introduction 32m MVS 4b ★★
A delightful slab climb up the elegant slim groove in a fine position. Easy ground on the right leads round into a short corner at the foot of the slab. Climb the left edge of the groove in the slab. Surmounting a bulge high up the groove is the crux.
DJ Cameron, AB Durrant 23.04.1948

16 Herdwick Buttress 27m VD ★★
A pleasant route and the easiest way onto the front face.
1 12m Scramble up rightwards into the open corner. Climb this on good holds, pulling out right onto the rib which leads to a ledge.
2 15m Climb up a left-facing flake and follow the thin twin cracks above which lead to the terraces and belays. Scrambling then leads to Ash Tree Ledges and the alphabet routes.
F Graham 18.03.1925

West Face
The centrepiece of the crag, this fine sweep of clean rock catches most of the sun. The routes start from a series of ledges running across the face known as Ash Tree Ledges, though all signs of the trees have long gone.

Approach: Climb one of the routes on the lower section or scramble, with care, up the vegetated ledges of the Bilberry Chute.

Descent: Abseil from the top of the face between 'A' Route and 'C' Route. This area is often busy so beware of climbers below. Alternatively, descend South-East Gully. ⚠ This is exposed in places and loose. Enter from behind the summit block. Initially narrow with perched blocks; some 30m down across the central rib then scramble down short walls to finish down the left-hand corner (facing out).

South-East Gully can be avoided. From behind the summit block, traverse right on ledges then, well-back from the crag, descend steep grass.

17 Kipling Groove 52m HVS 5a ★★★★
A magnificent and popular classic route taking an impressive and 'Rudyard' line up the steep front face of the buttress. Start from the left end of Ash Tree Ledges.
1 10m Scramble easily leftwards to the ledge below the overhangs.
2 11m 4c Traverse the undercling left beneath the roof to a crack which leads to an overhung recess. Clipping both ropes into protection placed in the crack beyond the roof will avoid them jamming in the crack at the left end of the undercling.
3 31m 5a Climb the right wall of the recess, past a dubious block, to the overhang. Step right onto the edge and follow a crack to a resting place beneath the bulge. Now for a choice of cruxes. Pull up and reach strenuously rightwards to a diagonal crack (protection). Then, either continue along a horizontal crack which gives a fingery traverse right, or pull up again and stand on a small ledge and then foot traverse the horizontal crack. From the ledge, ascend a crack to easier ground and the top. A first class pitch.
Photo page 89.
AR Dolphin, JB Lockwood 17.05.1948

18 Equus 40m E2 5c ★★★
Another excellent and varied pitch. A difficult initial overhang, technical bridging up the slim groove and a bold finish, combine to give a sustained outing. Move up leftwards to the centre of the roof. Pull over and continue up the groove on small holds until forced left to a junction with *Kipling Groove*. Up this a short way to a resting place beneath a bulge. Swing left to a small ledge and climb the groove and exposed wall on the right to gain a horizontal crack which is followed leftwards to finish.
E Cleasby 21.04.1976

19 Eastern Hammer 38m E3 6a ★★★
A masterpiece of excellent fingery climbing up the bulging wall. Start by scrambling up to the ledge below the overhangs. Pull over the overhang onto the steep wall and climb (peg) to a crack and a good hold beneath the final bulges. Step up, move to the left end of the bulge and pull across it rightwards to a small ledge. Finish more easily up cracks.
P Livesey, A Manson 22.05.1974

20 Poacher 45m E1 5b ★★
Splendidly exposed and bold climbing. Start left of a prominent left-slanting flake crack.
1 10m Scramble leftwards to a ledge below the overhangs; as P1 *Kipling Groove*.
2 23m 5b Climb the crack rightwards, pull across the overhang and climb to a second square-cut roof. Holds above this allow bold moves left (spike), then climb a slim groove to a well-positioned ledge.
3 12m 5b Traverse a break rightwards to the arête. Crucial moves up the wall on the left lead to easier climbing. The groove above the stance is 4c.
JA Austin, E Metcalf 21.07.1963

21 'F' Route 40m VS 4c ★★★
A classic crack climb with the crux fittingly near the top. Scramble leftwards as for *Kipling Groove*. Climb rightwards beneath an overhang and up onto small ledges. A flake now leads left to a small ledge beneath the overhangs. Move up right into the corner proper and follow it to a fine and bold finish.
RJ Birkett, V Veevers 4.05.1941

22 Whit's End Direct 38m E1 5b ★★★ ◆
An enjoyable route with some fine slab climbing and a neat section through the roof. Start at a slanting flake crack. Ascend the crack and continue direct up a line of slim cracks to a resting point a couple of metres below the overlap. Step right and move up to reach left to the left end of the overlap. Climb into the hanging corner and make an exhilarating move right onto the slab; finish more easily on small, but positive holds.
JA Austin, R Valentine 2.10.1972

23 Spring Bank 38m E2 5c ★★★
The brilliant 'non-line' up the centre of the blank slab and through the middle of the overlap gives a superb well-protected pitch. Start at the bottom right-hand corner of the smooth slabs. Follow the rib and then thin cracks in the slab to the middle of the roof. Arrange yourself around the lip and pull over on small holds to continue more easily up the slab to the top.
Photo page 76.
MG Mortimer, E Cleasby, MG Allen, M Lynch, J Lamb 1.06.1979

24 'D' Route 30m S ★★★
A brilliant pitch, with character despite its brevity. It follows the fine crackline delineating the right-hand side of the smooth slab-like wall that sweeps up to a square-cut roof. The initial section is quite delicate. Start 5m right of smooth slabs, on a small terrace some 20m above Ash Tree Ledges, gained by scrambling up from a point 6m left of a perched flake. Climb up easily, then make a dainty 5m traverse left to gain the right-slanting groove. Follow this for 5m to a ledge. Climb the Forked Lightning Crack above to join *'A' Route* below its final crack. Finish up this.
GS Bower, PR Masson 31.05.1919

25 Oliverson's Variation 56m VD ★★★
and Lyon's Crawl
This is the easiest way up the front of the crag and provides varied and interesting climbing on superb rock. Start from Ash Tree Ledges, 12m left of a short wall scratched with the letters ABCE, at a spike belay just right of a prominent detached flake perched against the face.
1 10m Climb easily rightwards to a belay on a narrow ledge.
2 16m Traverse right for 5m, then up more directly to gain the left edge of the Forty Foot Corner. Climb this for 7m to an obvious rightwards crack; the start of Lyon's Crawl.
3 15m Traverse up and right to a large ledge.
Continue rightwards into Green Chimney, then across its right wall into the Crow's Nest.
4 15m Step right and follow pleasant slabs to the top.

26 'A' Route 75m MS ★★★
A great climb on excellent rock, so typical of this part of the crag. It takes a series of steps rising to the left. Start left of the letters ABCE on the rock.
1 18m Scramble up and right to gain a spacious platform. Belay 9m further right, below a polished crack.
2 5m Climb the crack to gain the midpoint of a ledge.
3 9m Traverse left along the ledge to the foot of the Forty Foot Corner.
4 18m Delightful climbing just left of the corner leads to a spike then traverse left and slightly up to a ledge at the foot of an open groove, traditionally known as Lichen Chimney.
5 11m Climb Lichen Chimney to flake and crack belays.
6 14m The rock staircase on the left leads across to a steep finishing corner crack.
E Rigby, D Leighton, J Sandison 7.04.1903

27 'C' Route 62m S ★★★★
A classic route giving some fine climbing in good positions, following a fairly direct line. Start by the letters.
1 18m Scramble up and right to gain a spacious platform. Belay 9m further right, below a polished crack.
2 27m Three metres left of the belay, a short but steep wall containing a flake leads into a steep recess, which is climbed with difficulty to a large ledge. Move right to a flake at the foot of a groove. Enter this groove via the right side of the flake and climb it, eventually trending up left to belay at a small ledge below a prominent square-cut overhang.
3 17m Climb to the overhang and pull round left beneath it to a ledge. Climb the groove above, moving right at a flaky spike to finish direct in an exposed position.
AP Wilson, CH Jackson, A Brundritt 3.08.1918

28 'B' Route 69m S ★★★
An entertaining and ever popular climb. Towards the right end of Ash Tree Ledges, where it slopes down to the right, a large platform can be seen up on the right, guarded by a short wall with the letters ABCE scratched on it. Start left of the letters.
1 18m Scramble up and right to gain a spacious platform after 9m. Belay 9m further right, below a polished crack.

2 10m Climb the crack to gain the midpoint of a large ledge. Follow this easily rightwards for 6m to the foot of the formidable impending corner. The evidence of engineering work on the crack was the consequence of releasing a jammed knee - be careful!
3 5m Amen Corner. This is it; the battle you have been relishing. The overhanging and leaning corner is awkward but succumbs to a positive approach. A polished climbing technique is the best antidote to the equally well-polished veneer on the holds. Belay.
4 9m Ascend a broad ramp leftwards to a ledge beneath the corner.
5 12m Climb the slabby left wall of the corner until a short traverse across its right wall leads round the corner to a stance; The Crow's Nest.
6 15m Step right and follow pleasant slabs to the top.
HB Lyon, J Stables, AS Thomson 7.07.1907

South-East Face
The right side of the crag is split by South-East Gully, a main descent route. The wall to the left is the **South-East Face**.

Approach: Scramble up steep ground above the gearing up point or follow the gully further to reach the start of your chosen route.

Descent: South-East Gully.

29 Bracket and Slab Climb 97m S ★★★★
An excellent long and varied route. Start at a slabby rib leading up to a large spike-flake.
1 31m Climb the easy-angled rib to its spike-flake top. Step left into a groove and follow this, or the rib on its right, passing several awkward steps up into a grassy bay. Continue to the back of the bay behind the large blocks and belay beneath an overhanging V-groove.
2 12m The Bracket is the large block stuck on the wall up and right. Climb up to the right of the groove leading to the niche and make a devious traverse horizontally rightwards for 6m. Traversing the Bracket gains a groove just to its right which leads up and leftwards to a stance in an alcove.
3 26m Climb out rightwards from the alcove and traverse diagonally rightwards over easy ground, well below the overhanging Amen Corner, to just before the left edge of the first chimney pitch of *Gimmer Chimney*. The Neat Bit follows a leftwards-rising ramp, then climb the steep wall to a huge sloping ledge system, The Gangway. After placing gear to protect the second, traverse easily rightwards along this to the foot of the left-hand of two chimneys.
4 9m Amen Chimney - the narrow, slightly overhanging left-hand chimney is better protected than it appears, best suited to thin masochists who will bury themselves in it seeking security of sorts. Stouter individuals or those preferring a more consistent grade will opt for the easier chimney round to the right.
5 19m Traverse onto the rib on the left of the gully and follow it keeping close to its right-hand edge, but moving left a little just below the top.
HB Lyon, J Herbert 8.08.1923

30 Crow's Nest Direct 91m HVS 5a ★★
Good climbing that stretches most people. Start at a clean slab, split by a prominent right-to-left slanting crack.
1 26m 4b Climb the crack, passing an overlap at 9m; continue to belay in the rocky corner beneath an overhanging V-groove.
2 14m 4c An easy crack leads into a niche level with an open groove on the left. Gaining this groove proves problematic; once achieved, climb it to a ledge.
3 17m 5a At the back of the ledge, just right of the crack, is a small pedestal. Starting on this, climb the difficult bulging wall above to a large ledge. Just to the right, a narrow layback crack (5m left of Amen Corner) leads to a broad ramp; The Gangway. Move up to belay below a prominent thin crack in the wall above.
4 10m 4c A sensational rising semi-hand traverse across the overhanging wall on the right leads to an exit onto a small ledge above the overhang. Move up left to a belay above the traverse. Alternatively, climb the steep thin crack above the start of the hand traverse.
5 24m Climb leftwards and up into The Crow's Nest. Step left into a corner and follow this and the slabs above to the summit.
S Thompson, P White, A Mullan, V Bolton, J Ashton 1940

31 Remembrance 105m HVS 5a ★★
A varied route with a distinct crux. The route is usually still climbable if P2 is wet and the rest looks dry. Start at the clean slab, split by a prominent right-to-left slanting crack.
1 35m 4b Climb the crack, over the overlap and up into a groove which leads after 3m into another grooveline running back diagonally right. Pull into this and follow it until it steepens. Traverse delicately right to join *Gimmer Chimney* P1 and follow this to the belay.
2 20m 5a Climb the short rib above by its right edge to a ledge. Step right to start the

South-East Face | **Gimmer Crag** | 89

Langdale

overhanging groove above (large cams). Good holds in the groove lead via a further step right after a couple of metres to a belay below the right-hand twin chimney.
3 35m 4b On the right is a turf ledge. From its right end, climb along a fault and up over a bulging wall. Once established on the slab above, follow the flake crack leftwards to a smooth slab. Up this and the short crack in the steepening buttress above. Continue in the same line to a narrow heather ledge.
4 15m Climb the short crack and buttress above.
SJH Reid, JR Grinbergs 14.03.1990

32 Gimmer Chimney 80m VD ★★★
A classic route up the striking twin cracks. Start at a broken rib under the main line.
1 32m Climb the rib and ensuing easy chimney to a steep section at 23m which proves awkward. Easy climbing then leads to a stance on the right.
2 17m Traverse left for 3m into a tricky groove which leads into a sentry box. Climb the deep crack, using holds on its right rib, to a stance at the right end of a broad ramp and beneath the black depths of the narrow chimney so obvious from below.
3 11m Ignore the narrow chimney and traverse 5m right into the parallel chimney, which leads amenably to a belay in the open gully above.
4 20m Quit the gully bed for the rib on the right and finish up this.
E Rigby, J Sandison, AS Thomson 2.11.1902

33 Chimney Buttress 64m S 4a ★★
Agreeable climbing with a short dynamic crux. Start below the corner.
1 13m Climb a short crack and scramble up and leftwards to a spacious ledge below a chimney.
2 27m 4a Climb diagonally rightwards to a small ledge overlooking South-East Gully, then back left to a higher ledge. Now 'piano play' your way over the centre of the bulging wall, after which enjoyable slabs trending slightly rightwards lead to a good ledge.
3 24m More slabs above lead pleasantly to the top.
HB Lyon, G Ackerley, J Herbert 3.09.1923

34 Bachelor Crack 54m MVS 4b ★★
Varied climbing up the right edge of the face.
1 18m 4b Climb the corner to a small ledge. Move left to surmount the bulge and traverse delicately back right, crossing a crack to gain the far rib; belay a short way higher at a small ledge.
2 36m Pleasant climbing up the walls and slabs above, over several grassy ledges.
RJ Birkett, V Veevers, J Craven 3.08.1941

Kipling Groove HVS (page 84)
David Simmonite

NECKBAND CRAG

OS Grid Ref: NY 256 062
Altitude: 550m

Cravat VS (page 92) Nigel Hooker — Nick Wharton

Superb single-pitch outcrop style climbing. The immaculate rough rock is seamed with corners and cracks. Slow to dry, yet it's a cool refuge when the sun gets too hot.

Approach: From the ODG, walk over to and up The Band, passing through Stool End Farm. Follow the good path up The Band until it levels out with a large boulder on the left. A vague path branches off right, going anti-clockwise round the summit knoll to descend steeply to the left end of the crag. If you find yourself climbing steeply up the ridge to Bowfell, or if the Climbers' Traverse is reached, you have gone too far.

Overview page 94.

Descent: *In-situ* abseils are usually in place above *Razor Crack* and *Mithrandir* or scramble up and left then down steep ground to the foot of the crag.

① Cravat 35m VS 4c ★★
Exposed adventurous and quite tough on its steep lower section. Start below the wall at a short vegetated corner. Climb the corner to a ledge. From its right end, climb a short crack until a line of holds lead rightwards to a scoop in the arête. Move up this to a ledge. Go round the rib on the right and follow a thin crack in the slab diagonally right to reach a good crack 2m left of the corner. Finish up this crack.
Photo page 90.
H Drasdo, N Drasdo 1950

② Aragorn 40m E3 5c ★★
An excellent pitch with interesting exposed and varied climbing. Start in the large corner of *Mithrandir*. Follow the corner for about 4m. Traverse the undercut slab left to a spike and enter a niche. Leaving the niche leftwards to gain the easier groove is tricky. Climb the groove and finish up the thought-provoking left-slanting crack.
A Evans, D Parker Sep 1971

③ Gandalf's Groove Direct 36m E2 5b ★★★
A magnificent outing across the left wall of the large corner and up the left arête. Delicate balance climbing on beautiful rock, it requires steadiness on the upper section. Ascend the corner for about 16m until a descending traverse leads easily out left to a very shallow right-facing corner near the rib. Climb delicately up this and step left onto the rib. Continue boldly up the right-hand side of the rib, the difficulty slowly easing towards the top.
JA Austin, FP Jenkinson 4.07.1964

④ Mithrandir 33m HVS 5a ★★
This tough classic climbs the commanding left-facing corner. Slow drying yet technical, it is much harder in less than perfect conditions.
J Hartley, R Sager Aug 1972

⑤ Glorfindel 35m HVS 5a ★★★
Stitching together surprisingly good holds this finds an improbable way up the centre of the crag. Really handy if *Mithrandir* is wet. Climb the corner to half-height then traverse across the right wall to the groove of *Gillette Direct*. Move up and right, and pull into the slanting crack around the corner. Finish up this.

⑥ Gillette Direct 35m E2 5c ★★★ ◆
A brilliant well-protected route up the compelling line of narrow hanging grooves in the right wall of *Mithrandir*. Start at the ragged crack. Climb the crack to the overhang (thread). Traverse left onto the slab and enter the groove with difficulty. Continue delicately to a small ledge. Gain a better ledge and climb the steepening groove above to good finishing cracks in the final bulge.
K Wood, JA Austin Jul 1968. Direct Finish W Lounds 1969

⑦ Tracheotomy 35m E2 5c ★★
An excellent sustained and evenly-graded route. Climb the ragged crack then traverse left onto the slab and into the groove. Pull right into a small niche in the rib and make an awkward move into the crack above which is followed to the top.
M Berzins, B Berzins May 1978

⑧ Razor Crack 35m E1 5b ★★★ ◆
A marvellous climb tackling the superb crack and several impressive overlaps. Technically modest, giving strenuous and sustained climbing with good protection and resting places. Start at a ragged crack running up to the left end of a band of overhangs at 5m. The crack is immediately strenuous up to the overhangs. Traverse right beneath these until a thin crack leads back left into the wider main crack. Follow this over several overlaps and the odd jammed flake to the top where you can sink thankfully amongst the bilberries.
Photo this page.
JA Austin, K Wood 26.08.1966

Razor Crack E1 (this page) Calum Grant & Steph Marshall — 📷 Nick Wharton

Neckband Crag | 93

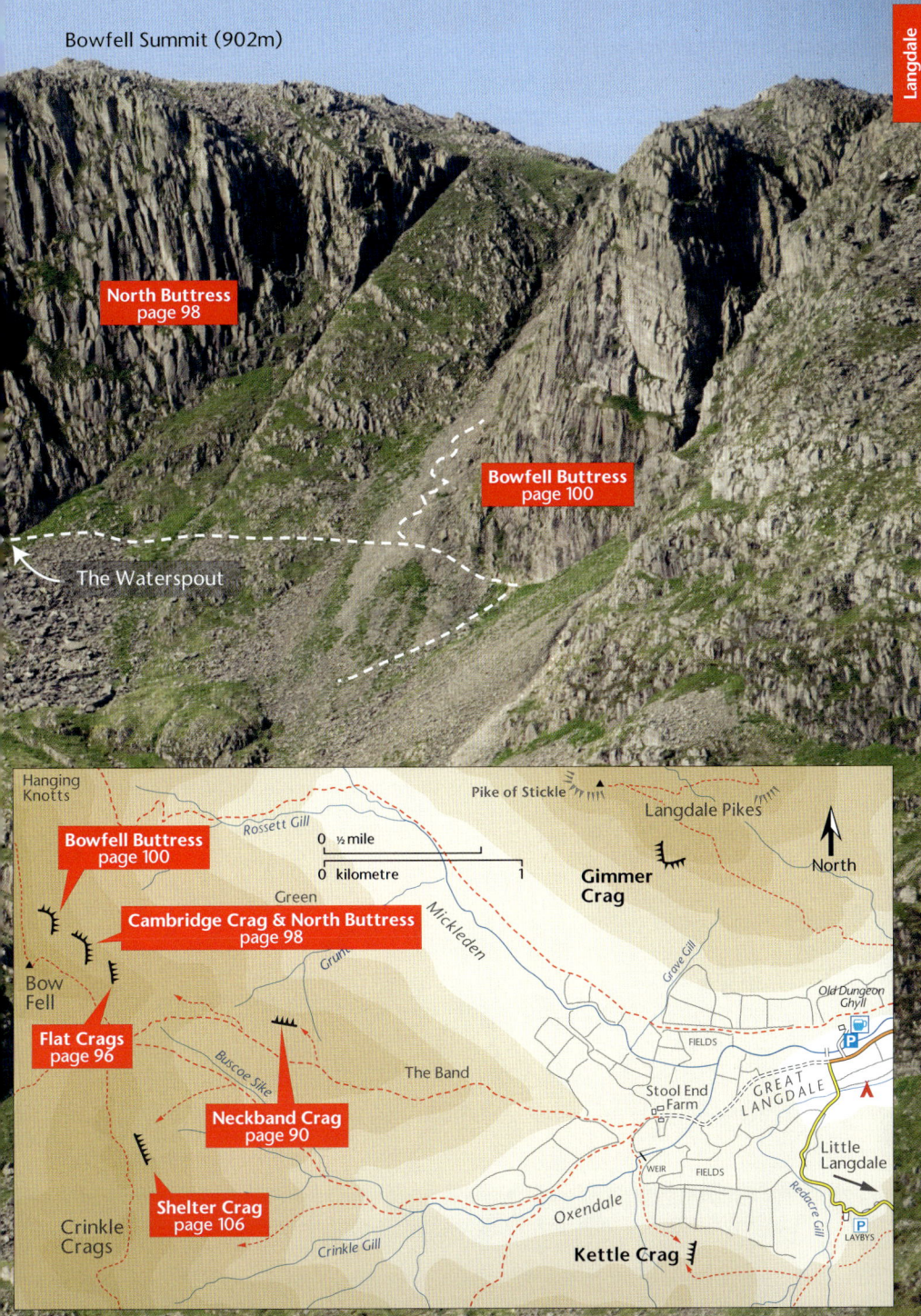

FLAT CRAGS

OS Grid Ref: NY 249 065
Altitude: 750m

A deceptive crag that is even steeper than it looks. Home to some hard routes plus some excellent middle grade options.

Approach: From the ODG, follow The Band. Where the path forks at a scree-covered section (tiny cairn), take the path on the right heading for a flat shoulder; here a well-marked path, The Climbers' Traverse, contours rightwards below the crag.

Descent: Either down the Great Slab or head up the hillside to the left end of the crag to get back onto the upper part of the sloping rock terrace.

1 Mary Ann 42m VD ★★
A good route on immaculate rock. Start just right of a large flake some 6m right of a mossy cave near the top of the rock terrace.
1 22m Climb a short crack and step right to another crack which is followed to a line of overhangs. Traverse left below these and go up into a slabby bay. Huge flake belay up on the right.
2 20m A short crack on the left gives access to a rising traverse leftwards across the slabby wall. Finish steeply on good holds.
J Umpleby, P Grindley, J Slockett

2 Slowburn 33m E3 5c ★★
A good route, steeper than it looks, which follows the left-bounding wall of the bay on sloping holds. It has got harder since a large chunk fell out of the arête. Start just below the toe of the slab at a short corner. Climb up easily then up the wall to the right before traversing back left on small edges with feet at the level of the obvious small pocket in the wall. Pull out left to the arête. Follow a ramp rightwards to its top. Traverse delicately up and leftwards to a ledge on the arête. Pull up and follow the edge of the wall up and right in an exposed position to easy slabs.
B Berzins, M Berzins 11.07.1979

3 Flat Iron Wall 43m E1 5b ★★
An excellent first pitch which finds the easiest way up the undercut white wrinkled wall so prominently visible from the approach walk. The wall looks holdless but is just off-vertical and covered in little edges. Protection is better than might be expected - sufficient to allow one to savour the excursion. Start in the corner.
1 22m 5a Make a rising traverse rightwards to a small ledge above the overhangs. Step right and climb the wall trending slightly rightwards. Towards the top, cross the left-hand of two slight bulges to a ledge on the right arete then move up to belay on the higher ledge.

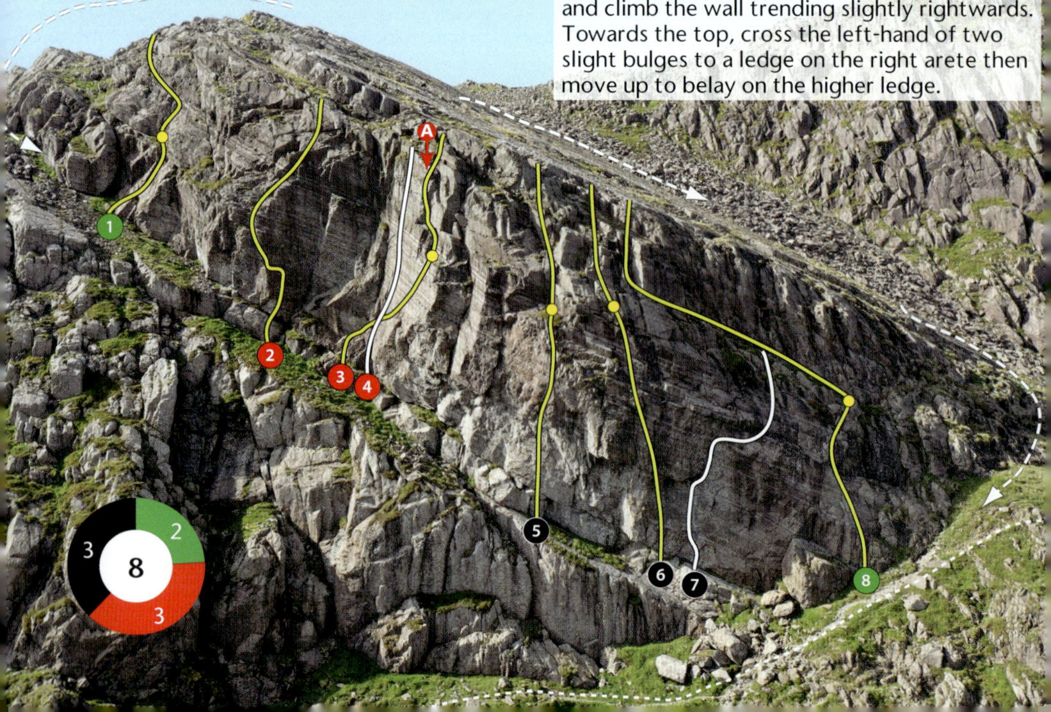

2 21m 5b On the left is a succession of three little corners. These prove to be disproportionately awkward for their size.
J A Austin, F Wilkinson 18.07.1971

❹ Fastburn   36m   E2 5b   ★★★
This superb pitch directly up the *Flat Iron Wall* provides a contrasting combination of strenuous crack and delicate wall climbing. Start at a hanging crack. Climb the crack and hollow flake above to a ledge. Continue delicately up the wall, trending left to join the thin slanting crack. Follow the crack, moving out right at the top to a ledge. Move immediately back left and climb the wall to easier ground.
E Cleasby, I Greenwood Jun 1979

❺ Redundancy of Courage   45m   E5 6b   ★★
The prominent hanging groove above the smooth lower wall halfway up the rock gangway is gained from below and left. Start at a recess left of the line of the groove.
1 20m 6b Climb the thin crack almost to the break. Traverse right to a sloping hold below the groove. Pull into the groove and climb it to a belay.
2 25m 4c Easy slabs to the top.
M Berzins, CP Smith 1992

❻ Ataxia   46m   E5 6b   ★★★
An incredibly sustained pitch up the vague crack groove line at the right-hand end of the central wall. Start about 5m up the rock terrace, below an audacious gritstone-like roof crack.
1 23m 6b Attack the roof and crack to gain a ledge on the right. Step back left and follow the steepening crack to a narrow ledge below a short groove. Pull into the groove and make some hard moves to reach good holds at its top. Move up to a small ledge and belay.
2 23m 4c The slabs above trending leftwards.
M Berzins, B Berzins 12.07.1979

❼ Exposure   33m   E5 6a   ★★★
A sustained and well-protected route up the grooveline formed by the prominent curving overhang which defines the right side of the imposing central wall, marred only by its slightly gloomy appearance. Start directly below a green streak under the overhang. Climb the short wall to a slab, step left and gain a slim groove leading to the lower overhang. Step right and gain the main groove then up to the top overhang (peg) with difficulty. Move right on small holds to a ledge then gain the slabs above which lead more easily to the grass terrace.
B Berzins, M Berzins 3.05.1980

❽ Flat Crags Climb   43m   S   ★★
A surprisingly good climb at an amenable grade, venturing into some impressive terrain. Start at the slabs part way up the slope on the right of the crag.
1 16m Climb the excellent slab for 7m when a short traverse left gains a ledge. Traverse diagonally rightwards and up past another ledge to reach the large grassy terrace.
2 27m Walk up the terrace to where it steepens. Re-belay and look left. A sloping ledge beneath the steep wall leads out towards the edge of the crag in a very exposed position. Follow this to its end and move delicately round the edge to discover a fine deep crack. Climb this and the corner above, which finishes steeply. The route can be continued a little way by scrambling up the pleasant ridge on the left to an obvious summit.

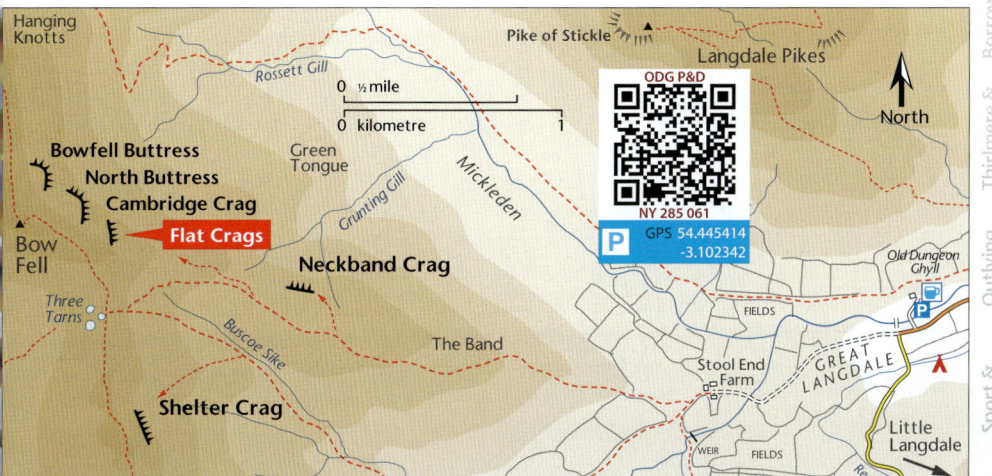

CAMBRIDGE CRAG & NORTH BUTTRESS

OS Grid Ref: NY 246 066
Altitude: 775m

Sitting high up, right beneath the summit of Bowfell, this rambling buttress is made up of a jumble of walls and pinnacles giving something of a mountaineering feel.
Approach: From the ODG, follow The Band. Where the path forks at a scree-covered section (tiny cairn), take the path on the right heading for a flat shoulder; here a well-marked path, The Climbers' Traverse, contours rightwards below crags to The Waterspout.
Descent: Either left and down the Great Slab or right and down the steep gully. You probably ought to get the full summit experience on Bowfell before heading back down!

❶ The Cambridge Climb   77m   VD   ★★
A very good climb, a classic of its era and genre, with some excellent positions. Start about 10m left of The Waterspout at the foot of a broad slab sloping upwards to the right.
1 11m Climb the slab to a corner.
2 9m Step round the rib on the right and climb up to a ledge with an overhanging block belay.
3 14m Traverse left to the second of two grassy niches, above which a sharp jutting flake is climbed to another grassy corner.
4 15m Climb the pleasant flake chimney to a ledge on the right.
5 11m Step back left into the chimney and climb to a large terrace.
6 17m A giant's three-step staircase leads up and rightwards with increasing difficulty to an exit onto the ridge. Easy scrambling remains.
WT Elmslie, A de St C Walsh 6.09.1922

❷ Riboletto   43m   E4 6a   ★★★
A brilliant pitch; an excellent line on perfect rock, one of the highest-finishing routes in Langdale. Graded for its bold start and tough crux. High in the centre of the steep ground between **Cambridge Crag** and **North Buttress** will be seen a fine arête rising to its own summit. Approach by scrambling up the broken vegetated gully line directly beneath it. Start below the smooth groove on the right side of the rib.
1 33m 6a Climb the groove for 5m to a good hold and protection on the right, then make delicate committing moves left to gain the narrow hanging slab below the rib. This leads left round the corner to a good rest below a thin groove and crack (small runners). Continue, with difficulty, up the left side of the rib (crux), useful hidden hold right of the rib, to reach a ledge. Follow the right side of the rib past another small ledge to belay below a short wall.
2 10m 4c Easily up the wall. The summit of the mountain lies just behind and an effort should be made to visit it and enjoy the view!
Photo page 111.
P Rigby, A Greig 19.06.1988

The Waterspout

3 The Gnomon 63m E1 5b ★

A good main pitch up the left-hand of the three big grooves, currently somewhat mossy. Start from a grassy platform and large spike belay below twin cracks.

1 40m 5b Climb the crack in the corner into a niche. Step left and climb a short wall to a larger niche. Move left to a small ledge on the left rib, swing back right and climb with difficulty (peg) to a ledge. Follow the steep groove above to broken rock. Scramble up to a belay below a tower.

2 23m 4b From the centre of the tower, move up and then follow a line of holds rightwards to the edge. Climb directly to the top.
L Brown, G Lund 23.04.1960

4 Mindbender 28m E2 5b ★

The central groove provides a fantastic pitch with better protection than appears from below, but the start is a bit of a shock. Start from the ledge directly below the groove. The short initial groove can be very stubborn but the fist crack up on the right provides a good home for a large cam (or as a pleasant alternative, climb *The Gnomon* and move right). From the sloping ledge thus gained, climb the main groove on immaculate rock, past a difficult bulge to a steep airy finish.
RJ Kenyon, R Bennett 10.06.1979

5 Sword of Damocles 56m E1 5b ★★

A classic route from the 1950s, which climbs the right-hand and largest of the three grooves. The 'Sword', a wedged rock spike which gave the climb its name, has long since gone. Start from the ledge below the groove beneath a prominent overhung curved crack, actually the base of a huge pinnacle.

1 23m 4c Climb the crack to enter the groove on the right. Move up easily to the foot of a groove behind the pinnacle. Go up the groove until a long stride right can be made to gain a ledge on the edge of the buttress. Move up a little until a dramatic semi-hand traverse can be made leftwards across the groove to a stance on the left wall.

2 33m 5b Climb the groove (where the Sword was) passing to the left of an awkward bulging nose. Climb the steep impressive flake crack to a resting place; continue up the crack, until a move right leads to easier climbing and the top.
PJ Greenwood, AR Dolphin, D Hopkin 23.08.1952

6 The Scabbard 61m VS 4c ★

A reasonable route with some good positions and a crack pitch of esoteric qualities. Start at a thin crack in a short wall below the base of the main crackline and about 12m right of *Sword of Damocles*.

1 22m 4c Climb the thin crack to a grass ledge at 7m and scramble up to belay below the line of the main crack.

2 13m 4c Above the belay on the left, and curving down towards the left, is a shallow scoop near the edge of the left-hand rib. Climb steeply for a couple of metres then make an awkward move to gain this scoop. Follow it to a stance and high thread belay.

3 26m 4c Climb the widening crack above, interestingly precarious, to finish up broken grooves.
JA Austin, E Metcalf 28.05.1960

OS Grid Ref NY 246 066 — Cambridge

BOWFELL BUTTRESS

OS Grid Ref: NY 246 067
Altitude: 750m

The prominent buttress standing proud of the fellside dominates the top of the valley. Good rock and long routes make for an excellent day out, especially with the morning sun.

Approach: From the ODG, follow The Band. Where the path forks at a scree covered section (tiny cairn), take the path on the right heading for a flat shoulder, here a well-marked path, The Climbers' Traverse, contours rightwards below crags. Continue on this path past The Waterspout crossing a broad scree chute to the foot of the buttress.

Descent: Walk over the top of the buttress and down into the col. Descend the loose gully on the left. Or if seeking the summit experience, head up the other side of the col and on up to the top of Bowfell.

Woolly Jumper E1 (page 104) Tim Whiteley — 📷 DAVID SIMMONITE

Langdale

1 Bowfell Buttress 106m HS ★★★
A classic mountain route which takes the easiest way up the front of the buttress. Book early to avoid the queue. Generally VD except for the notorious crack, which becomes even harder in the wet. It is very popular in winter conditions hence all the axe and crampon scratches. Start below a small ridge 3m left from the edge of the smooth wall forming the foot of the crag.
1 23m Climb the ridge to a belay. Climb the short smooth polished chimney on the right and easy ground to a terrace.
2 30m Tackle the steep wall above moving diagonally leftwards to a sentry box in a chimney. Follow the chimney for about 12m and continue up easy ledges to a large terrace sloping down to the right; follow this for about 7m and belay at the foot of a highly-polished crack.
3 17m The slippery crack is very steep, shiny and awkward, but there is a comforting ample green terrace below. Once standing on the rock ledges above, slabby rock leads back left to a pinnacle belay.
4 18m Continue left and ascend a groove leading to a chimney. Go up to a slab and continue up the wall above until a short traverse left across the corner leads to a platform and large belay.
5 18m Step back to the right and follow a groove and its left-hand branch to finish.
Photo page 104.
T Shaw, GH Craig, GR West, C Hargreaves, LJ Oppenheimer 24.05.1902

2 The Central Route 93m VS 4c ★★
An interesting route with some good climbing. Start at the left edge of the smooth wall forming the foot of the crag. The route keeps left of *Bowfell Buttress* after the first pitch.
1 13m Pleasant climbing up the broken groove.
2 16m 4c Attack the left-facing chimney corner and gain good holds on jammed flakes when it starts to impend. From these, step out right onto the arête, move up and then back into the corner. Its easier continuation now leads to block belays.
3 20m 4b Move left a couple of metres, then up and back right onto a slabby rib. Follow this, eventually reaching a block belay (peg) below a long thin groove line.
4 27m Step onto the block and climb the thin groove with increasing difficulty to an awkward finish into a recess. The steep right corner and rib is then climbed to a crevassed ledge; step back left and go up another rib to grass shelves.
5 17m Move a few metres up to the left to the slab and finish up this.
HM Kelly, B Eden-Smith 20.05.1931

3 Bowfell Buttress Eliminate 108m E2 5b ★★
A good route with some bold climbing. Start below the right-hand of the cracks which split the smooth wall forming the foot of the crag.
1 25m 5b The crack is harder and bolder than it looks and has no protection until the difficulties ease at a niche after 5m. Step right and continue more easily to a grassy ledge 5m left of a long slim groove.
2 25m 4c Climb the groove to a belay below the slippery crack of *Bowfell Buttress*.
3 12m 4a Step down right and climb the deep V-groove to a ledge below a steep wall.
4 23m 5b Climb the corner on the left for 3m before swinging back right onto the steep wall above. Go up easier rock to a small niche on the left. Head boldly up the smooth white wall heading for a short thin crack slanting up left onto a fine narrow ledge.
5 23m 5b Traverse right and upwards then, with a few delicate moves, gain the far edge of the buttress. Round the corner is a steep crack which is climbed to easier ground.
JA Austin, DG Roberts 21.06.1964

4 Ledge and Groove 102m VD ★★
A fine mountaineering route optimistically attacking the right-bounding arête of the White Wall only to be forced right before gradually reasserting itself. To label it 'rambling' is to neglect the traditional aspiration of seeking out the line of least resistance up an uncompromising piece of rock! All the pitches except the last can be shortened if required. Start about 20m right of the right-hand of the cracks which split the smooth wall forming the foot of the crag and some 4m left of the gully.
1 17m A short wall and groove lead to a large ledge at 5m from where a rib leads to another ledge; belay at its right-hand end.
2 21m A short wall is followed by a staircase to the right to a ledge at 9m. Above is a right-facing corner with an overhanging right wall. Just round the corner on the left, a line of good holds leads up left for 4m and then back right across the top of the groove to a stance overlooking the chockstone of North Gully.
3 12m Step up and traverse right to a short groove which is climbed to a sloping ledge. From the left end of this, climb the ridge to a stance.
4 15m Crux - make a delicate traverse right into a chimney corner formed by a small sub-

Bowfell Area | 103

1. Bowfell Buttress — HS ★★★
2. The Central Route — VS 4c ★★
3. Bowfell Buttress Eliminate — E2 5b ★★
4. Ledge and Groove — VD ★★
5. Air on a Bowstring — E3 6a ★★★

sidiary buttress. Climb this to a ledge and large belay on top of this buttress.
5 20m A shallow groove on the right leads to an awkward landing on a grass ledge at 7m. Much harder if wet. Traverse easily left for 6m to the foot of a steep crack in a corner. Up this for 2m then make an awkward move onto a small ledge on the left, followed by further awkward moves past a projecting boulder guarding entry to a large grassy terrace.
6 17m Move left along the terrace and climb a crack to a ledge and up the short wall above to the top.
RD Stevens, G Stoneley 5.05.1945

⑤ Air on a Bowstring 50m E3 6a ★★★
A magnificent route, up the centre of the White Wall giving varied climbing, bold in its middle section and having a well-positioned crux. Start at the left end of the narrow terrace at a crack 3m right of the corner on P3 of *Bowfell Buttress Eliminate*.
1 15m 5c Climb the stubborn right-leaning crack. Either continue up the crack above and step right to a block belay or move right into a corner and climb it to the same point.
2 35m 6a Climb the short corner to ledges at its top below an impending wall which guards entry to a continuation corner. Move left for 2m (runners) and boldly work up right to gain the foot of this corner. Climb it more easily to a rest. At the top of the corner, step left round a neat triangular rib into a slim groove and from its top, use an upside down spike on the left to pull onto the final headwall. Climb this to the top.
J Cooper, T Walkington June 1992

⑥ Woolly Jumper 60m E1 5b ★★★
Excellent; a minor classic which climbs the right arête of the White Wall. Modest protection makes the exposure well felt. Named after a sheep with short-lived aeronautic ambitions. Start at the right-hand end of the big terrace halfway up **Bowfell Buttress**, easily reached by scrambling up North Gully for 25m, then out left onto the ridge to below the first of two short grooves in the arête. The right wall of this groove is heavily undercut.
1 30m 5a An obvious layaway hold on the lip of the overhung right wall is gained from the left and used to pull confidently round onto the slab above. Continue more easily up left to the attractive groove in the arête. Climb this to a ledge at the foot of the main arête.
2 30m 5b Starting below the left side of the arête, make an awkward move round it to gain a niche in the right wall. Delicate moves up the right rib of the niche gain a ledge. Step left and climb up to a small quartz ledge on the arête. Stand on this and follow a shallow flake rightwards to a narrow ledge. Step back left and layaway up the arête on superbly rough rock and great exposure, until the angle eases below a wide crack. Climb this to a large ledge and belay. Scramble off to the left.
Photo page 101.
P1: RM Biden, G Halliwell; P2: J Cooper
P1: Mid 1990s; P2: Aug 1990

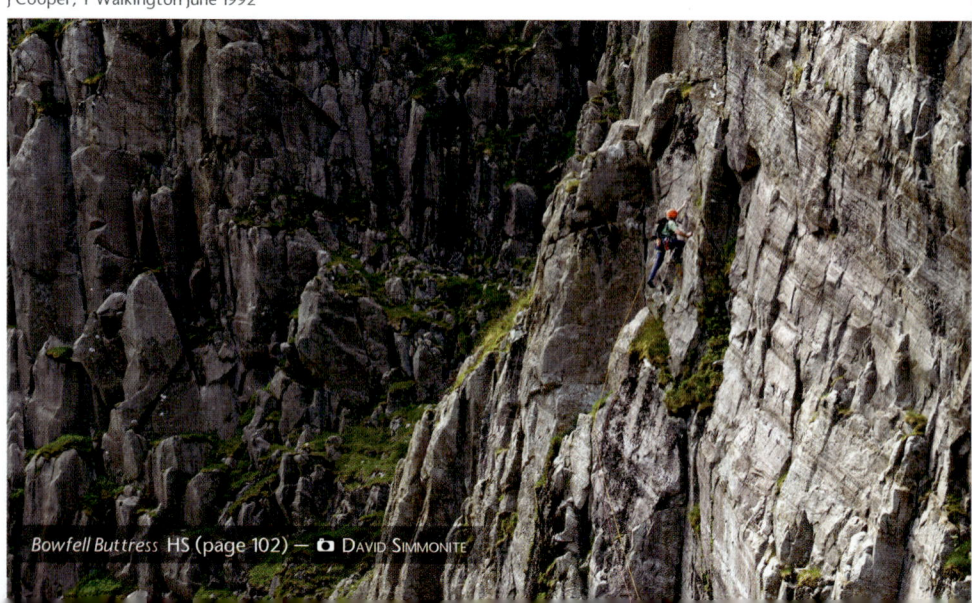
Bowfell Buttress HS (page 102) — David Simmonite

Bowfell Area | 105

1. **Bowfell Buttress** — HS ★★★
3. **Bowfell Buttress Eliminate** — E2 5b ★★
4. **Ledge and Groove** — VD ★★
5. **Air on a Bowstring** — E3 6a ★★★
6. **Woolly Jumper** — E1 5b ★★★

Langdale

North Gully chockstone

SHELTER CRAG

OS Grid Ref: NY 250 056
Altitude: 720m

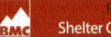 RAD Shelter Crag
 OS Grid Ref NY 250 056

Hidden away and quiet, this high crag has abrasively rough rock and dries relatively quickly. There's great scope for climbers operating between VS and E2.

ODG P&D
NY 285 061
P GPS 54.445414 -3.102342

Approach: From the ODG, climb The Band to the Three Tarns. Turn left and follow the main path along the ridge for 10-15 mins until after a series of slabs, the summit of the highest of the Crinkles comes into view. Head diagonally left and down onto a prominent terrace. Worth gearing up here.

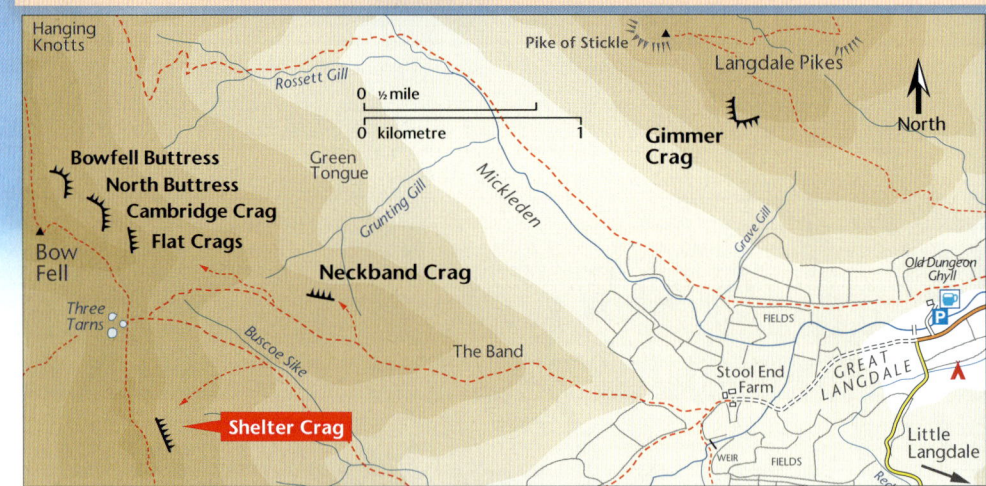

Buscoe Buttress

Approach: From the terrace head steeply down a rocky grass slope then descend a rock ramp on the left. Skirt round the first buttress then zig-zag down steep grass to **Buscoe Buttress**.

❶ Panjandrum 63m E1 5b ★★★
Takes a line up the crest of the buttress. Start at the lowest point of the buttress below a conspicuous hanging groove.
1 20m 5b Climb directly up to the bottom of a shallow hanging groove. Climb this and the fault line on the edge to a stance and spike belays.
2 23m 5b Climb directly above the stance then rightwards above the overhung corner of *Moonstruck;* ascend strenuously to gain a groove. Step left onto a rib and follow this to block belays.
3 20m 5a Climb the steep headwall using the crack near the right edge stepping left and up to the reach the top.
C Read, GL Swainbank 31.07.1999

❷ Moonstruck 60m E1 5b ★★
The arching corner makes a sustained and intricate exercise. Slow to dry.
1 40m 5b Climb leftwards into the corner and follow it as it curves right, with a final swing right round a blunt rib before entering the groove above. Move up and left, to climb a series of grooves to reach block belays on the edge of the large ledge above.
2 20m 5a Scramble up to the foot of the steep headwall. Climb directly up to gain and follow the crack near the right edge then step left and up to reach the top.
C Read, GL Swainbank 01.05.1999

❸ Diplodocus 60m HVS 5b ★
Steep strenuous climbing. Start at a rightward-slanting open groove.
1 40m 5b Climb the groove; at its top, move left into a second groove and up to an overhang. Make a committing move left (crux) to a niche. Continue up to a corner then move right onto the arête. Climb to a short groove, then a wall trending left to block belays.
2 20m Scramble rightwards up the grass ledge to the foot of a narrow rib; follow it to the top, passing the right side of the headwall.
C Read, GL Swainbank 11.07.1999

Oxendale Buttress

Approach: The left-hand side is approached from Buscoe Buttress. For routes 7-10 on the right descend below **Buscoe Buttress** then head left (facing out).

❹ Island of Dreams 46m E2 5c ★★
An excellent main pitch up the bulging buttress. Start 2m left of the cave at a short groove.
1 33m 5c Climb straight up, passing a doubtful spike, to beneath a small bulge. Move first right and up to gain a foothold on the wall, then back left and up to the foot of a short steep hanging groove, left of the main overhang. Climb this with difficulty to a resting place and continue up the vertical crack above, pulling out right at its top. The rightward-slanting fault leads to a ledge then move left into a short capped groove, pull up out left onto a sloping ledge and ascend more easily to block belays.
2 13m 4b Ascend directly onto the top of the large block and climb the vertical fault line above to a ledge. Finish via the short thin crack directly ahead.
C Read, GL Swainbank 29.07.1999

❺ Pleasure Zone 46m E1 5b ★★★
Excellent climbing up the right-facing open corner which defines the right-hand side of the upper bulging section of the buttress. Start immediately right of the cave beneath a small square-cut overhang.
1 30m 5b Climb past the left-hand end of the overhang (spike) then pull out left to gain a sloping ledge. Ascend to an overhang beneath the bulging wall, where a step right leads to the obvious rightward-slanting corner groove. Follow this to a horizontal ledge beneath a short steep wall split by a crack. Climb the crack to the left end of a long grass ledge. Thread belay in the corner on the left.
2 16m 5a Step out left and up onto the large slab. The steep narrow crack immediately above is followed to the top.
C Read, GL Swainbank 13.06.1999

❻ Footlights 60m VD ★★
Start 2m right of the cave at the foot of the right-slanting gangway.
1 22m Step across right to climb a series of gangways leading up rightwards until, near the top of the wider upper section, moves right gain belays at the left edge of a large sloping grass ledge.
2 21m Climb onto the easy-angled slab above.

Step up left and ascend diagonally leftwards to a small ledge. Move out left then up directly to a thread belay in a corner at the left end of the grassy ledge.
3 17m Ascend the corner and the crack up the wall above, until a step up left gains a short groove leading to the top.
GL Swainbank, C Read 03.04.1999

❼ Arcanum   68m   VS 4c   ★
Finds a way up the buttress left of and overlooking the corners of *Showtime*. Start some 7m up steep grass ledges left of the vegetated bay, beneath a short steep pillar with a crack in its left side.
1 7m 4b Ascend the left edge of the pillar until a pull right gains a small ledge. Move up and left to a large ledge.
2 30m 4a From the right-hand edge of the ledge, move up and swing round right into a recess. Move right again onto the arête and follow it to a platform. Continue up passing a prominent hollow blade of rock on its right then swing out right and continue up to The Balcony. Scramble up to belay at the foot of a wide crack formed at the back of a huge block.
3 17m 4c Climb the crack by its right wall to a ledge, move up left and make a steep pull up the short wall to gain The Circle. If the final moves are wet move further right then up.
4 14m 4c A sharp arête defines the right edge of the wall above, to the left of the open chimney of P4, *Thespian*. Gain the crest of the arête by some bold moves up its left side and gain the crack emerging from the chimney behind. Climb up and left to follow the broad rib to the top.
GL Swainbank, C Read 25.07.1999

❽ Showtime   76m   E1 5b   ★★★
Good well-protected climbing. Start 3m right of the vegetated bay, at the foot of a clean wall.
1 14m 5a Climb the wall to a thin crack, where a pull up and left leads onto a large slab and stance.
2 30m 5a From the top of the slab move left and climb the main corner until a move right leads to beneath a large hollow flake guarding access to an overhung corner. Move right onto the steep wall and climb to the foot of the final groove. Climb this to a ledge.
3 15m 5b Climb over blocks onto a slab in an overhung recess. Pull up and right onto the steep wall. Traverse right onto the front and up to enter an open groove leading to a ledge.
4 17m 4c At the left side of the headwall is a short steep corner topped by an overhang. Climb the corner, pulling out left to ascend the groove above to the top.
GL Swainbank, C Read 02.05.1999

❾ Thespian   72m   VS 5a   ★
Start at a sloping ledge beneath a shallow corner with a short crack in its left side.
1 12m 4a Climb the corner to a large recess. Step onto the left wall and ascend to a belay at the foot of the ramp.
2 30m 4c From the right end of the ramp, move up then right and ascend to a groove. Move up left to beneath a hanging chimney groove; climb it and move left. Ascend the wall above, trending right to enter the right-hand of two prominent grooves and climb it to a ledge. Scramble up and belay beneath a wide crack.
3 16m 5a To the left of the wide crack is a leaning groove. Climb this to a ledge at its top and make a steep pull up the short wall.
4 14m 4c An open chimney splits the wall above. Climb the crack up its left side.
C Read, GL Swainbank 16.05.1999

❿ Oxendale Arête   77m   VS 4c   ★
Follows the right-hand arête of this buttress. Start 5m left of the right-hand toe of the buttress, below a shallow corner.
1 23m 4c Climb the rib on the right to a resting place beneath a steep wall, at about 15m. Step to the right then up to a ledge and step left to belay on the arête.
2 19m 4c Step up into the sentry box on the left and pull up awkwardly then right to regain the arête. Continue up a right-slanting groove then up left onto an easy-angled slab.
3 21m 4c From the right end of the wall above, climb a groove. Good holds in the niche above allow a swing round left onto the front. Up into the niche and thence onto an easy-angled slab. Trend right across the slab and pull over overlaps to gain the large ledge. Belay on the right.
4 14m 4c Climb the right side of the open chimney and the easy-angled arête.
C Read, GL Swainbank 24.04.1999

Buscoe Buttress

1. Panjandrum — E1 5b ★★★
2. Moonstruck — E1 5b ★★
3. Diplodocus — HVS 5b ★

Riboletto, Cambridge Crag E4 (page 98) Nick Wharton — 📷 David Simmonite

KETTLE CRAG

OS Grid Ref: NY 278 049
Altitude: 300m

This secluded crag has a range of easy to mid-grade routes that catch the afternoon sun.

Approach: Follow the main Pike of Blisco path from the Blea Tarn Road that links Great and Little Langdale. After 800m, head rightwards for a col in the ridge. Once through this, a fence leads down into a steep grass gully and the routes.

Descent: A slanting rock terrace leads back to the grassy gully - Take Care! For routes above the terrace, scramble to the top of the crag and so back into the approach gully.

Red Slab S (page 114) Andy Lloyd & Theo Cassani — 📷 Ron Kenyon

① **Tea Time Arête** 25m MVS 4a ★★
Boldly climb the arête on good holds with poor protection to a ledge. Avoid the heather by stepping airily right to finish on the front face.

② **Semerikod** 22m VS 4c ★
Climb ledges leftwards then the overhanging crack. Turn the roof on the right entering a niche then a second niche. With hands above, exit left.

③ **Orange Pekoe** 20m VS 4c ★
Start at a deep crack 15m down from the slab and vegetated corner. Pull left then climb the wall and bulging arête.

④ **Heather the Weather** 30m S ★
The left side of the wall presents a steep start, ascend on positive holds.

⑤ **Major Slab** 30m VD ★
Climb rightwards to gain the central crackline and follow this to the top.

⑥ **Serendipity** 30m S ★★★
Start at the bottom of the gully. Climb easily at first on large blocky holds then slightly right and up a blunt rib. Climb the crack to an arête and exposed finish.

⑦ **Red Slab** 18m S ★★★ ◆
A gem of a pitch up the side wall forming the right edge of the big slabby wall. Excellent rock and gear. Pull out left from the cave and climb the slabby wall direct.
Photo page 113.

⑧ **Minor Melodic** 25m VS 4b ★★
Climb the left side of the slab to the break. Optional belay. Continue left and up to finish.

⑨ **Minor Slab** 30m VS 4b ★★
Delightfully delicate; quite bold. Climb the slabby wall to finish via a thin crack. Optional belay. After a problem start, continue up the slab and the short wall.

⑩ **Singing Kettle** 20m VS 4b ★★
Climb the left-hand crack to a heathery bay. Pull over the overhang and teeter up the left edge of the slab.

⑪ **Rose Pouchong** 20m MVS 4b ★
Climb the right-hand crack system across the left end of the overhang, finish up the knobbly slab.

⑫ **Earl Grey** 20m VS 4c ★★
Delicate climbing up the vague crack (crux) leads to better holds and a tiny V-groove. Float over the overhang left of the groove on big incuts. The final slab goes easily left, with care by a loose flake.

from Stool End Farm

CONISTON

The jewel in the crown hereabouts is the mighty **Dow Crag**, one of the most accessible mountain crags in the Lake District. It provides some terrific routes - both ancient and modern - to suit all levels. The other crags in the area complement their expansive neighbour by providing quieter, shorter routes in delightful surroundings.

Easter Rising, Dow Crag E2 (page 136) Nick Wharton — 📷 David Simmonite

BLIND TARN CRAG

OS Grid Ref: SD 261 967
Altitude: 590m

A delightful venue with rough compact rock sitting above the mysterious Blind Tarn with no obvious inlet or outlet - great for a swim on a sunny afternoon.

Approach: From Coniston, at the crossroads just south of the garage in the village, head west up the hill on Station Road. A left-hand bend is followed by a very steep section of road. Continue for approximately 1km to a gate. Through this to a large Pay & Display car park. Follow the Walna Scar Road west past the turn-off for **Dow Crag** and over the small bridge. After 1km, an old quarry track on the right leads up the hillside and across spoil heaps to the foot of the crag.

Map page 117.

Descent: To the right of the crag.

❶ See Ordinary 30m E6 6b ★★
Brilliant climbing straight up the centre of the crag, tackling the slightly overhanging headwall head on. Bold in the lower reaches, good gear can be arranged before the powerful and strenuous upper section. From the lowest point of the crag, climb up the slabby wall to the left of the groove. Mantle onto a narrow ledge and continue up and right, climbing a slightly bulging wall to reach an unaccommodating ledge. Make thin and committing moves up and right to a good hold at the top of the slanting groove (gear). Powerful moves above, passing a hold in a square-cut hole, lead up the headwall to an awkward top out.
C Moore 4.07.2021

❷ Cinderella 36m VS 4b ★
A pleasant clean open climb up the left-hand side of the main wall. Start at the lowest point of the crag.
1 13m 4b Move diagonally leftwards to reach an obvious perched block. Pull onto the wall above and boldly follow the steep diagonal runnel leftwards to the arête. Step round the arête to a belay in a large grassy notch.
2 23m 4b Up the steep groove behind the belay then stride left, crossing a grass ledge, to the base of a thin crack. Follow this, pulling out left with difficulty, to finish up the easy rib.
RJ Birkett, T Hill 1944

❸ Snitch 36m HVS 4c
Varied and thought-provoking. From the lowest point of the crag, climb to the perched block. Continue up the hanging corner directly above to reach a clean ledge at 12m. Traverse delicately horizontally left across the wall to the left edge then go up to a ledge. Pull over the cracked bulge above to gain an obvious pod. Climb directly out of this and follow the leftwards-slanting crack across the steep headwall to finish.
TW Birkett, CW Brown 18.08.1973

❹ Goldscope Direct 34m E3 5c ★★
An excellent line following the central arched hooded groove. From the lowest point, climb to the perched block. Continue up the hanging corner directly above to reach a clean ledge at 12m. Climb the thin wall above to gain a sloping ledge. Follow the arched groove to a large sloping hold at a blank section. A bold long reach right on flat holds is made to gain a diagonal quartz band which is followed diagonally left to finish up a short groove. Belay well back.
S Wood, A Phizacklea 29.04.1993

❺ Blind Vision 33m E3 6a ★★★
A brilliant wall climb, fingery and sustained. Start at a small pinnacle at the foot of the arched overhangs. Climb up then trend left on quartzy holds to reach a short groove. Go right (peg) then climb the wall above and right, past a horizontal slot, to gain the shallow scoop below the hanging block. Continue up the wall to reach the excellent thin crack for a steep finish.
A Phizacklea, S Wood 29.04.1993

❻ Blindingly Obvious 35m E3 6a ★★
Start below the capped groove 3m right of the small pinnacle. Climb boldly up the wall and hanging groove until it is possible to make a hard move left and over the overlap just below the hanging block. From the block, traverse left to the ledge beneath the arched groove. Climb this then tackle the "blindingly obvious" steep thin crack in the wall directly above.
C Moore, J Flanagan 16.05.2020

❼ Blind Pugh 37m E3 5c ★
Start below the capped groove 3m right of the small pinnacle. Climb boldly up the wall and hanging groove until it is possible to make a hard move left and over the overlap just below the hanging block. Move up to the block and continue up the arête to finish.
B Davison, A Smith 25.04.1987

DOW CRAG

OS Grid Ref: SD 264 977
Altitude: 610m

A magnificent crag with brilliant routes at grades to suit everyone. The rock is clean, generally dries quickly and, despite relatively easy access, it has the atmosphere of a high mountain crag.

Approach: From Coniston, at the crossroads just south of the garage in the village, head west up the hill on Station Road. A left-hand bend is followed by a very steep section of road. Continue for approximately 1km to a gate. Through this to a large Pay & Display car park. The continuation of the track is called the Walna Scar Road which leads eventually to the Duddon Valley. Follow this on foot for 1500m to a fork. Head right (north) uphill following the well-trodden path to Goat's Water. Cross the beck to paths leading up steeply across scree to the crag.

Eliminate 'A' VS (page 124) Tom Edwards & Joe Farnell — 📷 David Simmonite

'A' Buttress

A large impressively steep and intimidating buttress with masterful long routes at all grades.

Descent: South Rake provides the best descent; it is loose and care should be taken especially if a team is below. Walk south along the ridge passing Easy Gully which is steeper, loose and not recommended.

1 Trident Route   93m   HS   ★★

A good route which provides three sections of enjoyable open climbing separated by easier sections. Start at a vague hollow below an obvious small buttress, just where the rocks bend round in to the very foot of Easy Gully.
1 21m From the hollow, traverse rightwards across the steep wall to an open groove and move up to a rock ledge (peg). Traverse back left on to the front of the buttress and follow the right-hand crack above to a grass ledge. Scramble 8m leftwards across an open gully and belay beneath the steep left wall.
2 13m Climb easily leftwards up a slabby ramp to reach a flake at 4m. Traverse delicately right across the steep wall to reach a crack. Climb this to a grass ledge.
3 36m Follow the broken buttress above, inclining left at the top, to reach a grassy bay at the head of a small gully (the quick way down). Above lies the final steep section of the buttress.
4 23m A narrow grass ledge leads horizontally leftwards for 10m onto the exposed edge of the buttress overlooking Easy Gully. Pull up and right to a rock ledge and climb the ragged crack in the steep wall above, on good holds, to the top.
GS Bower, JB Wilton 10.10.1920

2 Arête, Chimney and Crack   97m   S 4a   ★★★★

A traditional and very popular climb combining all three elements of its name. Start below the clean left-hand arête of 'A' Buttress, marked by an edging of quartz.
1 27m 4a Climb the crest of the arête using the quartz edging to start until a rock ledge is reached at 12m. The wall above is steeper and the holds smaller. Climb up and slightly right then continue directly up an exposed crack to grass ledges.

2 21m Climb left of a broken groove, running up and slightly right, passing a couple of large flakes, then step right and climb the groove passing to the left of a prominent pinnacle to a well-worn ledge in a recess below steeper rocks.
3 15m 4a Using the flake below the bulging rock, climb up and right until a short hand traverse leads into an open chimney on the right. Climb direct over a bulging chockstone to a large ledge immediately above.
4 10m Traverse horizontally right across the exposed narrow ledge into the centre of the buttress. A couple of metres before a grass ledge is reached, a conspicuous crack cleaves the face of the buttress. Belay below this.
5 24m 4a The crack is tricky to start and leads to easy ground. Less worthwhile, but useful for overtaking, after 10m, transfer to the left-hand rib. Scramble to the summit ridge.
TC Ormiston-Chant, THG Parker, SH Gordon 18.09.1910

3 Gordon and Craig Route 101m S ★★
Deservedly popular. When high winds and mist wreath the rocks dropping away below your feet, this atmospheric route can justly claim to be the most exposed climb of its standard in England. Scramble up a grassy groove for 4m to a flat ledge at the base of a left-trending line.
1 22m Climb the clean delicate scoop leftwards to reach a little recess below a final steepening. Either climb the steep crack above or move right to a flake which leads back to a stance.
2 21m P2 of *Arête, Chimney and Crack*.
3 15m P3 of *Arête, Chimney and Crack*.
4 13m Traverse horizontally right across the exposed face of the buttress to a small grass ledge. Belay below a ramp in the wall above.
5 18m Crux. Climb onto the ramp and follow it round a corner on the right to a small niche. Continue up to a ledge of dubious blocks, overlooking Great Gully. Climb the exposed and awkward corner, pulling out left to a welcome landing on ledges.
6 12m Move easily left for 6m then back right up a slab to reach the narrow neck at the top of the buttress. Scrambling remains.
SH Gordon, A Craig, JP and R Rogers, J Hanks, R Gregson 26.09.1909

Dow Crag — AL PHIZACKLEA

❹ Abraxas 85m E4 6a ★★★
A serious and impressively steep route that takes a lot of scalps. Scramble up to the base of a right-facing corner and belay on the left.
1 18m 5c A bold pitch with little protection. Move right for 3m to a flake then climb the steep wall above to a recess. Pull over the bulge onto a mossy slab above with difficulty. Cross the slab leftwards to a stance below the overhanging wall.
2 25m 6a Climb the wall rightwards beneath the overhang then pull into the groove above which leads to a resting place on the right. Step back left and climb the crack with difficulty to reach an undercut flake; an exhilarating move right leads up into a groove above the steepest section. Climb this to a roof then traverse right to blocks.
3 12m 4c Climb the steep groove left of the blocks then directly up the wall over a bulge into a short V-groove. Climb this to a belay.
4 30m 5b Approach the steep shallow groove directly (to the left of the hanging arête) and climb it on small holds. Move left and follow the groove line and easier walls to the top.
R Matheson, JR Martindale 27/28.06.1975

❺ Isengard/ 102m E2 5b ★★★
Samba Pa Ti
This brilliant combination creates an amazingly enjoyable direct. A technical and reasonably well-protected first section is followed by bold and strenuous space walking. Start on a ledge below a short right-facing corner.
1 9m 4b Climb the corner and move right.
2 39m 5b Cross the slab on the left and follow a diagonal line, passing an awkward bulge, to a long ledge. Move right a couple of metres then climb a steep crack up to and over an overhang. Follow a slab to the large cave.
3 30m 5b Climb the right edge of the slab to the overhangs and boldly pull over the first bulge on excellent holds. Move up the groove 2m and pull out rightwards onto the steep wall above. Climb directly to the bulge and skirt it on the right, moving left to easier ground and belays below a crack.
4 24m 4b A weakness 9m right of the main crack leads to a narrow neck at the top.
L Brown, A McHardy Apr 1962 / A Hyslop, RO Graham Aug 1977

❻ Eliminate 'A' 103m VS 4c ★★★★
One of Britain's greatest routes; cunningly conceived, of absorbing interest and with a superb atmosphere. Impeccable climbing weaving through impressive rock architecture. The pitches can all be split. Either start from the gully bed or from a ledge some 6m higher.
1 38m 4b An absorbing pitch. From the ledge climb rightwards onto a steep wall overlooking Great Gully. A short groove leads onto a ledge. From the left, trend rightwards following a shallow depression in the steep wall until a move right (awkward) and mantelshelf lead onto a small ledge. Follow the groove above and exit delicately left onto a slab. The recess above is the Raven's Nest; head right, round the exposed corner, and swarm up a wide crack to a commodious sloping ledge.
2 25m 4c Traverse left across a very exposed wall and move up to a sloping shelf in a corner. Step delicately down and round the rib on the left where a ledge runs across a sloping slab. The impressive diagonal flake is followed up and left beneath the roof, until an exposed bulge (look down!) at the far end leads to a recess.
3 40m 4c Traverse rightwards until larger holds lead up to a ledge system. Move 3m left until below a steep shallow corner. Climb this then traverse right using a flake bridged across a little overhang to a rib just left of a wide crack. Pull leftwards over an overhang and follow a clean shallow groove slightly leftwards to a grass terrace. Scramble to the summit ridge.
Photo page 121.
HS Gross, G Basterfield 17.06.1923

❼ Side Walk 91m E2 5c ★★★
An adventurous expedition offering exposed climbing up the steep grooves and walls overlooking Great Gully. Start just below the first chockstone of Great Gully.
1 16m 5c Climb the crack on the left of the boulder to the top of the pillar. Traverse left on small holds to a small ledge, where a hard move up the wall leads to a grass ledge below a large corner. Belay or, better, combine with the next pitch.
2 9m 5a The sustained corner is climbed to a large sloping ledge.
3 12m 5b Traverse right on to a slab beneath an impressive steep wall overlooking the gully. Climb a small overhang into a corner containing a thin crack. Climb to another overhang, pulling out rightwards to a large ledge.
4 27m 4b Climb above the belay to some perched blocks, slightly to the right. Go above these, trending first left, then right until a large triangular grass ledge is reached. Climb up to the right for 3m to some blocks.
5 27m 5a Climb to the right to beneath a large bulging groove. The groove is climbed direct to an overhang at 12m, passing a large insecure flake. The overhang is turned on the left by climbing an awkward crack past some doubtful blocks to the top.
L Brown, B Stevens 06.04.1960

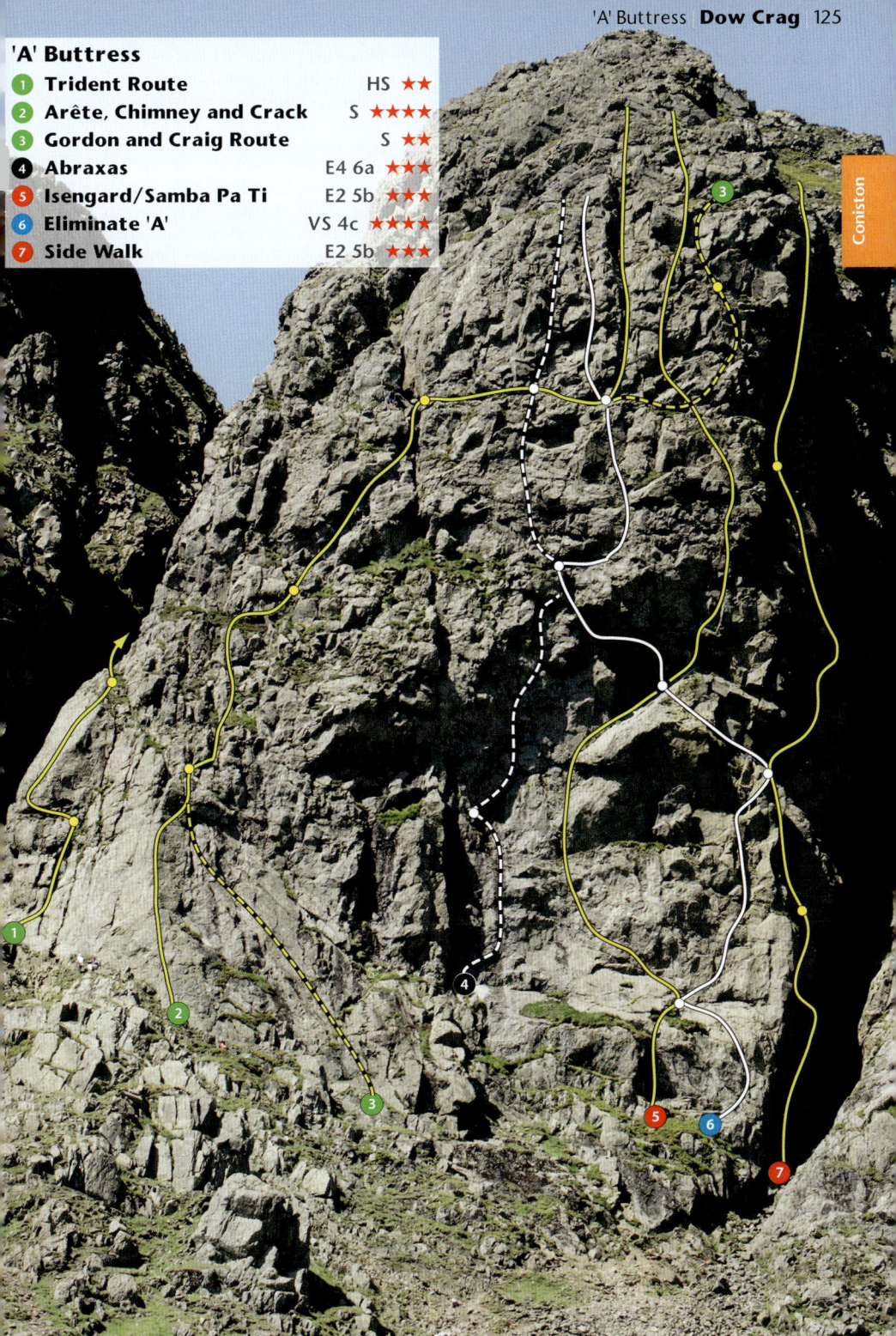

'B' Buttress (Upper Section)

An array of aspirational climbs are found on this dome-shaped section of the crag soaring above the slanting descent rake of Easy Terrace. The most striking line is that of the excellent and popular *Giant's Crawl*, a large diagonal slab crossing the buttress from the foot of Great Gully. Despite some seepage, most routes dry quickly. Beware of the potential for rocks being knocked off from above.

Descent: Descend the upper section of *Giant's Crawl* and continue right to join Easy Terrace.

8 Broadrick's Direct   64m   VS 4c   ★

Unlocking the correct way can be a challenge.
1 21m From the gully, 5m below the chockstone, take a steep wall on the right, a slab and a groove.
2 10m 4b Climb the groove directly above to a ledge below a bulge.
3 12m 4c Pull up the right-hand groove, cross into the left-hand groove and follow this steeply to block and flake belays.
4 21m Move diagonally right over easy ground to a final wall.
R Matheson May 1980

9 Giant's Crawl   115m   D   ★★★

An excellent inescapable route climbing the wide slabby gangway running diagonally rightwards from the foot of Great Gully. Serious accidents confirm that using the old flake belays is dangerous. A desperate route in poor conditions! **Take great care not to knock rocks off the ramp as there will often be others climbing below.** The pitches are only a guide - many can be run together.
1 18m Climb easy slabs and move left to a sloping ledge at the foot of a crack.
2 15m Climb the crack, passing a final quartz section, to a good ledge. The quartzy slabs to the right give a bolder variation at VD.
3 14m Traverse the ledge and easy ground diagonally rightwards to a stance on the edge.
4 12m A short wall leads to a ledge at the 'narrows'. Continue up slabs to a stance beneath a crack.
5 8m Continue to easy ground. Scramble rightwards to Easy Terrace.
6 18m Follow a well-marked grassy terrace leftwards to an awkward corner. This leads to a large ledge on the edge of the buttress.
7 12m Round to the left is a groove. Climb the crack up this and exit on the right.
8 18m Easier climbing leads to scrambling.
ETW and OJ Addyman, RF Stobart Easter 1909

10 Nimrod   84m   E1 5c   ★★★★

One of the best routes in The Lakes; increasing difficulties and some wonderful positions make this a memorable outing. Start on a large grass ledge at the foot of a cracked blocky ramp.
1 30m 5a Climb the wall to flakes below a shallow groove. Enter this and pull over the left-hand side of a small overhang to a flake. Traverse right, at first horizontally, then diagonally up, to small ledges beneath a bulging wall. Climb down these ledges to a large grassy terrace at the top of the ramp from where the pitch started.
2 15m 5b Move back up to the ledges and climb the steep wall on the right until an awkward traverse left leads into the main groove. Move up to a small spike and exit left on large finishing holds. Belay on *Giant's Crawl*. Alternatively, but harder, the groove can be climbed directly.
3 26m 5c Behind the belay is an open, left-facing corner. Climb to a small ledge below this then to a thin light-coloured crack in the left wall. Traverse delicately left across the steep wall then up to a prominent small blocky ledge on the arête with awesome exposure. Turn the bulge above on the right to reach easier ground and a grass ledge.
4 13m A short wall above leads rightwards to a large ledge.
D Miller, D Kirby 2.06.1962

11 Holocaust   72m   E4 6a   ★★★

A great climb, requiring confidence and impetus on the crux - the most fallen from piece of rock on the crag. Start below the centre of the steep wall, by an embedded flake on a grass ledge. This ledge is easily reached by scrambling across from half-way up Easy Terrace.
1 36m 6a Climb the shallow groove above to a down-pointing fang. Pull up to a thin diagonal crack before moving boldly right across the leaning wall to excellent holds; move up into a shallow depression. Follow a steep slab diagonally right to stand below steeper rock. Traverse delicately left to reach *Giant's Crawl*.
2 36m 5b Above is a smooth overhanging wall. Follow the groove on the right of this until a swing left around a rib leads to a quartz-riddled slabby gangway. Climb this to a recessed grass ledge. From the left end of the ledge, climb a steep crack to a ledge.
R Matheson, G Fleming, J Poole 2pa 20.07.1971

⓬ Tumble 36m E4 5c ★★★★
A very fine climb, one of the best of its grade in the district, providing sustained, rather than technically exacting, climbing accepting the challenge of the slim groove in the steep wall. Start directly below the groove. Step up left to a slight bulge then traverse rightwards and enter the groove. Climb to the top of the groove to reach a short crack in a small overhang. Traverse left, round the nose, and climb directly up past the left end of the overhang to reach a traverse. Climb over the capping roof at its narrowest point and continue to *Giant's Crawl*.
Photo page 131
P Livesey, J Lawrence 15.06.1975

⓭ Pandora's Box 37m E5 6b ★★
A brilliant route up the shallow groove 2m right of *Tumble*. Start below the groove, at a thin flake pressed against the face. From a standing position on the flake, very bold climbing leads to a jug at the bottom of the groove. Continue up this (2 pegs) until a step left can be made into the top of a groove. Move up and traverse right below the bulges to reach a sloping niche. Pull back left immediately and mantelshelf on to a fine rock ledge, just below the line of large overhangs. Climb round the large roof flake to reach a good hold in the headwall and then climb through the final bulges to reach *Giant's Crawl*.
A Phizacklea, JL Holden, R Knight, D Kells 5.05.1990

⓮ Catacomb 60m E1 5c ★★★
An extremely enjoyable and varied outing which traverses below the line of overhangs capping the wall. Start at the right-hand end of Hyacinth Terrace, at the foot of a mossy slab, below a wide steep crack.
1 36m 5b Climb the short slab and wide crack until a committing move left on flakes leads to the rising traverse line below the overhangs. Follow this all the way to *Giant's Crawl*. Belay up on the right.
2 24m 5c The left-slanting line in the steep wall is followed strenuously to reach the right-hand side of a grass ledge. Step up right and surmount the over-hang with difficulty, to enter a groove. Follow broken cracks out right to reach a grass terrace. Move down this and right to reach Easy Terrace.
R Matheson, MR Matheson 15.04.1972

'B' Buttress (Lower Section) 1 hr
A great selection of routes make this the most popular section of the crag. Fast-drying and enjoying the sun the longest. Beware of the potential for rocks being knocked off from above.

Descent: All routes end on Easy Terrace; follow this leftwards.

⓯ Pink Panther 40m E2 5c ★★★
An excellent diagonal line up the immaculate wall, with fingery climbing and adequate protection. Start on a flat-topped pedestal 3m left of the bridged block. Step right to a flat ledge and climb a scoop to reach a slight depression in the middle of the face. Move right beneath steeper rocks to reach a truncated spike below a rounded bulge. Stand on this with difficulty and enter a groove on the right. Climb this to its top and then pull out left on to a slab below the large roof. Skirt round the right-hand end of this and climb a scoop to easier ground.
R Matheson, MR Matheson 28.06.1973

⓰ Leopard's Crawl 48m HVS 5a ★★★
Superb open climbing on perfect rock. A masterpiece of its generation and one of Jim Birkett's best routes. Start where a large flake is propped against the wall.
1 28m 5a Step up from the block and traverse right to better holds. A short ascent then leads to a crack on the left of a brown crinkly wall. Cross this delicately rightwards and enter the base of a scoop, awkward and not well-protected. Climb the scoop to a ledge below the top crack of *Murray's Route*.
2 20m 4c Traverse right along the flake system and then climb a shallow groove in the wall above to easier ground.
RJ Birkett, L Muscroft, T Hill 9.09.1947

⓱ Tarkus 53m E2 5b ★★
A testing pitch with a serious start. Protection at the start is marginal (micro-cam and small wires). Start off a little ledge a couple of metres below and to the right of the bridged block.
1 33m 5b Step boldly right across the bulging wall using a conspicuous flake as a hand or foothold then move up, with haste, to a horizontal break. Traverse right to a little ledge below a steep crack. Or (6a) start directly below the crack and climb up to the ledge. Follow the crack and the wall above, trending leftwards to reach a ledge.
2 20m 4c Traverse right along the flake system and then climb a shallow groove in the

'B' Buttress (Lower Section) | **Dow Crag** | 129

wall above to easier ground.
R Matheson, MR Matheson 18.04.1972

18 Murray's Direct 48m VS 4c ★★★
Three contrasting variations make a classic with its own distinct character matching that of its easier partner. Start at a vertical embedded flake by a conspicuous right-slanting ramp.
1 22m 4c Tiger Traverse: Step boldly right and work along the ramp to an open corner. The Link: Step right and climb a wall above to a stance on a small ledge below the final steep corner.
2 26m 4c Direct Finish: The thought-provoking corner leads to an easing below the overhang. Take a diagonal line rightwards to cracks and easier ground.

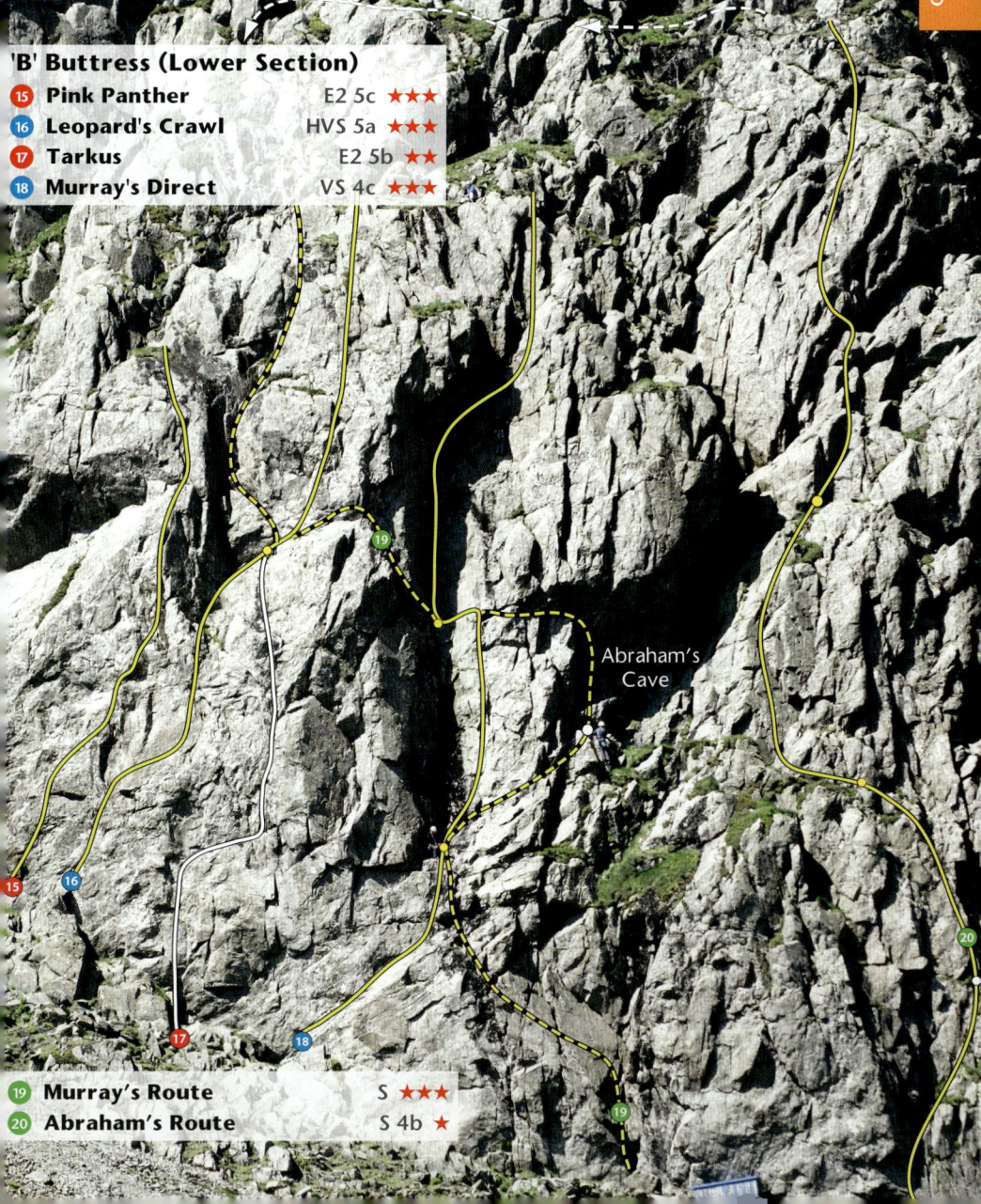

'B' Buttress (Lower Section)
- 15 **Pink Panther** E2 5c ★★★
- 16 **Leopard's Crawl** HVS 5a ★★★
- 17 **Tarkus** E2 5b ★★
- 18 **Murray's Direct** VS 4c ★★★

- 19 **Murray's Route** S ★★★
- 20 **Abraham's Route** S 4b ★

Hopkinson's Crack, HS (page 136) Rachel Burr — David Simmonite

Tumble E4 (page 128) Nic Brierley — 📷 Nick Wharton

⑲ Murray's Route 74m S ★★★
A classic, threading a way up an impressive area of rock with the most delightful situations. Start at an open V-chimney just to the left of the stretcher box.
1 23m Climb the chimney to an overhanging wall then cross the polished slab on the left with difficulty (crux) to a crack. Continue under bulging rock, round a corner and up to a ledge. The best belays are to be found on the large ledge directly below the corner.
2 12m Traverse rightwards over the obvious detached flake and follow the arête above for a few moves before stepping right into a short chimney. Climb this and the blocks above to a comfortable stance in a large cave (Abraham's Cave).
3 21m Exit leftwards up the fine steep crack and traverse horizontally to a possible belay below the steep corner. Climb the short flake chimney in the left wall and swing along the exposed flake line, descending slightly to a stance below a flake, about 2m right of another steep corner.
4 18m Move up the flake above which is followed leftwards back into the corner. Climb the wide crack above which leads awkwardly to a ledge. From there a V-groove on the left leads towards Easy Terrace.
DG Murray, WJ Borrowman, BL Martin 25.04.1918

⑳ Abraham's Route 62m S 4b ★
A fine classic route of increasing interest. Start up a wide broken groove which is the first easy break right of the stretcher box.
1 13m Climb the rightwards-trending groove to some grass ledges. Continue up the groove to a recess. Belay on the right.
2 12m Step onto a rock ledge on the right and stride left across the recess to follow fairly easy rocks up and leftwards to a long grassy ledge. This ledge runs leftwards into an open cave known as Abraham's Cave; escape is possible across the slabs up and right.
3 13m Climb the very shallow open groove on the left side of the steep wall above. Easier rocks lead to a grass terrace.
4 24m 4b Climb a series of short grooves and walls to a ledge below a blocky spike, towards the left end of the overhangs. The step left onto a slab is not easy, but good small holds lead to a spike where a groove continues rightwards to the crest of the buttress. An easy pitch leads up to Easy Terrace.
GD Abraham, AP Abraham, FT Phillipson March 1903

㉑ Woodhouse's Arête 35m E6 6b ★★★★
One of the finest hard pitches in the Lakes. Aspiring leaders are often seen taking huge but very safe falls into space on their first attempt. Follow the arête above Woodhouse's Pinnacle with growing anticipation from the crowds watching-on. Start below and left of the huge pinnacle on a grass ledge. An easy groove and pleasant flake crack lands you in a polished leftward-slanting groove. Climb up this a short distance to stand on a flake. From here, lean round the steep arête on the right to find a good jug. Swing round on this then up steeply to a small ledge. The short flake and wall lead to a step right beneath an overhang (peg and small wires). Hard moves rightwards round the overhang gain a finger pocket. Swing left on to the undercut arête in a brilliant position and climb it to the top, an undercut pocket and a flat hold being most helpful.
K Phizacklea, R Matheson 13.05.1998

㉒ The Shining Path 40m E5 6b ★★★
Superb climbing! Natural protection is available without resorting to the pegs; they were replaced in 2012. The first peg is very low and could easily be overlooked. Bridge up the right edge of the pinnacle until it is possible to establish oneself on the wall. Climb up, with a particularly desperate move past the fourth peg, to reach a pocket. Finish leftwards up the short corner below the headwall. From here either abseil from the top of *Woodhouse's Arête* or continue up the top pitch of *Hesperus*, which is very worthwhile.
A Hyslop, D Kells 16.06.1992

㉓ Paths of Victory 59m E6 6c ★★
This provides a sustained and extremely fingery extension to *The Shining Path*. Follow *The Shining Path* to the pocket. A desperately difficult sequence follows. Step right and climb straight over the bulge using the right-hand pocket to get established on the featureless wall above. A traverse right brings holds near the arête overlooking the deep chimney into reach (peg). A final hard move leads to a diagonal ramp and some respite! Step right onto the upper slab (peg), then continue directly up the centre, crossing an overlap.
S Wood, D Kells 5.08.1993

㉔ Hesperus 36m E2 5c ★★
Steep and strenuous climbing. Start up the striking right-facing chimney between **'B'** and **'C' Buttresses**.
1 24m 5c Climb the crack, passing a smooth section at 10m, to a small overhung ledge on the left wall. Step down left from here onto

'B' Buttress (Lower Section) | **Dow Crag** | 133

Eliminate 'C' VS (page 134) — 📷 Peter Sterling

the face and climb to a small fragile pocket then move left with difficulty to better holds. Follow the corner above, pulling out awkwardly leftwards onto a large sloping ledge.
2 12m 5a From the top of the right-hand block, climb a couple of metres up the wall until it is possible to step down and rightwards onto an exposed traverse. Follow this on good holds to easier ground.
R Matheson, MR Matheson, J Poole 4.07.1973

'C' Buttress
This rounded slabby buttress offers one of the most popular lines at **Dow Crag**. Water is available just to the right, where there is a small but constant flow out of a crack in the rock - absolute nectar!
Descent: Easy Terrace leftwards.

㉕ Southern Slabs 40m MS ★
A delightful route taking the sweep of quartz-splashed slabs. Scramble up and right to a ledge below the quartz-marked slab. A pleasant upward traverse leads to a small grass ledge. Climb the slab directly to reach a well-scratched rock ledge just below the 'large slab' on *'C' Ordinary Route*. Move left and climb the mossy slab to reach a grass ledge and belay. Go right and finish up the *'C' Ordinary Route*.
GS Bower, AW Wakefield, G Basterfield 6.06.1920

㉖ 'C' Ordinary Route 100m D ★★★
A classic route of outstanding quality. Start just left of the lowest point of the buttress.
1 15m Climb the crest of the buttress to the top of a partially detached flake. Alternatively, head up and right, then leftwards finishing up a steep crack.
2 16m Follow the slabby scoop, leading to easier ground. Scrambling leads to a big ledge, with a fallen flake, below a steep wall.
3 10m Traverse left to the end of the ledge then follow a scoop up right to a ledge. The steep wall above the belay can be climbed direct (harder).
4 16m Trend left across the slabs to reach a ledge on the edge of the buttress. Follow this directly to another large ledge.
5 13m Climb the large slab above which leads rightwards to ledges. Continue to the one at the top of a chimney which has spectacular views into *Intermediate Gully*.
6 13m Follow the flake system in the steeper wall on the left to a rib. Move left around this and climb a crack (awkward). Stance and belay up and right.
7 17m Follow a gangway rightwards round a bulge to a ledge. Pull up to the left and traverse horizontally left; easy rocks lead up to Easy Terrace.
GF Woodhouse, AJ Woodhouse Aug 1904

㉗ Charmer 52m HVS 5a
A fine open route taking the steep arête just left of *Intermediate Gully*. Start 10m up the bed of the gully, below a series of curving scoops in a slab on the left.
1 16m 4b Climb the scooped slab to a short right-facing corner overlooking the gully; this leads to a grass ledge.
2 24m 5a Traverse right to reach the foot of the arête. Climb this direct, bold and on good holds, to reach a ledge at 12m. Move up to a grass ledge and follow the easier rib above to a belay.
3 12m 5a Directly above is a steep hanging corner, just to the right of a large nose of rock. Climb this past some awkward shelving holds to reach a ledge. Scramble up to Easy Terrace.
A Phizacklea, JL Holden 13.06.1992

㉘ Eliminate 'C' 46m VS 4c ★★
A very enjoyable route, providing delicate climbing in an exposed position high on the left of *Intermediate Gully*. Start from the large ledge at the top of P1 of the Gully.
1 14m 4c Climb the slab leftwards using a diagonal (often greasy) crack beneath an overlap to start. Step left onto the wall to reach a small ledge. An awkward traverse left leads to an exposed ledge on the arête. Climb a crack above to reach a grass ledge.
2 12m 4a A shallow groove on the right leads up the wall above and around the arête on the right. Follow this easily to reach a large ledge.
3 20m 4c Move into the steep corner on the right. Traverse delicately right across the rough wall to reach an obvious and slightly loose spike on the arête overlooking the gully - a very exposed position! Climb up the arête to a gangway which runs back left towards easier ground and ledges. Scramble up *'C' Ordinary Route* to Easy Terrace.
Photo page 133.
HS Gross, G Basterfield 9.07.1922

㉙ Intermediate Gully 52m MVS 4b
This gully, one of the great, classic Victorian climbs, becomes a titanic struggle in greasy or wet conditions. Scramble some 30m up the lower section of the gully to a cave.
1 9m Climb the awkward crack and the right wall of a short chimney to a large ledge.
2 8m The troublesome chockstone above is climbed direct. Continue more easily to a ledge and a belay on the right.
3 21m 4a The wide crack leads strenuously to

'C' Buttress | **Dow Crag** | 135

Spring water

easier ground. Where it steepens, climb the left wall to a recess below a jammed chockstone.

4 14m 4b Another unsympathetic chockstone leads with considerable difficulty to a deep cave. From a small ledge on the right, stride left into a groove on the left wall. Follow a crack to Easy Terrace.
EA Hopkinson, JH Hopkinson Campbell 14.04.1895

Easter Gully
The Amphitheatre

Excellent routes hidden away from the crowds. **Easter Gully** divides **'D'** and **'E' Buttresses** and is a vast funnel. About 35m above the scree, it is spanned by a huge chockstone, beyond which is The Amphitheatre. The place is atmospheric and sunny and is the starting point for the many excellent routes.

Approach: Scramble up the gully. The huge chockstone can be passed on either side - the way left is easier.

Descent: Scramble up and left until a shallow grassy chimney leads down onto a broad grassy dome (the true top of **'D' Buttress**). Walk left into the easy top section of *Intermediate Gully*, and descend this to a well-worn platform on the left. This is the end of Easy Terrace which can be followed to the bottom of the crag.

30 Great Central Route 60m HVS 5b ★★

A climb of immense character offering a superb blend of strenuous and delicate climbing in a position of great exposure. A major breakthrough for its time even with the use of combined tactics, a method still occasionally employed today, it follows the imposing pillar in the centre of **The Amphitheatre**. Start at the foot of the pillar.

1 24m 4c Climb the nose and follow pleasant slabs rightwards to a ledge below a steep crack. The infamous South America Crack.

2 24m 5b As delicate as the previous pitch was strenuous. Step from the sloping left edge of the ledge, left of a slight nose, onto the thin crinkly wall to reach slightly better holds; move right and up to a handy little ledge (crux). Follow the crack above to a large diagonal overhang. Traverse left under this, across the mossy slab, to reach the crack. Up this for a couple of metres then step right onto a ledge on the front face of the pillar.

3 12m 4b Traverse rightwards along the ledge and move round the grossly exposed corner. Finish up the pleasant slabs above.
JI Roper, GS Bower, G Jackson, AP Wilson Sep 1919

31 The Norseman 57m E4 6a ★★

Difficult climbing in a fine situation.
1 24m 4c Climb the nose and follow pleasant slabs rightwards to a ledge below a steep crack. P1 of *Great Central Route*.
2 33m 6a From the right end of the ledge, a thin crack is followed to the diagonal overhang. Pull over this rightwards to a ledge. The wall above is very committing (peg). Move up again and step left around the arête. Climb the crack on the left side to easier ground.
I Greenwood, P McVey 17.06.1979

32 Hopkinson's Crack 45m HS ★★

A superb old-fashioned crack climb. First ascent on the same day as his brothers were doing the first ascent of *Intermediate Gully*. This Hopkinson got the better deal!
1 15m The crack is climbed directly to a ledge on the left. Thread belay or, more likely these days, continue.
2 12m Step back into the crack and climb with greater difficulty, exiting left onto the Bandstand ledge (phew!).
3 18m Follow the wider crack to easier ground. Beware of loose rocks in the steep gully.
Photo page 130.
C Hopkinson, O Koecher 14.04.1895

33 Easter Rising 46m E2 5c ★★

Continually interesting climbing taking a direct line up the wall to the right of the corner.
1 25m 5c Climb the wall on the right directly to an overlap (thread). Move left and surmount the overlap and smooth quartzy wall above to ledges below a crack. Climb the wall 3m left of this crack, moving slightly left, to reach ledges and a belay above.
2 21m 5a Move left into the vague crack in the upper wall and follow it to the final hanging rib. Step right into the groove which leads to the top.
Photo page 116.
A Phizacklea, R Matheson 30.05.1982

34 Black Wall 30m HVS 5a ★★★ ♦

This fine wall climb and an impressive achievement in 1920 tackles the steep right-hand edge. Well-spaced holds lead to the overhang. Use a crack on the left side to gain the wall above then continue to ledges.
Descent: Scramble off rightwards.
JI Roper, G Basterfield 24.06.1920

GREY CRAG

OS Grid Ref: SD 283 988
Altitude: 330m

 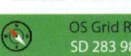

Enjoyable slab climbing on impeccable rock. Welcome shade on hot days or early sunshine. With obstinate seepage, the routes are at their best after several dry days. Other than a couple of ancient junipers, belays at the top are difficult to find.

Approach: Park in Coniston and follow the vehicle track alongside Church Beck, passing the Coppermines Youth Hostel, to Levers Water Beck. Cross the beck and climb steep grass to the crag.

Descent: With care by abseil. Or, walk to the right then descend the incline to Levers Water Beck.

4

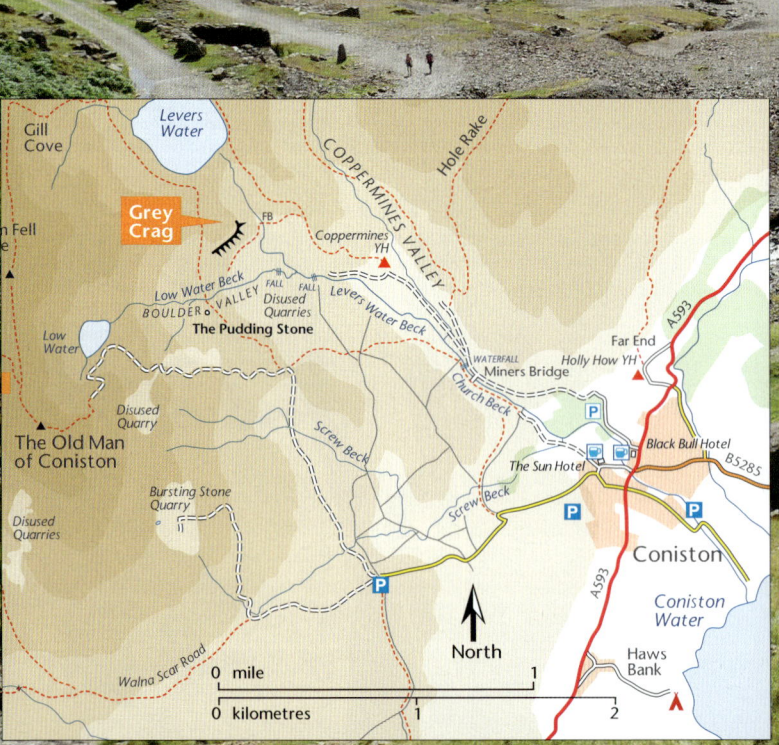

Drought VS (page 140) Astrid Saxby — Keith Sanders

1 Glasnevin Wall 44m VS 4b
A route of some character. Start at the foot of the ramp.
1 9m Scramble left along the ramp to a large ledge.
2 12m 4b Just to the left of the top of the ramp there is a steep wall with an overhang at 6m. Climb the wall to the overhang then traverse left along a heather ledge to a small rock stance; spike belay.
3 23m 4a Traverse left to the top of two large partly-detached blocks and move up to a small ledge. Climb the wall above and move right to a sloping ledge. Continue up shelving rock.
JP Hool, WL Barnes 7.06.1963

2 Catalyst 51m VS 4b
An interesting route. Start at stepped ledges below a cracked bulge some 6m right of the ramp.
1 31m 4b Climb the wall for 5m crossing a bulge to reach a shallow scoop. Traverse left until below a ledge. From the ledge, climb the slab above then traverse left to another ledge and a flake belay.
2 20m 4b Climb diagonally left to a scoop, climb this for 3m then continue leftwards to flat sloping holds that lead rightwards to the top.
JP Hool 12.09.1969

3 Drought 42m VS 4b ★
When dry this enjoyable sparsely protected pitch follows the light-coloured clean streak of rock in the centre of the slab. Start at stepped ledges below a cracked bulge. Climb the wall, over a bulge; cross a shallow scoop and continue up the pleasant slab. Juniper belay.
Photo page 139.
JP Hool, WL Barnes 10.06.1962

4 Snowdrop 35m VS 4b ★
A shallow scoop above the start of a blocky ramp leads to better holds (crux). Continue to the left of a prominent prow. Juniper belay.
A Phizacklea, JL Holden 6.04.2013

LITTLE HOW CRAG

OS Grid Ref: SD 274 996
Altitude: 550m

Great climbing on sound rock. Beautifully positioned above the north-western shore of Levers Water. Catches the sun for most of the day. All of the routes are worth climbing.

Approach, Coniston: Up the Coppermines Valley to Levers Water and up to the crag.

Approach, Walna Scar Road gate: Follow the path on the right. This leads through what is known as Boulder Valley (home to some good bouldering) and eventually to the dam at Levers Water. Walk clockwise round the west shore of Levers Water. The crag is on the flank of Brim Fell a short way up the fellside.

Descent: Well to the left.

❶ Black Moss Route 32m HVS 4c ★
The slabs to the left of, and parallel to, *Black Moss Crack* give pleasant climbing. From the base of the crack, climb for a couple of metres and then make a long traverse left and slightly upwards to an obvious block left and below the curving crack. Climb the slab and vague rib above to a steep finish.
WJ Borrowman 11.05.1919

❷ Black Moss Crack 39m HS 4a ★
The curving crackline.
1 30m 4a Move up the crack and follow it in its entirety, finishing up a steep wider section. Belay on the right.
2 9m Leftwards up a scoop then right to the top.

❸ Greased Lightning 31m VS 4c ★
Another good route. Move up to the curving crack and follow it for 6m. Step up to the right onto the slab and climb it, just right of the curving corner, and passing a little overlap on its left to the top.
A Phizacklea, JL Holden 17.10.1992

❹ Thunderclap 31m VS 4b ★★ ♦
A good route with sustained interest taking a direct line up the centre of the slabs. Start at the base of the curving crack. Climb the wall directly, passing to the left of a grass ledge at 9m, and taking the line of bulges at the top by the groove line on the left.
Photo page 142.
R Matheson Jul 1983

OS Grid Ref
SD 274 996

RAD
Little How

Coniston
SD 300 978
GPS 54.370667
-3.077451

Thunderclap VS (page 141) Astrid Saxby — Keith Sanders

Little How Crag

5 Thunder Slab 42m HS 4a ★
An enjoyable open climb, taking the easiest line up the right side of the slab. Start at the base of the left-facing corner.
1 30m 4a From the chockstone, climb the corner for a couple of metres and move left across the slab using a thin diagonal crack to reach a small grass ledge. A few moves back right lead to the base of a short shallow corner, 3m left of the main corner. Climb it, exiting left and move up to the line of bulges. These are avoided on the right by following the main corner to grass ledges.
2 12m Follow the easy line leftwards to the top. The left-hand crack in the steep wall above is a most entertaining alternative.
GS Bower, WJ Borrowman, TC Ormiston-Chant 11.05.1919

6 Sunshine Arête 41m VD ★
Very enjoyable - the easiest line up the arête right of the corner. Start at the base of the corner.
1 8m Make an awkward move to start a rising traverse rightwards onto the arête and up to a ledge and block belay.
2 21m Climb the left edge of the steep slab to a large grass ledge.
3 12m Traverse left across the ledge and follow a slab up to the left.
GS Bower, WJ Borrowman, TC Ormiston-Chant 11.05.1919

7 Trouble and Strife 41m S ★
Start at a wide left-slanting crack at ground level: this is just right of the arete.
1 20m Climb into a niche with a dubious flake at its top. Climb the wall above and through a bulge 3m to the right of the arête. Belay on the first grass ledge; there is a spike 4m above the ledge.
2 21m Climb the slab to a higher grass ledge. Climb the short left-facing corner on the right and then break through the bulge via the vague groove above.
S Reid, B James, C King 23.06.2005

Little How Crag

① Black Moss Route	HVS 5a	★
② Black Moss Crack	HS 4a	★
③ Greased Lighting	VS 4c	★
④ Thunderclap	VS 4b	★★
⑤ Thunder Slab	HS 4a	★
⑥ Sunshine Arête	VD	★
⑦ Trouble and Strife	S	★

DUDDON

The Duddon valley is a delightful backwater, well off the beaten track for most Lake District visitors. As such the climbing, while predominantly short, can provide some great days out in an idyllic setting.

The Plumb, Wallowbarrow VS (page 152) Peter Sterling & Laetitia Sterling — 📷 DAVID SIMMONITE

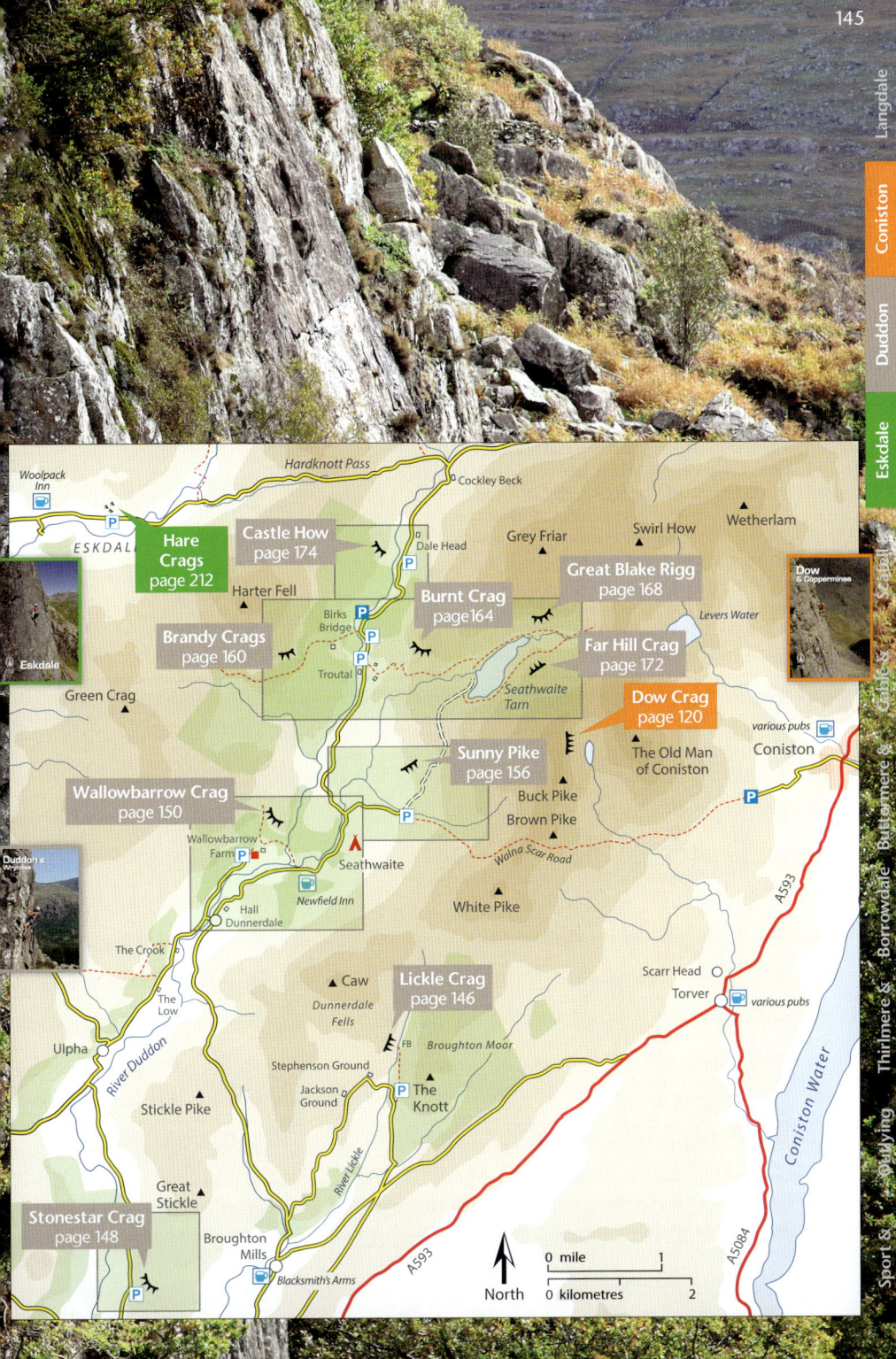

LICKLE CRAG

OS Grid Ref: SD 240 941
Altitude: 280m

Delightful climbing in a lovely secluded valley. Tucked away to the east of the Duddon is the beautiful hidden valley of the River Lickle. **Lickle Crag** is the largest of a number of small crags on Caw, overlooking the river.

Approach: Approach from the A593 Torver to Broughton Road. Take the moor road from either end to the 'scissors' junction. Head north up the narrow road towards Stephenson Ground. Just after the first bridge there is a parking area on the right called The Hawk; keep going. 400m further on is a gated track on the right; keep going. After another 400m, there is another gated track on the right with space to park. If you get to another bridge, you have gone too far. From the gate, follow a path north to join the forestry road. Hike along this for a kilometre until the crag can be seen to the west across the river. Head left down a wet path and cross a slate footbridge.

Descent: To the left and down grass. Abseil.

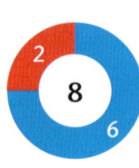

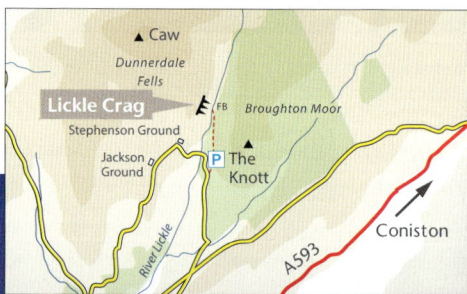

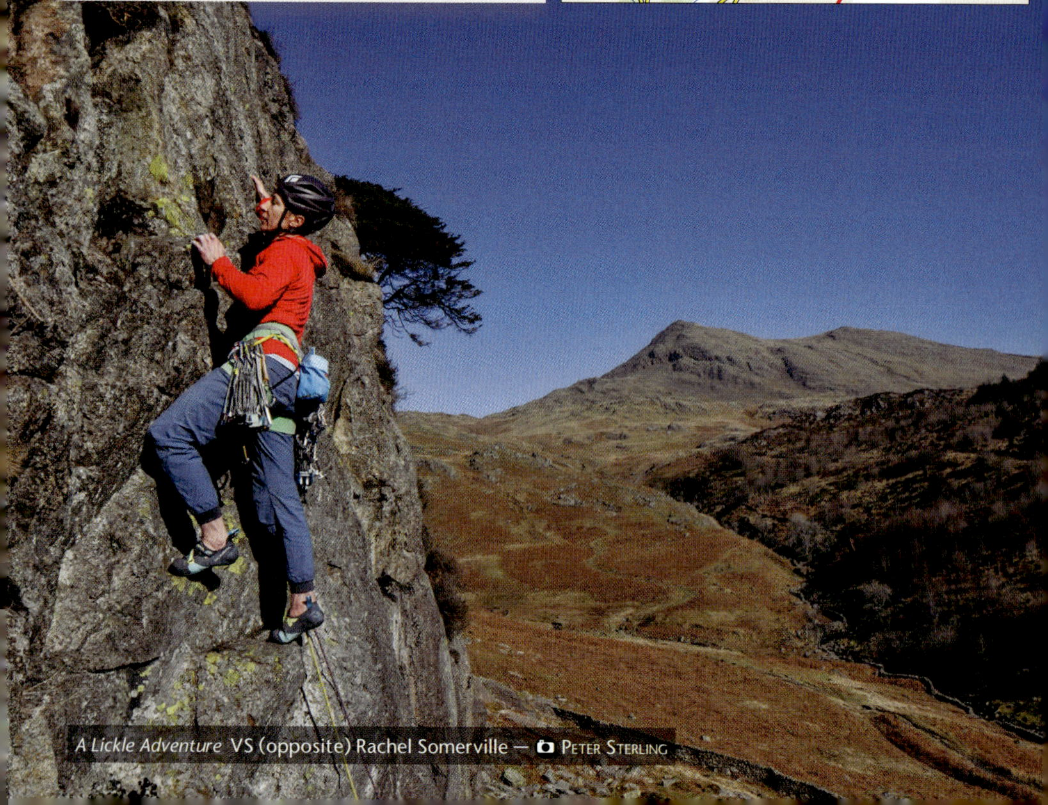

A Lickle Adventure VS (opposite) Rachel Somerville — 📷 Peter Sterling

① **Tickle**   25m   VS 4b
A stubborn start through a pod leads to a groove. Climb this to ledges on the left. Finish up the cracked wall.
E Rogers, RO Graham, SR Scott 2.03.2021

② **Lick Down**   25m   HVS 5a   ★
Climb the slab left of the small prominent block (micro-cam right of block). A tricky move leads to a ledge. Continue following grooves and cracks to a block belay.
RO Graham, E Rogers 28.02.2021

③ **A Lickle Adventure**   25m   VS 4b   ★★
A fine pitch. Climb the clean central wall starting from a prominent embedded flake and finish at the highest point.
Photo opposite.
D Hannah 1977

④ **An Almost   25m   HVS 4c   ★★
Pleasurable Sensation of Fright**
An unwavering direct version of *A Lickle Adventure* gives the best climbing on the crag.
Feb 2021

⑤ **Morning Sun**   25m   VS 4b   ★★
Enjoyable climbing on positive holds with abundant protection. Follow a white streak for 7m to a ledge and continue up clean slabs to finish.
E Rogers, RO Graham 28.02.2021

⑥ **Reet Petite**   27m   VS 4b   ★
Climb the slabs to the right of the white streak and trend left to finish.
E Rogers, P Sterling, R Somerville 1.03.2021

⑦ **Sterling Crisis**   25m   E1 5b   ★
Climb a slab to the roof. Heave across rightwards then climb a crack and slabs trending left.
RO Graham, E Rogers, SR Scott 2.03.2021

⑧ **Gold Standard**   18m   E1 5b
Start up the easy-looking (!) ramp. Move right at the break (cam and nut low on right). Take the first weakness in the overhang and climb the tricky wall above.
RO Graham, E Rogers 5.03.2021

STONESTAR CRAG

OS Grid Ref: SD 202 907
Altitude: 150m

A great single-pitch venue close to the road. Quick-drying with afternoon and evening sun, this is a popular crag once the normal bird restriction is lifted.

Seasonal restriction: 1st Mar to 30th Jun.

Approach: A large layby below the crag is available for parking. A well-marked path heads up the hillside next to the fence.

Descent: Either side.

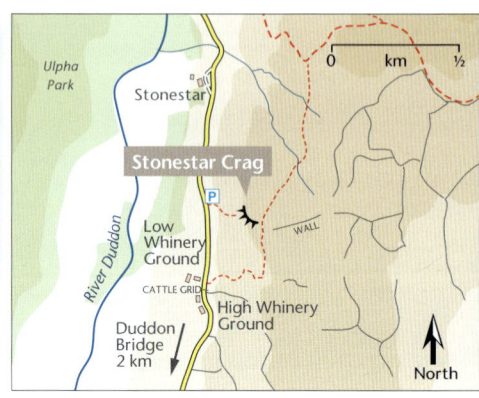

Quarry Layby

SD 201 907

❶ Last Chance Saloon   23m   VS 4b
Starts beneath the right end of the square-cut overhang. Climb onto a fin of rock and continue up the crack above. A tricky move gives access to the right-trending crack running parallel to, and just left of, the top crack of *Venezuela*; follow this then finish up the wall above.
D Geere, J Daly 25.10.1997

The impressive steep slab on the right has several very good climbs.

❷ Venezuela   24m   HVS 5a   ★★
Steep climbing with a distinct crux. Start on a grass terrace below a rounded rib, about 9m above and right of the large tree. The rib leads to a block at 9m below a steep wall. Climb up and leftwards onto the wall crossing a thin leftwards-slanting crack to gain a right-slanting grassy crack with some difficulty. Follow this to the top.
R Matheson, MR Matheson Aug 1968

❸ Columbia   27m   E1 5b   ★★★ ♦
A superb satisfying climb with ample protection. Start at light-coloured twin grooves. Climb the right-hand groove to the overhangs (doubtful block); step left onto the upper wall. Follow a clean diagonal crack rightwards across the slab with a delicate fingery sequence then up to the top.
Photo opposite.
A Phizacklea, M Lynch 13.04.1981

❹ The Challenger   30m   E3 6a   ★★
The slab below the leftwards-slanting overlap gives delicate technical climbing. Scramble above a smooth sloping boulder, avoiding the vegetation. Pull over a small overhang to stand in the diagonal slots above. A tough delicate sequence rightwards leads to a good crack below the main overlap. The challenge is to continue diagonally leftwards, using the overlap, to reach *Columbia*. Cross this and take a direct line up the slab, past a small flat-topped flake, to finish.
A Phizacklea, P Donnelly 4.07.1989

❺ The Breech   27m   E2 5c   ★★
A good strenuous route. Start directly below the right-hand side of the overlap. Climb easy ground then a steep crack to reach the overlap. Pull over rightwards and move boldly up the diagonal crack until it eases; a direct line is taken to the top.
E Cleasby, A Phizacklea 8.02.1981

❻ Anchor Handling   27m   E2 5c   ★★
A worthy counter-diagonal with some technical climbing. Follow *The Breech* to a good slot below the lower overhangs at 3m. Traverse right to reach substantial holds above the overhang. Pull onto the slab leftwards to gain the crack of *The Breech*; continue leftwards to gain a good hold then finish directly.
A Phizacklea, P Donnelly 4.07.1989

Columbia E1 (opposite) Peter Sterling — David Simmonite

WALLOWBARROW CRAG
OS Grid Ref: SD 222 968
Altitude: 210m

An impressive crag with an extensive selection of enjoyable mid-grade multi-pitch routes. Fast-drying, steep, clean and solid rock make this a popular refuge when the higher crags are wet. Presiding imperiously above the valley as it narrows towards Seathwaite, its array of steep buttresses forms a mountain in itself, with an appropriately precipitous skyline.

Approach: High Wallowbarrow Farm - reached by following a narrow No Through Road along the west bank of the River Duddon. Parking is on hard standing or grass near the farm; a donation, which goes to both MRT and *Médecins sans Frontières*, is courteous. Pass quietly through the farmyard and take the gated track immediately to the left. Follow this up through trees, fording a beck, to a drystone wall at the base of the **West Buttress**. A path leads up rightwards through the trees to the **East Buttress**.

Bryanston VS (page 152) Peter Sterling & Laetitia Sterling — David Simmonite

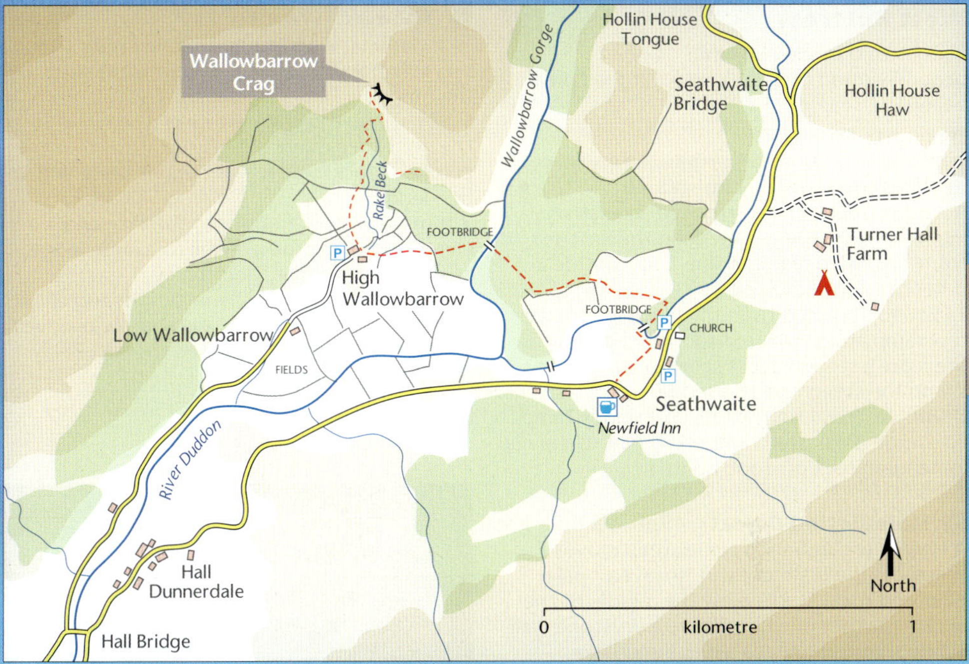

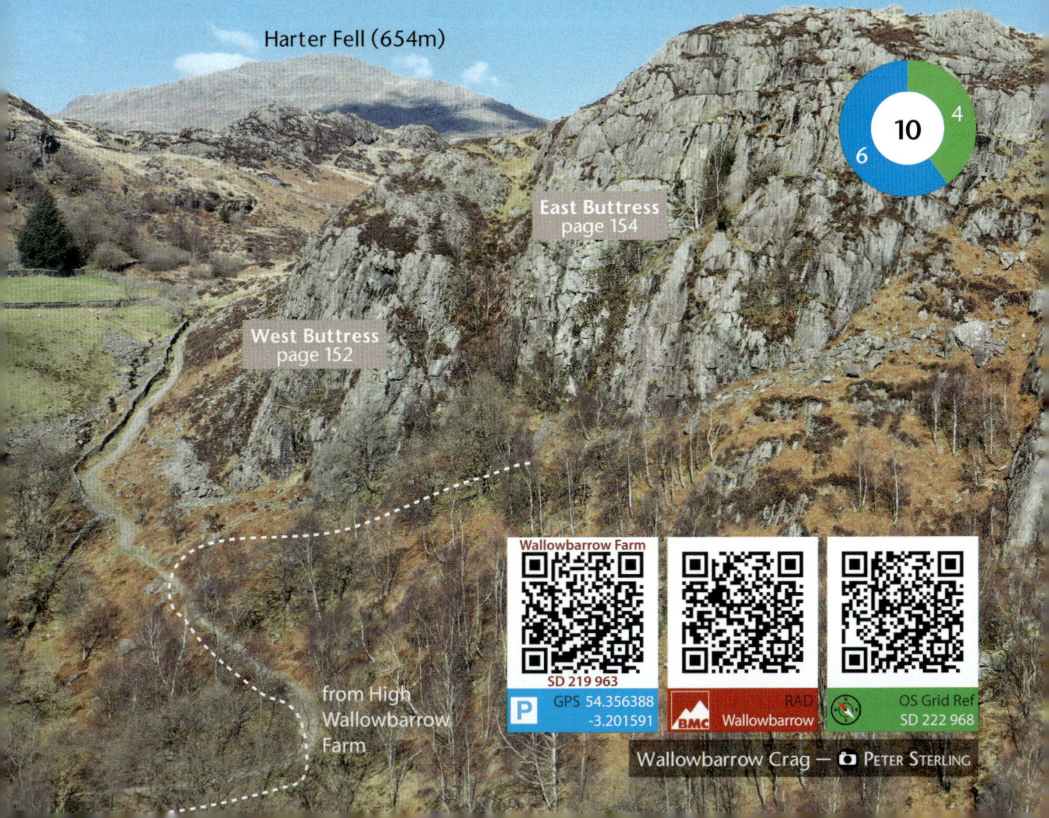

151

Wallowbarrow Crag

Hollin House Tongue
Seathwaite Bridge
Hollin House Haw
Wallowbarrow Gorge
Rake Beck
FOOTBRIDGE
High Wallowbarrow
Low Wallowbarrow
FIELDS
FOOTBRIDGE
CHURCH
Turner Hall Farm
Seathwaite
Newfield Inn
River Duddon
Hall Dunnerdale
Hall Bridge

North
0 — kilometre — 1

Duddon

Harter Fell (654m)

East Buttress
page 154

West Buttress
page 152

10 / 4 / 6

from High Wallowbarrow Farm

Wallowbarrow Farm
P GPS 54.356388
SD 219 963 -3.201591

BMC RAD
Wallowbarrow

OS Grid Ref
SD 222 968

Wallowbarrow Crag — Peter Sterling

West Buttress

Popular mid-grade climbing; generally good rock; be careful at the top as belays are scarce.

Descent: To the left.

1 Western Wall 33m VS 4b ★★
A connoisseur's climb, exposed and satisfying, traversing the grey wall on the buttress front in a rising diagonal line. Start beside a detached-looking block.
1 15m 4b Stepping from the block, gain a narrow ramp and traverse diagonally rightwards (delicate), stopping just short of a crackline. Climb the steep wall to a ledge.
2 18m 4a Trend rightwards up a slabby ramp to a large flake, step right and move steeply up impending rock on good holds.
LG Sullivan, PE Wilson, J Jenkinson 20.05.1963

2 Malediction Direct 49m VS 4c ★★
A fine little climb with some steep moves following the distinct incut groove of pale-coloured rock. Start below the middle of the buttress at a broken rib above a drystone wall.
1 24m Climb the rib to a niche and flake.
2 25m 4c Climb bulging rock left of the small roof to gain the open groove and follow this steeply taking the left branch towards the top.
AJ Simpkin, AH Greenbank March 1959

3 The Plumb 51m VS 4c ★★
An uncompromising line with an uncertain finish.
1 24m Climb the rib to a flake.
2 27m 4c Move a couple of metres right of the niche and climb the open groove to the chimney crack. Follow this surmounting the hanging flake with difficulty; improving holds lead upwards.
Photo page 144.
D Miller, JA Austin June 1967

4 Bryanston 53m VS 4b ★★★
A good climb of increasing difficulty with an exhilarating final pitch tackling the conspicuous crack near the right-hand side of the headwall.
1 24m Climb to the flake.
2 16m Go diagonally right, following a weakness, for 9m. Traverse horizontally right and ascend to a small ledge next to a detached block.
3 13m 4b Enter the crack from the left, climb to a recess then step left and climb the wall. Belay well back.
Photo page 150.
J Smith, WF Dowlen 8.04.1956

5 Thomas 57m HS 4a ★★★★
Fine climbing with an improbable finish; deservedly popular. Start at a well-worn patch on the ground.
1 21m Climb the crack slanting steeply up to the right then move directly upwards to some perched blocks; move right under these and up to a ledge.
2 18m Move back right onto the face and climb the steep cracked wall to a large ledge at the top of a pillar. Block belay.
3 18m Make an awkward move right and climb the wall into the exposed and shallow grooves above. Generous holds lead to the top. Belay well back.
Photo below.
WF Dowlen, D Stroud 26.06.1955

Thomas HS (above) — 📷 David Simmonite

West Buttress | **Wallowbarrow Crag** 153

Duddon

East Buttress

Satisfying routes on sound rock; mossy in places.

Approach: From the base of the **West Buttress**, walk right through trees.

Descent: Cross the top of the crag to the right to reach a wide grassy gully. Descend this with care.

6 Nameless 90m HS 4b ★★

A very good climb; exposed and satisfying. Begin up a prominent groove avoiding the triangular-shaped overhang by an entertaining detour.
1 32m 4b Climb the groove and make a decidedly awkward exit onto a ledge. Climb leftwards across the mossy slab to a definite impasse at a groove. Move up then swing onto the steep face on the left. Climb this slightly left for 3m then delicately turn a bulge on the right to enter a shallow groove. Continue up and left to a stance.
2 18m Climb the shallow groove on the right, to a grass ledge, then step left across a slab and follow the cracked wall to a good ledge with a flake belay.
3 40m 4a Traverse diagonally leftwards to a large poised block on the arête. Surmount this to gain a slab then climb rightwards to an arête. Climb the arête on its left side and the easier rib above to a small roof. Pull directly over this and go up leftwards to a stance.
WF Dowlen, J Hollin 1.06.1956

7 Digitation 48m VS 4c ★★

A thrilling well-protected climb directly up the slab and breaching the distinctive overlap. Start from the three poised blocks.
1 30m 4c Step right off the topmost block and climb the wall to a small ledge. Move left, and climb the shallow right-facing corner to the overlap. Pull boldly over leftwards and continue to the oak tree. Alternatively, pull over rightwards and climb straight up the left side of the bulge to the belay.
2 18m 4b Climb a thin crack in the centre of the steep wall at the back of the ledge to a horizontal flake. Pleasant walls lead to the top.
DG Heap, JR Amatt, CB Greenhalgh 3.04.1963

8 Agitation 60m VS 4c ★

Flanking *Digitation* this daring companion climbs the wall to the right. Start from a distinct recess with a sloping floor 3m right of the leaning blocks.
1 30m 4c Climb the recess, pulling out leftwards and moving up left to a small ledge. Continue, unflustered, across ledges diagonally rightwards to reach the long narrow overlap. Alternatively, instead of going left from the recess, climb the corner then step right and climb to a ledge. Surmount a bulge on the left and traverse leftwards to the long narrow overlap. Pull over a couple of metres right of a shallow corner in the slab above, then continue up and leftwards to the large oak tree.
2 18m 4c Thin climbing via a series of sloping steps up the right-hand side of the grey wall, stepping left before the final section.
3 12m 4a Climb into a grassy niche and step onto a square block on the left. Continue up the short wall to a grassy ledge. Step left and finish up the clean right wall of the mossy V-groove.
C Childs, G Saxon (1 pa) 24.08.1973

9 Trinity Slabs 60m S 4a ★★

A super route that has a number of thought-provoking moves following the stepped buttress. Start by a flake capped with an overhang.
1 18m Climb the wall, left of the flake, and where it steepens move leftwards to below a short shallow corner. Continue directly to a large flake.
2 12m The bouldery wall on the left of the flake leads to a leaning block. Step off the block onto a second short wall leading to a large ledge. Belay over to the right.
3 15m 4a The groove on the right is awkward and leads to the next ledge system. Or, at the same grade, up and right an exposed undercut rib leads directly to the same ledges.
4 15m Pull into an incipient groove with some difficulty. The groove is followed to a step right onto the final arête. **Photo below.**

Trinity Slabs S (above) — 📷 David Simmonite

East Buttress | **Wallowbarrow Crag** | 155

10 Wall and Corner 58m VD ★★
Could this be the most popular climb on the crag? The mix of short pitches and engaging moves provides an absorbing climb of no mean difficulty. This wall of clean rock, distinguished by a massive feature in the shape of a blunt handgun, is an attraction in itself. Begin at a bare patch below a short smooth wall near the right-hand end of the crag.
1 10m Climb onto a small rock ledge and continue up the centre of the wall on small polished holds to reach a large ledge below the 'handgun' overhang.
2 15m Climb the shallow groove and crack past the left side of the overhang until easier rocks lead leftwards to a large flake.
3 12m The wall above the flake is climbed for 5m until a short traverse left brings you to a drystone wall. Climb past this to a bridged block.
4 21m Step left off the block, up the steep wall, and move right across the corner to a grassy recess. Follow the right-hand wall of the large corner above to the top.

SUNNY PIKE

OS Grid Ref: SD 242 974
Altitude: 200m

The clue is in the name. Easy access and plenty of easy routes make this an idyllic location.

Approach: From the bottom of the Walna Scar Road, walk 500m up the Seathwaite Tarn track. On the left is a lone Scots Pine; to its right is a hurdle closing a gap in the wall. Go through this gap then head 200m north across damp ground to the crag.

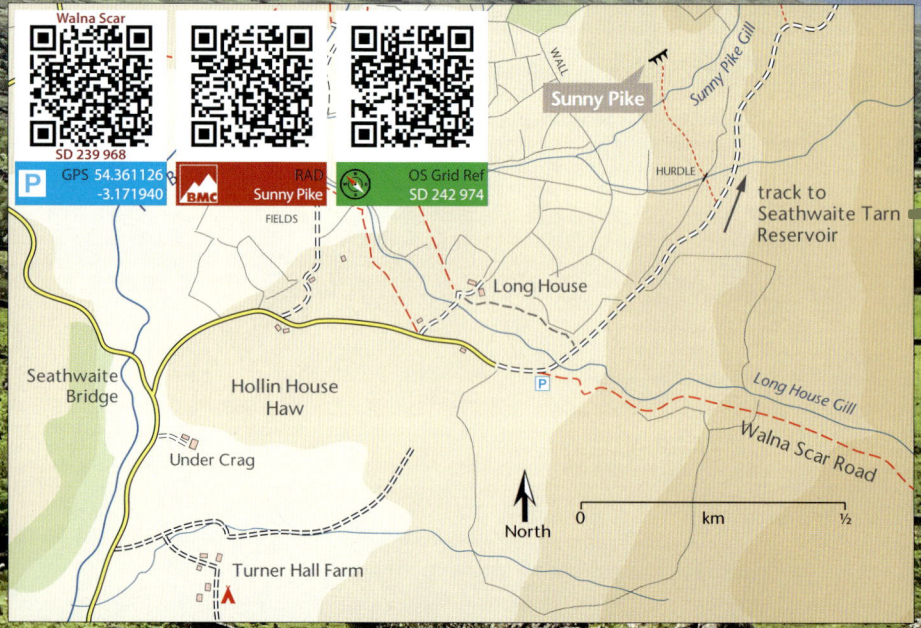

Birthday Crack S (page 159) Laetitia Sterling — 📷 Peter Sterling

The Main Crag

① Sol 30m MVS 4b
Start at the base of a shallow corner some 10m left of a hanging pod. Climb the shallow corner to a mossy slab which is traversed up to the right to the base of a steep wall. Climb this to the left side of a small roof and above.
PC Bennett, D Baker 3.11.2021

② Arvakr 25m MVS 4b
Start slightly to the right of the hanging pod at a series of ramps trending up to the left. Follow the ramps to the left arête of the pod and climb it on spaced jugs to finish.
PC Bennett, D Baker 3.11.2021

③ Alsvior 25m VS 4c
Climb directly to a large block. Surmount the block to continue up the steep obtuse corner on spaced jugs to the top.
PC Bennett, D Baker 3.11.2021

④ Aska 25m VD
The lower diagonal line rising across the crag beneath the hanging pod.
PC Bennett, D Baker 20.03.2022

⑤ Svalinn 25m E1 5b ★★
Start below the waist-high shallow niche. Climb into the niche and directly up to an overhang. Up the ochre-coloured rock to a flake then left to holds on the grey rock. A long reach gains the left-slanting crack to finish.
Photo opposite.
PC Bennett, D Baker 24.03.2022

⑥ Avsugning 30m VD ★
A joyous romp across the right-to-left rising line above *Aska*.
PC Bennett, D Baker 8.03.2022

⑦ Lipsill 25m E1 5a ★
The steep broken crackline. Start just to the right of a shallow niche at knee height and follow the left wall of the crack to good finishing holds.
PC Bennett, D Baker 20.03.2022

⑧ Moninn 25m HS 4a
Starts below the hanging corner. Climb to the hanging corner; at its top, step left to finish.
PC Bennett, D Baker 22.11.2021

⑨ Skoll 25m HVS 5a ★
Take the crack and flakes. Difficult moves at the small roof gain a narrow ledge; flakes lead to the top.
PC Bennett, D Baker 13.11.2021

⑩ Sunny Boy 20m HVS 5a ★
Climb the wall leftwards to the base of a flake. Steep moves above lead to the top. An easy second pitch is available above [D].
A Phizacklea, JL Holden 18.11.2018

⑪ Fizzle 20m S 4a ★
The line of big holds.
RO Graham, E Rogers 12.07.2020

⑫ Hati 25m VS 4c ★
Follow juggy flakes up and left, crossing just below the block, then follow a line of flakes trending leftwards to the top.
PC Bennett, D Baker 13.11.2021

The Main Crag - Upper

13 Gleipnir 12m HVS 5a
The crack on the left offers well-protected but intense climbing.
PC Bennett, D Baker 20.01.2022

14 Birthday Crack 18m S 4a ★★
The next crack which is easier than it looks.
Photo page 157.
A Phizacklea, JL Holden 7.10.2018

15 Sunny and Share 18m E1 5b ★
The right-hand side of the thin wall gives sustained climbing.
A Phizacklea, JL Holden 18.11.2018

16 Sunny Sunday VD
Climb the multiple crack system avoiding the dirty crack.
I Bradley, A Salisbury 12.07.2020

17 Bring Me Sunshine 18m VD
Climb the wall. Good holds enable a pull onto the slab. Easy climbing leads to the top.
JL Holden, A Phizacklea 18.11.2018

Svalinn E1 (opposite) Fin Leather
David Simmonite

BRANDY CRAG

OS Grid Ref: SD 225 989
Altitude: 450m

Rough clean rock with a good selection of routes, a sunny aspect and an attractive view down the valley make this a worthwhile venue.

Approach: The forest road from the Forestry Commission car park can be conveniently and quickly used to get closest to the crag on foot or by bike. Follow the forest road across the bridge, passing Birks, continuing until the track loops back to the west, by a junction, below the crag. Alternatively, on foot, follow the track to a footpath marked by a fingerpost, just before the Birks junction. Head right up a wet footpath through trees keeping left at a junction to eventually reach open ground below the crag, then thrash across rough ground to the base. Some 2.5km from the car park.

Descent: Walk down either side or abseil.

Lower Brandy Crag

Rough clean rock, a great selection of routes and a sunny outlook make this a popular venue. Well worth the walk.

Descent: Either side or by abseil

1 Napoleon 12m E2 5b ★
Climb the rib and leave the scoop steeply and with difficulty to finish up the slab.
E Rogers, K Forsythe 18.07.2004

2 Snake 15m HVS 5a ★
The right-to-left diagonal ramp.
E Rogers, K Forsythe 31.10.2004

3 Slim Groove 12m E3 6a
Small wires. The groove is climbed using the rib on the right to a swing left at the top.
E Rogers, K Forsythe 18.07.2004

4 Stumpy and His Friends 12m E1 5b ★
Climb a broken groove with a conspicuous V-slot at its top.
B McGowan, G Wilks 20.06.2004

5 Summer 14m E2 5b ★★
Small wires. Start below a sickle-shaped groove 2m left of *The Groove*. Climb direct to finish right of the prow.
P Strong, B McGowan, G Wilks 21.06.2004

6 Solstice 14m E3 5c ★★
Small wires. Start below a sickle-shaped groove 2m left of *The Groove*. Climb directly to gain the sickle-shaped groove. Move left, cross the heather and grass ledge rightwards and finish directly above.
P Strong, B McGowan, G Wilks 21.06.2004

7 Left Rib 19m E3 5c
Follows the arête to a flake finish.
K Forsythe, E Rogers 18.07.2004

8 The Groove 19m HVS 5a ★
Terrific line. The deep clean groove is a satisfying challenge.
B McGowan, G Wilks 20.06.2004

9 Right Wall 12m E2 5b ★★ ◆
Technical with fiddly gear. Climb the centre of the wall to a hard sequence up left then rightwards to a slab; finish over the bulge on the right.
Photo this page.
E Rogers, K Forsythe 18.07.2004

Upper Section
Combine the lower routes with one of the following upper pitches to enjoy longer routes.

10 Brandy Sour 12m E1 5b
Delicate with interest. Climb the centre of the wall to reach a slim groove.
K Forsythe, E Rogers 18.07.2004

11 Brandy Bitter 12m HVS 5a
Head rightwards across the stepped ledge into a steep groove. Climb this passing an intimidating bulge.
K Forsythe, E Rogers 18.07.2004

Right Wall E2 (this page)
Clare Reading — Neil Foster

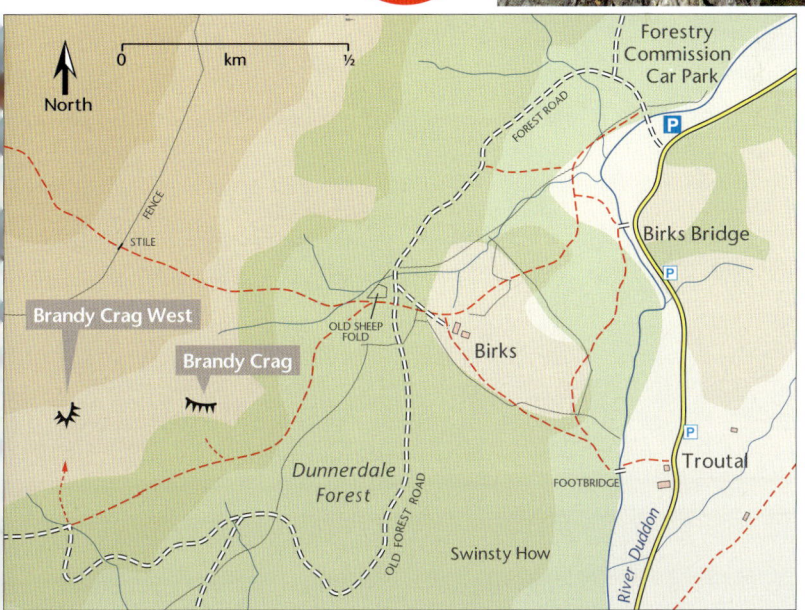

BRANDY CRAG WEST

OS Grid Ref: SD 222 989
Altitude: 450m

A good selection of easier routes on clean rough rock in an idyllic location.

Approach: From the car park, follow the forest track over the bridge, past the turning for Birks and beneath **Brandy Crag**. Keep going until beneath the crag then head up across rough ground.

See map page 160.

Descent: Easy walk/scramble down either side.

Birks Bridge
SD 234 996
P GPS 54.385717 -3.179396

BMC RAD
Brandy West

OS Grid Ref
SD 222 989

The Main Crag – Left Side

① Family Affair 30m VS 4c ★★
Start behind the jumble of boulders at the left end of a rightward-sloping gangway, 15m right of the tree. Climb the gangway rightwards over a small step then move steeply back left to enter the bottom of a V-groove. Climb the groove and the continuation groove on the right of a large detached pinnacle. Step off the top of the pinnacle to finish up slabs.
J Kay, D Kay 26.05.1997

② **Scimitar Slab** 50m HS 4a ★
Start at the left end of the gangway. Climb the gangway for 10m to a steepening and move delicately up to a mossy ledge. Traverse right across a mossy scoop. Continue up the right-hand side of a slab to its top. Step up to more slabs and follow these easily to a large ledge.
M Biden, I Gray, J Daly 1.04.2007

The Main Crag – Right Side

③ **Parable** 22m S 4a ★
Starts at a fine easy-angled slab just right of a pointed flake on the wall. Up the slab rightwards and delicately up into the continuation groove. Climb it to a heather ledge and a continuation easy broken groove to the top.
C van der Velde, D Kay 15.06.1997

④ **Anecdote** 30m VS 4c ★
Immediately right of the slab section is a steep crack. Climb the crack (not as easy as it looks) and blunt rib above then move left to the lowest point of the V-shaped headwall. Climb directly to the top.
M Lynch, D Kay 27.07.1997

⑤ **Fable** 20m VS 4c ★★
Ten metres right of the slab section is a fine striking corner. Climb the corner and pull out left at the top then follow the rib more easily rightwards to the top.
M Lynch, D Kay, J Kay, C van der Velde 7.06.1997

⑥ **Aesop** 20m VS 4b ★★
Two metres right of the corner is the smaller of two hanging slabs below two V-grooves. Climb on to the small hanging slab, move right and then pull up the short wall into the left-hand V-groove. Follow this to the top.
M Lynch, D Kay, J Kay, C van der Velde 7.06.1997

⑦ **The Weathermen** 20m HS 4b ★
Five metres right of the striking corner is a hanging slab. Pull on to the larger hanging slab, follow it to its right-hand end then pull up the rib into a groove. Follow this groove to broken ledges.
C van der Velde, D Kay 15.06.1997

BURNT CRAG

OS Grid Ref: SD 243 991
Altitude: 350m

The best crag in the valley, if climbing well enough to appreciate the steep lines on perfect rock. Catching the sun all day, it dries quickly and provides an excellent, if tiring, day out.

Approach: From the cattle grid south of Troutal Farm, follow the track along the wall, passing through several gates before heading up the hill towards a gate in the wall. The crag lies diagonally leftwards up the fellside.

Descent: Either side.

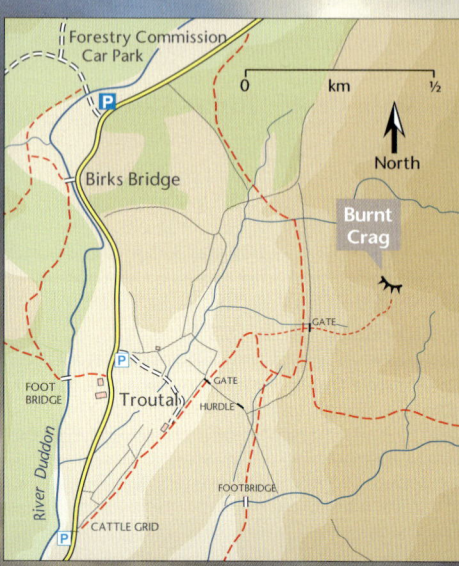

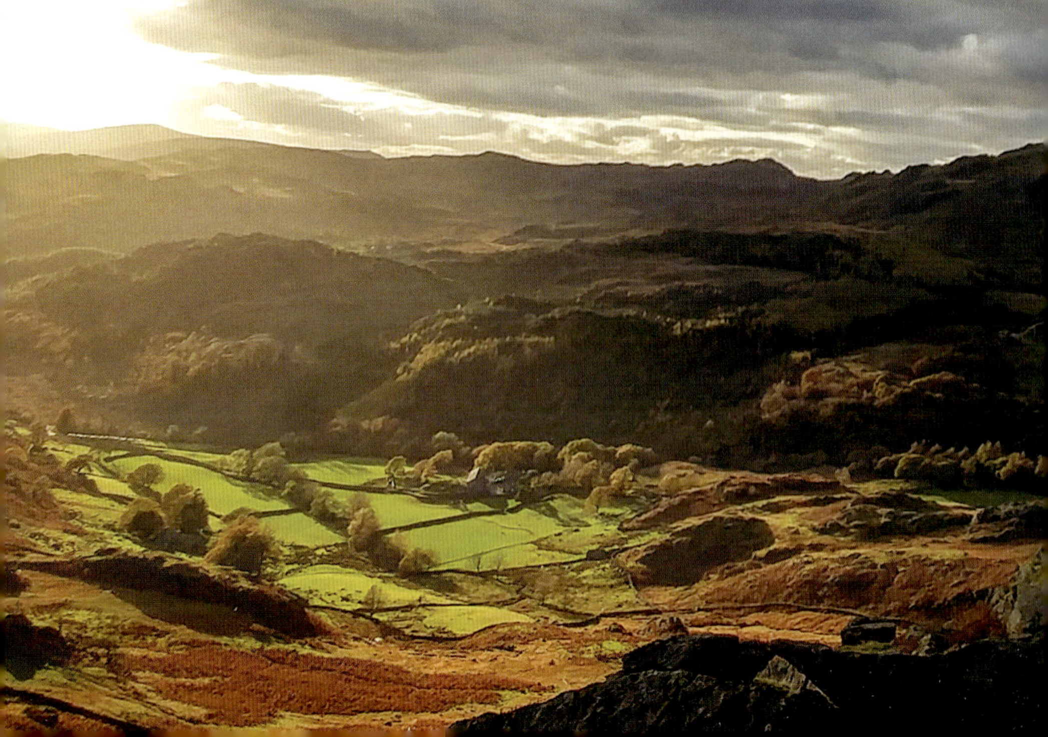

Innocenti E3 (page 166) Scott Quinn & Tom Priestley — 📷 Chris Moore

Duddon

1 Breaker 24m E2 5c ★★
A steep strenuous route up the left wall of the crag. Climb the left-slanting diagonal crack then the wall via breaks to a chockstone below a prow of rock. Traverse right along a ledge to a small cave then, using the large flake above, move left to finish up a groove.
RO Graham, G Smith 20.07.1983

2 Double Trouble 27m E3 6a ★★
This fine unyielding climb starts below the right arête of the overhanging left-hand wall of the crag. Step off the boulder and climb across the steep wall, passing two horizontal slots (cams), to a niche. A difficult technical groove follows.
I Greenwood, A Hyslop, A Phizacklea 21.10.1979

3 Innocenti 30m E3 6a ★★★
A good sustained climb up a thin left-trending flake which starts below a square-cut corner capped by an overhang. Using a flake, awkwardly enter a shallow niche then follow the strenuous flake crack out leftwards until a resting foothold can be reached on the left wall. Move up to a patch of heather then follow a slanting line back right, above the big overhang, where a good sharp flake continues in the same direction through the final bulge.
Photo page 165 & opposite.
RO Graham, A Hyslop 27.10.1979

4 Waking the Witch 29m E4 6b ★★★
A brilliant route (once the start dries up) taking the leg-pumping corner below the roof. Start below the square-cut corner. Bridge into the groove and precariously climb it to the overhang. Pull out right and follow the easier continuation to a resting place. Either climb the cracked headwall above directly or via a detour out left (slightly easier).
M Radtke, A Ledgeway 27.10.1985

5 Shifter 30m E3 6a ★★★
An excellent climb, strenuous and well-protected. Climb the central rightwards-facing corner. The upper bulge is bypassed on the left.
RO Graham, I Greenwood 29.09.1979

Burnt Crag | 167

6 S.P.C. 28m E3 5c ★★
An enigmatic one-move climb which could leave you smouldering with frustration. The shallow groove, parallel to and just right of the central right-facing corner. Climb a steep wall and enter the main groove. Up this to a bulge then move right to stand on a small protruding nose below the upper corner (peg circa 2013). Use small flakes on the right rib to finish.
RO Graham, I Greenwood 29.09.1979

7 Scorched Earth 30m E4 6a ★★
A pleasantly delicate route starting at a protruding block. Pass the block to reach the base of a smooth rightwards-trending ramp and climb this using a vague rib on its right edge (peg). Cross the ramp leftwards to a large block and move up to the overhangs. Step on to another block on the left then, using a tiny flake on the edge of the groove, pull into the corner and finish directly.
A Phizacklea, JL Holden 14.05.1989

8 Burning Desire 30m E5 6b ★★★★
A scorcher! Start below a steep pink groove. Enter the groove using a large flake and climb it to good holds where it peters out. Traverse slightly left and move up to the overhang (peg) then step right and reach for a flat hold in the small groove immediately to the right. Stand on this and finally drift delicately right to enter the prominent bottomless groove which leads easily to the top.
A Phizacklea, JL Holden 1.04.1989

9 An Alien Heat 26m E5 6b ★★
Another blistering route. A large selection of small wires is essential. Start below the left-hand end of a glacis some 6m up the crag. Climb the groove to the glacis and follow a leftward-trending ramp to where the rock bulges. Difficult climbing slightly rightwards leads to a jug at the foot of a right-facing groove and finish up this.
M Radtke, J Cooksey 23.07.1989

Innocenti E3 (opposite) Esther Foster — 📷 Ed Luke

GREAT BLAKE RIGG

OS Grid Ref: SD 259 995
Altitude: 350m

An extensive area of good clean rock on the hillside overlooking the head of Seathwaite Tarn.

Approach: Park at the foot of the Walna Scar Road then follow the track to the tarn. Cross the dam before deciding the approach you want to take, depending on which buttress you intend to visit first. Once at the crag, it is easy enough to scramble between the two buttresses described here.

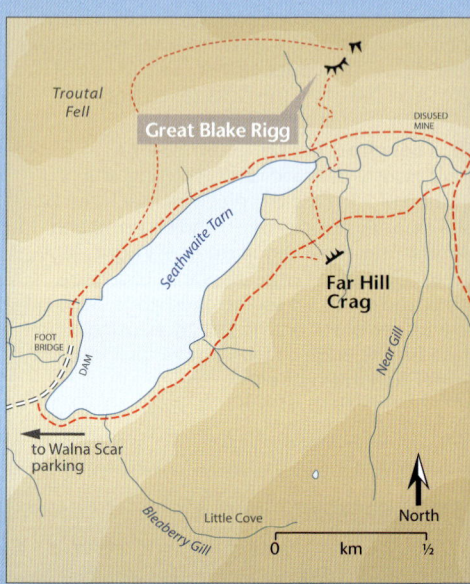

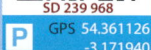

The Upper Wall
page 171

Main Buttress
opposite

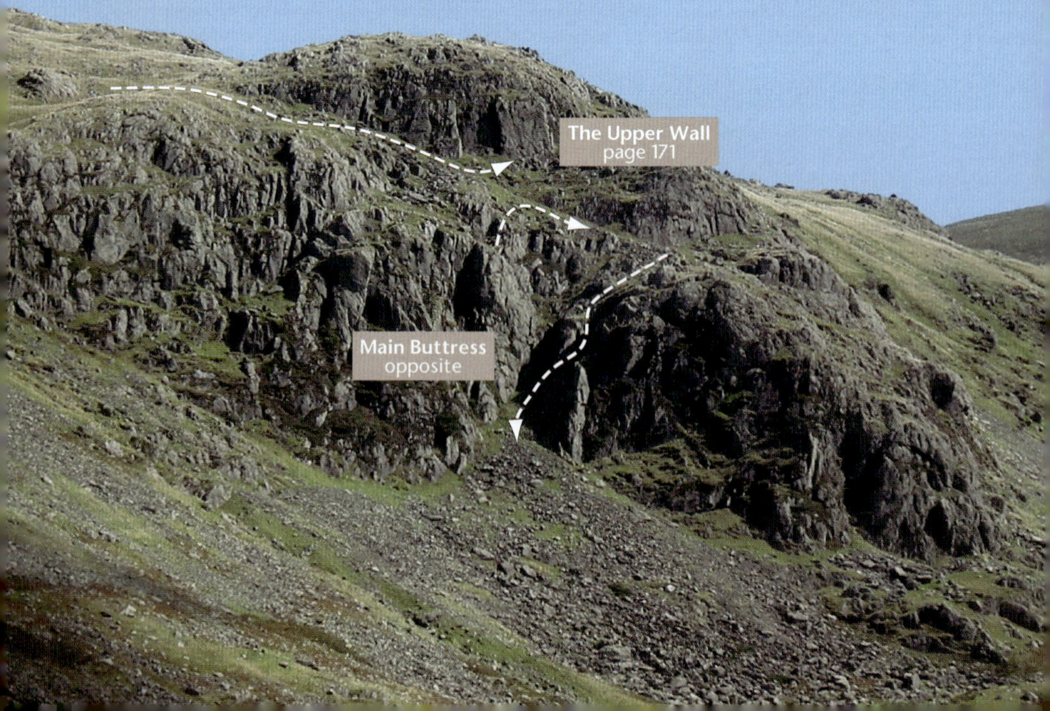

Main Buttress

An amazing buttress of perfect rock on what is the best part of the crag. Forming the wall of the wide gully, there is a large detached block at its foot. The two central routes give some of the longest pitches in the valley with the added benefit of an abseil point: lower off with 60m ropes or abseil.

Approach: From Seathwaite Tarn, strike up the fell towards the most extensive clean rock lying to the left of a wide grassy gully. This is to the left of and some way above the toe of the crag.

Descent: Descend well to the right down a wide grassy gully; further than the horrid wet one.

❶ Against All Odds   60m   E2 5c   ★
From the toe of the rib 3m right of a block.
1 23m Climb the rib and grass ledges to a flake in the highest grass recess. Move up and right to belay on a grassy ramp below a large pinnacle.
2 25m 5c Climb the front face of the pinnacle (sustained and fingery) to its crest, then follow the rounded rib above, trending left below the headwall to belay beneath a right-slanting corner.
3 12m 5a Climb the corner to the top.
K Phizacklea, D Geere 7.5.1984

❷ Dressed for Success   62m   VS 4b
1 18m Climb the buttress, passing a ledge, to belay below a steep clean wall.
2 14m 4b Traverse left below the wall to a dirty corner. An awkward move up this enables a right-slanting groove to be gained, which leads to a ledge.
3 30m 4b Climb the groove above to a small pinnacle and continue directly up a short steep slab on small holds to finish.
D Geere, K Phizacklea 25.03.1991

❸ Younger than Yesterday   44m   E4 6a   ★★★
A difficult slab pitch on superb rough rock. Crucial protection is from a peg.
1 28m 4b Pitch 1 of *Thor*.
2 16m 6a Pull left into a V-groove then step right immediately above the overhanging wall onto the slab. Climb the centre of the slab (peg) linking the horizontal breaks to finish with a heart-stopping sequence above the last gear. Brilliant!
K Phizacklea, D Geere 18.04.1991

A bit easier, superseded by *Younger than Yesterday*, is **Rumour** [18m E2 5c ★ 1981]. Above the slab traverse right above the lip of the overhanging wall to a small ledge on the edge; follow this to join *Thor*.

❹ Thor   49m   HVS 5a   ★★
A steep route up the left side of the clean right-hand buttress. Start at a large detached block lying against the toe of the buttress.
1 28m 4b Climb the arête of the block and continue up some short walls to the bulging rock. Step left and belay on a sloping heathery ledge below a square-cut overhanging wall.
2 15m 5a Traverse right with difficulty to reach a small scoop which leads steeply to a resting place beneath a small overhang. Climb the crack above to a perched block then step left to a ledge by the arête.
3 6m 4c Climb the arête on the left.
D Geere, S Spence 25.08.1968

❺ Yggdrasil   44m   E2 5b   ★★ ♂
Start below the left-hand side of the slab. Climb the slab and the left-hand of two shallow grooves to a grassy ledge. Continue, past some heather, to a spike below a bulging wall. Climb a shallow corner on the right to a bulge at 4m. Step left and make a tough pull into a shallow hanging groove; this leads to a ledge. Climb another groove above to a large flake. Finish out right. Abseil.
A Phizacklea, JL Holden 14.05.1989

❻ Valhalla   46m   E2 5b   ★★★ ♦ ♂
An amazing long pitch on clean rock. Climb the slab and right-hand of two shallow corners to a rock ledge. Pull onto the rock fin on the right, bridge the prominent corner/sentry box right again then climb the continuation finger crack above to a flake (*Odin*). From its top, climb up rightwards to another good flake edge then climb the slab direct passing just left of two grass ledges to finish up the right side of a rock nose above. Or abseil.
J Daly, K Phizacklea 2.09.2002

❼ Odin   39m   VS 4b   ★
Start at the foot of a small gangway which rises rightwards to a chimney.
1 21m 4b Climb the gangway to a niche at the foot of the chimney. Swing out left, round a flake, which is climbed on the left. From the top of the flake, make a rising traverse to the left to a large foothold on the corner. Climb the wall above to the bulge then traverse right for 3m until it is possible to climb up to a large ledge.
2 18m Traverse left for 5m on good holds until the wall above may be climbed to a large ledge with a big detached flake on the left. The crack behind the flake is climbed to the top.
TW Birkett, B Heslin 27.08.1972

Main Buttress

1. Against All Odds — E2 5c ★
2. Dressed for Success — VS 4b
3. Younger than Yesterday — E4 6a ★★★
4. Thor — HVS 5a ★★
5. Yggdrasil — E2 5b ★★
6. Valhalla — E2 5b ★★★
7. Odin — VS 4b ★

The Upper Wall

A hard climber's dream. Steep, clean, sunny and fast-drying with some very interesting problems.

Approach: The best approach is to follow the path up Grey Friar, which strikes northwards up the steep fell after crossing the dam. Once the ridge leading up to Grey Friar is reached and the crag can be seen across to the right, traverse the fell towards the crag.

Descent: To the right.

1 Laypincher 15m E3 5c ★
A fine strenuous pitch up the left-hand arête of the main face. Climb the crack up the arête and make an awkward move right to finish.
C Gregg, JL Holden, A Phizacklea 2.09.1989

2 Just Good Friends 15m E2 5c ★★
The obvious crack 8m right of the arête. Climb a crack to a tree then move up to a down-pointing fang. A hasty pull left leads to a good flake which is followed to the top.
A Phizacklea 15.10.1988

3 The Lutine Bell 15m E5 6b ★★
An a-peal-ing route that is not a-toll easy! Climb directly to a small flake/pod at 6m and follow the thin crack above to a shallow 'cave'. Exit left up a short flake.
A Phizacklea 15.10.1988

4 Bowel Howl 16m E4 6a ★★
Start at a small pinnacle below and left of a slim corner high in the wall. Climb past the pinnacle to the pod. Go right and stand on the ledge below the slim corner (runners in the crack on the left). Climb the corner to a jug then escape left to a large flake; follow this easily to the top.
A Phizacklea, JL Holden 10.09.1989

5 The School of Hard Knocks 16m E5 6b ★★
A sustained problem up the right-hand side of the wall. An awkward start leads to a flat hand-hold; move right (peg) then gain the break with some difficulty (peg). Climb directly up the flake and follow the crack leading left (microwire in a pod) to easier ground.
A Phizacklea, JL Holden 2.09.1989

FAR HILL CRAG

OS Grid Ref: SD 259 989
Altitude: 450m

Another good crag with tough routes on steep clean rock across the tarn from **Great Blake Rigg**.

Approach: Park at the foot of the Walna Scar Road and follow the track to the tarn. On reaching the dam, head right and follow a path along the south shore for approx. 1.3 km. The crag lies up the fellside, 300m or so after crossing a small col.

Descent: To the left.

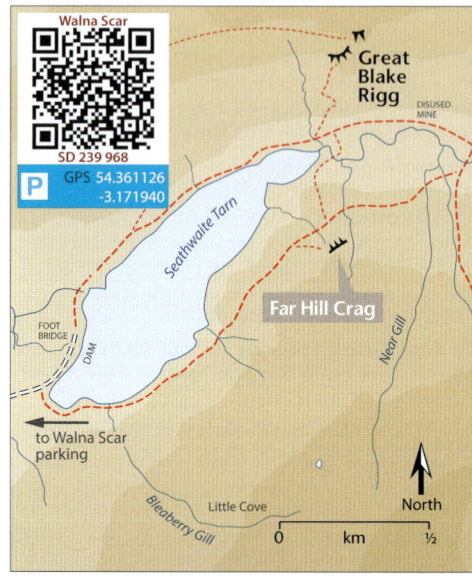

1 Olive 22m E1 5b ★★
The fine crack. Climb a short wall to a huge down-pointing flake then follow the steep left-hand crack to the top.
RE Wightman, M Lynch, I Wall 27.09.1987

2 Drum Roll 30m E2 5c ★★
A very good pitch up the bottomless central groove. Climb up to the huge fang and follow the right-hand crack strenuously to gain the groove. Climb this and pull out left at the top then head rightwards to finish.
E Cleasby, R Matheson Jul 1983

Sparkle in the Rain E4 (opposite) Chris Wallis — CHRIS WALLIS

❸ Double Gravity 28m E3 6a ★
The double gravity geophysical anomaly makes the initial crack desperate. Climb the steep thin crack to a break on the left (peg); pull up and right to good holds. Continue directly up a steep wall to a ledge below the easy finishing slab.
A Phizacklea, JL Holden, A Rowell 24.04.1990

❹ Sparkle in the Rain 25m E4 6a ★
The steep capped corner. If wet, start up a short groove on the left. Climb the corner with increasing difficulty to the stubborn capping roof which obstinately prevents access to the easier ground above!
Photo opposite.
RE Wightman, A Phizacklea 28.05.1988

❺ First of Class 26m E4 6a ★★★
A brilliant route. Climb the thin ramp to the roof (medium cam) and pull round its right-hand side to a crozzly pocket (nut). Step left above the roof to a small corner and climb directly (peg) to the overhang. Fingery moves left from the niche lead to a shallow groove, with easier climbing above.
A Phizacklea, A Rowell, JL Holden 24.04.1990

❻ Machiavellian Paragon 26m E5 6a ★★★
A bold route up the shallow scoop, starting just left of a mossy streak. Climb the rough wall to a slot in a little overlap (medium cam) then trend leftwards up the vague scoop to reach a diagonal overlap. Follow this rightwards with increasing trepidation (peg) after which the difficulties ease.
RE Wightman, A Phizacklea 28.05.1988

❼ Lagonda 25m E3 5c ★★★
A marvellous pitch up the Y-shaped crack in the centre of the slightly mossy right wall. Follow the crack. Where it divides, utilise the right-hand branch to a greater extent to finish, the final move probably being the hardest!
E Cleasby, R Matheson July 1983

❽ Satyriasis 25m E4 6a ★
Good though poorly protected climbing. Climb a vague crinkly scoop to a tiny overlap at 11m (wires); pull out right and move up to a good hold (peg). Trend up and right to reach better holds below the final groove above the right edge of the wall.
A Phizacklea, B McKinley 16.08.1988

Duddon

OS Grid Ref
SD 259 989

BMC RAD
Far Hill Crag

CASTLE HOW
OS Grid Ref: SD 237 004
Altitude: 250m

Southern Jessie E4 (page 176) Anna Taylor — 📷 Marc Langley

A short compact crag with some good routes on clean rock and the added benefit of a short flat walk-in.

Approach: Park off the road by the river just north of Hining House. Cross the river using the stepping stones and into a field through a gate. Cross the field to reach the crag.

Orange Wall

Steep wall climbing with sometimes sketchy gear.

Approach: Turn right from the path towards the south side of the crag and head through the short outcrops to the overhanging orange wall on the second tier.

Descent: Leftwards.

① Gavin's Horror 15m HVS 5a
Start at downward-pointing block. From the left-hand side of the block, gain and climb a corner to a leftward-slanting ramp. Finish up a crack in the headwall on good holds.
R Guise Jun 1996

6m right is a large block at head-height.

② Dash Riprock 18m E3 5c
Easily up the left side of the block to a ledge. Climb to the right-hand side of the cutaway above where a thin rightward-slanting flake leads to a flat ledge. Gain this then up the edge to the top.
B Ebsen, I Ryan 6.07.2003

3m further right is a flake/block

③ Southern Jessie 17m E4 6a
A serious lead with awkward protection. Climb blocks and ledges to the wall. Ascend an otherwise smooth face with a powerful crux to reach a ledge. Continue up the wall directly above.
Photo page 174.
A Wilde 1.08.1995

④ Elle May 16m E5 6a
A very bold route starting below a dark mouth right of the crescent overlap. Easily up to the left-hand side of the mouth then up the wall above to the sanctuary of a ledge. Step left to finish up a corner.
D Birkett Jun 1996

⑤ Donna's Variation 16m E3 5c
From the mouth, bridge right to reach a good hold then climb straight up on reasonable holds to reach the right-hand side of a ledge. Finish direct.
I Cooksey, JC Hudson 1.08.2019

⑥ Bryn's Route 16m HVS 5a
Start at a rightward-slanting ramp. Move left across the wall to a spike and follow steep cracks above to a ledge. Finish up the crack on the left.
A Wilde, C Cowe 8.05.1995

Zelda's Wall

Zelda's Wall is the lowest buttress facing the river on the east side of **Castle How**.

Approach: Head right towards the lowest rocks.

Descent: Leftwards

⑦ Zelda's Face 15m HVS 5a ★★
Start at the lowest point of the crag right of the dirty groove. Climb to the left-hand end of the prominent horizontal break then finish up cracks above.
A Wilde 11.05.1995

⑧ Intensive Care 15m E1 5b
Start on the left-hand side of a niche at the base of the wall. Climb direct to the break by way of a thin crack then continue up bearing slightly left; bold but short.
J Turner, W Spain 21.05.2010

⑨ Why Study 18m E5 6b
Straight up to mantel into a horizontal break and reach a crack in the headwall.
A Hocking, A Wilde 10.04.1997

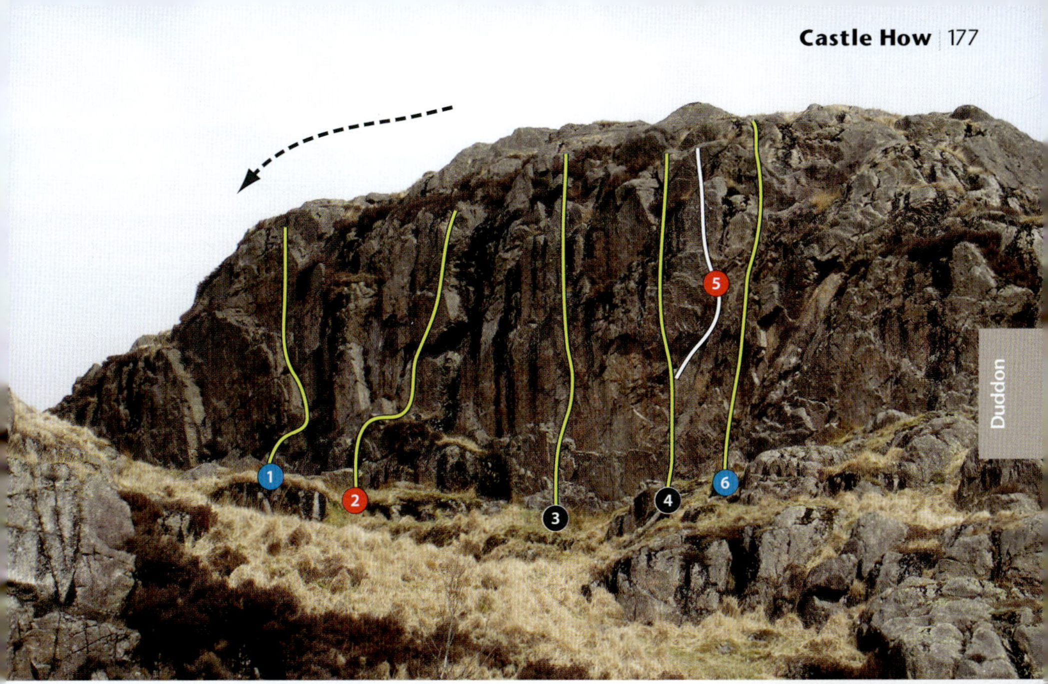

Castle How | 177

Duddon

10 A Dog in a Hat 14m E1 5b ★
A short ramp leads into the groove on the right-hand side of the wall. Swing right at the top to avoid heather.
K Phizacklea, D Geere Jul 2019

WRYNOSE

Immaculate rock, south facing and with a stunning outlook; with only a short stroll to reach them, unsurprisingly these crags are very popular. These outcrops provide single pitch routes at all grades, with plenty for the beginner and improver.

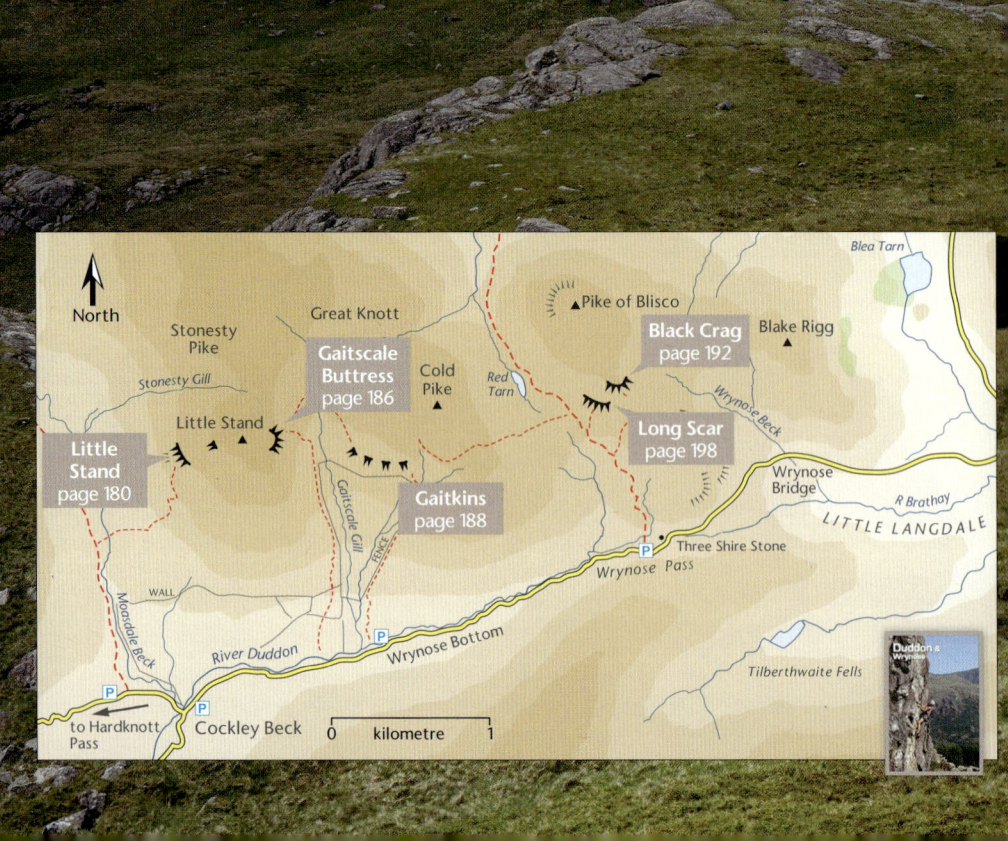

Ratbag, Gaitkins VS (page 189) Steph Marshall — 📷 David Simmonite

LITTLE STAND

OS Grid Ref: SD 248 033
Altitude: 580m

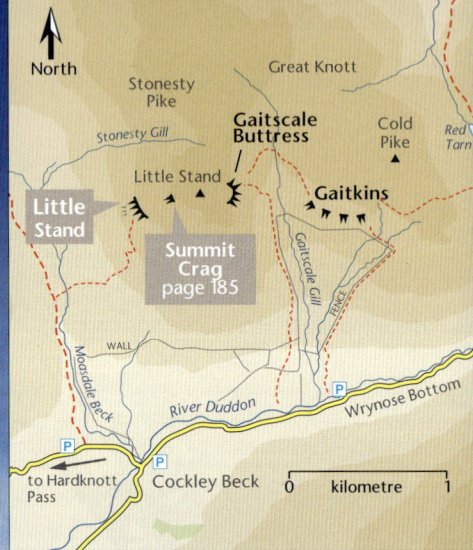

A series of small buttresses spread over the west side of the hill known as Little Stand. There are many small outcrops with a wide range of routes at all grades. The routes are short and the slog up the hillside is tough BUT the rock is amazingly rough and a pleasure to climb on. A selection of the best are provided here.

Approach: Park at the bottom of Hardknott Pass and take the substantial bridleway up Mosedale. After about 1km, head east to cross the beck and a large fenced-off area, using the stiles. Head up the hillside following a vague trod.

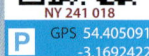   

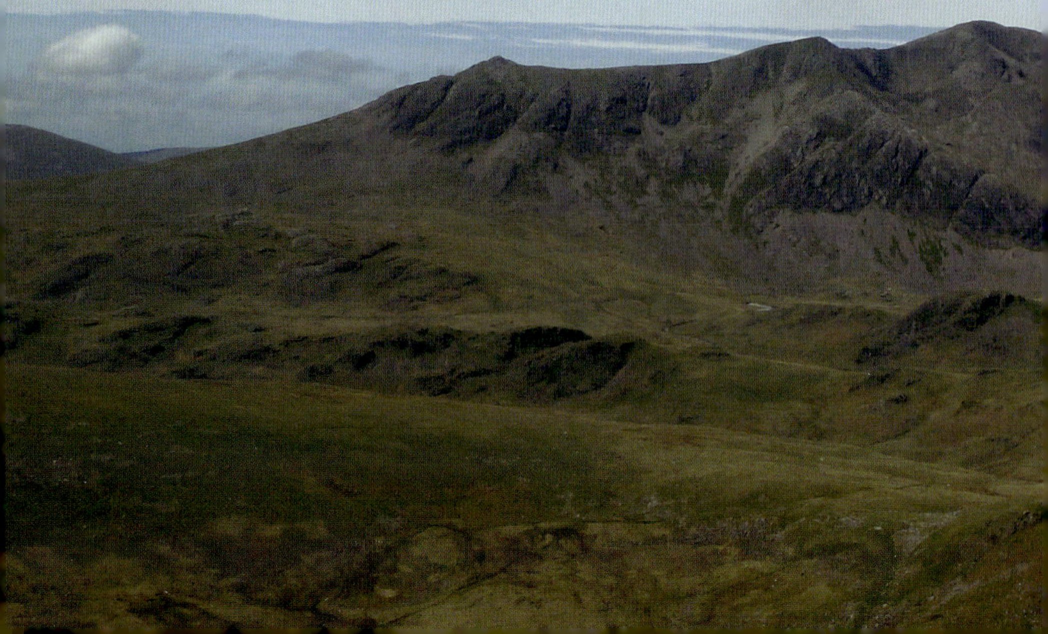

Gringo E2 (page 183) James Dickinson — 📷 Cath Sullivan

Bookend Wall

1 The Mission 15m E2 5c ★
A good route up the centre of the moss-speckled wall. Climb a short corner then trend leftwards following vague cracks to finish directly up the middle of the wall.
J Daly 31.08.1991

2 Family Affair 16m S ★
A mossy crack leads to a scooped groove and pleasantly to the top.
J Daly, R Daly 31.08.1991

3 Marathon Crack 15m HS 4a ★★
The S-crack gives a fine climb. Follow the crack in its entirety; gaining the slab is the crux. More nuts than a nutty chocolate bar!
D Woolcock, P Wright, D Rotheray 14.07.1991

4 Madam Butterfly 18m E1 5a ★★
Flutter your way up the beautiful rock of the blunt arête. Start just right of three perched blocks. Climb up easily; where the rib steepens, climb to the right of a triangular roof then move back left to finish up the slab on the left of the upper arête.
Photo page 185.
J Daly, K Phizacklea, K Daly 29.07.1991

Nose Buttress

Stiff starts crossing a barrier roof at head-height mix it with easier slab climbing.

Descent: Scramble down to the left.

5 Gringo 23m E2 5c ★★
A fine strenuous route starting directly below the nose. Overcome the stubborn roof using a thin crack to enter the left-hand groove. Climb this for 3m then trend left and follow the arête to the top.
Photo page 181.
K Phizacklea, J Daly 15.12.1990

6 Hi-Fi 23m E2 6a ★
An interesting route with a boulder problem start. Pull over the overhang to enter the groove right of the nose. Pull up the arête on the right then follow the groove above.
D Armstrong 25.06.1996

7 Black Watch 22m HVS 5a ★★
A pleasant route which starts below a black mossy groove in the slabs right of the nose. Climb the groove for 4m then traverse left onto the arête. Follow this and the corner above.
K Phizacklea, J Daly 15.12.1990

8 Sundance 23m S ★
From the foot of the broken corner, pull out left to gain good holds then move up to a ledge. Climb the right-trending slabby scoop to the top.
J Daly, K Phizacklea 15.12.1990

Central Buttress

Strenuous climbing on an impressively steep buttress easily identified by the superb finger crack in its overhanging right wall.

Descent: Head rightwards

9 Little Big Man 18m E1 5b ★
Climb a short groove to the overhang. Strenuous undercuts lead through to the left-hand V-groove to finish.
J Daly, K Phizacklea, K Daly 29.07.1991

10 Calamity Jane 19m E2 5c ★★
Another fine strenuous route starting below the left-hand V-groove. Climb up to the overhang and swing right to enter an open niche at the foot of the central groove. Follow the crack to the top roof and pull directly over this to reach easier ground.
J Daly 2.09.1991

11 Custer's Last Stand 21m E1 5b ★★
A great route starting just left of the left-hand arête of the overhanging wall. Climb a short wall to the roof and pull rightwards over this to gain a shallow diamond-shaped niche above. Continue directly over the next overhang then trend right to finish.
J Daly 7.06.1991

12 Tomorrow's Hero 21m E6 6c ★★★
The steep crack line. Heroics needed to finish.
D Birkett 23.06.1996

13 Malteser 17m VS 4b ★
Climb steeply to a protruding ledge at 4m. Follow the sharp arête above.
P Wright, D Woolcock May 1990

Little Stand Summit Crag ⏱ 55 min

Steep climbs on superb rough rock in a beautiful location high up on the hillside

Descent: To the left

14 Cabin Boy 18m E3 6a ★
The difficult crack followed by a harder step right to hopefully finish up an easy continuation rib.
C Thorpe, RO Graham 22.06.1995

15 Captain Crater 11m E4 5c ★★
The beautiful protectionless wall. Start behind the large block on the floor. Climb steeply to pull onto the ramp at a tiny overlap. Step left and climb the slabs above, pulling directly through the top bulge.
A Phizacklea 24.04.1993

16 A Vroom with a Ewe 22m E2 5c ★★★ ♦
A brilliant well-protected route. Follow the crack, but using many holds on the featured wall to reach the halfway ledge. Continue directly, pulling through the short overhanging crack in the headwall. The best short route in the area!
A Phizacklea, JL Holden 24.04.1993

17 Teardrop Explodes 22m MVS 4b ★★
Good climbing up the corner. Climb the corner to a ledge. Pull out left then climb up pleasantly to finish up the right side of the headwall.
D Geere, J Daly 27.10.1997

18 Toots 20m E3 5c ★★
A pleasant route with a thin start. Climb the crack then continue over a bulge to easier slabs above.
D Armstrong, M Hetherington 14.09.1996

19 Blackbeard 20m MVS 4b ★
Climb the right edge of the wrinkly slab to the grass ledge then climb the deep groove bounding the right side of the face.
J Daly 19.10.1997

Madam Butterfly E1 (page 182) Nick Wharton
📷 Keith Sanders

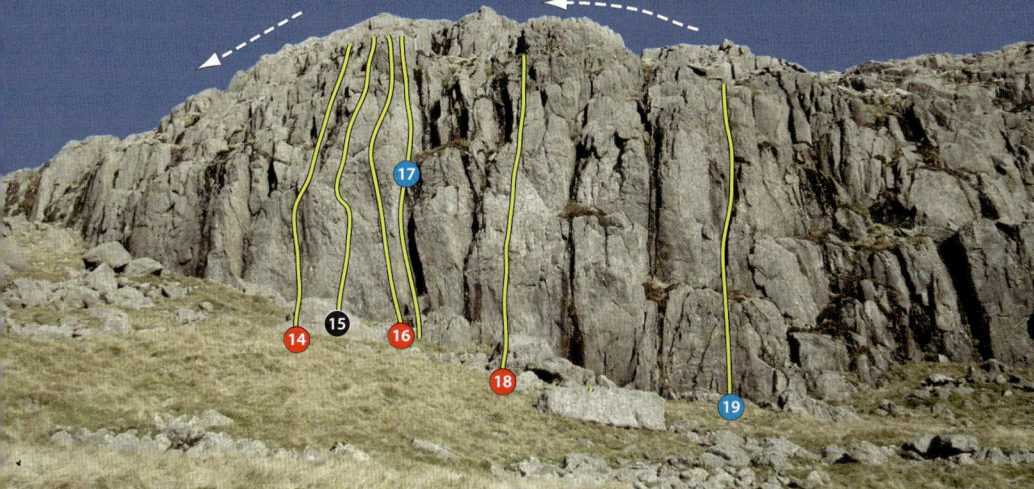

GAITSCALE BUTTRESS

OS Grid Ref: NY 253 034
Altitude: 670m

Slim Slow Slider VS (opposite) Steve Scott — Nick Wharton

Rough solid rock enjoying morning sun. Some areas do run to moss. This prominent pillar overlooks the head of Gaitscale Gill, about 2km north east of Cockley Beck. To make the most of any sunshine, it is best visited early in the day. The most prominent feature is the rounded brown pillar towards the right-hand end. To the right of this is a steep clean wall which ends at a dirty corner.

Approach: Park off road in Wrynose Bottom. Ford the river and wind through walls taking a sketchy trod northwards alongside a fence on the west bank of the gill, keeping west of the plantation. Alternatively, approach from the top of Wrynose Pass as for **Gaitkins** and contour round the hillside. Combine here with **Gaitkins** for a great full day out.

Descent: Either side of the crag.

1 Slim Slow Slider 35m VS ★
A fine varied route that improves with height. Start in the grassy recess at the lowest point of the nose. Climb steeply onto the lowest rib then trend left and up keeping left of a short V-groove to reach the base of the main groove. Follow this pleasantly to where it curves left and peters out into moss. A step right onto the upper rib of *Gaitscale Buttress* leads airily to a belay.
Photo opposite.
JL Holden, A Phizacklea 3.05.1993

2 Gaitscale Buttress 33m E1 5b ★
A pleasant delicate route up the rounded pillar at the left side of the steep right wall. Start on a ledge 3m above and right of the grassy recess at the lowest point of the nose. Climb up and left to reach a short groove. Climb this and the slab above to the steep nose. Follow the prominent crack strenuously through the bulge to a good hold, from where the rib on the left is gained. Climb this to a grass ledge and good belays.
A Phizacklea, JL Holden 3.05.1993

3 The Masterplan 38m E4 5c ★★
The seemingly blank wall gives a superb intricate route. Start as for *Crack of Dawn*.
1 26m 5c Climb up and left to a vague green groove (nut and spike). Traverse leftwards delicately into the centre of the wall (peg and nut). Pull up to reach an incut hold (skyhook), then move right to gain a tiny shallow groove. From this, a fingery traverse left leads to a good hold. Pull up onto the large shelf; flake belay below the upper rounded pillar.
2 12m 5b Climb the thin crack directly up the nose and over a bulge then continue to the top.
A Phizacklea, A Rowell 26.08.1993

4 Crack of Dawn 32m HVS 5a ★★
An excellent route climbing the rounded pillar above the steep wall. Start 4m down and left of a dirty corner, below the right-hand of two short green cracks high on the wall. Pull up on flake holds to reach a short groove then climb directly past the quartz to reach the crack. Follow the crack to just below the grass then step right and continue up to a heathery crack. Climb the rounded slab above (sparse protection) to gain a niche; finish directly above this.
A Rowell, A Phizacklea 26.08.1993

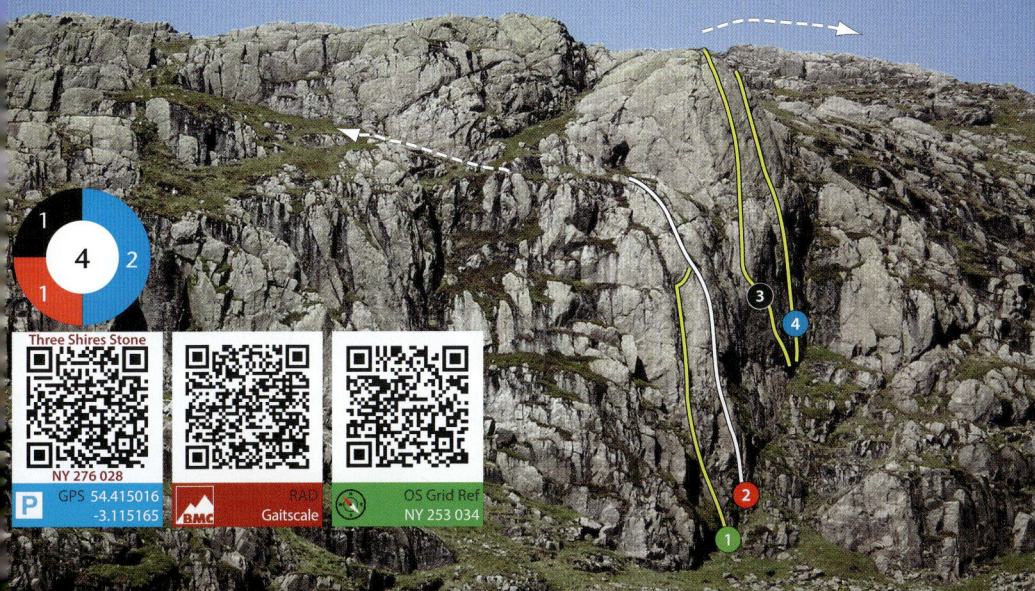

GAITKINS

OS Grid Ref: NY 260 033
Altitude: 670m

Three Shires Stone
NY 276 028
GPS 54.415016 -3.115165

BMC RAD
Gaitkins

OS Grid Ref
NY 260 033

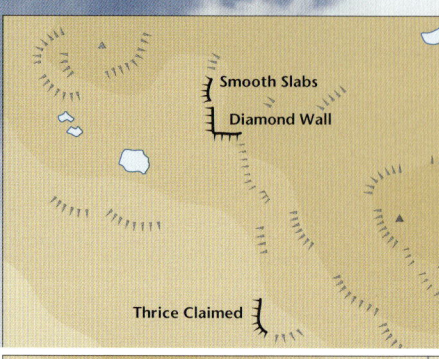

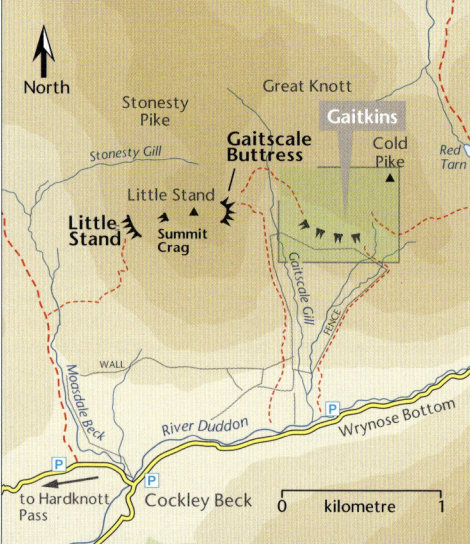

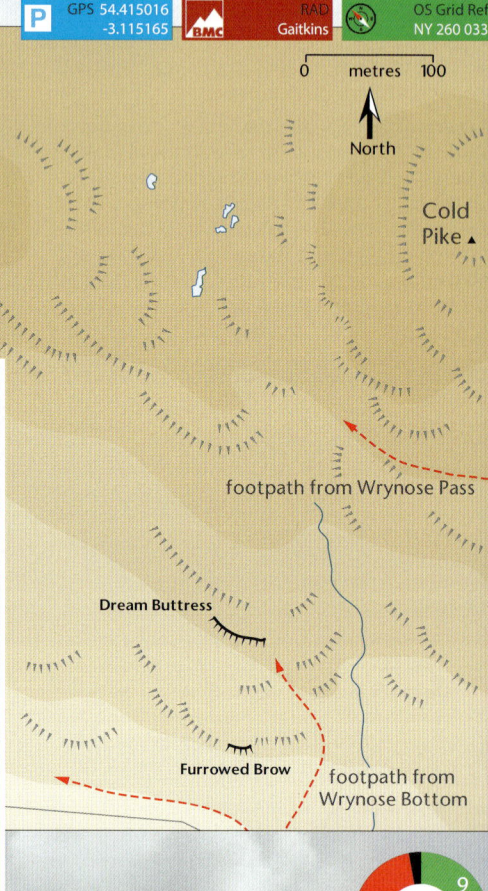

Many short climbs on immaculate rock in a delightful sunny setting overlooking the upper Duddon valley. This range of craglets, spread over the hillside can make for an idyllic day out.

Approach: Park at Wrynose Pass and follow the good path towards Red Tarn and the Wrynose crags. Where the land levels out head left towards a dip in the shoulder of Cold Pike (boggy in places). Once over the ridge, the two sections **Upper Gaitkins** and **Lower Gaitkins** are spread over the hillside.

1 The Mountain Ringlet 16m E3 5c
Climb the central short crack then move up, using the crack on the right, to a hard rockover left onto a small edge and gain the centre of the slab.

2 Seriously Smooth 16m E4 6a
Very bold. Climb to stand on a thin flake then step up and left to a sloping hold below a rightwards trending scoop (nut on left). Enter the scoop then climb precariously rightwards to a good foothold. Step back left into a depression to finish.

SMOOTH SLABS 10 .. 16m
- 3 Smoothly Severe — S ★
- 4 The Scoop — S
- 5 Nick's Route — VD
- 6 Runny Nose — D

DIAMOND WALL 15m
- 7 Ratbag — VS 4b ★
- 8 Jilted John — E2 5b ★★
- 9 Mossy Crack — HVS 5a ★ 🌿
- 10 John Shuttleworth — E3 5c
- 11 Thar She Blows — VS 4c ★
- 12 Iced Diamond — E2 5c ★★

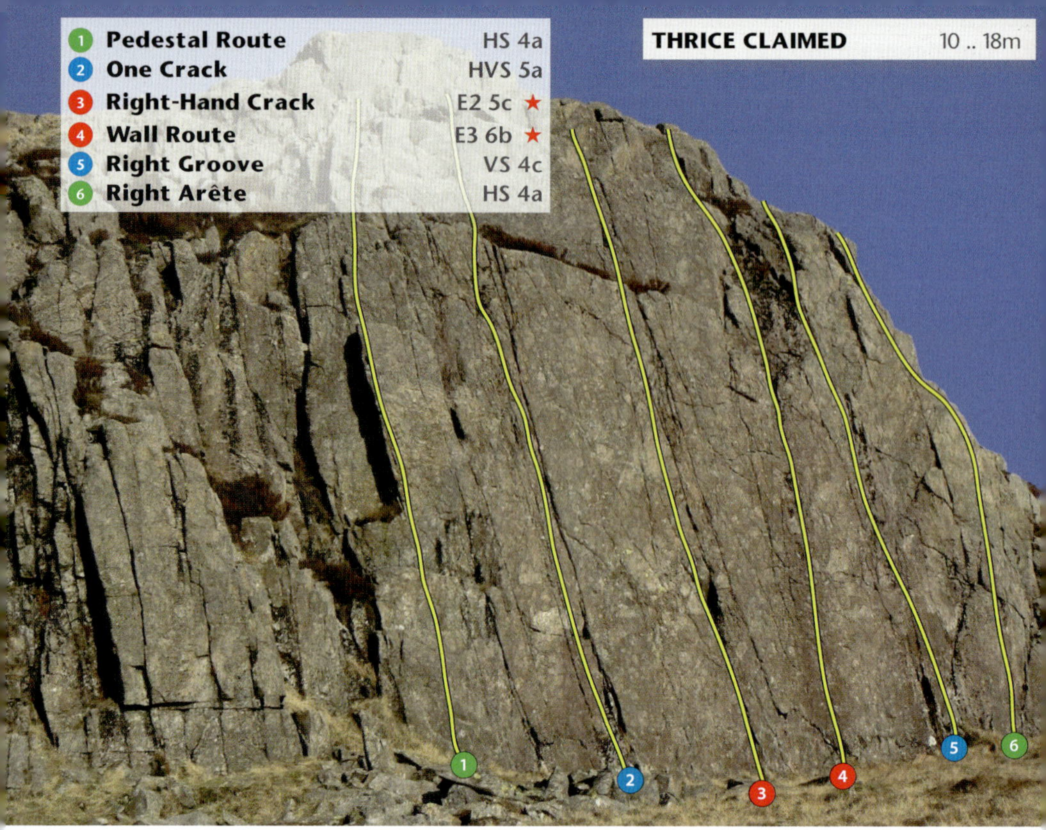

THRICE CLAIMED   10 .. 18m

1. Pedestal Route — HS 4a
2. One Crack — HVS 5a
3. Right-Hand Crack — E2 5c ★
4. Wall Route — E3 6b ★
5. Right Groove — VS 4c
6. Right Arête — HS 4a

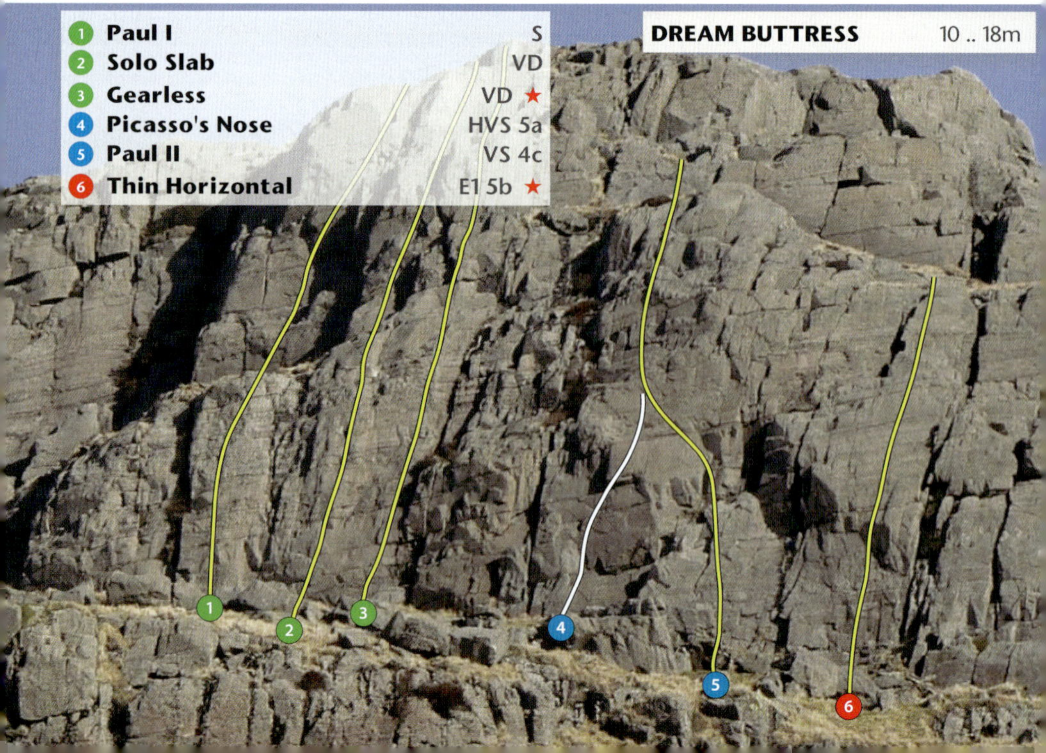

DREAM BUTTRESS   10 .. 18m

1. Paul I — S
2. Solo Slab — VD
3. Gearless — VD ★
4. Picasso's Nose — HVS 5a
5. Paul II — VS 4c
6. Thin Horizontal — E1 5b ★

Furrowed Brow E1 (below) Tony Mawer — 📷 David Simmonite

FURROWED BROW 14 .. 20m

1. Easy Edge Direct — VS 4c ★
2. Faulty Tower — HVS 5a ★
3. Tup's Purse — E1 5b ★
4. Furrowed Brow — E1 5b ★★
5. Take Three — E3 6a ★
6. Lost Generation — E2 5c

BLACK CRAG
OS Grid Ref: NY 274 037
Altitude: 580m

25 mn

Glass Slipper E2 (page 196) Nick Wharton & Chloe Parker — David Simmonite

A fabulous set of buttresses offering a good range of short climbs. The rock is tremendous - rough and solid. This is a delightful sunny venue for a full day or just an evening.

Approach: From the top of Wrynose Pass, follow the well-marked path north for about 750m. Just beyond a small rocky stream follow a vague path rightwards. Pass a fenced-off boulder in the general direction of the fell summit to the crag.

The West Face

The clean broad face clearly visible on the walk-in has a great selection of routes. A smooth overhanging wall of pocketed rock at the extreme left-hand end with a short chimney to its left marks the first routes.

Descent: To the left or right.

1 Pocket Crack 10m E3 6a ★★
The line of thin discontinuous cracks. Strenuous and fingery yet well-protected.
T Walkington 2.10.1987

2 Blind 16m HVS 5a ★
Climb 4m to a grass ledge then move up rightwards to a second ledge (crux); continue to the top.
T Walkington 23.06.1988

3 Slipshod 16m HVS 5a ★★
A deservedly popular route. Climb the wall direct to the niche. Follow the fine crack to the ledge, step right and up the short wall.
R Greenwood, R Cooper, P Donnelly 14.07.1984

A slim terrace now runs rightwards to the platform beneath The Needle.

4 Yellow Fever 16m E2 5b ★★★
Superb climbing. The thin discontinuous cracks in the smooth wall offer fiddly gear.
R Greenwood, C Ensoll, P Donnelly 2.07.1984

5 Yellow Peril 16m E5 6a ★
Climb up to the prominent overlap, pull over its right-hand side onto the smooth wall above and continue up this to a second smaller overlap. Hard moves past this lead to the top. Protection is negligible; side runners can be arranged to reduce both the risk of death and the grade!
T Walkington 10.07.1990

6 The First Touch 16m E1 5b ★★★
An attractive line with great climbing that's no pushover. Protection is available where it matters. Gain the right-facing, hanging groove which is followed to a leftwards finish.
R Greenwood, C Ensoll, P Donnelly 2.07.1984

Above the middle of the rock terrace are two thin straight cracks converging at the bottom to form a V-alcove. The next route starts here.

7 Hold On 10m S ★
The left-hand crack is tricky near the top.
J Cooper 27.09.1987

8 Mind of No Fixed Abode 10m E1 5a ★★
Effectively a bold solo on friendly brown rock with a hostile landing, especially if you bounce. Climb just left of the rib then up right to follow a short open groove.
J Cooper, T Walkington, B Rogers, D Birkett 9.04.1988

The South Face

The left-hand end of **The South Face** overlooks the gear base on a terraced platform.

⑨ The Needle   12m   VD   ★★
The Needle itself is a striking 8m javelin of rock which provides a memorable experience. Climb the wide corner-crack to gain the gap between the pinnacle and the crag. Climb the chimney above and up to the pointed summit. This can also be gained by a bold step from the mainland.
E J Hodge, J Lynam circa 1955

⑩ Needle Arête   12m   E3 6a   ★★
The south-west arête of the The Needle gives a superb pitch at the lower end of the grade. Climb the wall below the outside face of The Needle to a ledge at 4m. A committing move left (peg under tiny overlap) gains the arête which is climbed using holds on either side. The arête can also be climbed entirely on its left-hand side at E4 - the arête further left being out of bounds.
T Walkington, J Cooper 24.04.1988

⑪ Hang the Gallows High   12m   E6 6b   ★★
The south-east arête of The Needle provides a very difficult, protectionless and serious route. Climb easily up to the terrace at 4m. Armed with positive thoughts, work precariously up the left-hand side of the arête to a blind finish.
D Bates 17.05.1988

⑫ Skye Ridge   12m   VD   ★★
Follow the grooved rib 2m right of the corner. 40m right there is an impressive leaning wall with two hanging grooves in its upper half which provide the following routes. This wall can take some seepage and is slower to dry.

⑬ Bilko   12m   E4 6a   ★
Start below the line of weakness in the centre of the wall. Climb the thin cracks directly up the wall to a good jug level with the bottom of the short groove on the right. Move right and enter the groove. Climb it finishing with a good hold up on the left.
T Walkington, J Cooper 2.10.1987

⑭ Doberman   12m   E3 6a   ★★
Bridge up the deep corner until you have to commit yourself to its left wall in order to gain the right-hand groove above which is followed strenuously to the top.
T Walkington 2.10.1987

⑮ Just a Minute   20m   VS 4c   ★
Two sections of good climbing but rather disjointed. Climb up the wrinkly wall on its right and scramble up to below the undercut buttress above. Pull up to gain scoops above the left-hand side of the overhang and follow these onto the central arête. Either climb this, or move further right and climb a shallow groove.
K Lunt, T Madden 10.07.2005

Wrynose

Glass Slipper Area

50m right of *The South Face*, across a very broken area of rock, is the challenging slab taken by *Glass Slipper*.

Descent: To the right.

16 Not So Jolly 16m D ★
Climb the left arête to the easy-angled slab above. Step left and follow the clean arête to finish.
M Bebbington, I Knight 21.04.2010

17 Jolly Roger 16m VS 4c ★★
Climb the slanting cracks in the slab, which feel steeper than they appear from below, until an easier slab on the left can be gained leading to the top.
J Cooper Sep 1987

18 Fun Run 16m S ★
Climb leftwards to a ledge at 3m. Continue directly up the right wall of the corner, avoiding a perched flake at the top by a move right.
J Cooper, A Soper 16.09.1990

19 Second Generation 16m E4 5c
An eliminate with very poor protection taking the wall and arête just left of *Ann's Agony*.
I Tilney, A Tilney 21.05.2000

20 Ann's Agony 16m HVS 5b ★★
The prominent crack makes for a great route. Unfortunately, the start is frequently wet although this does not always make it impossible. Gain the crack by a strenuous undercut start and follow it direct.
T Walkington, A McWatt 2.10.1987

21 Glass Slipper 16m E2 5b ★★★
Lovely climbing on fantastic rock. Although low in its technical grade, minimal protection on the slab means it is often soloed. From the corner, step left above the overhung base. Work left and upwards to climb the slab slightly left of its centre until beneath the short headwall. Step right and finish direct. Side runners reduce the grade to a more relaxing HVS 5b.
Photo page 192.
T Walkington, A McWatt 2.10.1987

22 Pumpkin Corner 15m VD ★
The corner defining the right side of the slab provides a reasonable route. Climb the corner direct, passing the cracked flake with care.
pre-1997

㉓ **Sharp as Glass** 16m S ★★
Delightful climbing up the right-hand side of the arête.
Photo this page.
N Franklin, N Reid 28.08.1989

㉔ **Glass Clogs** 14m S 4b ★
Climb the centre of the knobbly slab, generally following the obvious seam.
D Bates 28.09.1987

The west-facing, easy-angled slabs to the right provide fun for parents with small children.

Wrynose

Sharp as Glass S (this page) Chloe Parker – David Simmonite

LONG SCAR

OS Grid Ref: NY 273 036
Altitude: 550m

Katie's Dilemma MVS (page 201) Steph Marshall & Tony Mawer — David Simmonite

A friendly location with a fine collection of pleasant routes in the lower grades on good rock. The approach is easy and the sunny aspect makes for a delightful experience.

Approach: From the top of Wrynose Pass, follow the good path towards Red Tarn for about 1 km. A well-marked path at the top of a small rise leads rightwards to the crag.

Descent: Either end or down one of the diagonal rakes that split the crag.

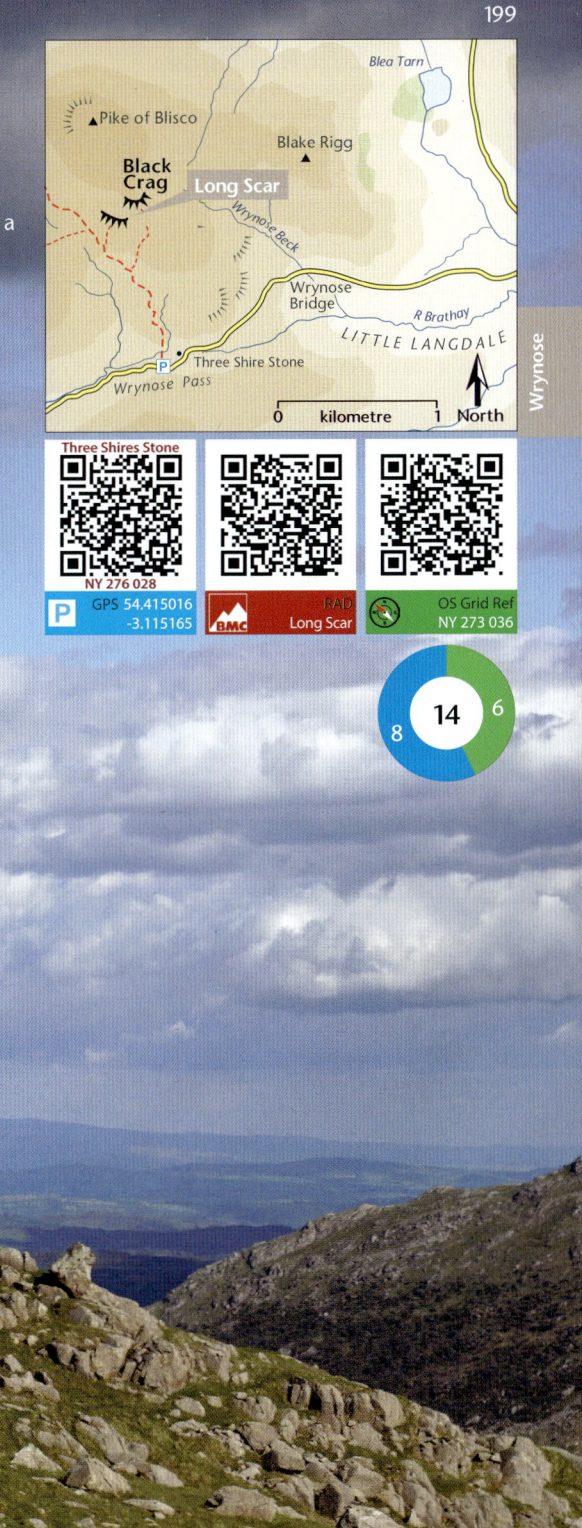

Long Scar - Left Hand Side

1 Great White 22m VS 4c ★
Interesting climbing taking the rounded pale area of rock. Start up the pale section on the left, boldly moving rightwards to finish up the thin steep crack.
BJ Clarke 6.06.2008

2 Long Scar Groove 22m S 4a ★★
The excellent continuous groove has a tricky start.
R Whitham, T Walkington 4.04.2009

3 Monster in a T-Shirt 20m HVS 5a ★
Without the crucial runner this is serious, if indeed you can reach it at all. Climb straight up the cracked wall to a ledge. Move up left (blind placement in the crack). Finish up the crack.
J Cooper, B Charlton 25.07.1998

4 The Singing Cowboy 20m MVS 4c
A very good route gaining the short right-facing hanging groove. Climb up and into the corner which is followed to an exit left.
J Cooper, S Harth Aug 1996

5 Trigger 18m S ★
Start from the ramp that forms the descent route. A metre up, make a short traverse right and climb up the clean wall and grooves.
J Cooper, B Charlton 17.07.1998

6 Green Treacle 28m HS 4a ★★
Start at a crack in the clean wall below the narrowest part of the descent rake. Climb the cracked weakness in the wall to the rake. A strenuous move allows the crack line to be gained and followed to the top.
J Green, W King 5.04.2009

Three Shire Stone — 📷 John Holden

Three stones have traditionally marked the adjoining boundaries of Cumberland, Westmorland and Lancashire. The monolith was carved from Cartmel limestone in 1816 for the Furness roadmaster William Field. Curiously, it wasn't erected until after his death in 1860.

A car hit the stone, which broke into four pieces, in 1997. It was repaired by Troutbeck stonemason, Gordon Greaves, and re-erected by the National Trust in 1998, with local support. Three County stones were also laid at that time: L to the south, W to the east and C to the west. To avoid further mishaps, the parking area was re-located.

Right Hand Side

7 Heart of the Matter 20m VS 4b
A bold but pleasant climb. Gain a grassy ledge and climb the right-leaning groove above to a platform. A mantelshelf leads to the top.
J Cooper, J Kelly 1992

8 Katie's Dilemma 20m MVS 4b ★
Start at the toe of the buttress beneath a perched block at one-third height. Climb up to the block and continue up the groove above.
Photo page 198.
R Linton, D Worrall 1982

9 Step to the Right 20m VS 4b ★
Climb a flaky crack until forced left towards the perched block. Step right and climb up across the right wall to mantelshelf into a groove which leads to the top.
J Cooper, J Kelly 1992

10 Something Stupid 18m HVS 5a ★
Rightly popular. Start at a crack in the middle of the long ledge at the foot of the wall. Gain the ledge and follow a thin crack past a small overhang and flake crack to the top. The crack is hard to start but has bomber gear.
D Oddy, D Potter 1982

11 Sam's Saunter 15m HS 4b ★
Starts below the left end of the slabs. Climb the shallow groove leftward on small holds and continue in the same line to the top.
R Linton, D Worrall 1982

12 Llywndyrys 17m VS 4b ★
Good climbing yet rather indirect. Climb *Sam's Saunter* to a prominent hold at about 4m. Move up right into a niche and then back left to gain the base of the layback groove. Follow this to easier ground.
D Davies, A Maughan 11.10.2002

13 Platt Gang Groove 16m VD ★
Very popular. Climb the right-slanting groove in the centre of the wall directly to the top.
D Worrall, R Linton 1982

14 Intruder's Corner 18m VD ★
Start below the left end of the easy ramp. Climb the line of weakness leading to a rock ledge at 12m. Finish up the fine corner.
D Worrall, R Linton 1982

ESKDALE

Medusa Wall, Esk Buttress VS (page 228) Steve Scott — 📷 David Simmopnite

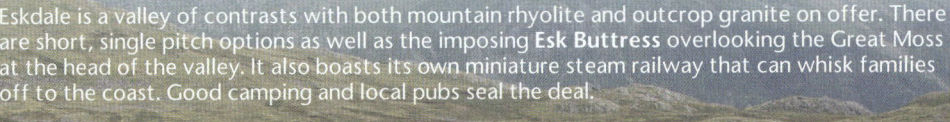

Eskdale is a valley of contrasts with both mountain rhyolite and outcrop granite on offer. There are short, single pitch options as well as the imposing **Esk Buttress** overlooking the Great Moss at the head of the valley. It also boasts its own miniature steam railway that can whisk families off to the coast. Good camping and local pubs seal the deal.

BRANTRAKE
OS Grid Ref: SD 145 984
Altitude: 90m

This handy outcrop of immaculate granite is just a short walk from the road. In the spring or early summer check the RAD to see if there are restrictions in place.

Central Crack VS (opposite) Bridget Glaister & Paul Cox — 📷 Mark Glaister

Main Crag

Clean and impressive, this striking piece of rock, split by three distinct cracks, is easy to spot.

Approach: From Eskdale Green take the road to Birker Fell, passing the King George IV, then turn right along the narrow Birkby road for 500m to a small parking area on the right. A steep path opposite leads up to the crag.

Descent: Either side.

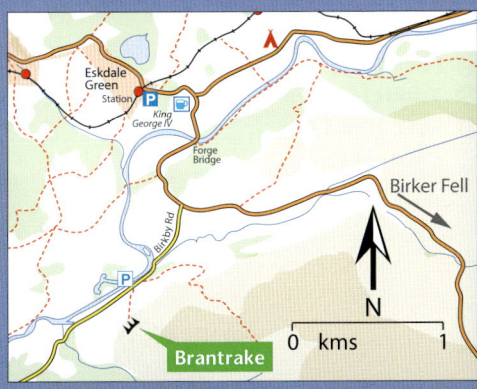

1 Left Edge 33m VS 4a ★
A good but rather bold route which follows the rounded rib on the left of the face. Start in the middle of the gully below the face. Climb leftwards up the wall to a ledge then continue up to below the main rib. Follow this directly to the top.
A H Greenbank, J Peacock 1959

2 Tunnel Vision 18m E2 5c
An eliminate which strictly avoids both the *Left-Hand Crack* and the arête. Ascend easily to a thin crack; up this to a good hold and runner before continuing up to the edge above.
P Strong, J D Wilson, A Wilson 3.06.1986

3 Left-Hand Crack 18m E1 5c ★
Climb the faint crack, which is difficult to protect, but relents with height.
J Lamb, R Allen June 1981

4 Central Crack 20m VS 5a ★★
After an awkward start, climb the crack to the top.
Photo opposite.
Eskdale OB staff 1950s

5 Art for Art's Sake 20m E5 6b ★★
One of the best slab pitches in the Lakes despite its contrived nature. Climb the blank wall between *Central Crack* and *Right-Hand Crack* (without recourse to either for protection) to a diagonal crack and runners. Climb the slab above to some chicken-heads, stretch right for a good hold in a break and finish easily.
A safer option is to use side runners in *Central Crack*. This allows the headwall above the chicken-heads to be climbed directly.
P Whillance, J Lamb 3.07.1981

6 Right-Hand Crack 15m HVS 5b ★★
The thin crack, just left of the rib, is climbed with awkward moves at 6m. Excellent protection.
Eskdale OB staff 1950s

7 Abstract Arête 12m E3 5c ★
An excellent delicate pitch up the sharp right edge of the wall, a long reach being a distinct asset. A runner at half-height is available, though a high side runner reduces the grade to E2.
G Smith Summer 1982

Upper Crag

This pleasant 10m high face lies just above and right of **The Main Crag**. It is a popular venue for groups and beginners. In addition to the routes described, many variations exist; these do not merit description - make up your own.

8 Block and Tackle - Right-Hand 10m VD
Climb the right side of the block then follow a line of short grooves.
Outward Bound Staff Pre 1991

9 Face Route 11m HVS 5a ★
Start just right of the block and climb the face direct. It all gets rather artificial near the top. The blank **Right-Hand Start** is E1 5c.
Outward Bound Staff Pre 1991

10 Terrace Crack 11m VD
The crack just to the right leads to the left end of Big Ledge. Continue up the corner groove or climb the blunt arête to its left.
Outward Bound Staff Pre 1991

11 Slim Line Tonic 10m VS 4c
A pleasant eliminate. Climb directly up the wall in between *Terrace Crack* and *The Middle Way* to Big Ledge. Continue in the same line, moving right near the top.
Outward Bound Staff Pre 1991

12 The Middle Way 10m S ★
The crack in the centre of the wall leads to the middle of Big Ledge then take the central crack above.
Outward Bound Staff Pre 1991

13 Dog Leg Crack 10m VD ★
The crack towards the right side of the wall leads to Big Ledge. Finish more easily up the right side of the wall above. **Photo below.**
Outward Bound Staff Pre 1991

Dog Leg Crack VD (above) Izzy Stothert — Jon Read

BELL STAND

15 mn

OS Grid Ref: NY 163 007
Altitude: 120m

A sunny quick-drying face of rough rock which bears a close resemblance to a natural gritstone edge. This little granite outcrop is situated high on the hillside above **Beckfoot Quarry** and is clearly visible from the King George IV pub, although from here it looks deceptively small.

Approach: Limited off-road parking is available at Stanley Ghyll House. Walk west along the road, passing **Beckfoot Quarry** on the right, to reach an old railway hut. From here, a sketchy path leads alongside the left of the quarry to the crag.

Descent: To the right.

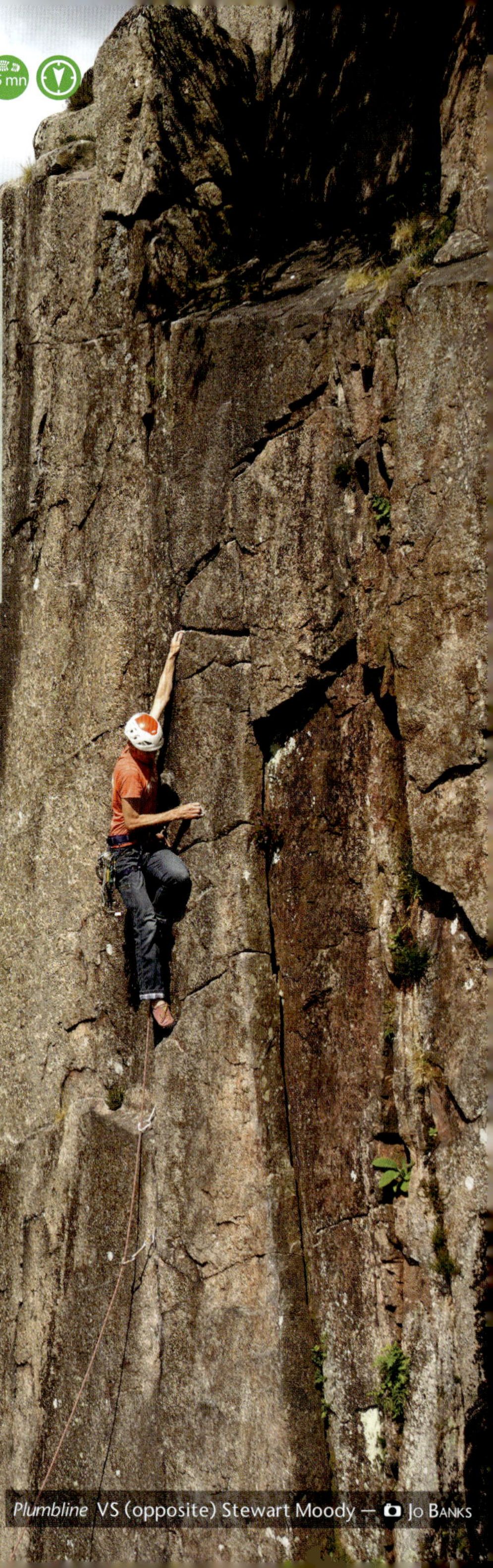

Plumbline VS (opposite) Stewart Moody — Jo Banks

Beckfoot
NY 168 005
P GPS 54.392785 -3.281962

BMC RAD Bell Stand

OS Grid Ref NY 163 007

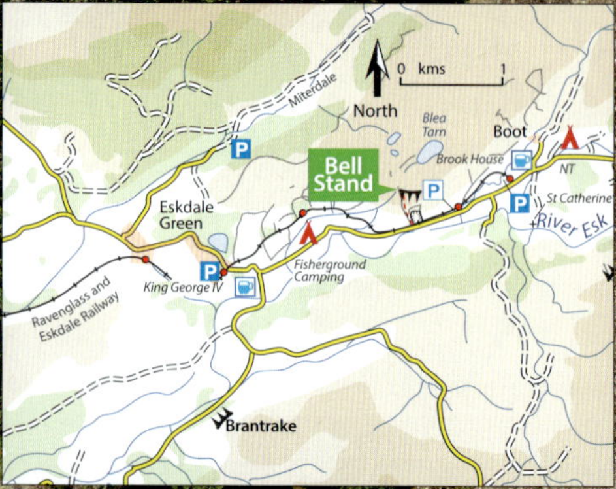

① The Seams 12m HVS 4c
Climb the left-facing corner then steep rounded cracks to join the fluted crack system.
P Whillance 16.12.1991

② Terminator 12m E3 6a ★
An eliminate up the slim pillar, using the right edge all the way. Stepping left for a runner at half-height reduces the grade to E2 5c.
P Whillance (solo) 16.12.1991

③ Innocuous Corner 12m HVS 5a ★
Climbs the slim right-facing corner directly.
P Whillance 6.04.1991

④ Sideslip 17m E2 5c ★
A good route 2m left of the holly. Climb to a small triangular overhang, then follow the slim groove on its left and continue up cracks to below the nose. Traverse right to a ledge, then step up left and climb a thin crack to the top.
P Whillance, C Fanshawe 15.12.991

⑤ Ladies Day 16m HS ★
Climb the corner to the right of the holly and exit onto a steep slab. Move up this to its top, step left and finish up a wide corner crack.
P Whillance 8.12.1991

⑥ Anniversary Waltz 16m E2 6a ★
A very fine route. Start below the centre of the wall at a thin crack. Climb the crack and move left to a ledge on the arête; easily gained by a direct, but inferior start. Step up right to a thin crack with difficulty and follow this to the top on better holds.
P Whillance 20.04.1991

⑦ The Birthday Present 16m E5 6a ★
A fingery and committing route; poorly protected throughout. Climb the crack to reach a ledge on the right. Small, widely spaced holds lead to a tiny flake high on the wall. Gain the thin crack above with difficulty and follow this to finish.
P Whillance 20.04.1991

⑧ Plumbline 15m VS 4c ★★
The direct crack forming the right-hand side of the wall, exiting leftwards above the sloping ledge. There is an alarmingly loose, but seemingly mechanically sound hold above the ledge.
P Whillance 15.04.1991 **Photo opposite.**

⑨ Hollow Flakes 15m MVS 4b ★
Start a couple of metres right of the crack at a slim corner formed by a large flake. Climb the flake to a small overhang. Use the horizontal break above to swing right and pull up to a sloping ledge. Exit leftwards.
P Whillance 15.04.1991

⑩ Tipsy Crack 14m HVS 5b ★
A good route starting below a Y-shaped crack 2m left of the large corner. Climb the leftward-slanting crack to a sloping ledge. Step right below the tree and finish up a slot on the right.
P Whillance 5.04.1991

⑪ The Puzzle Book 14m E2 5c ★★
Excellent. Taking the open corner which is deceptively awkward; the start is often wet. Follow the corner with escalating interest.
P Whillance 27.04.1991

⑫ Enigma Wall 12m E5 6b ★★
A very difficult proposition starting off the higher ledge around the arête. Climb up to a small niche, pull up left and follow a thin crack to the top with difficulty.
P Whillance June 1992

GATE CRAG

OS Grid Ref: SD 183 997
Altitude: 200m

20 mn

Steep climbs, on mostly solid rock, along a line of buttresses spanning the hillside across the valley from Boot. The crag has a lovely outlook and gets the sun from mid-afternoon. The right-hand buttress is the largest, though most offer an impressive line or two and both sides of the crag offer worthwhile climbing. The crag tends to be overlooked; this lack of traffic often doesn't detract from the climbing and many of the steeper routes retain a naturally semi-clean state. The groove and crack lines can remain damp after rain.

Approach: From Boot, take a narrow track to St. Catherine's parish church; park in the car park by the river bank. Walk upstream for ½km and cross the river via a footbridge. Immediately, take a path on the right through the trees then across the open fellside (bracken in summer) to the foot of the crag.

Descent: Numerous descents between the buttresses are possible - it is worth assessing options as one approaches the crag.

St Catherine's
NY 175 002
GPS 54.390888
-3.270337

RAD
Gate Crag

OS Grid Ref
SD 183 997

3 7 4

① **The Rats Tale** 21m E2 5b
An enjoyable route up the left side of the arête. From left of the arête, awkward moves lead to better holds on the bulging wall. Follow these rightwards onto the arête then continue to the top.
I Turnbull, A Wilson 26.03.1989

② **Rock Aid** 22m E5 6b ★
A bold, strenuous and intimidating undertaking. Climb to a right-sloping gangway then up to a rest under a small overlap. Make hard moves up and left to an awkward escape left onto the arête. Follow this to the top.
D Hall, D Hinton 25.07.1985

③ **The Sassanach Direct** 25m E6 6b ★★
A serious direct finish to *Rock Aid*: powerful and committing. Follow *Rock Aid* to the overlap. Move right to a jug on the lip; make hard moves up a groove on layaways to an undercut then reach a downward-pointing flake (protection). Power up and left to a finger pinch (crux) then crank your way to the top on small edges.
I Turnbull, J Carradice Jul 1989

④ **The Niche** 20m E4 6a ★★
An excellent clean route which climbs the obvious niche in the wall. Start in the (nearly always) wet groove directly below the niche. Climb the corner on the right to a ledge then move delicately into the niche from the left (poorly protected). Exit with difficulty using a thin crack and follow this up rightwards, with interest.
D Hall, P Strong Jun 1985

⑤ **Hysteria** 24m E3 6b
A fierce test-piece. Start at the left edge of the wall. Climb the arête then pull right to a break in the roof. Follow the break (2 pegs) to awkwardly gain a thin crack in the upper wall which is followed to the top.
P Strong, D Hall 10.08.1983

⑥ **Hydrenalin** 24m E2 6a ★★
A good, technically interesting roof problem, un-reliant on the pegs. Start directly beneath the centre of the long roof. Climb the wall (2 pegs) then surmount the roof with difficulty to enter a shallow groove which leads to the top.
D Hall, P Strong 30.05.1983

⑦ **The Golden Bow** 42m E2 5c ★★
Follow the crack to the bulge then make an exciting traverse left to gain a shallow groove around the rib, just right of the ivy. A step up the groove leads to a spike (sling), then follow the arête delicately and directly.
P Strong, D Hinton Aug 1984

Eskdale

HARE CRAGS

OS Grid Ref: NY 200 013
Altitude: 170m

A popular crag, clean and fast-drying. Several buttresses of delightfully rough granite give walls and blank open slabs with good climbing at all grades and a contrast of styles. The crag stands out on the fellside behind the Youth Hostel as one drives up the valley.

Approach: From the west end of the small car park opposite Wha House Farm, go through the kissing gate and take a 5 minute walk over a low hill northwards to the crag.

Easy Slab VD (page 217) Fiona Sanders — David Simmonite

Alternator Buttress

This short steep wall lies 120m left of **The Central Slabs**, and is identified by a large holly on its right-hand side.

Descent: To the right.

1 Magnetron 15m E2 5c ★★
A sustained line. Climb the shallow groove and follow the increasingly strenuous crack above; finish out right.
J Daly, K Daly 27.11.1987

2 Alternator 17m E4 6a ★★
A superb strenuous pitch. Climb a faint rib to an amazing blocky foothold then balance across right to finish up a shallow hanging corner.
K Phizacklea, J Daly 14.11.1987

3 Black Death 15m E6 6c ★★
Good climbing taking a direct line up the centre of the face. Climb the faint rib of *Alternator* to just below the blocky foothold. Step right below this (RPs); technical and committing climbing up the front of the wall gains a welcome side hold. Finish up the shallow hanging corner.
M Edwards, T Thompson 16.08.1997

- Alternator Buttress this page
- The Upper Wall page 214
- The Central Slabs page 215
- The Lower Buttress page 216
- Right-Hand Slabs page 217

The Upper Wall

This lies directly above **The Central Slabs**.
Descent: To the left

4 Upper Slab Route 1 17m VS 4b ★
Great moves from the prominent chicken head on a rising leftwards line reach a ledge. The short walls above lead to the top.
WE Pattison, AW Dunn 1974

5 Spiked Hare 16m E2 5c ★
A neat problem tackling the centre of the slab. Pass right of the large chicken head to reach better holds. Tackled direct, the blind shallow crack provides an awkward and difficult finish; making a step left reveals a less stressful solution [E1 5b]. The steep wall above maintains the interest.
B McKinley, A Rowell, A Phizacklea S Wood 21.04.1990

6 Hare Today, Gone Tomorrow 11m E5 6c
With no gear and a high crux, this is very bold. The right-hand side of the slab slab is climbed straight up the middle to a desperate smear.
S Wood

7 Labyrinth Route 20m S
A pleasantly delicate route starting below the right-hand rib. Follow a shallow depression diagonally leftwards across the slab to reach the grass ledge. Finish directly up the slab above.
WE Pattison 1974

The Central Slabs

Magnificent smooth slabs above a steep lower wall make a striking feature.

Descent: To the left.

8 Jugged Hare 28m VS 4b ★★
This popular varied route kicks off with a bold lower slab. Climb the centre of the slab to a grass ledge. The next objective is the curving flake which provides a great handrail to reach the final rounded cracks.
DN Greenop, T Baldwin, M Woods Jan 1971

9 Hareless Heart 24m E1 5b ★
Climb the flake and wall above to reach the slab. Climb directly up this until a faint diagonal crease runs up right. Follow this to a tiny overlap (runner), then step back left and finish directly up the rippled slab. Judicious meandering will reveal better holds and reduces the grade to **HVS**.
A Phizacklea, E Cleasby 8.11.1981

10 Butterballs 2 22m E5 6b
A steep fingery problem with ground-fall potential. Climb the wall to reach the centre of the prominent diagonal crack (small cams). Continue strenuously rightwards to reach the upper slab where the slab just right of an easy crack leads to the top.
TW Birkett, AN Other 13.05.1990

11 Slit Wall 23m E1 5b ★★
The prominent central crack in the steep lower wall gives the classic dilemma; whether to hang around for more gear or push on for the jug! Climb the crack with an enigmatic move where it deepens to reach the slab. Taking the clean bold slab, left of the cracks, is the most satisfying finish.

12 The Tortoise 23m E2 5c
Interesting climbing in its lower half. The short curving flake in the steep wall presents an awkward exit onto the slab.
A Phizacklea, AH Greenbank 23.04.1994

13 Birthday Boy 23m HVS 5a
Well-protected climbing. Climb a series of thin cracks slightly leftwards to land on the upper slab. Climb the dirty cracks above before following clean rock on the right near the top.
TW Birkett 13.05.1990

The Lower Buttress

This is the steep wall capped by a slab. The most obvious feature on this section of the crag is *The Groove*.

Descent: To the left

(14) Fireball XL5 20m VS 4b ★★
A very fine route starting at the left side of a large finger of rock. Climb the crack to the top of the finger then follow short rounded cracks above to a sloping ledge. The slabby corner above provides the finish.
Photo opposite.
J Daly 6.11.1987

(15) The Groove 15m E1 5b ★★
A fine challenge. Protection is more than adequate, but is difficult to arrange, on this sustained pitch. Climb the groove; at its top move right into a finish up the wide crack.
E Cleasby, A Phizacklea 8.11.1981

(16) Thunderbirds 18m HVS 5a
Good climbing on surprising holds. Climb the slab to enter the steep bird-speckled sentry box then escape right onto the slab. Follow the diagonal crack rightwards to finish.
J Daly 6.11.1987

(17) International Rescue 16m E3 6a
A great little problem. Gain a diamond-shaped hanging slab from the left then pull leftwards with difficulty into a short groove to reach a small spike (thin sling). Finish up rightwards via the easier cracked slab.
A Phizacklea, B McKinley 21.04.1990

Right-Hand Slabs

A clean open slab on the right.

Descent: Descend well to the left.

18 The Rib 22m D ★

This pleasant open route starts from a well-trodden bare patch immediately below the left-hand rib. Follow the crest of the rib. There's a thread in the grass gully on the left. Scramble to the top.
J Daly Oct 1987

19 Celebration 23m HS 4a

A delicate unprotected eliminate.
A Phizacklea 23.04.1994

20 Easy Slab 24m VD ★

A lovely route, not too well-protected, that follows the jagged 'lightning crack' up the centre of the slab to a triangular niche then trends leftwards.
Photo page 212.
J Daly Oct 1987

21 Pleasant Slab 26m S

A fine line on the clean upper slab. Climb the slab via a vague crack just to the left of two grass patches then trend leftwards across the slab to the top of the rib.
J Daly Oct 1987

Fireball XL5 VS (opposite) Bridget Glaister & Paul Cox — 📷 Mark Glaister

HERON CRAG
OS Grid Ref: NY 222 030
Altitude: 250m

Gormenghast E1 (page 220) Luke Jones — Ian Parnell

Quick to dry and with an easy approach, this impressive pillar dominates the west side of the valley a short distance from the foot of Hardknott Pass. *Gormenghast*, taking a direct line on the steep central wall, is probably the best and most enjoyable route of its grade in the area. Even steeper, the combination of *Iago* with *Titus* is a stern test of strength and technique. Together with the flanking VSs, a day here is definitely worthwhile. Recently, peregrine falcons have not nested allowing restrictions to be eased earlier in the year, but always worth checking beforehand.

Seasonal restriction: 1st Mar to 30th Jun.

Approach: From the bottom of Hardknott, walk up and past Brotherilkeld farm, following the way-marked path north. Cross the river by a footbridge then across a field to join a path on the west bank at Taw House Farm. A well-marked path follows the valley crossing Scale Beck bridge then, where the path starts to descend towards the river, continue ahead on a trod which can be difficult to spot in summer due to bracken. This contours the hillside to the foot of the crag. Following the more obvious path back down towards the river will necessitate an arduous climb up to the foot of the crag over scree and boulders.

Descent: Abseil 50m from above *Sidetrack*. Or, walk leftwards from the top of the crag to reach a wide scree gully.

Eskdale

1. Sidetrack 55m VS 4c ★★
A popular route with an enjoyable main pitch making an ascending traverse beneath the overhangs.
1 18m 4b Climb a stepped groove and slab rightwards to a belay.
2 35m 4c Gain a ledge, above on the left, and make an ascending leftward traverse until beneath a steep wall which leads to a groove beneath the overhangs. Continue delicately up left to a sloping ledge and second groove; follow this over a small overhang and pass a second overhang on the right. An easy wall leads to an oak tree.
3 12m 4a Climb the rib above.
RB Evans, IF Howell Aug 1960

2. Gormenghast 53m E1 5a/5b ★★★★
Arguably the best climb of its grade in the Lake District and a classic climb of great character - especially if climbed in one magnificent long pitch which is just possible with 60m ropes and careful gear placement. The line is stunning, the positions are superb, the rock is delightfully clean and solid and protection is plentiful, except for one short section. Start under the central crack.
1 28m 5a Climb the steep clean grey wall directly to a ledge below the soaring crack. Move left onto the steep wall where adequate flat holds, with inadequate protection, lead up to a traverse right to a niche. Trust yourself - the holds are all there! Following the crack direct to the niche is a less exciting more technical 5b. From the niche, continue up the crack then step left into a groove which leads to a flake belay 6m below the holly tree; or continue to the tree.
2 25m 5a From the tree, step to the right and climb past a prominent block. A crack leads to the centre of the headwall where more cracks are followed to improving holds leading right to a ledge. Finish direct.
L Brown, AL Atkinson 26.3.1960

3. Iago/Titus Combination 51m E3 6a ★★
This combination of pitches, starting up *Iago* and finishing up *Titus* gives a tremendous harder alternative to *Gormenghast* on the right of the pillar.
1 33m 6a Climb the groove until a crack near the top allows a large hold to be reached. Move up to a large grass ledge. Boldly climb the very steep wall to an overhang below a slim groove (peg), then climb the crack in the groove with difficulty to reach good holds before moving up to a ledge. Follow the crack first right, then left, to the top of the needle.
2 18m 5c Stand on a 'musical' (very fragile) flake on the right and step up to obvious undercuts where a long reach above the overhang reveals a good flake. Step left and climb directly to a tree, finishing up cracks in the headwall.
I Singleton, A Jackman (Iago) / A Phizacklea, DR Lampard (Titus) 4.07.1965 / 30.05.1989

4. Bellerophon 57m VS 5a ★★
An excellent route taking the long deep groove defining the right side of the main pillar. The route has positive holds, good protection and an inescapable line. Unfortunately, it does hold an abundance of moss and is slow to dry. Fortunately, despite appearances, the holds are clean. Start at the toe of the arête.
1 10m 4b Climb the shallow groove in the arête, left of a square-cut chimney, to a large grass ledge.
2 12m 4c Make a delicate move to the right to the foot of a steep crack. Ascend the crack to a large grass ledge.
3 13m 4c Climb the groove to a step left onto the pinnacle.
4 22m 5a Either step off the top of the pinnacle, or move round a nose on the right and work up a crack until good holds permit a strenuous pull-up. Easier climbing leads to a ledge. Climb an overhanging crack on small holds finishing rightwards.
ORD Pritchard, BS Schofield May 1958

ESKDALE ENCHAINMENTS

The Lakes is a fine place to enjoy big enchainments, linking routes creating a rock climbing way from the valley floor on to the summits. Eskdale is no exception and provides plenty of opportunity with loads of variation possible.

Heron Crag, *Gormenghast* E1 or *Bellerophon* VS continue to the Great Moss for bouldering on **Sampson Stones**. From here eye up a line on **Esk Buttress**, *Bridge's Route* HS or *Square Chimney/Medusa Wall* VS. This takes you from a valley setting into the high mountains. If that hasn't been enough of a day, the crags of Scafell are just over on the Wasdale side of Mickledore and will be in the sun until last light, so continue up *Botterill's Slab* VS a perfect evening climb during summer.

Heron Crag | 221

ESK BUTTRESS

OS Grid Ref: NY 223 065
Altitude: 490m

The Central Pillar E2 (page 228) Katy Forrester — David Simmonite

One of the finest crags in the district. The crag sits above the head of Upper Eskdale in a magnificent position, catching the sun for most of the day and remains largely clean and dry. The rock is solid and the wide range of grades means this is a must for everyone. The ground below the crag is steep and broken with easy scrambling to reach the start of the routes.

Approach, Cockley Beck: Park off the road at the foot of Hardknott Pass and walk up Moasdale on a distinct, yet often boggy, path. Descend to and cross Lingcove Beck, then follow a narrow path which contours round the hillside beneath crags. **Esk Buttress** comes into view across the Great Moss. To avoid the wettest sections, head round to the north (right) then climb steeply to the crag. Although this approach can be a bit boggy and looks a long way, it is quite easy with a lot less height gain.

Approach, Eskdale: Park in the roadside lay-bys near Brotherilkeld and follow the River Esk north to the outlet from the Great Moss. The dark forbidding **Cam Spout** is in front of you with **Esk Buttress** a further 500m to its right beyond the beck and path coming down from Scafell. Alternatively, cross the River Esk and head past Taw House Farm to cross Scale Beck Bridge. Just beyond this, a good path rises up the hillside then levels out before arriving at the Great Moss under Cam Spout. **Esk Buttress** is 15 mins beyond.

Descent: All routes require a scramble beyond the top of the crag before heading left and gradually walking/scrambling down broken terrain, hopefully picking up a faint path. Some *in-situ* abseil points might be in place to save a great deal of time and effort.

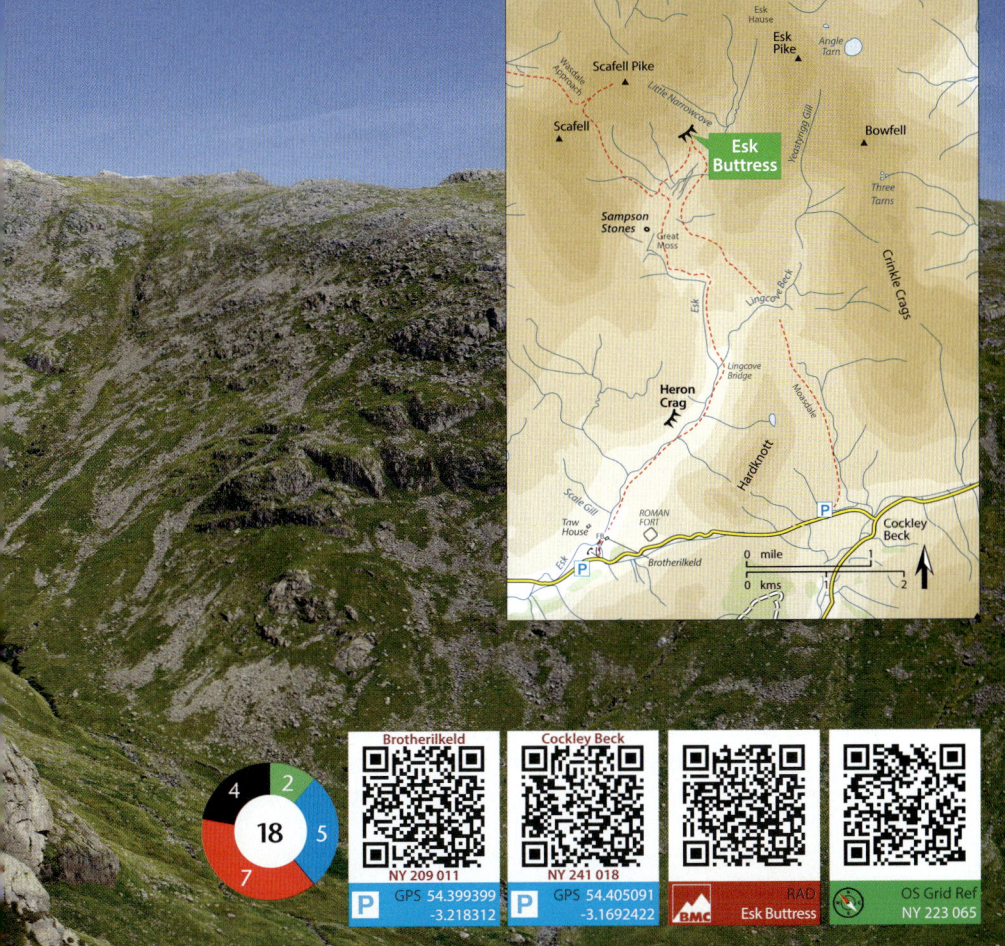

Gargoyle Wall

The steep clean wall at the left-hand side of the main crag easily identified by The Gargoyle, a curious protruding block overlooking the left side of the wall. There is a large expanse of steep broken ground below this wall which must be negotiated to reach most of the routes.

Approach: The usual approach is to follow the first pitch of *Gargoyle Direct*, or by scrambling up from either end of the ledge. Another way to reach the foot of the wall is to climb a route on the main crag and then walk down to the top of the wall where an abseil point can be fixed.

Descent: Abseil from a thread found at the top of *Gargoyle Groove*. Caution: 50m ropes do not quite reach the base of the crag. Alternatively, the wide open gully just left of the wall can be descended with care.

1 Gargoyle Groove   55m   VS 4c   ★
A good route which gives better and harder climbing than its apparently broken appearance would suggest. It follows the long well-defined groove at the left end of the wall, to finish just left of The Gargoyle. Start at the foot of a small buttress directly below and left of the groove, at a triangular wedged block.
1 19m 4b Climb the buttress to ledges and scramble up to the foot of the main groove.
2 18m 4c Go up the groove until forced onto the left wall by an overhanging nose. After a strenuous move on the left, move right to the tip of the nose above the overhang; easier climbing leads to a pinnacle belay on the left.
3 18m 4c Step back right and follow the remarkably sustained groove to the top, finishing just left of The Gargoyle.
AR Dolphin, LJ Griffin 9.08.1947

2 Alehouse Rock   42m   E4 6a   ★★
A superb steep route finishing up a thin crack just right of The Gargoyle. Start below the left-hand side of the wall, directly above the crevassed block. Climb a shallow groove to a small overhang at 5m, step right on undercuts and pull up the short wall to reach a spike. Step left and climb directly up the fingery wall until it eases by the arête. Traverse right for 5m across a narrow rock ledge then climb the shallow groove and the superb thin crack splitting the headwall to finish.
A Phizacklea 16.08.1988

3 Gargoyle Direct   81m   HVS 5a   ★★
The main pitch offers delightful open wall climbing with good protection. Start well down to the right at a narrow rock rib directly beneath The Gargoyle. (This is the only continuous line of rock leading to the foot of the wall.)
1 42m 4a Climb easily up the clean rib to grass and heather ledges. Steep scrambling, passing a rock crevasse, leads to a spike belay directly below The Gargoyle.
2 39m 5a Climb the wall, trending left slightly to reach a large spike at 8m, then move back

right to a sloping ledge. Follow a strenuous crack in a shallow groove for 5m, when a move left enables a rest to be taken. Continue left to a rib and follow it to a ledge beneath The Gargoyle. A short crack on the left leads to a block belay.
DW English, M McKenzie, K Brannon 3.06.1962

Gargoyle Wall

1. Gargoyle Groove — VS 4c ★
2. Alehouse Rock — E4 6a ★★
3. Gargoyle Direct — HVS 5a ★★
4. Wild Bunch Left-Hand — E3 5c ★
5. Grand Slam — E1 5a ★★

④ Wild Bunch Left-Hand 38m E3 5c ★
This is a fine route, piecing together several variations to create an outstanding steep pitch with a strenuous crux. Start below a thin crack. Climb the thin crack to a small ledge at 9m. A shallow groove above is climbed for a couple of metres, until a swing left gains a narrow ramp line. Follow this slightly rightwards to a roof, where a strenuous crack leads up to a large ledge out right. Pull back left onto a short nose which runs to the top.

⑤ Grand Slam 39m E1 5b ★★
Start below the thin crack. Follow the crack until it steepens then follow a rising line up right to a spike. The wall above leads to a square-cut overhang; pull out of the left side of this on small holds to thankfully gain a ledge. The wall on the right leads to the top.
W Young, I Singleton 12.08.1973

The Red Edge Area
This section of the crag consists of the steep clean wall below and left of the **Central Pillar**. It is bounded on its left-hand side by the deep-cut chimney.

⑥ Desperately Sea King 40m E6 6b ★★
An excellent sustained route up the corner culminating in a desperate overhanging crack. Abseil approach recommended.
Climb the awkward corner to its top then swing boldly left to enter a bottomless recessed scoop (peg). Step left to reach a thin crack and climb this, avoiding a suspect block, to an outrageous finish.
N Foster, M Berzins 26.05.1991

⑦ The Red Edge 60m E1 5a ★★★★
Superb climbing up the exposed grooved rib forming the right edge of the chimney. The difficulties are continuous but nowhere excessive and protection is good throughout. Start at the foot of the chimney.
1 39m 5a Ascend the chimney for 5m, until a thin crack on the right wall leads to the rib. Follow the rib for a short distance until a shallow groove on the left can be entered. Climb the steep groove to an overhang which is turned on the right; an easier groove above leads to a belay on the right.
2 21m 4c Move back left and follow a crack and then large flakes, slightly leftwards, towards the top.
Photo page 230.
JA Austin, NJ Soper, E Metcalf 17.06.1962

⑧ Hydra 54m E2 5c ★★
A good route, with a well-deserved reputation for difficulty up the shallow left-facing corner in the steep wall right of the edge. (The route is not as dirty as it appears, as the moss in the corner is avoided during the ascent.) Scramble up from the foot of the crag to a small tree on a well-worn ledge then move left to a belay directly below the corner.
1 33m 5c Climb diagonally leftwards towards the arête overlooking the chimney and follow it to a good ledge. Traverse right to the foot of the corner and climb it by interesting bridging moves (good RP) to where it gets dirty. Pull out right onto a good foot ledge and climb the wall above to a ledge on the left. Follow a groove above to a ledge on the right.
2 21m 4c A short corner and wall on the left lead to the top. P2 can be avoided by using the abseil point on the right above P1.
RJ Isherwood, CH Taylor 1967

⑨ Humdrum 38m E3 5c ★★★ ♦
A tremendous climb which boasts the best pitch of its standard on the cliff. Scramble up to the belay ledge at the foot of the wall. Climb steeply up towards some stepped grooves and follow these, with several bold moves, to a resting position. Go diagonally up leftwards to the top of the groove. After a couple of metres of ascent, traverse the wall on the right to a flat hold in the middle of the wall. Follow a thin crack above into a groove then pull directly over the square-cut overhang above to finish at a grass ledge. Abseil descent, or follow pitch 2 of *Hydra* to the top.
RH Berzins, M Berzins 8.08.1977

⑩ G.T.I. 42m E4 5c ★
A rather contrived but high quality pitch squeezed onto this fabulous piece of rock. Start from the ledge below the wall.
Climb the wall to a spike then continue directly to a good hold at the foot of a shallow groove, just right of an overhang. Follow the groove to good runners, then step left onto a committing brown crinkly wall which is climbed slightly rightwards to a sloping ledge. Move up to a good ledge then pull across right using an obvious rock scar to gain a poor resting place below a bulge. The final pull through this gives an excellent finish. Abseil descent.
I Turnbull, J Robinson, S Miller 1.09.1993

⑪ Black Sunday 63m HVS 5a ★★
A popular climb up the steep groove/crack system near the right-hand edge of the wall. The lower sections are rather mossy and need

Esk Buttress | 227

time to dry out after rain. Scramble up to a small tree beneath the main pitch.
1 33m 5a Move up to a prominent mossy crack and climb it to a slab on the right. Regain the crack and follow it for a couple of metres to where it fades, when a step left leads to a thin slanting crack. Follow this to a resting place beneath an overhang. Traverse right, back into the main crack line and pull rightwards round an overhang then ascend a short wall to a ledge.
2 17m 5a Climb the corner above until more broken rocks lead to a belay on the left.
3 13m 4b The wall to the left of a mossy scoop is climbed; belay well back.
J A Austin, E Metcalf, NJ Soper 17.06.1962

The Red Edge Area

12 Square Chimney/ Medusa Wall Combination   VS 4c ★★★
14 Bridge's Route   HS ★★★★

Central Pillar

Central Pillar is the unmistakable towering wall in the centre of the crag. It is bounded on its right by the deep corner of *Trespasser Groove*, and on the left by a mossy groove line.

12 Square Chimney/ 79m VS 4c ★★★
Medusa Wall Combination
An excellent combination finishing in a spectacular position above the main wall.
1 15m 4c Climb the chimney to a sloping ledge on the left.
2 15m 4b Cross a mossy slab on the left to enter a groove with a crack in the back; follow this to a small stance.
3 9m 4c Continue up the groove to a sloping ledge on the left. Alternatively, if the groove is wet, climb the left rib to the same point. Belay on a second ledge slightly higher.
4 13m 4c Climb the shallow groove up the left side of the wall, directly above the belay, to the top of a pinnacle. Traverse right to an exposed stance on the edge. The mossy V-crack on the right, in the centre of the wall, gives a strenuous alternative at (5a).
5 13m 4b Go up the groove above the belay for 5m, then traverse right to the edge, which is followed to a good ledge. Easy climbing and scrambling remains.
Photo page 202.

13 The Long Good 96m E3 5c ★★
Friday
A good sustained route climbing the shallow crease and headwall to the left of the. Start at the bottom left of the wall as for *Square Chimney Route*.
1 33m 5b Move up to a good spike at the very base of the chimney then step right on a heathery ledge to an incut hold on the steep wall. Pull up to gain a thin crack in the front of the pillar which is followed delicately to the top of a large flake. Climb the thin crack just right of the flake corner to a stance just right of the pinnacle.
2 38m 5c Follow the thin crack which leads directly to the junction between the slab and the headwall. Follow this junction rightwards, passing an awkward overhang, (crossing the *The Cumbrian* where it starts to go left on the headwall - take a good look for future reference!), and continue up into a delicate scoop. Step right across a slab and belay in a corner.
3 25m 5c Start up the thin crack directly above the belay to a good hold at 4m then pull rightwards across a fingery wall (poor Rock 2 in a horizontal crack) and lurch for a doubtful block. Pull onto the higher ledge then reach a higher ledge which is hand-traversed left to a point directly above the initial crack. Finish straight up.
A Phizacklea, JL Holden 4.04.2003

14 Bridge's Route 71m HS ★★★★
One of the classic routes of the district, providing a great introduction to the crag. The route initially follows a direct line up the lower part of the pillar, before traversing leftwards across the crag to finish above *The Red Edge*. Start by scrambling up vegetation and short rock walls to a cleaned ledge, just below, and 9m right of the base of the square chimney.
1 21m Move slightly right from the belay and follow steep rocks passing an awkward pinnacle to gain a very shallow cracked corner which leads to a grass ledge. Climb a crack above to a good flake which leads leftwards to a ledge.
2 13m Climb a steep groove above the left-hand side of the ledge and continue directly to a spike belay.
3 12m Traverse delicately left to a mossy ledge below an open chimney. A groove on the left leads to a block belay.
4 9m Continue traversing left along the sloping shelves to a small stance by a pile of flakes on the edge of the buttress.
5 16m Climb a mossy groove to a large grass shelf; belay well back.
AW Bridge, AB Hargreaves, M Linnell, W S Dyson 10.07.1932

15 The Central Pillar 98m E2 5b ★★★★
One of the best routes of its grade in the district with some exciting positions. Confidence pays on this superb climb. Start by scrambling up vegetation and short rock walls to a cleaned ledge.
1 40m 5a Climb slightly right then steeply up, passing an awkward pinnacle, to a shallow cracked corner which leads to a grass ledge. Continue up the crack above then climb a flake leftwards to a ledge. Climb a thin crack directly up the wall for 9m then step left to a continuation crack; follow this to a narrow ledge.
2 16m 5a Continue up the slab above, in the same line, then traverse rightwards across the wall to a narrow ledge. Move up left then step airily right around a nose to a hanging stance on a small ledge on the light-coloured rib.
3 13m 5b A good pitch to second. A shallow groove is climbed to a small ledge on the right. Go up left, over a small overhang, onto a slab and follow this rightwards to a small ledge

The Red Edge E1 (page 226) Nick Wharton & Ian Turnbull — 📷 David Simmonite

below an open corner.
4 21m 5b Traverse delicately across the exposed wall on the right and pull up to a small ledge (peg runner). Climb up the steep wall on the left past a doubtful block to a higher ledge then move right and climb up to reach a grassy bay on the right.
5 9m 4c Climb the undercut flake crack on the right of the bay or, alternatively, the easier wide crack on the left also leads to the top.
Photo page 222.
P Crew, M Owen 17.06.1962

⓯ The Cumbrian 89m E5 6a ★★★★
This climb boasts an awe-inspiring main pitch which takes the sensationally positioned, left-slanting corner, high on the front face. Technically sustained and strenuous on the crux but the protection is good. It starts as for *Bridge's Route*.
1 40m 5a Follow P1 of *Bridge's Route* to the top of the flake crack. Climb a thin crack directly up the wall for 9m and step left to a continuation crack; follow this to a narrow ledge.
2 16m 5a Continue up the slab above, in the same line, to join the traverse on P3 of *The Central Pillar*; this pitch is followed rightwards to a small ledge on the rib.
3 33m 6a Traverse left from the belay towards the steep wall (wires). Step left onto the impending wall to reach a shallow groove. Move up and left again with increasing difficulty, to enter the base of the slim corner. Climb the corner, surmounting a bulge near the top, and follow a slabby groove rightwards to a final bulge. Overcome this with difficulty.
R Valentine, P Braithwaite (alt) 5.05.1974

⓰ Trespasser Groove 121m HVS 5a ★★★★
A deservedly popular route which offers well-protected climbing, often of a strenuous nature. It follows the deep corner, bounding the **Central Pillar** on the right, before steepening rocks force the climb out right to finish.

1 30m Climb clean slabs to a heathery ledge.
2 20m Traverse up to the left to a ledge and then follow a groove above to the foot of the main corner.
3 27m 4c Ascend a slab for a short distance until moves left lead into the main corner; follow this to a recess. Go over a bulge to a second recess and continue steeply to a tiny ledge and spike belay.
4 10m 5a Climb onto a ledge on the right wall of the corner; continue up a thin crack in the wall above to a large flake. Move up right to a good ledge.
5 10m 5a A corner on the left is followed to an overhang; pull awkwardly up to the right and step across rightwards to better holds. Climb directly to a good ledge.
6 24m 5a Frankland's Crack leads onto a slab with some difficulty. Finish up a steep crack out of the top left-hand corner.
A R Dolphin, D Hopkins 6.09.1952

⓱ Bower's Route 116m HS ★
The original classic of the crag; more difficult than *Bridge's Route* but not as fine. Start below a sweep of slabs reached by scrambling 20m up an easy rake, from scree at the right-hand side of the crag.
1 30m Climb the centre of the clean slabs to finish rightwards onto a sloping heather terrace.
2 20m Climb diagonally leftwards to a small ledge; a right-slanting groove above leads to a clean ledge below a steep crack.
3 18m Climb the crack; belay on the left.
4 15m Climb steep rock for 10m until moves up to the left lead to a ledge: The Waiting Room.
5 15m Climb a steep awkward chimney on the right then follow a V-chimney out right to a rock ledge. Kirkus's Variation avoids the chimney: traverse the wall, right of the chimney, for 3m then climb a flake leftwards to the top of the chimney.
6 18m Slabs on the right lead easily to the top.
GS Bower, AW Wakefield, PR Masson 16.05.1920

Esk Buttress & Upper Eskdale — TOINY STEPHENSON

HARDKNOTT CRAG
OS Grid Ref: NY 228 016
Altitude: 440m

A popular crag that lies a few minutes walk from the Eskdale side of the top of Hardknott Pass. It faces west, dries quickly and offers some excellent climbing, often of a strenuous nature. The centre of the crag consists of steep grooves and cracks, whilst on the right, a blank-looking wall gives climbing of a bolder ilk.

Approach: Several pull-in options exist at the summit of the pass - park sensibly here and take a 5 minute stroll north to the crag base.

Descent: The best descent is to the right.

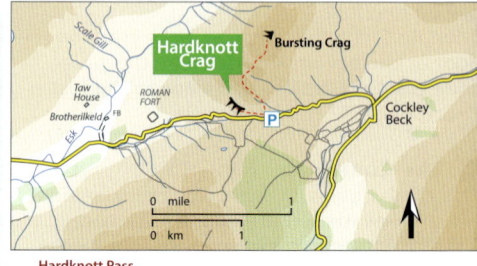

❶ **Caesar**   30m   E4 6a   ★★
An excellent route up the slim corner (small wires). Climb the wide initial corner to a ledge. The slim corner is followed with escalating difficulty and only relents once a good flake is reached. Finish up the groove above.
T Rogers, RO Graham 14.09.1989

❷ **Earl Boethar**   33m   E2 5c   ★★
Strenuous and a good test of fitness, albeit very well protected. Top end of the grade. The largest of the square-cut grooves in the centre of the crag. Start at a platform below a wide corner. Climb a wide crack in the right wall of the corner to a broken ledge. Ascend the corner above, passing a rectangular block, to reach a bulge. Overcome this with difficulty to a cheeky rest below the final roof. Pass this on the left into the final short corner. A clever detour to the left into a hanging groove (wire), up to a roof (peg) then back right, avoids the most strenuous section through the bulge.
E Cleasby, M Lynch 19.05.1982

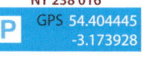  

❸ **Not Hard**   30m   HVS 5b   ★ 🌿
An excellent pitch which, despite its green appearance, provides sustained climbing with a technical finish. Climb the long green groove immediately left of the steep wall.
CJS Bonnington, M Thompson 1964

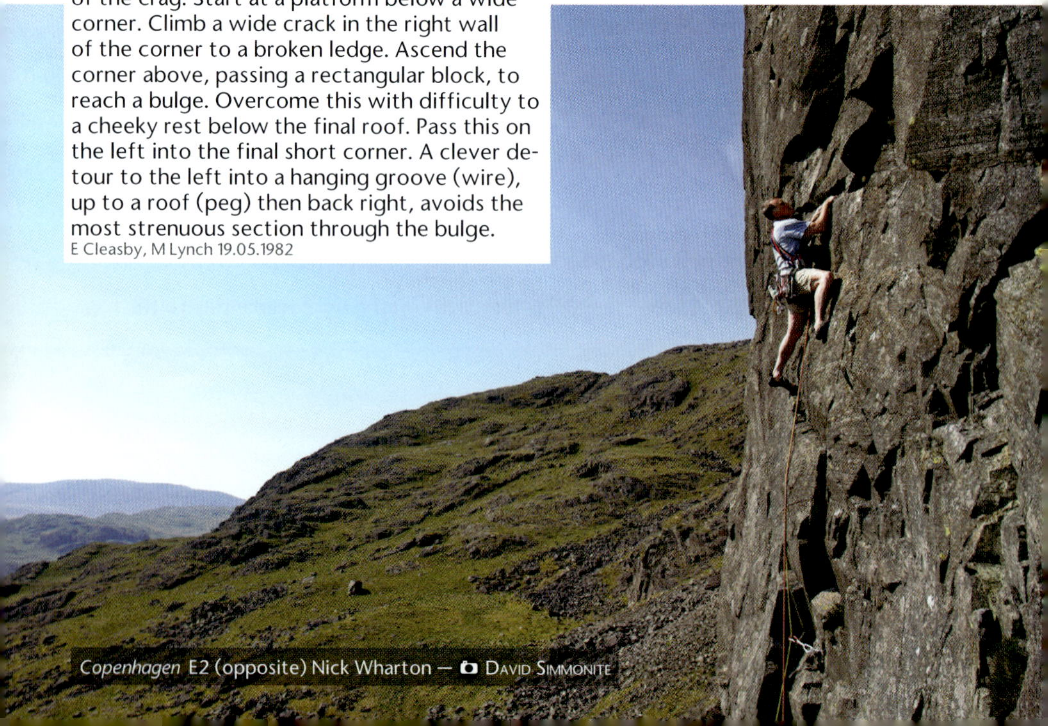

Copenhagen E2 (opposite) Nick Wharton — 📷 DAVID SIMMONITE

4 Powerglide 30m E4 6a ★★★
A superb sustained pitch. Start at the left-hand side of the wall below a slim bottomless groove. Climb the wall on the right for a couple of metres (wire), then step left to a sloping ledge below the groove. Enter the groove, with difficulty, and continue boldly to a good hold out left. Climb directly up the wall, passing a good spike, then span to an undercut, below a left-facing flake. Step left to a thin crack and follow this to better holds by the left arête; finish above.
E Cleasby, K Gibson 7.06.1982

5 Copenhagen 27m E2 5c ★★
A great line up the centre of the wall. It is no push-over and is quite bold in places. Climb a short wall for a couple of metres then follow a shallow right-slanting groove to good holds in the centre of the wall. Continue into the shallow inverted-V directly above then struggle onto a sloping ledge and second niche above. Step right to a small rib, go up then back left boldly over the roof, finishing slightly leftwards.
Photo opposite.
R Matheson Jul 1976

BURSTING CRAG

OS Grid Ref: NY 231 025
Altitude: 535m

This delightful crag is one of a few dotted around the north-west side of Hardknott summit. The outcrops are small but the rock is superb - rough and pocketed, and the outlook is magnificent, looking over Upper Eskdale, across the Great Moss to Bowfell, **Esk Buttress**, Scafell Pike, **East Buttress** and Scafell. With easy access and generally good grassy terrain, this would be an ideal venue for a family picnic on a nice afternoon or evening.

Approach: From the cairn at the top of Hardknott Pass, take the path north then go left, cross a stream then take the right-hand path gradually rising towards the north end of the ridge. Pass over the first peak then, once beneath the true Hard Knott summit with its distinctive cairn, veer off left beneath a low crag which turns a corner to become **Summit Crag**. Follow the base of this leftwards and **Upper Bursting Slab** comes into view about 100m ahead. Just beyond this **Bursting Crag** is visible, at a slightly lower level.

Descent: Descend to the right (south).

1 Wonderful Land 18m VS 4c
Climb a short wall and bulge at the right end of the overlap then the centre of the slab above.
D Geere, K Phizacklea 15.04.2021

2 Hargreaves Swing 19m HS ★
Climb through a small bottomless niche at 3m, traverse left above the slanting overlap then climb past some perched flakes higher up.
AT Hargreaves, GG MacPhee 1931

3 Mac's Crack 18m HS
Start up the bottomless niche then climb the crack above passing a protruding block at the top. Alternatively follow flaky jugs out left near the top (the original finish).
GG MacPhee, AT Hargreaves 1931

4 Ghost Riders in the Sky 18m VS 4b ★
Start 1m right of the pool. Climb the pocketed slab above direct.
D Geere, K Phizacklea 15.04.2021

5 See for Miles 18m MVS 4b ★★
Boldly climb the clean slab.
D Geere, K Phizacklea 15.04.2021

6 Broken Crack 18m S
Climb the heather-choked crack.
AT Hargreaves, GG MacPhee 1931

7 1931 18m VD ★
Start 2m left of the blunt rib. Climb the slab to beneath a smooth patch then follow a stepped weakness up left to join and finish up the crack.
GG MacPhee, AT Hargreaves 1931

8 Shindig 16m D
Climb the blunt rib in the centre of the crag either direct or on its left side.
Photo opposite.
AT Hargreaves, GG MacPhee 1931

9 Bursting Out 7m D
A route on the upper slab that climbs up through a rock scar. A pleasant extension to *Shindig*.
GG MacPhee, AT Hargreaves 1931

10 Slainte 17m MS
Take a diagonal line up the centre of the slanting slab right of the blunt rib then up the slab above staying left of the arête.
J Daly 13.07.2023

Hard Knott Summit — Peter Sterling

⑪ Rabble Army 12m S
Start at the base of a grassy ramp and climb the left-hand side of the slabby wall above.
D Geere, K Phizacklea 15.04.2021

⑫ Kon-Tiki 10m HVD ★
Start 1m right of the grassy ramp and climb the slim corner and crack.
D Geere, K Phizacklea 15.04.2021

⑬ Foot Tapper 9m VS 4b
The rounded rib. Start 2m left of the corner.
D Geere, K Phizacklea 15.04.2021

⑭ Dance On 8m D
Climbs the prominent short corner on the right-hand side of the crag.
D Geere, K Phizacklea 15.04.2021

⑮ Blinkers 8m MS
Climb a slanting line up the centre of the right wall of the corner. Avoid the diagonal break coming in from the right.
J Daly 13.07.2023

⑯ Side Swipe 7m MS
10m up to the right is short wall with a thin central crack; climb it.
J Daly 13.07.2023

Shindig D (opposite) Steve Scott – 📷 Nick Wharton

SCAFELL

Scafell is one of the finest crags in the country dripping with the early history of the sport and bang up to date with modern test-pieces. This is a true mountain crag that requires either good weather or great determination - or both. It sits high above Wasdale, a dramatic valley with the deepest, most sombre body of water - Wastwater. The valley provides some fabulous crags of its own.

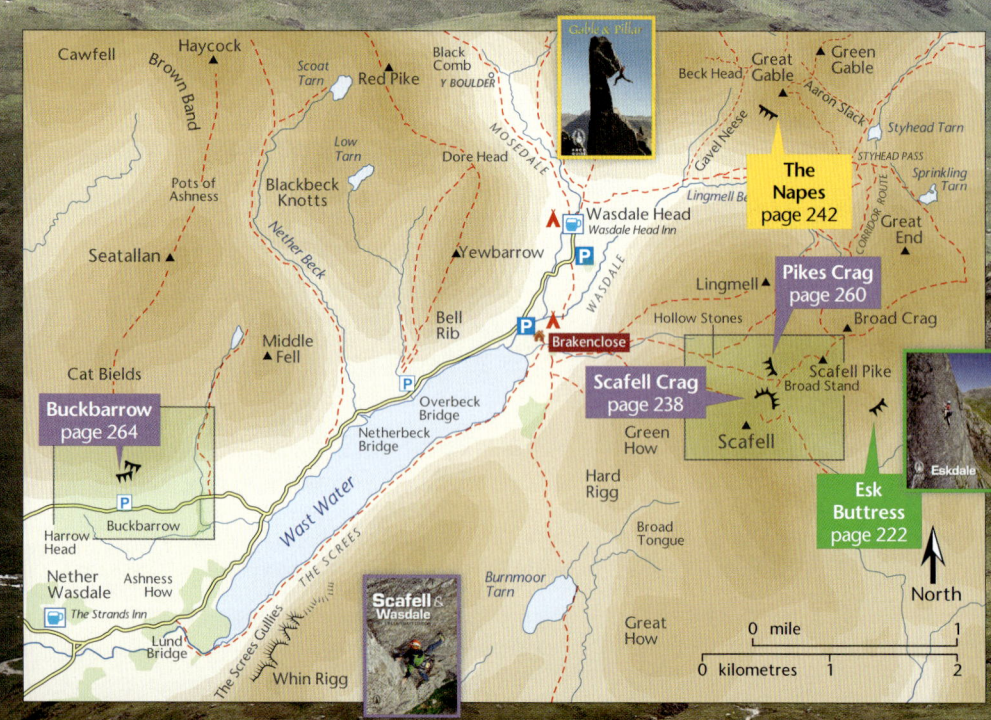

Dyad, The East Buttress E3 (page 256) Leo Houlding — Tom McNally

SCAFELL CRAG

OS Grid Ref: NY 209 068
Altitude: 790m

Approach: Scafell Crag is normally accessed from Wasdale Head by following the very popular track from the National Trust car park and campsite, used by many going up Scafell Pike. Where the main path to Scafell Pike branches off left, go right and up into the bowl of Hollow Stones with Pikes Crag up to the left, the dividing ridge of Mickledore ahead and the area of **Central Buttress** and **Scafell Pinnacle** on the right. The distinctive Woolworth Boulder is a welcome rest point before the final push up right to the base of the **Central Buttress** etc area. There is usually a small stream here to fill water bottles. The area can be approached from Borrowdale by Sty Head and the Corridor Route and contour up under Pikes Crag but it will take considerably longer.

Descent: Leftwards to reach Mickledore by abseil is safest. From the top of the crag, walk across and down leftwards until a large shelving platform on the right (looking out) can be reached. Go left (looking out) to a large perched block 10m directly above the crest of Mickledore; abseil (thread). Alternatively, go right from the top towards High Man and descend Deep Gill.

Central Buttress E1 (page 241) Leo Houlding — Tom McNally

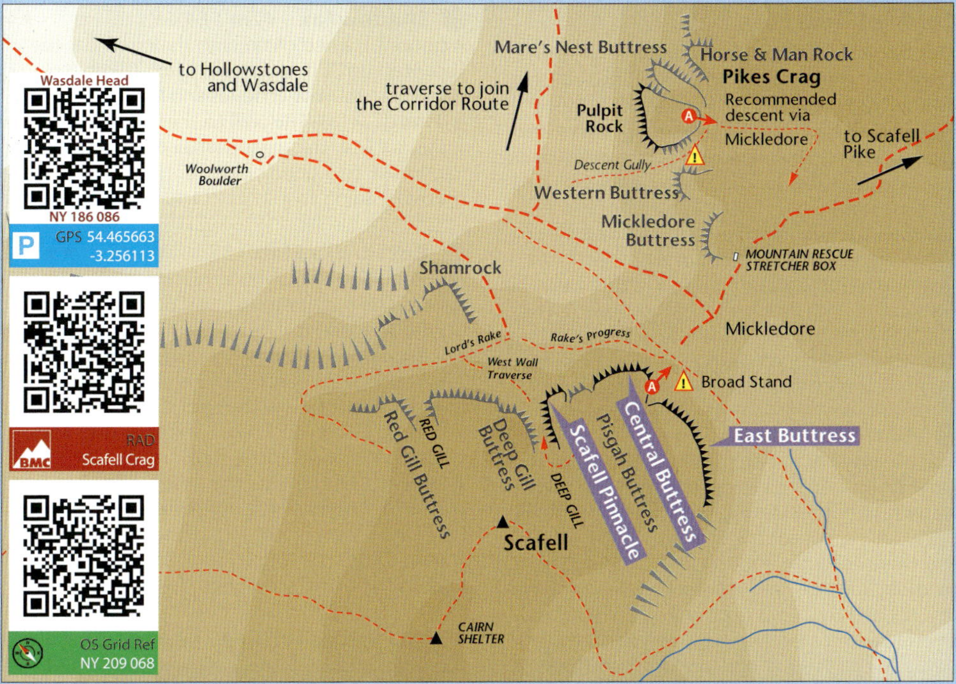

239

Wasdale Head
NY 186 086
GPS 54.465663
    -3.256113

BMC
Scafell Crag

OS Grid Ref
NY 209 068

Map labels:
- to Hollowstones and Wasdale
- Mare's Nest Buttress
- Horse & Man Rock
- Pikes Crag
- Recommended descent via Mickledore
- Pulpit Rock
- traverse to join the Corridor Route
- Descent Gully
- to Scafell Pike
- Woolworth Boulder
- Western Buttress
- Mickledore Buttress
- MOUNTAIN RESCUE STRETCHER BOX
- Shamrock
- Mickledore
- Lord's Rake
- Rake's Progress
- West Wall Traverse
- Broad Stand
- Red Gill Buttress
- RED GILL
- Deep Gill Buttress
- DEEP GILL
- Pisgah Buttress
- Scafell Pinnacle
- Central Buttress
- East Buttress
- Scafell
- CAIRN SHELTER

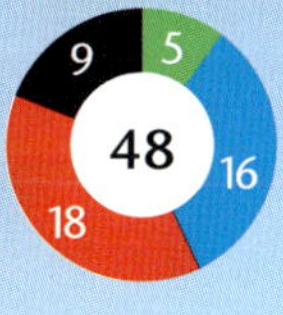

Scafell

9 | 5 | 16 | 18 | **48**

Photo labels:
- East Buttress page 250
- Moss Gill
- Steep Gill
- Deep Gill
- West Wall Traverse
- Botterill's Slab
- Central Buttress page 240
- Scafell Pinnacle page 245
- Lord's Rake
- Pisgah Buttress
- Shamrock
- Rake's Progress
- to Mickledore col
- Traverse to join the Corridor Route
- Woolworth Boulder
- Scafell Crag
- Al Phizacklea

Central Buttress

This large clean face is the highlight of **Scafell Crag**. The rock is generally sound and reliable on the trade routes of the main face; loose material will be found on the ledges and the aspect and some seepage produce areas of algae or moss. The face is characterised by many narrow, right-to-left slanting faults. These are used by many of the routes and all catch the evening sun. **Central Buttress**, with the distinctive huge flake perched in the centre, is flanked on the right by the deep dark cleft of Moss Gill. At the left-hand side of the buttress lies a prominent narrow light-coloured slab slanting across the face - *Botterill's Slab*.

❶ Black Rider 38m E5 6b ★★
Start below the centre of the wall. Climb to a large hold then rock-over to reach and climb a crack to ledges. Climb the wall to the small right-facing corner immediately right of the *Shadowfax* groove and the left-hand end of the overlap. Balancey moves lead to the good hold on *Shadowfax*. Climb rightwards across the overlap using a broken hold and small footholds to reach a jug on the right-hand side of the overlap. Climb directly up to gain a shallow cracked ramp which is followed to the top.
A Mitchell, N Pike 20.07.2013

❷ Shadowfax 42m E4 6a ★★
A good sustained climb with the crux near the top. Start 3m left of *Botterill's Slab*. Climb to where a system of grooves and ledges leads leftwards across the wall to the leftmost groove system. Climb this, past a small overhang and difficult wall, to a good hold. Continue up a shallow groove leading to a short crack.
P Botterill, S Clegg 7.07.1976

❸ Botterill's Slab 87m VS 4c ★★★ ♦
A compelling line of huge historical significance. The main pitch up the narrow light-coloured slab left of *Central Buttress* is outstanding for its technical merit, quality and position. The route dries quickly and is deservedly popular. Start below the slab.
1 15m 4b Climb up a short chimney and continue to the foot of the slab.
2 36m 4c Climb the slab by its left edge to a platform on the arête. Continue up a thin crack to belay in a recess on the left at the top of the slab.
3 36m Climb the left edge of the slab above, keeping out of the gully on the right.
FW Botterill, H Williamson, JE Grant 3.06.1903

❹ The White Wizard 96m E3 5c ★★★ ♦
A magical route with sustained, varied and interesting climbing, culminating in a tremendous finale holding you spellbound till the very end. It follows a line of steep grooves and

cracks up the wall right of *Botterill's Slab*. Start under *Botterill's Slab*.

1 15m 4b P1 of *Botterill's Slab*.

2 24m 5c Climb the corner of *Botterill's Slab* for a few metres. Make a long step right and follow a steep crack to a ledge (peg). Climb the shallow corner on the right until a move left and a crack lead to a ledge.

3 20m 5c Climb the continuation of the groove, with moves on the left wall at half-height, then take an overhanging crack to a ledge or follow the Original Route:

3a 22m 5a Make an awkward mantelshelf move onto a ledge on the arête on the right; then mantel again onto a narrow ledge which leads rightwards to a crack. Climb this to a gangway which leads diagonally left to the ledge.

4 15m 5b From the right end of the ledge, move across right and up to gain the bottom of a prominent crack. Climb this to a ledge.

5 22m 5c Pull round the arête on the right (peg) and climb the dirty awkward groove on the right to a small ledge. Either finish direct up cleaner rock (6a), or step up delicately round the bulge to the right to easy ground.
CJS Bonington, N Estcourt 11.09.1971

❺ Ringwraith 94m E6 6b ★★★★
A fierce route powering up the leaning wall and slender hanging corner to the right of *Botterill's Slab*. When clean, it is the best route of its grade in the Lakes.

1 18m 4a P1 of *The Nazgul*.

2 30m 6b Climb the short ramp on the left to a bulge (nut); then reach a series of layaway holds above (peg). Climb the smooth wall on tiny holds to a jug. Step left (runner) and up to a small ledge then continue directly on better holds to a pinnacle. **Or** take the original line (6b): climb to the layaways (peg) then traverse right along a handrail until a difficult move gains a dirty groove; hand traverse back left to reach the small ledge.

3 10m Easily up the ramp to a large ledge then down and right of a steep corner.

4 36m 6a Traverse right into the obvious overhanging corner and follow this strenuously to join another groove. Finish up this. A magnificent pitch.
M Berzins, RH Berzins, C Sowden 28.05.1977

❻ The Nazgul 84m E3 5c ★★★★
This tremendous climb cleaves a direct line up the full height of the crag. A superbly strenuous second pitch contrasts with the delightful airy last pitch. Start at a short crack just right of *Botterill's Slab*.

1 18m 4a Climb the crack and ascend easily rightwards to a flake below an obvious thin green crack slanting leftwards.

2 24m 5c Step left and climb the arduous crack to a resting place in a niche. Swing out left onto a narrow slab and follow it for a few metres until it is possible to climb the wall on the right into the obvious deep corner. Belay by some large flakes.

3 12m 5b Move up to reach a flake forming a detached pinnacle. Stand on this then step right into a surprisingly delicate scoop and climb up to a ledge.

4 30m 5a Climb the thin ramp on the left to where it widens. Continue up to a bulge then pull over rightwards to gain the higher parallel ramp line. Follow this in a superb situation to the top.
L Brown, K Jackson 12.07.1966

❼ Saxon 108m E2 5c ★★★★
A magnificent climb - a modern classic. The committing and strenuous main pitch climbs the exposed wall and slanting crack right of *The Great Flake*. Start just right of a short rock step on Rake's Progress.

1 30m 5c Climb the ramp for 8m, move into a shallow corner on the right and make a steep traverse rightwards to a corner on the left side of a triangular roof. Continue up the corner and trend right to belay below a corner, 8m right of the *The Great Flake*.

2 39m 5c Climb the corner and move 2m left (flake). Continue up the steepening wall and climb diagonally right to the arête and a small ledge. Traverse left on tiny stepped ledges then climb to the conspicuous left-trending crack. Climb the crack (awkward when wet) and the groove above to belay on the left (the V-ledge).

3 39m 5b Climb the mossy left-facing corner behind and continue to a second short corner; climb this to below an overhang and pull out right. Climb left onto the headwall above and up, or up and leftwards to the arête, and reach the top.
J Eastham, E Cleasby 10.07.1976

❽ Central Buttress 124m E1 5b ★★★ ♦
This route can justifiably claim to be the most famous rock climb in the country. Over the years, the centre of the main face has been probed and explored producing many variations. As befits its status, the route described, incorporating the direct start and finish, maintains the standard and offers continuously interesting exposed climbing of the highest quality. The traditional character associated with climbing The Great Flake was lost when the chockstone fell away with tragic consequences in 1994. Moving onto the exposed front face of the flake is now the standard route. Start just left of the foot of Moss Gill.

1 42m 5a Climb the corner then the rib and go up to a large ledge below a triangular roof. Traverse left for 4m to a corner and climb this and the wall above, bearing left, to The Oval.
2 25m 5b Marr's Variation. Climb easily to the foot of The Great Flake and continue for 5m to a sloping ledge on the left. An exposed traverse, using a horizontal crack, leads leftwards for 2m onto the front face of the flake. Step up slightly left and continue to a flat hold then move awkwardly up before trending right to a shallow crack from where the crest of the flake can easily be reached. Follow the flake leftwards to reach a spacious ledge - Jeffcoat's Ledge.
3 33m 4c Walk along the ledge and climb an easy ramp to a block and possible belay. Descend a little and traverse delicately right past a small pinnacle into a corner. Climb the corner and traverse easily right to the V-ledge.
4 24m 5a Climb the thin crack and gangway on the left for about 5m and traverse rightwards into an open corner. Climb the corner to the top and exit leftwards. Alternatively, starting from the left end of the ledge follow the fine top pitch of *The Nazgul*.
Photo page 238.
SW Herford, GS Sansom, CF Holland 20.04.1914

❾ CB - The Great Flake   26m   E3 5c
2a The original way up the flake crack can still be climbed; but, with the loss of the chockstone, and a resting place, this now means that attaining a layback position is extremely strenuous and committing. A very large cam reduces the grade to E2.

❿ Moss Gill Grooves   79m   MVS 4c   ★★★★
A magnificent delicate climb following the slanting groove just right of the main face. The crucial sections are short and well-protected. Start from Moss Gill, about 25m above Rake's Progress, where a slanting groove runs up to the left.
1 17m The groove leads to a good ledge. The overhanging block on the right is then climbed to a ledge below the main corner.
2 20m 4c Climb 3m up the corner and traverse delicately left to a small ledge overlooking the main wall of *Central Buttress*. Ascend the arête leading back to the groove. Go up this and the narrow slab to traverse right into the next groove.
3 24m 4a Wander serenely up the slab ahead first on its right then on the left and finally straight up to belay in a gully.
4 18m Climb the left wall of the gully for 5m and break out to a large ledge on the left. The steep wall above is delicate at its start and leads to the summit ridge.
HM Kelly, B Eden-Smith, JB Kilshaw 1.07.1926

⓫ Slab and Groove Route   72m   VS 4c   ★★
A fine route with a superb first pitch. Start up the big slab on the left side of Moss Gill.
1 33m 4c Climb the groove on the right side of the slab for 6m then traverse left to the foot of a thin crack which is climbed to a pocket near the arête. Follow the edge for a couple of metres and traverse left into a groove which is climbed until level with a recess on the left. Go back right into a corner immediately above the overhangs that cap the slab.
2 39m 4a Climb the groove then easily to the top.
RJ Birkett, LJ Muscroft 28.08.1948

⓬ Ring of Air   123m   E2 5b   ★★★
Enjoyable and exposed with a magnificent finale.
1 42m 4b Climb P1 and 2 of *Botterill's Slab* until possible to traverse right into the chimney and up to a ledge beneath an impending corner.
2 18m 5a Climb up rightwards across the steep wall on good holds to reach the ledge on the arête. Swing round onto the front face and move right to enable a mantel onto the ledge. Up and right onto a second ledge, which is followed right to a belay at the top of the ramp on *Central Buttress*.
3 9m Climb down the ramp and across to the left side of The Great Flake.
4 24m 5a Traverse the top of The Great Flake nearly to its end. Climb up into the horizontal crack and follow this rightwards, across the *Saxon* wall to *Moss Gill Grooves*. A really enjoyable pitch.
5 15m 5b Climb down *Moss Gill Grooves* for 4m. Make a committing traverse out right and across into a wide crack at a small chockstone. Make a precarious set of moves right into the next crack then up to a ledge in a niche.
6 15m 5a Climb down for 2m then step right and pull onto the left edge of the smooth slab of *Slab and Groove Route*. Climb up and right onto a ledge above the large roof. Continue up and right to reach a sloping ledge on the lip of the overhangs. Follow this rightwards and around a nose. Keep moving right on the same line until easier ground leads into the verdant Moss Gill.
M Berzins, C Sowden Aug 1983

Central Buttress

❷ **Black Rider**	E5 6b	★★
❸ **Botterill's Slab**	VS 4c	★★★
❹ **The White Wizard**	E3 5c	★★★
❺ **Ringwraith**	E6 6b	★★★★
❻ **The Nazgul**	E3 5c	★★★★
❼ **Saxon**	E2 5c	★★★★
❽ **Central Buttress**	E1 5b	★★★

Central Buttress | Scafell Crag | 243

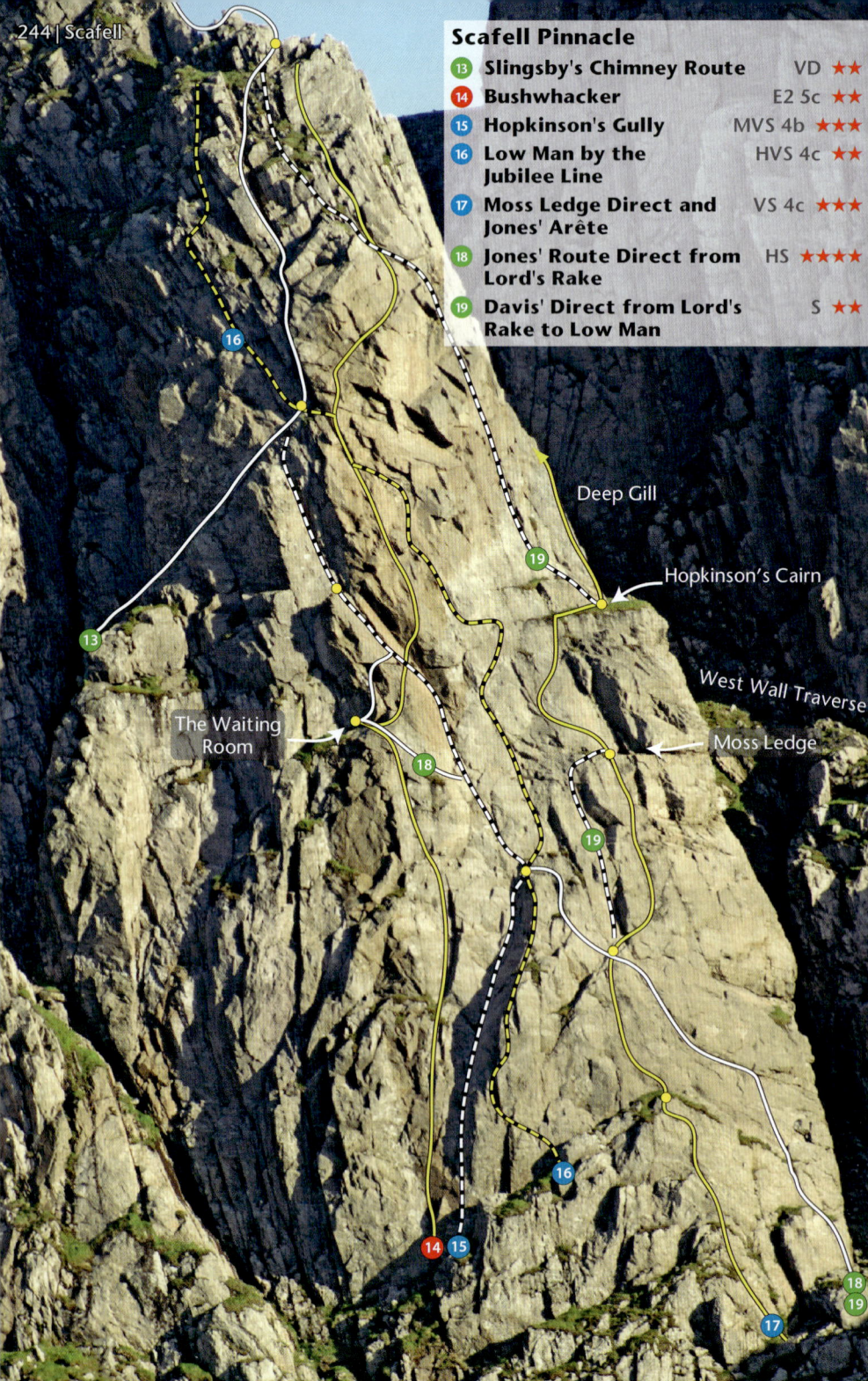

Scafell Pinnacle

Magnificent rock, very clean, solid and fast-drying, this is the conical buttress between Steep Gill and Deep Gill. Those routes facing Deep Gill receive the sun after mid-day and, in the early evening sunshine the slabs of the front face provide some of the most enjoyable climbing on the mountain. Those routes starting from Steep Gill are generally slower-drying and are prone to growths of algae and moss.

Descent: The Pinnacle has two summits High and Low Man. Gain the higher summit (High Man) then abseil or downclimb into the cleft which separates High Man from the summit plateau (Jordan Gap): 10m D. From here an easy traverse left leads on to the plateau. Mickledore can be gained by trending leftwards to pick up a faint rocky track leading down to the slabby area and abseil near Broad Stand. Use this to reach Mickledore.

Deep Gill and Lord's Rake: Head right for 70m to a cairn. Enter the gill at its head and descend loose scree for about 80m until it opens out by an impressive chimney on the left (looking out). The small cairned hump on the left indicates the start of the West Wall Traverse. Go down this until it meets Lord's Rake. Lord's Rake is loose and unstable - take great care especially when it is busy.

⚠ Avoid the descent from Jordan Gap directly into Deep Gill.

13 Slingsby's Chimney Route 97m VD ★★

The easiest way up The Pinnacle, this route has a fine classic atmosphere and good situations. Only Very Difficult for a few metres at the start of P2, the rest is Moderate. Start about 60m up Steep Gill just below where it steepens and narrows.
1 28m Easy rocks, ledges and slabs on the right wall of the gill lead to The Crevasse. Step awkwardly across this and climb a short slab to the foot of Slingsby's Chimney.
2 36m Climb the chimney - the undercut start is very difficult but soon relents. From its top, scramble to the summit of Low Man.
3 33m The Knife-Edge Arête is ascended, followed by fine climbing up the crest to reach High Man.
WC Slingsby, G Hastings, E Hopkinson, WP Haskett Smith 15.07.1888

14 Bushwhacker 90m E2 5c ★★

An interesting route on good clean rock which eventually finishes up the rounded rib to the right of Slingsby's Chimney. Start at the pyramid just left of the base of *Hopkinson's Gully*.
1 26m 5c Climb awkwardly into the scoop above then move left and climb a fine crack; continue to a ledge on the right.
2 18m 4c Take the flake crack and continue up the crack above to a line of good holds on the right. Follow these diagonally left to The Waiting Room.
3 46m 5b Step right across the slab of *Hopkinson's Gully* to gain the left edge of the upper slab. Climb this until level with the foot of Slingsby's Chimney then pull up and right to break out across the headwall, above the two dark niches, to the top.
A Phizacklea, R Knight 8.07.1984

15 Hopkinson's Gully 54m MVS 4b ★★★ ♦

An excellent delicate route on good rock which follows the well-defined shallow open corner running up the centre of the buttress. Sustained, with spaced protection on the first section. Start from the extreme left end of The Pinnacle Terrace about 10m from Steep Gill. The foot of the corner is guarded by a 2m wall which has a little pyramid of rock to its left.
1 24m 4b Climb the short wall into the corner. Continue with interest until this becomes a square chimney that leads to a ledge on the right.
2 21m 4a Follow the shallow bed of the gully, finishing up a wide crack which splits the slab forming the left flank of the gully.
3 9m The chimney above leads to The Crevasse on *Slingsby's Chimney Route*, finish up this to the summit.
SW Herford, GS Sansom 19.06.1912

16 Low Man by the Jubilee Line 104m HVS 5a ★★

Thin climbing on immaculate rock. Start at a square block 6m right of *Hopkinson's Gully*.
1 25m 4c Step off the square block onto the wall then traverse left into a short corner which leads to the rib just right of *Hopkinson's Gully*. Move up and step right then follow a short groove to an easy rib which leads to the belay overlooking the groove of *Hopkinson's Gully*.
2 45m 5a Go straight up following a thin crack to below a steepening where a rising flake leads right to a grass ledge (runner). Traverse immediately left to reach a small rock spike just above the steepening. Continue directly to reach the detached block in the centre of the face then step right and climb to a small

overlap. Traverse left, with difficulty, to the rib which leads to the ledge below Slingsby's Chimney.
3 34m 5a Climb the corner just left of the chimney to reach a thin smooth slab. Climb this to an awkward finish out right then scramble to the top of Low Man.
A Phizacklea, JL Holden 26.05.2012

17 Moss Ledge Direct 93m VS 4c ★★★
and Jones' Arête
A beautiful route which combines several individual pitches to create one of the finest outings of its standard in the Lake District. Start 6m left of the edge of Deep Gill at the top of a grassy trod, found at the foot of a small buttress lying below the line of the uppermost grass ledges.
1 12m The face of the small buttress is climbed to reach a grass ledge.
2 9m 4c A couple of metres to the left a bold rib on the wall leads with difficulty to a stance. Protection is reached after 6m of climbing.
3 15m 4b Follow a diagonal fault cutting up through a nose on the right and step onto slabs which are followed to Moss Ledge.
4 12m 4a Climb the steep slab ahead, Herford's Slab, bearing slightly left, then back right to Hopkinson's Cairn Ledge; belay on its left side.
5 27m 4c The rock on the extreme edge of The Pinnacle overlooking Deep Gill is climbed to a short shallow corner, The Bad Corner. This leads to a sloping ledge on the edge of the buttress.
6 18m 4a Jones' Arête is poorly protected however you approach it. Go straight up, usually on the left. A second steepening soon eases and leads to the top of Low Man.
F Graham, GM Wellburn 6.09.1925

18 Jones' Route Direct 54m HS ★★★★
from Lord's Rake
This classic line runs diagonally leftwards from the bottom right of The Pinnacle. It is reached by scrambling up slabs and ledges from The Pinnacle Terrace to some detached blocks and a thread on the edge overlooking Deep Gill.
1 15m The Gangway. Go delicately up to stand on the slabby ramp, then follow this leftwards and continue up a slab to a grassy niche. Care is needed to protect the second.
2 21m Go straight up, making for a rock scar at 9m. Step left into the shallow corner of *Hopkinson's Gully*; climb this to a vibrating flake then cross diagonally left to The Waiting Room.
3 9m Climb into the cave on the right. A triangular ledge projects from its roof, the mantelshelf move onto this gives the traditional precarious entertaining crux. The Toe Traverse follows and leads to the wide crack on P2 of *Hopkinson's Gully*. Or, avoid all the excitement by making a hand-traverse from the cave.
4 9m P3 of *Hopkinson's Gully*.
Photo page 248.
OG Jones, GT Walker 19.04.1898

19 Davis' Direct from 96m S 4a ★★
Lord's Rake to Low Man
A fabulous combination at a very amenable grade. Start by the thread overlooking Deep Gill.
1 15m Climb delicately up to and stand on the slabby ramp - The Gangway. Follow this then up a slab to a grassy niche. Try and protect your second!
2 18m Climb the shallow corner on the right, through a bulge and up a second left-facing corner where a steep move leads to some doubtful flakes. Step up right onto a ledge.
3 12m 4a Climb the steep slab ahead to reach the next big ledge - Hopkinson's Cairn.
4 21m Start from the centre of the ledge. Climb up a shallow groove just left of the arête which trends slightly left up to a ledge and then follow a shallow corner above to make a difficult finish onto a grass ledge on the left.
5 30m A slanting gangway to the left, followed by scrambling, leads to Low Man.

20 Right-Hand Edge 99m HVS 5a ★★
and Pinnacle Face Direct
Another very fine route which gives interesting and rather intimidating climbing throughout. Start at the blocks and a thread.
1 25m 4b Climb onto The Gangway of *Jones' Route Direct*. Step onto the slab above and continue directly through a break onto the next slab. Climb this diagonally rightwards until Deep Gill is overlooked; large cam belay.
2 20m 5a Step round right on to the wall overlooking Deep Gill and ascend diagonally right, up a series of overlaps, until it is possible to move back left to the edge and climb up to Hopkinson's Cairn.
3 28m 4c From the left end of the ledge step up and traverse horizontally left for 12m to a large block. From the left edge of a block, climb the grooved wall, delicately, to the edge of the platform under Slingsby's Chimney.
4 18m 5b Step down and traverse to the right onto a slab below two dark niches. Step up through the overhangs between the niches onto another slab. From its right end, ascend very delicately to easy ground.
JJS Allison, CJF Rowbotham 21.05.1961

Jones' Route Direct HS (page 246) 📷 David Simmonite

Scafell Pinnacle **Scafell Crag** 249

The next routes start from Deep Gill. These are best reached by following Lord's Rake and the West Wall Traverse to a sloping ledge below their starts.

㉓ Woodhead's Climb 45m MS ★★★
One of the best climbs of its length in the area. Start at the base of the blunt arête.
1 24m Follow the arête, very delicately at first, to a large grassy recess beneath the huge overhangs.
2 21m Climb into a corner on the left and cross the slabs above to the right to a small ledge. Continue straight up for a few metres, over a bulge, and trend left to turn the next overhang. Steep and exposed but well-protected. Follow easier rocks up the crest to High Man.
AG Woodhead, WL Collinson 24.08.1907

㉑ High Man by the Central Line 48m HVS 4c ★★★
A long sustained pitch on amazing rock. Climb a short crack to a slab then climb directly up through a V-niche in an overlap to a second overlap. Pull over just left of a moss streak and continue to a vague nose which is climbed directly to a break below an overhang. Climb onto the headwall and continue straight up through several overlaps to the top of High Man.
A Phizacklea, T Moore, JL Holden 8.06.2013

㉒ Central Route – Deep Gill Slabs 51m HS ★★
A fine route. Start below the blunt arête.
1 18m Go diagonally left across the slab with little protection, crossing a small overlap before trending left to reach a pile of blocks.
2 18m 4a Climb the slab to a niche, in the line of overhangs, at 9m. An awkward pull over gains a narrow slab on the face on the right which leads to a grass ledge.
3 15m Steep overlapping slabs immediately left of the grassy groove give an interesting finish.
HM Kelly, GS Bower, REW Pritchard 29.08.1920

The East Buttress

One of the finest stretches of high-mountain rock in the country providing many superb routes for anyone climbing above VS.
Overview page 258.

Approach: The crag extends leftwards from Mickledore which is usually reached from Wasdale as for **Central Buttress**. It is also possible to approach from Eskdale heading up the steep valley to the left of **Esk Buttress** from the Great Moss. This leads eventually beneath the imposing crag to Mickledore.

Descent: There are usually some *in-situ* abseil points that serve some routes. For others, go right to the rocky path that makes its way in steps down to Broad Stand. Take care, especially if wet. From the left-hand side of the crag, head back and left to descend an awkward gully to reach a path beneath the crag.

❶ Trinity   67m   HVS 5b   ★★★
Towards the left end of the crag is a mighty right-facing groove. This is the line of *Hell's Groove*. On the wall to the left is a thin groove that gives interesting and enjoyable climbing.
1 30m 5a Climb the groove to an overhang turned on its left to a ledge.
2 28m 5b Climb the bulge in the corner onto a slab. Follow the slab and the fine corner crack above to a resting place. Move diagonally left to the foot of a short wall and belay on the large grass ledge above.
3 9m 4c The corner above.
DD Whillans, J Sutherland 5.06.1955

❷ Hell's Groove   68m   E1 5b   ★★★
A good climb which follows the crack and wall right of a large open corner bounding the left side of the overhanging wall. Start below the short overhanging crack.
1 8m 5b A problematic crack; belay in the groove.
2 22m 5a From the sloping ledge in the groove, climb rightwards into a crack and ascend to another sloping ledge. Continue to a further ledge with a block at its right edge. A short wall and crack lead to a belay.
3 18m 4b Climb a crack in the wall to the right of the overhang to ledges and continue directly to belay below the obvious green crack.
4 20m 5a Climb the overhanging crack above and continue to a small cave. Climb straight over the roof of this to the top. If the crack is dank, it is possible to finish by climbing the slab on the left then traverse back right to a chimney, or escape up *Morning Wall*.
P Greenwood, AR Dolphin 24.05.1952

❸ The Almighty   18m   E5 6b   ★★★ ♂
The thin fierce and overhanging crack up the wall right of *Hell's Groove* provides a thankfully short but sensational climb. Start on a large block. Climb the very strenuous crack on small layaways to a blunt spike; here, improving holds lead to a block belay.
P Botterill, J Lamb 28.08.1981

❹ Morning Wall   72m   VS 4c   ★
Follows the easiest line diagonally left from the foot of *Ichabod*, with good climbing in an impressive situation. Start at the foot of the right-hand ramp.
1 20m Climb the right-hand ramp until about 4m short of the *Ichabod* belay where a descent can be made onto the lower ramp. Follow this left to a stance in the corner below a crack.
2 15m 4c Climb the vertical crack in the wall left of a V-corner (crux). Move up then step over a rib to the left and continue the traverse to a spike at the foot of a chimney.
3 22m 4a Step up left then back right into the chimney which is followed into a grassy bay. The sloping slab on the left leads to belays.
4 15m 4a Climb up a slab to the left to its top then pull up and traverse back rightwards along the block to an easy chimney. Climb this and its continuation to the top.
AT Hargreaves, W Clegg, M Linnell 13.08.1933

❺ Phoenix   51m   E2 5c   ★★★ ♂
A superb well-protected climb following a strenuous groove up the front of the tower to the left of *Ichabod*.
1 27m 5b Enter the groove by the obvious jamming crack, just left of *Ichabod*, then climb the cracked corner above and pull out left with difficulty to a poor resting place. Continue up the groove and pull out left again. Climb the corner to belay on the ramp.
2 24m 5c **The Arête Finish**: Move down the ramp then climb the beckoning crack in the rib. Move right to finish up the airy arête.
R Moseley, DM Adcock (1pa) 1.08.1957

❻ Ichabod   45m   E2 5c   ★★★★ ♂
Excellent rock and thrilling positions have made this the traditional classic on this section of the crag. It climbs a line just right of the large corner at the left side of the overhanging wall. Start in the niche below the corner. Climb the right-hand of the two cracks, passing rightwards below a protruding nose. Pull up into a slot below a crack then traverse delicately right into a shallow corner. Follow the corner and gain a small ledge at the foot of a narrow V-chimney. Follow this to an awkward exit left into the larger mossy main corner.

Climb this more easily (often damp) and continue up a steep crack to the top.
G Oliver, G Arkless, L Willis 28.05.1960

❼ Roaring Silence 54m E3 5c ★★★ ◆

Excellent airy climbing up the immaculate walls and overhang to the right of *Ichabod*; a fast-drying route. Start in the niche.
1 36m 5c Follow *Ichabod* to the top of the shallow corner. Traverse right above the overhanging wall to a thin crack and climb it until it steepens. Step right again to a good crack and follow it, and the slab above, to belay on a good shelf.
2 18m 5c Climb up to the niche which splits the right-hand side of the overhangs. Pull through and continue to the top.
RH Berzins, J Lamb (alt), M Berzins 17.06.1979

To the right the smooth wall overhangs alarmingly, it is even steeper than it seems. Rope hanging down it will appear to hang out at a gravity-defying angle. The wall is bounded on its left by an arching flake line.

❽ Borderline 54m E7 6c ★★★

An awe-inspiring route which provides intricate sustained climbing. The lower part follows the incredible curving flake on the overhanging wall. Start below the flake.
1 36m 6c Gain the flake and climb it (peg); step left and climb the wall with difficulty (peg and nut). Continue up by moving right on improving holds then back left to a resting ledge (thread). Move up to join *Roaring Silence* which is followed to a belay.
2 18m 6b Climb to the crack which splits the overhang to the left of the niche. A desperate finish and, according to the first ascentionist, you can't claim the route if you miss it!
C Sowden, M Berzins 21.06.1986

❾ Overhanging Grooves Direct 75m E3 5c ★★

A good climb taking the prominent overhanging flake crack about 12m left of the waterfall.
1 21m 5c Climb up to the flake (thread); follow the flake and the exciting wall above (crux) to a ledge. Climb two ramp/grooves above to a belay. A sensational pitch.
2 30m 5b Climb a ramp diagonally right to reach a fine crack in a white corner (usually wet). Follow this until it steepens, a short traverse right can be made into a large niche.

To avoid the crack if wet:
2a 30m 5b P2 as far as the fine crack. Climb this for a short distance then traverse right into a shallow groove in the steep rounded pillar. Climb this to the top of P2.
3 24m 5a Step back left and follow the crack to a ledge, level with a layback crack. Traverse right and finish up this.
J Adams, C Macquarrie 07.1975

❿ Chiron 77m E3 5c ★★★

An excellent route making a way up a clean wall. Start 5m right of the lowest part of the crag.
1 25m 5b Scramble leftwards to reach a thin flake system in the steep wall just left of a groove. Follow the flake past a hollow section then traverse leftwards above the dripping waterfall. Pull up to belay in a sloping recess.
2 16m 5c Move right to the apex of the slab then pull up strenuously to reach a ledge system. Climb into a shallow recess above (small cam on left) and climb the wall on the left on small holds to exit precariously onto a smooth sloping slab. Step left and up to belay.
3 9m 5c Above a step on the slab is a short steep wall. Climb this to a horizontal ledge and overcome the bulge above on the right to another large sloping slab.
4 27m 5c Walk right and pull up to a crack running diagonally leftwards in the overhanging wall. Follow this strenuously to a point 3m short of the corner on the left. A short steep flake and crack above leads to a grass ledge. Follow the corner behind to the top.
A Phizacklea, A Rowell, JL Holden 5.05.1990

⓫ The Yellow Slab 79m HVS 4c ★★★ ♂

Superb climbing in a magnificent situation taking a long leftward-rising traverse from the toe of the buttress to the top of *Ichabod*. Start at an opening 5m right of the lowest part of the crag.
1 29m 4c Easy rocks are followed by a walk to the left. Ascend the cracked slab slanting up to the left to bulging rocks at 6m. An overhang is passed by using a layback move. A little higher is a ledge. Traverse left across the slab and climb the corner. Step round left onto the face and climb onto a stance.
2 30m 4c The crack on the left is climbed to a ledge at the foot of The Yellow Slab. Climb this directly at first then leftwards until it ends. Move left and follow an exposed crack until a belay can be taken on an obvious shelf on the left.
3 20m 4c Move left round the corner, carefully using a doubtful flake, then work diagonally leftwards across the exposed wall, keeping a few metres below the overhangs, to a delicate finish.
M Linnell, H Pearson 10.09.1933

⓬ Great Eastern 99m VS 4c ★★
A magnificent inescapable climb that wanders up the buttress in an impressive setting. The technical difficulty is not great but care should be taken to protect the second. Start at an opening 5m to the right of the lowest part of the crag.
1 5m Easy rocks then a walk to the left.
2 24m 4c Ascend the cracked slab slanting up to the left to bulging rocks at 6m. An overhang is passed by using a layback move; a little higher is a ledge. Traverse left across the slab and climb the corner. Step round left onto the face and climb up onto a stance.
3 9m 4b The steep cracks ahead lead to a stance below a nook.
4 24m 4b Cross the slab on the right and go up the step. Ascend a little on good holds and continue the rising traverse right to a crevasse.
5 15m 4a Three metres higher is a shelf below a corner; climb either the left wall or the chimney on the right to a ledge. Climb up and round the corner on the right to a ledge at the top of the white slab.
M Linnell, SH Cross 21.08.1932

⓭ The Centaur 93m HVS 5a ★★★★
A magnificent climb threading an intricate line, that can be difficult to read, up the left-hand set of grooves just at the point where the whole crag bends round to form the left-hand face. Start at an opening 5m to the right of the lowest part of the crag.
1 18m 4b Climb to the ledge on the left then step up right to a higher ramp and follow a light-coloured left-trending groove to a ledge. Continue up the cracked wall to a stance.
2 14m 5a Climb the corner for 3m and move left onto the very edge of the buttress. Follow this for 5m then traverse back right crossing the groove to a stance.
3 15m 5a Move right and climb a short corner parallel to the main groove until a ledge on the left can be gained. Traverse left along the ledge to re-join the main groove and climb this. Go up the step in the slab above and belay.
4 18m 4c Traverse 5m right and climb a short groove to a ledge which runs across an impending wall just above. Follow this leftwards and upwards to a large green slab near the corner.
5 28m 4c Climb steeply up to the left and traverse behind the detached pinnacle to a ledge. Step up to the left and climb back right to two poised pinnacles and a ledge. Layback the spectacular crack to the top.
L Brown, S Read 30.06.1960

⓮ Equinox 67m E4 6a ★★
Yet another good climb that starts up the slanting square-cut corner and faint cracks left of the striking corner of *Lost Horizons*. Start at an opening 5m to the right of the lowest part of the crag.
1 16m 4c Up then rightwards over slabs to a short wall. Up this then left to beneath the smaller corner.
2 16m 6a Climb the corner and overcome the bulge with difficulty to reach nut belays on the slab.
3 25m 6a Gain a ledge on the right, below a hanging flake, by an awkward move. Climb the frantic flake to a ledge and then follow flake cracks and ledges to a ramp.
4 10m 5b Climb the corner crack to a large sloping ledge on the left. Climb the flake crack in the steep wall to the right to easier ground.
J Lamb, P Botterill 29.05/4.06.1978

⓯ Lost Horizons 69m E4 6b ★★★
The central and largest of the leaning grooves on this section of the crag gives superb and varied climbing in very impressive positions. Start at an opening 5m right of the lowest part of the crag.
1 17m 4c Climb up then trend rightwards up slabs to a short wall. Up this and the slab above to belay at the foot of the largest corner.
2 37m 6b Climb the strenuous corner to a ledge which is deceptively unbalancing. Continue up (peg) to below the narrow V-niche and traverse left to a ledge. Move back right to regain the crack above the corner with difficulty and climb a ramp. Block belay on the right.
3 15m 5c Climb the crack which splits the overhanging wall above.
P Livesey, J Lawrence Sep 1976

⓰ Shere Khan 72m E5 6a ★★★★
This magnificent and bold climb takes the rightward-slanting groove and ramp line right of the *Lost Horizons* corner. Scramble up the groove then left across a sloping ledge to the base of a steep groove (2 old pegs at 6m).
1 24m 6a Climb the groove and pull out rightwards with difficulty to gain the sloping ramp (old pegs). Follow this to its end (low runner) and climb the serious groove to a pull out right onto a sloping ledge.
2 21m 5c Climb the steep groove above and continue up a mossy crack to belay on the ledge system.
3 27m 5a Move across to the mossy steep corner. Climb this and break out rightwards at its top.
E Cleasby, R Matheson 28.05.1977

17 Minotaur 75m E1 5b ★★
Varied interesting and initially very exposed. Start at an overhung ledge with a large boulder.
1 24m 5b Climb the corner to the left to a small ledge. Move up and traverse right and up to a protruding rib. Move straight up into a scoop and follow the moss-speckled wet ramp up left to its top. Pull over the bulge (crux) to another ramp and follow this to the white slab.
2 24m 4c Climb the white slab for 10m until a move up and right can be made onto a big wet gangway which is followed almost to its top to a restricted stance.
3 27m 5a Climb to the end of the gangway and ascend the corner to a slab on the left. Climb this and exit left to a ledge. Go over diagonally left up another slab then scramble to the top.
S Clark, G Oliver, H Loughran, G Lowes 16.06.1968

18 Overhanging Wall 60m HVS 5a ★★
A strenuous start across an exposed steep wall leads to pleasant climbing up the great white slab. Start at an overhung ledge on which sits a large boulder.
1 24m 5a Climb the corner to the left to a small ledge. Move up and traverse right and up to a protruding rib; descend on its right and climb a crack to a ledge. Swing round right to a crack amidst the moss and climb over a bulge. Climb up step right and up again to a ledge. Traverse left into a corner and belay above.
2 36m 4b Traverse left to the foot of the great white slab and climb it to a large square block in its centre. Go straight up to a ledge and climb up leftwards from its right edge.
M Linnell, AT Hargreaves 23.07.1933

19 Edge of Eriador 60m E4 6a ★★
A brilliant challenging route particularly when combined with the first pitch of *Dyad*. The soaring arête of the second pitch is very bold.
1 21m 6a Climb the delicate ramp and pull out right. Climb the crack above to a poor ledge and follow the thin crack above to a ledge on the left with a peg and low nut belays.
2 18m 5c Move back to the arête and climb it, initially on the left, then continue directly to a stance at the top of the corner.
3 18m 5a Climb the arête above.
R Matheson, E Cleasby 19.05.1977

20 Dyad 63m E3 6a ★★ ♂
A good strenuous climb, following an entertaining crack on P1. Start at a small steep ramp.
1 21m 6a Climb the delicate ramp and pull out right. Climb the crack above to a poor ledge and follow the thin crack above to a ledge on the left with a peg and low nut belays.
2 18m 5c Move up to the groove above and follow it until a step right can be made onto the rib. Climb this for 3m then step left and follow a slab to a ledge.
3 24m 4b The easy crack on the right.
Photo page 237.
K Jackson, C Read Jun 1968

21 Mickledore Grooves 67m VS 5a ★★★ ♦
A very classy VS. One of the best routes of its grade in the Lakes. Start at the foot of a right-slanting gangway.
1 25m 5a Climb the short overhanging wall to the gangway on the right which is followed to the foot of twin grooves. Follow the left-hand groove for 5m and make an awkward step right into the right-hand groove. This is climbed to a ledge with a large block.
2 42m 4c Move onto a ledge on the slab to the right. Step left and follow a diagonal crack to the right, over a bulge, on good holds. Climb up and right to a groove; follow it until it steepens and traverse right to a sloping ledge. Move around the corner on the right and continue horizontally for 9m to a mossy opening which leads to the top.
CF Kirkus, IM Waller, M Pallis 24.05.1930

22 Leverage 48m E1 5b ★★★ ♂
Good steep sustained climbing following a line of cracks with a reputation for being fast-drying. Start at a steep crack.
1 22m 5b Climb the stiff initial crack, crossing the ramp and follow the steep crack above to a slab on the right. Step left onto a bulge and follow the cracks and V-groove above to a stance.
2 26m 5a Take the groove above and move right into the corner. Climb this, traverse right under the obvious roof and climb up onto a slab. Continue to the top.
R Smith, D Leaver 3.05.1958

23 The Fulcrum 54m VS 4c ★★ ♂
A pleasant climb passing through a rather improbable area of steep rock. Start at the first break in the wall below a short open chimney.
1 15m 4c Climb for 5m then gain and climb a right-slanting groove on the right to a small stance.
2 18m 4c Climb the recessed wall on the left. Gain the slab (awkward) and traverse horizontally left, under an overhang, to twin cracks.
3 21m 4b Continue up the groove to the overhang and take the steep crack on the left. Pull out right at the top then move left and climb to the top.
K Jackson, J Adams 16.06.1968

The East Buttress | **Scafell Crag** | 257

24 Chartreuse E1 5b ★★

24 Chartreuse 54m E1 5b ★★ ☾
A serious slab combined with a strenuous and awkward top crack.
1 27m 5a Climb easily rightwards up a diagonal break above and parallel with the gully bed to a ledge. Follow the ledge leftwards and make thin moves across the slab then climb up using flakes to a large ledge.
2 27m 5b Move right onto a ledge. Step left and follow a diagonal crack rightwards over a bulge. Step back left and climb to a resting place on the left of the huge block. Traverse right and climb the brutal crack to the top.
R Smith, D Leaver 3.05.1957

25 The Lord of the Rings 342m E3 5c ★★★ ◊
A magnificent, engaging expedition: long and arduous, offering some of the best pitches and situations on the cliff. To some, this is England's finest route... Great care should be taken to protect the second on many of the pitches. Eight hours is the standard time taken; a fast competent party could complete it in six. Start in the square-cut corner with a crack at the back.
1 30m 5a Climb the groove for 12m then traverse right across sloping ledges to a pull up a wall to a stance.
2 24m 5c Head out right then go up a slim groove on the edge to an overlap (leave a sling here to protect the second). Climb down and rightwards to a ledge on the arête: high nut belays. (This pitch is very foreshortened on the photodiagram).
3 15m 5b Move right into the corner of *Hell's Groove*. Climb this to a stance up and right.
4 24m 5b Move right and climb down a groove until moves to the right lead to the ramp of *Morning Wall*. Descend the easy gangway to the base of a large flake and climb the left side of this to its top. Make a thin move right along the narrow ledge and pull up to the stance at the top of the gangway of *Phoenix*.
5 15m 5c Move down the gangway and climb the crack in the rib to a break where it is pos-

sible to move right into the groove of *Ichabod*. Traverse right across the easy slab to belay on the shelf at the end of P2 of *The Yellow Slab* beneath the overhang.
6 30m 5b Climb straight down the easy slab to a recess. Descend the bottomless groove on the right of this for 2m to a tiny ledge. Move right around the arête to join *The Yellow Slab* at the foot of the crack. Move right and descend the rest of *The Yellow Slab* to a belay.
7 24m 4c Follow the horizontal ledge line across the steep wall on the right, crossing a groove to a stance.
8 30m 5b Move right and climb the corner above to pull onto a ledge above. Move right and pull onto a higher slab (peg). Continue traversing right into a white shallow chimney and climb this to a large ledge system.
9 27m 4b Follow a line of ledges round the corner to the large block in the middle of the white slab. Descend to the foot of the slab.
10 21m 4c Move round the rib on the right, move down and step to the right. Climb up a little and descend rightwards to the arête. Step round this to the stance beneath a large groove.
11 16m 5c Climb the crack above the belay before moving out onto the clean wall on the right, passing an overlap on its left side (this avoids the often damp corner on the left). Climb the fine twin cracks to the top of the arête and a ledge.
12 27m 5a Descend the slab, move below the overlap and traverse right into a groove. Move right round the rib and descend to below an overhang. Move right again and step down to a fine ledge on *Mickledore Grooves*.
13 42m 4c Step round the arête to another ledge on the slab. Follow a diagonal crack over a bulge on good holds then up and right to a groove which is followed until it steepens. Traverse right on a sloping ledge, move round the corner on the right and continue horizontally for 9m to a mossy opening leading to the top.
J Adams, C Read 14/15.06.1969

PIKES CRAG

OS Grid Ref: NY 210 071
Altitude: 760m

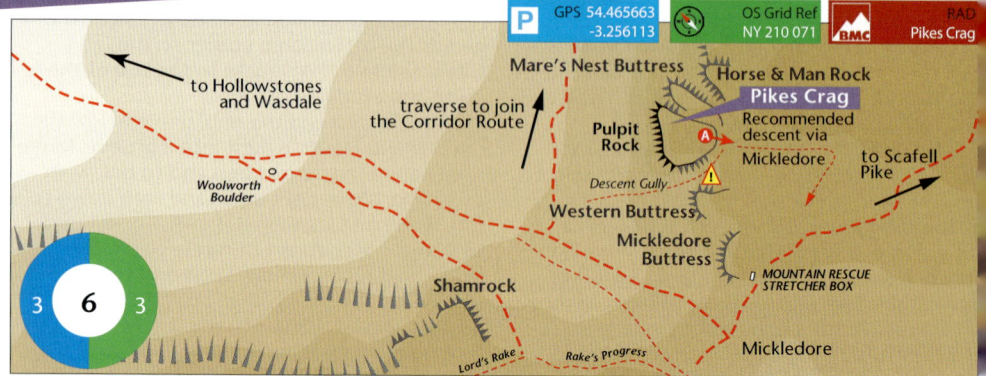

Pulpit Rock
The large crag to the left of Mickledore catches plenty of sun. The rock is rough and clean but beware of some ledges with vegetation and loose blocks. Carrying your kit with you, this makes a fine mountaineering way to ascend Scafell Pike, the highest summit in England.

Approach: The base of Pulpit Rock is a tier of broken rock topped by an almost continuous grass terrace from which the routes start. The right-hand end of this terrace can be easily reached from the scree below Descent Gully.

Descent: From the summit of Pulpit Rock, abseil or scramble east to a col. From here, contour south and east to join the path from Scafell Pike summit to Mickledore. Avoid the loose crumbling scramble down Descent Gully.

❶ Wall and Crack Climb 80m VD ★★
A clean route on very good rock with some polished problems. Follows the apparent left-hand ridge of Pulpit Rock.
1 10m Climb the ridge.
2 9m A steep wall is climbed to a ledge.
3 15m A vertical crack, or the face to the right, is climbed to a rock platform. From here, starting on the right, a staircase of rock leads to a terrace.
4 10m The wall above is climbed from right to left on improving holds.
5 10m Climb a zig-zag crack running up to the right in three risers.
6 11m A rock staircase leads to a ledge.
7 15m The almost vertical crack, or the wall on its left, is followed by easier rocks to the top.
HM Kelly, REW Pritchard, B Eden-Smith, G Wilson 19.04.1924

❷ Juniper Buttress 75m S ★★★
A satisfying route the cleanest on the crag. Start at a detached block at the foot of the crag.
1 18m From the block, a ledge is reached and a traverse made to the right into a corner below a crack. Climb the crack; near its top, move left onto the arête. Follow this to a ledge then climb a furrow slanting up the wall to the right to a grass ledge.
2 10m Climb a series of blocks to the left, finishing up a rather difficult crack.
3 15m Ascend rightwards to the edge of a grassy gully.
4 17m A groove, above and to the left, followed by a crack leads to a shelf with a recess at its back.
5 15m The exposed wall above is climbed by a difficult thin crack, starting at a rib just to the right. Easy scrambling to the top.
HM Kelly, REW Pritchard, NL Eden-Smith, W Eden-Smith 22.04.1924

❸ The Sentinel 77m VS 4c ★★
This route is easily identified by the striking face crack which splits a square-cut pillar 20m up the crag. Start at the right-hand edge of the steep rib which lies immediately to the left of the green mossy gully.
1 18m 4c Steep delicate climbing first up the rib, then trending left, leads to a grass ledge.
2 24m 4c Climb the corner above the ledge for 5m to an overhang split by a crack. Climb the striking and bulging crack to the top of the pillar.
3 20m Easier climbing straight up to a stance below and to the left of an obvious overhanging crack which can be seen on the skyline.
4 15m 4c Climb carefully up doubtful rock to the overhang and pull over strenuously. Continue straight up the crack to a stance.

Alternatively, the overhang may be avoided by climbing the corner above the stance and traversing right across the clean wall above.
P Fearnehough, J Wright Easter 1960

④ The Steeple to the Nave 141m VS 5a ★
An adventurous mountain route that takes a direct line from the lowest point to the summit prow, culminating with fine open climbing on the headwall. Start in a grassy bay on the left of, and just above, the lowest rocks of a rib, directly below the summit block.
1 42m 4c Climb up and into a short groove, topped by a small overhang. Turn it on the right and continue up the left edge of a clean rib to where it meets a mossy slab. Move up then step left. Climb up then right to gain a ledge and crack (thread). Move right and climb a clean wall near the edge; this leads to a large ledge and chockstone belay.
2 39m 5a A good pitch. Go left across the ledge for 5m and climb diagonally leftwards for 7m up the slabs to a black mossy streak. Move back rightwards and straight up the centre of the slabby pillar to a bold finish.
3 30m 4b The slabs, starting on the left, lead more easily to a stance.
4 30m 4b Climb the slabs and cracks above, heading for a conspicuous notch in the skyline, right of a large overhang and finish on the summit of the crag.
P1 GL Swainbank, C Read Aug 2003;
W Young, J Wilkinson Jun 1974

⑤ Grooved Arête 114m VD ★★★★
A good clean route with sustained and varied situations. Start from the well-worn ledge.
1 12m Enter the easy grassy groove running back to the left and belay in the V-shaped recess at the foot of a steep crack.
2 15m The left-hand crack is climbed for 8m then traverse to the arête on the left. Climb this past the end of the overhang to a grass ledge. Belay in the chimney a little distance back.
3 24m The chimney is climbed passing a bulge at 8m. Continue up a broken groove until grassy ledges lead rightwards into a rectangular corner.
4 20m The crack in the right-hand corner is hard to start. Continue up to a pile of blocks, pass them, and make a pleasant traverse to the right, to a prominent block on the edge of the ridge.
5 18m Climb the slab, working to the left, then cross over to a series of ledges on the edge.
6 12m Step over the corner on the left and continue up a slab to a ledge below a huge block. Climb the chimney on the left of the block.
7 13m Go along a ledge, running down to the left, on the wall above the gap and regain the slabby front of the buttress which is climbed direct to the summit.
Photo page 261.
CF Holland, GR Speaker 23.04.1924

Grooved Arête VD (above) James Berwick — 📷 Ron Kenyon

6 Megalith 130m HVS 5a ★★

A long route following a series of clean protruding ribs to the right of the big corner. Good sustained climbing. Start just right of a large grass bay beneath a prominent rib of rock.

1 23m 5a Climb the rib to a small overhang; step left to turn it. Move up and rightwards onto the steep slab to reach a crack in an overlap. Move up then to the right edge and follow it to a ledge with a block.

2 42m 5a Climb directly up the slab above to reach easier ground. Continue towards some large blocks on the right arête and go through them with care, onto the wall above. Step left and follow a deep crack; continue directly to ledges. Belay in a crack up on the left side of the next tier.

3 22m 4c Climb directly up the centre of the wall just right of the belay and, passing some cracked blocks, continue to a ledge. Follow the line of the crack up the wall above to a ledge.

4 26m 4c From blocks up on the right, pull left onto the arête then delicately move up it. Alternatively and much harder, climb the crack in the right wall and swing left at its top. Move left to a short crack, follow it and continue leftwards up an easy stepped ridge, to take a belay at the chockstone behind a megalithic block.

5 17m 5a Start just right of the chockstone. Climb directly up the steep stepped wall, turning the final step on the left, to reach the summit.

GL Swainbank, C Read 3.08.2003

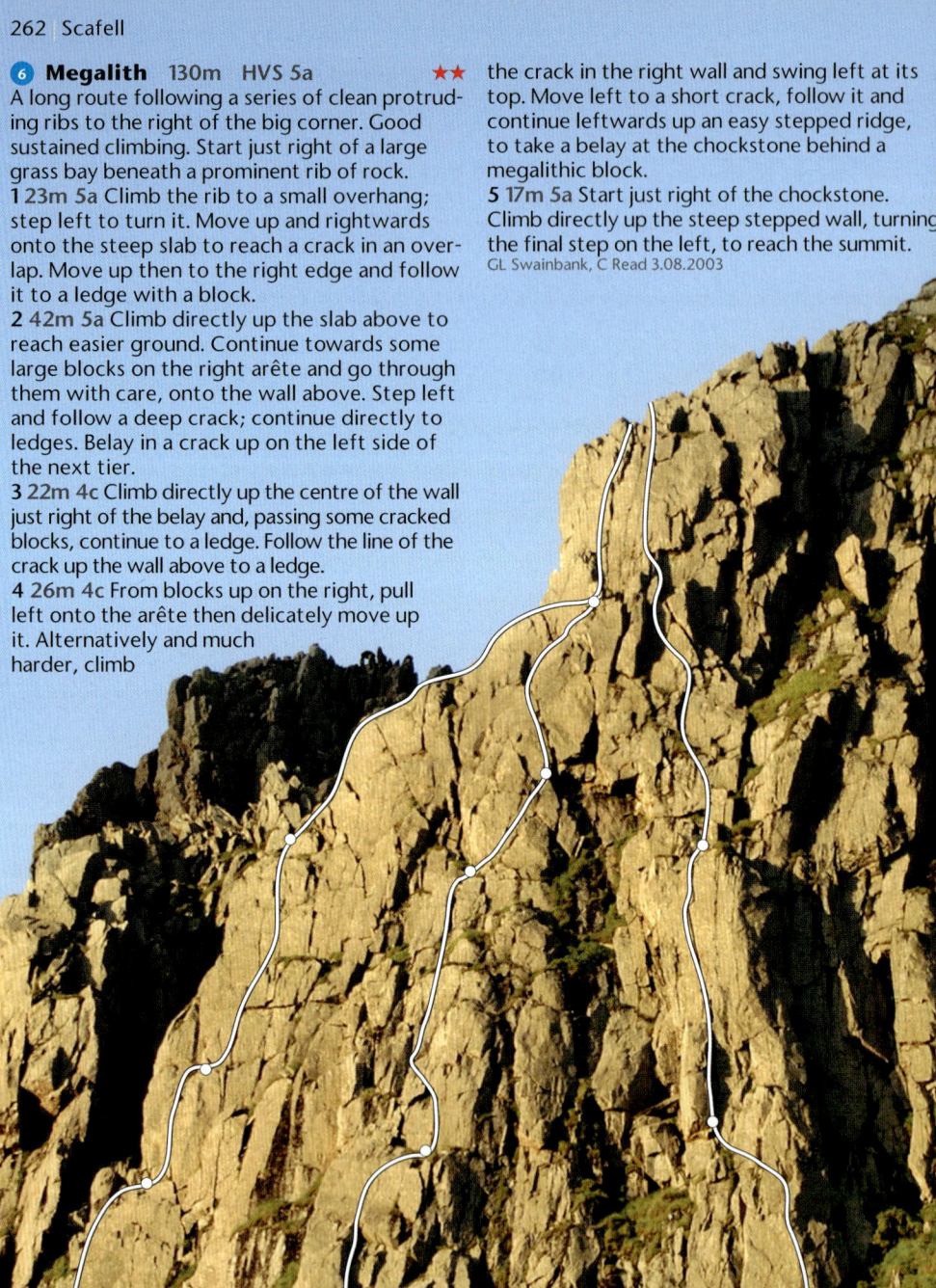

BUCKBARROW
OS Grid Ref: NY 135 058
Altitude: 300m

The Buckbarrow Needle VS (page 268) Roger Everett — David Simmonite

Buckbarrow has some excellent climbing on fast-drying rock. It provides a good alternative to the higher crags in the area and gets any sun on offer all day. The crag sits in a great location overlooking the west end of Wastwater. There are many crags on the fellside; the two best are described here.

Approach: Park off the road near Harrow Head Farm (either just before or 150m after the bridge over Gill Beck). Take a good path which starts just east of the bridge and follow this to a point where it's possible to trend right below **Pike Crag** (Upper Crag). Continue to a pleasant grassy platform at the very top of **Witch Buttress**, near the Buckbarrow Needle area. Climbs on **Witch Buttress** can be reached by a 45m abseil from here or a scramble to the left, looking down. A short section of rigging rope may be useful; take care with sharp-edged blocks. It is also possible to approach from directly below **Witch Buttress** by way of the steep rocky hillside.

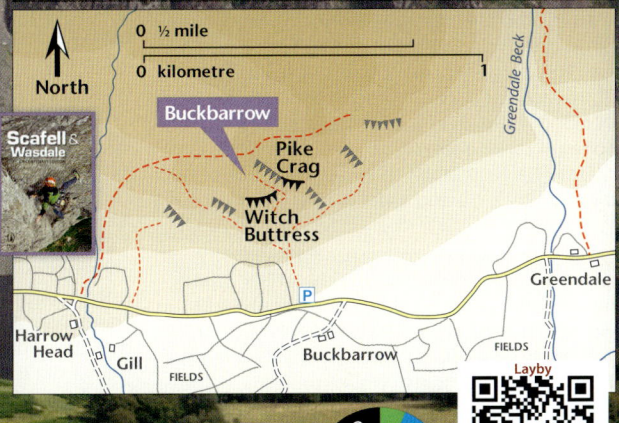

Layby
NY 130 055
GPS 54.436911
-3.341346

RAD
Buckbarrow

OS Grid Ref
NY 135 058

Witch Buttress

Excellent quality routes in the harder grades on rock that is generally good and quick-drying. This is the largest, cleanest piece of rock on the hillside, easily identified from the road by its fine central detached pillar with a pleasant grassy ledge below. Just above **Witch Buttress** lies the long outcrop of **Pike Crag** and **The Needle** which makes it possible to link together pitches on the lower and upper tiers resulting in some excellent long combinations.

Descent: Follow the grass rake rightwards to a small path trending left and down a rock step to the base.

1 Gagarin 60m MS
Start at the base of a rib just above the path.
1 23m Climb the rib up and right to a ledge. Climb the short wall then step up left onto a slab; the corner above leads to a stance.
2 17m Move left to the edge then climb up, breaking right, over mossy slabs to a clean rib. Move up to a corner.
3 20m The easy ridge then a conspicuous crack followed by a rib and slabs lead to the top.
AH Greenbank, P Moffatt 1957

2 A Cut Above 25m E1 5b ★
Start 4m right of the foot of the arête. Climb the shallow corner to the groove at the left end of the large roof. Make an awkward move into the groove where a diagonal crack leads out left onto the arête; finish up this.
Photo page 268.
A Stephenson, W Young 16.05.1983

3 The Mysteron 35m HVS 5b ★★
A good climb with a very challenging but well-protected crux. Start below a large corner left of the central detached pillar. Climb up and left to a large flake below the overhanging corner of *Imagine*. Traverse left below a green wall to the base of a groove. Climb this with a committing move left onto a tantalisingly high small ledge. Follow the crack up and right until a step left can be made into a crack that leads to the top.
WS Lounds, JC Eilbeck 1960s

4 Imagine 38m E2 5b ★★
An excellent route giving steep and sustained climbing. Climb left to a large flake and pull into the steep groove on the right. Difficult moves lead to the roof (thread). Pull over on undercuts and jugs into the easier continuation corner which is followed, trending right, to below an undercut crack. Possible belay. Awkward moves give access to the crack which leads to the top.
A Stephenson, J Wilson 15.04.1981

5 West Side Story 39m E4 6a ★★★
An tough route giving sustained and committing climbing. The climb takes the groove line in the face right of the central corner.
1 27m 6a Climb left to the flake below the steep corner. Pull up right across the wall onto a sloping ledge. Protection high up on the gangway, placed blind. Make committing moves up the rightwards-sloping gangway to gain a shallow groove that leads up to a small overhang. Step left and follow a crack then an easier rib to a sloping ledge below the undercut crack.
2 12m 5a Climb the crack above to easy ground.
P Whillance, M Hamilton, D Armstrong 4.05.1991

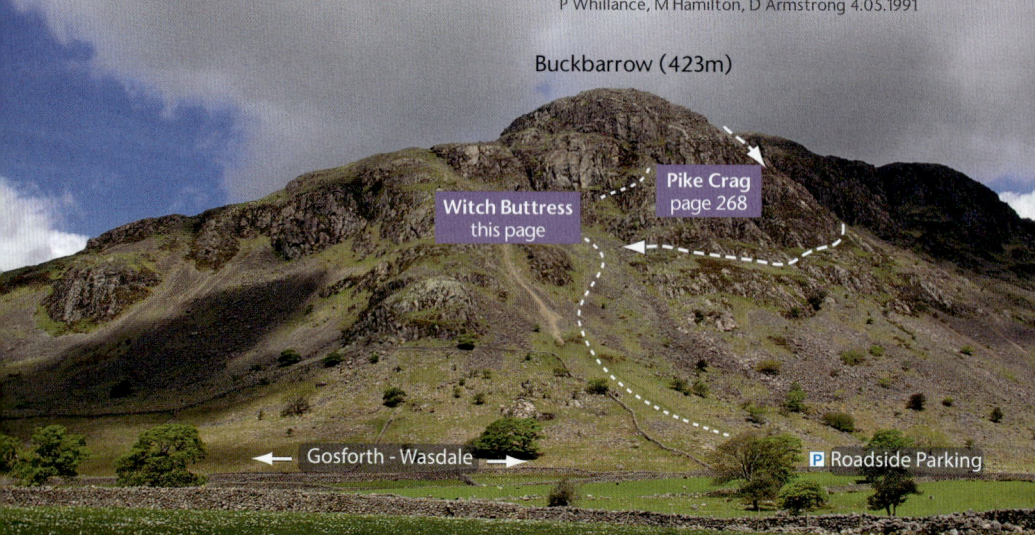

Buckbarrow (423m)
Pike Crag page 268
Witch Buttress this page
← Gosforth - Wasdale
Roadside Parking

Witch Buttress | **Buckbarrow** | 267

6 Harmony 35m HVS 5b
Don't be fooled by the beguiling name: the wide crack on the left side of the central pillar is very strenuous with a difficult and frustrating start.
1 23m 5b Climb the wide crack to a niche below a dirty groove. Continue up the groove and pull out right at the top, or climb the rib on the right.
2 12m 4c Step up and left into the open groove that leads to the top.
WS Lounds, JC Eilbeck 1960s

7 Wild West Show 40m E5 6b ★★
The left arête of the pillar has sustained exposed technical climbing requiring a confident approach.
1 27m 6b Climb the arête for 5m (protection round left of the arête but not obvious). Make a long reach right then move up and back left onto the arête. Continue up the arête until forced right again onto the wall at 12m. Step up then regain the arête and continue more easily to the top of the pillar. A precarious pitch.
2 13m 4c Climb the open groove.
D Armstrong, P Whillance 25.04.1981

8 Witch 40m VS 4c ★★★
A justifiably popular route of traditional style taking the enticing chimney line on the right-hand side of the central pillar.
1 27m 4c Climb the chimney for 10m then move right with difficulty into a small niche. Good holds lead up the wall to regain the crack above the overhang. Follow the crack to the top of the pillar.
2 13m 4c Step up and left into the open groove that leads to the top.
P Walsh, M Burke 2.03.1961

9 Too Many Hands 40m E2 5b ★★
A steep pitch with spaced protection now spoilt by vegetation lower down. 4m right of the chimney and 15m from the ground is a large wedged block. A thin crack runs up the right-hand side of this block and through the overhang above. Start just left of the crack and enter and follow this to the large wedged block. Climb the continuation crack to a pinnacle then step off this into a hanging corner. A long reach gives access to the next short corner which is exited, at its top, by a step left onto a ledge. Exposed moves now lead right across the steep slab to the arête where easier climbing leads to the top.
A Stephenson, C Sice, J Wilson, W Young 2.05.1981

10 Moffatt's Route 40m VS 4c ★
An enjoyable pitch starting at the bottom of the left-facing corner at the right end of the crag. Climb the corner to a bulge, step left into the next corner and follow this until forced out right to the rib that leads up to a ledge. Step diagonally left to a spike then up to a ledge below a steep corner. Finish up the corner which is difficult to start.
P Moffatt, P Hogg 1940s

A Cut Above E1 (page 266) Nick Wharton
📷 Peter Sterling

Pike Crag - The Needle

Descent: Traverse left below the upper part of the crag.

① Sunset Strip 50m VS 4b ★
Climbs the crack running up the slab.
1 20m 4b Climb the crack to a ledge, then step left onto a steep slab which is followed with increasing difficulty to a grassy bay.
2 30m 4a Up the corners above and over a doubtful block to a crack. Climb this to the top.
WE Pattison, AW Dunn Sept 1975

② Last of the Summer Wine 22m E1 5b ★★
Good climbing up the steep wall finishing with an intimidating crack. Start just left of the pinnacle. Climb the groove and step right onto a flake. Continue up the wall trending right until it is possible to swing across left into the base of the overhanging crack - straight up this to the top.
J Wilson, B Smith May 1982

③ The Buckbarrow Needle 23m VS 4c ★★
An interesting climb of traditional character. Climb one of the cracks, on either side of the pinnacle, to its top. Step off the pinnacle onto the wall above and make a bold move up on small holds to easier ground. For the left-hand crack the best way of starting it is up the rib just to the right, then step left to the large hold at the top of the initial pod. Climbing the crack direct is unpleasant.
Photo page 264.
P Moffatt, P Hogg 1947

④ Needle Front 23m E1 5b ★
Bold climbing on good rock up the left-hand side of the pinnacle. Start just right of the left-hand crack. Climb the wall then follow a line of footholds onto the right arête and up to the top of the pinnacle. Finish up the wall.
J Earl, P Stewart 23.06.1979

⑤ Needless Eliminate 22m E1 5b ★★
A fine pitch climbing the groove and crack just right of The Needle. Start in the corner just right of the pinnacle. Hand traverse diagonally left to a large spike then move up and pull onto a ledge on the right. Step back left and climb the crack, well-protected by small wires, direct to the top.
P Stewart, J Earl 23.06.1979

Pike Crag - The Needle | **Buckbarrow** | 269

6 Attic Stairs 1 20m MVS
Climb the arête and short wall to a recess, then climb the wall to the top.
WE Pattison, AW Dunn 1974

GABLE

The mighty bastion of Gable, one of the higher summits in the central part of the Lakes, is bedecked with crags on three sides. To the south, **The Napes** with its historic Needle; to the east, the imposing **Tophet Wall** and on the colder, north face, the immaculate **Gable Crag**. Anyone making the effort to get to these fine venues will be rewarded with some tremendous climbing at all levels.

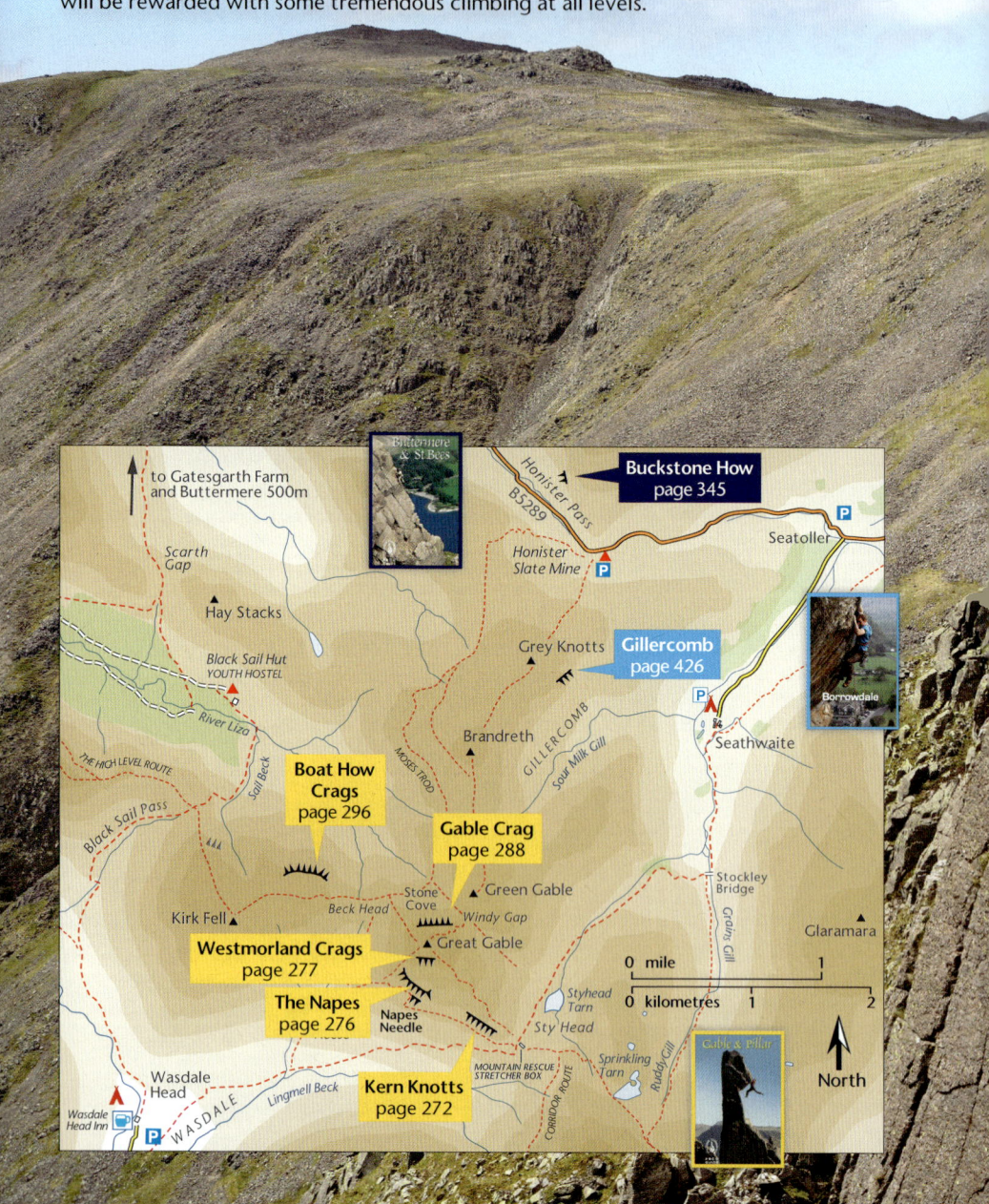

The Cayman, The Napes E2 (page 281) Paul O'Reilly — David Simmonite

KERN KNOTTS

OS Grid Ref: NY 215 096
Altitude: 520m

A superb crag with high-quality single-pitch climbing on steep rough rock which dries quickly. The commanding panoramic situation looking over the majestic terrain of Great End, Broad Crag, Scafell Pike, Lingmell and down Wasdale is possibly the best outlook of any Lakeland crag.

Approach: Depending on your start point, the best approach is from Seathwaite in Borrowdale. Take the popular path to Scafell Pike as far as Sty Head. From the Mountain Rescue Box, a small indistinct path rises across the fellside between the larger paths down into Wasdale and up onto Great Gable. This is the start of the Climbers' Traverse which leads on to **Tophet Wall** and the **Napes**. The path improves after the initial rise. Follow it until you reach the crag. The first part to come into view is the cracked wall with *Kern Knotts Crack* and *Innominate Crack*.

An alternative approach is to make the steep ascent from Wasdale to Sty Head.

See map page 270.

Descent: For the routes in the **Cracks Area**, there is an abseil point at the top of the wall. For other routes, head back and left to walk easily down the left side of the crag.

Cat Wall

❶ Feline Crack 35m VS 4c ★
Interesting climbing up the obvious vertical crack at the left end of the crag.
1 25m 4c Ascend easy slabs to the steep crack which is climbed with interest to a sloping ledge; step left to a good rest. Step back right and continue up the thin finger crack above, followed by easier climbing to a large open book corner on the right.
2 10m. Climb the corner to the top.
J Lamb, M Hetherington, J Fotheringham 1979

❷ Grimalkin 44m E4 6a ★★
Bold climbing up the banded wall. Start directly below a prominent short hanging corner at a thin ragged crack. Climb the crack using small holds on the left and make committing moves rightwards to reach the corner and good runners. Climb up and rightwards across the fingery bulging wall to reach a slim groove. Climb the groove more easily to a good ledge. Climb a short wall to a large glacis then another wall right of a corner to easier ground and the top.
K Telfer, J Gillespie, P Morgan 12.05.1997

Seathwaite
NY 235 124
P GPS 54.500832
-3.181496

RAD
Kern Knotts

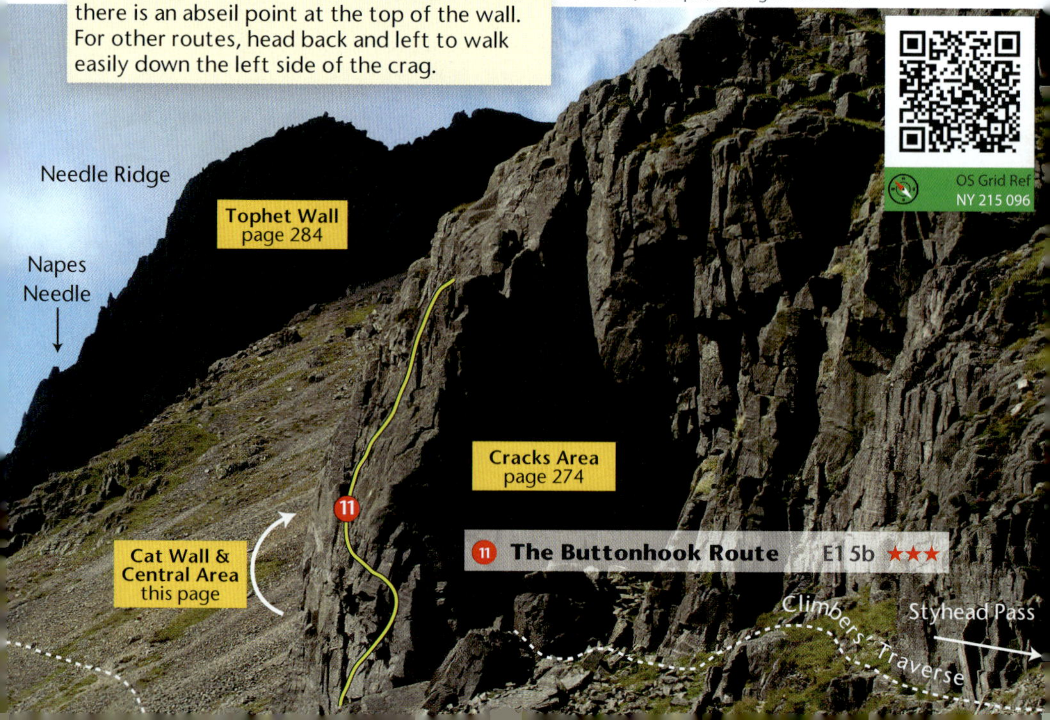

Needle Ridge

Tophet Wall
page 284

Napes Needle

Cracks Area
page 274

Cat Wall & Central Area
this page

11 The Buttonhook Route E1 5b ★★★

Climbers' Traverse

Styhead Pass

The next two routes share the same start and the first 10m of climbing. Start just left of a blunt arête which is bounded by a shallow groove on the left.

3 Pussy 40m E4 6a ★★

No soft touch! An intriguing route on perfect rock that makes a right-to-left rising traverse of the banded wall. Run out towards the top. Climb the groove to a large spike. Step right onto the steep cracked wall and climb up to a prominent square-cut overhang. Pull leftwards with some difficulty around the overhang into a shallow scoop. Make puzzling moves leftwards to reach a short hanging corner (junction with *Grimalkin*). Climb the corner to a small flake and continue leftwards, following the narrow ramp, until forced to make delicate moves to gain a good ledge above. Climb the rounded rib, on the left of the corner above, to the top.
A Phizacklea, PW Cox 25.04.1989

4 Sylvester 25m E3 5c ★★★

A problematic pitch which requires a cool approach. Climb the groove to a large spike. Step right onto the steep cracked wall and climb up to a small sloping ledge. Step back left and climb the awkward groove to reach good holds at the top.
PC Rigby, T Furniss 28.06.1981

5 Kern Knotts West Chimney 32m VD ★

The prominent chimney bounding the right-hand side of **Cat Wall** gives a traditional route requiring some old-fashioned techniques. Start below the chimney.
1 16m Easy rocks lead to the chimney; this is climbed to a platform using a variety of classic contortions.
2 16m Climb the crack above to a ledge at 8 metres followed by easier rocks to the top.
OG Jones, CW Patchell 27.04.1897

Central Area

6 Kern Knotts West Buttress 33m MVS 4b ★★

Start at the toe of the steep buttress. Climb the steep broken crack to a large spike below a V-groove. Pull up the groove and make an awkward step left onto a good foothold then follow a crack leftwards to a flat ledge. Move up left until a step back right can be made on jugs to a large broken ledge then easier ground to the top.
GS Sansom, SW Herford 12.04.1912

Gable

7 The Kraken 35m E1 5b ★★
Better than it looks: a puzzling start leads to a fine finish. Start in the centre of the the prominent lower corner in the middle of the buttress. Climb the short corner and make a long reach right to good holds. Pull up steeply on flat holds and move leftwards to a small ledge below the mossy corner. Ascend the corner until good holds lead out to the left arête in a fine position. Climb up more easily to a small corner and the top.
S Miller, A Stephenson 6.04.1974

8 The Crysalid 30m E2 5c ★★
An excellent exercise in steep fingery climbing with the crux at the top. Start at a blunt rib 4m right of the corner. Climb the rib to reach a long diagonal crack in the steep slab and follow it rightwards to the base of the steep upper groove. Climb the steep groove with commitment to a good hold on a doubtful flake. Step left onto a slab and follow this to the top.
S Clegg, J Lamb 24.10.1976

9 Triffid 30m E3 5c ★★
Climb the finger crack left of the chimney past a pinnacle and up a short wall to reach the bulging crack on the left, followed by a narrow V-groove. Pull over the small overhang and head for the top.
P Botterill, J Lamb April 1978

10 Kern Knotts Chimney 50m HS ★★
The prominent chimney on the Wasdale (west) side of the buttress. Climb the chimney negotiating a chockstone and passing under a leaning block.
OG Jones, WH Fowler, JW Robinson Dec 1893

11 The Buttonhook Route 30m E1 5b ★★★
Steep and exposed climbing - impressive for its time. Start at the foot of the buttress at a small rock pillar. Climb a short slab to the first overhang, pull right to a welcome jug and follow the crack to a small ledge. Good holds lead left to a short groove which is followed then trend right to a pinnacle on the right edge of the buttress. Follow the shallow stepped groove above.
G Balcombe, CJA Cooper Jun 1934

Cracks Area
The next routes start below the fine wall of rock set at right-angles to the rest of the crag. This is split by the twin lines of *Kern Knotts Crack* and *Innominate Crack*.

12 Kern Knotts Crack 42m VS 4c ★★
The wide left-hand crack gives a climb of great character. Start directly below the crack. Climb the crack to a sentry box at 8m. Either jam the walls of the sentry box to a narrower crack above (only good technique or sheer determination will pay off this way), or climb the right wall on small holds until a long step back left can be made to reach the narrower crack. Follow the fine crack to finish on top of the pinnacle.
Photo page 280.
OG Jones, HC Bowen Apr 1897

5 **Kern Knotts West Chimney** VD ★
6 **Kern Knotts West Buttress** MVS 4b ★★

13 Innominate Crack 42m VS 4b ★★★
The right-hand crack, and one of the classic crack climbs of the Lake District. Start directly below the crack. Follow the twin cracks until forced into the right-hand one. Climb the crack above until awkward moves can be made to gain a wide crack just below the top of the pinnacle. Climb the crack to the top.
GS Bower, B Beetham, JB Wilton Apr 1921

14 Innominate/ 35m E1 5b ★★★
Sepulchre Combination
A fine pitch which makes good use of the bottomless groove at the right-hand side of the wall. Start as for *Innominate Crack*. Climb *Innominate Crack* for 7m to a line of good holds; follow these diagonally right to the base of the large bottomless groove and climb the groove and wall, on small positive holds, to the top.
J Lamb 1975

THE NAPES

OS Grid Ref: NY 210 101
Altitude: 650m

Considered to be the birthplace of English rock climbing with apocryphal tales passed down from Victorian gentlemen in tweeds and nailed boots, **The Napes** now provides a varied range of mountaineering routes and modern hard classics. The unique **Napes Needle** is one of its main attractions but the crag has lots more to offer at all grades, including some very airy climbs; all climbers, whatever their ability, will find something to enjoy here.

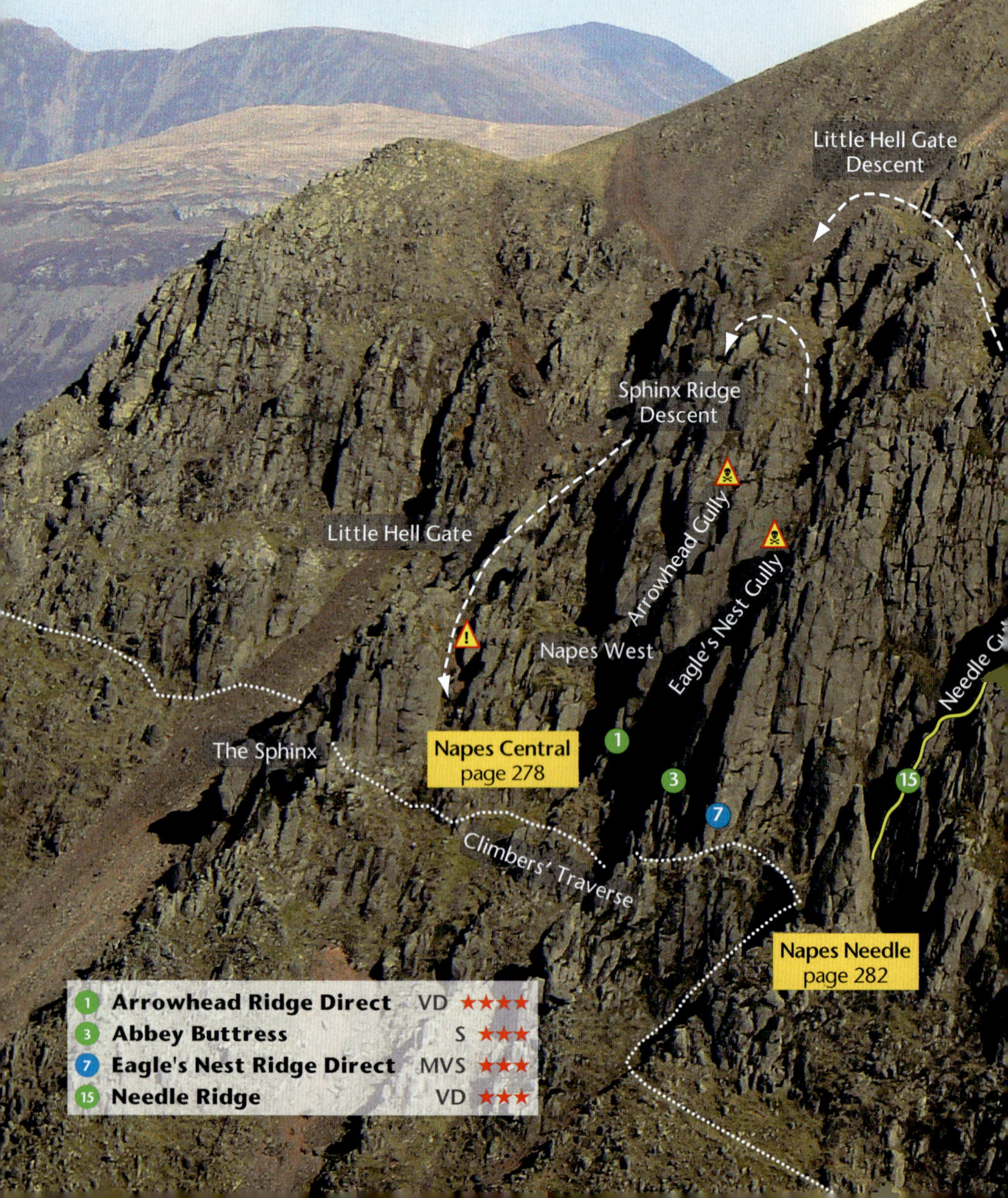

1	Arrowhead Ridge Direct	VD	★★★★
3	Abbey Buttress	S	★★★
7	Eagle's Nest Ridge Direct	MVS	★★★
15	Needle Ridge	VD	★★★

THE NAPES

Approach, Seathwaite in Borrowdale: Take the popular path to Scafell Pike as far as Sty Head. From the Mountain Rescue Box, a small indistinct path rises across the fellside between the larger paths down into Wasdale and up onto Great Gable. This is the start of the Climbers' Traverse. The path improves after the initial rise. This leads beneath **Kern Knotts Crag** and across scree slopes and fellside to reach first **Tophet Wall** and then **The Napes**.

Approach, Wasdale: Make the steep ascent to Sty Head before joining the Climbers' Traverse. It may look like you can take a short cut by heading straight up the hill - feel free but you will undoubtedly regret this choice by the time you drag your weary body to the foot of the crag and it won't have been any quicker after all!

See overview page 276.

Napes Central

❶ Arrowhead Ridge Direct 130m VD ★★★★

An excellent airy climb, characterised by the distinctive Arrowhead at the top of the steep section. Start at the lowest point of the ridge on the left.
1 15m Easy scrambling leads to steeper rock. Climb up to a ledge.
2 25m The steep ridge above is climbed, either direct, or round the corner from the right, to reach a pinnacle. Step off the pinnacle onto a slab then climb up steeply on good holds to the top of the Arrowhead. It is also possible to traverse left around the base of the Arrowhead to the gap behind but this misses the point!
3 10m Stride across the gap and traverse a horizontal section of the ridge.
Enjoy 80m of interesting, yet easy, scrambling along the ridge passing The Strid en route.
AG Topham, H Walker, WC Slingsby 14.03.1896

❷ The Tormentor 35m E4 6a ★★
Technical and intimidating climbing up the centre of the slab. Gain the lower left edge of the slab by climbing the short crack and stepping left along a grassy ledge. Pull

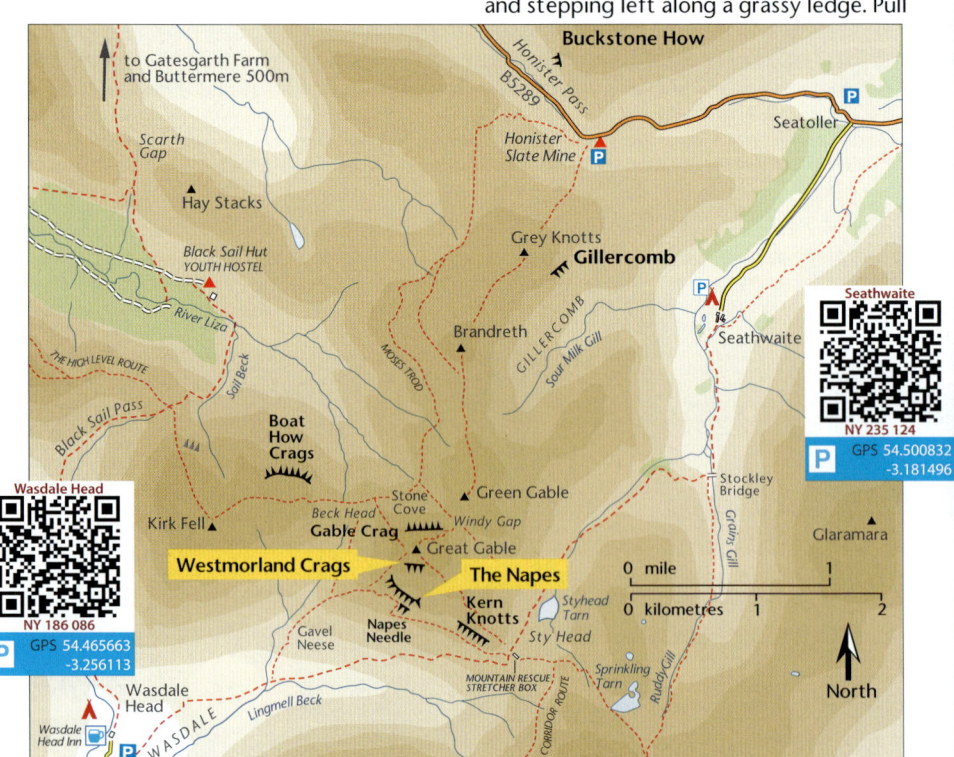

onto the slab and, after 2m, follow a faint weakness up and right (runner) then pull back to good holds at the foot of a diagonal crack. Follow the crack until in the centre of the slab then make some very scary moves straight up to the overlap (undercut hold and runner). Pull over and right on improving holds to another diagonal break and finish up the thin crack above.
A Phizacklea, AH Greenbank 8.08.1987

3 Abbey Buttress 58m S ★★★
A classic climb with a devious and intimidating second pitch. Start at the foot of the buttress behind the large detached flake.
1 20m Climb straight up to a ledge, step right and follow a steep crack to a ledge.
2 20m Climb steep rock above to a wide ledge at 4m. Traverse left for 5m and then go straight up for 8m then traverse back right below an overhang onto an arête that leads on good holds to a large ledge.
3 18m Climb the cracked blocks immediately right of the grassy gully to a ledge. Ascend the corner on the left to a junction with *Eagle's Nest Ordinary Route (West Chimney)*.
F Botterill, J de V Hazard 7.04.1909

4 Eagle's Nest Ordinary Route (West Chmney) 107m VD ★★
A fine old traditional route. Start below the grassy chimney.
1 30m Easy rocks lead to the bottom of *West Chimney* which is climbed, either by bridging, or by the right wall (*Pope's Variation*).
2 12m Climb up and right through a crevasse then go up a smooth slabby groove to belay in the corner.
3 12m The awkward chimney above is followed by the ridge on the left.
4 18m A chimney on the left is followed by easy scrambling up broken rocks to the foot of a tower.
5 35m Pull up the short steep crack to an exposed rock ledge and move right into the boulder-choked chimney. Follow the scratches and scramble along the ridge.
GA Solly, M Schintz 17.04.1892

5	Long John	HVS 5a	★★
6	Longbow	E1 5b	★★
7	Eagle's Nest Ridge Direct	MVS	★★★
8	The Cayman	E2 5b	★★★
9	Crocodile Crack	HVS 5a	★★★
10	Aligator Crawl	HS	★
11	Amos Moses	E1 5b	★★
12	The Wasdale Crack	HS	★★★
14	The Obverse Route	MVS	★★★
15	Needle Ridge	VD	★★★

Kern Knotts Crack, Kern Knotts VS (page 274) David Simmonite — 📷 David Simmonite

⑤ Long John   42m   HVS 5a   ★★
Delicate climbing up the strip of rock dividing the two chimneys. P1 on its own gives a superb climb at VS. Start below a pinnacle just right of the left-hand chimney.
1 33m 4c Climb to the bottom of the chimney then step left and climb the centre of the slab until forced out left onto the edge. Climb to a ledge which leads back right into the centre of the slab. Ascend the slab trending left to a platform.
2 9m 5a From the top of the pinnacle, a poorly protected and difficult move is made onto the wall above. Climb the wall more easily to a ledge.
HG Knight, HM Kelly 11.04.1928

⑥ Longbow   40m   E1 5b   ★★
The bow-shaped wall left of *Eagle's Nest Ridge Direct* gives some sustained climbing on clean solid rough rock. Start by the large pillar block. Step right and follow the rib up rightwards to a triangular overhang. Cross this and continue to a good foot ledge (runners on the right arête). Step left and climb the wall to join a right-slanting crack which leads to the Eagle's Nest. From the top of this crack, move left again to reach thin blind cracks and climb straight up the wall to where the angle eases and leads to a belay in the corner.
D Rogers, A Leece 16.06.2014

⑦ Eagle's Nest Ridge Direct   45m   MVS 4a   ★★★
A bold Lakeland classic giving delightful open and delicate climbing up the blunt arête overlooking the Dress Circle. Start directly below the arête on a sloping ledge. Climb steeply on good holds bearing right to a ledge. Climb up and left to the arête using two parallel cracks, then step up to the Eagle's Nest (a small platform); continue up for 5m to the Crow's Nest (another small platform). Climb the slab above boldly on sloping holds to a ledge. Belay in the corner. Either descend or continue up the ridge.
GA Solly, WC Slingsby, GP Baker, WA Brigg 15.04.1892

⑧ The Cayman   60m   E2 5b   ★★★
An excellent climb up the slender face right of the easy-to-spot *Crocodile Crack*. Start just left of *Crocodile Crack* below an overhang.
1 45m 5b Climb the overhang and crack above to where *Crocodile Crack* crosses the face. Step right and climb the thin diagonal crack to an overlap. Surmount this and continue up the wall above to the next overhang. Pull over and move up and right to a ledge on the arête. Ascend the steep arête in a fine position to a large ledge. Abseil, or:
2 15m A grassy chimney leads to the ridge.
Photo page 271.
P Whillance, DW Armstrong 9.08.1977

⑨ Crocodile Crack   58m   HVS 5a   ★★★
An excellent climb up the obvious wide crack above the Dress Circle. Start at the bottom of a flake crack to the right of the main crack above.
1 43m 5a Climb the flake crack for 8m then make a long step left into the main crack. Ascend the crack to an overhang at 15m. Continue up the widening crack, past a small ledge on the left, and then move up the crack again to a ledge.
2 15m Climb a grassy chimney on the right to join the ridge.
G Oliver, G Arkless, P Ross, N Brown 23.04.1960

⑩ Alligator Crawl   57m   HS   ★
A good climb that finds the easiest way up this part of the buttress. Start below the wide chimney which is bounded by an oblique overhang.
1 15m Climb the chimney to a ledge.
2 27m Step off the top of the block onto the wall then climb the fine crack to a ledge.
3 15m Climb a grassy chimney on the right to join the ridge.
G Oliver, G Arkless 22.05.1960

⑪ Amos Moses   60m   E1 5b   ★★
A direct line up the buttress on the right. Start below the right-hand end of the Dress Circle. The buttress is split by a wide right-slanting crack.
1 25m 5a Gain the crack from the left using a small rib and climb it past two bulges to a slab. Climb to a large grass ledge and pinnacle.
2 35m 5b Climb the pinnacle and step onto the wall below a prominent finger crack. Ascend the crack with difficulty to a small ledge and move up and left to the foot of an obvious groove above a bulge. Pull rightwards into the groove with difficulty and climb more easily to a stony ledge.
P Long, T Parker 20.06.1987

Napes Needle

Lakeland's celebrated pinnacle is a great attraction for many climbers and provides a unique experience and memorable day for teams as they sit, stand, do headstands and pose on its tiny flat top! Many of the routes share the same belay below the top block on the Shoulder and use a common final pitch for both ascent and descent. The top moves have acquired burnished sheen and require care.

Descent: Take great care. An abseil is not recommended. It is strongly advised that the climber(s) are lowered to the Shoulder and belay. The last man downclimbs. From here the climber(s) are lowered again to the ground. The last man downclimbs via The Arête, with the runners placed on the ascent, and left in place, clipped to the rope whilst descending, or placed by the climbers being lowered.

Warning: There have been a number of accidents to parties attempting to abseil from the summit.

12 The Wasdale Crack 17m HS ★★★
The original way and a very popular route with two entertaining and contrasting pitches. Start below the obvious wide crack down and right of the Gap.
1 13m Climb the awkward crack, facing left, then right to its finish; then ascend an easy slab to the Shoulder.
2 4m Mantelshelf onto a narrow ledge (easier from the right). Traverse left onto the face and climb delicately to the top.
WP Haskett Smith 27.06.1886

13 The Arête 20m HS ★★★★
The west arête gives a delightful pitch; start at the bottom of The Wasdale Crack.
1 16m Traverse delicately horizontally right until a pull round onto the arête can be made. Climb the arête to the Shoulder.
2 4m As for The Wasdale Crack.
Photo opposite.
WH Fowler 17.09.1894

14 The Obverse Route 24m MVS 4b ★★★
A fine route with a brilliant top pitch well worth seeking out. Start just right of the large crack on the east side facing Lingmell.
1 18m 4b Climb the steep slab right of the crack on small holds to the Platform, then a large flake, followed by a slab, to the Shoulder.
2 6m 4b Hand traverse right, along the horizontal crack under the top block (and over the Gap) to gain its north-west arête (opposite Needle Ridge). Soak up the exposure then make steep moves on good holds up the arête to gain the top.
SW Herford, WB Brunskill 26.08.1912

15 Needle Ridge 114m VD ★★★
A classic and justifiably popular route that is frequently used, both as a beginners' introductory climb, and as part of a mountaineering route to the summit of Great Gable. Start from the Gap behind the Needle.
1 12m Climb the very polished slab above the Gap to a short shallow chimney that trends left to a block belay on the edge of the ridge below a steep wall.
Alternatively, start from Needle Gully (to the left of Needle Ridge), at the lowest point of the ridge, and follow the arête on good holds to the same stance.
2 18m The crack in the steep wall above, followed by easier rocks, leads to a blocky ledge. Scramble along the crest of the ridge for 7m to a stance.
3 15m Climb the chimney above for 4m then step left onto the edge and follow this to a ledge. Either climb the short corner on the right, or pull delicately direct to a large ledge.
4 34m Climb the groove above which leads to the crest of the ridge, step around this (possible belay) and follow a straight crack in the wall overlooking the gully which leads back onto the crest. Alternatively, climb the groove for 3m then traverse right under the overhang and finish direct.
5 35m Easy scrambling along the gendarmed crest to the main ridge of The Napes. The descent down to Great Hell Gate lies 20m along the main ridge, down a red scree chute.
WP Haskett Smith, JW Robinson 1.09.1884

The Napes | 283

Tophet Wall HS (page 286) — 📷 Tom McNally

Gable

The Arête HS (opposite) Nick Wharton — 📷 David Simmonite

Tophet Wall

Tophet Wall is the large and impressively steep buttress which rises abruptly out of the sweeping screes of Great Hell Gate. A magnificent mountain crag with an unforgettable atmosphere. In mid-summer this south-east facing crag gets the sun until mid-afternoon but can suffer from a chill wind later in the day - early start recommended. There are a great range of routes at all grades sitting side-by-side including the classic *Tophet Wall*, one of the best routes in the Lake District, to hard extremes and a bit of everything in between.

Descent: From the top of the climbs, follow the ridge north until it joins the broad saddle which connects **The Napes** and **Westmorland Crags**, then descend west into Great Hell Gate which is followed down to the base of the crag. A shorter alternative is to descend The Back Staircase (Mod), which follows a narrow diagonal scramble from near the top of *Tophet Wall* into Great Hell Gate.

16 Tophet Bastion 82m VD ★

A good mountaineering route up the left side of the crag. Start at the bottom of a broken arête on the left-hand side of the ramp.
1 20m Easily up the arête to a grass ledge then climb the steep corner on the right to a rock platform. It is possible to by-pass the corner by the steep wall on the right.
2 17m Climb the slab above for 8m to a ledge then step left around the corner and up a steep arête to a stance.
3 12m Step right and climb straight up to the bottom of a groove at 7m. Climb the groove direct (crux, and awkward as it is easy to face the wrong way!) to the top (the groove can be avoided on the left).
4 6m Scramble up steep grass to the obvious feature of the Shark's Fin high on the left.
5 17m Starting from the right, climb the edge of the rib to the foot of a crack in a V-groove. Climb the crack by its left wall, exiting left at the top.
Kelly, EH Pryor, AR Thomson, Mrs Kelly, CG Crawford 13.06.1919

17 Tophet Grooves Direct 78m E1 5b ★

Needs a good spell of weather to dry. Start below the diagonal groove at the left side of the crag.
1 18m 5b Climb the groove with interest to a ledge on the right.
2 18m 5b Climb the scoop above passing a doubtful block to the overhang; step right a metre and climb directly over the bulge to a stance.
3 24m 5b Step right and climb the mossy wall direct to a ledge. Move left and climb leftwards back into the main groove then tackle the puzzling overhanging cleft through the roof. An easier groove above leads to a large grass ledge.
4 18m 4a Scramble over easy ground to the foot of a prominent rib and climb it to the top.
SJH Reid, J Grinbergs 18.07.1991

18 The Vikings 57m E3 5c ★★★

The archetypal Lakeland crack climb: it requires a determined approach. Start directly below the crack at an upstanding block. It is better to combine the first and second pitches.
1 15m 5b Climb leftwards to reach a steep crack. Ascend the crack then step right into another crack and make an awkward pull into the corner above. Climb the corner and pull out left at the top to a ledge.
2 27m 5c Move back right and climb the overhanging crack with increasing difficulty to gain the obvious flared niche. Pull steeply out of the niche and climb directly to a grassy crack. Climb the crack to a large pedestal belay.
3 15m 4b Continue up the crack and groove.
AR McHardy, P Braithwaite 15.06.1969

19 Incantations 87m E6 6b ★★★

A superlative test piece with two powerful pitches. Start below the nose rib 3m right of the prominent block.
1 22m 5b Climb the rib then rightwards up an easy groove to a large sloping ledge.
2 35m 6b A serious and sustained pitch. Difficult and bold moves lead up the overhanging wall (difficult to place wires). Continue up the wall (wires behind expanding flakes) to reach a thin right-slanting crack in the steep slab above. Climb the crack to ledges then move rightwards over a bulge and step up right onto the Great Slab. Climb up the slab then move left to a pinnacle belay.
3 30m 6b Climb the rib above the belay then step right to below a thin right-slanting crack in the overhanging wall. Climb the wall to a jug (old peg above), move right and pull up into the groove. The groove and its right-hand branch lead to the top.
P Whillance, DW Armstrong 15.08.1984

20 Supernatural 82m E5 6a ★★★★

A magical route with a committing and serious middle pitch which follows an intricate line up the steep wall right of *Incantations*. Start at the steep shallow groove just right of a large grassy groove.
1 25m 5c Climb the groove, moving right at the top onto the wall. Move up and make a difficult pull left onto the rib and ascend it to a good ledge and pinnacle.
2 32m 6a Climb the steep wall above the pinnacle to a bulge. Pull onto the steep hanging slab above and traverse it leftwards with difficulty to reach the base of a steep groove; climb the groove to a welcome spike and rest. Step right and climb a rib and groove that lead to good holds on the Great Slab. Step left and climb the slab until an easy traverse can be made leftwards to a ledge and large pinnacle belay.
3 25m 5b Climb directly up the rib above the belay to a ledge on the right then up a mossy slab on the left to a sloping ledge. Traverse right along the ledge then move up and right round the rib on good holds. Climb the wall and V-groove to the top.
P Whillance, DW Armstrong 1.07.1977

21 Tophet Wall 75m HS ★★★★

A magnificent mountain outing winding its way through very impressive rock architecture. Probably the best route of its grade in the Lakes. Take several slings and start to the right of a rightward-leaning corner crack in the centre of the wall.
1 20m Climb the thin wall just right of the steep crack (thin tape runner on flat spike just right of the start of the hard bit), until a step left can be made into the crack which is followed awkwardly to a ledge. An ascending traverse right leads to a ledge at the foot of a short dark wall.
2 17m The short wall above is climbed boldly to a broken ledge. Traverse left to a groove and climb it to a slab and spike belay on the right.
3 38m A fantastic pitch! Semi hand-traverse 10m rightwards in a sensational position to a crack and climb up to a small ledge then follow the crack up rightwards. Alternatively, continue the traverse a bit further and climb directly up to the same point. Climb the small pinnacle on the right then step left into the crack which is followed to an airy pull out right onto a flake pinnacle. Easier climbing up the wall leads to a belay on a narrow footpath. Descend by following the footpath rightwards to a scramble down to Hell's Gate Screes.
Photo page 283.
HM Kelly, REW Pritchard 14.07.1923

22 Demon Wall 76m VS 4c ★

A delicate counter-diagonal escaping left below the headwall. The initial pitch of *Tophet Wall* provides a more balanced outing. Start below the centre of the wall right of a right-leaning corner.
1 20m Climb the wall and crack; *Tophet Wall* P1.
2 18m 4b Step right round a bulging corner into a grassy recess. Climb its left wall on small holds to a ledge which is followed back left to a junction with *Tophet Wall* below a large corner.
3 20m 4c The Great Slab. Ascend *Tophet Wall* until a line of good flake holds encourages a break out left onto the open slab from the relative security of the corner. A rising traverse is made across the slab in a superb position to a spike belay on the edge.
4 20m Traverse left, then step left round a corner onto easy ground. Follow the pock-marked slab to the finish.
AR Dolphin, AB Gilchrist 10.04.1945

23 Sacrificial Crack 66m E4 6a ★★★

A very intimidating crack climb of great character. The route takes the frighteningly overhanging crack at the top right-hand side of the crag. Start below the right-slanting ramp.
1 20m Climb the wall and crack; *Tophet Wall* P1.
2 25m 5b A poorly protected pitch. Climb the rib just left of *Demon Wall* P2 to a broken ledge, move right then pull over a bulge into the right-hand of two short grooves (directly in line with the crack on P3). Climb the groove to a belay just right of the crack at a shattered pinnacle.
3 23m 6a Climb the crack with a dynamic move left at half height, followed by a long reach to a sinking jam below the recess. A strenuous pull gives access to the recess and a possible rest. Follow the crack with interest to the top.
J Lamb, P Botterill, J Taylor 18.06.1978

24 Tophet Ridge 52m VS 4c ★

A good climb up the steep right arête of the crag. Start below an obvious groove on the right side of the ridge, opposite Hell Gate Pillar.
1 30m 4c Climb the left wall and a groove to gain the ridge and follow it to a good rock spike and grass ledge on the right. Make an awkward move onto the spike and climb the steep wall (crux) to reach better holds. Climb more easily to a grassy corner.
2 22m 4b Climb up, past a large block, to a horizontal crack. Hand-traverse this to a short corner (junction with *Tophet Wall*), pull up onto the top of a pinnacle on the right and climb more easily to the top.
S Watson, R Holmes, B Porter, C Cowen 1.06.1932

GABLE CRAG
OS Grid Ref: NY 212 105
Altitude: 800m

Engineer's Slab Left-Hand Finish VS (page 292) Paul O'Reilly — David Simmonite

A superb high-level mountain crag with an imposing buttress of excellent rough rock. Steep and exposed from the outset the routes challenge. As **Gable Crag** sits high and is north-facing bring plenty of warm clothing and choose a dry spell.

High in the centre of the crag is the classic but inappropriately named **Engineer's Slabs**; there is nothing 'slabby' about this steep wall with high quality and sustained routes, most of which follow well-protected cracks. Between the cracklines are a number of superb and intricate wall climbs requiring a high level of commitment.

Approach: The easiest approach is from the summit of Honister Pass. Follow the old tramway incline west up the hillside behind the quarry car park for one kilometre then turn south onto a well-marked track that runs along the side of Grey Knotts. Keep on the main track below Brandreth then break off right to a small stile. Follow a vague path beyond the stile to join the lower path of Moses' Trod which leads to Stone Cove below **Gable Crag**. Climb directly up the boulder slope to the crag or follow a good path to Windy Gap and an easy traverse below the crag.

Approach, Wasdale Head: Follow the track to Burnthwaite then take the Sty Head path. After the bridge over Gable Beck, turn left and follow the Moses' Trod path up the steep south-west shoulder of Great Gable (Gavel Neese). Just below the prominent Moses' Finger boulder, follow a rising traverse line leftwards across the scree to the col at Beck Head. Ascend the shoulder of Great Gable for 200m, where a narrow track (North Traverse) leads off left under the crag.

Approach, Seathwaite: Take the path to Sty Head then turn north up Aaron Slack to the col of Windy Gap, between Great Gable and Green Gable. A short descent leads to the North Traverse path below the crag.

From Black Sail Youth Hostel, an easy walk leads to Stone Cove and Windy Gap then join the North Traverse below the crag.

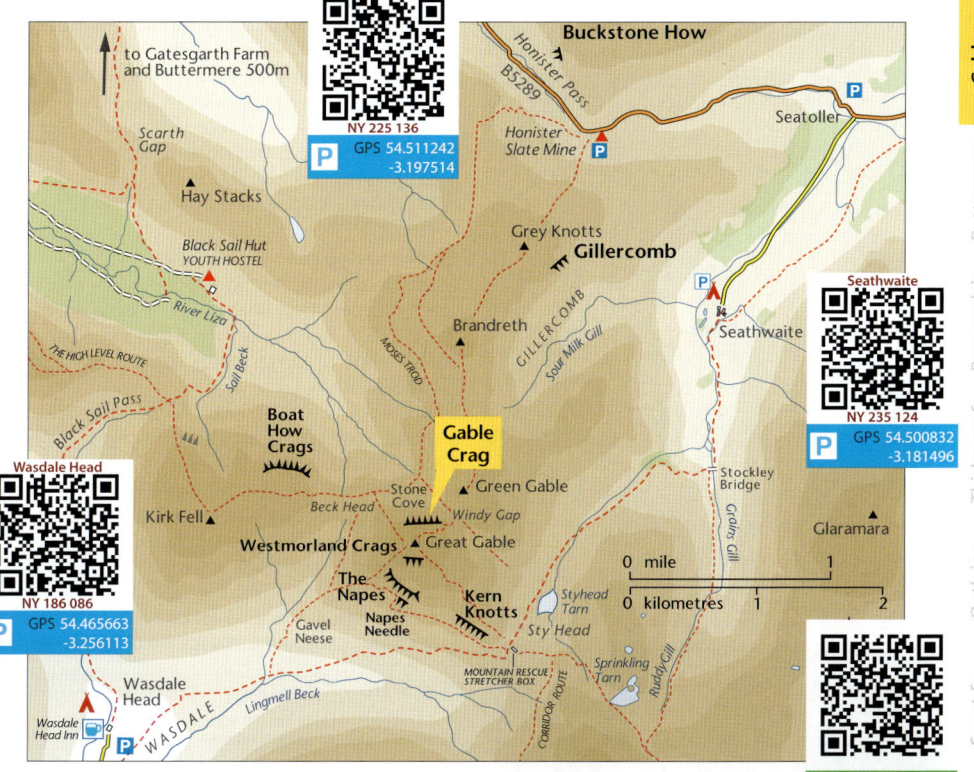

Sledgate Ridge

Approach: This slim buttress of rock rises above the path well below and left of the Engineer's Slabs Area.

Descent: Carry sacks and scramble up. Or, scramble carefully rightwards then descend a short gully to the foot of Engineer's Slabs Area.

1 Sledgate Ridge 73m HS 4b ★★
Three fine pitches. Start at the obvious crack (crux) in the steep little wall.
1 20m 4b The difficult crack can be avoided by an easy chimney on the right. The water-worn grooves on the right are followed for 10m then the wall on the left to a large ledge.
2 18m From the left end of the ledge, climb the wall then grassy slabs on the right to a large grass platform.
3 35m Climb the wall above to a ledge below three vertical cracks. The central crack leads to the top.
AH Greenbank, J Wilkinson, AE Wormell 15.06.1958

Engineer's Slabs Area

Well worth the walk to this unremitting crack-seamed wall offering brilliant climbing.

Approach: Scramble up steep ground to the right of a small broken buttress.

Descent: Abseil 60m with respect for those below. Walk north-west off Great Gable to Beck Head then follow the path south-east to the base of the crag.

2 Dream Twister 45m E3 5c ★★
Fine open well-protected climbing with a sustained crux section. Start just right of the chimney. Easy rocks lead to a ledge and loose blocks. Pull into the groove on the right, exiting right at the top onto the wall and a ledge. Climb the wall to the overhang. Pull over using the crack, moving left at its top into a wider crack curving rightwards to a ledge. The short crack above leads to a large grass ledge and thread belay.
C Downer, A Hall 13.07.1987

3 The Angel of Mercy 60m E1 5b ★★
Excellent tough crack climbing. Start directly below a jammed-block overhang at about 25m.
1 25m 5a Climb to a belay below the block overhang.
2 35m 5b Move up and traverse rightwards across the sandwiched slab to gain the crack. Follow the crack, to where the angle eases then climb the ramp up and right to below a wide overhanging crack splitting the headwall. Difficult moves lead up the crack to the top.
J Lamb, P Botterill 3.06.1979

4 Interceptor 65m HVS 4c ★
Gratuitously committing sequences with spaced protection linking reasonable holds trace a disjointed way into *Engineer's Slabs*. Start below a line of larger holds some 3m left of the central groove.
1 30m 4c An awkward and involving pitch; arrange adequate protection for the second. Climb the wall to the left end of a grass ledge then continue to the right-hand end of a second grass ledge. Follow a line of holds ascending rightwards to reach the twin cracks of *Engineer's Slabs* and climb into the sentry box.
2 35m 4c Continue up the fine groove to the overhangs, traverse left into two parallel cracks and climb to a stance by a huge flake. Climb the flake then traverse right to a groove. Follow the groove, moving right to a prominent spike, then finish up the rib.
PL Fearnehough, NJ Soper 1.06.1967

The Tomb E2 (page 292) 📷 David Simmonite

Gable Crag | 291

1. Sledgate Ridge — HS 4b ★★
2. Dream Twister — E3 5c ★★
3. The Angel of Mercy — E1 5b ★★
4. Interceptor — HVS 4c ★
5. Snicker Snack — E3 5c ★★★
6. Engineer's Slabs — VS 4c ★★★★
7. The Tomb — E2 5c ★★★
8. Sarcophagus — E3 5c ★★★★
9. Unfinished Arête — HVS 5a ★
10. The Jabberwock — HVS 5a ★★

5 Snicker Snack 57m E3 5c ★★★
Superb well-protected climbing taking the thin crack up the steep wall to the left of *Engineer's Slabs*. Start in the middle of the wall just left of the central groove.
1 45m 5c Climb the wall for 12m, step left and follow the straight crack through the overlap then continue up the thin crack above to belay at the huge flake.
2 12m 5b Climb the flake, traverse right and surmount a small overhang to gain a thin crack and follow this to an awkward finish.
C Downer, A Hall 15.07.1986

6 Engineer's Slabs 60m VS 4c ★★★★
An outstanding Lakeland climb of great character, taking the obvious crack and groove up the centre of the wall. Start just left of a groove in the middle of the face.
1 26m 4c The wall leads past a small pinnacle to the foot of a crack. Climb the crack for 5m to twin cracks on the right which lead to a chimney and sentry box.
2 34m 4c Traverse 2m to the right to a crack. Climb the crack crossing a ledge to reach a second ledge. Climb the chimney then savour the well-positioned final groove.

Variation - Left-Hand Finish - Many teams see sense and avoid the classic delights of the final groove and follow the jagged crack on its left wall. This leads to the arête then the ridge above.
Photo page 288.
FG Balcombe, JA Shepherd, CJA Cooper 8.06.1934

7 The Tomb 68m E2 5c ★★★
A superb exciting route demanding a lot of confidence. Protection is very good but you do move away from it. Start at a foot traverse where the ground falls away, 5m right of the central groove.
1 38m 5c Traverse right and up to a groove and sentry box. Exit leftwards onto the wall and continue to a ledge. Climb the wall on the left for 6m to a slot and solid protection. Step down and make a thin traverse right under the overlap to its end; then move up, crossing the overlap, to a reach a small ledge. Traverse right into a steep crack which leads to a stance.
2 30m 5a Climb the groove above to the overhang and step left into the large open groove which provides a fitting finale.
Photo page 290.
AG Cram, W Young 30.09.1966

8 Sarcophagus 64m E3 5c ★★★★
A technically absorbing face climb which rewards single-minded concentration. Start at a foot traverse where the ground falls away 5m right of the central groove.
1 36m 5c Make an ascending traverse right to the sentry box. Exit right to a large flake. Step up left to a small block at the right end of a grass ledge. Step off the block and make a series of increasingly committing moves up the wall to reach the right end of the overlap. Move left to a thin crack, climb to the next overlap and pull over strenuously, stepping right onto a narrow ledge. An exciting pitch.
2 28m 5b Move up and left into a groove. Follow this and climb the filthy crack above to finish up a vegetated groove. Cleaner rock will be found by moving right to climb the groove of *The Tomb*.
P Whillance, DW Armstrong 10.07.1977

9 Unfinished Arête 63m HVS 5a ★
Interesting climbing up the obvious arête that marks the right edge of the face. Start just right of the foot traverse where the grass ledge begins to fall away to the right.
1 15m 4b Traverse right to below a sentry box. Climb up and right to a small groove that leads to a grass ledge below the arête.
2 23m 5a Climb the arête to a small overlap. Traverse right then up to a grass ledge. Continue up the arête to a sloping ledge with shattered blocks. A bold pitch.
3 25m 4c The short slab on the left leads to a very exposed final groove well-endowed with holds and loose blocks.
FG Balcombe, JA Shepherd 10.06.1934

10 The Jabberwock 75m HVS 5a ★★
A great route with a wild finish - it takes the steep crack and grooved headwall at the right end of the face. Start from the lowest point of the wall, just right of the final gully on the approach scramble.
1 22m 4c Climb the cracked wall to ledges on the right of a large flake.
2 28m 5a Climb the crack, passing a large ledge at 18m, to a sloping ledge and shattered blocks.
3 25m 4c The short slab on the left leads to a very exposed groove which is climbed to the top on good holds (beware loose blocks).
R Valentine, J Wilkinson 4.06.1970

The FRCC Great Gable summit memorial plaque

THE GREAT GIFT

On the summit of Great Gable is a plaque commemorating 20 members of the FRCC who died in The Great War. The memorial to them is a tract of land, containing twelve majestic Lakeland mountains, purchased by the Club in 1923 to preserve our freedom to venture among these fells. This gift to the nation was entrusted by the Club to the management of the National Trust for the benefit of everyone.

The bridge over the Liza in Ennerdale is a memorial to the 13 members killed in World War II.

Every November the Club holds a simple Act of Remembrance by the summit memorial plaque, lest we forget the 'freedom we have to follow our dreams...'.

This section of the guidebook is dedicated to all those who gave their lives.

The Sphinx Rock, Great Gable — RON KENYON

ENNERDALE

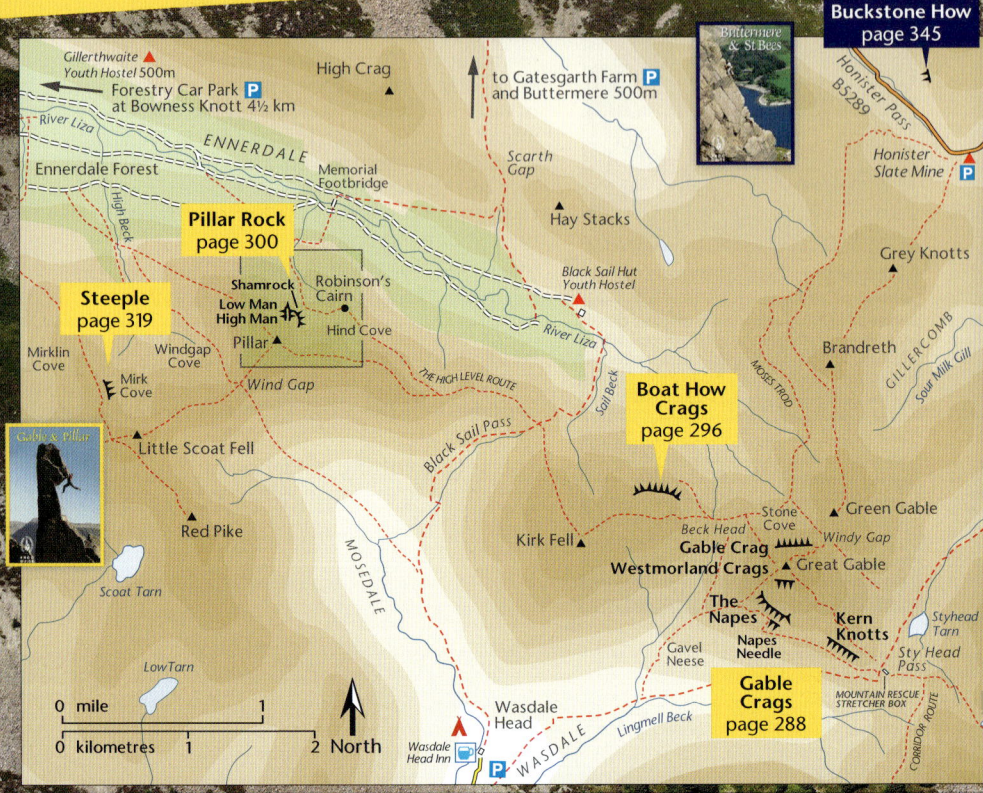

Ennerdale is a remote valley with little in the way of easy access. Sitting proud, high above the valley is **Pillar Rock** with its fortress-like towers and imposing walls. Here is a crag soaked in history that requires a determined effort to reach and then conquer. Further up the valley sit **Boat How Crags** while round the corner is **Steeple**, providing a true mountaineering feel to your day out.

Mirror, Mirror ..., Pillar E1 (page 315) Nick Wharton & Stephen Reid — David Simmonite

BOAT HOW CRAGS

OS Grid Ref: NY 200 110
Altitude: 700m

The long approach adds a feeling of remoteness, overlooking the upper reaches of Ennerdale. However, the effort is well worthwhile with some great climbing on tremendous rough rock. Due to a lack of traffic, some of the routes may be a bit dirty and may benefit from a quick clean. It gets the sun in the afternoon.

Approach: From Honister Pass. Follow the well-trodden path to Stone Cove below **Gable Crag**. Head up to the col at Beck Head then follow the path that contours round the northern slopes of Kirk Fell before heading up the steep ground below the crag. Alternatively, if heading for the top of the crag, walk up the shoulder of Kirk Fell until just beyond the top of the steep section and descend rightwards to the top of the crag.

Beck Head can also be reached by a stiff climb from Wasdale.

See map page 294.

Descent: Various abseils are available (check the condition of these as they don't get a lot of use) or take the wide gully to the right of the main crag.

Breakwater Slabs

The following routes, which can all share the same finish up the *Lighthouse*, are situated on **Breakwater Slabs** where the rock is good and dries quickly. The top pitches can be avoided by abseiling from a block on the right of the slabs.

1 Breakwater Slabs and Lighthouse   65m   S   ★
Start below the crack in the centre of the slabs.
1 30m Climb directly up the crack to a large grass ledge.
2 15m Up the grass trending right to below some broken slabs.
3 20m Climb the broken slabs, after which the climb steepens at the Lighthouse, the slabby rib overlooking the gully on the right. The holds remain good to the top.
G Basterfield, G Lee, T Graham Brown 31.05.1925

2 Groyne Strain   26m   E1 5b   ★★ ⚲
Excellent well-protected climbing. Start at the top of a large block. Step delicately left to reach a small triangular niche then smear leftwards to gain a higher recess in the slab. Follow the thin crack, moving left where it eases. Traverse right to finish up *Topsail*, or abseil off.
A Phizacklea, J Holden 3.06.2006

3 Grooved Arête   30m   VS 4c   ★ ⚲
An excellent pitch up the right-hand arête of the slabs, starting above a jammed block. Make an awkward step onto the arête from the right and follow a stepped groove on the right edge, pulling left over a bulge to the traverse line below the broken slabs. Either finish up *Breakwater Slabs and Lighthouse* or abseil.
HS Gross, G Basterfield, B Tyson 28.05.1928

4 Topsail   12m   E2 5b   ★★
The arête overlooking the Lighthouse makes a good top pitch to *Groyne Strain*. Climb slabs until they meet the arête. Pull across left for a good hold then move back up right on hidden pockets. Climb straight up the wall with long reaches to ledges on the arête. Finish direct to a ledge and large block belays.
E Rogers, K Forsythe 15.06.2006

Main Wall - The Boat

The steep face looking directly across the head of Ennerdale only receives the sun late in the afternoon. The rock is sound but areas remain lichenous and some routes may require cleaning before an ascent.

5 Numenor with Direct Finish   50m   E3 6a   ★★ ⚲
Steep and strenuous climbing up the thin ragged crack and bulges. Well-protected throughout with rests between the steep sections. An excellent line which greatly improves in proportion to the amount of cleaning done before the ascent. Start below a shallow leaning corner.
Climb the awkward leaning corner to a bulge.

Pull out right onto the steep wall, move up to the foot of the sharp crack and climb it over one bulge and up to the next. Continue over two more bulges to the top.
RO Graham, E Rogers 29.07.1999

6 Voyager 40m E3 5c ★★
Start from a hanging stance about 15m up *Numenor*. Traverse sensationally rightwards heading for a peg; two hidden right-facing ramps provide holds and runners. From the peg, climb delicately upwards to gain the base of a groove and finish up this.
E Rogers, RO Graham 29.07.1999

7 Flagship 50m E5 5c ★★★
The pride of Ennerdale and a very bold line directly up the front of the main wall. Despite numerous microwire placements between pegs, using skyhooks is possibly the only way to avoid a ground fall from the crux at 12m. A side-runner can be placed in *Numenor* to mitigate the seriousness. Climb a small slab (peg at 4m). Sustained technical climbing continues past three short grooves for 15m (peg on right). Move back from the peg and make a series of delicate moves left to reach small cracks (gear). Continue up the small steep groove, pull out right and follow slabs to the top. Superb!
D Birkett, S Wood, P Ross 25.06.1995

8 Voyager Direct 50m E6 6a ★★
The right-hand line up the front face. Cast off and gain the obvious ledge by a thin seam in the centre of the face. Step right and climb direct to reach an undercling. Reaching a good foothold above and left brings calm (small gear). Layback the square flake to reach a high sidepull to the left. Further sidepulls and crimps gain the slab above and the sanctuary of the end of the *Voyager* traverse. Finish up this.
S Litchfield, G Read 5.07.2013

9 Fanghorn 50m E3 5c ★★★
Tackles the proud arête between **Main Wall** and the **West Face**, starting at the toe of the blunt arête on the right. A classic route with excellent rock and situations.
1 20m 5c Climb to a small corner to the right of the rib then make an awkward pull left onto the arête. Go straight up passing a difficult sequence (old peg) to reach a shallow groove. Follow this to a stance.
2 30m 5b Traverse left across a flake and make a delicate move around a bulge into a hidden groove. Follow the groove directly to the top.
I Roper, NAJ Rogers 14.06.1969

West Face

This steep wall of excellent clean rock looking down towards Ennerdale receives the sun shortly after mid-day.

10 Jolly Roger 50m E2 5c ★★
An entertaining and varied climb. Start below the open groove, 9m right of the arête.
1 20m 5c Climb the groove past a spike and move up to an awkward slot in the overhang. Step left and climb a groove to a grass ledge.
2 30m 5a Climb the wide open groove above then left to a shallow corner and up this to the top.
Alternatively finish up the P2 of *Fanghorn* for a better balanced route.
E Rogers, RO Graham 29.07.1999

11 Trim and Incline 28m E3 5c ★★
Takes the centre of the wall, a few metres right of the groove. Climb to a hanging flake with a loose block at its top (poor nut). Make a series of long reaches up a set of 'steps' (skyhook) then go right to (second skyhook, wire). Traverse left and up to reach a good hold (gear). Move up and make a blind long reach left above the diagonal roof then climb directly up a shallow scoop to a ledge. To avoid the blind move over the roof step left from the good hold then climb a shallow groove to the ledge.
Either abseil off, or finish up *Poseidon Adventure*.
A Phizacklea, K Phizacklea 22.07.1997

12 Poseidon Adventure 50m E4 6a ★★
Start below the next groove up the slope.
1 25m 6a Climb the shallow chimney groove and exit left at the overhang. Move left to a skyhook placement and wire (on *Trim and Incline*). Climb directly up the wall above with difficulty to the apex of the roof and pull over this on dramatically improving holds to a good ledge.
2 25m 5a Climb the rib defining the edge of the buttresses, gaining it from the right.
RO Graham, A Jones 28.08.1999

13 Scenic Cruise 45m HVS 5a ★★★
A direct line up the steep **West Face**. Sustained climbing on excellent quick-drying rock. Starting just to the left of the chimney, climb a left-leaning scoop for about 6m then make a couple of interesting moves right to a crack line. Step right and climb straight up, heading for the base of the steep groove at the highest point of the buttress. Pull out left and climb a delicate slab which leads to the top. The groove may be climbed direct but is harder.
P Ross, P Greenwood 2.08.1996

The Boat

5	Numenor with Direct Finish	E3 6a	★★
6	Voyager	E3 5c	★★
7	Flagship	E5 5c	★★★
8	Voyager Direct	E6 6a	★★
9	Fanghorn	E3 5c	★★★

West Face | **Boat How Crags** | 299

PILLAR ROCK

OS Grid Ref: NY 172 125
Altitude: 600m

2½ hr

 RAD Pillar Rock
 OS Grid Ref NY 172 125

An impressively striking remote and complex crag with a rich history, hosting the first recorded climb in England, *The Old West Route*. Ennerdale has no public road and approaches are long, yet using a bike on the network of forest tracks significantly cuts down access time.

Approach, Wasdale: Park at Wasdale Head and take the path north towards Black Sail Pass. After crossing a beck the path forks, follow the upper right-hand branch to a high point with a small cairn (NY 184 117). Take the narrow well-worn path to the north-west, the start of the High Level Route, that contours the northern slopes of Pillar into Hind Cove then on to Robinson's Cairn and the east face of Pillar Rock.

Approach, Ennerdale: A bike is recommended. Park at Bowness Knott (P&D), no vehicles are allowed beyond. Take the track east passing Gillerthwaite Youth Hostel after 3.5km then, after a further 2.5km, fork right over a concrete bridge (6km). By bike, continue for 500m to a junction with the upper forest road. Turn right and after 450m stash the bikes then take the unsigned path south-east. On foot, 50m past the concrete bridge, some wooden steps mark the start of a wet path to the rock.

Approach, Buttermere: Park at Gatesgarth Farm then cross Scarth Gap into Ennerdale. At a fork walk in a westerly direction to reach the valley bottom. Cross the Memorial Footbridge then turn right to join the Ennerdale approach at the junction with the upper forest road.

Camping: On the ridge to the north of the stream in Pillar Cove on the Ennerdale approach are small areas of flat ground only 15 minutes from the crag. They catch the sun early, keep it late and have a water supply.

⑥	Walker's Gully	VS 4c	★★★
⑳	The Old West Route	M	★★

Pillar Overview — 📷 TONY STEPHENSON

North-West Climb MVS (page 311) Nigel Hooker & Stephen Reid — 📷 David Simmonite

Ennerdale

Bowness Knott
NY 109 154
P GPS 54.525599 -3.377036

Gatesgarth
NY 195 149
P GPS 54.523799 -3.245950

Wasdale Head
NY 186 086
P GPS 54.465663 -3.256113

Also see approach map page 294 & photo-plan page 303.

Pillar Rock

- West Face of Low Man
- North Face of Low Man
- East Face of High Man
- Shamrock
- West Face of High Man
- Ennerdale
- Green Ledge
- Waterfall
- Low Man
- High Man
- Pisgah
- Western Scree
- Western Gully
- Walker's Gully
- Shamrock Gully
- Shamrock Traverse
- Pillar Cove
- Robinson's Cairn
- The High Level Route
- Shelter
- Pillar Fell
- Great Doup

0 — 250m North

Buttermere & Newlands | Borrowdale | Thirlmere & Ullswater | Outlying | Sport & Slate

7 | 8 | 11 | 27

Pillar Overview — 📷 Tony Stephenson ✎ Peter Sterling & Stephen Reid

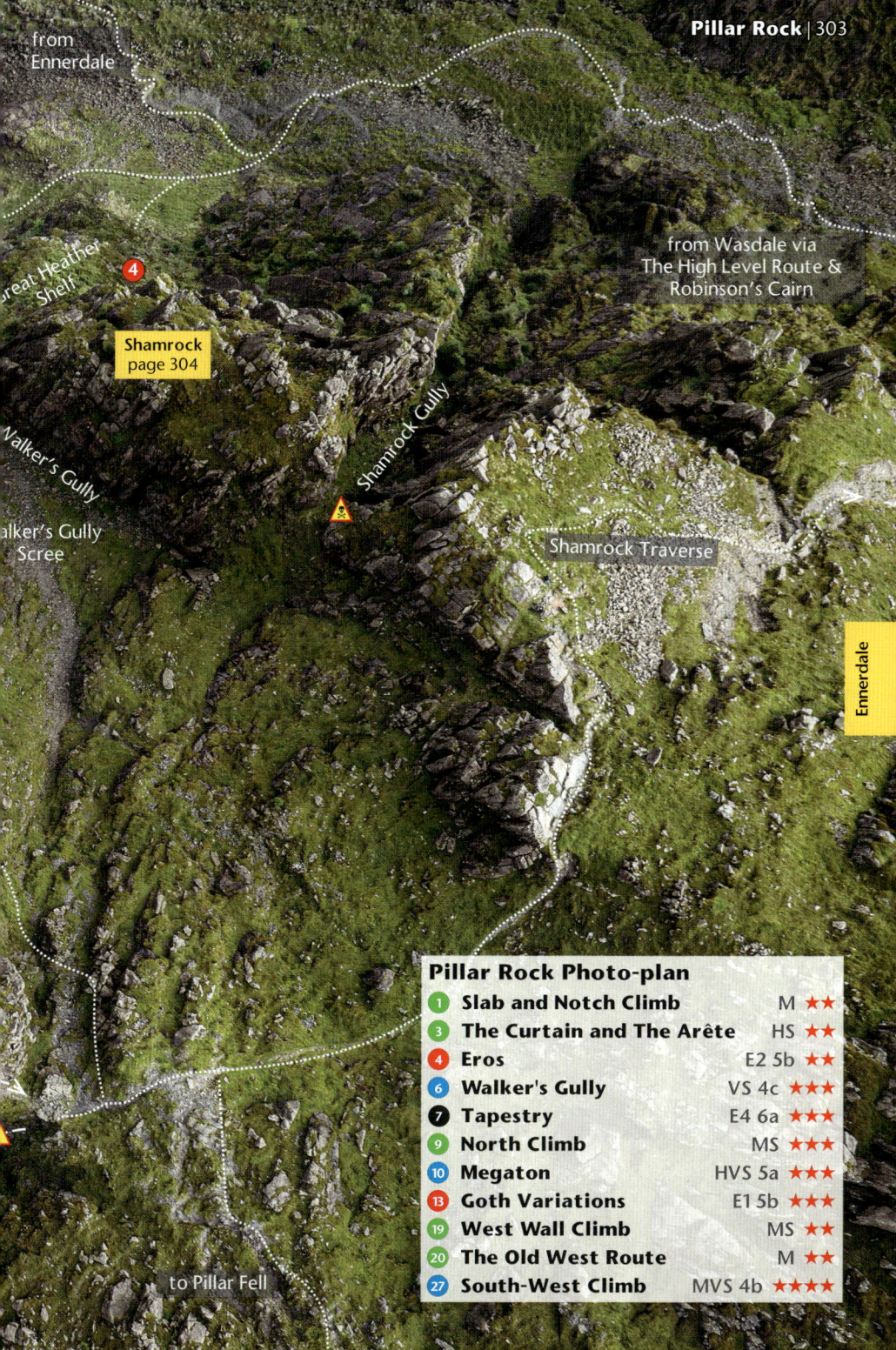

East Face of High Man

Approach: Follow Shamrock Traverse from the east towards Pisgah then scramble down to the start of the routes.

Descent: Reverse *Slab and Notch Climb* M (page 306). Or, abseil 16m from a block near the summit cairn into Jordan Gap. From the highest point of the gap climb an exposed line rightwards **10m M** on the South Face of Pisgah (opposite) to its right edge then on to the top. Scramble down the other side.

1 Slab and Notch Climb 60m M ★★
A popular historic climb finding the easiest way up and down. From the foot of East Jordan Gully climb onto the easy-angled Slab on the right, descend slightly, traverse across the base of the slab then climb either steep groove to the Notch. Move right along a narrow ledge then climb the steep rib to another ledge. Move right and climb slabs, step right to finish up the upper section of a large gully.
JWE Coneybeare and party. 14.08.1863

2 Stalingrad 30m E3 6a ★★
Strenuous sustained technical climbing. Start below the arête at the top of the Slab. Make an unprotected boulder problem start up a smooth groove to the right of a pinnacle. Step left to the pinnacle (high cam), then continue up the groove until it eases. Finish up and rightwards, keeping to the right of the arête.
P Winterbottom, JA Daly 2.09.2021

3 The Curtain and The Arête 78m HS ★★
This alpine style ridge runs up the arête between *Slab and Notch Climb* and its final chimney. Start by a wall on a flat grassy ledge (cairn), just above the lowest short wall of the arête.
1 26m The Curtain. The wall with good if dodgy holds is followed by an awkward wide crack which starts from a precariously poised block on the right. Climb rightwards on good holds following the narrowing ridge to a spike just before a large flat ledge.
2 7m Traverse the ledge leftwards and up to the Notch.
3 45m The Arête. Just right of the Notch, climb the slightly overhanging right-hand corner on good holds. Follow this to a headwall which is overcome via a thin left-slanting crack. The arête leads to the top. This pitch can be climbed from the Notch in its own right **MS**.
WP Haskett Smith 1884

Shamrock

A large rambling crag on the north-east side of Pillar that catches the morning sun.

Descent: Scramble down to the head of Shamrock Gully above the scree funnel of *Walker's Gully*, then scramble up rightwards and back leftwards to emerge at the top of the well-marked left-slanting diagonal rake of the Shamrock Traverse. Follow this down to the left.

4 Eros 167m E2 5b ★★
A bold climb with interesting but disjointed pitches. Start at the base of the rib, right of a groove.
1 25m 5a Climb the rib to a slab, which leads to a ledge on the right of the next sharp arête. Bold.
2 30m 5b Gain the steep rib which is climbed on its right side. Continue up the slab above to a ledge then traverse left to a grassy corner - even bolder.
3 22m 5b Climb the corner above with some difficulty, using the rib on the right as necessary.
4 20m 4a Continue to a ledge on the right. Step left across the groove and climb the left edge of a slab to a ridge which leads to beneath the final tower.
5 20m 4b Climb up a couple of metres to the left of the steep wall of the final tower, then traverse left along a grass ledge into Shamrock Gully, emerging by a huge flake. Belay on the opposite side of the gully.
6 20m 5a Stepping off the flake, climb slightly right then back left to an off-width chimney. Hard moves up this lead to easier ground and a final steep corner.
7 30m Easily along the ridge to the Tea Table.
WS Lounds, JC Eilbeck 18.08.1968
P6 P Winterbottom, SJH Reid 22.6.2024

5 Thanatos/Electron 182m HVS 5b ★★★
In dry conditions, this combination is one of the best and longest routes on this part of the crag. The layback crack on the penultimate pitch is bold but not technically difficult. Start just right of the lowest part of the crag, directly beneath the large roofed corner.
1 27m 4b Climb a slab and vegetation to a corner. Go up this for a couple of metres, then move left onto the steep slab which leads to a bilberry ledge. Continue up to a second bilberry ledge at the base of the main corner.
2 30m 5b Climb the corner until just below the first overhang. Traverse left onto a rib and enter a groove below the second overhang. Make difficult moves on the left to reach a good ledge.

3 25m An easy groove leads to the Great Heather Shelf; scramble down and left, around the corner, to the foot of a large left-facing corner with a short hour-glass shaped chimney on its right.
4 26m 5a Climb the vast right-angled corner to a small chockstone at 6m. Overcome an awkward bulge and continue up the corner with another awkward move higher up. Belay on a large grass ledge.
5 24m 4b Climb up the broken groove for 12m to a grass ledge and surmount the wall beyond to a large block. Belay at the foot of the imposing (not to mention intimidating) off-width crack.
6 20m 4c The crux! Climb the crack with determination.
7 30m 4b Move right and go up the grey arête to a slim ledge 2m below the top of a pinnacle. Traverse 6m right to the foot of a continuation arête and ascend this to the foot of the Tea Table.
WS Lounds, JC Eilbeck May 1968;
AG Cram, JC Eilbeck Sep 1966

PILLAR MULTI-ACTIVITY

Linking activities: cycle, hike, climb, summit, abseil, scramble, and water... Using a bike not only saves time but also kicks off a big adventure on Pillar. Climbing on the **West Face of High Man** is best in the sun after lunch. Options for a long day:

- ☐ Low Man via **North Climb** S 4a,
- ☐ Descend **The Old West Route** M then either
- ☐ High Man via **New West Climb** VD or
  South-West Climb MVS 4b

Abseil into Jordan Gap, then savour the exposure gaining Pisgah. If you have the energy, and the summits of High Man and Pisgah weren't enough, the views from the top of Pillar Fell are worth the extra effort. Finally, perhaps on the longest and hottest summer days, enjoy a cool down on the shoreline of Ennerdale Water.

⑥ Walker's Gully 182m VS 4c ★★★

A superb imposing and atmospheric traditional gully, one of the best of its type in the district. An exciting challenge that, in anything other than bone-dry conditions, will be at least a grade harder. Helmets should definitely be worn due to the loose scree above the gully.

1 32m 4a Climb an easy chimney followed by scrambling to the foot of a high green chimney. Climb the short wall right of the chimney and step out right onto a sloping grass terrace. Descend slightly and belay from a crack in the smooth right wall.

2 45m 4b A bold pitch. Return to the edge of the chimney and climb an exposed groove with poor holds until it is possible to step round left on to the first chockstone in the chimney. Chimney up to another chockstone and surmount this with difficulty. Scramble up the bed of the gully, overcoming a large chockstone en route, and belay at the foot of the steep continuation of the gully.

3 30m 4b Climb the chimney to a cave in the gully: usually wet. Climb behind, then over, a chockstone; bridge the gully until a sloping chockstone is reached. Another chockstone just above gives access to a short easy scree section.

4 25m 4b Above, a cave in the gully is formed by a large chockstone. The Through Route is strenuous but short. It can be avoided by climbing the left wall outside the cave but that would miss the fun.

5 15m 4a A further through route is followed by an awkward chockstone.

6 35m 4c Overcome another chockstone to gain the final cave. Climb the right wall until forced right to avoid the final capstone. Strenuous moves gain the top. Scramble up scree a further 20m or so to find a belay.

OG Jones, GD Abraham, AE Field 7.01.1899

Slab and Notch Climb Descent

From the summit of High Man head north for 10m then descend a cleft into the easy chimney splitting the East Face. After a few metres move left (facing in) onto a slab, down this to a ledge. Descend a short steep arête for 5m to another ledge. Move left (facing in) to the Notch. Descend either of two grooves beyond to the Slab; cross easily leftwards, up a little, then downclimb to the foot of East Jordan Gully.

North Face of Low Man

Seamed with ribs, cracks and grooves this imposing shady buttress has great rock. The frequent grass ledges hold water, so climb here in a dry spell.

Approach: From *Walker's Gully* along Green Ledge.

Descent: From routes 7, 8 and 9 up and left across vegetated ledges. Cross the scree at the top of Walker's Gully then down Shamrock Traverse.

From the top of Low Man climb *The Old West Route* M to High Man then descend *Slab and Notch Climb* M. Or, from Low Man descend the lower section of *The Old West Route* M for access to Western Scree and the West Face routes. **See photo-plan page 303.**

⑦ Tapestry 70m E4 6a ★★★

This excellent route weaves its way up the buttress in good situations but with a serious second pitch. Scramble 12m up from *Walker's Gully* to start at the foot of its steep right-bounding wall.

1 25m 5b Climb the centre of the huge pinnacle and finish by its left edge. Follow the groove leftwards to a ledge beneath an overhang.

2 20m 6a Climb the overhang and immediately step right to a shallow corner. Follow this almost to the top (last gear, tricky to arrange), then gain the wall on its left and climb rightwards to a ledge.

3 25m 5b From the right-hand end of the ledge, a groove in the arête leads to a soaring leftward hand-traverse. Follow this and then climb a crack back right to a ledge below final wall: belay. Climb a short V-groove with a chockstone at its base to reach the descent.

A Stephenson, C Sice, W Young, RG Willison 20.04.1980

⑧ Grooved Wall 124m VS 5a ★★

Despite the vegetated first section this is a tough rewarding climb with a well-protected crux running up the right wall of *Walker's Gully*. Start on the path just right of the foot of the gully.

1 45m 4a Scramble 15m up high grassy ledges to a wide broken chimney with a vast flake for its left-hand side. The chimney is followed to its top.

2 35m 5a Climb the left-hand groove to a ledge. Optional belay. Overcome the short overhanging crack (crux) to gain the groove then climb to a spike.

3 20m 4b Continue up the sustained groove to belay by a corner on the side of the groove.

4 24m 4c The final groove above is not without interest, but ends after 12m. Continue up ledges and grass to a rock gateway which opens onto the scree just above *Walker's Gully*.

HM Kelly, HG Knight, WG Standring 28.04.1928

Shamrock

- **4** Eros — E2 5b ★★
- **5** Thanatos/Electron — HVS 5b ★★★
- **6** Walker's Gully — VS 4c ★★★

9 North Climb 104m S 4a ★★★

A superb classic Diff with a Severe finish which is considerably harder in wet. Take lots of slings and start from Green Ledge, at a patch of gravel, where a short wall leads to a square platform.

1 10m An easy mantelshelf and short slab lead to a large ledge at the foot of a broken groove.
2 25m Follow the groove until it steepens at a small grassy bay.
3 34m Climb the Twisting Chimney on the right, then trend left up an open groove. Scramble up to a small ledge at the meeting of two narrow chimneys.
4 9m The Stomach Traverse. Squeeze up into then thrutch the right-hand chimney as it curves right in its upper half.
5 18m Climb the chockstone filled corner via a capstone. Walk left for 6m to the Split Blocks. Climb into the Split, turn left and wriggle up the chimney to the top of the Blocks. Traverse left, making an exposed stride across the void of the Strid, to a big ledge below and right of the Nose.
6 5m 4a The Nose. Go left along the ledge to a corner (high runner) then out left to stand on a projecting flake. Boulder up and left to reach better holds and a ledge.

6a 8m HS **The Hand Traverse Finish**
Useful when the Nose is wet: strenuous yet with tremendous holds. From the right end of the ledge, climb the steep wall for 3m to a sharp-edged flake then traverse boldly left to the top of the Nose.
WP Haskett Smith, G Hastings, WC Slingsby 27.07.1891

Descent: Up and left across vegetated ledges. Cross the scree at the top of Walker's Gully then down Shamrock Traverse. Alternatively, the grassy gully above, Stony Gully, leads to the summit of Low Man where *The Old West Route* can be joined. Take great care not to dislodge any stones.

10 Megaton 120m HVS 5a ★★★

Varied, interesting and sustained. Start towards the right-hand side of Green Ledge, some 7m left of Bounding Buttress, below the steep grassy bay.

1 18m 4b Climb a 3m rib to grass. Make the best of the rock rib above to the lower end of a rightward-rising grass ramp under a steep slab. Belay at its far end.
2 26m 4c Start 2m left of the belay and follow a thin crack directly up the slab until about half-height then head up and diagonally leftwards to a stance well up on the left by a pile of blocks.
3 36m 5a Step off the pile of blocks and traverse right along two rock ledges to a groove. Climb this for 2m then move leftwards up a gangway to a thin crack which soon widens and is followed until the angle eases. Climb rightwards for 12m or so to a recess identified by a dubious spike and loose pebble in a corner.
4 20m 4c Pull directly over the bulge into a groove and follow it to a mossy shallow niche. Avoid the moss by stepping left and moving up to easier ground under a steep crack.
5 20m 4c Climb the crack to the top of Low Man.
W Young, WA Barnes 20.05.1972

11 Goodbye To All That 124m E1 5b ★★★

A direct line on excellent rock taking in the prominent ragged crack right of the main pitch of *Megaton* and culminating in a sensational top pitch. Low in the grade. Start as for *Megaton*,

1 18m 4b *Megaton* P1.
2 26m 5a Two metres to the left is a thin crack in the slab. Climb this direct to a narrow bilberry ledge and huge block.
3 36m 5b Climb into an overhung scoop just left of the belay and pull out awkwardly onto a small ledge on the left. Climb to and up the crack pulling out rightwards to easier ground. Climb directly over bulges and slabby rock to belay in a recess identified by a dubious spike and loose pebble in a corner.
4 20m 5b Stride onto a ledge on the right (spiky block). Climb the arête into a rock bay then the wall on the right to reach a square pocket then traverse right to a flake on the arête. Go straight up to easy ground and a small quartz ledge on a superbly exposed rib out on the extreme right, well below a deep chimney. Oppenheimer's Chimney.
5 14m 5b A bold pitch. Climb up to the base of the chimney (gear). Traverse horizontally leftwards on blocks to some tiny footholds on a rib and make a long reach up and left for a jug. Climb the wall in an exposed position on good holds but with no further protection until a runner can be placed under a block on the left. Move back right and follow more jugs up a rib: it's best to belay immediately or your second may have trouble with the ropes.
6 10m Easy ground to the top.
SJH Reid, SR Stout 8.09.1996

Western Scree to Green Ledge Descent
⚠ From the Western Scree descend with great awareness of the gaping dangers of the Waterfall, keeping left (west) of the chasm and the very loose scree above it, until almost level with Green Ledge. Very carefully scramble across the Waterfall then on to Green Ledge; see detailed approach notes on page 312.

North Face of Low Man | **Pillar Rock** | 309

North Face of Low Man
- **6** Walker's Gully — VS 4c ★★★
- **7** Tapestry — E4 6a ★★★
- **8** Grooved Wall — VS 5a ★★
- **9** North Climb — MS ★★★

12 North-West Climb 130m MVS 4b ★★★

A fine route giving varied climbing and good situations. Start at the right-hand end of Green Ledge, underneath Bounding Buttress, at a short rightwards-slanting grassy gangway.
1 20m Climb the gangway to a ledge and follow a chimney for 10m to a slab. Traverse left across the slab to belay at the foot of a much wider chimney.
2 36m 4a The wide chimney is taken direct to finish on a grassy slab in a corner (possible belay). Climb a short crack on the left onto the crest of the buttress and follow another crack up this until the angle eases at a terrace. Cross the large platform rightwards for 9m to belay at the base of a smooth easy-angled slab.
3 25m 4b Ascend the slab and a short grassy corner to a grass ledge under a prominent steep V-groove. Traverse the ledge leftwards around a rib and climb into the first of a series of three recesses. Carry on up into the second recess below an undercut groove.
4 25m To the left of the undercut groove above are three vague grooves. To gain the first groove step left to a nose and climb it to a ledge with a large block. Climb the groove above, mainly on the left, then pull out left at its top. Stride immediately back right and go up to a belay below an impending crack.
5 24m 4b Oppenheimer's Chimney. Traverse rightwards under bulges and go up to the foot of a deep chimney-crack. After an awkward start, it becomes more reasonable and easy scrambling then leads to the top of Low Man.
Photo page 301.
FW Botterill, LJ Oppenheimer, A Botterill, JH Taylor 8.06.1906

Ennerdale — Jon Allison

West Face of Low Man

Excellent rock which dries quickly in the afternoon sun. A route here is best combined with a route across on High Man.

Approach:
From Ennerdale, climb the fellside well to the right of **Pillar Rock** then follow a rising horizontal path left to the Western Scree.

From Wasdale, follow the High Level Route and Shamrock Traverse to the top of Pisgah. Descend Western Gully to the Western Scree.

From Green Ledge, the tricky barrier formed by the Waterfall needs to be crossed. Follow Green Ledge rightwards to where it drops away into a wide gully. An awkward sideways scramble leads, with a one metre rock step, across the gully and up a short slimy wall onto the scree. All very serious and poorly protected. A slip here could be fatal! Or, before the rock step, scramble down from Green Ledge crossing the gully lower down using a steep grass trench then continue until you gain the open fell side. Scramble up to join the path crossing the scree.

Once on the Western Scree beneath the West Face, the routes can be reached by following the West Wall Traverse. This exposed traverse starts 10m up the scree from the top of the Waterfall, almost opposite the point where the approach path from the valley meets the scree. ⚠ Rope advised, the huge chasm of the Waterfall cannot be seen from directly above: take great care. At the far end a huge block on a grass ledge marks the start of *The Appian Way*.

Descent: Scramble down the lower section of *The Old West Route* M. **Take great care not to knock rocks off the ramp as there will often be others climbing below.**

13 Goth Variations 75m E1 5b ★★★
A very well-positioned climb; meagre protection from small wires on the crux. Follow West Wall Traverse to a huge block on a grass ledge. Scramble down and left, passing a smaller block, to another grass ledge at the foot of an open-book corner with an undercut arête on its left.
1 20m 4b Move right to a short greasy groove. Climb to the right of this then the left-slanting slab above, to a ledge in a V-groove below a big roof.
2 35m 5b Traverse left for 2m to the foot of a mossy groove. This is climbed until a dubious block in the roof of a small overhang is reached then break out left across a small slab to an arête (gear). Climb the overhanging wall above, poorly protected by tiny wires, to a narrow sloping ledge and move left to the fine arête and follow this to a stance.
3 20m 4a Climb up to a short curving crack on the right. Ascend this and finish up rough slabs taking a line almost on the left arête.
M de St Jorre, N Hannaby 13.06.1959

14 The Appian Way 65m HS ★★
A very pleasant and exposed route with delicate wall climbing and good situations. Follow the West Wall Traverse leftwards, first downwards slightly under a long low wall, then diagonally upwards over grassy ledges for some 70m, to a huge block on a grass ledge.
1 20m Climb grassy rock 3m left of the mossy groove then traverse to the right across the top of the groove to gain a grassy corner ramp. This is followed to its top; flake and crack belay.
2 15m Climb the thin corner crack. From its top, traverse delicately left across the imposing wall to a worrying spike on the skyline. Belay on wires just left of the base of the spike and back this up with gear in a crack on the left.
3 12m Move left and ascend a series of steep ledges (bold) to a grassy terrace and a large block leaning against the wall.
4 18m Climb the slightly overhanging, right-hand branch of an 8m crack on the left of the block followed by slabs.
REW Pritchard, HM Kelly 16.07.1923

15 Appian Wall 77m VS 4c ★★
Start at a large block reached via the West Wall Traverse.
1 25m 4c Bridge the mossy groove direct and continue up the clean groove until just below the right end of an overlap. Step right onto the arête and follow cracks up the wall to the traverse on *The Appian Way* which is followed leftwards to a dodgy spike. Belay on wires just left of the base of the spike and back this up with gear in a crack on the left.
2 25m 4b Move carefully up off the spike and traverse boldly rightwards towards the middle of the wall before climbing to grass ledges. Go rightwards up these to a crevasse stance. A virtually runnerless pitch!
3 27m Climb the blunt arête above the stance then scramble to a spike.
CJ King, SJH Reid 9.09.2004

South-West Climb MVS (page 318) Nigel Hooker — 📷 David Simmonite

16 Mirror, Mirror ...   70m   E1 5b   ★★★

Excellent wall climbing on very rough clean rock. There are some lengthy runouts on both pitches. Take several thin slings and a cool head. Start from a flat rock platform on the West Wall Traverse, just right of a bottomless chimney towards the left-hand end of a smooth vertical wall.

1 33m 5b Climb a short crack up into the chimney, but step immediately left onto the buttress which is climbed to a terrace. Climb the wall directly above to gain a rightward-slanting grassy ramp. On the wall above the ramp is a flange-like projection - hand or foot traverse this to a tricky move left around the arête. Bold but easier climbing up the wall leads to easy slabs; trend left to belay on grass in the leftward-facing corner.

2 30m 5b From the corner, step one metre left then climb the middle of the wall to a break (*The Appian Way*). Move right to the left-hand end of a slim overhang then climb through the bulge (hidden wire). Boldly climb the wall aiming for a tiny overlap up and to the left (hidden micro-cam above and left). Continue straight up, passing a small spike, to a break below the steep headwall. Step right and climb directly through the headwall to a crevasse stance.

3 27m Climb the blunt arête above the stance then scramble to a spike.

Photo page 295.
P1 CJ King, SJH Reid 10.05.2006;
P2 CJ King, SJH Reid, J Preston, K Wigglesworth 10.06.2005
P2 Upper section A Phizacklea, R Wightman 14.05.1988

17 The Devil's Entrance   65m   VS 4c   ★★

Start at the steep dark right-hand crack in the smooth vertical wall which slants down slightly leftwards just above the West Wall Traverse.

1 25m 4c Climb the crack and move up right onto the slab then back left immediately onto a rib. Climb the rib to grass and step right into a slim rightward-facing cracked groove; follow this to a flake.

2 40m 4b Step off the flake and climb the left edge of the slab for one metre before traversing left into the left-facing corner. Climb the corner to a small quartz ledge at the apex of the slab on its right. Continue up the steeper corner above, moving right at a bulge near its top, to a chockstone on *The Old West Route*.
R Bennett, R Lavender 15.08.1972

West Face of Low Man | **Pillar Rock**   315

18 Thor   65m   VS 4c   ★★

An enjoyable climb with good situations and excellent rock. Start at the steep dark right-hand crack.

1 30m 4c Climb the crack and move up and right to ascend an easy-angled rightward-slanting slab using a flake crack. Climb directly up a steeper slab above (just right of a corner), to just below a slim open groove on its right-hand side. Traverse right 2m, past a large flake, and up to a small rock ledge.

2 20m 4c A tough pull up a steep crack gains a groove which leads to a small overhang. Turn this on the left and continue up to a grass ledge and huge block.

3 15m 4c Step up off the top of the block and make an airy rising traverse across the wall on the right to a grass ledge; scramble up to a belay.
R Schipper, CJS Bonington 13.06.1967

19 West Wall Climb   65m   MS   ★★

A good route with continuous interest. Follow the West Wall Traverse for a few metres to a platform below a 3m wall.

1 15m A short crack leads to a grassy rake. Cross this and make a hard start up a groove until able to pull left to a sloping ledge. Bold.

2 15m Step right; steep rocks then lead to a slab. The crack in the wall on the right leads to a small sloping ledge 3m below the end of the crack. Belay on the pedestal on the right.

3 15m Descend left from the pedestal and make an awkward traverse left, well under a mossy groove, to a short groove on the left. Climb this to a large scoop and belay at the base of a cracked pinnacle.

4 20m Climb the left arête of the pinnacle and from its top, up a short awkward groove or the wall on its left. Easier rock leads to the top.
HM Kelly, CF Holland, CG Crawford Jul 1919

20 The Old West Route   M   ★★

Low Man and High Man are separated by this obvious well-marked scramble - the original route of ascent of Pillar in 1826. From the Western Scree, follow the left-slanting rake to the summit of Low Man. From here move to higher grassy ledges until a more rocky right-to-left diagonal line leads to a short steep corner and a small pinnacle. A determined heave-ho will gain easier terrain that leads to the summit of High Man.
J Atkinson Jul 1826

West Face of High Man

The most impressive face of **Pillar Rock** and the quickest to dry.

Approach: As for the West Face of Low Man. See page 312.

Descent: Reverse *Slab and Notch Climb* M (page 306) then scramble up to a path and down Western Gully. Or, abseil 16m from a block near the summit cairn into Jordan Gap. From the highest point of the gap climb an exposed line rightwards **10m** M on the South Face of Pisgah (opposite) to its west rib then on to the top. Scramble down the other side then down Western Gully. Alternatively, *The Old West Route* M could be downclimbed with care.

21 Gondor 70m E2 5c ★★★
Impressive and exposed with strenuous and delicate climbing. Start 40m up *The Old West Route* at the base of a striking rib, left of a prominent groove.
1 25m **4a** Follow the rib to a green ledge on the left then up a wall and slab to block belays.
2 18m **5b** Climb the groove in the arête to a bulge. Pull up and boldly right until the angle eases. Belay in a corner below a grass ledge.
3 27m **5c** Climb down for 2m and traverse delicately right round the nose onto the wall. Go up and left to easier climbing, following a groove to a large ledge.
AG Cram, K Robson Apr 1967

22 Gomorrah 80m VS 4b ★★
Start 40m up *The Old West Route* at the base of a striking rib, left of a prominent groove.
1 25m **4a** Follow the rib to a green ledge on the left then up a wall and slab to block belays.
2 20m **4b** Step up right, round the rib and across the corner to ledges. Step down and climb an awkward right-slanting cracked groove on the right to a ledge below the big groove. Up the groove, taking care with the blocks to a stance under the roof.
3 35m **4b** Overcome the bulge and finish up the groove.
3a Ridge Variation 4c ★★★ Traverse left then climb a steep crack over a slight overlap onto a slab. Move left into a groove which leads to a ledge and easy climbing.
HM Kelly, CF Holland Aug 1919
Ridge Variation M Linnell, AS Piggott 15.05.1932

23 Vandal 80m HVS 5a ★★
A fine route. Steep and better protected in its lower half. Start below the large triangular overhang.
1 25m **4c** Climb the grassy corner to 5m below the triangular roof where a line up the wall on the right leads, with a difficult move, to a small ledge. Take the short curving crack on the right to a good stance.
2 35m **5a** Climb the main crack passing a large overhang on its right to a small overhang at 12m. Move left round this then left to the arête. Climb boldly up the slab above until a traverse right leads to a grassy bay. Go up 6m and move left to a small stance at the foot of a flaky hollow rib: poor belay.
3 20m **4a** Avoid the rib by stepping down to cross the slabs rightwards, then climb through a break in the arête to finish up a chimney. Or, **4b** traverse down leftwards to enter and finish up the groove (*Gomorrah*).
G Oliver, JM Cheesmond, L Willis 13.06.1959

24 Pillar of Salt 85m E2 5c ★★
Clean and rough rock. Start below the triangular overhang.
1 25m **5a** Climb the grassy corner to 5m below the triangular roof where a line up the wall on the right leads, with a difficult move, to a small ledge. Take the thin crack on the left to a stance.
2 30m **5a** Step up then make a rising traverse rightwards along a series of holds on the wall to the arête. Up the arête to a bulge then traverse right along a slim ramp to the foot of a chimney.
3 30m **5c** Pull up the short wall on the left to a ledge then make a series of hard moves up the wall above (micro wire) to get established on a sloping ledge on the arête. Follow the arête to a slab on the left. Reach and mantel onto a huge jug on the arête then continue to another break. Finish up the edge above.
SJH Reid, J Preston Sep 1997

25 Rib and Slab Climb 90m HS ★★★★
One of the best of its grade and an excellent way to the summit of Pillar Rock. Start just above the start of a right-slanting intrusion of pale rock, 2m below a large block embedded in the scree.
1 26m Traverse left along a footledge and keep going to a steep rib with a groove. Climb this to break out left at a small ledge. Climb the slab right of the groove or the rib on its right to a ledge. Bold.
2 20m The groove above is hard to start but soon eases. Climb the steep rib to a stance at the top.
3 20m Traverse right and up, crossing a groove onto a superb rough slab. Climb this, heading rightwards to a rib which is followed to a pile of blocks.
4 24m Follow the crack for 3m then head leftwards via a block. Climb the slab and rib above.
CF Holland, HM Kelly, CG Crawford Jul 1919

26 New West Climb 87m VD ★★★★

A very fine route that provides some great climbing. Start just below a large block lying on the scree, and above an equally big block embedded in the scree, 25m or so down from West Jordan Gully.
1 20m Follow an easy shallow chimney, trending left to a rib which leads to a small corner. A staircase on the right leads to a ledge.
2 10m Climb a wide shallow chimney to a small platform then move 4m left to step down to a ledge.
3 17m Follow the obvious groove to ledges then make an awkward traverse left to the foot of a chimney with a chockstone.
4 20m Climb the imposing chimney to a chockstone at 9m. Head right, round a rib, continue right then up to a pile of blocks.
5 20m Climb the crack and slab to a ledge then the slab on the left.
GD Abraham, AP Abraham, CW Barton, JH Wigner May 1901

27 South-West Climb 65m MVS 4b ★★★★

Delightful climbing on small but positive holds. Start just left of West Jordan Gully
1 35m 4b A short groove leads to a small ledge under a slab with a deep-cut hold. Gain the hold from the left, move awkwardly right then continue up the slab to where it steepens. Pull up on good holds to a small ledge and up the rib on the edge of the gully for 10m to a square ledge.
2 22m 4b Traverse diagonally left for 3m then step up, back right and up the slab, keeping to the right until a steepening. Climb boldly up the slab until just below a short crack. Traverse right under a large block and move up to a flake.
3 8m 4b Step airily out left and pull steeply up the arête to easy ground and the top.
Photo page 314.
P1 HR Pope, WB Brunskill Sep 1911;
P2 CF Holland, RF Stobart, DE Pilley Jul 1919;
P3 HM Kelly, CF Holland, CG Crawford, NE Odell Jul 1919

Steeple Buttress VD (opposite) Emily Brooks & Fiona McCarthy — Stephen Reid

STEEPLE - EAST FACE

OS Grid Ref: NY 158 116
Altitude: 700m

A fine multi-pitch mountain route with a summit finish in one of the most beautiful and remote coves in the Lake District.

Approach, Ennerdale: From the car park at Bowness Knott, follow the forest track, take a right turn over a bridge, then bear left over a footbridge to join a forest track on the other side of the valley. Follow this track past Moss Dub until you reach a stream on the right - Low Beck. Take the path on the east (left) of the stream until a small path leads off diagonally left. Follow this, crossing the upper forest track, until you arrive at the boundary of the forest and another stream - High Beck. A faint path on the west (right) side of High Beck leads into Wind Gap and Mirk Cove.

By bike follow the approach for **Pillar Rock** then keep cycling west along the upper forest track until, just after crossing High Beck, a path will be seen leading up through the trees. Take this, or more pleasant, the firebreak just to the right (2½hrs - 3hrs).

Approach, Wasdale: Park just before Bowderdale. Head north along the valley for about 5km to the ridge between Haycock and Scoat Fell. Head east, across Scoat Fell, then a few hundred metres beyond pick your way carefully down the steep fellside into Mirk Cove. Steeple summit sits at the tip of the ridge to the north of Scoat Fell.

Map page 294.

Bowness Knott
NY 109 154
GPS 54.525599
-3.377036

Bowderdale
NY 160 065
GPS 54.447185
-3.295442

1 Steeple Buttress 180m VD ★★
Remote and unfrequented. This route will always provide a memorable mountain day. Start towards the back of the cove where a clean grey ridge descends from its right-hand side almost to the floor.
1 45m Scramble easily leftwards up broken rocks to a slightly undercut rib. Follow the rib on superb rough rock to a square ledge where the rib widens to a flat wall with a crack in its centre.
2 45m Climb the rib at the left edge of the wall, or the crack, then follow the rib to a recess. Optional belay. Continue up the rib on good holds to a grassy ledge.
3 35m Scramble up the right edge of the buttress to more grass, then move left to the base of a hanging rib leading to the summit.
4 25m Make an awkward step up the left side of the rib then follow the crest, avoiding a large block on its left, or climb straight over it, then scramble up to the foot of two repulsive chimneys.
5 30m Climb the slim V-groove to the left, avoiding the chimneys. Initial tricky moves lead up and airily left to superb holds; easier rock then leads to a fine finish at the summit cairn.
DA Elliott Apr 1957 **Photo opposite.**

RAD Steeple

OS Grid Ref
NY 158 116

BUTTERMERE

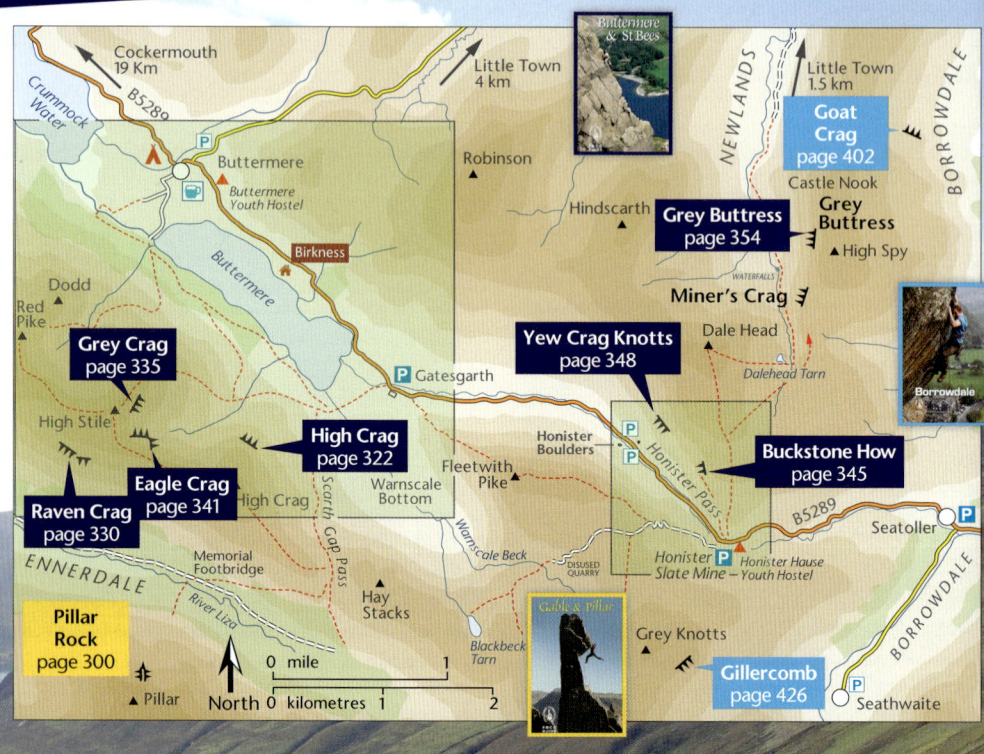

A beautiful valley with its two lakes, Buttermere offers both low-level climbing and high-mountain options. There are some true classics to be discovered here.

Cleopatra, Buckstone How HVS (page 347) Justin Shiels & Chris Shiels — 📷 David Simmonite

HIGH CRAG

OS Grid Ref: NY 182 145
Altitude: 450m

45 mn

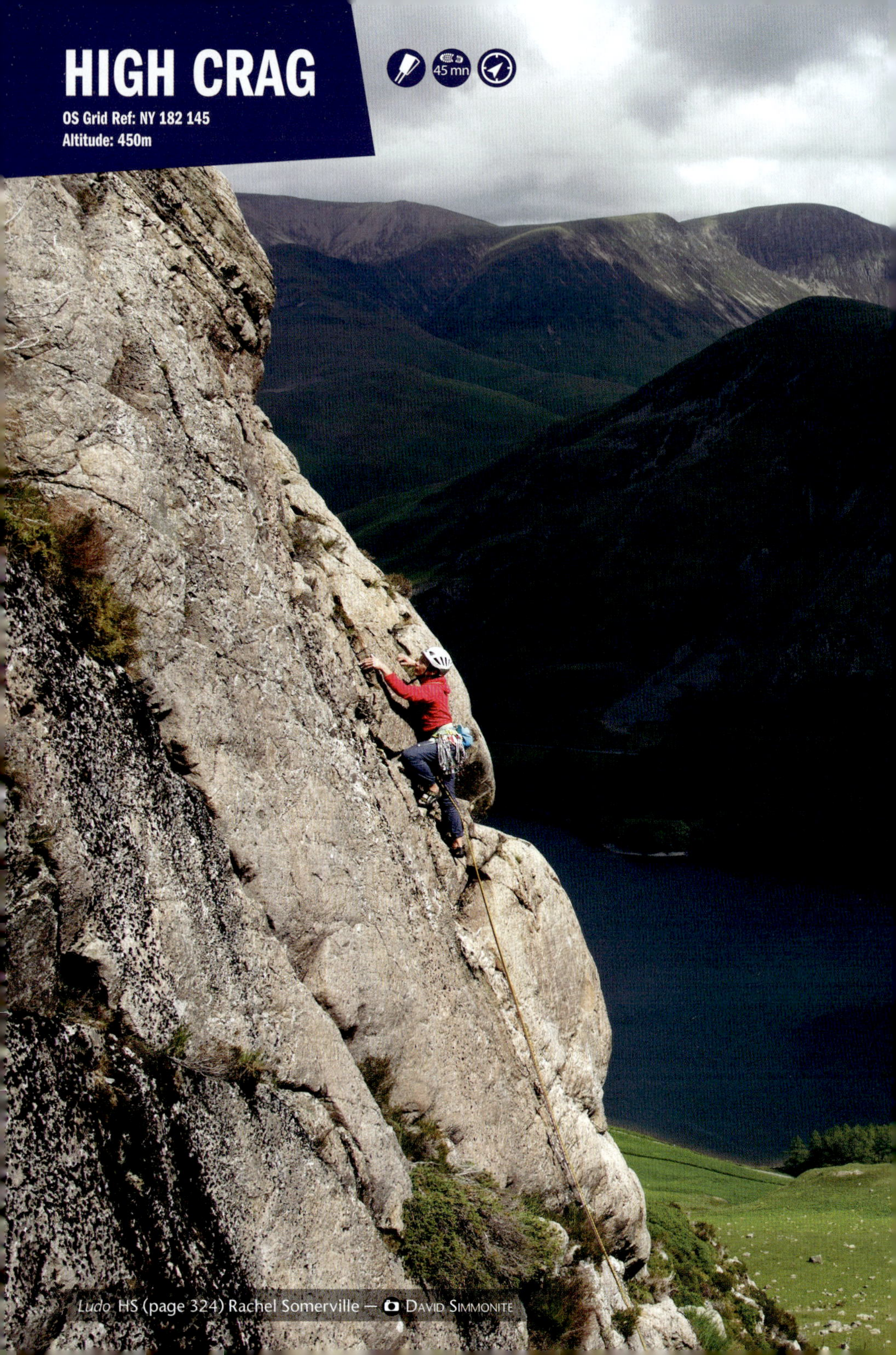

Ludo HS (page 324) Rachel Somerville — DAVID SIMMONITE

A great, surprisingly accessible, crag that gets the morning sun.

Approach: P NY 195 149 From Gatesgarth Farm, follow the path past the top of the lake. Follow the Scarth Gap path up the hill past the trees to a gate, then take the left side of a fence on the right, directly up to the crag.

See overview page 342.

Descent: Abseil.

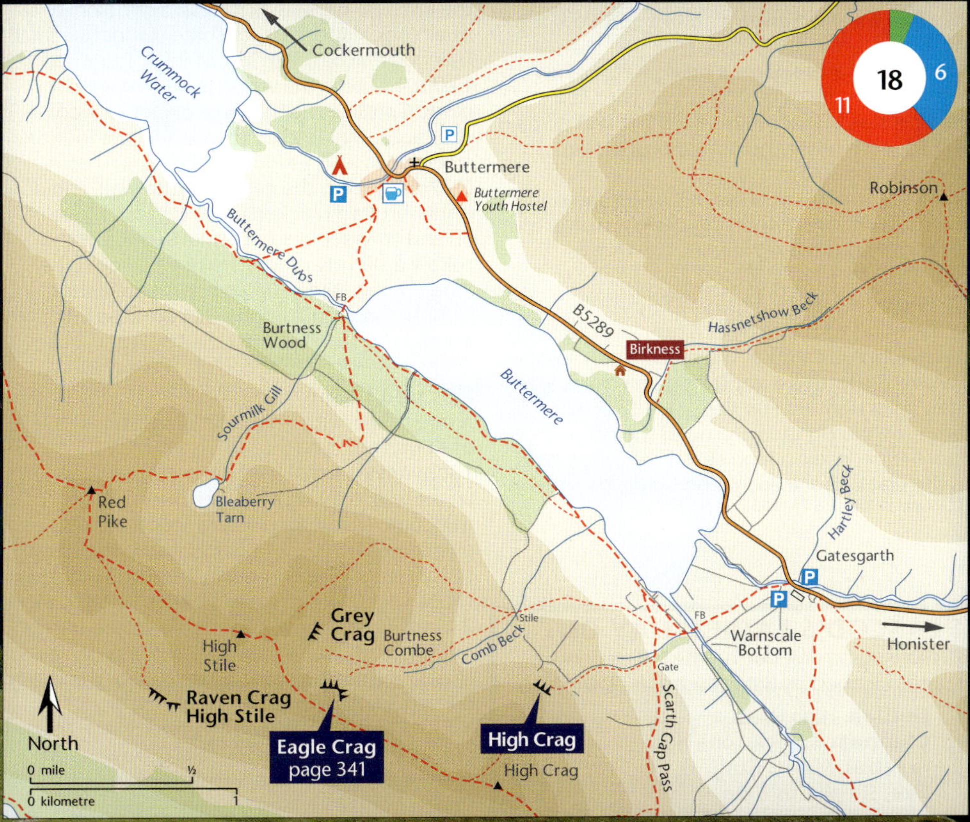

Left-Hand Crag

Several excellent pitches, though some have become very mossy.

Approach: Walk 100m up and left of **Main Buttress**.

Descent: To the rightl.

1 Indecent Obsession 20m E3 6a ★★
Sustained and a good test of technique and footwork. Start 4m right of the corner. Climb the wall to a small overlap. Move left then back right above it to a small ledge. Finish up the thin crack, hard at first.
C Downer, M Scott 24.05.1986

2 Foul Play 20m E1 5b ★★
Absorbing crack climbing on positive holds with abundant gear.
S Swindells, P Read 27.04.1986

3 Red, Raw and Itchy 20m E3 6a ★★
Between the central crack and the right arête is a thin crack. Climb the crack and then the wall direct.
W Williamson, B Shaw 18.06.1992

4 The Executioner's Song 20m E3 6a ★★
The striking arête gives a bold pitch. Follow the arête to the overhang (small wire in a vertical slot.) Hard moves back left and up gain a crack with better holds and protection.
Variation Finish 5c
From the top of the arête, move up and rightwards to the crack splitting the overhang; a few strenuous moves lead to the top.
C Downer, C Bacon 30.05.1986

5 Short Circuit 20m E1 5c ★
Start round to the right at a break in the overhang. Pull through the break then move awkwardly left to a good ledge on the arête. Step back right and up the crack to another ledge. Swing rightwards round the rib to a foot-ledge, make a long reach to a good hold in the crack above and climb boldly to the top.
C Downer, R Royce 8.06.1986

PEASCOD'S LADIES' DAY OUT

A challenging day-out on the ladies-named routes climbed by Bill Peascod in 1950/51.

☐ **Delilah**, High Crag   VS 4c
☐ **Cleopatra**, Buckstone How   HVS 5a
☐ **Jezebel**, Miners Crag   VS 4c
☐ **Eve**, Shepherds Crag   VS 4c

Main Buttress

Here are some of the most enjoyable routes in the valley. Start early to catch the sun; start later to avoid the heat.

Approach: This fine crag is in three sections. Routes on the left-hand face start from the toe beneath a sloping table of rock, perched up on a ledge, Rock Table Ledge. 15m right is the Gearing Up Stone, another flat boulder. The central section, a smooth undercut wall, sits above a large glacis and is reached from the Gearing Up Stone by scrambling. The main face, with its twin caves of the Goblin's Eyes, is bounded on the right by the cleft of Gatesgarth Chimney.

Descent: From the top of **Main Buttress**, descend well to the left (east). This starts as a well-defined path. A short steep corner (easier than it looks from above) gives access to a long clean groove leading back to beneath Rock Table Ledge. Abseil with care down *Dry Trim*.

6 The Three Kings 42m VS 4c ★
Interesting climbing up the first steep wall at the left side of **Main Buttress**. Start from a small rock ledge beneath three distinctive small triangular niches, 15m left of Rock Table Ledge.
1 20m 4a Climb the wall crossing a diagonal crack. Continue via the three niches to reach easy slabs, that lead up then left to the foot of a steep clean wall, just left of the capped corner.
2 22m 4c From the centre of the wall, trend rightwards to cracked blocks (care). Move up and traverse diagonally left to reach and follow a slightly cracked groove to gain the ledge above. Move up and pass the first of two overlaps on its right. Pull up, step left then ascend the steep wall to the top.
C Read, BR Shackleton 6.05.2000

7 Ludo 55m HS ★★
A direct line with good climbing. Start 4m left of Rock Table Ledge.
1 30m A fine pitch. Take a leftward-rising line up the wall, crossing a heather-filled fault, to gain some whitish layers and a scoop. Step left, overcome a bulge moving rightwards, then climb to easy ledges. Belay beneath, and just right of, a capped right-facing corner, and just left of a crack.
2 15m Climb the right edge of the slab, to the right of the corner, via a slim groove. Move up steeply to gain and climb a scoop on small holds then belay on a sloping rock ledge beside a huge block.
3 10m Move up the ledge leftwards for 2m and pull into a shallow bottomless groove in the final tier. Head up rightwards.
Photo page 322.
B Masson, P Gomersall 10.06.1984

8 Artefact 67m MVS 4b ★★
A popular route reached by scrambling up from the left. Start on Rock Table Ledge
1 24m 4a Climb the corner crack at the back of the ledge, step up right and exit by a grass mantelshelf. Continue to the large sloping ledge below a crack.
2 16m Follow an easy slabby ramp diagonally left to a ledge below an overhung corner.
3 27m 4b Climb the corner capped by an overhang. Turn this on the right and climb an easier groove to a sloping rock ledge below an undercut crack. Climb the crack to easier rocks.
NJ Soper, JA Austin, S MacLean, BL Griffiths 19.06.1965

9 Dry Trim 33m E1 5b ★★
Very good climbing. Start just right of the corner crack. Climb to a thin crack and then the wall.
S Howe, R Cassidy 21.07.1984

10 Samson 33m HVS 5b ★★★
A fine pitch up the centre of the smooth central wall. Start by the corner crack. Make an ascending traverse right, just above the overhang to the crack in the centre of the wall. Climb the crack which fortunately eases.
Photo opposite.
L Kendall, A Clarkson 21.05.1963

11 Close Shave 33m E1 5b ★★
A steep climb squeezed between the other lines. Start under the overhang, directly beneath the crack of *Samson*. A difficult pull left through the overhang (easier than it looks) gains the foot of the crack. Right to a thin crack then make tricky moves rightwards to the arête. Move back left and climb the wall to step right onto a small ledge. Climb the thin left slanting crack on the left then follow further cracks though the bulges.
SJH Reid, SR Stout 15.06.1999

12 The Philistine 35m E1 5b ★★★★
A great climb up the blunt arête. Protection is only good when it is most needed. Start below the large overhang, 3m left of the arête. Climb to the overhang and traverse right to a big foothold on the arête. Climb the crack to a poor resting place, then step delicately down and left to gain the left side of the rib. Finish up the arête in a superb situation.
Photo front cover.
E Cleasby, TW Birkett 23.06.1975

13 Lost Colonies Direct 46m E3 6a ★★
Excellent climbing starting 4m right of the blunt arête. Move delicately right (gear in a shallow corner). Traverse left and up (thread), move right and climb the superb crack and capped groove to finish up the fine wall and easy slabs.

14 Psycho 50m E1 5b ★★
Technical climbing with a hard pull out of the final groove. Start beneath the left-hand cave.
1 15m 4c Gain the top of the detached flake and climb cracks above to the left-hand cave.
2 35m 5b Move left from the cave and climb a difficult shallow groove (thread). Move up and left with difficulty to gain a V-groove. Climb this and easier rock.
L Brown, JS Bradshaw 12.09.1964

15 High Crag Buttress 55m HVS 5a ★★
Fine climbing taking a direct line up the main face passing between the caves. A magnificent single pitch climb; 60m ropes. Start beneath the right-hand cave.
1 15m 4c A short corner on the right leads to a grass ledge then an awkward wall gives access to the two caves; belay in the left cave.
2 15m 4c Pass the overhangs using the rib between the caves and continue up the chimney-crack above to a small square cave.
3 25m 5a Climb the rib on the right of the cave (thread), make a delicate diagonal traverse right to a slab and ascend easy grooves to a grassy shoulder at the top.
JJS Allison, L Kendall 23.09.1962

16 Nebuchadnezzar's Dream 54m E1 5b ★★
Another good route following the thin crack between *High Crag Buttress* and *Gethsemane*. Start beneath the right-hand cave.
1 18m 5a Climb to the cave and exit rightwards onto ledges. Belay down and right.
2 36m 5b Climb the thin crack to where the angle eases. Step right to a groove and climb it over an overhang to easy ground.
J Lamb, M Hetherington, A Dunhill 10.07.1979

17 Gethsemane 47m E1 5b ★★★
The prominent crack in the centre of the right-hand wall gives an excellent climb. Start at the right side of the wall.
1 9m A wall to a grass ledge; move left to belay.
2 38m 5b Take the main crack to a resting place below an overhang. Pull onto a hanging block in the overhang then swing left to a groove that leads to the top.
JA Gosling, JA Brooder 9.05.1970

18 Delilah 50m VS 4c ★★★
Sustained and delectable climbing, the upper section takes the fine groove. Start at the right side of the wall.
1 18m 4a Move left onto the grass ledge then gain a narrow rock foot-ledge just above. Traverse this back right to an excellent crack that is climbed to a stance in the chimney.
2 32m 4c Ascend leftwards into the groove and climb this exiting right.
W Peascod, B Blake 10.08.1951

Samson HVS (opposite) Andy McVittie — David Simmonite

Main Buttress | **High Crag** | 329

#	Route	Grade	Stars
12	The Philistine	E1 5b	★★★★
13	Lost Colonies Direct	E3 6a	★★
14	Psycho	E1 5b	★★
15	High Crag Buttress	HVS 5a	★★
16	Nebuchadnezzar's Dream	E1 5b	★★
17	Gethsemane	E1 5b	★★★
18	Delilah	VS 4c	★★★

RAVEN CRAG HIGH STILE

OS Grid Ref: NY 164 144
Altitude: 610m

The rough solid rock and sunny aspect overlooking Ennerdale below the summit of High Stile make the routes here well worth the effort of the walk from Buttermere.

Approach: From Buttermere, follow the well-constructed path up Red Pike then descend the other side of the ridge in the direction of **Pillar Rock**, seen across the valley.

Spearhead Buttress

The largest and steepest buttress.

Descent: Descend to the right and down scree beside the buttress.

❶ Daddy Short Legs   33m   E1 5b   ★★
Delightful. Climb the arête, 4m left of *Butterfly Crack*, to a smooth section at 13m. Step left then, using the edge, up on small holds for 4m, to improving holds on the arête. Move up and left to a large foothold then back right to finish up the arête.

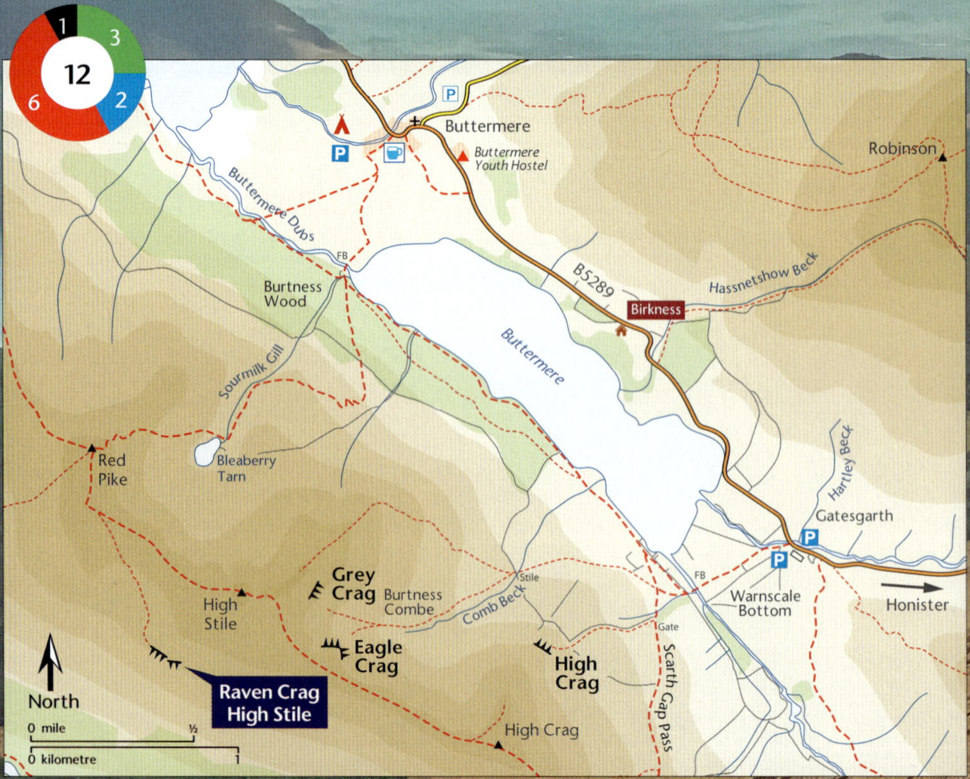

Painted Lady E3 (page 332) Rachel Somerville — 📷 Laetitia Sterling

② Butterfly Crack 33m S ★

Direct and steep, up the centre of the buttress. Start below the crack. Gain the crack by awkward moves slightly to the right, then climb it on good holds to a poised block. Work carefully past it and climb the crack at its narrowest part until it deepens into an easier final chimney.
J Carswell, A Barton 8.09.1935

③ Painted Lady 33m E3 5c ★★

Exposed and exhilarating climbing taking an intricate line of least resistance. Start in a recess beneath a bulge, 3m left of the right-hand edge and above an embedded flake. Pull over the bulge to holds on the right, move left then up passing a perched flake on the left. Step onto the flake and ascend the left side of the wall, continuing up steepening rock, to outflank the first band of overhangs (dubious hold). Pull up to beneath the second band of overhangs and traverse right (peg above). Climb the wall and move up the corner (peg). Continue to the third overhang, pull over to finish up a hanging groove.
Photo page 331.
B McGowan, G Wilks 13.09.2003

④ Alpine Ringlet 30m E4 5c ★★

Excellent steep and bold climbing taking the right edge of the arête and the impressive crack. Start a metre or so above the right edge of the front face, beneath a shallow groove. Climb the groove easily until it steepens. Up on the right is an obvious handhold (skyhook). Make a long reach for big flat holds on the left (peg). Step left around the arête (peg) then up and make a difficult step right for a small flat spike. Gain a jug on the arête, pull up and make a long reach for a block hold. Climb the crack until a ledge is reached on the left. Balance to the arête and a finely positioned move to the top.
E Rogers, K Forsythe 16.07.2006

⑤ Apatura 30m E3 5c ★★

Start up the large corner (*The Emperor*). Once over the first bulge, move left on flat holds then steeply up the right side of the arête to a flake at the base of the right slanting crack of *Alpine Ringlet*. Climb the arête direct to finish.
T Millen, D Armstrong 9.08.2020

⑥ The Emperor 33m E1 5b ★★

Sustained well-protected climbing up the fine bulging groove on the right flank of the main buttress. Start 4m above the right edge of the front face, beneath the prominent wide crack. Climb initial rocks below the crack then step left off blocks to climb the wall via the steep narrow ramp. Overcome the first bulge and continue up a second steep ramp. Pull over the second bulge to gain a long wedged block in the groove above. Continue more easily to the final overlap, climb the crack above this, then continue up the groove through the notch at the top.
C Read, SW Pollington 12.06.2005

Spearhead Buttress | **Raven Crag High Stile** | 333

7 Family Plot 35m HS 4a
A difficult first pitch leads to easier climbing. Start 4m above the right edge of the front face, beneath a prominent wide crack.
1 10m 4a Climb the crack then make a short traverse right to a corner; small stance with chockstone.

★ **2** 25m Climb the wall and pull up into the looming well-cloven groove which widens into a chimney. Pull over blocks with care and continue up the wall on the left.
DN Greenop, CJ Crowther 1.05.1965

Eighty Foot Slab Buttress

About 30m vertically lower and to the right of a small subsidiary buttress, is a fine sweep of slabby rock.

Descent: Descend to the left, down scree beside **Spearhead Buttress**.

8 Outside Edge 25m VD ★

Start immediately right of an overhang at the left side of the face. Climb steeply and awkwardly over a bulge to a slab, pull out left, and traverse up left to the edge of the buttress then follow this to a small ledge on the west face (possible belay). Climb a short scoop and continue rightwards.
IM Banner Mendus, J Carswell, A Barton 29.09.1935

9 Zig Zag 30m VS 4c

Use the *Outside Edge* entry to reach the foot of a right-facing corner. Climb the corner to a short traverse left to ledges and the top.
J Carswell, A Barton 8.09.1935

10 Crazy Diamond 25m E1 5a ★★

Excellent climbing up the centre of the face. Start 2m right of the low overhang on the left at some blocks. Step off the blocks and climb directly for about 12m to a large hold on the left. Move up and diagonally to the right then continue up the steepening wall, moving slightly leftwards to easier rocks.
C Read, P Fleming 27.09.2003

11 Shine On 25m E2 5b ★

Thin bold escapable climbing up the right edge of the face.
A Phizacklea 24.09.2005

12 Kona Nu Nu 27m VS 4c ★

Good climbing up the conspicuous crack on the right side of the main slab. Start beneath the thin crack. Climb the crack which runs up the left side of a subsidiary slab to reach a glacis beneath an impending groove. Pull up and follow the crack above until it ends. Continue more easily up the walls above to the top.
C Read, NF Tonkin, GL Swainbank 12.10.2003

GREY CRAG

OS Grid Ref: NY 171 148
Altitude: 700m

A series of short buttresses arranged in tiers that allow many natural link-ups. The quick-drying rock is very clean and incredibly rough, all sitting in a magnificent position at the top of the combe.

Approach: From Gatesgarth Farm, follow the track across the head of the lake. Head uphill. Where the path kinks left continue in the direction of travel, following a faint path that slowly rises across the hillside beneath the craggy ground above. Once the far end of this is reached, the path heads more steeply uphill, eventually reaching and crossing a stile. Then take an indistinct path along the line of the beck, heading up and right across scree slopes to the foot of the crag.

See overview page 342.

Harrow Buttress

The lowest buttress and the usual point of arrival.

Descent: Descend to the right. Head left to reach routes on **Mitre Buttress**. For **Chockstone Buttress**, scramble up rocks above to a saddle, then descend rightwards.

1 Harrow Buttress   45m   D   ★★
A good climb with a steep start, just left of the toe of the buttress.
1 10m Climb the corner, or the arête on its right, to a roomy ledge.
2 15m Climb the chimney then traverse 3m left and move up to a ledge below a broken groove.
3 20m Climb the groove then scramble to an overhung corner. Pull up left and climb to the top of the buttress.
W Bishop, WA Woodsend 1912

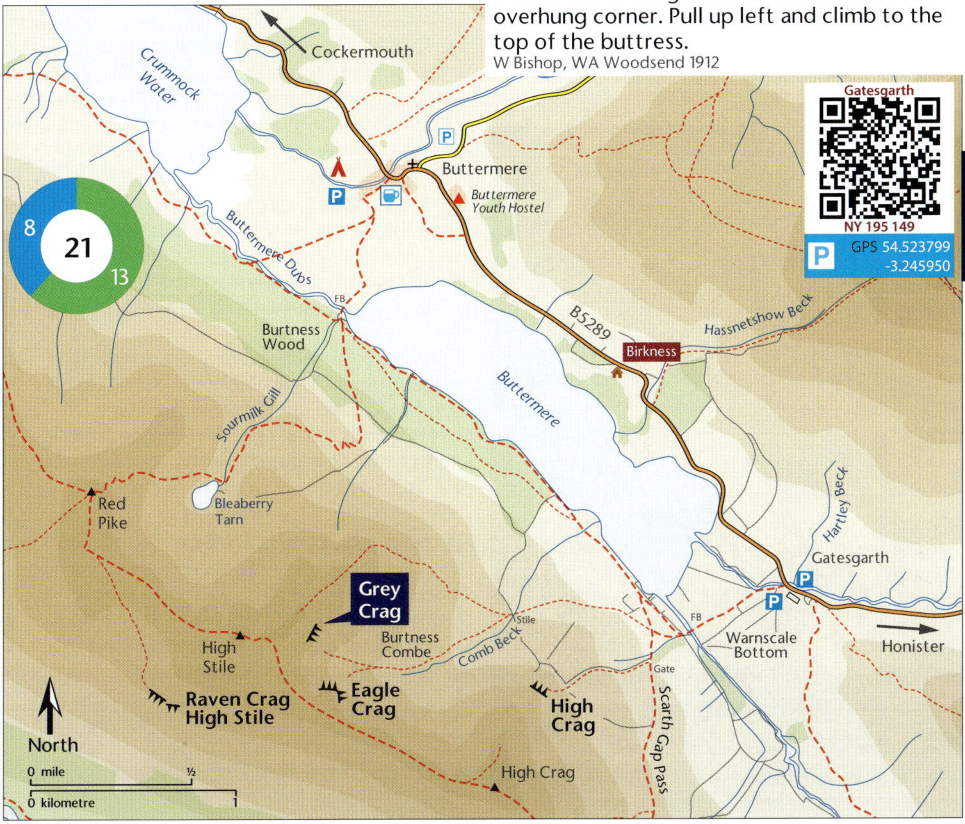

② Spider Wall 40m VS 4c ★★

An ingenious way up with one strenuous pitch and the other delicate with poor protection.
1 8m Climb the steep vegetated groove 4m right of the toe of the buttress to a ledge below an overhanging crack.
2 19m 4c Climb the crack and gain a hold out on the right wall. Move right and up, then cross back left to a platform. Climb a shallow groove on the right.
3 13m 4b Traverse the steep wall diagonally right to a small bracket in the middle; continue to the top.
W Peascod, GG Macphee 5.08.1945

③ Harrow Wall 46m VD ★★

Steeper and more continuous than *Harrow Buttress* following a zigzag line up the face. Start near the right-hand side.
1 18m Climb the flat rib beside a left-facing corner to the right end of a narrow sloping ledge that runs across the face.
2 8m Traverse left across the ledge over a block to a small ledge below a groove.
3 20m Climb the groove and move right up easier-angled rock.
W Peascod, A Barton 13.09.1942

Mitre Buttress

The left-hand buttress of the lower crag.
Descent: Descend down the badly eroded scree-chute to the left, or continue up to below the upper tier of **Oxford and Cambridge Buttress**. The gully immediately to the right is not recommended.

④ Mitre Arête 35m MVS 4b ★

A well-shaped climb; steep and serious. Start well up the scree.
1 20m 4a Climb the arête over several bulges to a small ledge below a steep wall.
2 15m 4b Step left onto the exposed wall and climb a ladder of ledges.
J Greaves, F Poulter 22.04.1946

⑤ Mitre Mouse 37m HS

A disjointed climb with a good second pitch. Start above the scree where a pinnacle rests against the face on the left side of the broken ground beneath the overhang.
1 25m Step left and climb the pinnacle to a triangular roof. Move left and move daintily (without protection) up to the pinnacle top. A short wall on the left and easy blocky ground leads to the foot of a chimney.
2 12m A steep jug-infested pitch. Climb the crack right of the chimney. Continue up a slight groove and pull up into a wider crack; go up this to easier ground. Finish by scrambling.
BJ Clarke 23.06.2005

⑥ Mitre Buttress Ordinary 64m M ★

The easiest line up the wall. Start where a pinnacle rests against the face at the left side of the broken ground beneath the overhang.
1 20m Climb easily to a cave with a pointed roof.
2 8m Traverse left and slightly down to a ledge, then move left to its end. Pull up on good holds and climb to block belays.
3 14m Climb a wall to a grass ledge, step left along the ledge and climb the steep chimney.
4 22m Climb the easy ridge to the top.
CA Elliott and party 1912

⑦ Mitre Buttress Direct 80m MS ★★

A varied route climbing the buttress from the lowest point.
1 13m Climb the wall leftwards to a ledge.
2 15m Climb a short wall then walk right to the steep east face of the buttress.
3 15m Climb the wall on its left side then mantelshelf onto a narrow ledge on the right and follow it left to the edge of the buttress.
4 22m Climb the steep exposed wall above to a ledge. Alternatively, climb the scoop on the

① Harrow Buttress D ★★

left to a cave then move right to the steep wall. Another short wall leads to a ledge and belays.
5 15m Traverse left to a steep chimney and a fine finish.
AC Pigou and party 4.07.1915

8 **Ribbon Wall**   46m   MVS 4b   ★★
Pleasant wall climbing reached by scrambling to a ledge.
1 25m 4b Climb blocky flakes on the left to a thin horizontal flake and pull up right then work up and left to a small protruding flake. Move up to a shallow corner which leads to the arête.
2 21m Step right and climb the cracked face to the crest of the rib. Continue up easy ground to jumbled blocks.
A Phizacklea, JL Holden 6.05.2006

9 **Rib and Wall**   96m   D   ★
Good varied climbing and the logical continuation to *Harrow Buttress*. Start at the foot of a rib in the gully between **Mitre Buttress** and **Harrow Buttress**.
1 25m Climb the right face of the steep rib to a grass nook and continue up to a large block.
2 7m Climb the block on its right and cross its top to the main wall.
3 15m Climb the mass of shattered rock, trending right to beneath a V-groove.
4 12m Move up the groove a few metres then pull right round the corner to a narrow ledge. Cross the wall to a cave formed by a big detached block.
5 12m Climb the wall right of the block then move right to gain and climb a short steep crack to a ledge.
6 25m Finish rightwards on easy-angled slabs.
W Peascod, GG Macphee 5.08.1945

10 **Sol**   36m   VS 4c   ★
Delicate fingery climbing leads to vigorous jamming. Start from near the saddle, beneath the blunt rib of a huge boulder, above which stands a prominent left-facing corner.
1 25m 4a Step off a block under the right side of the left face and climb the right edge on superb crinkly rock to the slab, then up to the top of the boulder. Continue up an easy slabby rib to a ledge beneath the prominent left-facing corner.
2 11m 4c Climb the superb corner.
C Read, SW Pollington 17.06.2006

Chockstone Buttress
The middle tier comprises The Slabs, which rise from the gully on the left and **Grey Wall**, the fine central section.

Approach: Ascend rightwards from the foot of **Harrow Buttress**, or by scrambling up from the top of the **Harrow Buttress** routes.

Descent: The gully immediately left of the slabs area is not recommended. To regain the foot of **Chockstone Buttress** and Grey Wall, traverse well to the right to reach an easy open scree gully. Descend (careful not to go too low) and traverse back close beneath the crag; or, continue down the scree to reach the foot of **Harrow Buttress**. To regain the foot of **Mitre Buttress**, traverse left over a saddle above that buttress and go down the badly eroded scree gully.

11 **Slabs West Route**   55m   HS   ★★★
A fine open climb. Start up the gully 9m below a small grassy bay.
1 32m Ascend a thin crack in the slab for 5m. Where it steepens climb the wall to the left then, where the crack ends, move up right to a ledge. Move left and slant up leftwards then straight up the slab to a ledge below a pile of blocks beneath an overhang which forms a jutting nose.
2 23m Climb left of the overhang into a shallow niche. Step out and right above the nose, make a few moves up and step left, to finish straight up the slabby wall.
W Peascod, A Barton 13.09.1942

12 **Slabs Ordinary Route**   61m   VD   ★★★
Intense varied climbing with an easy unprotected section on P2 that requires composure.
1 18m Make an ascending traverse to blocks. Climb the blocks to the left side of a large sloping ledge; belay at its right-hand end.
2 23m From the left-hand end of the sloping ledge climb easy-angled rock to a crack. Follow this, and the clean slab above, to the foot of a wide right-facing corner.
3 20m Climb the corner on excellent holds.
H Bishop, WA Woodsend 11.08.1913

13 **Return with a Vengeance**   69m   MVS 4b   ★
A particularly fine top pitch. Start at the lowest point at the right-hand toe of the slabs.
1 25m 4a Climb easily to a sloping grass ledge at 3m. Climb a thin crack on the right of the arête past the bulge. Step left onto the crest which is followed to the right side of a large

sloping ledge.
2 20m Climb the ramp on the right to the leftward-trending crack, follow the crack to a ledge. Trend right up slabs to a stance at the foot of a right-facing corner.
3 24m 4b Traverse 4m right to the edge of the buttress and climb as close to the arête as possible, with steep moves at mid-height (crux); protection is available only where most needed.
WF Hurford, CB Fitzhugh 21.08.2000

14 Chockstone Ridge 67m M ★
The stepped ridge beyond the gully right of the slabs. Start from a ledge a few metres up on the left side. Climb the crest and its easy-angled continuation, passing a *gendarme* at 30m to climb a steep chimney near the top.
JH Clapham and party Apr 1914

Grey Wall
The next routes are on **Grey Wall**, the fine wall 30m horizontally to the right.

15 Suaviter 48m S ★★
A delightfully exposed second pitch. Start at a bollard in a shallow corner, beneath the left end of a long ledge.
1 10m Climb the corner, move right then up to the long ledge.
2 16m Step down from the left end of the ledge, traverse delicately left to a crack with a protruding block. Climb the crack to a ledge, across doubtful blocks, to reach a roomy ledge on the left.
3 22m Climb the ridge above to an area of ledges and blocks then a groove with a wide crack at its back to the top.
W Peascod, SB Beck 12.07.1941

16 Grey Wall 45m VS 4c ★★
Steep and direct, through the niche at half-height.
1 9m 4a Climb the crack to the long ledge.
2 28m 4c From the left end of the ledge climb the crack in the shallow corner, step left onto the wall and follow cracks. Step right and

up into a niche. Move up and pull out right then ascend twin cracks to a small ledge. The corner-crack on the left leads to a large ledge with block belays.
3 8m Move right and follow an easy rib.
J Adams, C Read 19.02.1972

17 Fortiter 42m MVS 4b ★★★
Clean and direct, this climbs the prominent crack right of centre.
1 8m Climb a crack and blocks to the right end of the long ledge.
2 24m 4b Move up to the small ledge on the right, step left into the crack and follow it to an overhang. Pull over this (crux) and move right to a further crack. Climb it to a narrow ledge below a flake in a corner.
3 10m Climb the crack in the corner to a ledge; finish up an arête.
W Peascod, SB Beck 12.07.1941

GREY CRAG LINK-UPS
Grey Crag offers brilliant opportunities to link climbs. Some of the best are:
- ☐ **Mitre Buttress Direct** & **Oxford and Cambridge Direct Route** — MS
- ☐ **Fortiter** & **Dexter Wall** — VS
- ☐ **Harrow Buttress, Chockstone Ridge** & **Oxford and Cambridge Direct Route** — MS

Oxford and Cambridge Buttress

The upper compact buttress of excellent rock is a superb venue.

Descent: The gully to the left of the buttress is easy but heavily eroded. Alternatively, traverse above the crags to the extreme right-hand end (north), where easy ground leads down and back in.

⓲ Oxbridge Entrance 40m S ★★
Good clean climbing in the upper half. Start in the centre of the face. Climb a grassy cracked rib to a shallow right-facing groove then up grassy slabs to beneath a bulging crack (possible belay). Move up to the crack, traverse left along a thin crack in the slab to its left then go up to a ledge. Climb rightwards up the wall to the right-hand and most pronounced finishing crack.
Photo below.
SJH Reid, JE Reid 23.06.1999

⓳ Oxford and Cambridge Ordinary Route 42m D ★★
Start just left of the arête which forms the corner between the left and right faces of the buttress.
1 15m Climb stepped rocks to a good ledge.
2 10m Traverse left into the corner and climb the difficult overhang on good holds. Belay immediately above.
3 17m Climb the corner to the top. Alternatively, step up left to climb the arête.
HV Reade or possibly earlier by AC Pigou and friends. Sep 1914

⓴ Oxford and Cambridge Direct Route 42m MS ★★★★
A classic and exposed line on immaculate rock up the main arête of the buttress. Start at the junction of the left and right-hand faces.
1 15m Climb the arête, first on the right, then on the left, before pulling steeply onto the crest and following it to a ledge.
2 27m Move up left to a short bulging crack; climb it and move back right to a ledge. Follow the right edge over another bulge and the top.
HV Reade Sep 1914

㉑ Dexter Wall 42m VS 5a ★★★ 💎
A great single-pitch route. Well-protected and at the 'hard' end of **VS**. Start 5m right of the arête. Climb a crack to a V-niche beneath and just left of an overhang. Step right below the overhang and climb a crack for a few metres to a narrow ledge. Traverse right, climb a slim corner then move right again to a small ledge; or move down right to another ledge beside a large leaning flake. Optional belay, 4a to here. The thin vertical crack provides a testing finish.
W Peascod, SB Beck 16.03.1941

Oxbridge Entrance S (above) Steve Scott — 📷 Keith Sanders

EAGLE CRAG
OS Grid Ref: NY 172 145
Altitude: 600m

Eagle Front VS (page 344) Steve Scott & Nick Wharton — Keith Sanders

EAGLE CRAG

Home to the classic *Eagle Front* and a number of other cracking routes, this big imposing crag dominates the head of Birkness Combe. Its northerly aspect and elevation means that it needs a long dry spell before it is truly in condition. Some of the routes can be quite mossy, retaining moisture, although *Eagle Front* remains clean thanks to greater traffic.

Approach: From Gatesgarth Farm, follow the track west across the head of the lake. Head uphill. Where the path kinks left continue in the direction of travel, following a faint path that slowly rises across the hillside beneath crags. Once the far end of this is reached, the path heads more steeply uphill, eventually reaching and crossing a stile then take an indistinct path along the line of the beck, heading for the crag which is in front of you at the head of the combe.

See map page 323.

Descent: Gain some more height before heading, with care, down the steep open rocky gully on the right.

RAD Eagle Crag
Gatesgarth GPS 54.523799 -3.245950 NY 195 149
OS Grid Ref NY 172 145

1 Fifth Avenue/ Central Chimney 150m VS 4c ★★

This traditional combination has a long and sustained delicate pitch with adequate protection which links with the impressive upper pitches of *Central Chimney*. Unfortunately, in part overgrown and sometimes dank, in which case a really good alternative is to finish up *Carnival* from P4 **HVS**, or *Eagle Front* from P5 **VS**. Either way is worth the stars.

1 30m Climb steep grassy cracks and corners to the right-hand side of an alcove.
2 42m 4c Move left and make a difficult move up the wall. Trend rightwards to an open groove with delectable climbing leading to the Terrace.
3 16m 4b Traverse left into *Central Chimney*.
4 27m 4c Climb the intimidating cleft.
5 25m 4c Another steep chimney.
6 10m 4a Move easily to the top.

W Peascod, SB Beck, FJ Monkhouse 27.07.1940

High Crag Fell (744m)

High Stile (806m)

Grey Crag page 335

Eagle Crag page 341

High Crag page 322

From Gatesgarth

From Buttermere

Buttermere — Colin Read

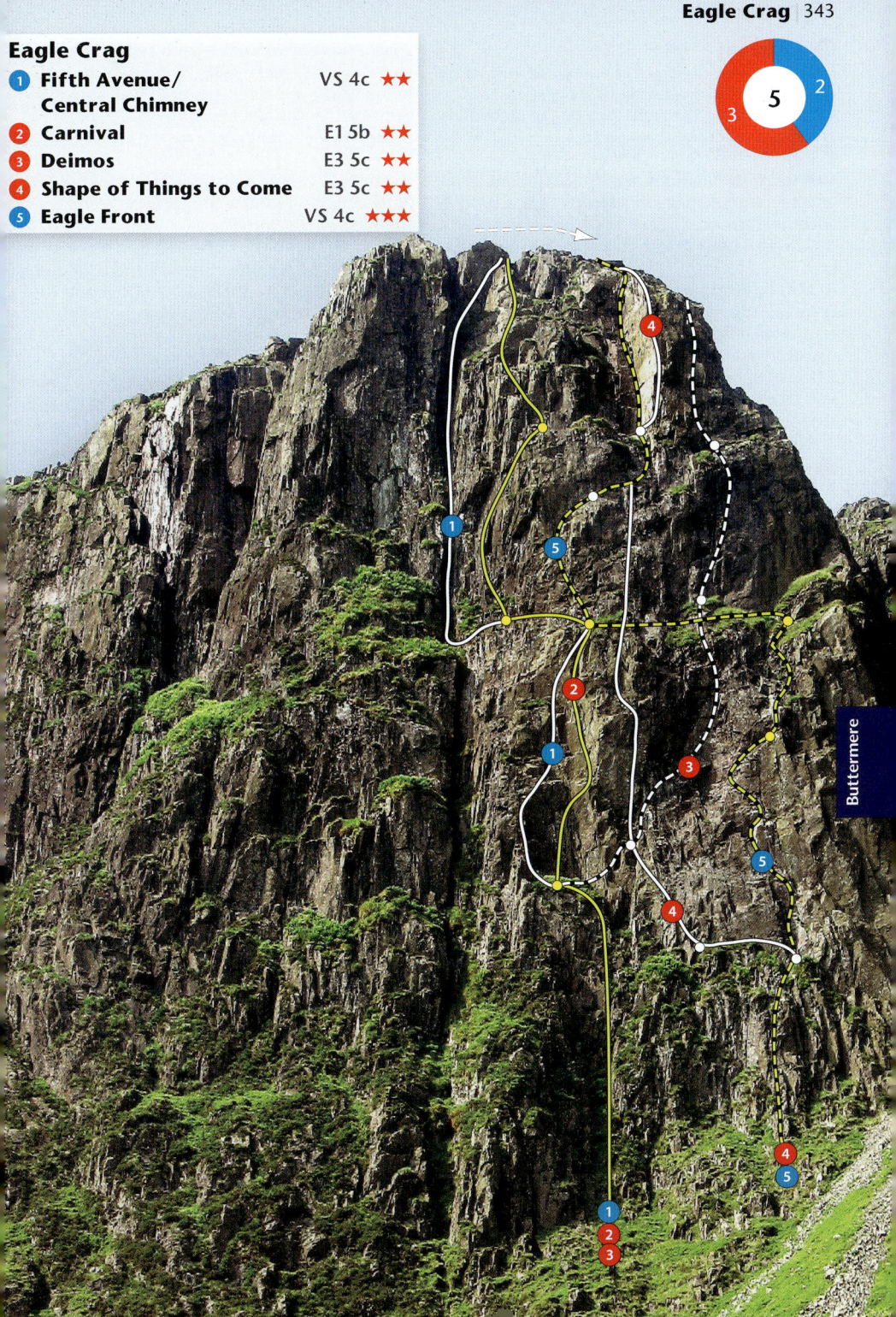

② **Carnival** 139m E1 5b ★★
Relatively fast drying, this enjoyable and varied route is at the lower limit of its grade.
1 30m Climb to the right side of the alcove via steep grassy cracks and corners.
2 35m 5b The steep crack at the back leads to a ledge. Move right across a little slab to another steep crack which leads to a V-groove and the Terrace.
3 12m 4b Traverse left to a stance in a grassy bay.
4 27m 5a A spooky pitch. Climb the shallow grooves above on the left and then move right to a small ledge. Move up and traverse right to a groove and belay on a ledge above.
5 35m 4b Follow the cracked rib and move left to climb the arête left of the grassy trench.
I Roper, JA Austin, NJ Soper 17.07.1965

③ **Deimos** 134m E3 5c ★★
A sustained expedition; solid climbing all the way from the alcove to the top.
1 40m 4c Climb to the right side of the alcove via steep grassy cracks and corners. Go round to the right and up a shallow groove to a small ledge.
2 36m 5c Climb into the corner below the overhangs slanting away to the right. A few delicate moves up the slab gain a line of undercuts and layaways; follow these rightwards with some difficulty to below a bulging groove with an excellent jug on its smooth left wall. Make a long hard move off the jug followed by further precarious moves to reach the terrace.
3 25m 5b Up on the right is a rightward-slanting groove. Enter this from the left and climb it to a ledge on the right. Climb the steep wall above on good holds to a good ledge.
4 33m 5b The bulging crack and groove above lead, without loss of interest, to the top.
J Adams, C Read 21.10.1972

④ **Shape of Things to Come** 115m E3 5c ★★
An excellent way up the crag, with some hard sections. It finishes in a great position on the superb arête right of *Eagle Front*. Start at a blunt spike below a rib.
1 30m 5a Climb the easy rib to the terrace then traverse left for 6m to a knobbly ramp which leads left. Climb a groove above and step left to a ledge.
2 30m 5c Make difficult moves to get established in the groove. Take a deep breath then launch yourself up the very steep groove with the confidence that the holds must improve soon - surely! Eventually, with some relief, a large spike is reached. Move left to a sloping ledge (peg) and climb the bold wall above and right to the Terrace.
3 25m 5a Climb onto a large detached flake on the right and up the bubbly groove above to a scoop. Continue delicately to a traverse line (*Eagle Front*) and follow it rightwards and up to the foot of the corner.
4 30m 5b Climb the right wall to a niche in the arête. Move back onto the wall and delicately balance out onto a small ledge above the overhang. Climb the arête, using both sides as seems most appropriate.
SJH Reid, TW Birkett 10.09.1986

⑤ **Eagle Front** 150m VS 4c ★★★
A fine outing taking the line of least resistance up the front of the buttress. It strings together a succession of excellent pitches on good rock which is cleaner than most parts of the crag thanks to the more frequent traffic. Start up a slight but obvious rib which protrudes from the foot of the face, about 20m left of the right-hand edge of this face.
1 18m Climb the rib then traverse right to a nook.
2 28m 4c Climb into the steep groove, move right to gain a ramp sloping back to the left and follow this to the 'Difficult Bit' up a steep shallow corner. Move up awkwardly to reach a small ledge, swing up right to a higher ledge then traverse back left across a sweep of tricky slabs. Flake handholds lead to a ledge up on the right.
3 20m 4c Pull up into the shallow groove above, step right around a rib to a grass ledge and ascend easily to the Terrace and a block thread belay.
4 22m The Long Green Traverse (The Terrace). Go horizontally left, crossing a mossy slab at 15m, to reach a prominent grass ledge on the skyline. Move up left to a small rock ledge.
5 14m 4c Climb the steep wall, trending slightly left, before stepping back right across a delicate slab into a groove. Climb this to Nail Ledge.
6 20m 4b Traverse right, crossing exposed ribs to the waterworn slab. Ascend the corner to a large stance below the fine corner-crack.
7 28m 4b Climb the crack, finally stepping right to a belvedere; top out by scrambling.
Photo page 341.
W Peascod, SB Beck 23.06.1940

BUCKSTONE HOW

OS Grid Ref: NY 222 142
Altitude: 400m

A very accessible crag; steep and exposed. Routes can feel challenging yet are comfortably sound and provide memorable experiences.

Approach: From the top of Honister Pass, take the old quarry track crossing unstable slate spoil and follow a descending path to the right end of the crag.

Descent: To the right on loose spoil. Take care!

❶ Catalyst 80m E2 5b ★
A sustained climb. Start up a shallow groove just right of an arête and 12m left of the large block.
1 20m 5a Climb a vague corner to a ledge at 8m, move right onto the wall and climb to an overhang. Cross the slab on the left and pull up over blocks to a ledge.
2 25m 5b Climb the recessed wall to a detached flake. Step up left into an easier groove and climb it to a spiky arête. Traverse left on bilberry ledges and move up to a tree.
3 35m 5b Go left round the corner to an embedded flake and step off it onto the wall. Move right over a bulge to climb an overhanging groove (peg), exit onto the left arête. Climb the steep grooves above trending right to the top.
C Read, J Adams 6.05.1972

❷ Sinister Grooves 80m VS 4c ★★★
A brilliant climb of unforgettable character; a benchmark at the top of the grade. Start beneath an open groove 10m left of the large block.
1 25m 4a Climb the groove, beside a heathery central crack, then move up through a more defined groove to step right to a stance below a deep V-groove.
2 25m 4c Climb the enigmatic groove to its top. Step right and go up round the arête. Climb a tapering slab until it is possible to traverse 4m left round a rib and go up into the bay below a long crack.
3 30m 4c Climb the crack (hard to start) and then the chimney.
W Peascod, SB Beck 31.03.1946

❸ Honister Wall 95m HS ★★
A fine series of typical **Buckstone How** pitches! Start just right of the large block.
1 20m Climb the wall to a stance below overhangs.
2 13m Traverse left and climb a steep arête to a niche behind a small oak tree.
3 14m From the bollard on the right, climb a short wall and groove to a large grassy corner.
4 13m The Black Wall. Traverse diagonally right then climb the rib.
5 20m Traverse diagonally left across a slab and under a small overhang before moving up to a ledge.
6 15m Climb the short wall on the right and scramble to the top.
Photo page 347.
W Peascod, SB Beck 19.05.1946

❹ Caesar 72m HVS 5a ★
Furnished with satisfying holds the central pitches are enjoyably steep. Start at a green groove on the left of the lower buttress 5m left of the foot of the lower buttress.
1 9m Climb the groove past a large jammed flake to a shattered ledge below the overhangs.
2 26m 5a Pull up into a niche then step up right and climb a fine groove to a niche with spikes.
3 13m 4c Move left to a ledge then up to a little overhang; turn it on the left and climb to a ledge.
4 24m 4b Climb a curved groove over thin flakes to the top of the crag.
L Brown, AP Turnbull 27.09.1959

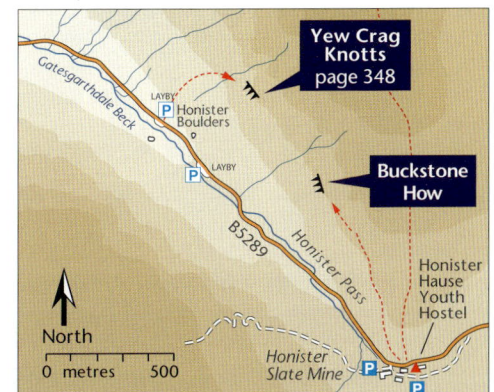

Buckstone How | 347

5 Alexas 64m HVS 5a ★★
Interesting throughout with a fine second pitch. Start at the foot of a lower buttress.
1 12m 4c Climb a shallow groove and move up to a shattered ledge.
2 26m 5a Traverse right below the overhangs to a perch at the foot of an undercut groove. Climb the groove steeply to a ledge on the right below the overhangs, then climb diagonally left until it is possible to move up right to a ledge.
3 26m 4b Move right to gain a bottomless groove then climb its left wall and the continuation to the top.
B Ingle, P Crew 2.09.1962

6 Encroacher 60m E1 5b ★
An enjoyable direct line starting just left of the smooth brown-stained wall.
1 35m 5b Climb steeply between jutting flakes to gain the end of a gangway. Follow this leftwards for a few moves then continue thinly up the groove to the overhang. Pull over this on good holds and cross the upper traverse of *Cleopatra* to gain a leftward-facing corner. Climb this and pull right onto the rib. Climb over an overlap to a ledge.
2 25m 4c Step left and climb over broken rocks to a spike. Swing left onto the face and climb up left to a groove that leads to the top.
D Knighton, M Brown 16.07.1978

7 Cleopatra 71m HVS 5a ★★★
The classic climb of the crag; an ingenious and airy way through the layers of overhangs. Start below the smooth brown-stained wall (*Cleopatra's* "tawny front"), 2m left of the V-groove.
1 25m 4c Climb onto a pillar then move rightwards over a bulge to a gangway. Follow this up leftwards to a crack and climb it for 3m. Traverse the wall on the right to gain a large ledge.
2 20m 5a Move delicately up the rib on the left then traverse left to the left-hand of two grooves. Climb this and step left to belays; poor stance.
3 26m 4b Move right to gain a bottomless groove then climb its left wall and the continuation, to the top.
Photo page 321.
W Peascod, B Blake 18.05.1951

8 The Asp 48m E2 5c ★★
Start just right of a small pillar.
1 16m 5c Climb the thin V-groove, 2m right of the smooth brown-stained wall, to the right end of the gangway then go up a smooth groove (crux) to a roomy ledge.
2 32m 5b Climb the open groove to an overhang then gain a crack on the right wall and climb it to a grassy ledge. Finish up the rib on the right.
J Lamb, P Whillance 24.06.1976

9 Groove Two 48m HVS 5a ★★
A classic pitch, made formidable by the stone-ground smoothness of its walls. Start 7m left of the tree-choked recess.
1 20m Scramble up to a worn chimney-groove and climb it to a stance beside a tree.
2 28m 5a Move right and climb the main groove; its very steep entrance can be avoided by the polished black groove on the left, which is a grade easier.
W Peascod, SB Beck, G Rushworth 20.07.1947

Honister Wall HS (page 345) Catherine Kenyon
📷 Ron Kenyon

YEW CRAG KNOTTS

OS Grid Ref: NY 219 146
Altitude: 350m

Short routes on clean quick-drying rock that catch the sun most of the day. The first buttress on the left when going up Honister Pass from Buttermere.

Approach: Park in a lay-by below and left of the crag. Take the conspicuous grass rib, well to the left of the scree, to a stony path leading right to the foot of the crag.
See map page 345.

Descent: Straightforward and obvious, down to the right.

BMC RAD
Yew Crag Knotts

Layby
NY 216 144
P GPS 54.519313
-3.212009

OS Grid Ref
NY 219 146

Hearth Direct E2 (opposite) Jesse Dufton — 📷 Molly Dufton

1 Face the Music 35m E1 5b
Good climbing up the prominent twin grooves on the left. Start directly below the main corner. Climb leftwards to climb the left-hand of the twin grooves to a ledge. Finish up another groove.
C Downer, E Rogers, RE Wightman 16.04.1987

2 Substitute 40m E1 5b ★★
Steep and sustained, yet well-protected climbing, up the main corner on the left side of the buttress. Gain the corner via a ramp from the right and climb to sloping rock on the right can be gained with difficulty. Continue up the steep corner above on excellent holds.
A Greig, J Moore Aug 1977

Below the main arête are two well-defined corners.

3 Poker 30m E2 5c ★
A direct line starting up the left-hand corner, finishing up the arête. Climb the thin crack in the right wall to a traverse. The hanging ramp above (crux) is climbed by its right edge onto the wall above. Finish up the arête on good holds.
RO Graham, W Williamson 12.03.1987

4 Hearth Direct 30m E2 5c ★★
Sustained with a tricky corner then an exhilarating bulge. Climb the corner then over the overhang on big flat holds. A wall and short groove above on the right lead to the top.
Photo opposite.
RO Graham, TW Birkett 26.03.1981

5 Chimney Buttress 27m HVS 5a
The buttress immediately left of the chimney. Climb a smooth wall for 4m to a ledge, make a 3m traverse left and climb an open groove until steeper rock forces a short traverse back right. Finish up the rib. Or, climb directly above the ledge to the rib E1 5b.
R Valentine, J Wilkinson 13.09.1969

6 Sweep 20m MVS 4b
A series of somewhat artificial but enjoyable variations. Climb the corner immediately right of the chimney exiting right to the gap behind *Yew Crag Needle*. Move back left by a large flake and step across the chimney to finish directly up the buttress on the left.
J Grinbergs, SJH Reid 7.10.1990

7 Yew Crag Needle 20m VS 4c ★
The miniature Napes Needle pinnacle. Pleasant.
1 10m 4c Start at the front of the pinnacle. Climb the left-hand arête to a small roof and hand-traverse right along the break to the right edge. Pull directly over the bulge to the top; pinnacle belay.
2 10m 4b Descend into the gap and traverse right to a corner that is followed past a loose block to the top.
SJH Reid, J Grinbergs 7.10.1990

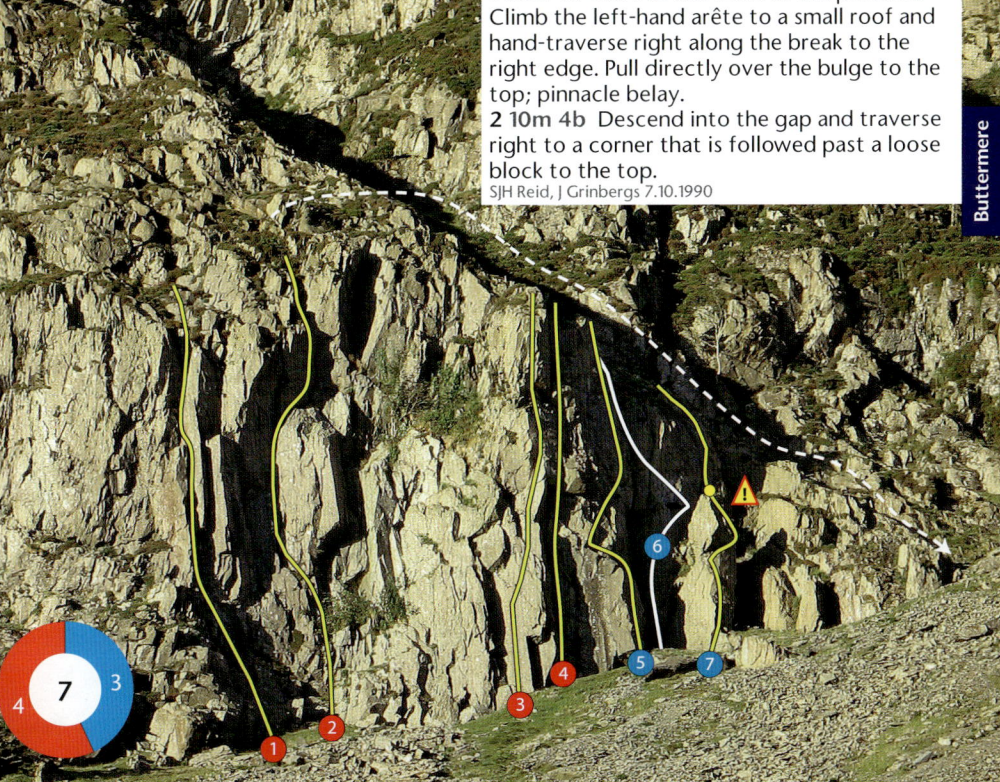

NEWLANDS

Unfrequented routes tucked away in a quiet valley, Newlands provides a respite from the crowds.

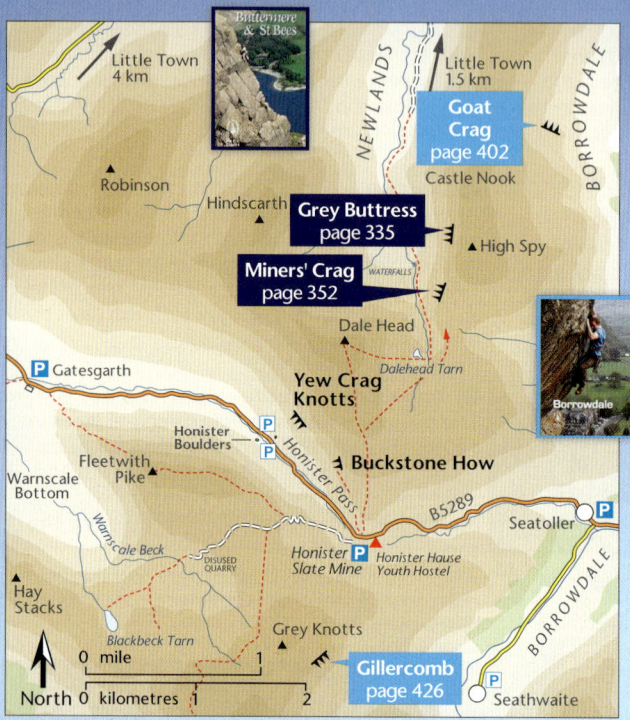

Jezebel, Miner's Crag VS (page 353) Ron Kenyon & Jonny Wilson — David Simmonite

MINERS' CRAG

OS Grid Ref: NY 231 157
Altitude: 480m

A large and complex crag. **Terrace Wall** offers the best climbs, often found stiff for the grade.

Approach: From Honister Pass, follow the fence heading for Dale Head until the angle eases at around 570m. A vague path forks right over a shoulder and bogs to Dalehead Tarn. The crag can be seen clearly just beyond Dalehead Tarn. From a short way up the start of the good ridge path to High Spy, the scree descent gully is located on the left. The top of the descent gully is a convenient spot to leave sacks. Exiting the gully level with the Quartz Rake, a careful scramble leftwards gains access to the routes.

Descent: From the top of the crag, walk down the right side down the first gully and scree below.

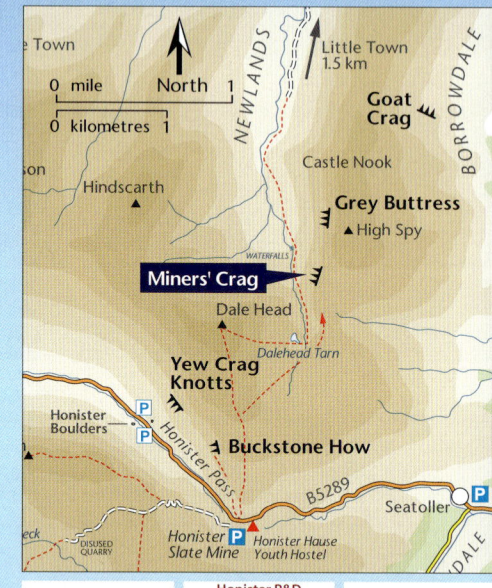

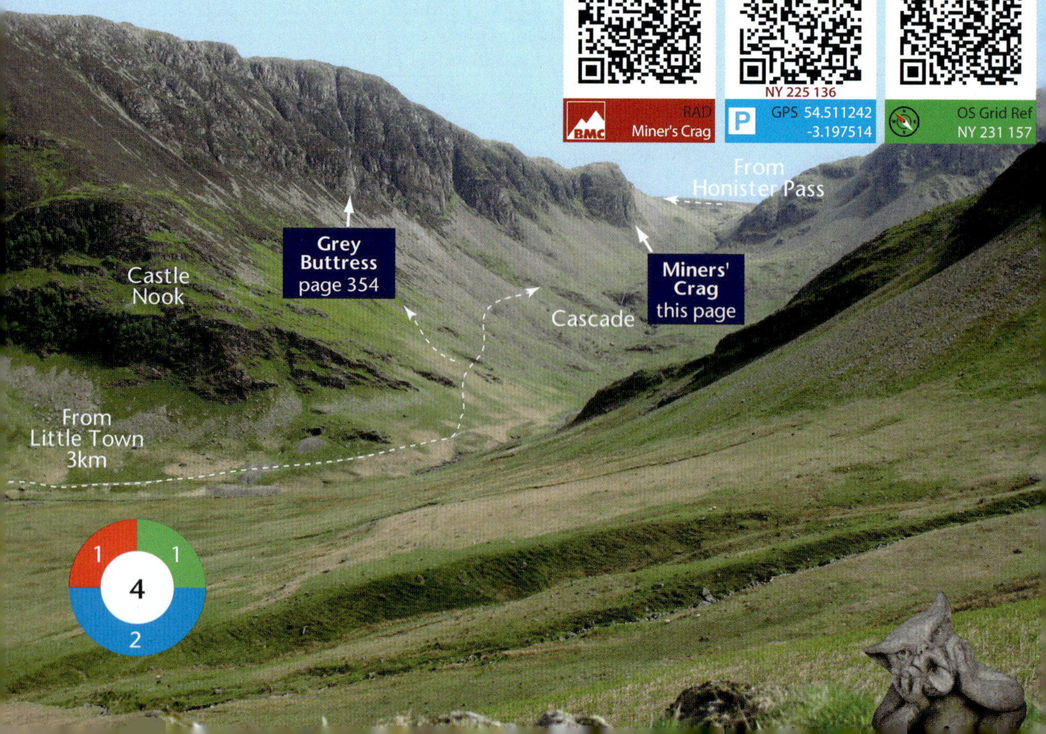

Terrace Wall

Steep exacting routes with a 'big' feel.

Approach: Exit the gully level with the Quartz Rake and carefully scramble leftwards to the routes.

① Jezebel 42m Vs 4c ★★
1 17m Climb the blocky corner to a ledge then move right below the corner; belay.
2 25m 4c Climb the corner past a tree to stand on cracked blocks below the steep upper section. Traverse airily left to the arête and climb this, initially steep, to finish.
Photo page 351.
W Peascod, SE Dirkin 29.07.1950

② Bathsheba 39m E1 5c ★★★
Excellent climbing, steep, with continuous interest. Start directly below the upper corner, at the base of a steep wall just right of an area of oozing black rock.
1 17m 5b Climb onto a triangular slab below a short impending groove, move up this and pull out left onto the steep wall to good holds. Continue up the wall to the base of a short open groove, traverse to its right edge and move up and back left to a ledge.
2 22m 5c The difficult corner.
C Read, P Fleming 5.11.2006

③ Harlot 37m HVS 5a ★★★
The steep central headwall. Start 8m right of the big right-angled corner below and just right of an open slabby groove where a quartz fault on the face runs down to meet the fellside.
1 20m 4a Step up and work steeply leftwards on good holds to gain the slabby groove; follow this line, over steps, to a ledge and spike.
2 17m 5a Climb to a sentry box, exit left then continue up the fault-line finishing through a V-notch.
GL Swainbank, C Read 16.05.2004

Upper Crag

Exposed slabs and grooves offer a warm up to link with the sterner climbing above.

Approach: Continue down the scree with care.

④ Corkscrew 63m HS
Winds its way up in superb positions. Start at a rib below and left os a large slab.
1 13m Climb the rib to a niche left of the slab.
2 23m Traverse left then climb the steep little slab and groove and continuation groove on the right. Step left across its top the up to a ledge below a sweep of slabs.
3 27m Cross the slab to the right arête and finish airily to reach the terrace.
Photo below.

Corkscrew HS Jonny Wilson
David Simmonite

GREY BUTTRESS

OS Grid Ref: NY 232 163
Altitude: 450m

Interesting routes on solid rock.

Approach: Follow the pleasant valley path from Little Town to Castle Nook, 3km. Soon after the mine buildings, the path forks; take the left branch following the main drainage towards Dalehead Tarn. Then when nearly below the crag, head steeply up on a vague path that soon vanishes amongst the heather and scree.

Descent: Abseil down the right side from a block. Alternatively, traverse with care, well above the gullies to the left (north) of the buttress before moving down through steep heather.

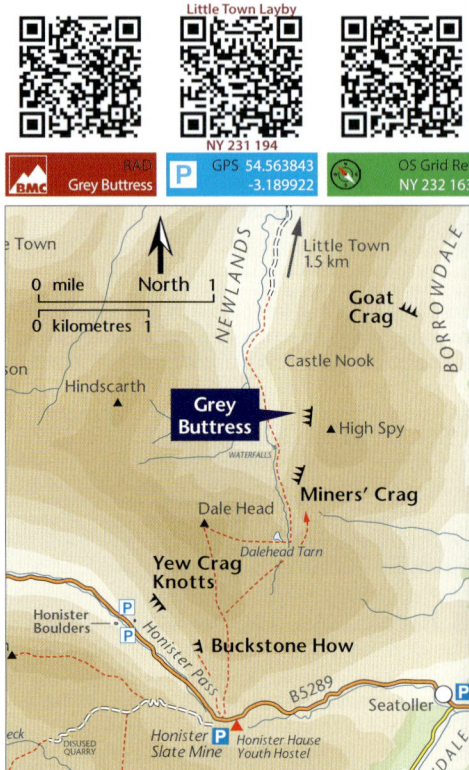

Brandywine VS (opposite) Rachel Somerville
DAVID SIMMONITE

① **Brandywine** 67m VS 4c ★★★
Intricate and technically demanding. Take care to protect the traverses. Start behind a perched block atop a broken rib.
1 23m 4c Step off the block into a steep corner then pull left over a large block onto a gangway. Climb the gangway, step left into a niche then move up and traverse left to a ledge.
2 20m 4c From the left end of the ledge, climb cracks to a traverse right across the wall to a triangular foothold. Continue boldly up to a slab on the right. Traverse rightwards up to the edge of the slab, step right and move down to a stance in a scoop; thread and nut belays.
3 24m 4b Move up rightwards on slabby rock into a groove climbed by its right edge before working back left over steep rock (minimal

protection) almost to the top of the heather-choked groove on the left, then pull up steeply rightwards to finish.
Photo opposite.
JA Austin, DG Roberts 25.07.1964

② Direct Route 44m HVS 5a ★★
Extremely fine on P1 and better than appearances suggest on P2.
1 24m 5a Climb the corner to the bulges. Move right then pull onto a flake; from its crest, climb the wall. Where it eases move left round a rib then up left into a scoop (thread and nut).
2 20m 4a Move up and right then climb the steep right-hand groove.

③ El Scorchio 47m E1 5b ★★
Nice climbing with a short crux. Start at the foot of a groove with a large flake on its left.
1 19m 4b Climb the groove then move up right to a block, pull right and continue up the slabby wall then trend rightwards to belay beneath a crack.
2 28m 5b Move up and traverse left onto a rock ledge. Make a difficult pull up the wall into an alcove (crux), move up a few metres then step left onto the fine clean wall. Continue, passing a flake on its right, to gain slabby rock then finish up a short rib on the left.
C Read, C Jones 18.07.2006

BORROWDALE

One of the most popular valleys in the Lake District with its roadside crags and proximity to the fleshpots of Keswick. Borrowdale has a wide range of excellent crags from little to lengthy, roadside to remote. There is something for everyone here. The valley can be busy with visitors and parking is limited so consider using the bus service up and down the valley from Keswick.

The Lost Boys, Steel Knotts HVS (page 399) Justin Shiels — David Simmonite

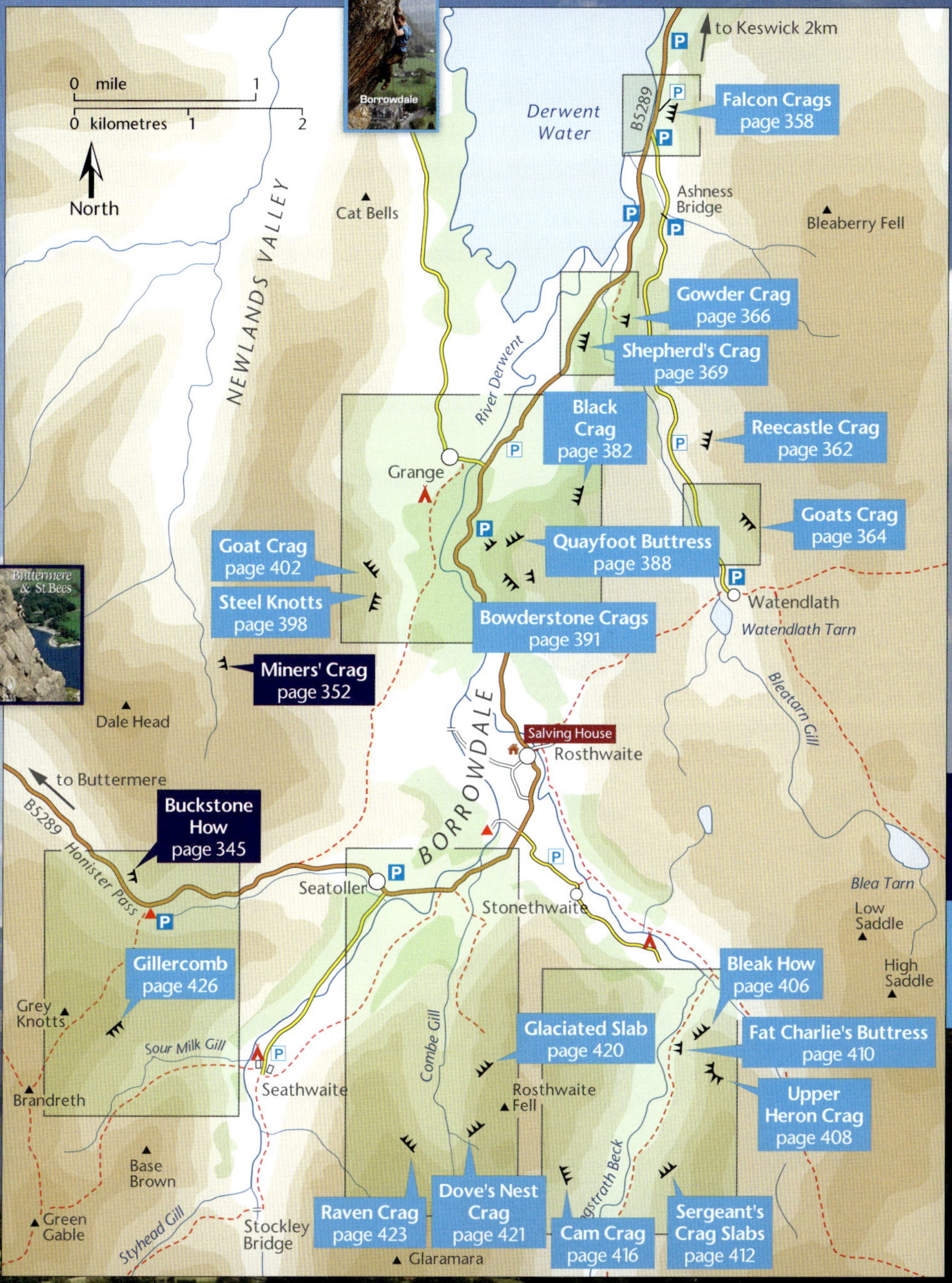
0 mile 1
0 kilometres 1 2
North
Borrowdale
to Keswick 2km
Derwent Water
B5289
Falcon Crags page 358
Cat Bells
NEWLANDS VALLEY
Ashness Bridge
Bleaberry Fell
Gowder Crag page 366
Shepherd's Crag page 369
River Derwent
Black Crag page 382
Reecastle Crag page 362
Grange
Goats Crag page 364
Quayfoot Buttress page 388
Goat Crag page 402
Steel Knotts page 398
Watendlath
Watendlath Tarn
Bowderstone Crags page 391
Buttermere & St Bees
Miners' Crag page 352
Bleatarn Gill
Dale Head
BORROWDALE
Salving House
Rosthwaite
to Buttermere
B5289
Honister Pass
Buckstone How page 345
Seatoller
Stonethwaite
Blea Tarn
Low Saddle
High Saddle
Gillercomb page 426
Bleak How page 406
Grey Knotts
Sour Milk Gill
Glaciated Slab page 420
Fat Charlie's Buttress page 410
Combe Gill
Seathwaite
Brandreth
Rosthwaite Fell
Upper Heron Crag page 408
Base Brown
Langstrath Beck
Green Gable
Styhead Gill
Stockley Bridge
Raven Crag page 423
Dove's Nest Crag page 421
Cam Crag page 416
Sergeant's Crag Slabs page 412
Glaramara

FALCON CRAGS

OS Grid Ref: NY 271 205
Altitude: 180m

Steep and well-featured all the climbing here is enjoyable and satisfying. The crag has two major sections with often slatey rock and gear is sometimes elusive. Both have a delightful outlook over the lake. The routes should be treated with respect.

Seasonal restriction: 1st Mar to 30th Jun.

Approach: From Great Wood car park follow the path south to below **Lower Falcon Crag**. **Upper Falcon Crag** can be reached from this path by finding a way up and left through the bracken which can prove to be an obstruction in the summer. Beware of ticks.

Descent: Generally, it is best to abseil. There is a path to the left.

Lower Falcon Crag

Steep, technical climbing. Check for restrictions. The base of the crag is guarded by brambles, so come here earlier in the year and bring pruning gear. *The Niche* and the routes to the right, starting near the big tree, are always accessible.

1 Spinup 50m VS 4c ★★

Bold, yet straightforward, climbing and exciting positions make this a popular outing. Start at the back left corner of a grassy bay. This may be obstructed by vegetation.
1 20m 4c Follow a small slab leftwards and step left around a rib to a ledge. From its left end climb to a gangway leading left for 3m, then climb right to a stance just left of a black groove.
2 30m 4c Move up for 2m then step right into the black groove. Climb the groove for 5m

then step right and down to follow an exposed traverse line above the overhangs to its end. Continue straight above or climb diagonally right to finish up a short groove above a pedestal. Belay well back.
P Ross, D Sewell 1957

② The Dangler   40m   E2 5c   ★★
Steep thuggy climbing. Start 2m left of the back right-hand corner of a grassy bay.
1 10m 5a Climb a wall and small bulge. Move diagonally right past a prickly bush then straight up to a block belay.
2 30m 5c Climb the steep groove on the left then left to a ledge (peg). Pull up right (peg) then traverse right on large flat holds. Move up and right into a groove line; climb this to the top.
S Clark, T Martin May 1963

③ Hedera Grooves   42m   VS 4c   ★★
The best easier route and a good introduction to the crag. Start in an alcove left of a large tree.
1 24m 4b Gain a grass ledge and climb the short groove above. Traverse boldly right to a groove and climb this to the holly tree.
2 18m 4c Gain and climb the groove above the holly then the ramp leftwards.
P Ross, P Lockley 10.08.1956

④ **The Niche**	E2 5c ★★★★	
⑤ **Interloper**	E1 5c ★★	
⑥ **Dedication Direct**	E1 5b ★★★	
⑦ **Kidnapped**	E2 5c ★★★	
⑧ **Plagiarism**	E2 5c ★★	
⑨ **Usurper**	E1 5a ★★	
⑩ **Illusion**	HVS 5a ★★★★	
⑪ **Lamplighter**	HVS 4c ★★	

All of the following routes are best descended by abseil from *in-situ* points on trees.

④ The Niche 59m   E2 5c   ★★★★
A hard classic offering surprisingly sustained and difficult climbing in excellent positions. Many people find P2 the harder. Start below the left end of the niche.
1 25m 5c Climb the bulging wall then step left and climb the rib until level with the niche. Traverse right with difficulty into the niche.
2 34m 5b Climb the back of the niche then traverse right to a break in the overhang. Pull over (peg) then climb the leftward-leaning groove over a slight bulge on the right and finish up the slabby wall.
A Liddell, R McHaffie 20.08.1962

⑤ Interloper 50m   E1 5c   ★★
An enjoyable route which takes the steep and well-protected groove 6m right of the niche.
1 29m 5c Climb to the large ledge with a steep groove at its left end. After an awkward start, climb the groove on good holds; belay on the left.
2 21m 4c Climb the gangway leftwards to a bulge. Move right then up the slabby wall.
A Liddell, R McHaffie 8.07.1962

The next two routes start behind the large tree.

⑥ Dedication Direct 48m   E1 5b   ★★★
A technical groove reaches the original route making a great way up the crag. Climb the groove to reach a cluster of small spikes. Traverse left into a fine slanting corner, follow this then left into the final groove.
P Ross, E Metcalf May 1957

⑦ Kidnapped 42m   E2 5c   ★★★
Tremendous sustained technical climbing in the upper part. Climb the groove to reach small spikes after 16m. Climb into the overhung niche then move up to the roof (peg). Traverse left to the arête then enjoy the final groove.
P Botterill, J Lamb 25.04.1978

The next three routes start right of the tree.

⑧ Plagiarism 48m   E2 5c   ★★
Always steady and justifiably popular. Climb to moves left into a slanting groove, finishing up its left rib to reach a small ledge. Traverse left across a steep wall (peg) to a shallow groove then up to a roof (peg). Pull over on the right to finish up the groove.
P Nunn, O Woolcock Aug 1962

⑨ Usurper 43m   E1 5a   ★★
Satisfying steep open climbing with great moves. Climb directly to, then follow, the obvious groove to a huge flake on the right.

Move up left to a ledge. The overhang up and right is overcome strenuously on ample holds to the final groove.
Photo below.
P Gomersall, N Bulmer 20.06.1975

⑩ Illusion 47m   HVS 5a   ★★★★
Exhilarating and exposed climbing with a big feel crossing the wall below the large overhang. Climb to the steep groove then continue to a juggy traverse right crossing several grooves to a corner. Climb this until forced right round the arête. Continue to a tree.
Photo page 15.
P Lockey, P Ross 10.06.1956

⑪ Lamplighter 40m   HVS 4c   ★★
An interesting and popular route. The short steep crack has a hard move, then up left to the groove. Follow this through a bulge and continue up and right, round the arête and up to a tree.
L Hewitt, S Glass 25.05.1964

Usurper E1 (this page) Adam Hocking — David Simm

Upper Falcon Crag

Brilliant steep wall climbs with an expansive outlook.

Approach: From Great Wood car park, a path leads south towards **Lower Falcon Crag**. Ascend the scree slope to the left of the lower crag then follow a fence rightwards. From Ashness Bridge, head north then to the top of the headwall.

Descent: Awkwardly, to the left.

1 Dry Gasp 60m E4 6a ★★

The final pitch is an excellent piece of climbing up the centre of the cracked wall that shouts at you from the road. Many people will abseil down the groove on the right and climb the final pitch only.
1 22m 4a Caution loose rock. Climb the broken groove past an old oak tree until a move right and a short right-slanting groove leads to a ledge. Belay below the groove on the left.
2 20m 5b Caution loose rock. Climb the groove over two bulges. Continue up leftwards via an easy groove to a stance below the headwall.
3 18m 6a Climb the crack diagonally left (peg) then directly up (thread). Holds lead up leftwards then back rightwards to a crack, up which the route finishes.
P Livesey 22.06.1974

2 Falcon Crag 60m E3 5c ★★
Buttress Route 1

A great route with a good second pitch finishing up the impressive corner on the headwall.
1 20m 4a Caution loose rock. Climb the broken groove past an old oak tree and belay at the right-hand end of the ledge below a bristly short wall.
2 22m 5b Caution loose rock. Climb the wall for 6m (peg) then move diagonally up left to climb an overhanging crack. Continue up via a groove to belay below the headwall.
3 18m 5c The corner is strenuous, keep something in reserve for the tricky finish.
P Ross, P Lockey. 4.05.1958

Falcon Crag Buttress Route 1 E3 (above)
Duncan Campbell — 📷 Jonathan Hughes

REECASTLE CRAG

OS Grid Ref: NY 273 176
Altitude: 300m

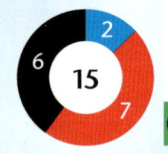

Steep clean rock for the strong-fingered to enjoy in a delightful setting close to the road. Every route is worth climbing and the short approach offers a very productive visit.

Approach: Take the steep road towards Watendlath. Limited parking on the bend beneath the crag. Walk NE to the crag.

See map page 357.

Descent: Abseil from the top of *The Rack* (don't get in anybody's way) or walk left.

❶ **The Executioner** 25m E4 6a ★
Short, with bold technical climbing. Steep moves lead up and left to boldly reach a shallow green scoop. Move rightwards and climb the easier wall.
P Whillance, D Armstrong 28.04.1979

❷ **The Torture Board** 25m E7 6c (F7c) ★★
This popular testpiece climbs the twin cracks. Climb steeply to gain the twin cracks (peg). Make hard moves up the cracks to the horizontal break, then continue directly with less difficulty.
P Cornforth 24.05.1987

❸ **Daylight Robbery** 30m E6 6c (F7b+) ★★★
Steep crimpy climbing. The crack is followed to its top (peg). Move right and make desperate moves up to a good hold. Continue up the easy cracked groove then slabs.
C Sowden, M Berzins 6.05.1984

❹ **Burn at the Stake** 30m E7 7a (F8a) ★★★
The central crack is bold, powerful and technical.
P Cornforth 1992

❺ **Penal Servitude** 30m E5 6b ★★
Brilliant wall climbing. Climb rightwards past quartz breaks (peg, RP2). Using tiny finger pockets move up then left and up to a rest. Step left and climb a slight groove.
D Armstrong, P Whillance 12.05.1981

❻ **White Noise** 30m E3 5c ★★★
Pumpy well-protected climbing. Climb to a small overhang; pull up left and follow the crack.
J Lamb, R McHaffie 9.08.1978

7 Rack Direct 30m E2 5c ★★★
A strenuous introduction to the crag; a bit of a soft touch. Climb to a break in the bulges. Pull over and climb the crack with a short deviation out right.
S Miller, R Parker 19.09.1977

8 The Rack 35m HVS 5a ★★
A good route which packs a lot in. Climb the short crack then ledges. A bold traverse left gains the crack.
R McHaffie, B Mallaghan 7.10.1973

9 The Rack - Finger Flake Finish 30m E2 5c ★★★
Fine steep climbing, well-protected with a short sharp section. From where *The Rack* traverses left, climb right into a white scoop and follow a thin flake. At its top, move left onto a wall, up to a large sloping ledge and then the tree.
P Whillance, D Armstrong 9.07.1981

10 Guillotine 30m E3 5c ★★★
A superb route giving sustained varied well-protected climbing. Never desperate but plenty of it. Climb to the ledge then continue up via a thin groove and rib to a bulge. Pull over this strenuously and up to a second bulge. Surmount this and continue up.
J Lamb 5.09.1978

11 Inquisition 30m E4 6a ★★★
An excellent route with independent climbing. From the ledge, boldly layaway a slight rib to a good hold on the left, and reach the niche. Move right then climb steeply to a rightwards-sloping ramp, follow this.
C Downer, R McHaffie 5.08.1984

12 Thumbscrew 30m E3 5c ★★★
A fine steep route, fingery and sustained, up the bubbly wall. Take the easy wall slightly leftwards to a ledge. Go up the steep wall to a flat hold between two parallel cracks. Climb the left-hand crack and groove above direct.
J Lamb, D Cherry 24.08.1978

13 The Gibbet Direct 30m E2 5c ★★
Sustained fingery climbing. Start directly behind the birch tree. Climb up left, then right, to below the short wall at the foot of a gangway. Make a hard move onto the gangway and immediately pull steeply left onto the wall. Climb this and the central crack.
C Downer, R McHaffie 24.07.1984

14 The Gauntlet 30m E1 5b ★
A worthwhile eliminate. Follow *The Noose* to a block 3m up in the corner crack. Finger traverse left across the steep wall to gain the gangway. Climb the wall above on improving holds.
C Downer, R McHaffie 5.08.1984

15 The Noose 25m HVS 4c ★★
Strenuous. Easy slabs lead up rightwards to a short corner. Climb the corner and crack to the top of the gangway. Follow the steep groove.
R McHaffie and party Apr 1972

Borrowdale

Layby
NY 270 178
GPS 54.550360
-3.128251

RAD Reecastle

GOATS CRAG

OS Grid Ref: NY 277 169
Altitude: 400m

Short routes of all grades in a sunny location.

Approach: Take the Watendlath road. Park on the right before the walls on both sides of the road begin. Go through the gate opposite then another just right. Up the left side of the field, through another gate then up the hillside passing the lower crag on your right.

Descent: Either side; to the right is better.

① Mort 15m E1 5b ★
Start to the left of the drystone wall. Climb easy rocks to a small triangular overhang. Pass this on the right, with difficulty, to gain a small ledge; finish up the easier shallow groove.
R Davies 3.09.1989

② Pussy Galore 14m E2 5c ★★
The leftward-slanting crack. Moving left to leave the niche is the crux but the upper crack maintains interest.
K Wilkinson, P Hirst May 1989

③ Munich Agreement 15m E1 5b ★
A good route with a sting in its tail. Start at the foot of a large slanting block. Climb the steep wall up and leftwards to the leftwards-rising traverse line. Move left then climb a rightward-slanting crack with a difficult finish.
N Brunger, J Gilhespy 3.09.1989

Inner Limits HVS (opposite) Peter Sterling — LAETITIA STERLING

4 Optional Omission 14m E2 5b ★
Quite stiff. Start left of a blunt arête and climb leftwards to a ledge; continue up the steep wall direct.
J Gilhespy, N Brunger 3.09.1989

5 Inner Limits 14m HVS 5a ★★
Climb the steep corner, step slightly left, then move right onto a slab. Continue up the left edge of the slab in a fine position.
Photo opposite.
R Kenyon, C Kenyon 30.09.1989

6 The Green 18m HS 4b ★
Move up left to stand on a spike then climb left again onto a ledge. Follow the leftwards-rising traverse line (decorated with green lichen) to finish up a short corner.
RA Smithson, D Heard 4.05.2004

7 Poland 15m VS 4b ★
Start up the slab, just right of the blunt rib, then go right to a corner. Move up right to pull onto the slab then climb the left side of the slab.
N Brunger, K Telfer 3.09.1989

8 Berlin Wall 15m E2 5b ★★
Starting just to the right of the tree, climb the slab to below the steep right wall. Climb the wall awkwardly (spike on the right arête).

9 Emma Line 16m HVS 5a ★★
Climb to the corner-crack then move left and follow the sharp arête in a fine position.
J Gilhespy, N Brunger, R Davies, K Telfer 3.09.1989

10 Son of Oz 15m HS 4b ★
Climb to the corner crack and follow this steeply to the top. Take large nuts/cams.
S Telfer, R Sharpe 3.09.1989

11 Rogue Herries 15m E4 6a ★
A poorly protected route with some dubious holds. The steep wall right of the corner, thankfully it relents towards the top.
K Telfer, R Davies, N Brunger, J Gilhespy 3.09.1989

12 The Colour of Magic 15m E4 6a ★
Start below the arête. Climb to undercuts below the overhang, span right then move up the shallow corner (protection), move back left then climb the arête.
R Davies, K Telfer, N Brunger, J Gilhespy 3.09.1989

13 Stranger to the Ground 12m E3 5c ★
Climb a short groove to a sloping ledge, just above a tree. Step left and climb the wall boldly on inconvenient holds.
K Telfer, R Davies, N Brunger 3.09.1989

GOWDER CRAG

OS Grid Ref: NY 266 187
Altitude: 200m

Clean and adventurous climbing. Despite first impressions and a reputation for loose rock, the fine buttress rising out of the trees behind the Lodore Hotel offers fine outings. A popular path below the crag is busy in summer, so it's best to come in the spring or autumn. Beware of the ants!

Approach: On the bend, a few hundred metres before the Lodore Hotel, is a small pull-in with a gate. Go through the gate and follow the path through the trees. The path steepens and soon the overgrown lower section of the crag appears.

Descent: Either side; left is further but easier.

Kaleidoscope HVS (opposite) Andy McVittie & Peter Sterling — David Simmonite

1 Fool's Paradise   103m   VS 4c   ★★
A popular classic offering varied climbing. Start at the lowest point of the crag.
1 39m 4c Climb the short, rather overgrown buttress to a ledge. Gain the groove above the tree then make a straightforward move left onto the arête. Climb just left of the arête on excellent holds, yet minimal protection, to a ledge on the right.
2 44m 4c Descend the groove on the right for a few metres, then traverse right to a tree. Move up and right awkwardly but with better gear. Move left and climb the steep groove past some very large perched blocks to a tree.
3 20m 4b Step left and climb a thin crack then the arête to a ledge. Finish up the short grassy corner on the right.
PW Vaughan, JDJ Wildridge 13.08.1951

2 Kaleidoscope   74m   HVS 5a   ★★
This enjoyable route starts about 10m up to the right of the toe of the buttress at a narrow ridge.
1 12m Ascend to a ledge and belay on a yew tree.
2 42m 5a Move right then climb up and pass to the left of a tree. Climb the wall above to a sloping ledge beneath the large overhang. Move left and climb the black groove to a large block on the left. Step right to the arête and climb the shallow groove and wall above to a ledge.
3 20m 4b Traverse a few metres right and climb a thin crack then the arête to a ledge. Finish up the short grassy corner on the right.
Photo opposite.
R McHaffie, C McCormick 23.12.1971

The Bludgeon E1 (page 375) Katie Mackay — 📷 Tom McNally

SHEPHERD'S CRAGS

OS Grid Ref: NY 263 185
Altitude: 140m

The most popular crag in the valley, and justifiably so: highly enjoyable routes across all grades, easy access and good quality quick-drying rock, along with a beautiful outlook - what more could you ask for?

Approach: Park at the Borrowdale Hotel - pay inside; Kettlewell or Bowderstone car parks; in a layby just beyond the Lodore Hotel; or a layby just after the bend on the way to Grange. A bus regularly runs up and down the valley.

See overview page 370.

Brown Slabs

Excellent, and very popular, single pitch climbs where many a climber has been introduced to the sport.

Approach: Through the trees from the road 200m north of High Lodore Farm. Alternatively, walk along the base from the south.

Descent: Looking out. Scramble down keeping to the right-hand side of the sloping ground. Cross a stile over the northern bounding wall and walk back round under *Brown Crag Wall*. Abseiling is discouraged - slings must be used to protect the trees.

① Brown Crag Wall 45m VS 4b ★★
A classic, varied and interesting, though rather polished, especially the first pitch. Start at a weakness in the wall at the twin-stemmed oak tree 8m left of the prominent right-facing corner.
1 30m 4b Climb the scoop for 3m then step right onto an arête. Move up boldly into a corner and onto a ledge. Move up, traverse left for 2m and ascend the slab to a sloping ledge. Continue up the slab and scoop then traverse right to a tree.
2 15m 4a Climb a shallow corner and continue, trending left.
R Wilkinson, KC Ogilvie, JDJ Wildridge 22.04.1950

② Conclusion 42m E1 5b ★★
A striking and strenuous route up the prominent right-facing corner. Climb the steep corner as it curves right. Continue up a V-groove heading right to an arête which is followed to the top.
P Ross, P Whitwell 2.10.1955

③ Brown Slabs Face 42m HVD ★★
A fine open route. Start just right of the oak at the left edge of the slab. Follow the scratched line up the shallow rib then climb a shallow broken groove to finish on the rounded rib.
B Beetham 1.09.1947

④ Brown Slabs Arête 44m D ★★★
A very popular route. Start about halfway between two obvious trees at the base of the slab where a line leads diagonally left.
1 16m Ascend the scratched line leftwards to a conspicuous notch in the arête.
2 28m Climb the crest of the arête in a pleasantly exposed position.
CD Frankland, B Beetham 1922

⑤ Brown Slabs Direct 38m VD ★★
A popular and now well-worn route. Start about halfway between two trees at the base of the slabs where a line leads diagonally left. Head straight up then rightwards and ascend a scoop to a large block on the left, level with a battered oak tree. Step off the block and climb the wall slightly leftwards on flakes.
B Beetham 7.04.1948

⑥ Brown Slabs 36m D ★★
Start at the well-worn line behind a tree, 5m left of the corner. Follow the most likely line to the top passing just right of a battered oak tree.
B Beetham 7.04.1946

⑦ Brown Slabs Scoop 35m HS ★★
Start one metre left of the corner groove. Climb the slab past the tree stump to a scoop. From its right-hand side continue on widely-spaced holds.
R Tolley, P Latimer 18.04.2007

⑧ Brown Slabs Crack 30m VS 4c ★★
Climbs the obvious corner-groove at the right-hand end of **Brown Slabs**. Climb the easy corner for 10m to a tree stump. Ascend the slippery corner above, with difficulty, to a tree. Continue up the corner to the top.
B Beetham 19.04.1947

North Buttress

Fine long pitches on this tall buttress split down the centre by the classic *Ardus*.

Approach: Follow paths rightwards from **Brown Slabs** or leftwards across the scree from **Fisher's Folly Area**.

Descent: Walk up the hill behind the crag to a path that leads north to the top of **Brown Slabs** from where an easy descent can be made to the left. Another way, which initially requires down-climbing at **VD**, is to descend to the right of the buttress.

⑨ Finale   34m   HVS 5a   ★★★
A great test piece giving strenuous and sustained climbing. Protection is excellent. Start at a short steep corner just left of the blunt arête.
1 21m 5a Climb the corner for 6m, step right and climb the bulge and crack above to a tree.
2 13m 4a Move right and finish up the open groove and crack in the slab on the right.
T Savage, P Ross 16.07.1965

⑩ Aaros   40m   E1 5b   ★★★
Outstanding with fine fingery climbing on the steep wall with the crux saved until the end. Start at the foot of the slabby ramp. Move up the ramp for 4m then follow the narrow right-slanting gangway for another 4m. Gain a shallow V-shaped sentry box in the wall on the left and follow the groove above for 3m. Move right and climb the steep wall. Continue in the same line leading to the traverse of *Ardus*. Follow this right a short distance then finish up a thin slanting crack in the headwall, 2m left of the corner.
R Graham, R McHaffie, TW Birkett, K Forsythe 22.10.1978

⑪ Ardus   42m   MVS 4b   ★★★
A wonderful and very popular climb up the large corner. Start at the foot of the slabby ramp leading right to the corner.
1 18m 4a Climb the ramp to a block at the foot of the corner.
2 12m 4a Climb the block and the corner above to a ledge.
3 12m 4b Make a tricky traverse left across the exposed slab for 5m then finish up a crack.
V Veevers, H Westmorland 15.05.1946

⑫ Delight Maker   40m   HVS 5a   ★★
An excellent direct line with a bold middle section. Start left of the split block and oak tree. Climb a shallow groove then move left onto the arête then follow this in an improbable position. Climb the overlap at a thin crack then the slab to a depression above grassy cracks. Climb the right-hand side then continue up and left to finish up the groove above.
R McHaffie, B Johnson 1982

⑬ Eve   50m   VS 4c   ★★★
A popular and memorable route weaving up the buttress. Start 8m left of the lowest point of the crag behind a large oak tree and beside a split block. P2 is quite serious and demands competence from the whole team.
1 13m 4b Climb the short slab and steep crack to a ledge.
2 22m 4c Ascend the groove for 2m; step left to a slab. Arrange protection, then cross the slab diagonally left to reach the top left corner.
3 15m 4b The short rib to the overhang. Move right onto the face and climb a crack to the top.
W Peascod, B Blake 11.08.1951

⑭ Adam   40m   VS 5a   ★★★
A superb well-protected companion to *Eve*. Start in the corner. Ascend the corner (junction with *Eve*) move right then back left and climb a short crack, past a holly tree, then slightly leftwards up the wall. The original way is a very good yet tougher proposition. From the holly tree move right then boldly climb the overhanging arête and steep wall.
P Ross, B Wilkinson 30.08.1955

⑮ True North   40m   E2 5b   ★★★
An excellent direct pitch with thin fingery climbing up the hanging slab and a magnificent finish, just warrants the grade. Start at the blunt arête just left of the prominent flake crack. Climb the arête and groove above to a broken ledge. Continue up the ragged crack in the black wall to a ledge, just right of a hanging slab. Step left onto the slab and climb it to a ledge. Swing up and right to finish the steep rib in a fantastic position.
J Lamb, R Allen 1981

⑯ North Buttress   45   E1 5b   ★★
A long and exciting pitch. Start a few metres up and right of the lowest point of the buttress on the left side of a large flake. Climb the flake and the bulge above. Continue up until a short traverse left gives access to a gangway trending back right. Immediately step left and ascend the obvious overhanging groove with difficulty, followed by easier climbing to finish.
PJ Greenwood, D Whillans, P Whitwell 1954

⑰ P.S.   38m   E1 5b   ★★
An exhilarating climb, starting at the broken groove 8m up and right from the foot of the buttress. Climb the groove to a ledge. Continue up the fault above to a wedged block then, using good technique or a long reach, move right to side-pulls to gain and climb the easy arête.
P Ross, B Aughton 19.04.1959

Fisher's Folly Area

A small steep compact buttress seamed with cracks and overhangs including the prominent wide *Kransic Crack* in its centre.

Approach: Round to the right from **North Buttress** or just down and left of **Chamonix Area**.

Descent: Carefully follow a clear path leftwards. Please do not abseil or top rope directly from the trees or they won't be there in the future!

18 M.G.C. 20m E2 5c ★★
This well-protected Shepherd's test piece is always well-chalked. To the left of the corner is a steep wall split by a thin peg-scarred crack. Yard up the overhung base and short crack to gain a flake. Move left and climb the crack to gain a ledge. Finish more easily up the wall.
B Roberts, G West 1958

19 Fisher's Folly 25m VS 4c ★★
A fine climb. Climb the right-facing corner then step left to a ledge (possible belay). Move delicately rightwards across the wall for 5m then climb to the overhang. Pass it on the right and continue to the top. Or, climb directly over the overhang HVS 5a.
M Thompson, P Nicol Easter 1955

20 Kransic Crack Direct 20m HVS 5a ★★
Excellent well-protected and varied climbing. Climb the left-hand crack to the top of the flake. Traverse the top of the flake to its right-hand end below a bulge. Climb up then right over the bulge then take the crack on the left on excellent holds.
D Peel 1956

21 Kransic Crack 22m VS 4c ★★
Climb the crack to the top of the flake then cross the flake to the right. Make an awkward move onto the wall then traverse rightwards to reach the finishing wide crack. For those of a perverse inclination, an alternative start climbs the off-width right-hand crack of the flake VS 4b.
GB Fisher, D Oliver, F Bantock 6.07.1952

22 Creeping Jesus 24m HVS 5a ★★
A testing direct pitch of continuous interest; some say E1. Start below the middle of the flake. Climb on positive holds to the top of the flake, move up the scoop above then go right to finish up the wall.
J Healy, A Mitchell 22.07.1978

23 The Grasp 24m E2 5b ★★
Good but bold climbing. Start by the huge flake. Climb the left-hand side of the large flake and move up to the scoop, right of the black overhang. Move left to a good hold then make a committing move over the overhang onto the wall. Continue carefully up the wall above moving ever further from your gear to gain a leftwards-slanting gangway which is followed to the top.
D McDonald, R McHaffie, N Robinson 5.10.1978

24 True Cross 30m VS 4c ★★
A rising leftwards traverse giving steep, sustained, well-protected climbing along a natural break. Start on the very large boulder on the right-hand side of the buttress. Step onto the blunt arête and climb it for 10m to gain the juggy break that cuts across the crag. Make a rising traverse leftwards, passing below the roof. Move up to the next roof and continue left to its left-hand end. Climb diagonally leftwards to finish at the top of *M.G.C.*
Photo below.
SJH Reid, W Phipps 3.04.1996

25 Chamonix 25m HS ★★
A rather devious route starting at the right-hand end of the huge flake that dominates the buttress. Climb the wall rightwards to gain the arête. Climb this then go rightwards to a pinnacle (possible belay). From the pinnacle climb the wall up and left into a wide crack, or climb the crack direct (harder). Continue more easily to a tree.
B Beetham 10.04.1946

True Cross VS (above) Alex Berry
Ron Kenyon

Chamonix Area

Classic multi-pitch routes including possibly the most famous climb in the Lake District.

Approach: Up and right from **Fisher's Folly Area** or, from **Jackdaw Ridge Area** follow paths leftwards across scree.

Descent: Go right across The Belvedere and down Jackdaw Terrace or further south - see *Jackdaw Ridge* descent and overview diagram. Alternatively it is possible to descend to the left by a steep path.

26 Crescendo 68m MVS 4b ★

A challenging route starting at the chimney just right of the large pinnacle.
1 35m 4b Climb the chimney to a platform then boldly up the polished wall, trending first left, then right, to reach an easier line of grooves leading to a ledge. Move left, climb over blocks then scramble through trees to a large oak tree below a triangular block with a steep wall behind.
2 33m 4a Climb past the block to a steepening in the wall then move left for 3m on good holds to reach another tree-covered ledge. Climb the ridge on the right to reach The Belvedere.
B Beetham 14.08.1948

27 The Bludgeon 54m E1 5b ★★★

A magnificent well-named climb with a strenuous and spectacular final pitch. Start at the base of a black slab to the right of the chimney forming the right-hand side of the prominent pinnacle.
1 30m 4c Climb to a groove at 15m; follow this, finishing up the flake on the left to a tree.
2 24m 5b Move left then climb the left side of the easy-angled rib to the right of the large dirty central groove. Step right around the rib, climb a short groove until below and right of a large overhanging pinnacle. Climb the crack on the right of the pinnacle and manoeuvre onto its top. Finish directly using the crack and flakes.
Photo page 368.
P Ross, P Lockey 14.04.1957

28 Little Chamonix 71m VD ★★★

Diverse climbing, great positions and a spectacular finale have make this a popular classic. Suffering the indignity of an ascent in roller-skates and boxing-gloves has only enhanced its status. A bit polished. Start 8m right of the prominent central pinnacle.
1 30m Climb to a groove at 15m; follow this, finishing up the flake on the left to gain a tree.
2 12m Scramble up right through trees to the left-hand of two conspicuous V-corners.
3 29m Ascend the left-hand corner to an overhang. The goal is to gain and cross the slab on the right to its right arête, then climb to the Saddle (possible belay). Ascend to the base of the pinnacle above, step right and up to gain its top. Make a couple of steep moves up and left to The Belvedere. A superb pitch.
B Beetham 26.05.1946

29 Stone Tape 34m E3 6a ★★

Good, steep climbing with an airy finish on the upper buttress.
1 12m 6a Follow the right-slanting break across the wall to a spike below the right side of the overhang. Step left and up to below the top of the overhang. Swing out left and up to belay on the Saddle.
2 22m 5b Descend a slab on the left and stand on a large block below an overhanging groove. Climb this, past a large dubious spike, to a ledge. Continue up the groove above to a sloping ledge and finish up the short wall.

30 Battering Ram 33m E3 6a ★★

A great route taking the right side of the arching overhang then the fine steep finger crack on the right. Start 8m to the left of the large oak tree below a large flake. From the flake, climb the wall first left then right to gain the right-hand end of the overhang. Follow the diagonal groove above the overhang to a ledge then traverse right to an oak tree. Climb the thin right-hand crack directly behind the tree to a groove which is followed to the top.
R Smith, J Earl 27.05.1984

Donkey's Ears HS (page 380) — 📷 Tom McNally

Wild Sheep Area

An area of ramps, grooves, steep walls and arêtes. Reference points are the upper arête of *Wild Sheep* and, 8m to the left, a large oak tree at the base of the crag.

Approach: Follow the base of the crag up and left to a large yew tree as for the **Monolith Crack Area**. Scramble up to broken ledges just above.

Descent: Via Jackdaw Terrace or further south - see *Jackdaw Ridge* descent and overview diagram.

③① Derision Groove 34m MVS 4b ★★
A popular route with some interesting moves. Start immediately right of the large oak tree. Climb the steep stepped groove on good holds to a ledge. Climb the gangway until a traverse left can be made to The Belvedere.
Photo opposite.
P Ross, JA Wood 27.02.1955

③② Wild Sheep 33m E2 5b ★★★ ◆
Takes the arête of *Black Sheep* on the left in its entirety. Similar to but more sustained than the original. Gain the pedestal and continue up steeply, just left of the arête, on superb incut holds.
K Wilkinson, D Booth, A Morris 31.03.1989

③③ Black Sheep 34m E2 5b ★★
A safe yet exciting route up the overhanging arête left of the deep chimney. A large bush grows at the bottom right-hand side of the arête. Start directly below this and climb easy ramps and corners to a ledge. A difficult move up leads to the bush. Move left onto the overhanging side of the arête. Climb onto a pedestal then gain and climb the right side of the arête.
P Botterill, D Hopkins 10.05.1977

③④ Shepherd's Chimney 32m VS 5a ★★
This direct version of the original gives a good line, finishing in a fine position. Start below a short corner at the left end of the steep smooth orange brown wall.
1 17m 5a Climb the corner to a grassy ledge. Up the groove above to an awkward exit.
2 15m 4a Climb the slanting chimney, steep initially, followed by easier climbing on the left wall.
B Beetham 31.07.1946

③⑤ Inclination 18m E5 6b ★★
Start at the belay at the top of P1 of *Shepherd's Chimney*. Climb the corner up and right of the belay (peg), move up (peg), then a hard traverse right leads to an easier finish up a groove.
J Lamb, P Botterill Jul 1979

㉘ Little Chamonix VD ★★★

Monolith Crack Area

Complex, with both hard and easy routes of one or two pitches, makes this area worth seeking out.

Approach: Follow the base of the crag up and left to a large yew tree. Now scramble up and right to a broken terrace beneath a steep smooth orange-brown wall. Continue scrambling up right over large blocks to Jackdaw Terrace. At the upper right-hand end of the terrace is an open corner and steepening.

Descent: Via Jackdaw Terrace or further south - see *Jackdaw Ridge* descent and overview diagram.

36 The Devil's Alternative 12m E6 6b (F7a+) ★★ ♂

A finger-tearing, serious and technical climb up the steep smooth orange-brown wall with poor protection which is difficult to arrange. Start below the centre of the wall. Step up onto a ledge then use a layaway to reach a ledge. Move left for a metre or so then move back up right to good pockets. Pull straight up to large oak and yew trees on the ledge above.
J Lamb, P Whillance 1.05.1981

37 The Black Icicle 30m E1 5b ★★★

An excellent route with a bold second pitch. Care needed to protect the start; on P2 protection is good but spaced. Start at the jumble of large spikes.
1 14m 5b Climb the thin black quartz crack running up the steep wall then move up to a tree.
2 16m 5a With or without the use of the tree, gain and climb the blunt arête. Move up and right to finish airily up the wall.
D Fielding 1958

38 Porcupine 28m E3 6a ★★

A pleasant first pitch leads to a short difficult corner. Start at the jumble of large spikes just to the right of the left-slanting V-groove.
1 18m 5a From the spikes, carefully pull directly up the overhanging rib on the right then follow the groove and wide crack above to a large ledge.
2 10m 6a Ascend the prominent short corner pulling up rightwards to finish. Intense but well-protected.
P Ross, E Ray 2.07.1955

39 Monolith Crack 32m HVS 4c ★★

A varied and popular route up the centre of the wall sporting a classic finishing crack. Start below the stunted tree.
1 12m 4c Climb the leftward-slanting break for 3m to a small niche. Move up using a small slanting foot ledge on the left to pass the tree and gain the ledge above. Ascend a short chimney to a tree.
2 20m 4c To the left is the Monolith. Climb the off-width crack just to its right then ascend a short corner and finish up the wall.

Monolith Chimney 23m S

2a For those not wishing to battle with the crack, it is possible to move to the left of the Monolith and ascend the chimney. Finish up the short corner and wall.
B Beetham 28.07.1947

40 Hee-Haw 16m VS 5a ★

A short but pleasant route. Start 2m left of a conspicuous rusty streak. Climb a faint cracked groove to gain a traverse line. Above is an obvious crack slanting left, with a faint crack on its right. Climb the right-hand crack to gain a ledge and continue to The Belvedere.
R Kenyon, C Eckersall 1983

Derision Groove MVS (opposite) Fiona Sanders
📷 David Simmonite

Jackdaw Ridge Area

Long relatively easy routes on this furthest right part of **Shepherd's Crag**.

Approach: Walk along the bottom of all the other sectors or, if approaching from High Lodore Farm, up the track and over the stile. *Jackdaw Ridge* is just beyond the stile.

Descent: Walk south from The Belvedere, the flat platform-like top of the crag. Descend slightly to the top of a gully and re-ascend the other side to a good path that leads back down to the stile.

41 Donkey's Ears 67m HS ★★

A classic climb with a decisive final pitch. Start 5m left of a conspicuous chimney where an ash tree is guarded by a slim flake.
1 26m Climb the easy wall then follow the scratched line into a wide grassy trough. Scramble up to a small cave below the huge projecting block.
2 8m From outside or inside the cave, climb onto an outward-pointing spike. Hand-traverse left and up or fight up between the donkey's ears to a ledge.
3 12m Ascend the pile of blocks above, trending right, to a tree.
3 21m Traverse left into a corner then delicately traverse to V-cracks. Climb these precariously and continue up to The Belvedere.
Photo page 376.
B Beetham 1.04.1947

42 Jackdaw Ridge 66m D ★

The high-polish shows how many people have enjoyed this route over the years. Start 7m left of the stile at a prominent well-worn rib.
1 26m Climb the rib for 8m and continue above to a ledge with a tree. Continue over blocks to a ledge with a large tree. Or, climb the less defined rib 3m left: VD.
2 23m Above the tree, climb the rightward-slanting V-groove to the easier-angled ridge and a tree.
3 17m Climb an awkward V-groove then continue on a rib to The Belvedere.
B Beetham 27. 08.1946

UPPER SHEPHERD'S CRAG

Ideal for families this attractive little crag offers short 10m routes with excellent belays, easily top-roped. The crag can be climbed on anywhere with some lines suggested.

Approach: From High Lodore Farm, follow the zig-zag path towards Watendlath, passing the approach to the main crag off to the left. The path levels out and once a low broken wall has been crossed, turn left and toddle to the base of the crag. Map page 369.

1 Tup D
2 Ram VD
Steep at the start.
3 Ewe D
4 Lamb VD
A difficult start; easy S with a direct line.
5 EZY D
6 Sheepdog D

Monolith Crack Area
- **39 Monolith Crack** — HVS 4c ★★

Jackdaw Ridge Area
- **41 Donkey's Ears** — HS ★★
- **42 Jackdaw Ridge** — D ★

MAC'S BORROWDALE ENCHAINMENT
A big day out round the valley on routes climbed by local climber Ray McHaffie.
- ☐ **The Niche**, Falcon Crags — E2
- ☐ **White Noise** or **The Rack**, Reecastle Crag — E3 or HVS
- ☐ **Aaros**, Shepherd's Crag — E1
- ☐ **Jubilee Grooves**, Black Crag — E1
- ☐ **The Crypt**, Quayfoot Buttress — HVS
- ☐ **Lakeland Cragsman**, Sergeant's Crag Slab — HVS

BLACK CRAG

OS Grid Ref: NY 263 172
Altitude: 260m

An excellent crag with routes for everyone. It sits above the trees in the delightful side valley of Troutdale.

Approach: Leave the valley road and head along the Leathes Head Hotel track; go through a gate then cross the delightful Troutdale making a steep well-marked short trek up to the foot of the crag. From the Bowderstone Quarry CP a path heads north dropping into Troutdale.

RAD
Black Crag

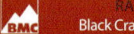

OS Grid Ref
NY 263 172

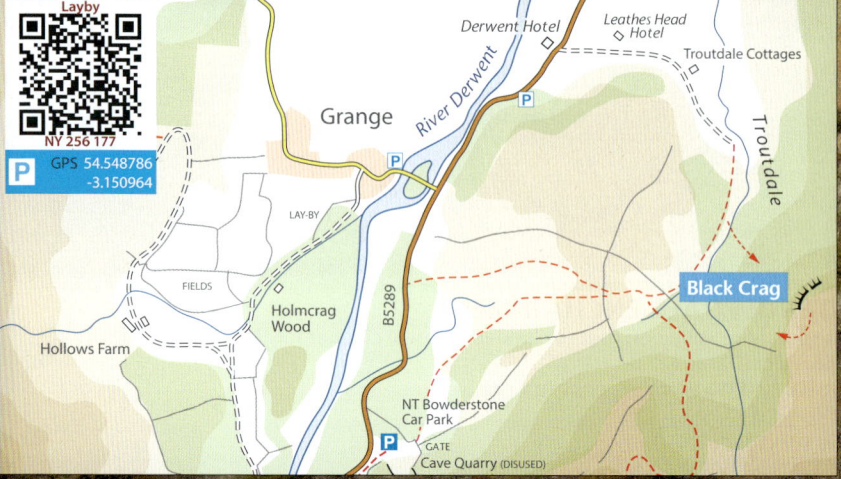

Troutdale Pinnacle S (page 386) Joe Gittins & Jack Overhill — 📷 David Simmonite

North Buttress

Impressive harder routes tackle the steep central wall and there's a fun juggy VS. Shrouded by trees, and prone to seepage lower down, the less well-travelled routes to the left have become vegetated. Take care moving across steep vegetation at the top.

Approach: Walk 50m up to the left from the base of the **Main Buttress**.

Descent: Walk up and back to the right to reach a stile, cross this then follow a steep path back to base.

① The Coffin 62m VS 4c ★★
A popular climb, committing and clean on its main pitch, vegetated on P1 and 3. Start at a slab left of the big corner taken by *The Shroud*.
1 10m Head left to climb a corner, apeing over a tree, to a vegetated ledge; move right to belay. Or, avoid the pitch by walking across to this ledge from higher to the left.
2 40m 4c Despite its appearance the steep wall on the left is climbed. At the overhang move left, up a gangway then right to a steep groove. Follow the groove, stepping left into its continuation, to a stance on a slab.
3 12m 4a Climb leftwards to the top of the slab. Move left around the edge to the final corner.
R McHaffie, D Brownlee 12.02.1967

② Jubilee Grooves 70m E1 5b ★★
Enjoyable; a strong line with a dirty finish.
1 25m 5a Climb the corner (*The Shroud*) then a short wall to a groove. Follow this left of the overhang to belay on the slab below the big overhang.
2 25m 5b Enter the groove left of the roof. At the top move right to continue up a long groove to reach a heather ledge; belay to the right.
3 20m 4a Go back left to finish up the rib.
W Freelands, R McHaffie 7.06.1977

③ The Shroud 72m VS 4c ★★★
A varied route of great interest.
1 12m 4b The corner to a stance on the right.
2 15m 4c Take the groove behind the belay to an overhang (peg). A couple of precarious moves right lead to glorious jug pulling. Belay below the big overhang.
3 21m 4c Cross the slab on the left for about 7m and then climb up left to a short groove left of a nose. Continue up to the right to another small overhang which is passed on its left. Go up the short groove above and step left to a ledge.
4 24m 4b Move right onto a rib then climb a series of mossy slabs and grooves towards bulging rock up on the right. Move right at the bulge then up easily to the top.
P Ross, P Lockey 1.06.1958

④ Grand Alliance 57m E4 6a ★★★★ ♂
A thrilling route following an intricate line; technical and delicate, an ascent demands competence and confidence from the whole team. Start below the arête to the right of the corner taken by *The Shroud*.
1 10m 4c Climb the blunt arête to a ledge.
2 15m 5b Traverse right to twin blocks on the ledge. Climb into the overhung corner above. Pull out right and climb the wall above to a slab and belay.
3 32m 6a Traverse right across the slab to the left end of a long overhang, mantelshelf onto a ledge on the wall on the left and traverse delicately right between the overhangs. Climb with less difficulty to foot ledges then trend left to reach small undercuts. Step right and make difficult moves up the wall to better holds. Easier climbing leads to a large ledge.
R Matheson, E Cleasby 28.07.1976

⑤ Vertigo 80m E3 5c ★★
A memorable and thuggy route taking a direct line through the mid-height overhangs. Start on a right-slanting gangway above a large holly tree.
1 12m Walk up the gangway, climb a short corner and step right to a yew tree.
2 14m 4c Step off a block into a corner on the left and climb to a large slab. Left for 5m to a block.
3 24m 5c Traverse right across the slab to the left end of a long overhang then mantelshelf onto a ledge on the wall on the left. Climb a series of short left-trending corners, pull over the final roof and move right to gain a small ledge. Climb left for 2m then the wall above to a small ledge on the left.
4 30m Climb the rib on the right then the groove above, over a hanging block, to finish on slabs.
P Ross, W Aughton 18.10.1958

The next route starts below the wet easy-angled black slab left of the gully.

⑥ Prana 54m E3 5c ★★★ ♂
A thrilling absorbing wall climb with good holds and reasonable protection.
1 12m 4b Climb the fault leftwards to a tree below the wall.
2 42m 5c Move right and climb the wall, 3m left of the gully, pulling up left onto the slab below the mid-height overhangs. Pull across on small holds; or use an easier alternative 2m right. Climb the wall until a step left can be made to a ledge. Climb the bulging wall above to where the angle eases and continue to a large ledge.
P Gomersall 4.09.1977

North Buttress | **Black Crag** | 385

Main Buttress

An array of classics, including the eponymous Pinnacle, make this a very popular spot. Routes converge at the summit, a stunning viewpoint.

Descent: Head up and right at the top of the crag then follow a well-worn path down the right side.

7 Obituary Grooves 100m HVS 5a ★★
Interesting sustained climbing. Start behind the fallen tree.
1 30m 4b Climb a steep slab to a ledge then move left and climb the crack, just right of a dirty corner, to a ledge. Move left and up a short corner then left again to a tree.
2 34m 5a Climb a groove to a tree below an overhang. Move out to the right and up to the top of a groove, where an awkward move leads left. Climb a short way up the groove then move left, up and out to the right to a tree.
3 36m 4c Easier rock leads to a large flake. Climb left into a leftward-slanting corner; exit on the right. Gain the groove above, move left to a holly tree and back right to finish via twin cracks.
PJ Greenwood, P Ross 30.07.1955

8 The Mortician 80m HVS 5a ★★★
A superb challenging route with a difficult well-protected crux.
1 30m 4b P1 of *Obituary Grooves*.
2 40m 5a Step up right then make enigmatic and committing moves to get established in the clean-cut groove; sustained climbing up this and the wide crack above leads to a belay.
3 10m 4c Move into a broken groove and continue directly to the top of the pinnacle. Climb the groove and wall to the top.
B Thompson, WA Barnes 7.08.1969

9 Troutdale Pinnacle Direct 99m VS 4c ★★★
An attractive and varied route, well-protected and a good introduction to the VS grade.
1 25m 4b Climb the steep slab behind the fallen tree to a ledge. Go up the flake crack over an overlap to another ledge and traverse right. Climb up 2m to a block belay.
2 25m 4c Move left a little and climb the immaculate wall on small positive holds; after 10m step left and continue more easily to a small ledge.
3 24m 4a Move right and climb a steep wall to a small ledge and belay.
4 25m P5 and 6 of *Troutdale Pinnacle*.
JD Oliver, M Nixon, K Pepper 27.07.1952

10 Troutdale Pinnacle Superdirect 97m HVS 5a ★★★
An entertaining combination of delicate and strenuous.
1 25m 4b P1 of *Troutdale Pinnacle Direct*.
2 25m 4c P2 of *Troutdale Pinnacle Direct*.
3 24m 5a Climb the steep crack, just left of the stance and pull out left at the top to a ledge.
4 10m 5a Climb a broken groove past a suspect block to reach the Finger Traverse. Move right to better holds in a groove then climb to the top of the pinnacle.
5 13m Follow big holds up the groove and wall.
P Ross, D Oliver 15.6.1959

11 Troutdale Pinnacle 105m S ★★★★
Originally known as *Black Crag Buttress*, this magnificent route offers continuously interesting climbing. Start at the lowest point of the crag, behind an old fallen tree at a short wide broken crack.
1 21m Climb the crack to a ledge then right to a birch tree. Climb the wall behind the tree for 6m to another ledge and continue up a broken groove to a large block.
2 28m Follow a groove on the right to slabs. Climb these rightwards to a large ledge and block belay below a shattered corner.
3 10m Ascend the steep corner then step left to a small stance on the right extremity of a sweep of slabs.
4 20m Traverse left and down the slabs to a corner. Swing across the steep left wall on polished holds and pull up to ledges.
5 13m Continue easily to the top of the pinnacle.
6 13m Climb the steep exposed groove then finally left to reach easier rocks.
Photo page 383.
F Mallinson, R Mayson 4.05.1914

12 Raindrop 90m E1 5b ★★★
This very direct line, probably the best E1 on the crag, gives great climbing in airy positions. Start in the centre of the steep slab at a left-slanting crack.
1 42m 5b Climb the crack to a ledge. Trend left up the slab to break through the left end of the heather moustache. Climb straight up to the left end of a small overhang then move left along a diagonal crack to below a shallow scoop; follow this to a stance.
2 33m 5b Climb the wall, just right of the crack, to a good foothold on the right. Move left then go straight up friendly cracks to gain a rightward-slanting groove. Climb this and the arête on the right to the top of the pinnacle.
3 15m 4c Climb a little way up the groove

behind then swing round the arête to the left and so to the top or, like most people, finish up *Troutdale Pinnacle*.
P Livesey, J Sheard Jun 1973

North Buttress
- **6 Prana** — E3 5c ★★★

Main Buttress
- **7 Obituary Grooves** — HVS 5a ★★
- **8 The Mortician** — HVS 5a ★★★
- **9 TP Direct** — VS 4c ★★★
- **10 TP Superdirect** — HVS 5a ★★★
- **11 Troutdale Pinnacle** — S ★★★★
- **12 Raindrop** — E1 5b ★★★

QUAYFOOT BUTTRESS
OS Grid Ref: NY 255 168
Altitude: 135m

Mandrake HVS (page 390) Keith Sanders — 📷 David Simmonite

This popular crag offers very accessible high quality climbing on superb compact rock: a paradise for **VS-E2** climbers! It is especially enjoyable to climb here in the afternoon or evening sun.

Approach: An easy path leads from the Bowderstone Quarry car park.

Descent: To the right side of the crag.

1 Quayfoot Buttress 56m VD ★★

Enjoyable varied climbing which becomes more interesting as height is gained. Start 3m right of the fence at the foot of the crag.

1 31m Climb a groove rightwards to a block overhang which is avoided on the left; continue to a ledge. Move left to a small tree then climb the arête and groove to a ledge.

OS Grid Ref
NY 255 168

Bowderstone P&D
NY 253 169

GPS 54.541288
-3.154773

RAD
Quayfoot

2 25m Climb the scoop on the left, make an awkward move onto a ledge then climb the slab above.
B Beetham 4.04.1946

2 The Crypt 40m HVS 5a ★★

Cracking climbing up the shallow scoop. From the left end of the ledges climb a few metres then move over an awkward bulge and continue to a tree. Move up to gain and climb the fine scoop; at the overlap move left to the final rib.
R McHaffie, JG Alderson 1.05.1969

3 The Crypt Direct 40m E1 5b ★★

This short and sharp alternative finish climbs the overlap and wall avoided by the original route.
K Rudd 17.04.1971

4 The Go Between 40m E2 5c ★★

A steep start leads to satisfying technical climbing. The crack leads to easier ground and a ledge. Follow a vague crackline in the middle of the wall above to a horizontal break; continue directly up the wall above to the top. If the initial crack is wet, start to the right.
J Lamb, P Botterill 20.06.1981

5 Aberration 44m VS 4c ★★

Technical and delicate climbing in good positions. Start below the right-facing corner in the centre of the buttress. Gain the corner, which gives interesting moves, leading to a short narrow chimney then an overhung ledge. Establish yourself on the rib to the left then go diagonally left to a dirty groove which is climbed, past a tree, to the top.
O Woolcock, P Nunn 2.05.1965

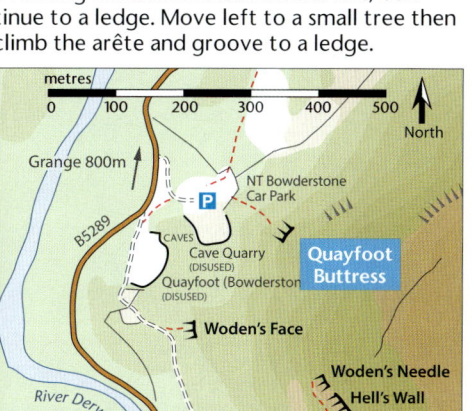

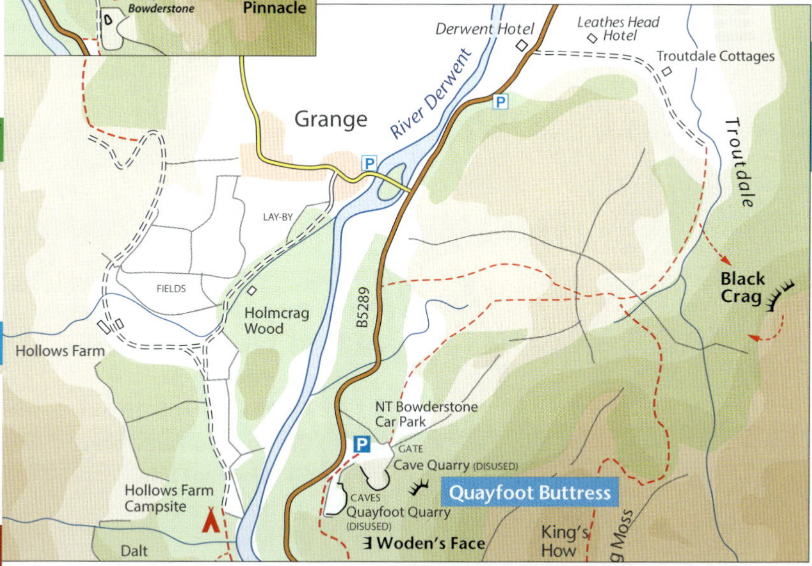

⑥ Mandrake 44m HVS 5a ★★★

One of the valley's finest single pitch HVSs. From the base of the corner, hand traverse left for 3m then climb up to a ledge. Continue up the thin crack leading to the bottom of the chimney-groove. Traverse right for 6m to another crack and climb this to an overhang; thrilling moves over this lead to a grand finish.
Photo page 388.
A Liddell, M Burbage July 1964

⑦ Irony 40m HVS 5a ★★

Sustained absorbing climbing leading to a memorable and spectacular overhang. The short stiff overhanging corner leads to a ledge. Follow a groove and slab on the left before moving slightly right to a crack which is climbed to a ledge. Cross the broken overhang and climb the thin crack; swing right at the top to another ledge. Move left under the large overhang and pull over with great difficulty; finish easily.
R Belden 1961

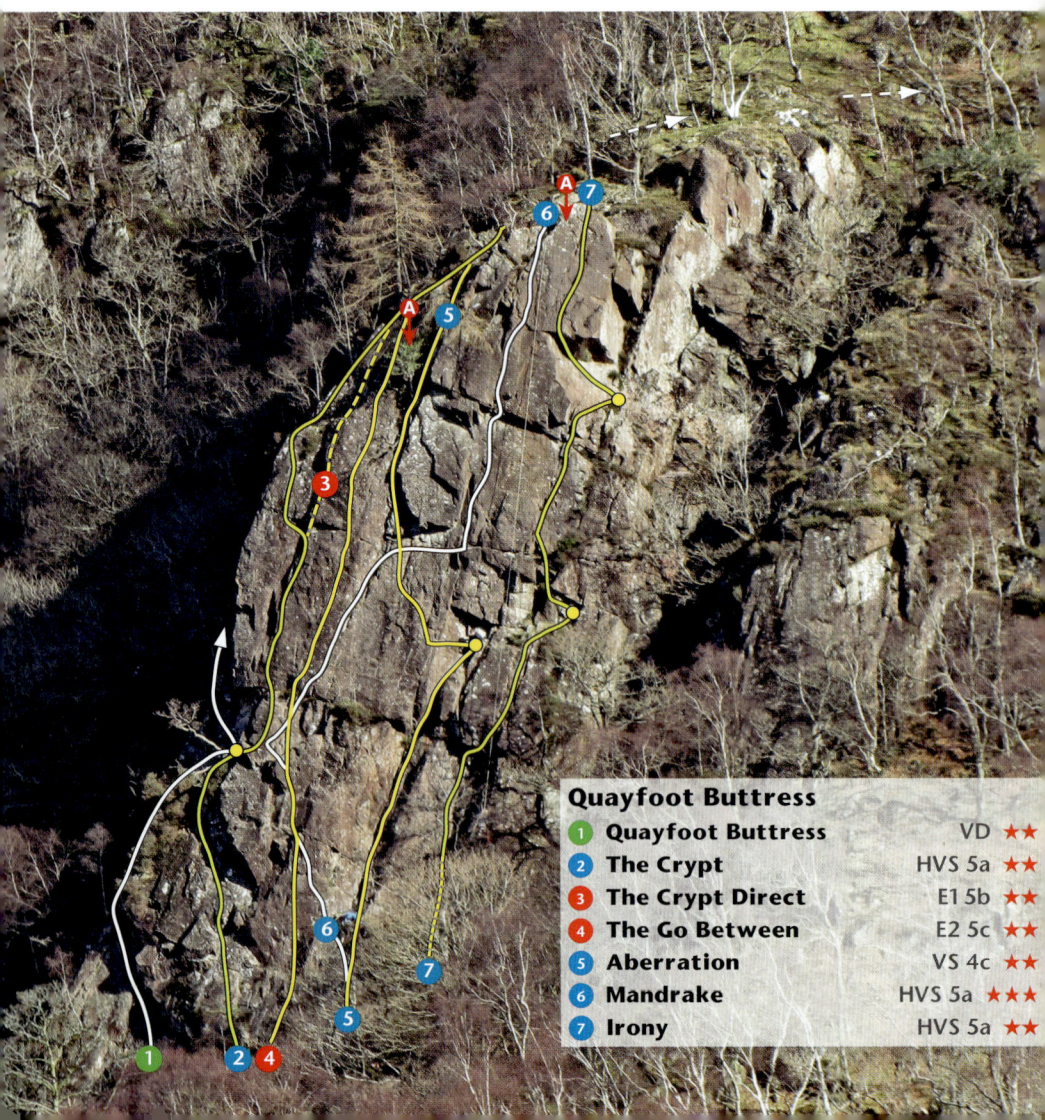

Quayfoot Buttress
① Quayfoot Buttress — VD ★★
② The Crypt — HVS 5a ★★
③ The Crypt Direct — E1 5b ★★
④ The Go Between — E2 5c ★★
⑤ Aberration — VS 4c ★★
⑥ Mandrake — HVS 5a ★★★
⑦ Irony — HVS 5a ★★

BOWDERSTONE CRAGS

OS Grid Ref: NY 256 165
Altitude: 220m

This cluster of buttresses above the iconic Bowderstone are home to very popular easier routes, bookending the fierce **Hell's Wall**.

Bleed in Hell, Hell's Wall E8 (page 396) Robbie Phillips — 📷 Marc Langley

WODEN'S FACE

OS Grid Ref: NY 253 166
Altitude: 110m

This delightful sunny wall has immaculate rock, a short approach and a nice selection of routes in the lower grades - plus a couple of others.

Approach: Take the track from the Bowderstone Quarry car park towards the Bowderstone. The crag is on the left.

Descent: From the terrace at the top of the routes, scramble with care left and down or gain more height before heading left.

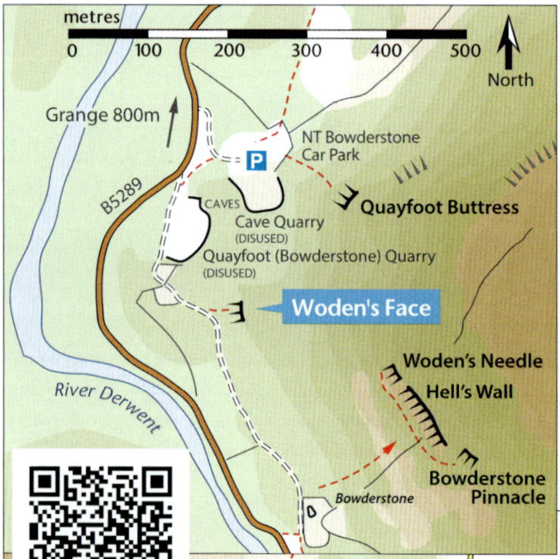

❶ Left Hand Route   13m   VD
The groove and crack on the left.
R McHaffie 1989

❷ Blue Riband   15m   HS 4b   ★
The enjoyable steep cracked face.
R McHaffie 4.06.1989

❸ Wimpey Way   24m   S   ★★
Start 3m right of the large tree and climb the stepped groove.
Photo opposite.
W Robinson, K Perry 1970

To the right is a large block overhang at 6m.

❹ Woden's Face   25m   MVS 4b   ★★
A popular route with exposed and exciting climbing in its upper half. Teeter up the wall to the overhang then move delicately left into a groove. A short distance up, step right and follow the precarious scoop in the edge of the buttress to the terrace. Alternatively climb to the right of the scoop; S.
B Beetham, CD Frankland 1921

❺ Woden's Face Direct   24m   S 4a   ★★
Good climbing up the centre of the wall. Climb to the overhang pass either side onto the block; left is easier. Step off the block, move right, then climb to the top of a shallow scoop. Move left then climb directly to the terrace.
B Beetham, CD Frankland 1921

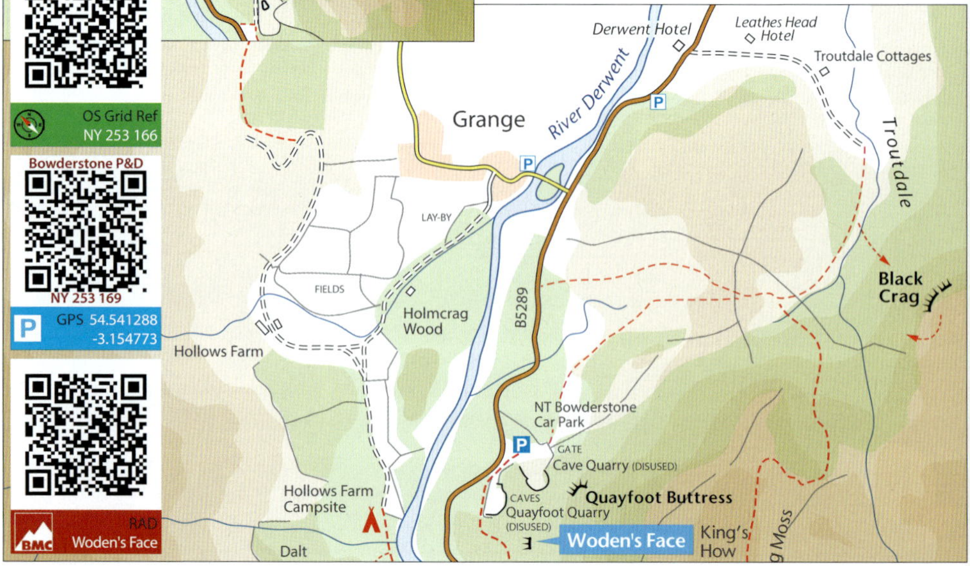

6 Woden's Wotsit 24m E2 5b ★
A direct route with good climbing yet no real line, or protection! Start from a ledge below the wall just right of a tree. A few stiff pulls up the wall lead to easier ground and a ledge. Continue up the wall and slab.
R Kenyon, C Eckersall 4.07.1984

7 Woden's Cheek 22m MVS 4b ★★
An awkward start leads to an airy finish. On the right side of the crag is a short groove above a small overhanging wall. Enter the groove by a decisive and difficult pull and follow it to a good ledge. Continue up the groove above moving right to finish.
B Beetham 12.09.1935

Wimpey Way S (opposite) Fiona Sanders & Keith Sanders — David Simmonite

Bowderstone Crags | 395

WODEN'S NEEDLE ⏱ 20 min

This small buttress fronted by a prominent pinnacle - Woden's Needle is worth the walk.

Approach: From the Bowderstone Quarry car park head along the track towards the Bowderstone. Just before the Bowderstone take the track on the left. Head off left below **Hell's Wall** to reach the start of the climbs.

Additional mape page 392.

Descent: To the left.

❶ Woden's Needle 30m VD ★★
An interesting climb. Climb the fissure on the left of the Needle to a ledge at 10m. Step down right then climb rightwards to the top of the needle. Finish up the wall. **Photo below.**
B Beetham 26.08.1936

❷ Creeping Bentley 30m VS 4c ★
A direct variation on *Woden's Needle*. On the front of the Needle move up right to a crack, climb this past a wobbling flake to reach the top via an obvious pocket. Step up then move left towards an oak tree and ascend the left edge of the wall.
R Smithson, D Heard 20.08.2004

BOWDERSTONE PINNACLE ⏱ 20 min

Directly above the Bowderstone, with the fierce modern routes to its left and hidden by trees, is the Bowderstone Pinnacle.

Descent: Well to the right.

❸ Thor's Entrance 40m S ★
An interesting climb with some good climbing in a great situation on the second pitch. It starts behind a large tree 5m left of the arête of the Pinnacle.
1 16m Climb the steep crack to a ledge and the crack above to belay on the Pinnacle route.
2 24m Climb the short V-groove onto the rib. Traverse delicately left to reach good holds in the shallow recess. Climb steeply to a spike on the arête and then to the top of the buttress.
R Miller, AC Cain 6.12.1953

❹ Bowderstone Pinnacle 36m D
A classic route that ascends the prominent buttress in the centre of the crag. Start 10m up the gully to the right of the buttress below the large tree.
1 12m Traverse diagonally left along polished ledges to a broken crack which leads to a stance on the arête.
2 18m Continue up the buttress, past a tree and dead stump, into the cleft between the buttress on the left and the Pinnacle on the right.
3 6m Either climb onto the Pinnacle, or climb the left arête of the buttress, then leap across the gap onto the top of the Pinnacle. Finish by crossing the ridge from the buttress and climbing a short step. The obvious gully on the right is not recommended for descent.
F Mallinson, R Mayson May 1914

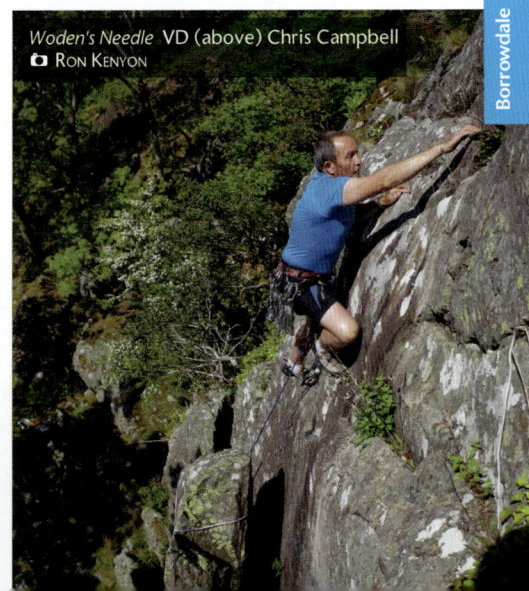

Woden's Needle VD (above) Chris Campbell
📷 Ron Kenyon

HELL'S WALL

🕐 20 min

An impressive area, for most just to be looked at, for some it provides several modern test-pieces.

Approach: From Bowderstone Quarry car park a track leads south; 50m before reaching the Bowderstone an indistinct path on the left, hidden by bracken in summer, leads steeply to **Bowderstone Pinnacle**, head left to **Hell's Wall**.

Descent: Follow a broken ramp to the left.

❶ Lucifer 30m E5 6a ★★
Takes the steep groove in the wall. Start left of the main wall and climb up into an open groove or more easily just right. Go up to a ledge then easily up left to the next ledge. Pull up right into the slim hanging groove (peg) and climb it, exiting left at the top.
P Whillance, D Armstrong 19.05.1981

❷ De Quincy 30m E7 6b (F7a) ★★
This poorly protected climb takes on the challenge of the impending wall left of the arête. Start right of the wide crack. Climb thin cracks in the left side of the wall then move left onto a ledge on the arête. Climb straight up above the ledge, just left of the arête (hidden peg), passing the final crack on the left.
J Moffatt, P Kirton Jun 1982

❸ Bleed in Hell 30m E8 6c (F8a+) ★★★
The stunning arête. Climb the wide crack to a ledge on the arête. Make the first few moves up the crack of *Hell's Wall* to a pocket (pegs) then left to the arête. Follow this to the top.
Photo page 391.
D Birkett 5.05.1992

❹ Hell's Wall 30m E6 6c (F7c+) ★★★★
The original testpiece of the wall - protected by *in-situ* pegs. Climb the wide crack to a ledge then go up to a ledge on the arête. Move up and right to gain a crack. Go up this then move out right and up rightwards to below a curving groove which is followed boldly to the top.
Photo below.
R Fawcett, C Gibb 1979

❺ Wheels of Fire 35m E4 6a ★★★
The awkward first corner leads to a very good top pitch above the impressive wall. Start in the slabby corner behind a large block.
1 15m 6a Ascend the corner to a ledge. Climb directly up the steep corner and crack above to a tree.
2 20m 6a Traverse diagonally left along the lip of the overhang. Pull up (long reach) then finish up the short wall and groove on the left.
P Whillance, D Armstrong 22.04.1979

❻ Valhalla 32m E1 5c ★★
The corner to the right of the wall.
1 18m 4c Climb the corner to a ledge. Move right across a slab and up steep cracked rock to a small tree below the corner.
2 14m 5c Follow the corner passing a square-cut overhang on the left.
W Barnes, D Elliott 22.09.1962

❼ The Bulger 36m E5 6b ★★★
An exciting and strenuous pitch and a must for fans of finger-jamming through roofs.
1 18m 4c P1 of *Valhalla*.
2 18m 6b Step down right and climb the vague crack in the wall above, until a pull out right can be made below the roof. Pull up to the thin crack and follow it rightwards to the top.
P Botterill, J Lamb 30.05.1981

❽ Heaven's Gate 35m E3 6a ★★
Climbs the arched groove on the right.
1 15m Scramble up past a holly and an oak to a large oak tree below the groove.
2 20m 6a Enter the groove above and follow it until forced out right at the top onto the rib. Climb the wall on the right of the rib to a ledge on the left.
J Lamb, P Botterill 1.06.1981

Hell's Wall E6 (this page) Karin Magog
📷 Steve Crowe

STEEL KNOTTS

OS Grid Ref: NY 246 164
Altitude: 240m

Excellent clean quick-drying rock with high quality climbing. It gets the morning sun so can be combined with one of the other crags that get the sun later.

Approach: From Grange, take the road next to the cafe, south. This eventually leads to a bridleway by the river which then climbs up a hill. Immediately after the gate, take a path up the fellside on the right next to a wall passing below **Steel Knotts Bluff** then up to the crag. Or, from Rosthwaite, take the lane west, cross the river then head up the path by Tongue Gill to join the bridleway. Cross over the col and head down. Just before the gate, take the path on your left.

Descent: Down scree to the left.

❶ **The Sting**   23m   E2 5c   ★★★
A fine route giving one of the best jamming exercises in the district. Start below a thin vertical crack, 5m right of the large holly tree. Climb the crack, past a small ledge at half-height, to finish up the short rib on the left.
RT Marsden, TE Dunsby 1973

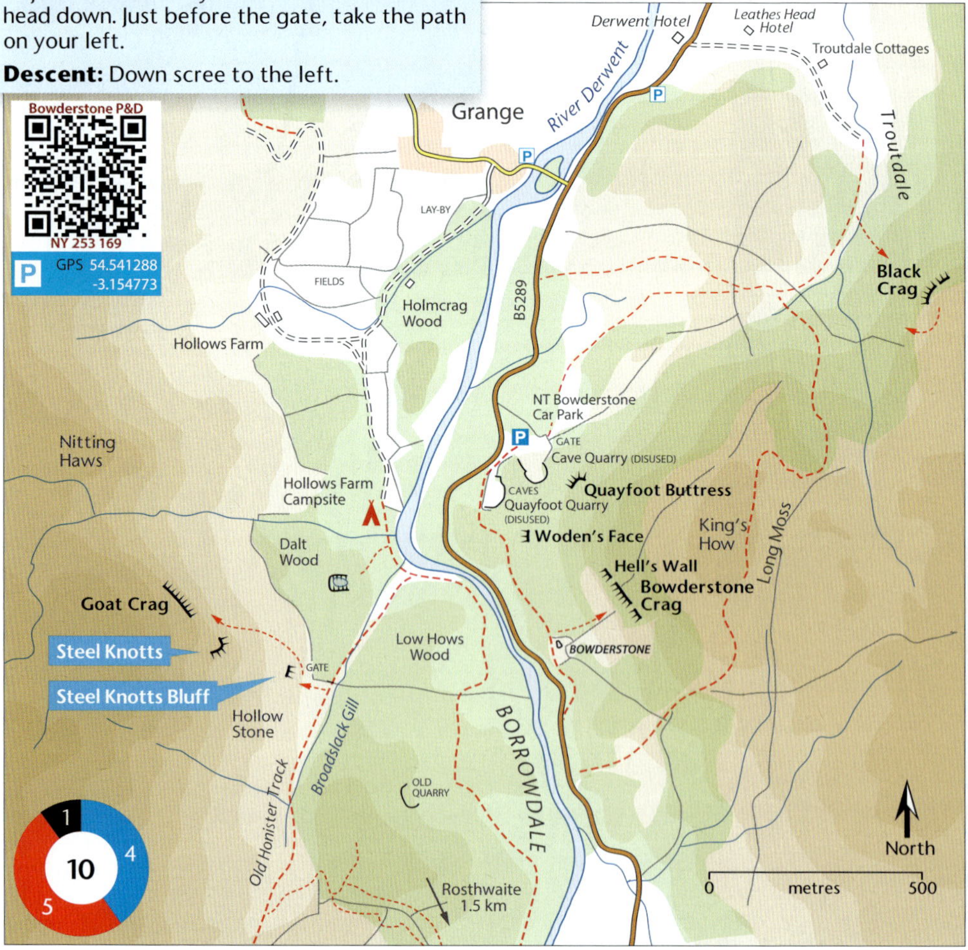

2 Meandering Maggot 30m E1 5b ★★
Start just left of a large block in the centre of the crag. Ascend a crack to gain the niche on the left, below an overhang. Climb up the corner, avoiding the overhang on its left, to follow pleasant cracks then the short arête.
R Kenyon, T Price 1984

3 Lurching Leech 30m HVS 5a ★★
Deceptively awkward. From the large block climb the crack to a corner. Finish up the wide crack.
K Leech, T Taylor 23.08.1965

4 Ambling Ant 30m MVS 4b ★★
A pleasant open climb starting on a block 6m down and right of the large block in the centre of the crag. Step off the block, then go up a corner to a ledge, just left of a holly tree. Pass the corner above by moves on the left to gain a ledge. Continue up the wall, passing a large detached block, to easier rock.
R Kenyon, T Price, L Jordan 20.10.1985

5 Route 2 30m VS 4c ★
The crack forming the left side of the pinnacle. Climb the crack exiting awkwardly, move up then climb the steep short wall just right of the corner. Move 2m left to the final slabby wall.

6 Tottering Tortoise 30m HVS 5a ★★
Entertaining. Climb the off-width crack forming the right side of the pinnacle then the steep short wall just right of the corner. Move 2m left and follow a slabby wall.
T Taylor, K Leech 23.08.1965

7 Loss Adjuster 30m E2 5c ★★
Start at the foot of the arête. Climb the wall on the right of the arête.
R Graham, P Graham 31.05.2013

8 The Lost Boys 30m HVS 5a ★★
The prominent arête right of the pinnacle. Climb a short corner just right of the arête with difficulty then climb diagonally left to step onto the pinnacle. Make a couple of moves up the wall and pull right to the arête. Climb this and the short wall above.
Photo page 356.
D Messenger, J Sharpe 21.05.1995

9 Paint it Black 30m E3 5c ★★
Climb the corner onto a large ledge on the right. Climb the black crack until it becomes thin. Move left onto the wall and make a hard move right up to a large hold. Stand on this and then continue to a big ledge. Climb the wall and crack, right of a holly tree.
B Davison, D Smart 24.07.1982

10 Free Falling 28m E4 6a ★★
Start in the centre of the steep wall. Climb the broken ribs to a small niche at around 4m. Make some awkward moves up and continue through the left-hand side of the shallow scoop to the large ledge. Finish up the wall and crack.
D Messenger, J Sharpe 17.09.1995

11 Terminal Velocity 28m E3 5c ★★
Start just left of the groove below an overlap at half-height. Climb the wall moving slightly left of the overlap to reach the large ledge. Finish up the wall and crack.
P Graham, R Graham 31.05.2013

Steel Knotts - Right
6	Tottering Tortoise	HVS 5a	★★
7	Loss Adjuster	E2 5c	★★
8	The Lost Boys	HVS 5a	★★
9	Paint it Black	E3 5c	★★
10	Free Falling	E4 6a	★★
11	Terminal Velocity	E3 5c	★★

STEEL KNOTTS BLUFF

OS Grid Ref: NY 247 164
Altitude: 160m

A handy little slab of textured rock that provides a great place for children or anyone in search of an easy introduction to rock. Bolt belays at the top.

Approach: As for **Steel Knotts**.
Descent: Easy walk off.

1 Picnic 11m D
The easiest route has nice flake holds.

2 Sandwich 13m VD
The easiest start is on the left.

3 Pop 15m S 4a
A delicate start then climb through the white scar.

4 Biscuit 15m HS 4c
Barely independent; a thin start but the upper section is easier than it looks.

5 Cake 15m HS 4a
Very pleasant.

GOAT CRAG

OS Grid Ref: NY 245 165
Altitude: 350m

D.D.T. E1 (opposite) Andy McVittie — David Simmonite

An impressive crag of excellent steep rock with an awesome collection of hard extremes. 60m ropes are recommended to allow some of the routes to be climbed in one single, magnificent long pitch.

Approach: Parking is limited so it may be best to park in the National Trust Bowderstone Pay & Display car park. From Grange, take the road next to the cafe, south. This eventually leads to a bridleway by the river which then climbs up a hill. Immediately after the gate, take a path up the fellside on the right next to a wall passing below **Steel Knotts Bluff**. Follow a vague path up the hillside with some short scrambling to below the upper part of the crag.

Descent: Abseil off a sling around one of the trees. Walking off is not recommended.

1 D.D.T. 65m E1 5a ★★★

The impressive corner shouts to be climbed and does not disappoint.
1 35m 5a Climb the corner; a short excursion onto the steep right wall sidesteps the bulge. The wide crack above leads to a ledge and tree on the left.
2 30m 5a A short wall on the right leads to a V-groove. Climb this past an awkward steepening onto an upper slab. Climb up and rightwards to an unprotected dirty finish into trees. The ab point is to the right.
Photo opposite.
J Lee, A Jackman, P Ross 17.10.1965

Once up the groove it's a lot less scary to traverse left to another tree and ab from here.

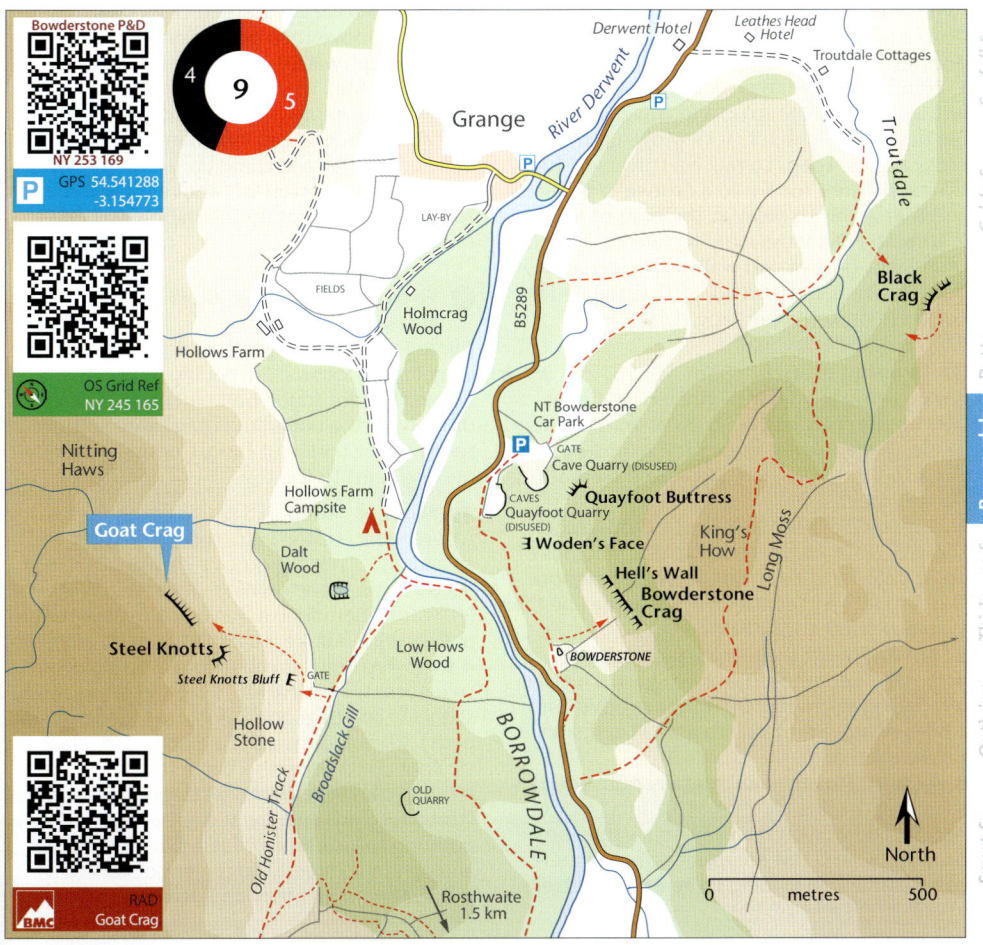

❷ The Voyage 83m E3 5c ★★★★
A magnificent involved trip, space-walking across very impressive ground. With sustained, absorbing, technical climbing, this passage ranks as one of the great E3s of the Lakes.
1 30m 5c Climb the initial corner of *D.D.T.* for 10m then step right to a junction with *Tumbleweed Connection* below a bulge. Go straight up (peg), traverse right to a groove in the arête and follow this onto the base of a ramp below a holly tree.
2 30m 5c Step down and traverse right below an overlap. Continue rightwards to reach and follow a higher ramp (aged bolt, pegs). Traverse down rightwards onto an easy slab to reach a ledge.
3 23m 5c Go up to and follow a flake crack over a bulge to a foothold below a corner. Climb the corner and wall above to finish.
S Clegg, P Botterill 26.06.1976

❸ Tumbleweed Connection 56m E2 5c ★★★★
Awesome climbing. Once engaged, the isolation requires total commitment. Best done in one massive pitch.
1 26m 5c Follow the prominent traverse line left to the arête. Step up and traverse left for 6m passing twin thin cracks. Move up then cross a bulge (peg) to reach a traverse. Move delicately right for 3m to a groove in the arête and follow this to belay at the base of a ramp.
2 30m 5b Follow the ramp leftwards. Take the prominent groove and wall until a sensational pull leftwards can be made across the undercut arête onto the finishing slab.
P Botterill, D Rawcliffe 25.06.1976

❹ Praying Mantis 85m E1 5b ★★★
A mega-classic insolently finding a devious way up the frowning buttress at an accessible grade. The apparent insecurity, exposure and circuitous route finding increase the emotional commitment.
1 25m 5b Climb the square-cut groove and slippery crack to a niche. Step left and move up to belay at the foot of a ramp... or ignore the step left and continue in the same line then step down left to the stance.
2 16m 4c Follow the ramp then work left across a steep smooth wall to reach a hidden left-facing V-groove. Climb the groove until a bold swing right leads to a small airy stance below overhangs.
3 44m 4c Traverse horizontally right (peg), selecting the line carefully, to a small ledge. Ascend the wall on the right to a vague depression. Climb this steeply, until a step left gains a final slab leading to heather and trees.
L Brown, S Bradshaw 30.05.1965

❺ Athanor 73m E3 6a ★★★
This fusion of technical and steep maintains the heat and sustains the pressure.
1 28m 6a The rib on the left of a dirty groove leads to a large flake. The blank-looking groove above gives access to a short steep crack; move up leftwards to traverse under a small overlap and up to the sanctuary of the belay at the foot of the ramp. Abseil or continue; it is well worth the effort to clean this pitch.
2 45m 5c Go right and up a prominent V-groove to overhangs (peg). Continue up to a small ledge. Climb directly up the groove above towards the top overhang until a pull right gains mossy slabs. Belay on a tree to the left.
J Adams, C Read 14.09.1968

❻ Footless Crow 56m E6 6c ★★★
Altered by the loss of crucial holds (and protection), it remains an incredible and audacious undertaking. Climb the rib and the blank-looking groove to below a steep crack. Pull up into the niche above then go up right to gain and follow a rightward-trending ramp (aged bolt and pegs). Step up and left below the overhangs (peg). Improvise to eventually gain the tantalising crack. Step left round the rib to a little green wall and climb up to the overhangs. Pull through and step left above the overhang to continue straight up the slabby wall and final short corner.
P Livesey 19.04.1974

❼ Footless Horse 60m E6 6b (F7b+) ★★★
Climb *Footless Crow* into the niche and up right to gain the rightward-trending ramp. Pass below the roof (aged bolt and pegs). Climb directly up the undercuts (peg) and continue (peg) to the undercut fang. Continue directly moving right to the top.

❽ Mirage 60m E5 6b ★★★
At first delicate and bold, then very steep and strenuous. Climb the groove 3m right of *Athanor* and gain the beckoning undercuts. Work up leftwards then climb a thin crack to an awkward pull up right. Above is a large flat hold; stand on it then step right, round a rib and up rightwards to a pocket. Traverse left from the pocket to a slight rib and then go straight up (aged bolt and pegs). Climb rightwards (old bolt) and move straight up to beneath a bulge (old bolt). Step left and climb the weakness through the bulges (thread) to pull into the scoop beneath a down-pointing spike. Climb the left side of the spike and continue directly on finger pockets to a ledge. Now more easily up leftwards to finish.
R Graham, D Lyle 15.04.1981

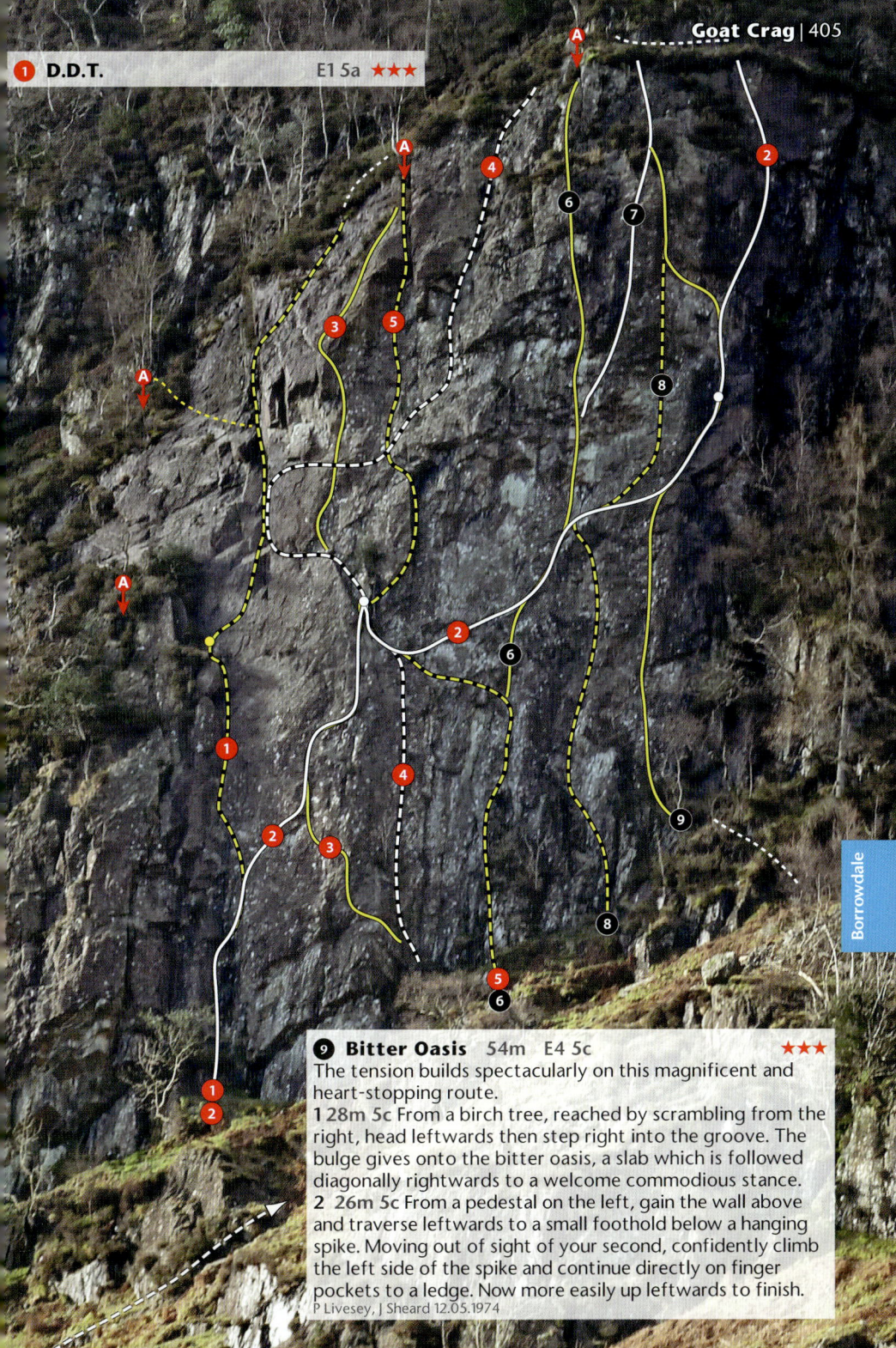

BLEAK HOW BUTTRESS

OS Grid Ref: NY 273 125
Altitude: 270m

Bold slabs and technical walls on this worthwhile crag with a good selection of routes.

Approach: The hamlet of Stonethwaite is reached by following the Borrowdale road beyond the narrowing at Rosthwaite. The bus comes past here or there is roadside parking. Follow the small road through the hamlet and onto the path through fields and a campsite beyond. This leads to Langstrath. The crag is situated a few hundred metres up the fellside above the footbridge over the lower reaches of Langstrath Beck. The best approach is to head left then follow a path rightwards below the crag.

Descent: Descend to the left or abseil.

Brush Off HVS (opposite) Peter Sterling & Nick Wharton — 📷 David Simmonite

① **Brush Off** 35m HVS 4c ★★
A bold route requiring a confident approach. Start just right of the small roof. Climb the featureless slab until forced left at 8m to a shallow triangular pocket. Move back right then go directly up to a ledge. Finish up the short wall above.
Photo opposite.
C Downer, C Bacon, S Kysow 24.05.1984

② **Fancy Free** 30m E1 5a ★
A striking route up the curving bold arête right of the slabs; sadly now becoming very mossy. Climb the arête from the right, with a short deviation to the left at half-height, to a small overhang. Pull over on good holds and follow the edge of a narrow white slab up rightwards to a tree.
C Downer, C Bacon, S Kysow 24.05.1984

③ **Bleak How Buttress** 36m E2 5c ★★★
A first class route with a distinct short crux. From the lowest point of the buttress, a short groove leads onto the oval slab. A couple of thin moves lead up and leftwards (spike). Start up a short groove then swing left to mantelshelf onto a huge jug. A series of easier grooves lead to a tree.
D Hellier 15.11.1983

④ **The Reiver** 36m HVS 5a ★★
A compelling climb, interesting throughout. From the lowest point of the buttress climb a short groove to an oval slab. Step right and climb a rib and reddish wall to a ledge. Where the wall steepens, climb slightly leftwards on decent holds then go directly to the top.
C Downer 5.06.1984

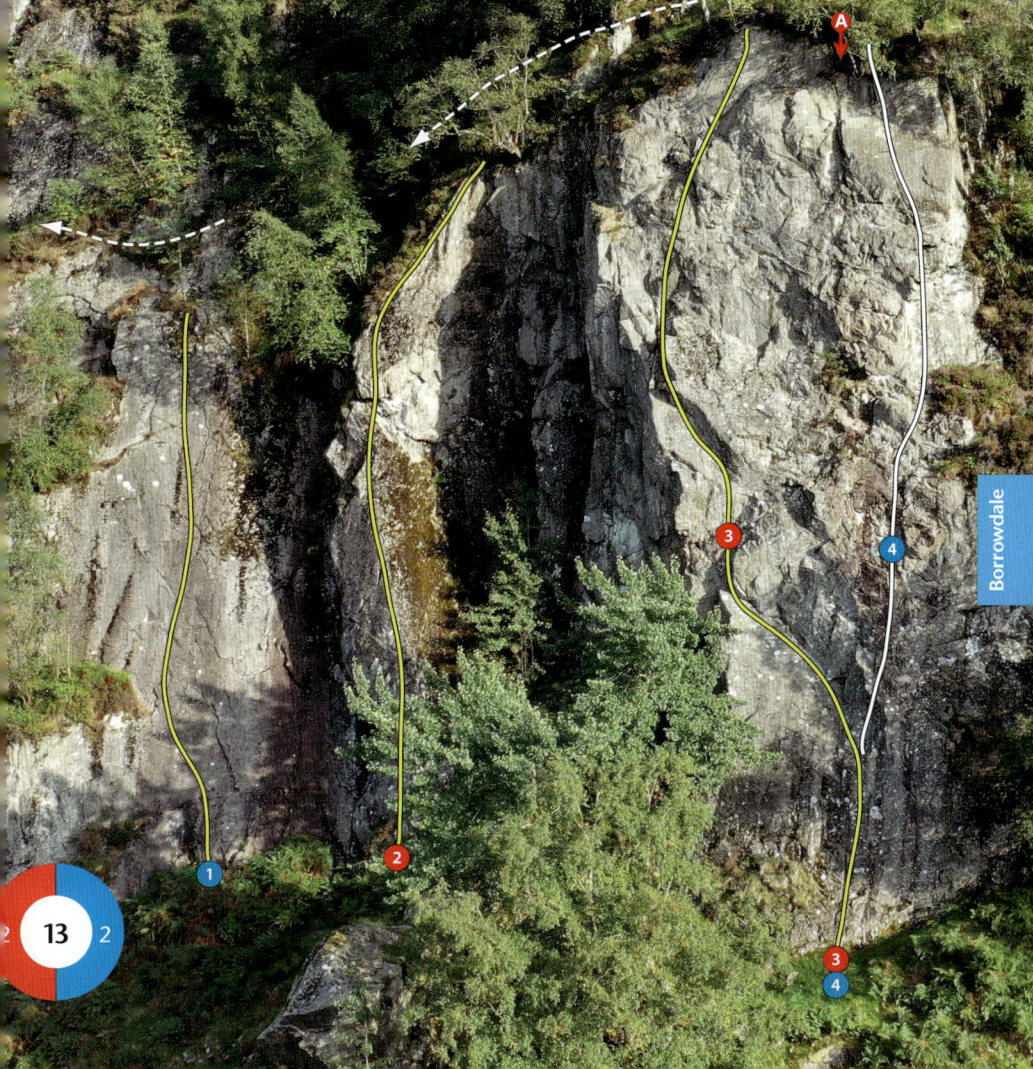

Borrowdale

UPPER HERON CRAG

OS Grid Ref: NY 274 123
Altitude: 440m

Big Foot E2 (opposite) Katy Forrester — 📷 David Simmonite

A short steep wall of very good rock with a concentration of excellent single pitch climbs. The superb situation, catching the afternoon sun, and the quality of the climbs make the walk very rewarding.

The hillside above the top of the crag is steep and very vegetated with heather and bilberry bushes. Belays at the immediate top of routes are limited so it is recommended to take an extra rope to set up a belay with anchors well back.

Approach: From Stonethwaite take the path (north-east) to Stonethwaite Bridge and follow the good path north of the beck through the village and campsite until reaching a bridge across Greenup Gill where it joins the main beck coming down Langstrath. Cross the bridge then follow a smaller path up the south side of the gill to the second drystone wall running up the fell. Follow a well-worn path steeply up the hill alongside this wall. Cross a stile and continue up for 100m to a shoulder. Traverse across and slightly down to a pleasant grassy terrace beneath the crag.

See map page 406.

Descent: Abseil or lower-off using the pre-placed belay or walk up and to the left to reach a good path.

❶ Traverse of the Frogs 30m E2 5b ★
A strenuous pitch with hard-to-place yet excellent protection. Start at the very left-hand end of the crag. Climb to the prominent rightward-slanting hand-traverse and follow this strenuously to finish up a vertical crack.
J Hughes, SJH Reid 26.06.1996

❷ Flamingo Fandango 22m E1 5b ★★
Climb a crack to a small ledge. Move up and left onto another ledge. Follow the flutings over a slight bulge to a ledge and finish up an overhanging crack in the nose above or, more sensibly, skirt to the left of the nose.
R Kenyon, C King 17.06.1984

❸ Big Foot 24m E2 5c ★★
A reachy route. A crack leads to a ledge and a little higher is a jug, beyond which a sinuous crack is followed. Finish up the nose on the left.
Photo opposite.
C Dale, R Curley 17.06.1984

❹ Little Nose 30m E2 5b ★★
A sustained route. Climb the shallow corner and the wall above to a hollow flake overlap. Stand on this then move right to a jug. From here, a long reach gains the groove above.
C Dale, R Curley 17.06.1984

❺ Shooting Fish in a Barrel 28m E4 6a ★
Good climbing up the great-looking clean wall. Pull left on to the ramp, step right and climb the wall past two horizontal breaks. Above the top break difficult moves left gain a crack. Step back right and climb the wall and slab with difficulty. Continuing up the crack of *Little Nose* makes an equally good **E3 5c**.
J Arnold, K Arnold, S Prior 23.06.2001

❻ The Question 28m E2 5c ★★
The technically demanding conspicuous grooved arête in the centre of the crag.
R Kenyon, C King 17.06.1984

Borrowdale

FAT CHARLIE'S BUTTRESS
OS Grid Ref: NY 272 124
Altitude: 160m

Cellulite E2 (opposite) Nick Wharton — David Simmonite

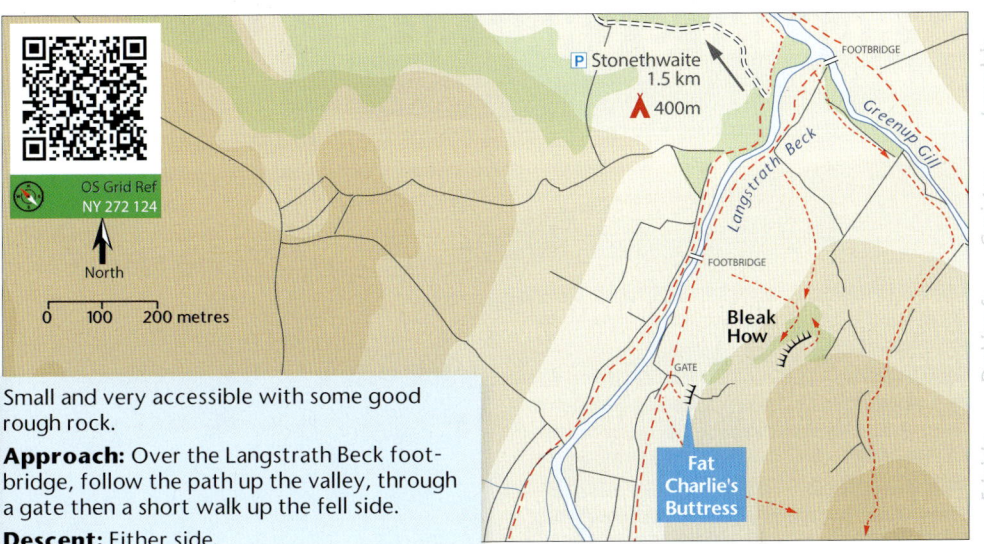

OS Grid Ref NY 272 124

Small and very accessible with some good rough rock.

Approach: Over the Langstrath Beck footbridge, follow the path up the valley, through a gate then a short walk up the fell side.

Descent: Either side.

① Myth of Fingerprints 20m VS 4b ★
Climb the delicate curving arête in a fine position.
M Boniface, N Wallis, C Phillips 26.02.1988

② Supermodel 15m E1 5b ★★
Climb the left side of the scoop then straight up.
A Hewison, G Baum 19.06.1996

③ Blubber 13m VS 4c
Following a vague crack.
G Baum, A Hewison 19.06.1996

④ Phantom Menace 13m HVS 5a ★
Gain the rightward-leaning diagonal crack at two-thirds height. Follow this to a monster jug finish.
M Lynch, D Kay 25.04.1999

⑤ Reassuringly Stocky 11m E2 5c ★
Climb the enjoyable slab to hard finishing moves. High runners possible on the left.
A Hewison, G Baum, J Meeks 11.07.1996

⑥ Cholesterol Corner 12m E1 5b ★
Climb the undercut corner 4m left of the arête and pull out onto a rounded ledge. Move up to gain good holds and (hidden) protection at the base of a depression. A hard move leads to better holds and the top.
A Hewison, G Baum 19.06.1996

⑦ Cellulite 10m E2 5c ★★
Move strenuously left to the arête and continue more easily.
Photo opposite.
A Hewison, G Baum 5.04.2000

SERGEANT'S CRAG SLAB

OS Grid Ref: NY 271 113
Altitude: 360m

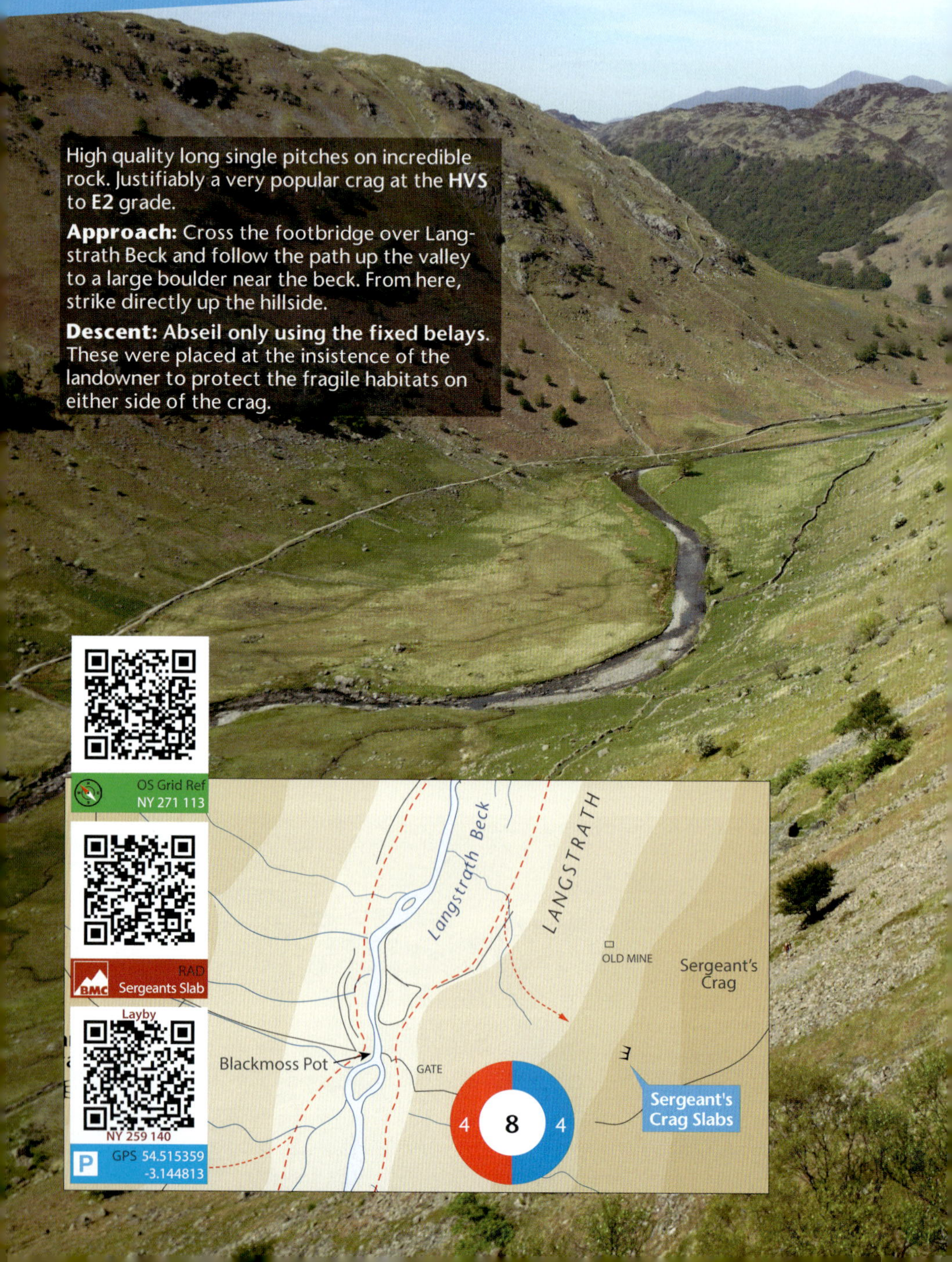

High quality long single pitches on incredible rock. Justifiably a very popular crag at the **HVS** to **E2** grade.

Approach: Cross the footbridge over Langstrath Beck and follow the path up the valley to a large boulder near the beck. From here, strike directly up the hillside.

Descent: Abseil only using the fixed belays. These were placed at the insistence of the landowner to protect the fragile habitats on either side of the crag.

Lakeland Cragsman HVS (page 414) Mary Grace Brown — David Simmonite

Borrowdale

1 Revelation 45m VS ★★
From the left-hand side of the main slab, climb leftwards towards a block step in the overhang, pull through this and follow the crack above until it peters out; move right and up a groove.
R McHaffie, J Bosher 7.07.1991

2 Endurance 45m HVS 5a ★★★
The thin crack left of the prominent central crack with an interesting sequence of moves through the overlap.
R McHaffie, J Bosher 7.07.1991

3 Between the Lines 45m E1 5b ★★
Climbs the slab and overlaps left of the prominent central crack. Start up the central crack; after a few metres, step left and climb between the two cracks without recourse to either. The pebbly pillar above gives a teasing finish.
J Campbell, SJH Reid 15.05.1995

4 Lakeland Cragsman 45m HVS 5a ★★★
The wider central crack has great moves and superb protection, sustained yet low in the grade. A good first HVS lead. Climb the slab passing a blocky overhang on the left. Continue up the crack over three small overlaps to finish up an easier corner.
Photo page 413.
R McHaffie, J Bosher 7.07.1991

5 Terminator 2 45m HVS 5a ★★★
Climb the thin crack right of the wider central crack through the left-hand of three breaks in the overhang. Delicate moves lead up and left to a right-slanting ramp groove leading to a narrow ledge. Pull into a corner on the right and follow the horizontal crack leftwards to finish.
R McHaffie, J Bosher 8.09.1991

6 Boris in Wonderland 45m E2 5b ★
A direct pitch starting just right of the previous route and giving similar but harder climbing. Climb to the central of the three breaks through the overlap and gain the slab above. Continue directly until moves left lead onto the rightward-slanting rampline. Move up then pull through the overlap and climb the slab leftwards to a ledge. Continue past another ledge to an easier finish on the left.
R Kenyon, C King 21.05.1995

7 Aphasia 45m E2 5b ★★★ ♦
The centre of the slab left of the groove gives one of Lakeland's finest slab pitches. Very sustained and intricate climbing with reasonable protection keeps your attention right to the top. Climb the short steep slab to below the right-hand break in the overlap. Pull up right and go straight up to a bulge where a hard move leads to a good hold. Continue up until moves right lead to a thin crack which ends at a narrow ledge. Pull up into the slight corner via a horizontal crack and climb the wall above directly to the top.
Photo this page.
C Downer, C Bacon, R HcHaffie 8.06.1992

8 Holly Tree Crack 50m E1 5b ★★
Start below a holly! Low in the grade and well-protected.
1 35m 5b Climb the groove past the holly to a niche. Follow the crack out of the top of the niche to a ledge.
2 15m 5a Climb the awkward corner to a ledge then follow a right-slanting crack to the top.
R McHaffie, J Bosher 17.07.1991

Aphasia E2 (this page) Nick Wharton & Peter Sterling — 📷 David Simmonite

Sergeant's Crag Slab | 415

CAM CRAG

OS Grid Ref: NY 262 111
Altitude: 340m

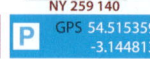

RAD Cam Crag
NY 259 140
GPS 54.515359
-3.144813
Layby

Superlative hard sustained and technical routes on impeccable rock. The easterly aspect and light traffic means the routes may need brushing prior to an ascent; the reward is worth the effort.

Approach: Follow the track on the west side of Langstrath passing through a gate opposite Sergeant's Crag Slabs, where the striking pyramid of Apex Buttress is conspicuous on the fell side to the west. Follow the south bank of the beck, with a wall on the right, to a col behind a craggy lump on the left. Contour south across the hillside, crossing a stile, and keep moving up and south (left) to the crag. Alternatively, strike up the fell directly beneath the crag to reach Cam Crag Boulders, the old hermit's cave and an excellent scramble up the ridge. In summer, bracken can be a problem.

Descent: From the top of both parts of the crag, head left to eventually come back round underneath the lower crag.

Lower Crag

Steep ground guarded by an overhang.

❶ Cameleon 20m E3 6a ★
Easy ground on the left to an overlap. Move right then make a committing pull through the overlap up and right to reach finishing cracks.
P Clarke, A Dunhill 12.08.2015

❷ 'Arry 'Ardnose 20m E3 6a ★★
Gain twin cracks left of an overhang with a step right at 6m. Continue up the wall.
K Wilkinson 23.05.1988

❸ Cam Crag Crack 15m E4 6b ★★
The striking crack through the left end of the roof presents sustained difficulty. Start at the foot of a groove. Overcome the roof then climb the crack.
K Wilkinson 23.05.1988

❹ Campaign 15m E7 6c (F7c+/8a) ★★★
Start up the steep groove of *Cam Crag Crack* to reach the roof (small wires and small cams). Move out to a spike undercut and make a hard sequence up to reach better holds. Keep your nerve and follow the crack to the top.
Photo opposite.
A Hocking, M Norbury, A Wilson, W Hunter 1.07.2011

❺ Campagnolo 22m E6 6b (F7b+) ★★
Climb the left side of the triangular recess then follow the horizontal break. Cross the wall to gain the right end of the capping roof to finish up a short groove.
K Phizacklea, C Matheson 22.08.2009

Upper Crag

Sustained and fingery climbing on this impressive sweep of immaculate rough rock covered in small edges, crystals and nubbins.

❻ Camouflage 25m E7 6b (F7b+) ★★★
Breaches the left side of the wall. Very bold in its upper section. Climb a short difficult overhanging groove, often wet; or, come in from the right. From a small ledge, move left then back right and climb a thin crack in the slab to a ledge (small cams in a small horizontal slot above a detached flake). Climb the wall above on very small holds and crystals; no protection.
M Dale 19.08.1998

❼ Camikaze 25m E6 6b (F7a) ★★★
Serious. Climb straight up to a sloping ledge (peg). Move up to hollow flakes and a horizontal break (stacked knife blades), then continue boldly up the wall to the left end of an overlap (cam 0.5). Pull through the bulge slightly left then continue to the top.
P Cornforth, G Cornforth 25.05.1994

❽ Teenage Kicks 25m E4 6a ★★
Start below a bulging wall 3m left of a shallow groove. Climb the wall to a large ledge and corner at 10m. Follow the thin crack on the left to a horizontal crack, then up to a small ledge on the right. Continue up under the overhang to a jug. Make a long stride left onto the wall then move up to the overhang and surmount this using a hidden side-pull on the right.
D Cronshaw, J Ryden, I Vickers May 1988

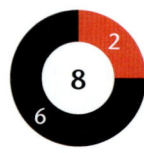

Campaign E7 (opposite) Adam Hocking
📷 David Simmonite

OS Grid Ref NY 262 111

Cam Crag

Blackmoss Pot

Borrowdale

COMBE GILL

Seatoller P&D
NY 245 138

GPS 54.513726
-3.166970

This offshoot of upper Borrowdale provides a selection of buttresses with, mainly, easier routes. From the relaxed **Glaciated Slab** to the long classics on **Raven Crag**.

BORROWDALE
River Derwent
B5289
Seatoller
Mountain View
Strands Bridge
FIELDS
Thorneythwaite Farm
FIELDS
High Buck How
Glaciated Slab page 420
GATE GATE
Seathwaite 1 km
Bessyboot
Thornythwaite Fell
Combe Gill
Rosthwaite Fell
Great Hollow
Raven Crag page 423
Dove's Nest page 421
North
0   ½ mile
0   kilometre   1
Combe Door

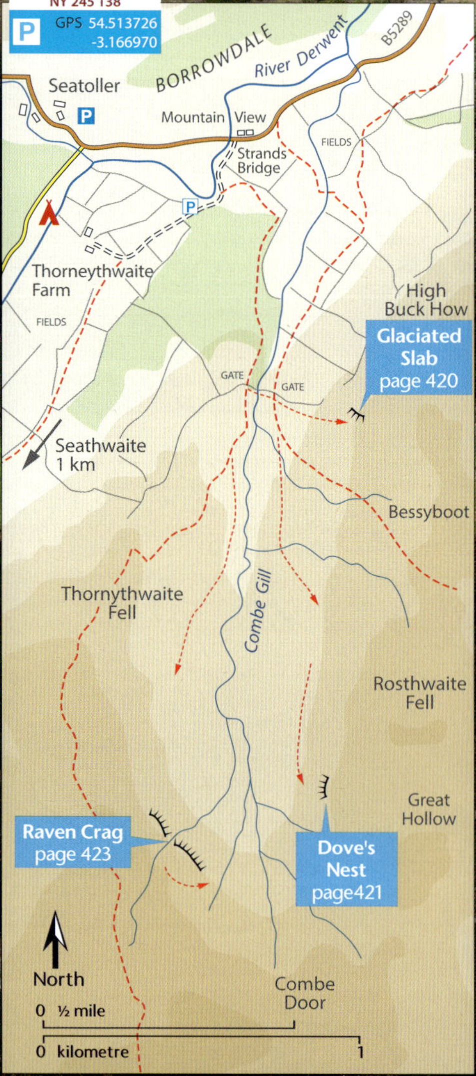

Trod Tethera, Glaciated Slab D (photo page 420) Katie Mackay — David Simmonite

GLACIATED SLAB

30 mn

2 8 6

OS Grid Ref: NY 254 128
Altitude: 300m

Excellent relaxed climbing on an ice-planed slab of immaculate rock.

Approach: Take a minor road on the left just after some cottages on the right, which leads towards Thorneythwaite Farm. Parking is available on the right of this road. Follow the path that leads from the road into Combe Gill. After a gate, cross the stream and up steep grass to the crag.

See map page 418.

Descent: Up and right.

1 Trod Pip 14m VS 4c ★
Bridge the corner behind the holly tree then pull directly over the bulge to easier ground.
D Byrne-Peare, P Ross Oct 1988

2 Trod Lethera 30m D ★
Climb the chimney then move left (exposed) to the ledge on the ridge. Finish on the right.
B Beetham 4.09.1944

3 Trod Too Far 28m HS ★★
Enjoyable delicate slab climbing.
P Latimer, R Tolley 18.09.2008

4 Trod Pimp 28m S ★★
Excellent climbing.
B Beetham 4.09.1944

5 Trod Methera 24m S ★★
Delicately climb the slab on great rock.
B Beetham 6.09.1944

6 Trod Tethera 22m D ★★
The enjoyable polished central crack.
Photo page 419.
B Beetham 4.09.1944

7 Trod 'A' Tween VS 4b ★
Delicately climb the slab with a necky start.
R Kenyon 31.10.1984

8 Trod Tan 16m D ★
Follow the leftward-slanting crack for 3m then rightwards to the top.
B Beetham 4.09.1944

OS Grid Ref
NY 254 128

RAD
Glaciated Slab

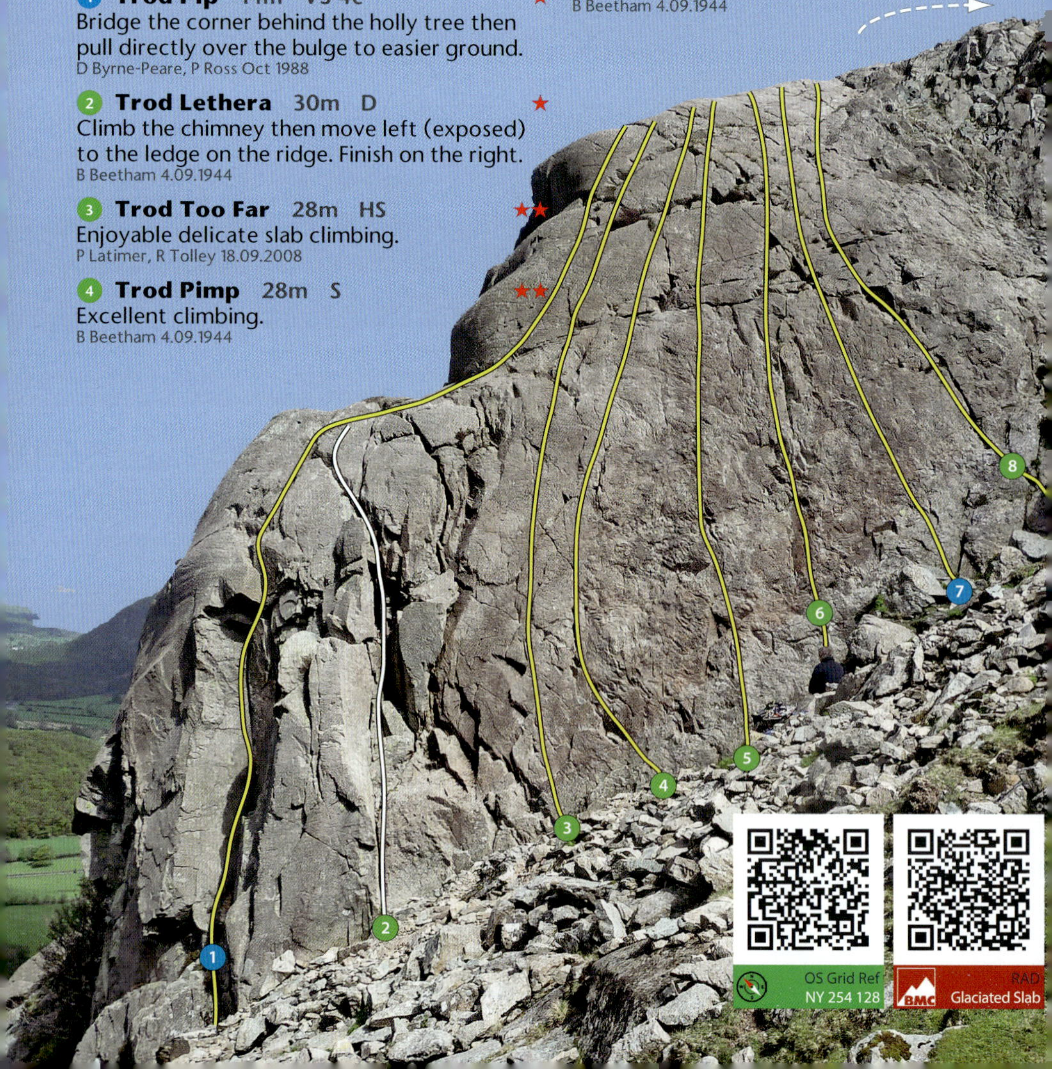

DOVE'S NEST

OS Grid Ref: NY 253 116
Altitude: 475m

In addition to the selection of normal routes, there is also the challenge of some deep chimneys that require more of a speleological approach. These were formed by rock slippage on a massive scale many years ago - even so, be very careful!

Approach: From the minor road to Thorneythwaite Farm, follow the path that leads up into the combe. At the head of the valley, take a line up the hillside on the left to the crag.
See map page 418.

Descent: Down either side.

Layby
NY 249 135

 OS Grid Ref NY 253 116
 RAD Dove's Nest
 GPS 54.511213 -3.160576

❶ Adam's Slab 38m MVS 4b ★★
An excellent pitch; poorly protected at the start. Climb the slab and the overlap then up to a heathery break. Climb the slab passing a block.
R Kenyon 8.06.1985

❷ Meet Your Maker 38m VS 4c ★
Good climbing but poorly protected in places. Start on the right-hand side of a downward-pointing block and climb the overlap. Continue directly and delicately to reach the prominent block. Climb the right edge to the top of the block, step right then straight to the top.
D Johnson, E Ostell 14.05.1997

❸ Horizontal Pleasure 80m HVS 4c ★★
An entertaining variety of moves in fine situations with a bold final pitch!
1 30m Climb a mossy scoop, trending right to the large ledge. Climb a short crack on the left then follow the left edge of the buttress to belay on the right at the entrance to the left-hand branch of the chimney.
2 20m 4c Climb the chimney to stand on a jug on the left arête. Swing across to the right wall then climb more easily to a pinnacle. Stride across the gap to a foothold at the base of the long narrow slab that forms the left arête of the chimney. Climb the slab then step onto the large chockstone on the right. Go up to a stance on the edge of the Attic Cave.
3 30m 4c A spectacular virtually unprotected pitch. Move up and left around the arête to stand on the foothold on the lip of the overhang. Foot traverse left to a small ledge on the left. Relax a little then trend leftwards up easier ground.
SJH Reid, JE Reid 20.09.1995

❹ Outside or Face Route 82m VD ★★
A pleasant and varied route requiring traditional techniques.
1 30m A crack in the slab trends left to a large ledge. From the right end of the ledge, climb up the arête to another ledge. Walk 8m right to below a chimney.
2 8m Follow the edge of the large detached block on the left to an interesting belay.
3 16m Drop down behind the block and disappear up the right chimney, to emerge in the Attic Cave. Belay on the left on the outside edge of the cave.
4 28m Step down from the belay and make a stride right across the top of the chimney. Move right a few metres then climb a fine crack. Continue up the wide crack above to a pinnacle on the right. Move left and up to finish.
RST Chorley, B Beetham, RW Somervell May 1944

❺ Clubfoot 70m VS 5a ★★
A pleasant climb reserving its sharp crux for the final moves.
1 26m Climb easy slabs to a short corner: belay below the chimney.
2 22m 4a Follow the diagonal line of weakness up to the left edge of the slab then continue to a stance below a small overhang.
3 16m Climb the rib to the right of the crack to a stance below a groove.
4 6m 5a Climb the steep and difficult groove.
B Evans, S Burns, B Hunt 1954

RAVEN CRAG

OS Grid Ref: NY 248 114
Altitude: 360m

Long atmospheric routes which provide a great day out with shorter options on **The Pedestal Wall**.

Approach: From the minor road to Thorneythwaite Farm, take the well-marked path on the west side of the beck before heading up right to the crag. For reference, *Raven Crag Gully* is the long deep gash in the centre of the rocky hillside.

See map page 418.

Descent: Head well left, taking care on the steep ground. If finished for the day and carrying your kit, follow the ridge on the right to the valley.

OS Grid Ref
NY 248 114

FA0
Raven Crag

Layby
NY 249 135
GPS 54.511213
-3.160576

The Pedestal Wall

Short pleasant routes at an amenable grade.

Descent: Scramble left.

1 Pedestal Wall 13m S ★★
A pleasant climb starting at the small pedestal. Climb the centre of the face, trending right up a crack near the top.
B Beetham 6.08.1940

2 Cock It 13m HVS 5a ★
Start right of the pedestal. Climb past the overlap on its right. Spaced protection.
T Langhorne 14.06.1987

3 For the Record 22m VS 4c ★
Climb the arête left of the prominent overhung corner to some cracks. Finish on the right-hand side of the nose.
T Langhorne 14.06.1987

4 Just A Quickie VS 4c ★
5 Crystal Slab MVS 4c ★★
6 Midge Ridge VS 4b ★
7 Raven Crag Buttress VD ★★
8 Corax HS 4a ★★
9 Corvus D ★★★★

④ Just A Quickie 13m VS 4c ★
Start 3m right of the overhanging corner and climb the wall and cracks.
R Kenyon 6.05.1984

Crystal Slab Area

Descent: Well to the left or up rightwards to follow the ridge.

⑤ Crystal Slab 94m MVS 4c ★★
An excellent route. Start at a groove below the slab.
1 45m 4c Climb a spiky groove and continue up a shallow scoop onto a light-coloured slab, below a wall. Step up the right-hand side of the wall then traverse left to a jug. Move up and continue more easily to ledges below an overhang (cams and nuts), or use a block belay on the left.
2 16m Go left on ledges for 5m then climb the left-facing overhung slab above to a grass ledge below a wide crack with a chockstone.
3 33m Climb the wide crack and final groove.
P Hirst, E Hirst 1.06.1985

Raven Crag Buttress

Long mountaineering routes.

Descent: Well to the left or right then down the long ridge.

⑥ Midge Ridge 120m VS 4b ★
The fine left-hand arête. Start at a short semi-detached pillar.
1 18m 4a Climb the pillar and pull right onto the arête. Climb this to a narrow ledge then a short wall leading to a scoop, a short groove then a large bilberry ledge.
2 30m 4b Pull out left and climb slightly rightwards up the wall to a ledge. Move left and climb a slab leftwards then round the arête. Boldly climb a narrowing ramp to a step left onto some dubious spikes then a short dirty chimney and wide bilberry ramp. Follow the ramp to its end.
3 19m 4b Climb a short wide slab then make a delicate traverse left across a scoop to a spike. Pull up into the scoop and emerge onto the ridge. Follow this for 7m to a ledge.
4 30m 4b Climb the leftward-slanting crack system above, passing a large flake on its left, then up the wall. Step airily leftwards to a block and bilberries. Avoid the short blank arête above on the left. Climb to, and stand on, the protruding block above and finish to the right.
5 23m Climb easy rocks.
SJH Reid, CAJ Reid, SA Baxendale 24.07.2006

⑦ Raven Crag Buttress 112m VD ★★
This classic and continuously interesting route starts 5m from the left end of the grassy shelf.
1 33m Climb the open chimney and ledges to a ledge.
2 26m Bear slightly left and climb to a ledge overlooking the gully. Continue past a projecting flake to a ledge.
3 30m Climb a groove and either follow the groove above, or move left and climb the groove overlooking the gully, until exposed moves up a short corner lead up to a large bilberry ledge.
4 23m Climb the easy rocks above.
B Beetham and members of the Goldsborough Club 6.09.1939

⑧ Corax 145m HS 4a ★★
An enjoyable climb starting just left of the gully.
1 30m 4a Climb to and follow the twin cracks leading directly to a large block.
2 30m 4a Climb past the block and follow a crack up the exposed buttress; slabby rock leads to a belay.
3-5 85m Move easily left to join *Corvus* at the top of P2 and follow it to the top.
B Beetham 1.07.1950

⑨ Corvus 147m D ★★★★
An extremely popular climb.
1 26m Start left of the gully up the slabs and move right at the top to a ledge in the gully. Climb the first V-cleft in the left wall of the gully to a ledge and large block.
2 36m Traverse left along a series of ledges to below a corner. Climb the corner which deepens into a chimney and a slabby scoop above to a stance.
3 35m Move right for 5m to the foot of a rib; climb the rib to gain a steep slabby wall. Belay on the right.
4 10m The Hand-Traverse - Move up right to a line of flakes then traverse left to a recess.
5 40m Climb to a large ledge and continue up a rib to below a scoop. Gain the scoop via a large flake and continue to the top.
B Beetham 10.06.1950

⑩ Raven Crag Gully 178m VD ★★★
The prominent deep gully in the centre of the crag; a classic in summer and winter conditions - though these are often difficult to tell apart! Scramble 25m to a cave formed by a chockstone.
1 23m Climb the groove on the right. Traverse left across the gully bed.
2 30m Climb the groove on the right. Avoid a cave by easy climbing to the left.
3 15m Scrambling.
4 23m Climb the rib on the right and turn a cave at 12m on the right.

5 60m Continue to where it steepens.
6 16m Climb the right side past a chockstone and move right.
7 11m Move up a short way then traverse across the gully below the capstone, passing to the left.
WA Wilson, JW Robinson, CN Williamson 1.09.1893

⑪ Summit Route 197m S ★
This pleasant mountaineering route initially follows the right edge of *Raven Crag Gully* then trends right to gain the large ledge below the final buttress. Start just right of the gully at a grass ledge, below a short wall.
1 16m Move left and climb a shallow corner to a ledge and block belay.
2 26m Move up left and climb a short steep wall. Continue up slabby rock to reach a belay on the right.
3 36m Move left to gain and climb a slabby groove overlooking the gully. Finish either up a short chimney or its left wall. Belay on a grass ledge below a corner-crack.
4 20m Climb the crack to a ledge on the right. Go diagonally left and up to a tree belay.
5 23m Move up a crack on the right. Climb a V-groove and crack up to the left, to a belay below a slabby corner.
6 13m Climb the corner and easy rock above to gain the right-hand end of the large terrace.
7 20m Walk left to a cairn below a square scoop in the final buttress.
8 8m Climb the scoop awkwardly to a sloping ledge on the left. Thread belay.
9 10m Traverse left along the sloping ledge and continue at the same level to a belay.
10 25m Climb up to a small overhang on the right. Climb an obvious crack on its left to a rock crevasse. Continue to the top up a short awkward corner, in the same line.
B Beetham, J Foyle 13.05.1951

⑫ Summit Route - 22m S
variation finish
7a Start 6m right of P7. Climb the groove on the front of the buttress and continue up to a saddle. Step down and right to the foot of a groove. Climb the crack in the slab on the left to the top.
D Murray, DA Crawford 3.10.1959

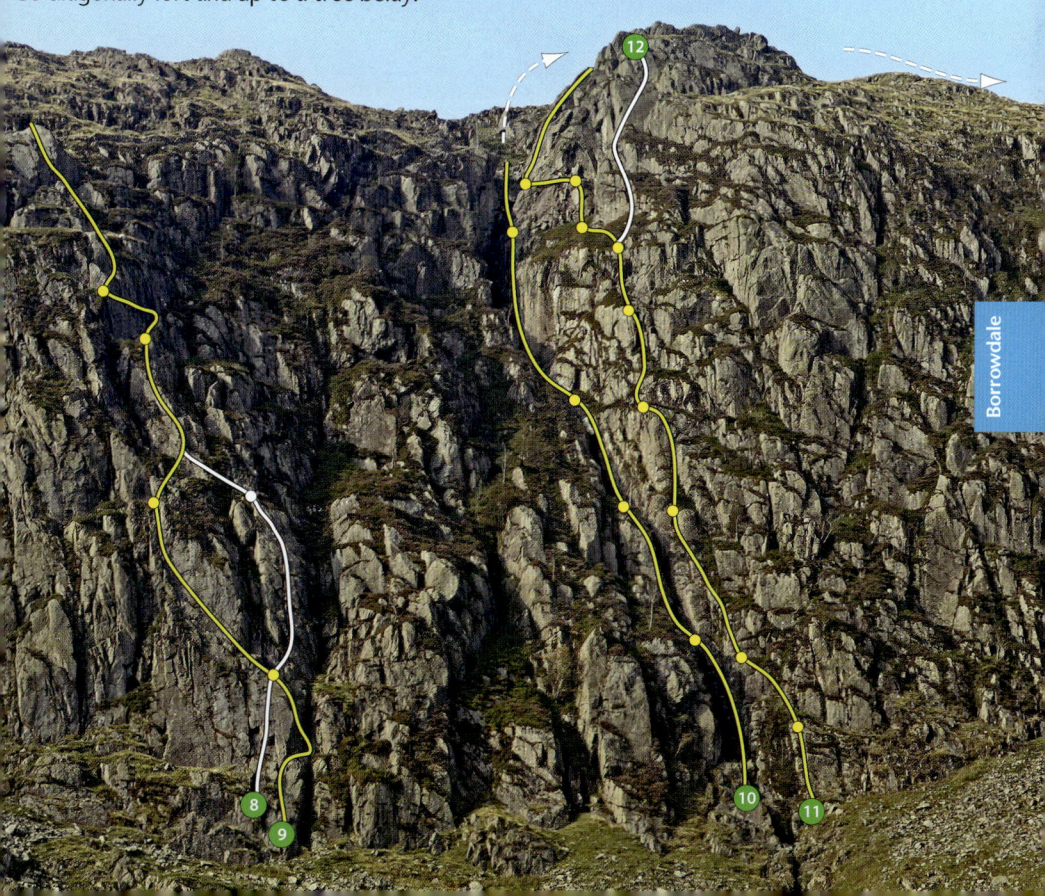

GILLERCOMB

OS Grid Ref: NY 223 125
Altitude: 480m

A sunny mountain crag with long routes on good rock.

Approach: From the top of Honister Pass. The bus stops here and there is plenty of good parking at the Youth Hostel and at the Honister Slate Mine. Take the steep path beside the wall heading south. A few hundred metres before the summit of Grey Knotts, head left and descend the wide gully to the north of the crag swinging round, across rough ground to the base.

Alternatively, from Seathwaite, follow the path up the left side of Sour Milk Gill then cross the very boggy base of the comb towards the crag.

Descent: The wide gully to the right (north) of the crag.

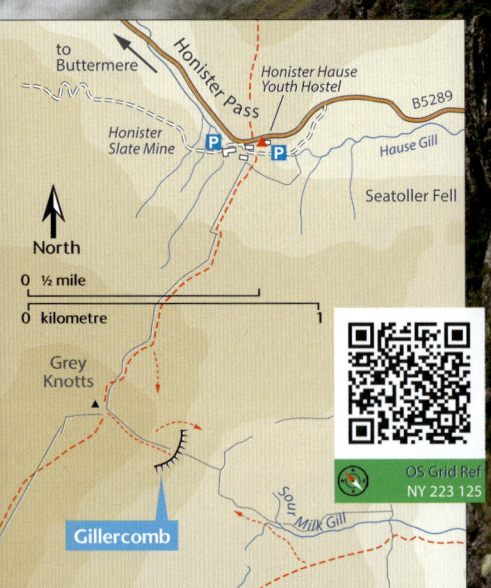

Gillercombe Buttress S (page 427) Mark Eddy — David Simmonite

1 Gillercombe Buttress 195m S ★★★

A popular classic on superb quick drying rock; it has a lovely sunny aspect. Start just right of the prominent gully at the lowest point of the buttress.
1 30m Slabby rock leads to a steepening; move left and pull into a square recess on the right wall of the gully. Climb the recess, then move right past a flake to an upper ramp which leads right to a stance.
2 40m Move up right and awkwardly traverse left for 7m. Climb easy rock to a steep wall; traverse left across ledges to a platform below an imposing corner crack.
3 20m Climb the crack then move up right to a stance.
4 40m Climb a short steep scoop on the right to a large ledge. Scramble up an open corner to a large ledge and wedged flake belay.
5 40m Step left from the flake and climb a difficult groove to a ledge. Continue up slabs passing a V-groove on the right, to easier ground.
6 25m Scramble to the top.
HB Lyon, W Woodsend 28.05.1912

2 Grey Knotts Face 131m VD ★★

A character-building mountaineering route with a traditional squeeeeeze; stout climbers will probably choose one of the two harder options. Start just left of the fence at the base of the crag.
1 13m Scramble to a large grass ledge.
2 25m Climb diagonally right into a corner and follow it past a square ledge to arrive at the Letter Box; post yourself through the slot and wriggle up the cleft to gain the top of the block. Having regained your composure move left and ascend to a large ledge. The Letter Box can be avoided, although these options are both slightly harder; S.
2a Climb the corner directly above the slot.
2b Move right from below the slot then climb a crack on the front face using a wedged flake.
3 13m Climb the chimney crack at the left of the ledge.
4 20m Continue up the chimney with a chockstone to a grass ledge.
5 & 6 60m Climb the right rib of the shallow gully.
B Beetham 18.06.1939

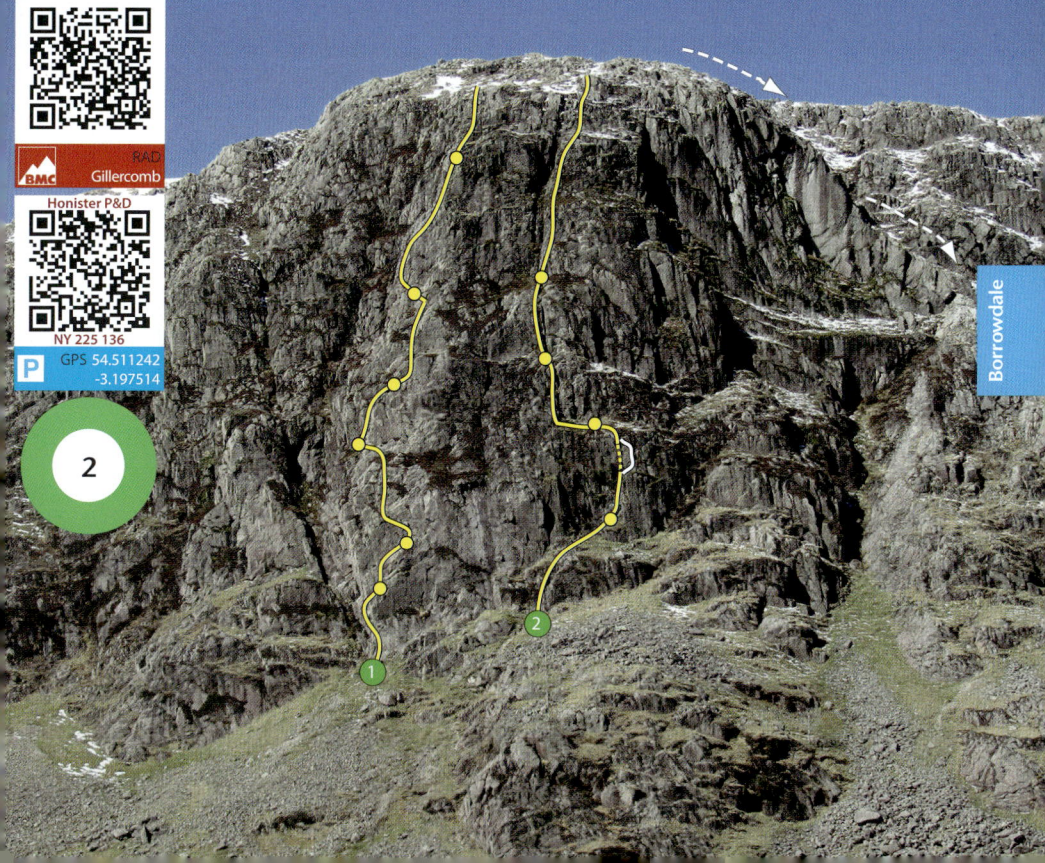

THIRLMERE

Running north south through the centre of the district, Thirlmere is home to some classic venues. The ever-popular **Castle Rock**, with its two very different faces, provides a wide range of shorter routes while the imposing **Raven Crag**, towering over the reservoir dam, is home to some big hard challenges. Tucked away in a subsidiary valley, **Iron Crag** is the preserve of the extreme climber with some of the steepest, hardest routes in the area. A regular bus service runs between Ambleside and Keswick.

Communist Convert, Raven Crag VS (page 440) Rachel Somerville & Andy McVittie — 📷 David Simmonite

CASTLE ROCK OF TRIERMAIN

OS Grid Ref: NY 322 197
Altitude: 275m

An important crag with a broad range of excellent routes. Very accessible with generally solid rock, despite the collapse of a massive chunk at the left! The two crags give very different yet complementary experience; steep and uncompromising, relaxed and friendly.

Approach: Parking on the A591 opposite the turning to the Thirlmere dam and Bridge End Farm is extensive and free, the bus also stops here. Head east towards the crag along the old road, through a gate on the right crossing Legburthwaite CP (P&D) taking a path on the left opposite the building. Cross the road into the field opposite then follow the path rightwards, across a track up a slope to a footbridge over the water course. Continue steeply up through the wood to the **South Crag**, on the right over the wall.

See map page 428.

Descent: To the right.

North Crag

The steep **North Crag** offers some of the finest middle grade climbing in the area. The rock is steep and juggy, although some of the flaky holds should be treated with caution. Protection can be sparse outside the comfort of the crack and groove lines and some routes call for a bold approach.

A massive rockfall occurred at the left end of the crag in 2019 with the aftermath still apparent.

Approach: From **South Crag**, traverse left beneath the crag to reach the **North Crag**. If you plan descending by the **South Crag**, you can gear up below the **South Crag**.

Descent: The easiest and safest descent is to the right over the top of **South Crag**. North Gully on the left provides a shorter but far more serious and dirty descent. Several abseil points can save time and effort, although: Do make sure of the line and Do ensure that you have sufficient rope - climbers have had epics!

Since the huge pillar collapsed, routes on the left have seen little traffic and have become vegetated - they will clean up with regular ascents.

RAD
Castle Rock

Legburthwaite P&D
NY 317 195

OS Grid Ref
NY 322 197

GPS 54.565626
-3.059450

① Zig Zag 100m VS 4c ★★
This interesting, varied route has become vegetated. It has some rattly flakes and the rock should be handled with caution. Start at a pedestal.
1 37m 4c Climb easily to an ash tree, follow the leftward-slanting gangway to a large terrace; poor belay.
2 15m Walk to the right descending slightly then traverse a big flake to an ash tree.
3 24m 4c Ascend the slab on the right then a steep crack and a second crack, moving onto the left wall to avoid debris from a collapsed ledge. Belay at the foot of the large slab. Walk to the right and abseil off or:
4 24m Follow the slab leftwards.
RJ Birkett, CR Wilson, L Muscroft 22.04.1939

② Agony 90m E2 5a ★★
A brilliant spooky unprotected wall climb demanding confidence and control. Start at the lowest point of the crag.
1 40 m 5a Start up *Overhanging Bastion* following the slab and cracked wall to a ledge. Head audaciously up leftwards to join a cracked groove. Follow this and the wall above rightwards to belay above a large tree.
2 36m 5a Very bold. From a shallow scoop above, move right to a blunt flake then up to a ledge (cam). Step left round the arête then climb steeply to a flake on the left. Move up rightwards to a scoop in the arête. Follow this more easily to the slab. Belay below an open groove in the wall above.
3 14m 4a Climb the groove.
G Oliver, N Brown 24.05.1959

③ Overhanging Bastion 75m HVS 5a ★★★★
The classic route of the crag, swaggering up the gangway which cuts the **North Crag** in such an obvious and exposed manner. Bold moves to start the upper gangway place the route at the upper limit of the grade. Start at the lowest point of the crag below an easy-angled slab.

1 30m 4c Climb the mossy slab then a crack on the left. Move right then up and right into the corner which leads to ledge above a tree.
2 25m 5a Climb the slabby gangway to a pinnacle where the gangway narrows. Follow this, boldly to start, to its top. Move left across a wall and up into a large niche. Climb a wide crack to a ledge. Abseil point to the right (tree), or:
3 20m 4a Climb a wall rightwards, pull onto a slab and head left to the top.
Photo below.
RJ Birkett, CR Wilson, L Muscroft 1.04.1939

4 Eliminator 92m E3 5b ★
Two good pitches of climbing. Start at a shallow groove beneath a vegetated ledge
1 10m Ascend the groove to the ash tree.
2 35m 5a Climb the fine tapering unprotected rib on the left. The climbing is easy enough but very bold. Traverse some way left to belay on the large ledge behind the ever-popular ash tree.
3 35m 5b Climb rightwards across the wall behind the ledge to the grass ledge. Step back left round the arête and go diagonally leftwards with little in the way of protection to the foot of a right-facing corner which is climbed to a slab (peg). Climb the slab for 5m then a ramp on the left to a block.
4 12 m 4b Climb the wall above.
W Freeland, K Rudd 24.06.1969

5 May Day Cracks 70m HVS 5a ★★★
This fine climb takes a series of cracks which divide the high left part of the crag from the lower right-hand section. The climb is sustained, well-protected and very worthwhile. Start at a shallow groove which leads to a vegetated ledge. There is an obvious deep V-groove above.
1 10m Ascend the groove to the ash tree.
2 36m 5a Climb the chimney and V-groove then continue to the base of the large slab.
3 24m Climb the big slab on the left.
RJ Birkett, L Muscroft 1.05.1947

6 Thirlmere Eliminate 55m E1 5b ★★ ♂
An enjoyable and sustained climb up ribs and corners. Protection is only just adequate. Start below a 2m high perched flake.
1 37m 4c Climb onto the flake and continue up a corner to the left end of a long narrow ledge. Traverse diagonally left into a corner and pull onto the arête. Follow the arête to a sloping ledge in an overhanging bay.
2 18m 5b Climb the steep corner moving onto the right wall at the top. A bold pitch.
P Ross, PJ Greenwood 26.06.1955

7 Rigor Mortis 57m E2 5c ★★★ ♂
A stiff climb with a fantastic exposed third pitch. Start at a shallow corner just right of the perched flake.
1 15m 4c Climb the wall to a small overhang in the corner. Swing right onto the front and follow a steep crack to a long narrow ledge.
2 20m 5c A thin corner which peters out into a crack rises from the left end of the ledge. Climb the corner and crack to the top of the White Cone. Step up and traverse the steep little wall leftwards into a shallow scoop. Climb the scoop and belay on the sloping ledge below the corner.
3 22m 5a Round the corner on the right, a line of interrupted gangways provides a sensational passage ending with a swing round a rib into the final chimney.
P Ross, B Aughton 18.04.1959

8 White Dwarf 30m E4 6a ★★ ♂
A technical and direct way up the crag. The corner is very bold with poor protection where it matters. Start at the top of the first pitch of *Rigor Mortis*. Climb the face of the White Cone and move into the corner above its apex. Follow this to the gangway then finish straight up the bulging wall.
TW Birkett, KW Forsythe 5.05.1978

Overhanging Bastion HVS (page 430) Fiona Sanders
David Simmonite

❾ The Ghost 30m E3 5c ★★★ ⚤

From *Rigor Mortis*, climb a short wall into the bottom of the groove to the right of the White Cone. Make hard moves right to gain the large flake and step into a V-groove. Follow this groove and the left arête then up the steep wall above moving leftwards.
AG Cram, WA Barnes, W Young July 1964

The following routes are best climbed as a single first pitch with a convenient abseil descent from trees.

❿ Harlot Face 50m E1 5b ★★ ⚤

A good climb with a short crux. Start 10m right of a 2m high perched flake at a line of shallow interrupted corners rising leftwards.
1 30m 5b Climb the line of corners to the right end of the long narrow ledge. Climb a short way up the overhanging corner then make a few difficult moves up and round the rib on the right. Continue steeply on better holds, then up a corner to carefully step onto a tree-covered ledge. Abseil from here or:
2 20m 4c Climb the open groove above.
RJ Birkett, L Muscroft 26.06.1949

⓫ Triermain Eliminate 49m E2 5b ★★★ ⚤

Strenuous well-protected climbing. Start at a crack just right of the line of shallow interrupted corners rising to the left.
1 31m 5b Climb to a small ledge and go up a corner above to a long narrow ledge. Ascend the overhanging corner at the right end of the ledge to a short chimney. Move up to a tree-covered ledge on the right. Abseil from here or:
2 18m Finish by the shallow groove above.
DD Whillans, J Brown, D Cowan 15.03.1953

⓬ Ted Cheasby 46m E2 5c ★ ⚤

A strenuous and sustained crack and groove in the left side of the blunt rib. Start just to the left of the rib.
1 30m 5c Climb the thin crack (two pegs) and the groove above to a step right above the bulge. Move back left and climb a shallow groove to a tree-covered ledge. Abseil from here or:
2 16m Climb the wall above.
P Gomersall Easter 1977

⓭ The Final Giggle 30m E2 5b ★★ ⚤

Great climbing tackling the pocketed wall. Protection is sparse. Start below the left end of a ledge capped by a brown overhang. Climb steeply through the left side of the overhang into a groove. Move neatly up and right (2 pegs) then continue towards a small tree. Traverse left onto a tree-covered ledge.
MA Toole, P Ross 12.07.1965

South Crag

An open sunny aspect and solid clean rock with extremely enjoyable climbs. This clean compact dome about 35m high is very popular. At the top, belays are difficult to arrange and great care is required ensuring they are solid.

Descent: To the right.

❶ Gazebo 38m HVS 5a ★★★

Superb climbing and a most enjoyable route. Start at the foot of a big groove 5m left of the stone wall. Climb the groove and exit right. Move right and climb the delightful wall.
G Lee, C Downer 1971

❷ Via Media 38m S ★★

A fine steep route with a tricky crux. Start at the foot of the big groove 5m left of the stone wall. Cross the right wall of the groove to the rib and climb it. Climb the slabs and then the crack on the left side of the wall.
GF Parkinson, W Rae 10.05.1945

❸ Romantically Challenged 36m E1 5a ★★

Start at the fence. Climb the short groove containing a stunted tree then up the wall to a rightward-rising crack. Follow this then climb the left-hand side of the wall to a ledge. Pull over the juggy sandwiched bulge.
S Reid, A Lywood 2002

❹ Direct Route 36m VS 4b ★★

A very good climb with an intimidating start 3m right of the stone wall. Climb the steep wall boldly for 6m then move leftwards and up to ledges. Climb the wall to a sentry box and follow the crack to a ledge. Climb the bulge and slab above.
AT Hargreaves, GG MacPhee 10.05.1930

❺ Failed Romantic 36m E1 5b ★★★

Very good climbing on small sharp holds. Rather bold. Start 4m right of the stone wall at a steep rib. Climb the rib to a small ledge. Climb the wall above direct to the right end of a leftward-slanting crack and follow this to the top.
S Hubbard 1.08.1984

❻ Kleine Rinne 36m VS 4b ★★

An excellent route. Start at the foot of a steep groove 5m right of the stone wall. Climb the groove passing a small tree on its left. Climb the slab to its left edge below a steep groove in the wall. Pull up into the groove and continue up the exposed wall to easier ground.
JJ Allison 1.04.1963

South Crag - Left

1. Gazebo — HVS 5a ★★★
2. Via Media — S ★★
3. Romantically Challenged — E1 5a ★★
4. Direct Route — VS 4b ★★
5. Failed Romantic — E1 5b ★★★
6. Kleine Rinne — VS 4b ★★
7. Yew Tree Climb — VD ★★
8. Gangway Climb — VD ★★

7 Yew Tree Climb 38m VD ★★
The inviting left-slanting wide slab as the crag turns the corner.
1 26m Climb the slab on the left to just below an overhung corner. Climb the broken rib on the right to a ledge and tree then move left and up the slab to a wall.
2 12m Climb the wall to the right of the crack and continuation slabs.
GG MacPhee, M Barker 31.03.1928

8 Gangway Climb 34m VD ★★
Superb yet serious. Climb on to the ledge on the left and ascend the rib. Climb the gangway on the left and continue up the slab.
Photo below.
GG MacPhee, JW Baxter 19.05.1928

9 Wall Climb 25m S ★
Start on a ledge on top of large blocks and below a large detached block. Climb onto the block. Step right on to the wall and up the short steep groove then straight up the slab to a slim groove which is climbed to a ledge. Follow easy slabs to finish.
D Armstrong 1978

10 Slab Climb 25m S ★★
A pleasant, reachy climb. Climb the slab then a short steep corner; easy slabs lead to the top.
M Barker, GG MacPhee 3.07.1928

Gangway Climb VD (above) Fiona Sanders — 📷 David Simmonite

RAVEN CRAG

OS Grid Ref: NY 304 188
Altitude: 350m

Classic testing routes on this prominent imposing crag overlooking Thirlmere. The huge cave is home to big substantial hard routes, whereas the wall to its right offers easier options.

Approach: Park at the junction with the dam road on the back road that runs to the west of Thirlmere, or in a layby 100m north of the junction. If the dam road is closed to traffic, continue north along the dual-carriageway towards Keswick. After 1 km make a left turn to come onto the back road. From here, a path goes through a gate and steeply up the hillside to join a forestry track. Go left to a sharp bend with the crag looming above you. From the bend, follow a vague path up the steep hillside. Gear up in the grassy bay beneath the crag. For the routes that start in the cave, make your way well up to the left until a short climb up a corner next to a tree and a scramble lead to a good ledge. Some climbing S - worthy of a rope - leads to the cave.

Descent: Abseil. Walk from the very top west through the woods until a good path is reached and followed to the right to the col where a path returns you more safely down the hillside. The steep vegetated gully on the right is not recommended.

 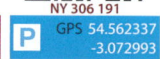 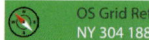

Thirlmere Dam Bridge — PETER STERLING

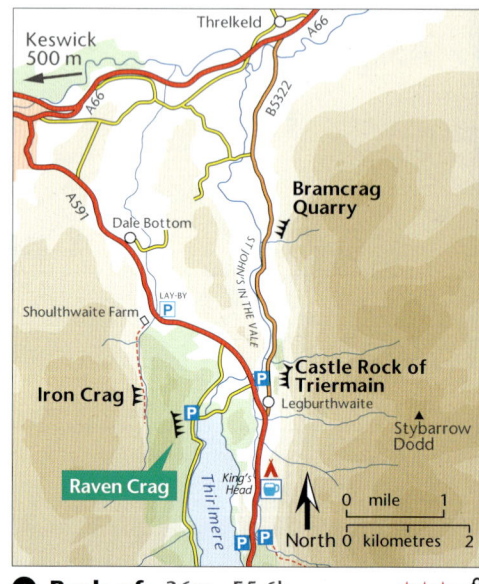

① **Peels of Laughter** 36m E5 6b ★★★
A superb route combining thin wall climbing with a brutal roof. Start directly below the middle of the wall, 3m left of a sycamore tree. Climb a very shallow loose groove to a large break. Move left off a block onto the steep wall. Step back right then follow a shallow scoop to the roof. Traverse left and climb through the roof at the obvious weakness to a good hold. Continue more easily up the groove above to a block.
P Livesey, P Gomersall 1.06.1977

② **Medlayer** 27m E3 5c ★★★
Great climbing all the way. Start on the left side of the cave. Climb the wall behind the tree on superb pockets and edges to the ledge at the bottom of the groove; from here, traverse out left to climb the rib.

③ **Close to the Edge** 37m E3 5c ★★★
1 16m 5c Climb the pocketed wall behind the tree to the foot of the groove. Traverse right across the overhung slab and pull round and up to a foothold stance (peg).
2 21m 5c Step up and swing left to the left arête of the groove then continue up the fine groove system to a large ledge.
S Clegg, P Botterill 15.05.1977

Das Kapital E6 (page 440) Matt Foot — 📷 John Hartley

❹ The Gates of Delirium 57m E4 6b ★★★★ ♂

A brilliant classic with a fantastic finish.. Start beneath the groove at the back of the cave.
1 18m 6a Climb the groove to the hole. Traverse left (old pegs) then up leftwards to a foothold stance in a groove (peg).
2 21m 6a Step up and right to stand in the groove. Climb the groove pulling out left with difficulty passing a sloping ledge to gain another ledge. Step back right above the groove and climb the wall moving right to a grass stance. Abseil.
3 18m 6b **Relayer** Step left and scramble up to the foot of the headwall. Climb 5m until it is possible to swing right across the overhanging wall to a good hold on the lip. Pull onto and climb the slab.
P Botterill, S Clegg 7.08.1976

❺ Das Kapital 46m E6 6b ★★★

A tremendous route with a burly start then hard technical climbing to finish.
1 28m 6b Climb the groove to the hole and follow the crack straight over the large roof (two threads; peg). Climb the intermittent crack until it is possible to swing right to a large thin flake which is followed to its top. Step up and left (two pegs) then traverse left for 3m with hands on a sloping ledge to a shallow groove. Make a sequence of difficult tenuous moves up the groove before moving left to the respite of a ledge; block 2m higher. Abseil off, or:
2 18m 6b Rarely climbed since the loss of a crucial nut placement. Climb the crack above to an overhang. Move right to follow an undercut slab rightwards to a niche. Move up a couple of metres (very limited protection) then step left to gain a thin crack. Climb the wall to the left of the crack to the final crack.
Photo page 439.
P Livesey, P Gomersall 1.07.1978

❻ Blitzkrieg 58m E4 6a ★★★

A fine strenuous assault on the cave headwall. Start beneath the groove at the back of the cave.
1 19m 5b Climb the groove to a hole below the roof, swing right and traverse rightwards (peg) to a recess.
2 24m 6a Traverse back left to a niche and climb the flake to the overhang. Move left and climb the break through the overhang with difficulty to belay below the chimney; or maybe better to continue.
3 15m 5c Climb the chimney and exit left. Move up and follow a line of flakes out left onto the wall. Follow this to the top.
P Gomersall, P Livesey 1.07.1977

❼ Communist Convert 42m VS 4b ★★

This left-to-right rising traverse is a popular climb; exposed, delicate on sound rock. The crux is slow to dry. Start at the right-hand side of the short wall below the cave.
1 15m 4a Climb slabs and move right onto the nose.
2 27m 4b Move diagonally right to an open groove, mantelshelf onto a small ledge then continue rightwards to a small rock ledge. Traverse right and upwards, step down into the crack and move up to a large ledge on the right; (large spike). Walk off to the right.
Photo page 429.
AR Dolphin, D Hopkin, M Dwyer, J Ramsden 10.05.1953

❽ Totalitarian 72m E1 5c ★★★ ♂

An outstanding route. Above the gearing up point is a shallow grassy bowl. Start at the top of this, at a large block, directly below the right-hand corner of the cave.
1 32m 5b From the block, move left round a rib and climb a shallow corner on the right and the wall above to a good ledge below an open groove. Climb the groove until forced to step up right with difficulty. Continue to belay on the ramp (peg).
2 22m 4b Move diagonally right to an open groove, mantelshelf onto a small ledge and continue rightwards to a small rock ledge. Traverse right and upwards, step down into a crack and move up to a large ledge (spike).
3 18m 5c Step left and climb the corner (peg) leading up to the roof. Step delicately out right to the edge to look round the corner where you will find a delightful crack; follow this more easily.
CJS Bonington, M Thompson 2.09.1964

❾ Empire 63m E3 6a ★★★ ♂

An excellent route with a tough crux. Above the usual arrival point at the crag is a shallow grassy bowl. Start at the top of this, just right of a large block.
1 18m 5a Move right and climb into a shallow groove. Continue straight up to the ledge system on the right (thread, peg).
2 33m 5c Go left into a niche then climb out of the right-hand side. Follow the ramp rightwards then climb to a small ledge. Continue up the slab to the obvious steep groove. Climb this and move left to reach easier ground. Continue rightwards to a stance below the roof.
3 12m 6a Climb to the overlap where an awkward move leads onto the wall above (peg), then continue to the top.
K Myhill, K Jones 1.09.1973

IRON CRAG
OS Grid Ref: NY 297 193
Altitude: 350m

Solidarity E1 (opposite) Graham Iles — David Simmonite

Two very different buttresses. The **Left-Hand** is a steep clean wall with a range of low-extremes plus a couple of harder ones thrown in. The **Right-Hand** looks steeper but is actually a LOT steeper. It is home to some very testing routes.

Seasonal restriction: 15th Feb to 31st May. Applies to Right-Hand Buttress and central section. Left-Hand Buttress is unrestricted.

Approach: The parking layby is the old road off the big sweeping bend by the entrance to Shoulthwaite Farm. Take the track towards the farm and small caravan/campsite. Follow the footpath between the farm buildings and, soon after the gate, take the smaller path through a second gate on the right. This leads up the hill to a forestry track. Go right, round the bend, until a path on the right leads through a gate and over a footbridge. Follow the beck up the valley until beneath the crag. Go straight up the steep grassy hillside to beneath the **Right-Hand Buttress**. If going to the **Left-Hand Buttress**, keep going round and up the hillside.

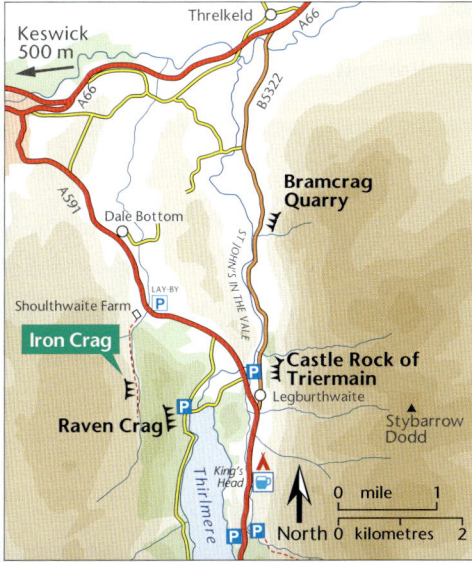

Left-Hand Buttress

Enjoyable technical wall climbing.

Descent: The only safe descent is down the left-hand side. There is also an abseil point at the top of *Solidarity/Granolithic Groove*.

❶ The Steel Band 45m E2 5b ★★
Pleasant, somewhat bold, climbing. Not well-protected although a good hold appears just when you want one making it low in the grade. Start at the foot of a small greenish ramp just right above the rocky ridge. Can be done in one long pitch with 60m ropes and plenty of long slings.
1 17m 5a Climb the short green ramp rightwards then straight up for 3m on pockets until holds lead rightwards across a wall to a rib. Move right across a groove then step down and right to a small ledge in the next groove.
2 28m 5b Climb right to the obvious horizontal break and follow this to a left-facing flake-crack. Step down and hand-traverse right to a sloping ledge. Good holds lead up the middle of a wall through the upper break to the top.
Photo below.
P Whillance, D Armstrong 18.07.1981

❷ Granolithic Groove 35m E1 5b ★★
Excellent climbing. Start from a ledge with a large block. Climb the groove for 3m then up the right-hand wall to the break. The steep groove and wall above lead to a cleaned rib which provides great climbing on positive holds.
P Whillance, J Loxham 12.06.1981

❸ Solidarity 35m E1 5b ★
Takes the next groove to the right starting at a small bush. Climb a thin crack rightwards to a small overlap then pull steeply into the groove. Follow this passing a small overhang to where it ends. Continue up a short wall and then finish up the short rib on the left.
Photo opposite.
P Whillance, J Loxham 12.06.1981

❹ Kryptonite 32m E5 6b ★
A tough route that takes the thin crack in the otherwise blank wall. Start by a small bush. Climb a thin crack rightwards to a small overlap then move right to a steep crack. Climb this until it is possible to move left to beneath the thin crack splitting the steep wall above the horizontal break. Follow the crack; where it peters out make a sketchy committing sequence on edges and smears to the welcome sanctuary of the break beneath the overhang. Surmount the overhang and follow the short groove above.
R Graham, C Downer 17.04.1982

The Steel Band E2 (above) Jon Stevens — PETER STERLING

5 Marble Staircase 32m E4 6a ★★★

A fine climb. Start below a steep corner to the left of the slanting gash. The corner slants rightwards steeply then kicks back left at an easier angle. Climb the steep corner to reach jugs and a small ledge on the left. Climb straight up to regain the corner where it heads left at an easier angle; follow it to a prominent horizontal break. Traverse right along the break for a few metres to the left-facing flake crack. Go up this then teeter delicately leftwards to reach the upper break below an overhang. Pull over to a short final groove.
P Whillance, D Armstrong 14.07.1981

6 Amabilite 32m E4 6a ★★

Good climbing with some significant run-outs between reasonable gear. Start beneath the steep corner. Climb the corner then step right into the continuation groove. Move up and right making a mantelshelf onto a ledge. From the left side of the ledge, climb the wall above arriving at the niche on the horizontal break. Make the first move right out of the niche, then gain a standing position in the break. Climb the wall above and left to reach the next break. Climb the wall directly above.
N Wharton, C Gore, T Whiteley 12.06.2009

7 Hiddenite 32m E2 5c ★★★★

A fantastic route with a serious, yet straightforward start and a tricky well-protected crux. Scramble up right over blocks until about 6m right of the groove behind a large detached flake. Step up and traverse boldly left along sloping ledges (cam) to below the groove; poor protection. Climb the groove to an overhang then move right to a faint groove in the wall. Climb the right wall to a thin horizontal break (nuts, cams). Now you need to figure out how you will reach the next holds at and above the small overhang. Once done, pull up and continue slightly leftwards to the top. A fantastic piece of climbing.
D Armstrong, P Whillance 16.07.1981

Left-Hand Buttress

1	The Steel Band	E2 5b ★★
2	Granolithic Groove	E1 5b ★★
3	Solidarity	E1 5b ★
4	Kryptonite	E5 6b ★
5	Marble Staircase	E4 6a ★★★
6	Ambailite	E4 6a ★★
7	Hiddenite	E2 5c ★★★★

Right-Hand Buttress | **Iron Crag** | 445

Right-Hand Buttress

Relentlessly steep climbing. French grades are purely indicative; these are very adventurous.

Descent: Down the gully on the left, well back from the crag.

❽ The Committal Chamber   57m   E5 6a   ★★

Exposed sustained and strenuous, a tremendous outing. The route provides an excellent isight into the nature of the climbing. Start at the left-hand end at a short crack in a corner.
1 12m 4c Climb the corner to the yew tree.
2 24m 6a Follow the crack to a niche then step down right (thread). From a big hold make a series of committing and strenuous moves to reach the obvious sloping ledge.
3 21m 4c Up from the end of the ledge then round the corner to finish.
R Graham, C Downer 27.07.1983

❾ Western Union   39m   E6 6b (7b+)   ★★★★

A magnificent direct line up steep and difficult ground. Start below a grassy ledge at 5m, just right of the lower of two trees. Reach the grassy ledge then climb a difficult wall - much steeper than it looks, (peg) onto a large sloping ledge on the right. Move left into and up a sentry box (peg). Step right, climb the crack and wall on the right to a rest in a niche in the diagonal break. Launch up the steep difficult groove (two pegs) to a brief respite. The final groove eventually eases and leads to the top.
D Hall 27.09.1986

❿ The Iron Man   36m   E7 6c (7c)   ★★★

An awesome route taking the line up the wall to the left of the top central groove. Climb *Western Union* to the break. At the base of the thin groove is a flake which sports a peg. Climb boldly up the thin groove onto the head wall, move left, peg, then up to and over the small overlap to a tiny niche. Hard moves left gain the arête which is followed to the top.
A Wilson, M Johnston 11.06.2008

⓫ If 6 was 9   40m   E9 6c (8a+)   ★★

This impressive route tackles the all-too-obvious blank wall in the centre of the crag. Start as for *Phoenix in Obsidian*. Climb the initial wall (passing a peg runner) to a large ledge. Move left to below the left end of a small overlap. Climb directly, passing three peg runners on the way, to a junction with the break. Finish up the steep V-groove above as for *Phoenix in Obsidian*.
D Birkett 20.08.1992

⓬ Phoenix in Obsidian   40m   E7 6b (7b)   ★★★

A fairly direct line up the right-hand side. Beware of rope drag when climbing the final groove. Climb the initial wall (peg) to a large ledge. Climb the wall (two poor pegs) then make some hard committing moves to gain a good hold (peg, wires). Move up into the niche. Swing right and make difficult moves to gain a good hold below the roof (Rock 5). Make a difficult traverse left and pull through the overhang at its narrowest point to gain the ledge below the V-groove. Climb the steep V-groove.
M Radtke 2.07.1989

ULLSWATER

Boy Racer, Raven Crag Threshthwaite E4 (page 460) Nick Wharton — David Simmonite

Great climbing in the side valleys feeding delightful Ullswater, away to the east. A popular spot for visitors to enjoy the water activities. **Eagle Crag** in Grisedale has a range of easy to mid-range routes while the mighty **Dove Crag** and the impressive **Raven Crag Threshthwaite** are home to many harder challenges.

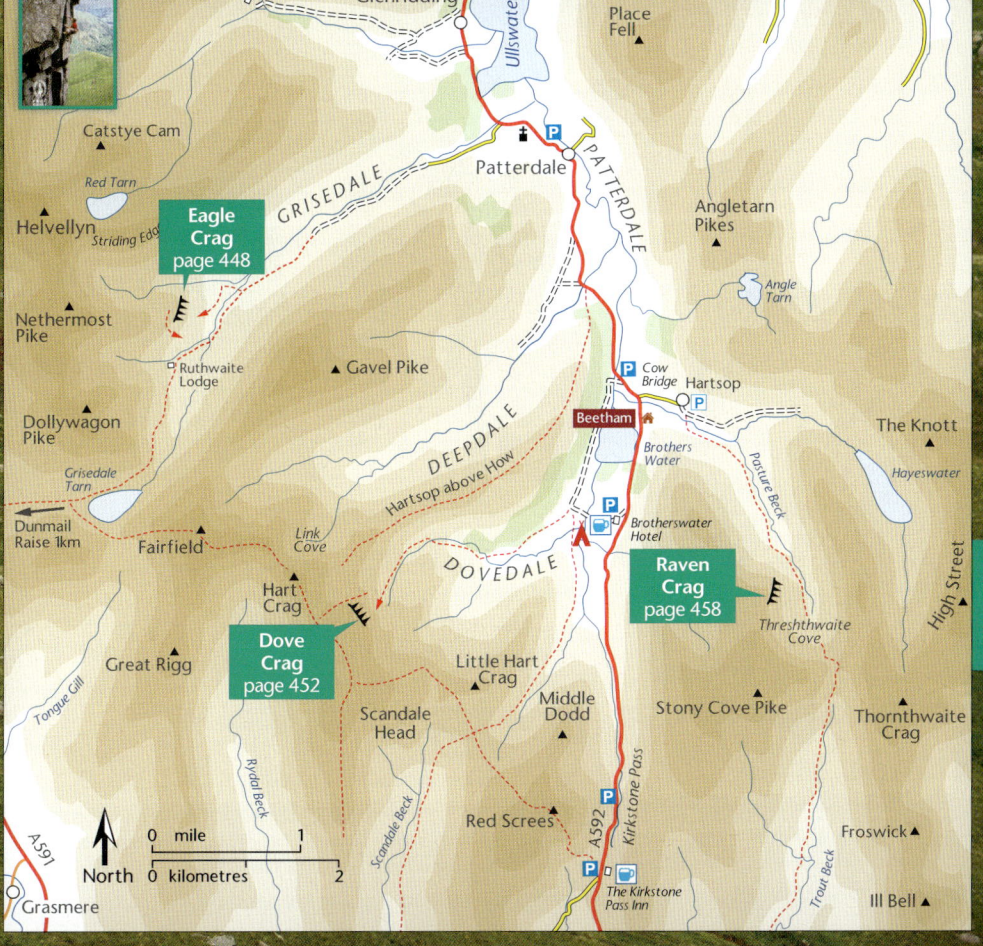

EAGLE CRAG

OS Grid Ref: NY 357 143
Altitude: 395m

Kestrel Wall S (page 450) Katy Forrester — © Keith Sanders

❶ Hawkeye 25m VS 4b ★★
An excellent pitch with good positions. Start below the left end of a broad ledge, below the left side of a large bulge. Climb the left side of the bulge into the shallow groove at 4m. Continue up the groove rightwards onto the rib, then up keeping to the left of the large perched block. Finish straight up to The Pasture.
T Marr, M Tooke 23.07.2008

❷ Kestrel Wall 45m S ★★★ ♦
A superb climb starting below a prominent flake crack.
1 27m Climb to the rock ledge and ascend the crack moving left at the top to a stance behind a perched block. Continue directly to The Pasture.
2 18m Climb the steep slab, 8m right of the stone wall, to the upper ledge. Climb into the scoop above the right end of the ledge, move right to the rib and up to the top.
Photo page 448.
RJ Birkett, AH Griffin 19.07.1954

❸ Pericles 45m HVS ★
A good route with an intimidating crux. Three metres right of the flake crack, a line of flakes forms a shallow groove leading to an overhang. Start directly below this.
1 27m 4c Climb to the groove and move up this until it is possible to step right below a big spike. Climb to this and continue to The Pasture.
2 18m 5a Directly above the highest blocks on the ledge is an overhanging V-chimney containing an obvious quartz jug. Surmount the overlap and move left on the slab below the chimney. Climb this to the final slab and the top.
O Woolcock, MS Wild Sept 1960

❹ Warbird 45m VS ★★
Good enjoyable well-protected climbing. Start at the foot of a V-corner.
1 27m 4c Climb the corner, step left at the top and gain a ledge. Follow the groove for 2m then step left and climb the wall just left of the arête to a small corner. Trend left to a corner-crack. Climb up the wall just right of the crack to belay on The Pasture.
2 18m 4a Climb the slab 2m right of the stone wall to the upper ledge. Finish up the final wall.
T Marr, M Tooke 25.08.2008

❺ Horse Power 65m E2 ★★
Right again is a large overhang with a groove on its right. Start up slabs below this groove.
1 35m 5c Climb the slab to just right of the V-groove. Use the crack to gain a flake on the right of the groove. Climb with interest to gain better holds then follow a crack up leftwards to a big spike. Step back right and climb the steep delicate slab boldly to The Pasture.
2 30m 5c Climb the black-streaked slab to gain the foot of a short hanging groove. Pull steeply out right and up with difficulty. Follow the steep corner above finishing out left.
D Musgrave, G Arthur, D Musgrave (Jnr) 28.05.1989

❻ Grand Day Out 37m HVS 5a ★★
Superb well-protected climbing with good positions. Start at the left of the slabs. Climb easily rightwards and gain a higher grass ledge. Step right and climb a steep rib-groove to pull leftwards onto the slab. Trend slightly left then onto a small shelf. Pull out left and follow a steep shallow groove direct to The Pasture.
T Marr, M Tooke, F Fitzgerald 26.06.1999

❼ Sobrenada 59m VS ★★
An excellent climb starting at the foot of the 15m slab beneath the buttress.
1 36m 4b Climb the slab. Move up into the cave, pull out to the left and ascend the corner. Move right to the nose, climb the short wall and follow the sharp rib to The Pasture.
2 23m 4c Starting to the right of the piled blocks, traverse 5m right to below a flat-topped spike. Climb up to this and traverse back left until it is possible to gain the large shallow chimney. Ascend the chimney with interest and pull out left to a slab. Climb the slab and ribs to the top.
MA James, GA Leaver, KA Brookes 11.06.1957

❽ Soliloquy 76m E2 ★★
The second pitch is superb though poorly protected. Start at the foot of the slab.
1 36m 4b Climb to the cave. Mantelshelf onto the right-hand rib. Pull out of the groove and, keeping to the edge of the rib, ascend to The Pasture.
2 40m 5a Climb to below the prominent rib. Up to an obvious flat hold and, using the groove on the left, ascend to a ledge leading back to the rib. Continue up the rib and then slabs
N Allinson, C Greenhow 21.06.1975

DOVE CRAG

OS Grid Ref: NY 376 109
Altitude: 580m

A huge and imposing crag that looms over the valley. The **North Buttress** is home to a fine collection of very hard routes.

Approach: Parking is available at the Brotherswater Inn where appropriate refreshment can be had at the end of the day. Take the track through Syke Side Campsite to Hartsop Hall then a good path up Dovedale to the crag. Or, park at Cow Bridge then take the track south towards Hartsop Hall.

Descent: Well to the right.

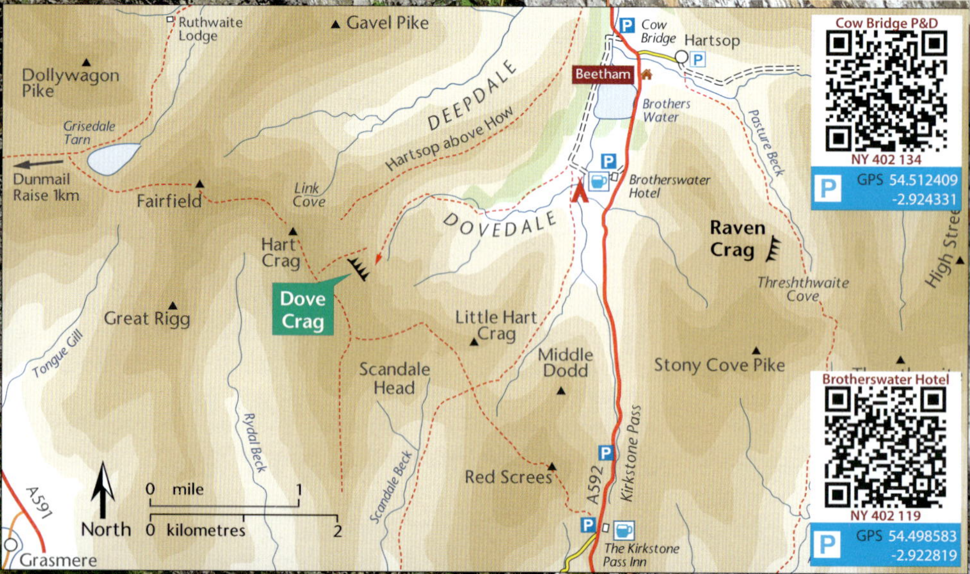

Extol E2 (page 454) Dave Birkett — Ian Parnell

The Main Crag

Steep, intimidating and adventurous, not often climbed, so may be quite dirty.

1 Westmorland's Route 110m MS ★★
An interesting mountaineering route which requires good dry conditions. Start at the foot of the ridge just below a huge boulder in South Gully.
1 21m Steps lead rightwards to the grassy ridge; follow this easily to a large ledge.
2 21m Ascend the ridge on its slabby right side to a sloping stance, on the ridge, by a pinnacle belay.
3 15m Follow the ridge directly to a grassy ledge below a wall.
4 20m Traverse right on spiky brackets for 5m, above a gully, and then ascend the mossy leftward-slanting slab to a grassy ledge on the ridge.
5 21m Climb the little wall and traverse up to the left to the end of a gangway. Move up to a large vegetated ledge and traverse this rightwards to a belay.
6 12m Climb the final wall.
H Westmorland, J Mounsey, WA North 3.10.1910

2 Dovedale Groove 54m E1 5b ★★
Very traditional and a tough proposition. Start at the foot of the crack behind a large boulder.
1 15m 5b From the top of the slab make an awkward move into the groove and continue to a stance below a conspicuous wide overhanging crack.
2 18m 5b Climb the crack to a chockstone then pull awkwardly left onto a slab. Continue more easily up a groove and slab to a large grass ledge.
3 8m Move up to a grass ledge below some overhangs.
4 13m 5a Above a short slab is a gap in the overhangs. Climb through this and step left into the left-hand groove to finish.
DD Whillans, J Brown, D Cowan 4.05.1953

❸ Hiraeth   75m   E2 5b   ★
A climb of contrasts; the bold poorly protected first pitch leading to a well-protected crux. Currently rather grubby. Scramble up to the base of a slab 6m below *Dovedale Groove*.
1 27m 5a Climb a thin crack to the top of the slab then follow the weakness rightwards to a small ledge. Up to grass on the left then continue up the steep wall to a small stance.
2 15m 5b Move up to a sloping ledge on the left. Climb the green groove above (crux)..
3 15m 5a Move left and ascend a short overhung corner. Traverse right for 10m to a rib then drop down a groove to a stance (or continue).
4 18m 5a Re-climb the groove then a steeper groove to the right of the rib. Move right, then finish leftwards up overlapping mossy slabs.
P Crew, B Ingle 10.06.1962

❹ Phobos   69m   E2 5c   ★
Steep wall climbing. Take at least six long slings to extend runners. Start where the path at the foot of the crag steepens and becomes a scramble.
1 30m 5c Climb vegetated rock to reach a crack on the left of an overhang. Follow this to a traverse line and move up right to the highest of the flat rock ledges. Climb the steep wall leftwards for 6m then move right to a shallow niche. Step back left then climb the groove, stepping left below the bulge, to the overhang. Turn this on the right and take a stance at the foot of the terrace.
2 15m 4b Step right and climb leftwards to follow a gangway parallel to the terrace, then the chimney above rightwards to a stance.
3 24m 5a Climb the short corner and move right past a large spike to below a large corner. Ascend the corner and hand-traverse right along a thin crack below a roof then move up to gain easier ground.
C Read, J Adams Aug 1972

❺ Extol   92m   E2 5b   ★★
Once a Lakeland icon finding a way up the centre of the crag. The top section is clean and provides an exposed challenge, yet the rest is disappointingly rather broken and dirty. Start at the right side of the triangle of slabs just left of a big boulder.
1 47m 5a Climb the grassy groove and then traverse right to below the corner. Climb the corner for 12m then traverse left with difficulty for 3m. Step up and re-enter the corner over a bulge. Move up and climb a small chimney then step round the rib to a good stance.
2 45m 5b The grassy leftward-slanting ramp 6m left of the stance is the initial objective. Cross the main groove and then swing left on a series of good jugs to the ramp. Climb this with a brief excursion on the right wall at its top to reach a position below a steep wall capped by an overhang. Climb the wall then, at the overhang, move right to pull into a bottomless groove splitting the overhang. Follow the groove until forced to move right to finish up the rib.
Photo page 452.
DD Whillans, C Mortlock 17.04.1960

❻ Hangover   72m   HVS 5a   ★
A fine route, now quite dirty, finding the line of least resistance up the centre of this daunting crag. Exposed with some suspect rock. Start at the right side of the triangle of slabs just left of a big boulder.
1 18m Climb the grassy groove then traverse right to a belay below a corner (or continue up the next pitch).
2 29m 5a Climb the corner for 12m then traverse left with difficulty for 3m. Step up and re-enter the corner over a bulge. Move up and climb a small chimney then step round the rib to a stance.
3 25m 4c Traverse right with care along the shattered ledge and climb a pinnacle. Move up to a groove, step right across a rib into a corner and climb the V-chimney.
JW Haggas, JK Booth, R Clough 20.05.1939

The Main Crag | **Dove Crag** | 455

The Main Crag
1. Westmorland's Route — MS ★★
2. Dovedale Groove — E1 5b ★★
3. Hiraeth — E2 5b ★
4. Phobos — E2 5c ★
5. Extol — E2 5b ★★
6. Hangover — HVS 5a ★

North Buttress
Brace yourself. This impressive wall leans continuously and offers spectacular strenuous climbing on generally good holds and adequate protection.
Descent: To the right.

❼ Bucket Dynasty 25m E7 6b (F7c) ★★★ ♂

A steep exciting climb on good rock. Start at the layback crack below the right end of the grassy terrace. Climb the crack to its top and follow the wall above until a move left leads to huge holds (med cam). Climb the intimidating wall above to a layaway (small cams). Pull up again to gain *Vlad* (large cam) and finish up this.
M Berzins, N Foster 27.05.1991

❽ Dusk Till Dawn 30m E7 6b (F7c) ★★★ ♂

This route climbs the huge leaning pillar on the **North Buttress**. An awesome route, one of the steepest lines in the Lakes. A double set of small cams is recommended. Start at the obvious layback crack below the right end of the grassy terrace. Climb the crack to its top and follow the wall above until a move left leads to huge holds (med cam). Climb the intimidating wall above to a good layaway (small cams). Pull up again to gain the traverse line (*Vlad*). Traverse right for a couple of metres to good holds (Friend 0.5 or Wallnut 6). Moves up and rightwards gain the right side of the pillar. A series of big moves on big holds following a leftwards-leaning ramp lead to a huge shake-out below a ramp. Make hard moves (peg) to superb jugs on the left side of the pillar. More huge moves upwards lead to a small ledge. The tricky groove above is climbed to another ledge.
A Wilson, C Hope 19.07.2003

❾ Vlad the Impailer 35m E7 6b (F7c) ★★★ ♂

Stupendous, bold and very strenuous climbing make this an unforgettable route. Worth checking the state of the pegs and *in situ* tat - they were replaced in 2010. Long slings are essential. Start at the foot of the rock step. Climb the flake crack to a rock shelf then up the wall from the right end to the good flake. Swing left to a jug and then another (0 Friend above), then traverse left (*in-situ* Rock 1, vital Friend 2.5). Undercut left to a downward-pointing spike and good footholds then pull up left (Rock 1, crucial Friend 0.5 or Wallnut 6). Swing down across left (Friend 3) then climb (peg) to a jug (Friend 1 or 1.5 on right). Gain the block and niche up and left; crux, (peg) and continue up the faultline (peg, thread) to gain a belay.
The leader can then reverse to the *in-situ* gear and, with the second up on the rock shelf, lower to the ground. Karabiners are in place.
M Berzins, N Foster 26.08.1990

❿ Fear and Fascination 48m E5 6a (F7a+) ★★★★

A classic climb; bold, strenuous, intimidating with maintained interest. Brilliant. Climb the flake crack to the rock shelf and pull up the wall at the right end of the shelf (old peg). Continue up the wall to a flake and then less easily to a short crozzly crack. Hand-traverse right and pull into a niche (old pegs). Step right and up, passing an obvious spike, to gain the right end of the ledge system and a good rest. Climb the fine groove above, making a sneaky step out right when all the holds seem to run out, and finishing via the deep groove.
R Graham, TW Birkett 26.06.1980

⓫ Bucket City 45m E6 6b (F7b) ★★★

Another tremendous pitch, this time taking the diagonal crack to the left of *Fast and Furious* and an intricate line up the superb headwall. Climb the flake then step left into a shallow cave. Pull over the bulge and climb to the break. Step left round the rib to the base of a thin diagonal crack (old pegs). Fight the stubborn crack to a rest in the niche then climb up and rightwards passing an obvious spike to gain the right end of the obvious ledge system and a good rest. Make a couple of moves up the groove above before breaking out left via a line of holds on the lip of an overlap. These lead to an obvious slot from which a line of reasonable holds, breaks and ledges lead directly up the wall (peg).
M Berzins, N Foster 28.05.1988

⓬ Fast City 37m E5 6a (F7a) ★★★

A direct line up **North Buttress** linking the start of *Fast and Furious* with the top of *Bucket City*. It follows *Fast and Furious* to the top of the groove and moves left to gain the prominent spike (junction with *Fear and Fascination/Bucket City*). Climb up to the ledge system then make a couple of moves up the groove above before breaking out left via a line of holds above the lip of an overlap. These lead to a slot (small cams) from which a line of reasonable holds, breaks and ledges lead directly up the wall, slightly right (peg).
S Crowe, K Magog, A Wilson 16.08.2003

North Buttress | **Dove Crag** | 457

13 Fast and Furious 45m E5 6a (F7a) ★★★★

A bold and sustained climb of great quality which takes the shallow groove and headwall directly above the starting flake. The name suggests the required approach! Several long-ish narrow tapes are useful for the small spikes. Climb to the flake then the short bold rib to the base of a smooth wall guarding entry to the groove. Neatly avoid this obstacle with a step up to the right before hand-traversing back left to the base of the groove (peg). Layback boldly up the groove to better holds and runners then trend rightwards passing a tiny spike to a long reach (crux) to gain a superb hidden jug on top of a short rib. The wall above is climbed boldly, first right, then left, then straight up, aiming for the obvious finishing chimney.
Belay above this or continue to better gear further up to the left.
R Graham, D Lyle, TW Birkett 30.06.1982

| **5** | Extol | E2 5b ★★ |
| **6** | Hangover | HVS 5a ★ |

14 Flying Fissure Finish E5 6b (F7a+) ★★★★

One of the best E5s in the Lakes. It follows the hanging groove right of the chimney of *Fast and Furious*. Follow *Fast and Furious* to the superb jug after the crux. Move right (peg) then race up the wall (*in-situ* thread) to gain a line of buckets which lead up the sensational groove to the top.
N Foster, M Berzins 11.08.1990

15 Explosion 30m E4 5c ★

A deceptive pitch which is very strenuous and poorly protected. Not a soft touch. Start at the very right of the buttress where an obvious easy gangway leads up and left. Climb the steepening gangway leftwards then climb more directly to the corner, a rest and an easier finish.
P Botterill, P Whillance 30.06.1976

RAVEN CRAG THRESHTHWAITE COVE
OS Grid Ref: NY 419 112
Altitude: 450m

G.T.X. E3 (page 460) Jim Gordon — David Simmonite

For those climbing at **E3** and above, this is one of the best crags in the Lakes. The rock is solid, compact and with compelling lines. More stars than a night at the Oscars.

Seasonal restriction: 15th Feb to 31st May.

Approach: From the tiny hamlet of Hartsop, leave the car park and turn right over the bridge. Follow the track into the lovely valley which is followed until the crag is seen slanting up the fellside on the right. Head steeply up the line of the old wall.

Descent: Abseil or down and right.

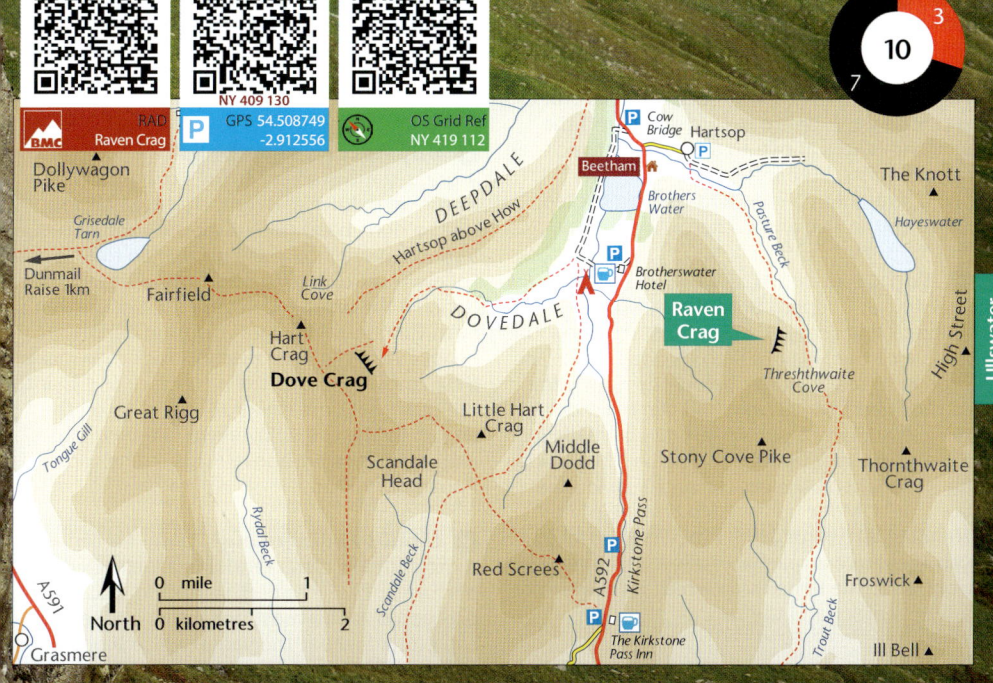

❶ Grand Prix 40m E3 5c ★★★
A great climb. Start up the left-hand of two grooves directly below the left side of the Shield. Climb the corner to a ledge below the overhang at the break. Move right slightly and climb the overhang (protection) to the leftward-slanting ramp which is followed to a short groove. Race up this and finish up the obvious crack system.
P Whillance, R Berzins, P Botterill Sept 1980

❷ Road Rage 40m E7 6b ★★
Try to stay calm! An exciting route with bold thin climbing. Climb the corner to a ledge below the overhang. Over the overhang to the ramp; arrange gear here. Step right onto the Shield underneath a small overlap. Move right to a flake then make hard committing moves up the wall on poor holds (peg on left). Continue directly up until the headwall is reached left of the final ramp of *Top Gear*. Step up and right onto a ledge (peg) before finishing directly up the crack.
N Wharton, H Davies, P Clavey, D Donnini 27.06.1995

❸ Internal Combustion 40m E6 ★★★
An excellent climb. Bold to start then technically very demanding and finger-testing. High octane fuel recommended.
1 8m 5a Climb the groove a few metres right of the corner to the break.
2 32m 6b Make committing moves over the first overlap (peg on the right). Surmount the next overlap by pulling leftwards towards the crack before stepping back right above the peg. Climb the wall to a short diagonal crack and follow this to cross *Top Gear*. Climb the wall and cracks above to a small overhang (peg up and right). Step left (peg on the left) then climb straight up - hard and well-protected. Finish up the slab and corner.
R Smith, JW Earl 21.06.1986

❹ Top Gear 40m E4 6a ★★★★
Top Route! A superb bold climb taking a diagonal line across the Shield. Start below the middle of the Shield. Climb the wall, crack and groove to reach ledges below the right edge of the Shield. Move right and climb a short flake-crack until a pull up left can be made into a steep groove. Swing left to gain a large sloping foothold on the bottom right-hand edge of the Shield. Move up to reach the line of holds trending leftwards across the Shield until a vague groove is reached. Follow this then step right onto the large ramp which is followed to a short corner and the top.
P Whillance, D Armstrong 30.05.1981

❺ Redex 30m E2 5c ★★
The prominent diagonal crack sweeping from left to right across the centre of the crag gives sustained climbing.
1 13m 5b Climb the diagonal crack to the horizontal fault.
2 17m 5c Follow the crack to the small tree. Step right into the steep groove and follow this to the top.
CW Brown, TW Birkett 31.07.1976

❻ G.T.X. 40m E3 5c ★★★
An impressive and sustained route taking a direct line up the centre of the crag. Start at a shallow groove. Climb the groove rightwards to the scoop, step left and climb steeply to the horizontal fault. Up to the small tree and then climb left to the overhang. Pull over this into the groove and up to a second overhang. Climb this on the right and up to finish.
Photo page 458.
P Whillance, R Parker 5.05.1980

❼ Running on Empty 35m E4 6a ★★★
You may well be by the time you reach the top! Excellent climbing taking the stepped groove right of the central groove. Start at the left end of the easy grassy ramp below a large overhang at half-height. Small wires will be found useful. Climb the groove (quite bold) heading for the right end of the large overhang where a large spike will be found. Use this to swing right with a committing move onto the wall above which is climbed delicately to a large groove. Follow the groove to the top with an awkward finish.
J Lamb, P Botterill 9.07.1981

❽ Boy Racer 37m E4 6a ★★★
A great climb starting at the right-hand side of the arch down and right of the easy ramp. Up the right-hand side of the arch and make a tough move into a slim groove on the right. Follow this boldly to a good ledge and up the ramp to the break, down and right of a raven's nest. Climb the short left-slanting ramp/groove past the first quartzy crack then make a thin move to reach the next crack and so into the groove. Climb the groove and rib on the left up to the break. Excellent climbing into and up the groove above leads to the top.
Photo page 446.
P Botterill, J Lamb 21.06.1981

❾ Liquid Engineering 38m E6 6b ★★★
A magnificent climb requiring a well-oiled performance. Sustained, steep and sparsely protected with a most deceptive and serious top pitch. Start at the vague white scoop a few metres down from the arch.

Raven Crag Threshthwaite Cove

1 24m 6b Climb into the scoop then move across left and up on layaways (peg). Move up then tentatively left across the blank slab to a good sidehold. Climb the wall above to a diagonal crack then more easily to a ledge. Step right to a scoop and follow the slab to a large block.
2 14m 6b Move up the ramp for 2m to below a large bottomless groove. Pull into the groove (tape) to some good footholds. Climb up the groove making some very technical moves and then continue with a little more ease to the top. Spike belays well back.
P Rigby, A Murray 2.09.1984

10 High Performance 40m E5 6b ★★★
1 25m 6b Climb into the scoop and then up to a thin diagonal crack. Follow this until it is possible to move up to the large slot that forms the start of the thin crack which is followed up the wall. Continue with ease to a horizontal break and large block.
2 15m 6a Climb into the large groove above then move across right to a good jug on the arête. Step back left into the groove which is followed to the ledge above the capping roof. Finish up the wall above. Belay well back to the left on spikes.
P Botterill, J Lamb 2.05.1981

OUTLYING

Missing Words, White Stone VS (page 484) Keith Sanders — David Simmonite

Sprinkled around the edges of the Lake District are a number of fine crags. Just because they aren't in the high fells does not detract from what they offer. **Armathwaite** is an idyllic riverside, sandstone crag with rounded cracks and imaginary holds, **Gouther Crag** and **Buckbarrow** are fine, easily accessible crags whilst **White Stone** is virtually roadside and a pleasant diversion on the way to or from its more impressive neighbours.

- **Armathwaite** 464
- **Gouther Crag** 474
- **Buckbarrow Crag** 480
- **White Stone** 484

ARMATHWAITE

OS Grid Ref: NY 505 452
Altitude: 50m

The Exorcist E4 (page 467) Nick Wharton & Roy Goddard — David Simmonite

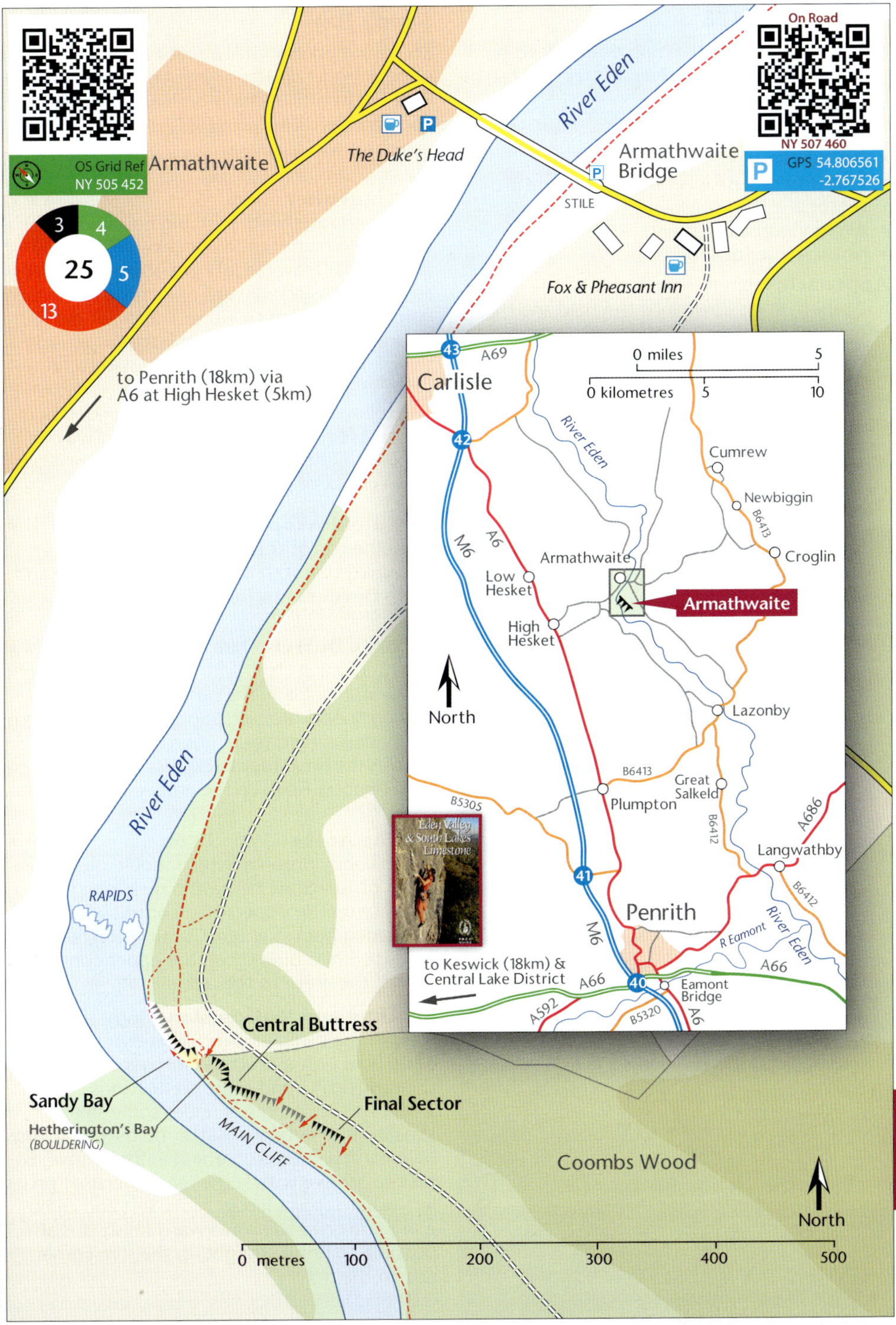

465

Armathwaite
OS Grid Ref NY 505 452

The Duke's Head

Armathwaite Bridge
STILE
NY 507 460
GPS 54.806561 -2.767526
On Road

Fox & Pheasant Inn

3 — 4
25
13 — 5

to Penrith (18km) via A6 at High Hesket (5km)

River Eden

RAPIDS

Sandy Bay
Hetherington's Bay
(BOULDERING)

Central Buttress

MAIN CLIFF

Final Sector

Coombs Wood

0 metres 100 200 300 400 500

Carlisle — A69
River Eden
Cumrew
Newbiggin
M6 / A6
Armathwaite
Low Hesket
Croglin
High Hesket
Armathwaite
Lazonby
B6413
B5305
Great Salkeld
Plumpton
B6412
Langwathby
A686
Penrith
R Eamont
River Eden
to Keswick (18km) & Central Lake District
A66
Eamont Bridge
A592 / B5320 / A6

North

Langdale | Coniston | Duddon & Wrymose | Eskdale | Scafell & Wasdale | Gable & Ennerdale | Buttermere & Newlands | Borrowdale | Thirlmere & Ullswater | **Outlying** | Sport & Slate

ARMATHWAITE

A different style of climbing on sculpted sandstone by a picturesque river. Protection can be hard to find and/or place.

The soft rock needs care:

- Do not climb when the rock is wet.
- Top-roping - use long slings and rope protectors.
- Avoid vigorous brushing.
- Not suitable for groups.

Approach: From the north side of the bridge, a footpath leads down into the field and back under the bridge. Follow the riverside path upstream to where it forks above the rapids. Take the left-hand fork to a steep descent to the river. **Sandy Bay** is on the right, the **Main Cliff** is to the left.

Glenwillie Grooves HS (opposite) Mel Adam & Roy Goddard — 📷 David Simmonite

Sandy Bay

Steep and pumpy with a soft landing. This popular area consists of an overhanging wall of rock to the left of the prominent slanting corner. The area is notable for its many boulder problems and traverses.

❶ Kingfisher 16m S ★★◆

Steep and satisfying, with big holds and deep water soloing potential. Access is river level dependent! Traverse left just above the river and climb to an awkward open groove. An easy corner is followed to either a difficult move over an overlap and up to the top, or alternatively, move left and up a tricky slab to finish.
S Wilson, A Yarrow 5.05.1973

The following three routes are extended boulder problems that gain the ledge halfway up the crag. Either finish up *Time and Motion Man*, down climb, or jump into the river!

❷ Kaleidoscope Eyes 15m E2 5b ★

From the top of the stump move up and leftwards to a step below the steep arête and climb this direct to finish on the ledge.
M Tomlinson 15.08.1986

❸ Grey Duster 15m E3 6a ★★

An entertaining climb with a steep start 2m right of the stump. Climb the centre of the bulging wall on finger-caressing edges and layaways into a very shallow groove. A good hold on the left enables the final crack to be first viewed and then climbed. Finish up the groove to the ledge.
J Lamb 1975

❹ The Arête 15m E3 6b ★★

A slap happy problem which should guarantee hours of fun! Start below the overhung rib. Levitate up the slopers to a conspicuous little blackened pocket at 3m. Continue on better holds to finish directly up the upper continuation of the arête to the ledge.

❺ Time and Motion Man 16m E2 5c ★★

Start in the damp alcove. Either dyno to a good hold or move up and leftwards with great difficulty and some contortions onto a very narrow gangway under some small square-cut overhangs. Better holds lead to jugs below a little bulge guarding a fine groove. Enter the groove with some relief then exit on its left wall to gain a ledge. Move left and climb a slight groove to an awkward finish. It is also possible to finish straight up the slim corner just to the right.
RJ Kenyon, T Dale, S Wilson 17.05.1973

6 The Exorcist 18m E4 6a ★★★
An excellent burly route best climbed quickly. Make a hard pull onto a ledge then move up (peg at 5m). Move right with trepidation to a pocket and make a strenuous and technical sequence back left then straight up (first ascent peg) to a ledge.. Leaving the sanctuary of the ledge, climb into the top groove best exited on the left.
J Lamb 1974

7 Glenwillie Grooves Direct 16m MVS 4b ★
The corner.
S Wilson, A Yarrow 12.05.1973

8 Glenwillie Grooves 18m HS ★★
The short sharp crux at the top is very safe. From a ledge 3m right of the corner, climb the wall just right of a thin crack to a ledge on the left. Take the slab on the right delicately to a foothold. Climb the wall to the left to gain another ledge below the final corner. Climb this then follow the ledge above with care to a tree.
Photo opposite.
S Wilson, A Yarrow 12.05.1973

Central Buttress

A fine buttress with stepped overhangs, sitting above the path.

Descent: Head left and back to the approach path.

9 Cally Crack 12m E3 5b ★★
A steep and intimidating climb. Climb the central corner to moves right past a dubious block to the foot of the crack - climb it!
J Lamb 1973

10 Princess Anne's New Ring 26m VS 4b ★
Start at the foot of the slab on the right of the bay.
1 13m 4a Climb the slab for 3m then move diagonally leftwards on shelving rock to a point below the oak tree on the ledge. From here, bear right then back left and surmount the final wall to the tree.
2 13m 4b Climb the corner at the back of the ledge gymnastically to a deep groove. Swing out left to a good ledge and finish up the corner above.
2a An easier option - climb the slab on the left then the short corner.
A Yarrow, S Wilson 29.05.1973

11 The Monkeyhanger 35m HVS 4c ★★
An excellent climb with a serious top pitch in a fine position. Start at the foot of the slab on the right of the bay.
1 16m 4a Climb the slab for 3m then move right onto a wall of good rock. Climb leftwards past a tree stump to the end of the long grassy ledge. Climb the steep wide crack on fantastic holds to a tree.
2 19m 4c Either, traverse right from the ledge, just above the wide crack, to near the arête then climb in an exposed position to the ledge above. Or climb the short overhanging wall at the back of the ledge to gain a shelf then traverse right for about 4m to the right arête. Continue up to a second ledge, more exposure. Move slightly right, over an overlap, to gain and finish up a delicate and unprotected slab.
S Wilson, A Yarrow 1973

12 Savage Simian 30m HVS 5a ★★
A fine and serious adventure taking a direct line up the centre of the buttress. Start at the toe of the buttress. Move onto the gangway then climb leftwards, passing the stump of a small tree. Climb the arête, on large suspect holds with no protection, to gain a ledge and a broken block on the right. Move leftwards off the block to holds over the overhanging arête then pull over to a ledge. Move slightly right, over an overlap, to gain and finish up a delicate and unprotected slab.
A Little, T Cornish 9.11.2004

13 The Bullgine Run 27m MS ★★
The superb big rightward-slanting slab in the upper part of the buttress. Start at the toe of the buttress.
1 7m Climb the ramp then continue up an obvious crack to gain Long Ledge; move right to the tree.
2 20m Climb the juggy slab, starting to the left of and running up behind the tree, easily up and rightwards. Climb a short crack to gain a detached horizontal block and continue moving rightwards (Walking the Plank) until an easy gully provides an escape.
S Wilson, A Yarrow 12.05.1973

14 Wildcat on the Swallowtail Line 23m HS ★★
A harder variation on *The Bullgine Run* taking the crack through the roof.
1 7m Climb the ramp then continue up the crack to gain Long Ledge.
2 16m Follow the groove behind the tree rightwards to a ledge. Climb the short crack to gain the horizontal break. Overcome the crack through the roof and continue to the top.
A Yarrow, S Wilson 12.05.1973

On the right side of the buttress, and at a higher level, is a very open and interesting face remarkable for its fine rock architecture; a soaring arête on the right and a gigantic block overhang to its left. The priapic appearance has informed the choice of route names.

15 Flasherman 30m VS 4b ★★★ ♦
A runout crux adds to the adventure. Start in a cave under an overhang below the big open-book corner. Climb the slab diagonally right then pull over the bulge on satisfying holds to a block. Climb the corner to the large flake at its top. Step right and climb boldly up the shallow groove to good holds then move left to finish past the downward-pointing tree.
Photo page 471.
A Yarrow, S Wilson 17.05.1973

16 Erection 26m E1 5a ★★★
A stiff undertaking heightened by the lack of protection. Start at a steep wall. Boldly climb the tricky wall then, more easily, move up to the overhanging block. The horizontal undercut flake is awkward; climb to its top. Follow the shallow scoop in the steep wall above in a wonderful position.
J Lamb, A Liddell 12.01.1974

Central Buttress | **Armathwaite** | 469

Outlying

17 Viennese Oyster 27m E3 5c ★★
An intimidating exciting line, with superb exposure. Climb the steep wall and slab to the block overhang (high runner in the horizontal flake-crack). Traverse right to a jug then pull strenuously over the bulge. Step left and move over a small triangular roof (first ascent peg). Either reach high and right for good holds then traverse steeply right round the arête, or climb the wall.
G Brown, H Loughran 10.09.1987

15 Flasherman VS 4b ★★★
16 Erection E1 5a ★★★

Flasherman VS (page 468) Mel Adam — David Simmonite

Barnacle Bill E1 (opposite) Nick Wharton — David Simmonite

Final Section

A long section of slabby walls and corners.

Descent: At either end.

⑱ Free 'n' Easy   12m   E5 6a   ★★★

An outstanding, absorbing and serious climb requiring technical competence and a cool approach. Climb the breaks to a rest (wires). Move up and left to the final crack with rising hopes of finishing.
P Whillance, A Greig 8.05.1974

A huge boulder forms a narrow passage between itself and the crag. At the top of the passage, a jammed block bridges the gap creating a tunnel.

⑲ The Crescent   13m   E3 5b   ★★

Start just left of the tunnel. Follow the curving shelf leftwards for 4m then the wall above to a jug. Pull up, stand up and move left, then finish easily up the slab and corner.
J Lamb, M Hetherington 1974

⑳ Jelly Terror   9m   E1 5b   ★★

A strenuous protectable climb. Start on top of the jammed block below the crack. Gain the ledge and climb the slim crack to pass a bulge. The wider cracks above are easier.
J Lamb, M Hetherington 1974

㉑ Y-Front   11m   E2 5b   ★

A bold climb on positive holds. Climb the corner. At the triangular roof pull left to gain side holds and step onto the rib below the hanging cleft. Climb the cleft, transferring onto the left wall, to finish at the top of the arête.
P Botterill, M Hetherington 25.03.1974

㉒ Barnacle Bill   13m   E1 5b   ★★

A superb classic with a delicate crux. Climb to the roof then traverse right under the roof to the final crack.
Photo opposite.
RJ Kenyon, S Wilson 1973

㉓ Scallop   13m   E7 6b   ★★★

Slabtastic! A direct line up the slab passing the scallop feature and other imaginary holds.
P Gunn 7.09.2014

㉔ Codpiece Left-Hand   12m   E1 5b   ★★

Climb the crack to gain the ramp by a difficult move.
A Yarrow, S Wilson 1973

㉕ Codpiece   12m   E2 5c   ★★

The prominent flaring crack. A test-piece of poor jams and layaways with awkward protection from small wires.
A Yarrow, S Wilson, R May 1973

GOUTHER CRAG
OS Grid Ref: NY 515 127
Altitude: 330m

Bloodhound E2 (page 478) Esther Foster — Tom McNally

Good climbing across the grades in an unspoilt secluded valley. Often dry when the central Lakes are wet; midges can be very irritating in summer.

Approach: From Shap, take the road to Bampton. Through Bampton Grange then over the bridge and turn left. From Penrith go via Askham and Bampton, turning right immediately before the bridge at Bampton Grange. Stay left then fork right and over a cattle grid. Follow this road to a large parking area before another cattle grid at the entrance to the Swindale Valley. **Do not** park any closer than this. Walk along the road to a bridge over the river. Follow the path up the hill then rightwards, by the wall, over another bridge, heading for the crag.

Gouther Crag — 📷 AL PHIZACKLEA

Truss Buttress

This excellent buttress lies off to the left, easily identified by the stepped ridge which gives the buttress its name.

Descent: Descend from near the top of the buttress to the right.

❶ Castration Crack 27m E3 6a ★★
A very good route tackling the thin crack in the centre of the face. Climb the wall to the crack and follow it with increasing difficulty to a ledge. Continue in the same line to the top.
P Whillance, P Botterill 9.06.1980

❷ Truss Buttress 38m VD ★★
A fine route on clean sound rock taking the prominent ridge. Start just left of the foot of the ridge.
1 20m Climb the arête using thin cracks in the middle section to a point where the angle eases.
2 18m Continue up a little slab to the left and ascend the rib.
Photo below.
RH Fidler, CE Arnison 7.08.1933

❸ Sam 20m S ★
An enjoyable pitch. 30m right of the toe of the buttress is an easy slab. Follow the slab leftwards then the obvious V-corner above.
S Miller, A Miller 1.07.1976

❹ Times of Stress 30m E3 6a ★★
Good well-protected climbing. From a small tree climb a short steep crack onto a slab. Pull up past a break to reach a thin crack which is followed to a spike. Move right then up left to regain the crack which leads to a ledge. The scoop left of the thin crack leads to a ledge and easier ground.
P Whillance, P Botterill 10.07.1980

❺ Hernia 22m E1 5b ★★
A strenuous and well-protected route with some entertaining moves. Only just worth E1. Start at a huge flake which leans against the foot of the rounded buttress to the right. Climb the flake by an easy slab on its right and, from its pointed top, climb steeply rightwards and round a bulge to a ramp and groove. Finish up this.
B Rogers, W Day 1.07.1976

❻ Scabby Horse 20m VS 5a ★
At the right-hand side of the buttress is a leftward-slanting ramp with a tree at its foot. This gives a pleasant route with one hard move. Climb to the top of the ramp and finish up a steep shallow groove. For a direct and much harder option, climb the steep poorly protected wall to the left. E3 5c.
RJ Kenyon, A Greenhow 27.08.1973

Truss Buttress VD (above) Rowan Hebblethwaite — 📷 David Simmonite

Fang Buttress

Cracks, bold slabs and walls define this steep popular buttress.

Approach: This steep clean buttress lies some 200m horizontally to the right of **Truss Buttress**. Just below the foot of **Truss Buttress**, a faint track leads rightwards over a shoulder through trees to a large buttress with a shallow cave at its foot.

Descent: Head back and right at the top of the crag then descend the grassy ridge on the right. A series of short rocky scrambles leads to the bottom. This is much better and safer than the dodgy gully immediately beneath the buttress.

7 Sostenuto 36m HVS 5a ★★
An exposed climb up the front of the buttress. Start from a rock gangway.
1 28m 5a Climb the flake crack just left of a thin leftwards-slanting crack and then the steep wall to ledges below an impressive smooth groove. Move left along a slanting crack to an easy rib which leads to a stance.
2 8m The easy crack on the right is followed to the top.
H Drasdo, RB Evans, NJ Soper, RP Harris 23.08.1958

8 Fang Direct 30m E1 5a ★★
A very good rather bold route. Start at the blunt arête. Climb the crack past the overlap to the traverse of *The Fang*. Continue in the same line to gain a shallow scoop then exit rightwards. Finish easily up the blunt rib.
RM Flood, JR Sutcliffe 7.07.1974

9 The Fang 40m MVS 4a ★★★
A fine steep climb. It is exposed with adequate protection. Start directly below a holly tree under an overhang at the right edge of the buttress.
1 20m 4a Climb to the holly and make a bold ascending traverse left to ledges on the front of the buttress. Ascend a steep thin crack to a ledge on the right on the edge of the face.
2 20m Ascend the steep arête at the right end of the ledge to a platform and climb the blunt rib above.
JS Williams, CR Wilson, T Nicholson, RA Ewin 27.10.1946

The buttress now bends round to form the slabby left wall of a gully.

10 The Doghouse 39m MVS 4b ★★
Start at the left-hand edge of the gully wall below a short right-facing V-groove.
1 24m 4b Climb the groove and walk along the ledge to a niche. Climb the steep crack to a narrow ledge. Step off the triangular block and climb the wall slightly leftwards on a series of ledges. Move back slightly right and climb boldly to the foot of the right-facing V-groove which is followed to a ledge.
2 15m Ascend the wall to a ledge (ring peg). Continue up the groove above.
R Wilkinson, B Peace 17.08.2003

11 Left Edge 39m S ★
A steep well-protected route. Start at the left-hand edge of the gully wall below a short right-facing V-groove.
1 24m Climb the groove and move out left to a patch of vegetation. Surmount the small overhang and climb a crack and wall to finish up the V-corner 3m left of a similar corner.
2 15m Ascend the wall to a ledge (ring peg). Continue up the groove above.
C Griffiths, G Oliver 20.03.1966

12 Kennel Wall 37m MS ★★★
This very good climb takes the middle of the slabs. Start at a large block at the top of the scree. Climb the indefinite crack to the right end of a narrow ledge. Ascend the crack and grooves and follow easier rocks above.
JS Williams, CR Wilson, T Nicholson, RA Ewin, GH Tyson 20.10.1946

13 Bloodhound 37m E2 5b ★★★ ♦
An excellent sustained bold route. Start in the centre of the slabs. Climb easily up right then left with difficulty to gain a prominent flake in the middle of the slab. Continue directly upwards then move right to the base of a groove in the right-hand side of the top overhang. Climb the groove and the wall above.
Photo page 474.
RG Hutchinson, JW Earl 2.07.1978

14 Hindleg Crack 22m S ★★
The steep chimney on the right of the slab provides an interesting experience.
JS Williams, CR Wilson, T Nicholson, RA Ewin, GH Tyson 20.10.1946

15 The Keswickian 28m E8 7a ★★
Start up the chimney. Climb the short wall and crack to a ledge underneath the left-hand side of the large roof and arrange gear in the corner (making sure you extend it well). Now make wild moves through the large roof until the slab can finally be gained. Follow the wonderful wall/arête (hidden wire on the slab/arête at half-height, in a pocket) to the top.
A Hocking, M Norbury 15.06.2011

Fang Buttress | **Gouther Crag** | 479

16 One Step Beyond 24m E3 6a ★★★
This superb climb crosses the hanging slab that sits enticingly above the gully. Start up the short off-width crack on the right. Follow the crack through the roof then traverse down across the lip of the roof to a good hold (low peg). Move up (peg) then down slightly to make a delicate series of moves to reach a resting foothold just right of the arête. Bold climbing on small holds just right of the arête leads to the top.
Photo opposite.
I Williamson, J White 5.05.1980

17 The Dalesman 20m E4 6b ★★
Takes the wall up the right side of the hanging slab. Start up the off-width then where the crack turns horizontally right, go left, directly through the roof, via a hard move to good holds (peg) then finish magnificently, straight up the right side of the slab.
R Patterson, A Scott 13.06.1998

18 Dogleg Crack 13m HVS 5a ★
The short off-width crack through the roof to the right of the hanging slab.
RJ Kenyon, S Howe 29.08.1977

One Step Beyond E3 (this page) Esther Foster
TOM MCNALLY

Outlying

BUCKBARROW CRAG
OS Grid Ref: NY 483 073
Altitude: 335m

The Clangers E1 (page 482) Justin Shiels — David Simmonite

Short single pitches and longer rambling routes all on good solid rock make a fine alternative to the central Lakes.

Approach: Turn off the A6 north of Kendal into Longsleddale and follow the narrow road to its very end. Park at the end of the tarmac. Follow the track up the valley for 2km until beneath the crag. A stile gives access to the fell and final steep approach.

Low Crag

The shorter buttresses to the left of the main buttress and nearest the track. The right-angled corner of *Express Crack* provides a good reference point.

Descent: To the left.

① The Blunder 25m HVS 5a ★
The steep chimney-crack just right of the large pinnacle. Climb the right rib awkwardly then follow the crack.
S Hubbard 13.03.1982

② Express Crack 33m E1 5b ★★
From afar the right-angled corner shouts to be climbed and doesn't disappoint. Strenuous and well-protected by large cams.
JA Austin, DG Roberts, JJS Allison 25.10.1969

③ The Clangers 33m E1 5b ★★
A very good climb which feels quite bold and reachy in its lower half. Start beneath the overhang 3m right of the corner. Climb up to the line of flakes and follow them to the large ledge and the slab above.
Photo page 480.
JW Earl, R Smith 12.07.1986

④ The Hog's Back 34m HVS 5a ★★
Climb to a slim groove entered with a difficult pull over a small roof. Follow this to a tree. Climb the rib on the right to a bulge. Turn this on the right and move back left to the arête which is followed to a ledge. Finish up easier rocks.
JD Llewellyn, A Sutton 16.09.1956

High Crag

This steep buttress lies to the left of the upper part of Cleft Ghyll. Its most obvious feature is a steep arête flanked on the left by a wide grassy gully. An 8m block stands at the foot of the arête.

Approach: Scramble up steep grass diagonally leftwards from the bottom of Cleft Ghyll.

Descent: To the left.

⑤ The Minotaur 42m HVS 4c ★★
A sensational climb up the main nose of the crag. It is sustained, exposed and not too well-protected but the holds are good. Start directly below the arête just left of the 8m block.
1 12m 4a Climb a little arête just left of a chimney and traverse right to the platform on top of the block.
2 30m 4c Climb a slanting crack to gain the arête at a flake. Climb the bulging arête to a prominent overhang. Turn this on the left (it can be climbed directly), regain the arête and follow it to the top.
I Roper, D Hall 15.07.1964

Low Crag — Buckbarrow Crag — Al Phizacklea

The Dandle

Mountaineering routes on the largest buttress on the crag.

Descent: Traverse the hillside to the right. This involves a climb down into and across the top of a grassy gully. It is graded Difficult for a move and can be awkward if wet. The slope and scree can be descended beyond this.

7 Sadgill Wall 100m S ★★

A very good climb. Start at the foot of a slabby rib.
1 20m Climb the slab until it steepens. Step right and ascend to a grassy ledge. Continue up to the left to belay at the foot of a steep wall.
2 20m Climb the rightward-slanting flake crack to a thread runner then climb the slab on the left to a stance.
3 30m Traverse sensationally right across the steep slab to its right edge. Ascend directly and continue up ledges to a rowan. Scramble up into the grassy bay above.
4 30m Cross the right wall of the bay and climb the broken ridge to a ledge by a 3m crack. Climb the corner and the easier rocks above.
AH Griffin, CE Arnison, T Philipson 1.07.1949

6 Dandle Buttress 46m S ★

A good climb up the left-hand ridge of **The Dandle**. The first pitch is considerably harder than the rest of the route. Start on the right wall of Cleft Ghyll, 6m below the large chockstone.
1 14m Climb polished slabs to a corner and then climb steeply up twin cracks to a stance on the edge of the buttress.
2 15m Follow the broad ridge to a ledge and climb a chimney on the left.
3 17m Continue to the top. The descent route now lies straight ahead. However, it is also possible to continue up the rock above and onto the fell.
JD Best, M Linnell, H Johnson 5.06.1926

WHITE STONE

OS Grid Ref: SD 390 848
Altitude: 200m

Good, easy and mid-grade routes on pocketed rock. This small accessible crag sits overlooking the A590 and Morecambe Bay south of Newby Bridge.

Approach: From the A590 take the most southerly turning signposted Staveley-in-Cartmel then immediately right onto a short stretch of abandoned road. Park here; walk south to a public footpath where the crag is conspicuous on the fellside. Walk to the top of the crag; gear up, then descend a well-marked path at the south end.

Descent: To the right.

Bird restriction may be in place Mar 1st to Jun 30th. Check the RAD.

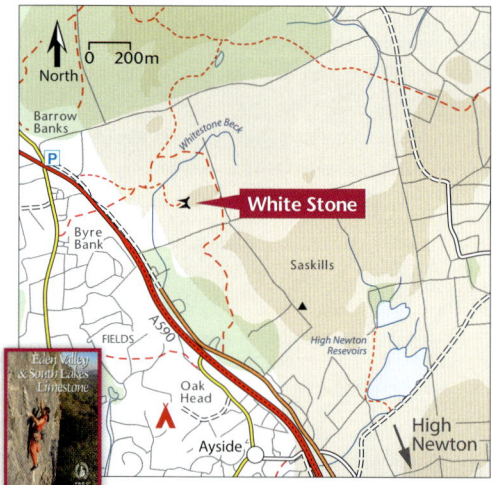

1 Missing Words 20m VS 4c ★
Start just right of the right-facing corner at left end of crag. Climb the wall to a ledge then flakes. Up the unprotected rib and the wall above, just left of the overhang. From the break go over the overhang and to the top.
Photo page 462.
I Greenwood 1983

2 The W 25m HVS 4c
Climb the pocketed slab left of the left-facing corner to a small block below a prominent V-notch. Step off the block and pull strenuously into the V-notch using a good pocket. Follow the easy groove to finish rightwards on slabby rock.
B Davison 30.05.1992

3 The V 25m HVS 4c
Start below the right-hand end of the main overhang where a projecting block creates a left-facing corner. Climb the corner and move left below the overhang to stand on a small block below the V-notch. Climb the overhang between the two notches and up the crack in the slab to finish up the wide twisting crack.
pre-1969

4 Direct Route 25m HS 4a
Start below the left-facing corner. Climb this then step up and right on to the hanging block. Climb the overhang between the gooves and continue direct up slabs.
Photo opposite.
pre-1969

5 Jess 37m S
A right-to-left girdle and a worthwhile route despite being a little vegetated in the middle.
1 23m Climb the sla bs at the start of *Chimney Route* then traverse below the full length of the central overhang until able slither to a belay at a loose spike.
2 14m Climb the slabby chimney above and easy slabs to the top.
L Ainsworth, Miss A Ainsworth 1988

6 Chimney Route 25m VD
Climbs the deep cleft using a variety of techniques. Start up a pocketed slab below and right of the line of the cleft then step left into an overhung V-niche. Bridge up past the overhang and pass the flake chockstone via a move onto the slab. Step back into the chimney to finish on jugs up the steep crack in the right wall.
pre-1969

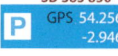

7 Wild Winds 25m HVS 4c ★

A bold route up the left edge of the central pillar. Climb the pocketed slab then right to the V-niche. Step right and climb the rib. Continue up the wall, right of the arête. Good pockets and protection eventually appear.
A Phizacklea 20.09.1981

8 Moose 25m VS 4b ★★

The best route on the crag which climbs the steep central pillar. Start directly below the pillar and climb the pocketed slab then follow a short diagonal crack leading to a niche below the overhang. Step up and left then make a difficult move right above the overhang. Continue boldly up the right side of the pillar.
pre-1969

9 Cracked Wall 23m MVS 4b

Follow the slab and crack to the niche below the overhang then step right. Awkward, but well-protected climbing leads diagonally right up the groove well to the left of a triangular niche.
pre-1969

Direct Route HS (opposite) Steve Scott
📷 David Simmonite

SPORT

Moonchild, Chapel Head F6C+ (page 504) Rachel Somerville — David Simmonite

As a sideshow to the fabulous trad climbing traditions of most Lake District venues, we can also offer some top-class sport climbing on limestone, sandstone and microgranite around the region. We'll provide the routes, you just bring clips and strong fingers.

- **Scawgill Bridge Quarry** — 488
- **Coudy Rocks** — 492
- **Bramcrag Quarry** — 494
- **Scout Scar** — 498
- **Chapel Head Scar** — 503
- **Millside** — 509
- **St Bees** — 511

SCAWGILL BRIDGE QUARRY

OS Grid Ref: NY 177 258

5 mn

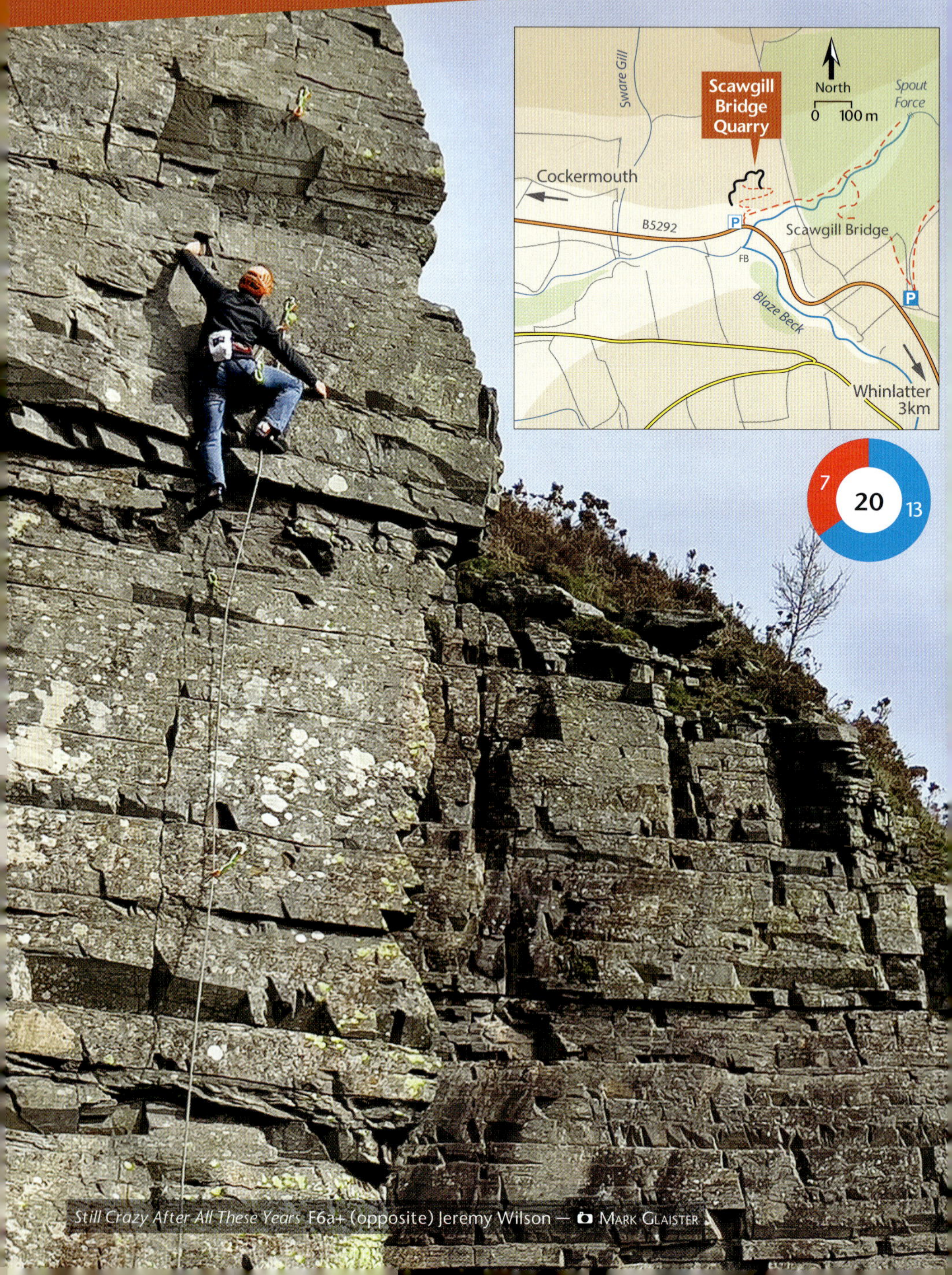

Still Crazy After All These Years F6a+ (opposite) Jeremy Wilson — 📷 MARK GLAISTER

Quick drying with a host of amenable grades.

Approach: The quarry is above and to the north of Whinlatter pass between Braithwaite and Lorton about 3km west of the top of the pass. Park carefully on the bend below the crag. Go through the gate and follow the path to the right of the gravel pit. Above the gravel, follow the path rightwards for 100m (ignore short cuts) and then jag back left along a path through gorse to the crag.

RAD Scawgill Bridge

Scawgill Bridge
NY 176 258

GPS 54.620116
-3.275842

OS Grid Ref
NY 177 258

① **Switchblade** 15m F6a ★
The short corner and crack.
C Downer, J Cameron 25.09.2021

② **Sarcopenia** 15m F6b ★★
The centre of the wall provides an excellent route.
C Downer, C Fowler 12.08.2021

③ **Still Crazy After All These Years** 15m F6a+ ★
A thin crack left of the arête.
Photo opposite.
A Evans 6.10.1991

④ **Wilderness Edge** 15m F6a ★★
An excellent climb up the obvious arête. A single bolt replaces the original single peg to preserve the integrity of the route. If ethics aren't important additional bolts are within clipping distance.
A Evans, F West 26.09.1991

⑤ **Kleptomania** 15m F6b ★
Superb climbing. The grade assumes you climb just right of the bolts. Easier options utilise the arête.
C Fowler, C Downer 15.08.2021

⑥ **The Azov Brigade** 15m F7a ★
Hard as nails - like the Brigade. Direct up the wall.
S Chadwick 13.05.2022

⑦ **The Book Thief** 20m F6a ★★
Gain the left-slanting ramp then traverse up left towards the arête. The wall leads to the overlap and a well-positioned crux.
C Downer, C Fowler 15.08.2021

⑧ **Jenga** 15m F6b ★
Follow the left-facing groove moving left at the overlap then steeply to the lower-off.
C Downer, B Young 3.04.2022

⑨ **Whinlatter Wall Direct** 20m F5c ★
Follow the stepped ramp leftwards to an overhung ledge. Climb straight up and then trend rightwards to an overlap and the lower-off.

⑩ **Fake News** 20m F6b
Start up a right-slanting groove then directly up the wall above to a perplexing move past the last bolt.
B Young, C Downer, C Wornham 2024

Scawgill Bridge Quarry

⑪ **Scawgill Grooves** 20m F5c ★★
An excellent route. Start up slabby ground then follow the two grooves above which lead to the overlap and a steep finish.
A Evans 2.10.1991

⑫ **Bootlegger** 20m F5c ★
Head right from the first bolt towards the overlaps above.
B Young, C Downer 14.04.2022

⑬ **Prohibition** 20m F6a+
Follow *Bootlegger* to its second bolt then head rightwards to a quartz-streaked wall. Climb this to a break in the overlap where unhelpful holds lead left to the lower-off.
C Downer, B Young 27.04.2022

⑭ **Kong Korner** 20m F6a+ ★★
The stepped corner provides a fine route.
C Downer, B Young, A Davis, C Wornham 22.05.2022

⑮ **Pickpocket** 20m F6b+
At the first ledge move right onto the wall finishing up a fine crack.
C Downer, B Young, C Wornham 17.08.2023

⑯ **Skull Island** 20m F6c ★
C Fowler, C Downer 25.04.2022

⑰ **King Kong** 15m F6c ★★
C Fowler, C Downer 26.08.2021

⑱ **Monkey Magic** 15m F7a
Sustained climbing between the cracks.
P Winterbottom 28.09.2022

⑲ **Border Force** 20m F6c ★
C Fowler, C Downer 27.03.2022

⑳ **Best in Show** 20m F6b+ ★★
An excellent route up the fine arête bounding the right side of the wall, unaffected by seepage. Climb to the ledge. Step up and left onto the face and climb the left side of the arête.
C Downer, B Young, C Wornham 7.08.23

COUDY ROCKS

OS Grid Ref: NY 688 200
Altitude: 160m

Perfect Weather to Fly F7a (opposite) Steve Broadbent — 📷 AILEEN ROBERTSON

An impressive sandstone wall in an extremely attractive setting located in the centre of Appleby, on the east side of the River Eden. A good place to retreat to if the central Lakes crags are wet.

The crag lies on private land and access has been granted on the understanding that:
- Only bona fide climbers.
- Any livestock should not be disturbed.
- The gate is always left closed.
- No litter.
- No damage to property.
- No dogs in the field below the crag.

Approach: From near the Royal Oak Inn on the B6542 follow Mill Hill, on the opposite side of the road, down to the car park next to the River Eden. Walk across the field to the crag.

① **Perfect Weather to Fly** 9m F7a ★★
Overcome the overhung base to gain the wall then ascend leftwards by the arête.
Photo opposite.
D Bush 2.03.2010

② **Periculo 'D' Sinister Manus** 9m F7a+ ★
Good fingery climbing. Slightly harder if climbed exclusively on the left of the bolts.
N Davies, S Leahy 6.08.2017

③ **Big in Japan** 9m F7a ★★
Sustained climbing up the wall leads to an obtuse finish.
J Hughes, T Dixon 29.10.2009

④ **Resisting a Chippy Tea** 9m F7a+ ★
Great slab climbing with a thin start, fingery middle and thuggy finish. It's not ticked until you reach the holds above the lower-off!
D Allen, N Davies 10.05.2018

⑤ **Resisting Chiptation** 9m F6c+ ★★
Interesting climbing leads to a crucial traverse left on crimps to finish.
D Robinson, MF Kenyon 27.06.2009

⑥ **Brown Eyed Girl** 10m F6a+ ★★
Glued-on flake by the third bolt.
N Davies, D Allen 19.10.2018

⑦ **Two Pints and a Packet of Crisps** 9m F6b+ ★★
Weave up the wall before or after refreshment in the Royal Oak.
E Parker, MF Kenyon, RJ Kenyon, D Robinson 27.06.2009

⑧ **The Sands of Time** 9m F6a+ ★★
Climb the vague arête.
RJ Kenyon, D Robinson, E Parker, MF Kenyon 27.06.2009

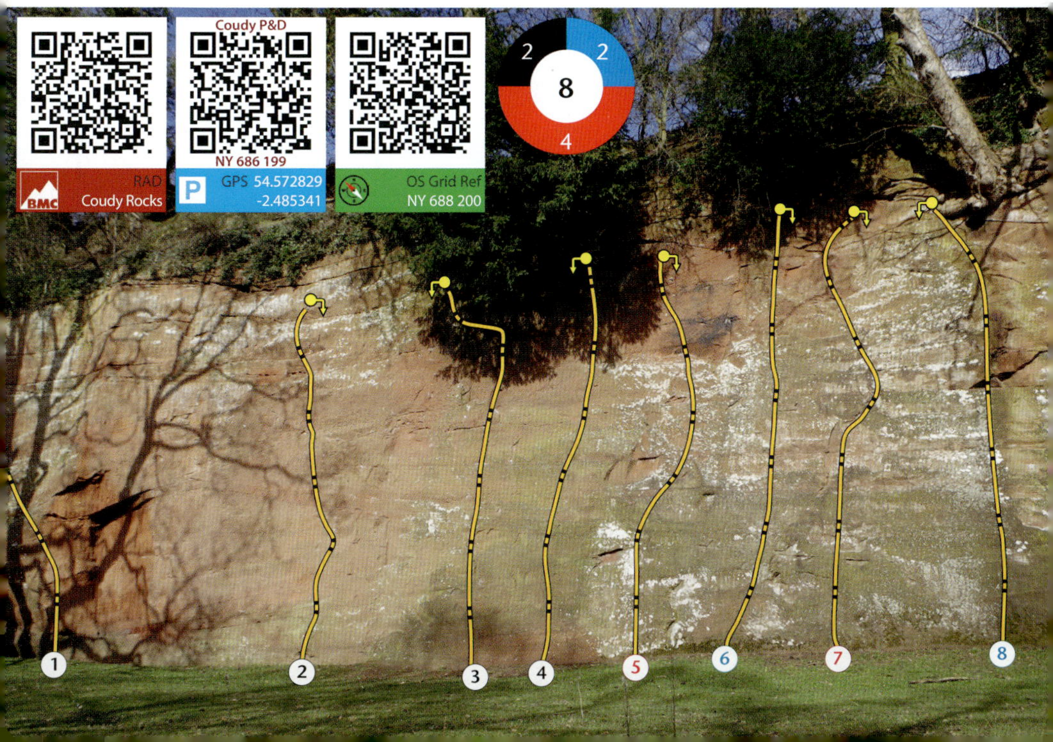

BRAMCRAG QUARRY

OS Grid Ref: NY 320 220

A popular sport-climbing venue with good rock and easy access. Large blocks have been pulled off, sometimes with serious consequences, so treat with care when climbing, belaying or just waiting for your turn. This venue is not suitable for children or groups.

Approach: Park sensibly off the road, not next to the access road. Do not block the main road or the access track. Walk up the track and across the access ridge. Head round to the right for the **Main Wall**.

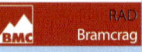 RAD Bramcrag
 GPS 54.588104 -3.056024
 OS Grid Ref NY 320 220

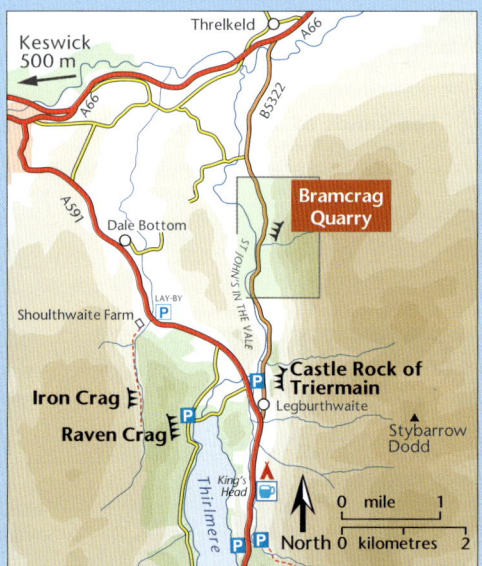

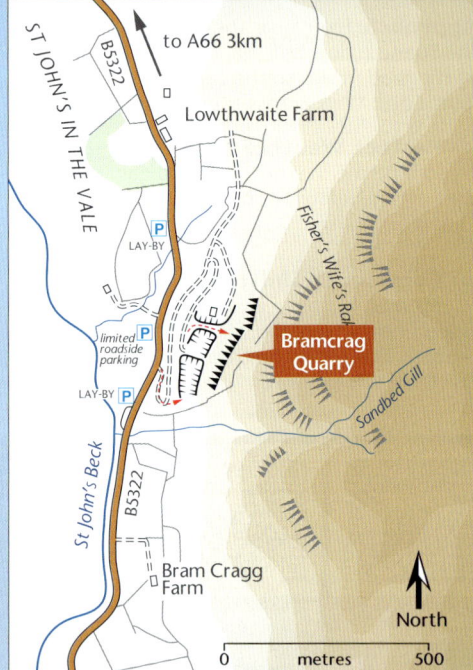

Bramcrag Quarry — Peter Sterling

Main Wall

High-quality routes with sustained absorbing climbing. **Main Wall** is the centre piece of the quarry. The left side is quick-drying with little seepage.

① **The Tipton Slasher** 30m F6b+ ★★
From the blocks at the left side of the wall climb the slim groove in the arête then cross an overhang into a groove. Move right round the rib using a quartz vein (tricky). Continue up in a fine position to a large ledge. Step left to finish by climbing the arête.
C Downer, L Jones, C Fowler 20.06.2012

② **Yorkshire Ripper** 30m F6b+ ★
Clip the first bolt on *The Tipton Slasher*. Using a dubious-looking flake, pull rightwards and continue steeply into a recess (crux). Move up and right and over a bulge. From the bolt, step right onto a large detached block and follow the groove above to the large ledge. Climb the wall.
Photo below.
C Downer, M Armitage 20.05.2014

③ **Usain Bolt** 30m F6b+ ★
The impressive cleaned corner. Climb the wall until awkward moves lead into the corner. Climb up the corner with difficulty onto a ledge. Continue until a pull out left leads to a large ledge. The tricky groove on the right leads to a lower-off on the left.
C Fowler, C Downer 10.08.2012

④ **Eastern Promise** 35m F6b ★★
An excellent climb. Climb the groove to its top then swing right using a shot-hole and move up to a small ledge. Continue straight up the wall (crux) to reach an easing in the angle. Climb a further 5m then trend left below the shallow grooves to reach the headwall.
A Phizacklea, J Holden 14.04.1991

⑤ **Coup de Triomphe** 30m F6b ★★
A fine hybrid which dries quickly. Climb the slab to the overlap by a block. Pull over the overlap to reach a shot-hole. Move up then left onto a ledge. Climb to the bolt then finish up the groove on the right.

⑥ **The History Boys** 30m F6b+ ★★
Climb easily to ledges and attain a standing position on the left end of the jammed block. Pull directly over the overhang. Climb the groove and slab to a projecting block. Move right to a bolt then pull out left to a ledge. Finish up the green-speckled groove.
C Downer, G Lee, G Proctor 8.05.2010

⑦ **Bobby Dazzler** 30m F6b ★
Climb the flake and move up through a rock scar. Step left and follow a groove to its top. Pull right onto a rib and climb the slab aiming for a large block. Step right and pull into a bay; lower-off.
C Downer, C Higgins, D Ferguson, C Fowler 21.07.2009

Yorkshire Ripper F6b+ (above) Chris King — David Simmonite

Center Parc

Fun routes in the easier grades make this a popular sector.

Approach: Keep walking beyond the **Main Wall**, over some worrying debris - result of previous rockfalls.

⑧ **Blencathra Badger** 27m F5c ★★
Delightful climbing, champion. This gem climbs the right side of the water-worn slabs.
A Phizacklea, J Holden 1991

⑨ **Ship of Fools** 27m F6a ★
Climb the black-streaked wall to a grassy ledge then easily to the foot of a black wall. Make a rising traverse to a grooved arête.
C Downer, K Forsythe, A Tilney 27.04.2014

⑩ **Brothers in Arms** 30m F6a ★
Follow the ramp and rib to the second bolt. Step up and left then climb to the overhang. Over this to reach and finish up the steep cracked slab.
C Bainbridge, S Bainbridge 7.06.1992

⑪ **Barrow Boys' Day Out** 30m F6a ★
Good open climbing. Climb a rounded rib, left of a shot-hole at 4m (bolt). Climb diagonally right to the conspicuous slim ramp then the corner above.
A Phizacklea, J Holden 23.03.1991

⑫ **Goodbye Mr Major!** 31m F6a ★
An excellent route at a consistent grade. Gain a ledge at 3m. Follow darker-coloured rock up and left to a ramp. Cross the ramp then climb a slab to a groove which leads onto a rib; finish up this.
RJ Kenyon, P King 1997

⑬ **Goodfellas** 27m F5b ★
Climb over the bulge, or the groove to its left. Climb the wall and groove.
P Botterill, A Davis, C Downer, C Fowler 16.07.2013

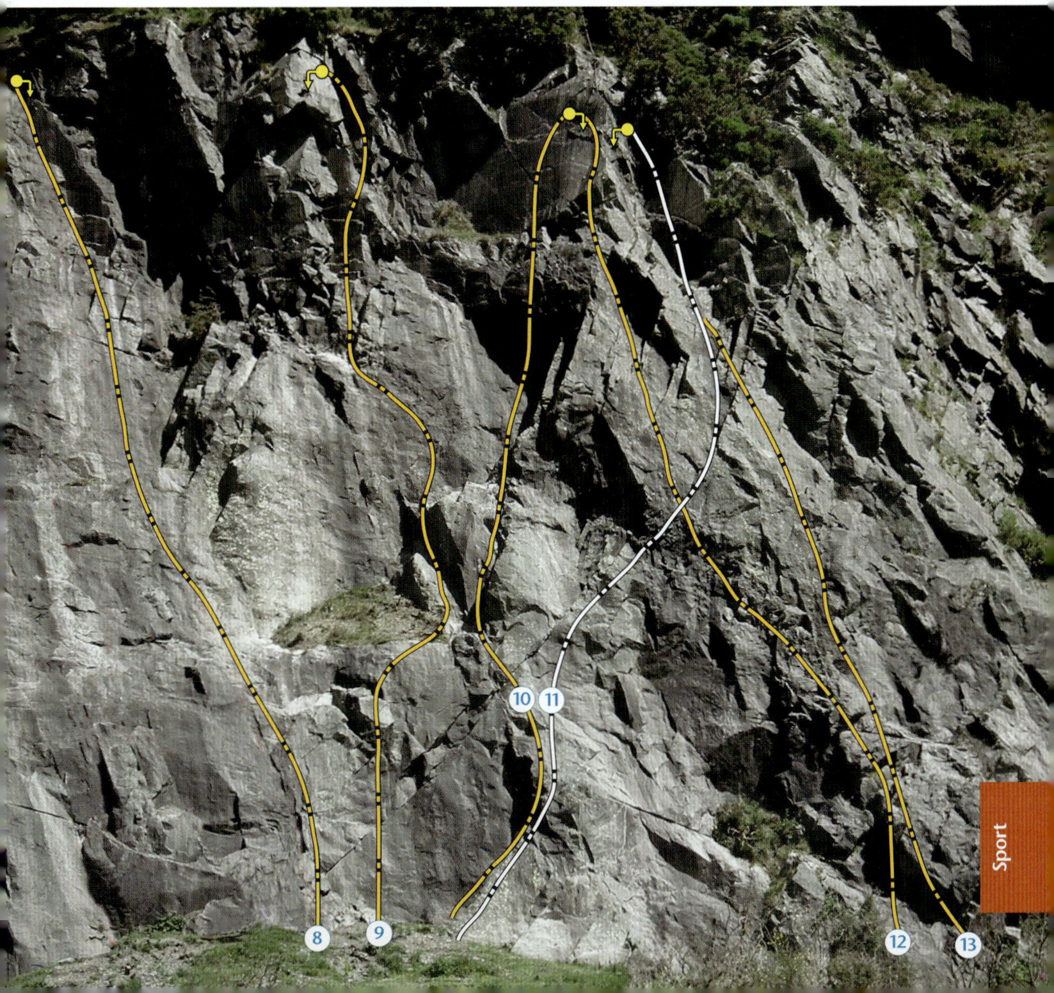

SCOUT SCAR
OS Grid Ref: SD 486 916

A Fistful of Steroids F6c (page 502) Olly Roberts — Nick Wharton

A handy sports venue with a wider range of grades than its fierce cousin, **Chapel Head Scar**. A lovely location with a view out across the idyllic Lyth Valley - once you are above the trees. Afternoon sun and very easy access from Kendal make this a popular venue

Approach: From Kendal, take the Underbarrow road crossing above the bypass. Just beyond the top of the hill there is a car park on the right in an old quarry. Cross the road then take the path south along the scar passing a shelter; the 'Mushroom'. About 300m past this, at a dip in the edge of the scar, drop down steeply to the west into trees then follow the path south until the crag appears.

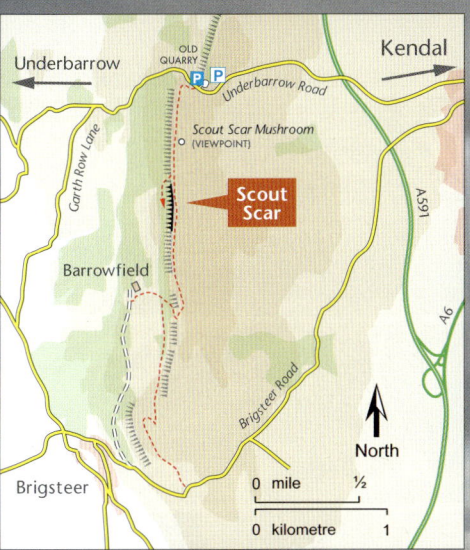

Born Free F6a (page 501) Chris Shiels
📷 Keith Sanders

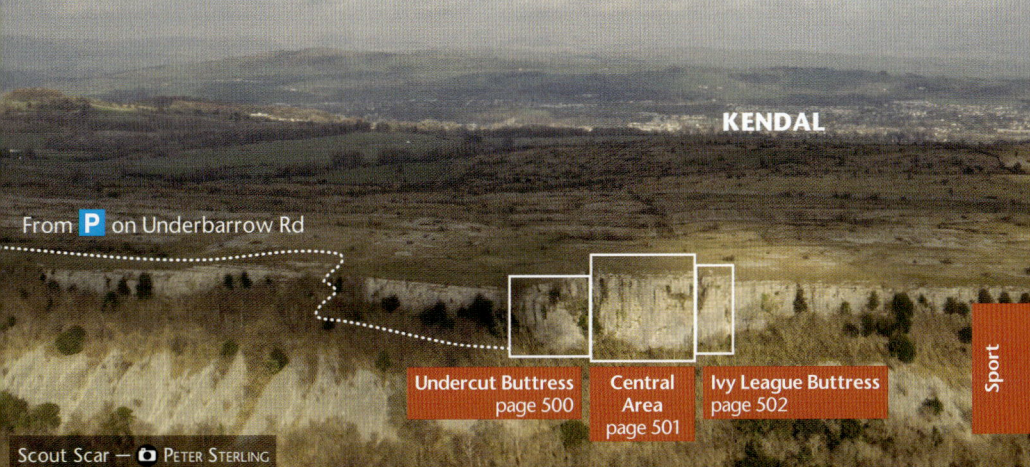

Scout Scar — 📷 Peter Sterling

Undercut Buttress

Short and fierce. The first substantial section of crag reached along the cliff-base path, it has a large overhang at the left side and a series of overlaps. There are some easier routes on the left although there may still be some loose rock.

① **Mr T** 11m F6a ★
Start behind the large ash tree at the left end of the buttress. Climb the short wall to the arête then continue up the left side.
N Wharton Feb 2020

② **Sheepwrecked** 11m F6a+
Climb the short wall, move rightwards then up the centre of the wall.
N Wharton Feb 2020

③ **Feral** 11m F6b+ ★
Start 2m right of the tree below a groove. Make hard moves on undercuts and sidepulls to get established on the wall. Move up into the groove and a ledge then move up and left.
N Wharton Feb 2020

④ **First Blood** 14m F7a+ ★
Powerful climbing. Boulder the roof at its widest point on undercuts and head for a good hold.
P Carling, M Glaister 13.11.1985

⑤ **Sylvester Straits** 12m F7c ★★
Another powerful climb. Battle your way up using strength and finesse.
J Bird, C Lewis 23.08.1986

⑥ **Meet the Wife** 12m F7b+ ★
Three stacked gymnastic boulder problems. Warm up before you try this one!
M Lardener 14.08.1991

⑦ **Telegraph Road** 15m F7a ★★
Takes the steep depression starting from the right.
P Carling, M Glaister 23.04.1986

Central Area

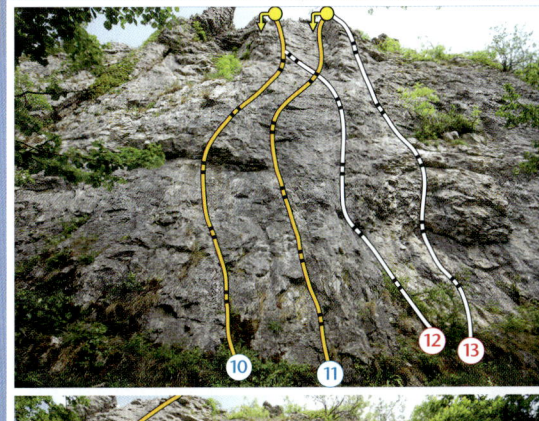

⑧ **Douglas** 13m F6b ★
Starts a little way up the overgrown gully. Follow the initial wall and groove before moving left to a scoop and fine wall to the top.
C Allen, R Allen 1.07.2014

⑨ **Good Medicine** 20m F5+ ★
Start below the cleaned slab right of Red Rock Gully. Pass a crux bulge at one third height.
S Halford 25.11.2023

⑩ **Born Again** 26m F6a+ ★
A good route providing a relatively easy way up the largest part of the crag.
J Bird 1992

⑪ **Born Free** F6a ★★
Climb to and pass the right end of the overlap then trend left up a vague groove before a traverse right to the base of the corner crack. Lower-off at the top of the tower.
Photo page 499.
E Cleasby, M Lynch, C Brown 1975

⑫ **Born to Run** 24m F6c ★★
A great technical route, using small pockets and fingery holds. Start from the right.
J Bird, D Seddon 11.03.1985

⑬ **A Fistful of Steroids** F6c ★★★
⑭ **Crimes of Passion** F7a ★
⑮ **Grave New World** F7b ★

⑬ **A Fistful of Steroids** 24m F6c ★★★
Whilst drug-induced rippling muscles may help power you through the initial bulge, the rest of this excellent route requires style and technique. Fantastic.
Photo page 498.
J Bird 21.05.1986

⑭ **Crimes of Passion** 15m F7a ★
A varied, technical and sustained route up the centre of the wall; the initial section is nails.
J Bird, F Booth 17.6.1986

⑮ **Grave New World** 13m F7b ★
Climb the wall left of the arête to the bulge, pull over this and up to the chain.
D Seddon, J Bird 21.05.1986

Ivy League Buttress

Approach: Round the arête is a corner and a cave at ground level.

⑯ **Ivy League** 16m F7a+ ★★★
Climb the line of pockets and continue up to a small bulge. Overcome this using smears and undercuts then feel the burn in the top groove.
T Walkington 1982

⑰ **A Vision of Things Gone Wild** 16m F7b+ ★★
Another fierce route and coveted flash. Visualise up and right over two bulges to the small overhang. Burst left through this and then straight up.
T Mitchell, D Bates 20.05.1986

CHAPEL HEAD SCAR

15 mn

OS Grid Ref: SD 442 862

This impressive steep crag which overlooks the secluded Witherslack valley is a delight. It gets the sun in the afternoon but the trees provide some shade. Some routes can be prone to seepage after prolonged rain. Please observe some simple requirements to maintain the good relationship with the National Park rangers:

- No climbing left of Central Gully.
- Use only the established paths.
- No gardening or damage to trees.
- Never top-out, only use the lower-offs.
- Do not leave any litter or waste - go before you go!

Beware of ticks.

Seasonal restriction: 1st Mar to 30th Jun.

Approach: From the A590, take the turning into Witherslack and follow the road for 5km north through the village up the valley to Witherslack Hall. Turn right and park here. The crag can be seen on the escarpment across the fields. Head towards the crag along a good path across the field, passing through gates and into woods. Follow the track round to the right and, after 200m, take the first path on the left. This leads through trees and across scree to arrive at **Moonchild Buttress**.

RAD Chapel Head

Witherslack School
SD 436 860
P GPS 54.266341 -2.865630

OS Grid Ref SD 442 862

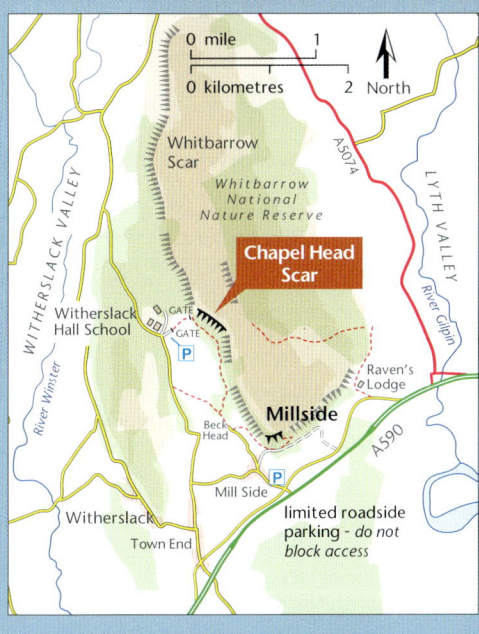

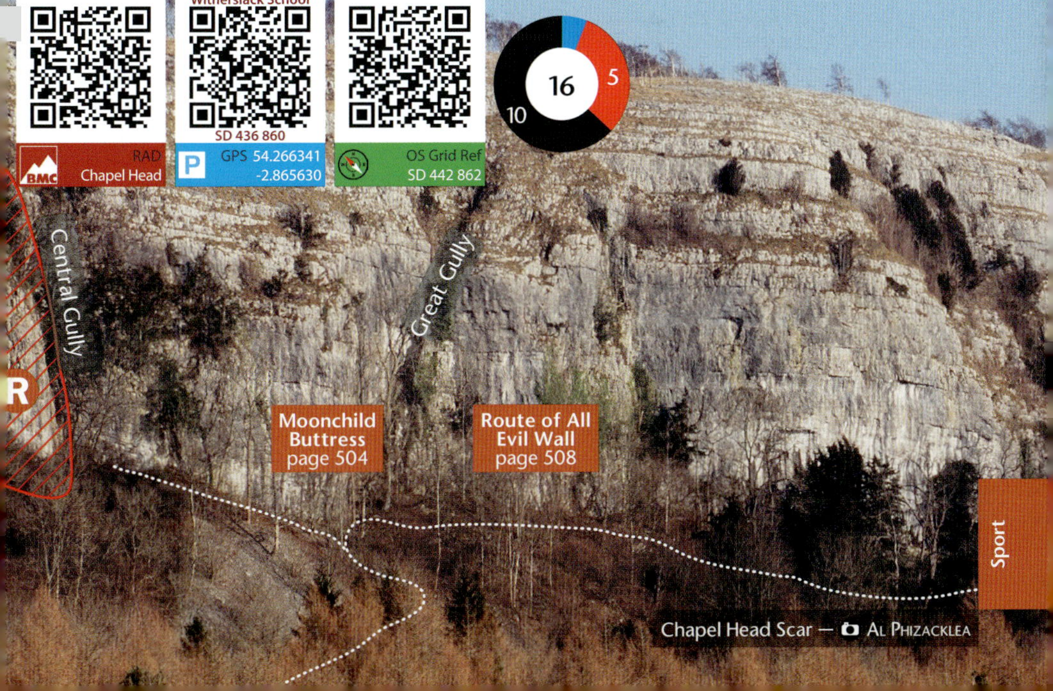

Chapel Head Scar — AL PHIZACKLEA

Moonchild Buttress

Steep climbing on solid clean rock offering some of the best routes on the crag.

Approach: Immediately above the point at which the path arrives at the cliff.

① **Jelly Head**   25m   F7a   ★
A left-hand finish to *Interstellar Overdrive*. Climb over the roof on the upper wall leftwards then up.
J Bird, A Tilney 1991

② **Interstellar Overdrive**   24m   F6c+   ★★
A victim of its popularity this is now very polished. Start a few metres left of the slanting groove. Climb the pocketed lower wall up a vague groove until the angle eases. Clamber over a dead yew tree and up to the roof then move right into the hanging groove. Follow this with increasing difficulty.
D Cronshaw, D Knighton 1979

③ **Sun God**   25m   F6a+   ★
A good warm up following the prominent flake. Follow the flake to the dead yew tree then continue up the groove and bulging flake behind.
D Cronshaw, L Ainsworth 1974

④ **Cement Head**   25m   F7a+   ★★
Although this is only really half a route, the top half, it does climb superb rock and can be combined with the start of *Interstellar*.
J Bird 1989

⑤ **Zantom Phone**   25m   F7c+   ★★
Thin fingery climbing up the steep wall right of the groove. Start below the wall and make hard moves, including a mono, to eventually reach *Cement Head*; finish up this.
P Ingham 1986

⑥ **Phantom Zone**   25m   F7c   ★★★
Brilliant! From the toe of the buttress, just left of where the approach path reaches the crag, make a hard rock-over to a tufa on the right. Move up and initially left then back right over steepening ground, to get through the bulge and into a vague groove. At the top of this is a small ledge offering a brief respite. Continue up the thin wall to gain and climb the smooth groove.
P Ingham 1986

⑦ **Bleep and Booster**   27m   F7a   ★
The shallow groove left of the more prominent groove of *Moonchild*. Climb the main groove to a helpful hold then move left to reach better holds at the bottom of the groove. Step up and right to something of a rest before pressing on up the groove until stopped by the capping bulge. Pass this on its left then head right to gain entry to the next groove. At the top of this, stand up beneath the left side of the prominent prow to reach the lower-off on its left.
S Hubbard, A Mitchell 1985

⑧ **Moonchild**   24m   F6c+   ★★
The striking groove just right of the toe of the buttress. Climb steeply to a scoop on the right. Pull up and left into another scoop then straight up, climbing the flake. Finish up and left at the yew tree. Alternatively, step left at the second scoop and climb a crack to a lower-off.
Photo page 486.
R Fawcett, A Evans, D Parker 1974

⑨ **62 West Wallaby Street**   27m   F7a+   ★
The residents of this famous address would probably find some ingenious way of getting to the top; you'll probably need to rely on power and technique! Tackles the steep wall to the right of the prominent groove. Climb the wall and steep bulge on small but positive holds to reach a ledge. Trend rightwards.
K Phizacklea 1997

⑩ **War Hero**   26m   F7a   ★★
A great route. Start by the first rock step. Climb straight up the wall to a shallow corner at 6m. Head leftwards over a bulge before climbing up and right to gain, first a small ledge then up again to a larger ledge with the remains of a tree stump. Continue up the wall to the left of the corner on fantastic rock.
S Whittall, K Phizacklea, A Phizacklea 1997

⑪ **Tricky Prick Ears**   27m   F7b   ★★★
A tremendous route with a lot of climbing. Start a couple of metres up the slope by the second rock step below a shallow blank groove. Climb the groove to reach the long, sometimes damp, flake. Make a difficult move out left and up to easier ground. Move up and right, over the next bulge, to reach a resting position on the left, adjust your cap. When you are ready, move up and right across the steep white wall to reach the overhanging groove. Make hard moves to enter and then follow this groove to the top. Awesome!
P Cornforth 1988

⑫ **Maboulisme**   16m   F7c+   ★★
Merveilleux
A spectacular route up incredibly steep rock. Start at a ledge with a bolt belay some way up the gully. From the ledge, traverse left across the gully, take a deep breath and fire yourself up the big holds. Keep heading outwards to a hard move on the lip. Pull over and finish more easily up and left.
P Cornforth 1986

Moonchild Buttress
- ⑦ **Bleep and Booster** — F7a ★
- ⑧ **Moonchild** — F6c+ ★★
- ⑨ **62 West Wallaby Street** — F7a+ ★
- ⑩ **War Hero** — F7a ★★
- ⑪ **Tricky Prick Ears** — F7b ★★★
- ⑫ **Maboulisme Merveilleux** — F7c+ ★★

Route of All Evil Wall
A solid wall of compact rock with an amazing headwall.

⑬ **Eraser Head** 25m F7b+ ★★★
A direct route up the wall. Start up the initial corner/groove but, instead of stepping right to the ledge, move left slightly and follow a direct line straight up, crossing the horizontal break and up the superb smooth pocketed rock of the headwall.
J Bird 1991

⑭ **The Route of All Evil** 30m F7a+ ★★
A great route that meanders up this excellent wall. Consider using twin ropes. Climb the groove on the left with a step right onto a small ledge. Move back into the right-trending groove and climb the centre of the wall to reach a large break. Go up to another break which is then followed leftwards to a reasonable rest. Step back right then finish up a shallow scoop in the left side of the headwall.
Photo this page.
G Smith, A Phizacklea 1983

⑮ **Mid-Air Collision** 25m F7b ★★★
Start up the thin wall right of the groove, briefly joining the groove then, where it curves right, go over the bulge and up to the horizontal break. Thin moves up and right to and then over the final small roof.
A Hyslop 1991

⑯ **The Borg** 25m F7a+ ★★
Start 5m right of the corner beneath a steep white groove. Climb this into a niche then a hard move to swing left to reach a flake. Head left to the central groove. Follow this to the break then climb up and right to climb the arête on the right.
I Cooksey, K Phizacklea 2011

The Route of All Evil F7a+ (this page) Ian Cooksey
NICK WHARTON

MILLSIDE

OS Grid Ref: SD 451 845
Altitude: 100m

Small yet worthwhile offering good sport climbs. The crag emerges like a ship's prow above the trees at the south-western tip of the Whitbarrow escarpment. The clean upper groove of *Cadillac* stands out from the road. Check for ticks after a visit.

Approach: Park immediately after crossing the cattle grid from the A590 on to the Mill Side road. Continue on foot into the hamlet of Mill Side and take the steep lane on the right by the phone box. Where the track levels, pass a path on the left (Beck Head) continuing for a few hundred metres to a path on the left rising through woodland. Follow this and after 200m take a less obvious path, at a finger post, left crossing over a scree chute easily to the crag.

① **Firebird** 20m F7a+ ★
Left of the large white patch of lichen, climb the lower wall to the ledge by a small low cave. Enter a short thin groove and climb the wall above.
J Daly, K Phizacklea Jan 1995

② **Mustang** 21m F6b ★
Rears up impressively just left of the pedestal. Cross the break to a small niche then left, passing a small tree, to break up and right to reach ledges below the tough top wall.
R Graham, E Rogers 28.06.1991

③ **Integrali** 22m F7a+ ★
Climb easily up the right-hand side of the short pedestal to the horizontal break. Crank the bulge and flake to reach the thin right-leaning yellow corner. Up this to a lower-off on the right.
D Donnini, K Phizacklea Feb 1995

④ **Cadillac** 24m F6c ★★
Committing technical climbing. Climb the line of bolts to the left side of the pinnacle to a ledge. Take the rightwards-trending groove on flakes and edges. Climb the immaculate smooth wall and the hanging groove to finish.
Photo page 510.
E Cleasby, A Phizacklea 12.04.1982

⑤ **Countach** 23m F7b ★★
Power up the bulges, grooves and cracks. Excellent.
P Ingham, P Botterill March 1985

⑥ **Straight-8** 19m F8a ★★
Start up the wall on the right to the cave below the roof. Move right and climb the bulge direct via a tough sequence to an independent belay.
J Freeman 29.04.2014

⑦ **Straight Tach** 20m F7b ★★
Link up... *Straight-8* into *Countach*. Makes for a really good combination.
D Eastham 24.09.2016

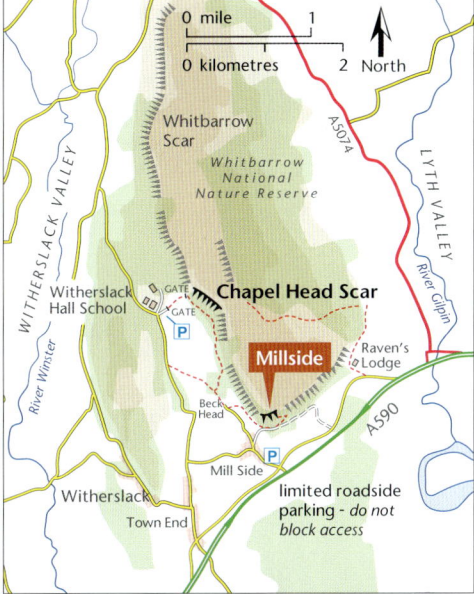

Millside

1. **Firebird** — F7a+ ★
2. **Mustang** — F6b ★
3. **Integrali** — F7a+ ★
4. **Cadillac** — F6c ★★
5. **Countach** — F7b ★★
6. **Straight-8** — F8a ★★
7. **Straight Tach** — F7b ★★

Cadillac F6c (page 509) Catherine Plum — Keith Sanders

ST BEES
OS Grid Ref: NX 940 145

An impressive headland of red sandstone next to the Irish Sea with views over to the Isle of Man. The weather is often much better than further inland and the crag dries quickly, although some routes will seep after prolonged rain. Routes are generally equipped with new, seaside-specific, stainless steel bolts and lower-offs. The route selection provided is not affected by tides but the rock platform can be extremely slippery when wet.

In addition to the sports routes listed, there are some brilliant bouldering opportunities.

Approach: Follow a long narrow track from Sandwith and park at Tarnflatt Hall Farm. Continue along the track to the lighthouse and from the Fog Station, just beyond, turn right, immediately cross the fence to find the descent on the left after 50m. Continue northwards under a small crag then steeply down vegetation and blocks, with some aid from knotted ropes, to reach a bare ledge. The first routes are 15m along the ledge to the south. Drop down towards large boulders to arrive at the left-hand, northern end of **Apiary Wall**. Other than at high spring tides, a less steep way from the foghorn is to turn right (north) and follow the landward side of the fence; at the second stile, cross the fence and drop down to the sea. Boulder hopping south, you arrive at **Apiary Wall**.

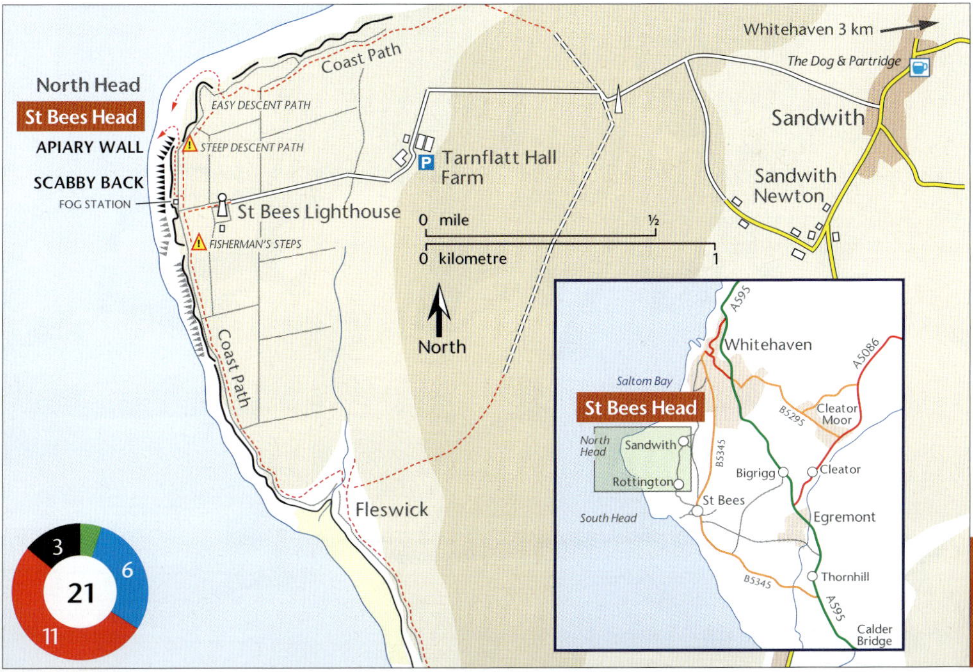

Apiary Wall

The prominent arête of *Nectarine* rises above massive boulders and provides a good reference. The first routes start from the grassy slope at the left.

① **Blooming Marvellous** F6c ★★
The square arête with a sting in the tail.
I Williamson 22.11.1993

② **Just Nice** F6a+
The wall right of the arête. Shared lower-off.
C Johnstone April 1994

③ **Ancient Mariner** F5+ ★
Good climbing up the corner-crack.
J Wilson 1993

The next lines start lower down, on the main wall, just above an excellent circuit of boulders.

④ **Nectarine** F6c+ ★★★
Mega classic. The impressive left arête of the big wall.
J Adams, S Scott April 1994

⑤ **Drone** F7a+ ★
Start in a leftward-facing corner.
A Jones 1989

⑥ **Virgin Queen** F7a ★★
Climb up the corner and into the second corner, exiting on the right to the lower-off.
A Jones 1989

⑦ **Royal Jelly** F6b
Wobble up the central flake (3 bolts) then traverse left along the ledge and follow the bolts up to the lower-off.
J Adams, P Cheung 6.05.1995

⑧ **Honey Pot** F6b+ ★
All of the way up the central flake.
A Jones 1989

⑨ **Beeswax** F6b
Start up the central flake then exit up the ramp passing the roof on its right.
A Jones 1989

⑩ **Swarm** F7a ★★
A technical start leads to a pumpy and spectacular finale up the open groove.
A Jones 1989

⑪ **Bee Line** F6b+ ★
A short route with a fierce start up to the ledge at 10m. Start at a rightwards-slanting crack with a small upside down V at its base. Climb the crack with difficulty then trend leftwards across the slab to the lower-off.
A Jones, W Hannah Sept 1999

⑫ **Bee Hive** F6c
Start up the groove right of the low roof then break out left after the second bolt. Follow the bolts to the lower-off.
J Adams, W Hannah 7.05.1995

⑬ **The Apiarist** F6b+ ★★★
Great sustained climbing with an alternating series of hard moves and good rests; the final layback corner is tackled in a spectacular position. Start just right of a low level roof and climb the series of grooves and corners.
A Jones 1989

⑭ **Bee Sting** F7a ★★
Below the left-hand end of the large roof on the right-hand side of **Apiary Wall**.
A Jones 1989

⑮ **Foul Brood** F7a+ ★
Direct over the right-hand end of the large roof.
A Jones 1989

St Bees — 📷 Paul Jennings

Scabby Back

Continuing south, **Scabby Back** offers a good range of climbing. The area is accessed above the step in the rock platform equipped with a chain.

The southern extremity is tidal.

(16) Recharge   F6a+
The left-hand line up the slab with a hard move for the short to finish.
J Adams 1994

(17) Feeling Groovy   F6c   ★★
The central line on the slab has a balancy crux.
S Wood 1992

(18) Stage Fright   F6b
The right-hand arête starting direct.
Photo opposite.
S Scott 1993

(19) Route Two   F4
Up the easy groove on the right with a step left at the top.
E Cleasby 1980

(20) Megadrive   F6b+   ★
Climb the left side of the wild leaning arête.
J Adams, S Scott 1994

(21) Dreaming of Red Rocks   F7a+ ★★★★
The St Bees must do! A stunning route up the overhanging right side of the arête. A good test of fitness.
A Hyslop 1992

Access groove from Apiary Wall

Stage Fright F6b (opposite) Nick Wharton — David Simmonite

SLATE

Everyone should climb on slate for the sake of improving their technique. The Lakeland slate crags provide a mixture of trad and bolted routes on this fine rock. Lake District slate tends to be a bit more coarse than that found in North Wales meaning that friction is merely poor as opposed to non-existent.

A number of the slate quarries have undergone regeneration. Many new routes have been created and old favourites brought back to life. Cleaning and re-bolting to high modern standards is ongoing. Much of this work is thanks to the enthusiasm and effort of local activists. New bolts and anchors are provided by the Cumbria Bolt Fund, in order for this work to continue, your donations are essential.

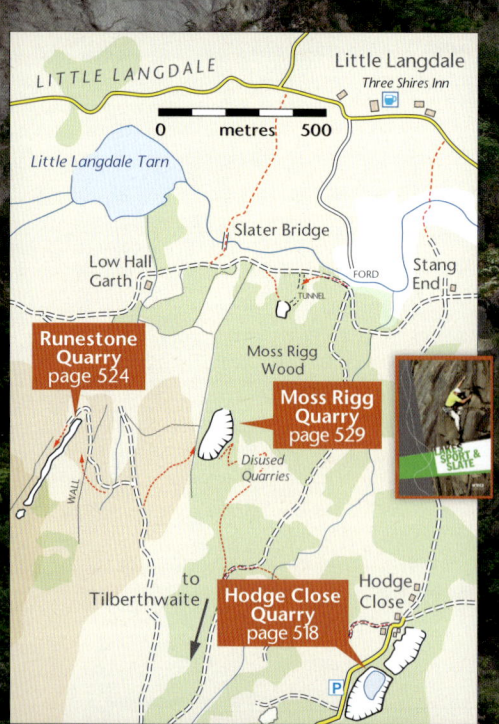

Malice in Wonderland, Hodge Close E4 (page 523) Theo Moore — Tom McNally

HODGE CLOSE QUARRY
OS Grid Ref: NY 317 017

Sky F6b+ (page 522) Molly Oliver — Jacob Smith

The Main Wall

This impressive 60m wall showcasing the best of Lakeland slate climbing extends the full length of the east side of the quarry.

Approach: Located in the Tilberthwaite valley just north of Coniston, it is approached by the narrow road, sign-posted Hodge Close, off the A593. The quarry is beyond a collection of cottages being a huge hole in the ground on the right with parking on the left. To the north (left) of the quarry is another quarry (Parrock Quarry) linked by a huge archway. Approach by walking along the road, passing some cottages then entering from the north and walking through Parrock Quarry and the archway or abseil, depending on start point.

See map page 516.

① **Joie de Vivre**   50m   F6c+   ★★
A climb of some elegance. Start left of a sycamore tree.
1 20m 6c Climb a short wall to a ramp. Initially stubborn, the crack eases with height then head left to belay (twin bolts) or continue (long slings helpful).
2 30m 6c+ Climb the fine groove and flake crack above to a coconut sized hole. Traverse right to a good foothold and thin crack then head left to the top.
A Towse, J Hool, S Harvey 6.09.2009

② **Blade Runner**   55m   F7a   ★★★
Brilliant climbing, classic slate-style: balancy, delicate and all on your feet.
1 25m 7a Start up the ramp as for *Joie de Vivre*. At the 3rd bolt, step up left into a shallow scoop then up to a ledge. Over a bulge and leftwards to reach better holds and the *Joie de Vivre* belay. Move up and right easily for 5m and step down right to a ledge; bolt belay.
2 30m 7a Make hard committing moves up the right edge to reach the first bolt then follow the edge with sustained moves for 10m. Overcome an awkward overlap until a left-slanting crack leads to a roof. Climb over the roof and up the wall above using a drill hole in the slab to gain better holds and up left to the top.
P Whillance, A Towse 1.04.2022

To the right is a large clean rock scar capped by an overhang. The shallow crease at the right-hand side is taken by the following route.

③ **Second Coming**   50m   F7a+   ★★★
Fabulous, well-protected climbing except for one easier run-out section mid-way. Start about 10m right of the highest point of the scree in an alcove with an iron spike. Step off the spike to climb a difficult first wall to reach the break. Go left then up into the groove. Step left again onto the speckled slab to reach a small ledge. Tricky moves lead up until a stride right reaches a flake ledge. From a good hold an acrobatic sequence leads up then right into a large bottomless groove. More easily up this before reaching a ledge in the easy-angled groove. Straight up the wall above to finish.
E Cleasby, P Short, JL Holden, A Towse 19.07.1992

④ **First Night Nerves**   50m   F7b   ★★★★
A sensational route with sustained, hard climbing tackling the left side of *The Main Wall*. Step off the iron spike and climb the initial wall with difficulty to reach the break under the roof then head left and up into a hanging groove. Climb up and right precariously and with great difficulty to eventually reach a small overhang at a short groove. Up this then delicate climbing leads up the slab. Make a tricky step left to the arête then back right for a few moves up the wall just right of a shallow groove.
RO Graham, A Phizacklea 13.09.1987

❺ **The Main Event**   73m   E5 6a   ★★
An impressive route. Its wandering nature, poor protection and difficulty add spice. Start below the overhanging wall, a few metres right of the iron spike, at the foot of a steep thin crack.
1 28m 6a Climb the crack, using a sloping ledge out left to reach a traverse line below the overhanging wall. Traverse right following the flake to reach a large ledge.
2 45m 6a Traverse back leftwards, along a ramp below the steep wall for 4m, pull up right then back left to gain the upper wall (peg). Follow the thin flake up and left then rightwards to good ledges. Climb the shallow groove on the left to a ledge (bolts). Climb up for a couple of metres before stepping right to finish more or less directly. The short open corner above the belay (to the left of the big flake) can be followed (peg); thin moves above lead to a junction with the main pitch at the good ledges reducing the grade to E4 6a.
P1 P Whillance, R Parker / P2 P Whillance, R Parker, P Botterill, D Armstrong, A Murray Spring 1980

The next route starts in the final little bay, just above the water's edge at the foot of a large corner adorned with two bent spikes.

⑥ **The Plunger**   15m   F6b+   ★
A technical problem up the striking arête. Climb the thin diagonal crack rightwards (wires) to the arête (bolt). Follow the arête above to a flake and continue to the ledge.
P Cornforth, A Phizacklea 4.05.1987

The Upper Main Wall

Arguably some of the best and boldest slate climbs in the country are found here. By today's standards they seem wild with absurd protection. Let's keep it that way.

The routes start from the ledge system which runs across the foot of the **Main Wall**, about 20m above the pool. Climb up from below or abseil to the ledge.

⑦ Stage Fright 50m E6 6b ★★★★
A superb sparsely protected and intimidating route demanding fearless determination. Its focus is the stark isolated groove. Start from a large flake on the left-hand side of the ledge. Traverse leftwards across a short ramp below the steep wall for 4m. Up right then back left to gain the upper wall (peg). Traverse delicately left across the slab to a rib (peg). Step left, using a hidden foothold, into the slim leftwards-leaning groove; climb to a poor resting place (peg). Move left and up to a good ledge then climb the wall trending rightwards for 10m until a thin flake leads directly to the top.
P Whillance, D Armstrong 21.05.1983

⑧ Ten Years After 45m E5 6a ★★★
Sustained elegant climbing above well-spaced gear. Start off the left-hand ledge, at the foot of the groove. Climb the groove then move leftwards onto the undercut wall. Step delicately left then climb up to better holds then rock over leftwards to reach some ledges (wires). Step right and use a hollow flake to reach a shallow stepped groove. Climb this (peg) then continue directly up the wall to a small groove; follow this to an awkward finish.
R Matheson, E Cleasby Easter 1980

⑨ Wicked Willie 45m E5 6b ★★★
A superb route with good widely spaced protection. Climb the groove before pulling left onto the undercut wall. Step delicately left then climb up to better holds. Make a hard move up and right (peg) then climb easier ground (bolt). The thin flake above is climbed (Friend 1/2) until a final wild move rightwards leads to a friendly ledge. Climb the wall above, first on the right, before moving left to a good hold directly below a tree at the top.
A Phizacklea, G Cornforth, P Cornforth 3.05.1987

⑩ Sky 47m F6b+ ★★★
Excellent climbing. Belay on the large ledge, below the left-hand end of the big roof. Climb to a ledge below a thin flake crack; follow this strenuously. Where it peters out level with the big roof make a hard move left into a short corner and out again to join a groove. Traverse the headwall rightwards across a ledge system to reach the final shallow groove.
Photo page 518.
E Cleasby, R Matheson Easter 1980

⑪ Life in the Fast Lane 45m E6 6b ★★★
A classic, audaciously climbing the prominent rib leading to the right-hand side of the big roof. A courageous and controlled approach is required to deal with the sparse protection. From the foot of the groove, a shattered flake runs up right to the rib (cam). A very difficult and committing smear leads to easier climbing directly up the rib to the right-hand side of the overhang. Step right into a dirty corner (runners), then traverse back left directly above the roof (peg) to reach and climb a shallow groove (peg).
P Whillance, A Murray, R Parker Apr 1980

The Central Wall West

Most routes start from a large tree-covered terrace reached by abseil - please use a sling around the tree.

⑫ Big Randolph 54m E2 5b ★★
A great introduction to **Hodge Close** climbing combining trad with sport. Wires 1-7; small-med cams. Start below a steep flake crack towards the left end of the terrace. Bolts.
1 34m 5b Climb the flake which leads strenuously to the ramp system. Follow this rightwards (bolt) then climb the continuation groove to a bollard and bolt belay.
2 20m F6a+ Move up then traverse left to finish up the steep left-facing groove.
P1 P Whillance, D parker Mar 1980
P2 K Phizacklea, JL Holden, J Daly, P Whillance Jul 2024

⑬ Limited Edition 33m E4 6a ★★★
An excellent route which feels distinctly trad. Abseil to the bolt belay at the top of the ramp. From the lower left point of the ramp, step across left to gain a shallow right-facing scoop and find the right sequence to reach an excellent hold. Traverse diagonally left across the wall to reach a flake then up and slightly right to better holds below the slight steepening of the headwall. A hard move on quartz holds leads to a tiny right-facing flake; finish up this.
P Carling, P Noble 24.05.1986

⑭ Randolph Scott 40m F6b ★★

5 or 6 long slings are essential or take a belay. Up then right along a ramp to a stepped groove and higher ledge. Stride left, up (spike) then back right and up onto a ledge; continue to a large ledge (belay). Move up then traverse left to finish up the steep left-facing groove.
J Daly, K Phizacklea 2.05.1987

⑮ Behind the Lines 45m HVS 5a ★★

A classic line with ample protection. Start at the right-hand end of the ledge by a large tree. Climb the wall then, using a massive suspect flake, head up and across left (blunt spike) into the corner. Climb the corner to the top bulge then traverse right (loose spike) to finish.
R Parker, A Murray, P Whillance 30.03.1980

⑯ Malice in Wonderland 43m E4 5c ★★★

A beautiful route climbing the bold graceful arête. Start at the pine tree, below the large groove. Climb the slab on the right then a rib to the overhang. Step right (poor peg) and pull directly through the overhang, on good widely spaced holds, to land on the slab above. Traverse left, just above the roof, to reach the arête. Climb the left side, passing a diagonal crack, to a tree on its right flank. Step back onto the arête and climb it with conviction, past a thin crack on the left (RP), to a delicate and gripping finish.
Photo page 517.
P Whillance, R Parker, E Cleasby 20.04.1980

RUNESTONE QUARRY
OS Grid Ref: NY 306 023

A mature sport climbing venue. Well-bolted with a wide grade spread.

Approach: From Tilberthwaite Quarry, walk north along the road past cottages on the left to the farm. Take the left-hand bridleway up the hill until it levels out with a fine view of Langdale. Just beyond, a path heads down and left in the direction of a huge spoil heap. Over a stile by the gate then up an inclined path to the bottom end of the Lower Quarry. From the entrance to the Lower Quarry, follow the path up the right (west) side of the quarry to eventually reach a flat area between the quarries, from which the **Middle Quarry** can be seen. On the left (east) side of the quarry there is a pathway which leads under an impressive slab bridged across the entrance gangway. *Belly Button Slab* area is about 30m up to the left.

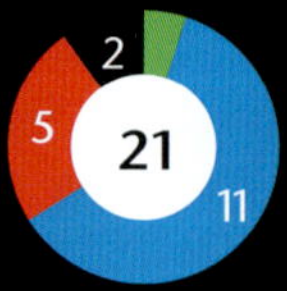

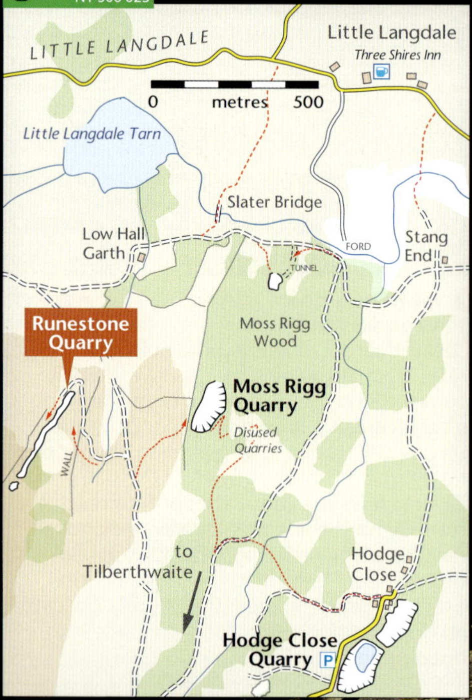

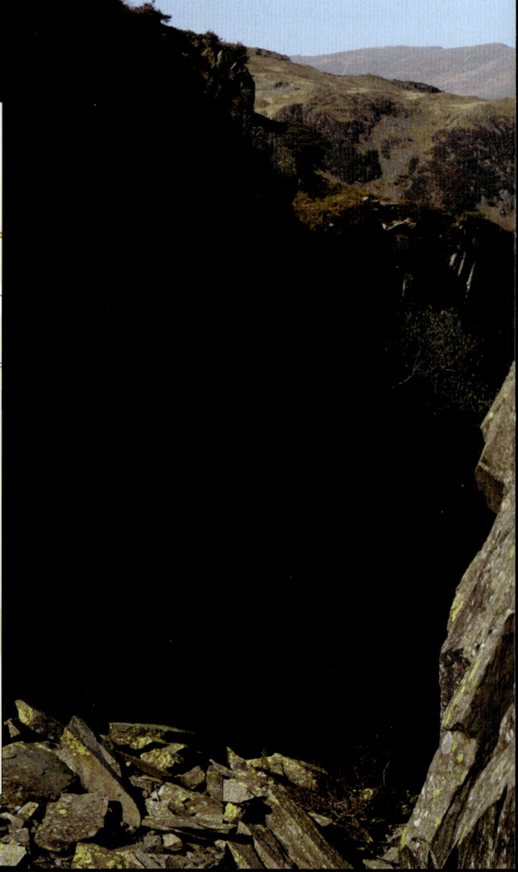

Self Isolation F6a (page 526) Matt Crawford — David Simmonite

Middle Quarry

A fine spread of routes at a mixture of grades. The selection here is at the lower end.

In the lower (northern) end of the quarry is the cave once used as an illicit whisky still by the notorious Lanty Slee. It was said that the resultant product was the best thing that ever came out of the quarry.

① **Coye Dog** 10m F6a+ ★★
A rib eases the step into the corner; climb this then continue up the groove to a lower-off.
V McClelland, E Blylock 9.04.1991

② **Moi Straws** 13m F6b+ ★
A hybrid. Clip the 1st bolt then make a delicate step left onto the slab above the overhang to join the upper groove.

③ **Belly Button Slab** 13m F5+ ★★
From a small walled enclosure, a diagonal flake crack leads into a broken niche; step left onto the large hanging slab and climb this directly up the shallow pillar.
M Bagness, L Harrison 18.04.1991

④ **Self Isolation** 11m F6a ★
From a pointed block, move left and climb the slab.
Photo page 525.
R Kenyon, R Illingworth 19.03.2020

⑤ **The Burning** 10m F6a+ ★
From a pointed block, pull onto the slab with difficulty. Climb a vague flake continuing past a small overlap.
V McClelland 9.04.1991

⑥ **Smile at the End of the Rainbow** 10m F6a+ ★
Pull over the right side of the overhang then follow the shallow groove.
R Kenyon, R Illingworth 26.05.2020

⑦ **Hats Off to Linten Miller** 10m F6a ★
The left-facing groove.
V McClelland 13.04.1991

⑧ **Hats Off Direct** 10m F6b
Follow the bolts directly up the slab to join *Hats Off to Linten Miller*.
R Illingworth 26.05.2020

⑨ **Runestone Cowboy** 10m F5b ★
A direct line up the fine slab.
R.Illingworth, RJ Kenyon 19.01.2020

⑩ **Greasing My Teapot** 10m F6a ★
Climb the slab with interest.
E Blylock, V McClelland 9.04.1991

⑪ **Wide Open** 11m F5a ★
The faint grooveline just left of the bolts.
V McClelland 9.04.1991

⑫ **Yodelling in the Canyon** 11m F4
The left-slanting groove; shared protection from bolts to the left.
E Blylock 9.04.1991

Down and right is a large impressive slab.

⑬ **Corona Nightmare** 15m F6a+ ★
A hard start leads to a faint crack.
R Illingworth, E McKenna Parker 20.05.2020

⑭ **Lucid Dreams** 16m F6b ★★
A great route following discontinuous grooves.
G Campion, A Campion 29.07.2018

⑮ **The Long Way Home** 24m F6c ★★
Start towards the right-hand end of the overhang barrier. Climb up via a jammed block then go leftwards through the overhangs to gain the slab above. Follow a ramp leftwards then climb a black-streaked wall and move right to finish up a clean groove.
P Whillance, A Towse 15.10.2021

Upper Quarry

Immediately above and south of **Middle Quarry**. Access is by abseil or via a hidden tunnel on its eastern flank. The most prominent feature is a huge arched cave at the southern (uphill) end.

The East Face features a long bow-shaped wall of steep slanting grooves ending at a low cave. The climbs typically have difficult lower sections easing with height.

Approach: Follow a path up to the right of **Middle Quarry** to reach a low wall and follow this then head left up to reach a grassy slope leading to the quarry top. Descend the steep eastern hillside with care, overlooking **Hodge Close**, to reach some ruined buildings. The tunnel entrance is behind the buildings; initially wet with stepping-stones, a drier section then emerges in a low cavern below the right side of the East Face.

Abseil: From the anchor at the top of *Whisky Galore*. This is located on a slab alongside a grassy bay in a distinctive cut in the rim - The Notch, midway along the eastern side.

① **Changing of the Guard** 8m F6a ★
Step off the block, traverse rightwards into a shallow groove and climb this on its right side pulling back left to a ledge.
D Geere, K Phizacklea, P Whillance 12.05.2022

② **Unrecalled Activists** 12m F6c+ ★
Start 5m down to the right of the prominent block, at a slabby groove in an alcove with a horizontal shot hole in left wall. Start easily for a few metres then climb a steep groove and over an overhang to gain a slab. Up this to the anchor.
K Phizacklea 12.05.2022

③ **Whisky Galore** 14m F6b+ ★★
Start at an undercut slab below a line of overhangs at 4m. Move up to undercuts and pull over the overhang to gain a slab. Step up then tiptoe right on a horizontal shot hole and pull around into a steep slim groove. Climb this over a small overlap and continue, exiting right onto a slab.
P Whillance, A Towse 27.05.2022

④ **Contraband** 14m F6c ★
Start at an undercut slab below a line of overhangs at 4m. Move up to the undercuts then traverse awkwardly right beneath the overhangs to reach a good hold in a groove. Climb the slim slabby groove trending rightwards and pull over onto the slab.
P Whillance, A Towse 16.06.2022

⑤ **Casting the Runes** 14m F7a+ ★★★
Start on the left-hand side of the wide cavern roof. From some blocks by a low shot hole, make a stiff pull up to gain a smaller shot hole then move right and up to an overlap. Pull straight over to a larger one, turn this on the left then climb a slab and short groove rightwards to the anchor.
K Phizacklea 12.05.2022

⑥ **English Summer** 16m F7a+ ★★
From blocks below the left side of the roof, boulder the roof to gain a groove and horizontal shot-hole. Make awkward moves right to reach better holds. Continue up and follow a slim groove, exiting right to a ledge. Move up and over an overhang then rightwards.
K Phizacklea 29.05.2022

MOSS RIGG QUARRY
OS Grid Ref: NY 312 026

Moss Rigg offers sport climbing in a setting of brutal beauty. Worked as recently as 1984, much unstable rock remains, so take extra care climbing and moving around the quarry.

Approach: From Tilberthwaite Quarry, walk north along the road passing through the farm. Take the gated bridleway branching up to the left and follow this, steeply at first, for about 1km, until it levels out. After the last gate, at a fingerpost, follow the footpath to the right heading right towards the wall and trees. Just over the wall, a smaller quarry can be seen. Keep walking along the wall round a small knoll. Climb the sturdy drystone wall with care to the quarry rim.

From **Hodge Close Quarry**, walk north to the cottages then west along the track descending through the quarries to the track between High Tilberthwaite and Little Langdale. Turn left/south towards High Tilberthwaite and right at the first junction (gated) following an ascending track passing crumbling quarry buildings to the rim.

See map on page 524 and overview on page 530.

Hodge Close
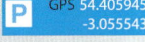
NY 315 017
GPS 54.405945 -3.055543

Tilberthwaite
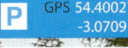
NY 305 011
GPS 54.400279 -3.070916

OS Grid Ref
NY 312 026

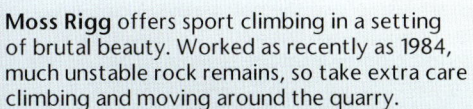

Titanic Arête F6c (page 532) Catherine Plum — Peter Sterling

530 | Slate

Dawn Wall

3D climbing in deceptively steep grooves and corners. This wall lies directly opposite the **Titanic Arête Area**. The climbing is on the top tier only, identifiable by a distinctive 'W' shaped slab when viewed from the opposite side.

Approach: Abseil to staggered flat grass ledges with bolt belay stations. All the climbs can be finished by topping out.

① **Morning Has Broken** 20m F7a+ ★
The overhanging thin groove and arête at the far left end of the wall. Abseil to a ledge and bolt belay at a slightly lower level than the other routes. Climb the overhanging wall via a slim groove exiting right to gain a ledge below the arête. Climb the right side of the arête for a few metres where difficult moves left lead around the arête and up the wall to gain better holds and the top.
K Phizacklea, P Whillance 20.07.2023

② **Living Daylights** 18m F6c ★★
Start from the far end of the ledge. Climb left into a groove line and follow this to a big ledge. Continue up then back rightwards to below a hanging arête. Climb a ramp leftwards to the final strenuous corner.
P Whillance, K Phizacklea 3.05.2023

③ **Twilight Zone** 18m F6b ★
Start just left of the bolt belays. Climb a stepped groove leftwards to a big grassy ledge. Continue up the steep wall on the left to gain the arête then follow ledges up leftwards; awkward moves back right gain a slab at the base of a steep corner. Up this to finish.
P Whillance, K Phizacklea 26.01.2023

④ **Dawn Chorus** 18m F6c+ ★★★
An excellent technical pitch. Start immediately right of the belays. Move up to a ledge then continue easily trending leftwards to below an overhanging wall. Move up right then climb the corner to reach a lower-off on the slab above.
P Whillance, K Phizacklea 3.05.2023

⑤ **Wake Up Call** 18m F6b+ ★
Start at a slight groove 4m left of the bolt belays. Climb the groove leftwards to reach a blank looking overhanging groove. Pull into this and out right to gain ledges. Climb the

Moss Rigg Quarry — Peter Sterling

steep corner above exiting left onto the slab, then up right to finish.
P Whillance, K Phizacklea 29.06.2023

⑥ **Morning Glory** 18m F6c+ ★★ ♂
The slim groove in the arête right of *Wake Up Call*. Start as for *Wake Up Call* then climb the slight groove to the first bolt. Move up right onto a slab below an overhanging wall. Pull across right into a thin groove and up this to a ledge on the right below a steep slim groove in the arête. Exposed and technical climbing up this leads to a slab. Easily up leftwards to the lower-off above *Wake Up Call*.
Photo this page.
P Whillance, K Phizacklea 9.05.2023

⑦ **Early Riser** 20m F6a ♂
The stepped groove line in the right-hand side of the wall. From the right-hand end of the ledge step up and follow a pleasant left-trending ramp to a steeper wall. Climb a short steep groove on the right and pull up to gain a groove. Follow this delicately right to reach better ledges, then go up another short steep groove to a slab then rightwards again to finish by a tree.
P Whillance, K Phizacklea 26.01.2023

Morning Glory F6c+ (this page) Steph Marshall
📷 Nick Wharton

Titanic Arête Area

The imperious soaring wall on the south-east side of the quarry has long, testing routes of great quality.

Approach: Either abseil from the large trees above the sector or alternatively it is possible to walk into the bottom of the quarry from the south-east corner - to the right of this sector.

⑧ **Heart of the Ocean**   58m   F7a+   ★★★★

An impressive climb, sustained, technical and fittingly with the crux being the final pitch. The two upper pitches tackle the imposing wall left of *Titanic Arête*. The first pitch, taking a hanging crack in the wall just left of *Titanic Arête*, provides a much better alternative start to that climb. Start at the cave entrance some 5m left of the foot of the arête.
1 30m F6c+ Boulder through the right side of the cave to gain a left-slanting ramp. Up this to broken ledges and back right to below a steep wall. Climb the wall and crack to the ledge and bolt belays on *Titanic Arête*.
2 8m F7a Step round left onto the wall. Traverse across the wall with tricky finger changes and tiny footholds, to reach a slight groove then up and left to the pinnacle.
3 20m F7a+ Step right to below a faint groove. Difficult climbing gains a right-slanting break. Up the wall trending rightwards to reach a lower-off or finish by stepping right to the arête.
P Whillance, K Phizacklea 30.08.2023

⑨ **Titanic Arête**   50m   F6c   ★★

A compelling line soaring skywards into the trees. Start up a short steep wall just right of the arête. Helmets and life-boats should be taken. The original first pitch has poor protection, loose rock and is vegetated so is not recommended. Avoid this by abseiling in to the bolt belay then climbing the top pitch, or if you want the full experience start up *Heart of the Ocean*.
1 26m F6a ⚠ The innocuous initial wall is awkward. Tackle the loose rib above with vigilance to reach the safety of a comfortable ledge.
2 24m F6c Climb the right-hand side of the arête. A tricky sequence above the peg may enable you to grab a large hold. From here reaching the top is inevitable.
Photo page 529.
P Ross, D Byne-Peare 8.07.1990

⑩ **White Star Line**   50m   F6c   ★★

Another great outing climbing the white slab and grooves up the wall to the right of the arête. Start 4m right of the arête beneath a short wall. The climb can be split at a mid-point belay or, better, climb the whole thing in one.
1 24m F6c Climb a short wall to reach a ledge at the foot of a large white slab. Climb the centre of the slab, avoiding the crack on the right, with a difficult move to reach a break. Continue to a ledge at its top then over broken ledges to a bolted belay below a prominent corner.
2 26m F6b Climb to the right then back left into the main corner. Step left and follow a crack in the slab to a ledge and airy perch on the arête. The headwall is climbed first direct then leftwards via a slight groove and left again to finish up a scoop.
P. Whillance, A Towse 10.09.2022

⑪ **Train Crazy Boy**   45m   F6b+   ★★★

An excellent and massive pitch, recently cleaned and re-bolted, this is one of the best routes here providing a lot of absorbing climbing. Up into a shallow corner stepping right to avoid steepening rock. Continue through steeper rock above trending left to enter a very smooth groove at 35m. The bulge provides an interesting entry to the steep final wall.
Photo below.
C Struthers, S Siddiqui 22.02.1998

Train Crazy Boy F6b+ (above) Peter Sterling
📷 Keith Sanders

BOULDERING

Carrock Fell — NY 361 310
St Bees — NX 938 145
Sour Milk — NY 231 123
Bowderstone — NY 253 164
Sampson — NY 217 054
Langdale — NY 313 059
Kentmere — NY 451 045
Eskdale — NY 147 002
Seathwaite — SD 238 968
Brant Fell — SD 409 962

Badger Rock, Kentmere   Mari Cole & Flora Wharton — Nick Wharton

The Lake District is home to a wealth of bouldering with problems to suit everyone, whatever your taste or standard. They are spread across the whole area. Details of all of these sites are available from www.lakesbloc.com and are covered by the excellent Lake District Bouldering written by Greg Chapman and published by Vertebrate Publishing.

Here is just a brief selection of the best locations, geographically spread across the area covered by this guide. This intends to only point you at the venues where you can at least make your own entertainment on a day off from the Trad or Sport. For details of specific boulders and problems see the Bouldering guide.

Kentmere

A fabulous area with a number of sectors located in the south-east of the district, readily accessible from Kendal, making an ideal stopping-off point when approaching the Lakes from the south. It is best suited to the mid-to-hard grades, but Badger Rock has some excellent easier options.

From Kentmere Village Hall/Church, walk up the road which leads to the Garbun Pass. Badger Rock sits alone in the field on the left after about 10 mins walk. Little Font is in the woods on the other side of the track just beyond Badger Rock. Other sectors can be found further up the fellside overlooking the track. **Photo this page.**

Brant Fell

This easily accessible, central location offers some easier bouldering with the best view in the Lakes. Situated above the tourist-trap village of Bowness, the small outcrops look out over Windermere and the Central Fells. The flat grassy area around the blocs make for a very family-friendly location. The Classic Traverse is the most popular problem but there are other straight-up problems that you can make up for yourself.

Take the B5284 (Crook Road) from Kendal to Bowness. Windermere Golf Club is on the left. A small crossroads marks the end of the golf course. Turn right (north) onto a smaller lane and park in a layby on the left after 300m. Go over the stile onto a track for 60m then head up left on grassy footpaths and tracks to the fell top. The crags are on the south-west of the summit.

St Bees

Located way out west, this is one of the best bouldering locations in the UK. A collection of superb sandstone boulders offering a wide variety of problem styles and grades sitting on flat platforms beside the sea beneath the sport climbs described on page 511.

Approach from Whitehaven as for St Bees crag. **Photo below.**

Eskdale

Inland from St Bees, the geology changes and presents us with a gift of wonderful granite bouldering in Lower Eskdale. There are many circuits as well as some outstanding lines on tremendous rough rock. Most is to be found in the area of Fisherground farm and campsite, not far from the King George IV pub.

Park at Eskdale Green station, walk back along the road towards the pub then take a footpath on the left. This takes you over the railway and on to and round to the left of Hollin How farm, through a gate and onto the fell. Continue on the path until the Diamond boulder appears in front of you. The areas further up the valley are more easily reached directly from Fisherground where parking can be found at a modest cost.

Sampson Stones

Much further up the valley in Upper Eskdale, the rock has changed back to volcanic. This is an idyllic location, only ½km south of the fabulous **Esk Buttress** on the southern slopes of Scafell Pike. The bouldering is magnificent and well worth the long walk-in.

Follow the approach to **Esk Buttress** (page 222) past Taw House Farm following the River Esk. The boulders come into view on the edge of Great Moss beneath the large crag of Cam Spout. The cockley Beck approach is handy from the south.

Toad Face, Seathwaite — Fin leather
📷 David Simmonite

St Bees — 📷 Nick Wharton

Langdale Boulders‡
Handily situated in one of our main climbing valleys and right next to the road, these boulders provide some excellent low-to-mid grade problems with good landings.

Please do not take dogs into the field and do not climb on the east face of the lower block due to the presence of ancient rock art.

Just beyond Chapel Stile heading into Langdale, the boulders can be seen in a field on the left. A layby is available just beyond on the right.

Sour Milk Gill & Gillercomb Boulders‡
Positioned at the head of Borrowdale, close to the hamlet of Seathwaite, these two closely located venues provide a fabulous range of easier and mid-grade problems, along with a few tougher options. The volcanic rock varies in nature across the boulders and all in a lovely setting.

From the road-side parking at Seathwaite, follow the path through the campsite and up the side of Sour Milk Gill.

Bowderstone
This iconic venue, a giant boulder at the heart of Borrowdale, provides steep hard problems that will test the best.

Follow the track south from the Bowderstone car park.
Photo below.

Seathwaite Circuit
Spread over the hillside on the way up to Seathwaite Tarn in the Duddon Valley, this area provides many problems in a delightful, easily accessible location. Handy for the numerous trad venues in the area and great for families with something for everyone.

Turn off the Duddon Valley road, north of Seathwaite and head up to the foot of the Walna Scar Road. There are boulders by the parking. For the remainder, walk up the track towards the tarn.
Photo opposite.

Carrock Fell
An amazing location with an endless supply of boulders, all just seconds from the road and 20 mins from the M6, Penrith and Keswick. The gabbro rock is superb and provides a wide range of grades to suit everyone.

Head north off the A66 at Hutton Moor End via Mungrisdale, Bowscale and Mosedale. The extensive blocs are scattered over the hillside on the left.

‡ Topo available on LakesBloc.

Picnic Sarcastic, Bowderstone, Borrowdale Caleb Reid — David Simmonite

TICK LISTS

By definition, this "Selective Guide" already contains all the best routes in the Lake District. However, some stand out from their peers. You can be sure that every route appearing in this collection is worthwhile. To help further distinguish between the almost 1300 routes described here, we have used the familiar star rating system from 'no' stars to ★★★★. Factors like position, variety, rock quality, interest and historical stature all play a role. This is challenging, especially when comparing a route on a world-class crag like Scafell East Buttress with those on a smaller outcrop such as Shepherd's Crag. A great deal of subjective opinion is at play too and no doubt you will disagree with some of our ratings.

To help you further, we have identified what we believe to be the "Best in Class" – two routes at each grade **D** to **E6** (excluding those already appearing in the next list).

☑ BEST IN CLASS

Route		Grade	Page
☐ **Middlefell Buttress**, Middlefell Buttress		D	64
☐ **Corvus**, Raven Crag Combe Gill		D	424
☐ **Arrowhead Ridge Direct**, The Napes		VD	278
☐ **Grooved Arête**, Pikes Crag		VD	261
☐ **Oxford & Cambridge Direct**, Crey Crag		S	340
☐ **Arête, Chimney & Crack**, Dow Crag		S	122
☐ **Bridge's Route**, Esk Buttress		HS	228
☐ **Thomas**, Wallowbarrow Crag		HS	152
☐ **Eliminate 'A'**, Dow Crag		VS	124
☐ **North-West Arête**, Gimmer Crag		VS	82
☐ **The Centaur**, Scafell East Buttres		HVS	254
☐ **Trespasser Groove**, Esk Buttress		HVS	231
☐ **Red Edge**, Esk Buttress		E1	226
☐ **Gimmer String**, Gimmer Crag		E1	80
☐ **Astra**, Pavey Ark		E2	57
☐ **Hiddenite**, Iron Crag		E2	444
☐ **The Voyage**, Goat Crag		E3	404
☐ **Sarcophagus**, Gable Crag		E3	292
☐ **Top Gear**, Raven Crag Threshthwaite Cove		E4	460
☐ **Tumble**, Dow Crag		E4	128
☐ **Fast & Furious with FFF**, Dove Crag		E5	457
☐ **Supernatural**, The Napes		E5	286
☐ **Stage Fright**, Hodge Close		E6	522
☐ **Ringwraith**, Scafell Crag		E6	241

You'll also discover the "gems" ◆. Routes that members of the team feel are special and merit highlighting.

The books Classic, Hard and Extreme Rock showcase the best of UK climbing. Produced by Ken Wilson and Bernard Newman, with an update of Hard Rock by Ian Parnell. These are the Lake District routes in those books.

☑ CLASSIC ROCK

Route		Grade
☐ **Murray's Route**, Dow Crag		S
☐ **Bracket & Slab Climb**, Gimmer Crag		S
☐ **Ash Tree Slabs**, Gimmer Crag		VD
☐ **'C' Route**, Gimmer Crag		S
☐ **Bowfell Buttress**, Bowfell Buttress		HS
☐ **Jones' Route Direct**, Scafell Crag		HS
☐ **Moss Gill Grooves**, Scafell Crag		MVS
☐ **Tophet Wall**, The Napes		HS
☐ **Needle Ridge**, The Napes		VD
☐ **The Wasdale Crack**, The Napes		HS
☐ **New West Climb**, Pillar Rock		VD
☐ **Rib & Slab Climb**, Pillar Rock		HS
☐ **Gillercombe Buttress**, Gillercomb		S
☐ **Troutdale Pinnacle**, Black Crag		S
☐ **Little Chamonix**, Shepherd's Crag		VD

☑ HARD ROCK

Route		Grade
☐ **Central Buttress**, Scafell Crag		E1/E3
☐ **Ichabod**, Scafell East Buttress		E2
☐ **The Central Pillar**, Esk Buttress		E2
☐ **Gormenghast**, Heron Crag		E1
☐ **Engineer's Slabs**, Gable Crag		VS
☐ **Praying Mantis**, Goat Crag		E1
☐ **Extol**, Dove Crag		E2
☐ **Totalitarian**, Raven Crag Thirlmere		E1
☐ **The Crack**, Gimmer Crag		VS
☐ **Kipling Groove**, Gimmer Crag		HVS
☐ **Nimrod**, Dow Crag		E1

☑ EXTREME ROCK

Route		Grade
☐ **Grand Alliance**, Black Crag		E4
☐ **Bitter Oasis**, Goat Crag		E4
☐ **Footless Crow**, Goat Crag		E6
☐ **The Gates of Delirium**, Raven Crag Thirlmere		E4
☐ **Saxon**, Scafell Crag		E2
☐ **The Nazgul**, Scafell Crag		E3
☐ **The Lord of the Rings**, Scafell East Buttress		E3
☐ **Lost Horizons**, Scafell East Buttress		E4
☐ **Shere Khan**, Scafell East Buttress		E5
☐ **Equus**, Gimmer Crag		E2
☐ **Eastern Hammer**, Gimmer Crag		E3
☐ **Trilogy**, Raven Crag Langdale		E5
☐ **R'n'S Special**, Raven Crag Langdale		E5
☐ **Fine Time**, Raven Crag Langdale		E5
☐ **Cruel Sister**, Pavey Ark		E3
☐ **Fallen Angel**, Pavey Ark		E4
☐ **Side Walk**, Dow Crag		E2
☐ **Holocaust**, Dow Crag		E4
☐ **The Cumbrian**, Esk Buttress		E5

INDEX

539

Symbols

62 West Wallaby Street	504
1931	234

A

Aardvark	51
Aaros	372
Abbey Buttress	279
Aberration	389
Abraham's Route	132
Abraxas	124
Abstract Arête	205
A Cut Above	266
Adam	372
Adam's Slab	421
A Dog in a Hat	177
Aesop	163
A Fistful of Steroids	502
Against All Odds	169
Agitation	154
Agony	430
Air on a Bowstring	104
Alehouse Rock	224
Alexas	347
A Lickle Adventure	147
Alligator Crawl	281
Almighty, The	250
Alpine Ringlet	332
Alsvior	158
Alternator	213
Amabilite	444
Ambling Ant	399
Amos Moses	281
An Alien Heat	167
An Almost Pleasurable Sensation of Fright	147
Anchor Handling	148
Ancient Mariner	512
Anecdote	163
Angel of Mercy, The	290
Anniversary Waltz	209
Ann's Agony	196
Apatura	332
Aphasia	414
Apiarist, The	513
Appian Wall	312
Appian Way, The	312
Aquarius	57
Aragorn	92
Arcanum	108
Arcturus	48
Ardus	372
Arête, Chimney and Crack	122
Arête, The	
Armathwaite	466
Napes Needle	282
Armalite	62
Armathwaite	**464**
'A' Route	86
Arrowhead Ridge Direct	278
'Arry'Ardnose	416
Artefact	326
Art for Art's Sake	205
Arvakr	158
Ash Tree Corner	82
Ash Tree Slabs	82
Aska	158
Asp, The	347
Asterisk	82
Astra	57
Ataxia	97
Athanor	404
Attic Stairs 1	269
A Vision of Things Gone Wild	502
A Vroom with a Ewe	185
Avsugning	158
Azov Brigade, The	490

B

Bachelor Crack	89
Barnacle Bill	473
Barrow Boys' Day Out	497
Baskerville	75
Bathsheba	353
Battering Ram	376
Beatles, The	30
Bee Hive	513
Bee Line	513
Bee Sting	513

Beeswax	513
Behind the Lines	523
Bellerophon	220
Bell Stand	**208**
Belly Button Slab	526
Berlin Wall	365
Best in Show	491
Between the Lines	414
Big Brother	48
Big Foot	409
Big in Japan	493
Big Randolph	522
Bilberry Buttress	70
Bilberry Buttress Eliminate with the Green Groove Finish	70
Bilko	195
Birthday Boy	215
Birthday Crack	159
Birthday Present, The	209
Biscuit	401
Bitter Oasis	405
Blackbeard	185
Black Crag	
Borrowdale	**382**
Wrynose	**192**
Black Death	213
Black Icicle, The	379
Black Moss Crack	141
Black Moss Route	141
Black Rider	240
Black Sheep	378
Black Sunday	226
Black Wall	136
Black Watch	183
Blade Runner	519
Bleak How Buttress	**406**, 407
Bleed in Hell	396
Bleep and Booster	504
Blencathra Badger	497
Blind	194
Blindingly Obvious	118
Blind Pugh	118
Blind Tarn Crag	**118**
Blind Vision	118
Blinkers	235
Blitzkrieg	440
Block and Tackle Right-Hand	207
Bloodhound	478
Blooming Marvellous	512
Blubber	411
Bludgeon, The	375
Blue Riband	392
Blunder, The	482
Boat How Crags	**296**
Bobby Dazzler	495
Book Thief, The	490
Bootlegger	491
Border Force	491
Borderline	252
Borg, The	508
Boris in Wonderland	414
Born Again	501
Born Free	501
Born to Run	501
Botterill's Slab	240
Bowderstone Pinnacle	**395**
Bowel Howl	171
Bower's Route	231
Bowfell Buttress	**100**, 102
Bowfell Buttress Eliminate	102
Boy Racer	460
Bracken-clock, The	52
Bracket and Slab Climb	88
Bramcrag Quarry	**494**
Brandy Bitter	161
Brandy Crag	**160**
Brandy Crag West	**162**
Brandy Sour	161
Brandywine	354
Brantrake	**204**
Breaker	166
Breakwater Slabs and Lighthouse	296
Breech, The	148
Bridge's Route	228
Bring Me Sunshine	159
Broadrick's Direct	126
Broken Crack	234
Brothers in Arms	497
'B' Route	86
Brown Crag Wall	370
Brown Eyed Girl	493
Brown Slabs	370
Brown Slabs Arête	370
Brown Slabs Crack	370
Brown Slabs Direct	370
Brown Slabs Face	370
Brown Slabs Scoop	370
Brush Off	407
Bryanston	152
Bryn's Route	176
Buckbarrow	**264**

Buckbarrow Crag	**480**
Buckbarrow Needle, The	268
Bucket City	456
Bucket Dynasty	456
Buckstone How	**345**
Bulger, The	396
Bullgine Run, The	468
Burn at the Stake	362
Burning Desire	167
Burning, The	526
Burnt Crag	**164**
Bursting Crag	**234**
Bursting Out	234
Bushwhacker	245
Butterballs 2	215
Butterfly Crack	332
Buttonhook Route, The	274
By Jingo	74

C

Cabin Boy	185
Cadillac	509
Caesar	
Buckstone How	345
Hardknott Crag	232
Cake	401
Calamity Jane	184
Cally Crack	468
Cambridge Climb, The	98
Cambridge Crag	**98**
Cam Crag	**416**
Cam Crag Crack	416
Cameleon	416
Camikaze	416
Camouflage	416
Campagnolo	416
Campaign	416
Capella	48
Captain Crater	185
Carnival	344
Carpetbagger	78
Cascade	57
Cascade Direct	57
Casting the Runes	528
Castle How	**174**
Castle Rock of Triermain	**430**
Castration Crack	477
Catacomb	128
Catalyst	
Buckstone How	345
Grey Crag	140
Cayman, The	281
CB - The Great Flake	242
Celebration	217
Cellulite	411
Cement Head	504
Centaur, The	254
Centipede	72
Centipede Direct	72
Central Buttress	241
Central Crack	205
Central Pillar, The	228
Central Route - Deep Gill Slabs	249
Central Route, The	102
Challenger, The	148
Chamonix	374
Changing of the Guard	528
Chapel Head Scar	**503**
Charmer	134
Chartreuse	258
Chimney Buttress	89, 349
Chimney Route	484
Chimney Variant	34
Chiron	252
Chockstone Ridge	339
Cholesterol Corner	411
Chopper, The	75
Cinderella	118
Clangers, The	482
Cleopatra	347
Close Shave	326
Close to the Edge	438
Clubfoot	421
Coati	51
Cock It	423
Codpiece	473
Codpiece Left-Hand	473
Coffin, The	384
Colour of Magic, The	365
Columbia	148
Committal Chamber, The	445
Communist Convert	440
Conclusion	370
Contraband	528
Cook's Tour	52
Copenhagen	233
Corax	424
'C' Ordinary Route	134
Corkscrew	353

Corona Nightmare	527
Corvus	424
Coudy Rocks	**492**
Countach	509
Coup de Triomphe	495
Coye Dog	526
Cracked Wall	485
Crack of Dawn	187
Crack, The	80
Cravat	92
Crazy Diamond	334
Creeping Bentley	395
Creeping Jesus	374
Crescendo	375
Crescent Climb	48
Crescent Slabs	48
Crescent, The	473
Crimes of Passion	502
Crocodile Crack	281
'C' Route	86
Crow's Nest Direct	88
Cruel Sister	50
Crypt Direct, The	389
Crypt, The	389
Crysalid, The	274
Crystal	82
Crystal Slab	424
Cub's Arête	29
Cub's Crack	29
Cub's Groove	29
Cub's Wall	29
Cumbrian, The	231
Curtain and The Arête, The	304
Custer's Last Stand	184

D

Daddy Short Legs	330
Dalesman, The	479
Dance On	235
Dandle Buttress	483
Dangler, The	359
Dash Riprock	176
Das Kapital	440
Davis' Direct from	
Lord's Rake to Low Man	246
Dawes Rides a Shovelhead	68
Dawn Chorus	530
Daylight Robbery	362
D.D.T.	403
Dedication Direct	360
Deimos	344
Delight Maker	372
Delilah	326
Demon Wall	286
De Quincy	396
Derision Groove	378
Desperately Sea King	226
Detour	82
Devil's Alternative, The	379
Devil's Entrance, The	315
Dexter Wall	340
Diamond Wall	189
Dight	80
Digitation	154
Diplodocus	107
Direct Route	355, 434, 484
Doberman	195
Doghouse, The	478
Dogleg Crack	479
Dog Leg Crack	207
Donkey's Ears	380
Donna's Variation	176
Do Not Direct	42
Double Gravity	173
Double Trouble	166
Douglas	501
Dove Crag	**452**
Dovedale Groove	453
Dove's Nest	**421**
Dow Crag	**120**
Dream Buttress	190
Dreaming of Red Hands	514
Dream Twister	290
Dressed for Success	169
Drone	512
Drought	140
'D' Route	86
Drum Roll	172
Dry Gasp	361
Dry Trim	326
Dusk Till Dawn	456
Dyad	256

E

Eagle Crag	
Buttermere	**341**
Ullswater	**448**
Eagle Front	344
Eagle's Nest Ordinary Route	
(West Chimney)	279
Eagle's Nest Ridge Direct	281
Earl Boethar	232
Earl Grey	114
Early Riser	531
East Buttress, The	**250**
Eastern Hammer	84
Eastern Promise	495
Easter Rising	136
East Raven Crag	**74**
Easy Edge Direct	191
Easy Slab	217
Edge of Eriador	256
Electron	304
Elevation	70
Eliminate 'A'	124
Eliminate 'C'	134
Eliminator	432
Elle May	176
El Scorchio	355
Elvis	30
Emma Line	365
Emperor, The	332
Empire	440
Encroacher	347
Endurance	414
Engineer's Slabs	292
English Summer	528
Enigma Wall	209
Enterprize	23
Equinox	254
Equus	84
Eraser Head	508
Erection	468
Eros	304
Esk Buttress	**222**
Ethics of Heather	42
Eve	372
Evening Wall	67
Ewe	380
Executioner's Song, The	324
Executioner, The	362
Exorcist, The	467
Explosion	457
Exposure	97
Express Crack	482
Extol	454
EZY	380

F

Fable	163
Face Route	207
Face the Music	349
Failed Romantic	434
Fake News	490
Falcon Crag Buttress Route 1	361
Falcon Crags	**358**
Fallen Angel	57
Family Affair	
Brandy Crag West	162
Little Stand	182
Family Plot	333
Fancy Free	407
Fang Direct	478
Fanghorn	297
Fang, The	478
Far Hill Crag	**172**
Fast and Furious	457
Fastburn	97
Fast City	456
Fat Charlie's Buttress	**410**
Faulty Tower	191
Fear and Fascination	456
Fear and Loafing	62
Fear Control	62
Feeling Groovy	514
Feline Crack	272
Feral	500
Fifth Avenue/Central Chimney	342
Finale	372
Final Giggle, The	434
Fine Time	68
Fireball XL5	216
Firebird	509
First Blood	500
First Night Nerves	519
First Touch, The	194
Fisher's Folly	374
Fizzle	158
Flagship	297
Flamingo Fandango	409
Flasherman	468
Flat Crags	**96**
Flat Crags Climb	97
Flat Iron Wall	96
Flying Fissure Finish	457
Fool's Paradise	367
Footless Crow	404

Footless Horse	404
Footlights	107
Foot Tapper	235
Forget-Me-Not	34
For the Record	423
Fortiter	339
For Whom the Bell Tolls	23
Foul Brood	513
Foul Play	324
Free Falling	400
Free 'n' Easy	473
'F' Route	84
Fulcrum, The	256
Fun Run	196
Furrowed Brow	191

G

Gable Crag	**288**
Gagarin	266
Gaitkins	**188**
Gaitscale Buttress	**186**, 187
Gamekeeper, The	64
Gandalf's Groove Direct	92
Gangway Climb	436
Gargoyle Direct	224
Gargoyle Groove	224
Gate Crag	**210**
Gates of Delirium, The	440
Gauntlet, The	363
Gavin's Horror	176
Gazebo	434
Gearless	190
Gethsemane	326
Ghost Riders in the Sky	234
Ghost, The	434
Giant's Crawl	126
Gibbet Direct, The	363
Gillercomb	**426**
Gillercombe Buttress	427
Gillette Direct	92
Gimmer Chimney	89
Gimmer Crag	**76**
Gimmer String	80
Glaciated Rib, The	31
Glaciated Slab	**420**
Glasnevin Wall	140
Glass Clogs	197
Glass Slipper	196
Gleipnir	159
Glenwillie Grooves	467
Glenwillie Grooves Direct	467
Glorfindel	92
Gnomon, The	99
Goat Crag	**402**
Goats Crag	**364**
Go Between, The	389
Golden Bow, The	211
Golden Slipper	50
Goldscope Direct	118
Gold Standard	147
Gomorrah	316
Gomorrah Ridge Variation	316
Gondor	316
Goodbye Mr Major!	497
Goodbye To All That	308
Goodfellas	497
Good Medicine	501
Gordian Knot, The	38
Gordon and Craig Route	123
Gormenghast	220
Goth Variations	312
Gouther Crag	**474**
Gowder Crag	**366**
Grand Alliance	384
Grand Day Out	450
Grand Finale	78
Grand Prix	460
Grand Slam	226
Granolithic Groove	443
Grasp, The	374
Grave New World	502
Greased Lightning	141
Greasing My Teapot	526
Great Blake Rigg	**168**
Great Central Route	136
Great Eastern	254
Great White	200
Green, The	365
Green Treacle	200
Grey Buttress	**354**
Grey Crag	
Buttermere	**335**
Coppermines	**138**
Grey Duster	466
Grey Knotts Face	427
Grey Wall	339
Grimalkin	272
Gringo	183
Grooved Arête	
Boat How Crags	296

Entry	Page
Pikes Crag	261
Grooved Wall	306
Groove, The	
Brandy Crag	161
Hare Crags	216
Groove Two	347
Groyne Strain	296
G.T.I.	226
G.T.X.	460
Guillotine	363
Gwynne's Chimney	51

H

Entry	Page
Hangover	454
Hang the Gallows High	195
Hardknott Crag	**232**
Hardup Wall	23
Hare Crags	**212**
Hareless Heart	215
Hare Today, Gone Tomorrow	214
Hargreaves Swing	234
Harlot	353
Harlot Face	434
Harmony	267
Harrow Buttress	335
Harrow Wall	336
Haste Not	36
Haste Not Direct	36
Hati	158
Hats Off Direct	526
Hats Off to Linten Miller	526
Hawkeye	450
Hearth Direct	349
Heart of the Matter	201
Heart of the Ocean	532
Heather Groove	45
Heather the Weather	114
Heaven's Gate	396
Hedera Grooves	359
Hee-Haw	379
Hell's Groove	250
Hell's Wall	**396**
Herdwick Buttress	84
Hernia	477
Heron Crag	**218**
Hesperus	132
Hiddenite	444
Hi-Fi	183
High Crag	**322**
High Crag Buttress	326
High Man by the Central Line	249
High Performance	461
Hindleg Crack	478
Hiraeth	454
History Boys, The	495
Hodge Close Quarry	**518**
Hog's Back, The	482
Hold On	194
Hollin Groove	40
Hollow Flakes	209
Holly Tree Crack	414
Holly Tree Direct	68
Holly Tree Traverse	67
Holocaust	126
Honey Pot	513
Honister Wall	345
Hopkinson's Crack	136
Hopkinson's Gully	245
Horizontal Pleasure	421
Horse Power	450
Humdrum	226
Hydra	226
Hydrenalin	211
Hysteria	211

I

Entry	Page
Iago/Titus Connection	220
Iced Diamond	189
Ichabod	250
If 6 was 9	445
Illusion	360
Imagine	266
Impact Day	54
Incantations	284
Inclination	378
Indecent Obsession	324
Inertia	80
Inner Limits	365
Innocenti	166
Innocuous Corner	209
Innominate Crack	275
Innominate/Sepulchre Combination	275
Inquisition	363
Integrali	509
Intensive Care	176
Interceptor	290
Interloper	360
Intermediate Gully	134
Intern	82
Internal Combustion	460
International Rescue	216
Interstellar Overdrive	504
Into the Light	24
Introduction	82
Intruder's Corner	201
Iron Crag	**442**
Iron Man, The	445
Irony	390
Isengard/Samba Pa Ti	124
Island of Dreams	107
Ivy League	502

J

Entry	Page
Jabberwock, The	292
Jackdaw Ridge	380
Jelly Head	504
Jelly Terror	473
Jenga	490
Jess	484
Jezebel	353
Jilted John	189
Jingo	74
Joie de Vivre	519
John Shuttleworth	189
Jolly Roger	
Black Crag	196
Boat How Crags	298
Jones' Route Direct from Lord's Rake	246
Jubilee Grooves	384
Jugged Hare	215
Juniper Buttress	260
Just a Minute	195
Just A Quickie	424
Just Good Friends	171
Just Nice	512

K

Entry	Page
Kaleidoscope	367
Kaleidoscope Eyes	466
Katie's Dilemma	201
Kennel Wall	478
Kern Knotts	**272**
Kern Knotts Chimney	274
Kern Knotts Crack	274
Kern Knotts West Buttress	273
Kern Knotts West Chimney	273
Kestrel Wall	450
Keswickian, The	478
Kettle Crag	**112**
Kidnapped	360
Kingfisher	466
King Kong	491
Kipling Groove	84
Kleine Rinne	434
Kleptomania	490
Kneewrecker Chimney	72
Kona Nu Nu	334
Kong Korner	491
Kon-Tiki	235
Kraken, The	274
Kransic Crack	374
Kransic Crack Direct	374
Kryptonite	443

L

Entry	Page
Labyrinth Route	214
Ladies Day	209
Lagonda	173
Lakeland Cragsman	414
Lamb	380
Lamplighter	360
Last Chance Saloon	148
Last of the Summer Wine	268
Laugh Not	42
Laypincher	171
Ledge and Groove	102
Left Chimney	45
Left Edge	205, 478
Left-Hand Crack	205
Left Hand Route	392
Left Rib	161
Left Wall	44
Left Wall Direct	44
Leopard's Crawl	128
Leverage	256
Lick Down	147
Lickle Crag	**146**
Life in the Fast Lane	522
Light Fandango	24
Limited Edition	522
Lipsill	158
Liquid Engineering	460
Little Big Man	184
Little Chamonix	376
Little How Crag	**141**
Little Nose	409
Little Stand	**180**
Living Daylights	530
Llwyndyrys	201
Longbow	281
Long Good Friday, The	228
Long John	281
Long Scar	**198**
Long Scar Groove	200
Long Way Home, The	527
Lord of the Rings, The	258
Loss Adjuster	399
Lost Boys, The	399
Lost Colonies Direct	326
Lost Generation	191
Lost Horizons	254
Low Man by the Jubilee Line	245
Lucid Dreams	527
Lucifer	396
Ludo	324
Lurching Leech	399
Lutine Bell, The	171

M

Entry	Page
Maboulisme Merveilleux	504
Machiavellian Paragon	173
Mac's Crack	234
Madam Butterfly	182
Magnetron	213
Main Event, The	519
Main Wall Crack	45
Main Wall Left-Hand	45
Main Wall Rib	45
Major Slab	114
Malediction Direct	152
Malice in Wonderland	523
Malteser	184
Mamba	74
Mandrake	390
Man of Straw	42
Marathon Crack	182
Marble Staircase	444
Mary Ann	96
Masterplan, The	187
May Day Cracks	432
Meandering Maggot	399
Medlayer	438
Medusa Wall Combination	228
Meet the Wife	500
Meet Your Maker	421
Megadrive	514
Megalith	262
Megaton	308
Mendes	64
M.G.C.	374
Mickledore Grooves	256
Mid-Air Collision	508
Middlefell Buttress	**60**, 64
Middle Way, The	207
Midge Ridge	424
Midnight Movie	80
Militant Tendency	25
Millside	**509**
Mindbender	99
Mind of No Fixed Abode	194
Miners' Crag	**352**
Minor Melodic	114
Minor Slab	114
Minotaur	256
Minotaur, The	482
Mirage	404
Mirror, Mirror ...	315
Missing Words	484
Mission, The	182
Mithrandir	92
Mitre Arête	336
Mitre Buttress Direct	336
Mitre Buttress Ordinary	336
Mitre Mouse	336
Moffatt's Route	267
Moi Straws	526
Moninn	158
Monkeyhanger, The	468
Monkey Magic	491
Monolith Chimney	379
Monolith Crack	379
Monster in a T-Shirt	200
Moonchild	504
Moonstruck	107
Moose	485
Morning Glory	531
Morning Has Broken	530
Morning Sun	147
Morning Wall	250
Mort	364
Mortician, The	386
Moss Gill Grooves	242
Moss Ledge Direct and Jone's Arête	246
Moss Rigg Quarry	**529**

Mossy Crack	189
Mother Courage	54
Mountain Ringlet, The	189
Mr T	500
Munich Agreement	364
Murray's Direct	129
Murray's Route	132
Mustang	509
Mysteron, The	266
Myth of Fingerprints	411

N

Nameless	154
Napes, The	276
Napoleon	160
Nazgul, The	241
Nebuchadnezzar's Dream	326
Neckband Crag	90
Nectarine	512
Needle Arête	195
Needle Front	268
Needle Ridge	282
Needless Eliminate	268
Needle, The	195
New Partnership, The	29
New West Climb	318
Niche, The	
Falcon Crags	360
Gate Crag	211
Nick's Route	189
Nimrod	126
Noose, The	363
Norseman, The	136
North Buttress	98, 372
North Climb	308
North-West Arête	82
North-West Climb	311
Not Hard	232
Not So Jolly	196
Numenor with Direct Finish	296

O

Oak Tree Wall	67
Obituary Grooves	386
Obverse Route, The	282
Odin	169
Oh Heck Direct	29
Old West Route, The	315
Olive	172
Oliverson's Variation and Lyon's Crawl	86
One Crack	190
One Step Beyond	479
Ophidia	74
Optional Omission	365
Orange Pekoe	114
Original Route, The	67
Outside Edge	334
Outside or Face Route	421
Outside Tokyo/Dight	80
Overhanging Bastion	430
Overhanging Grooves Direct	252
Overhanging Wall	256
Oxbridge Entrance	340
Oxendale Arête	108
Oxford and Cambridge Direct Route	340
Oxford and Cambridge Ordinary Route	340

P

Painted Lady	332
Paint it Black	400
Paladin	36
Pandora's Box	128
Panjandrum	107
Parable	163
Party Animal	25
Paths of Victory	132
Paul I	190
Paul II	190
Pavey Ark	46
Pedestal Route	190
Pedestal Wall	423
Peels of Laughter	438
Penal Servitude	362
Perfect Weather to Fly	493
Perhaps Not	38
Pericles	450
Periculo 'D' Sinister Manus	493
Persephone	24
Phantom Menace	411
Phantom Zone	504
Philistine, The	326
Phobos	454
Phoenix	250
Phoenix in Obsidian	445
Picasso's Nose	190

Pickpocket	491
Picnic	401
Pikes Crag	**260**
Pillar of Salt	316
Pillar Rock	**300**
Pink Panther	128
Pinnacle Ridge	277
Plagiarism	360
Platt Gang Groove	201
Pleasant Slab	217
Pleasure Zone	107
Plumbline	209
Plumb, The	152
Plunger, The	519
Pluto	68
Poacher	84
Pocket Crack	194
Poker	349
Poker Face	50
Poland	365
Pop	401
Porcupine	379
Poseidon Adventure	298
Powerglide	233
Prana	384
Praying Mantis	404
Princess Anne's New Ring	468
Prohibition	491
Prometheus	64
Proportional Representation	25
P.S.	372
Psycho	326
Pumpkin Corner	196
Pussy	273
Pussy Galore	364
Puzzle Book, The	209

Q

Quayfoot Buttress	**388**, 389
Question, The	409

R

Rabble Army	235
Rack Direct	363
Rack - Finger Flake Finish, The	363
Rack, The	363
Raindrop	386
Rake End Chimney	52
Rake End Wall	52
Ram	380
Ramrod	74
Ramsbottom Variation, The	31
Randolph Scott	523
Ratbag	189
Rats Tale, The	211
Raven Crag	
Combe Gill	**423**
High Stile	**330**
Langdale	**66**
Thirlmere	**438**
Threshthwaite Cove	**458**
Walthwaite	**22**
Raven Crag Buttress	424
Raven Crag Gully	424
Razor Crack	92
Reassuringly Stocky	411
Recharge	514
Rectangular Rib	51
Rectangular Slab	51
Red Edge, The	226
Redex	460
Red Groove	54
Red, Raw and Itchy	324
Red Slab	114
Redundancy of Courage	97
Reecastle Crag	**362**
Reet Petite	147
Reiver, The	407
Relayer	440
Remembrance	88
Resisting a Chippy Tea	493
Resisting Chiptation	493
Return with a Vengance	338
Revelation	
Raven Crag	70
Sergeant's Crag Slabs	414
Rib and Slab Climb	316
Rib and Wall	338
Ribbon Wall	338
Riboletto	98
Rib Pitch, The	52
Rib, The	217
Right Arête	190
Right Groove	190
Right-Hand Crack	190, 205
Right-Hand Edge and Pinnacle	
Face Direct	246

Right Wall	161
Rigor Mortis	432
Ring of Air	242
Ringwraith	241
R'n'S Special & Edge Finish	68
Road Rage	460
Roaring Silence	252
Rock Aid	211
Rogue Herries	365
Romantically Challenged	434
Rose Pouchong	114
Route 1	23, 31
Route 1.75	31
Route 2	23, 31, 399
Route of All Evil, The	508
Route Two	514
Rowan Tree Groove	74
Royal Jelly	512
Rumour	169
Runestone Cowboy	526
Runestone Quarry	**524**
Running on Empty	460
Runny Nose	189

S

Sacrificial Crack	286
Sadgill Wall	483
Sahara	42
Sam	477
Samba Pa Ti	124
Samson	326
Sam's Saunter	201
Sands of Time, The	493
Sandwich	401
Sarcopenia	489
Sarcophagus	292
Sassanach Direct, The	211
Satyriasis	173
Savage Simian	468
Savernake	70
Saxon	241
Scabbard, The	99
Scabby Horse	477
Scafell Crag	**238**
Scallop	473
Scawgill Bridge Quarry	**488**
Scawgill Grooves	491
Scenic Cruise	298
School of Hard Knocks, The	171
Scimitar Slab	163
Scoop, The	189
Scorched Earth	167
Scout Crags	**26**
Scout Scar	**498**
Seams, The	209
Second Coming	519
Second Generation	196
See for Miles	234
See Ordinary	118
Self Isolation	526
Semerikod	114
Sentinel, The	260
Sepulchre	275
Serendipity	114
Sergeant's Crag Slab	**412**
Seriously Smooth	189
Shadowfax	240
Shape of Things to Come	344
Sharp as Glass	197
Sheepdog	380
Sheepwrecked	500
Shelter Crag	**106**
Shepherd's Chimney	378
Shepherd's Crags	**369**
Shere Khan	254
Shifter	166
Shindig	234
Shine On	334
Shining Path, The	132
Ship of Fools	497
Shooting Fish in a Barrel	409
Short Circuit	324
Showtime	108
Shroud, The	384
Sideslip	209
Side Swipe	235
Sidetrack	220
Side Walk	124
Singing Cowboy, The	200
Singing Kettle	114
Sinister Grooves	345
Sixpence	54
Skoll	158
Skull Island	491
Sky	522
Skye Ridge	195
Slab and Groove Route	242
Slab and Notch Climb	304
Slab Climb	436

Entry	Page
Slabs Ordinary Route	338
Slabs, Route 1, The	34
Slabs, Route 2, The	34
Slabs West Route	338
Slab, The	29
Slainte	234
Sledgate Ridge	290
Slim Groove	160
Slim Line Tonic	207
Slim Slow Slider	187
Slingsby's Chimney Route	245
Slip Knot	40
Slipshod	194
Slit Wall	215
Slowburn	96
Smile at the End of the Rainbow	526
Smoothly Severe	189
Smooth Slabs	189
Snake	160
Snicker Snack	292
Snitch	118
Snowdrop	140
Sobrenada	450
Sol	
Grey Crag	338
Sunny Pike	158
Solidarity	443
Soliloquy	450
Solo Slab	190
Solstice	161
Something Stupid	201
Son of Oz	365
Sostenuto	478
Southern Jessie	176
Southern Slabs	134
South-West Climb	318
Sparkle in the Rain	173
S.P.C.	167
Speckled Band	74
Spider Wall	336
Spiked Hare	214
Spinup	358
Spring Bank	86
Square Chimney/	
Medusa Wall Combination	228
Stage Fright	
Hodge Close	522
St Bees	514
Stalag	50
Stalingrad	304
St Bees	**511**
Steel Band, The	443
Steel Knotts	**398**
Steel Knotts Bluff	**401**
Steeple Buttress	319
Steeple - East Face	**319**
Steeple to the Nave, The	261
Step to the Right	201
Sterling Crisis	147
Stickle Barn Crag	**44**
Still Crazy After All These Years	489
Sting, The	398
Stoat's Crack	54
Stonestar Crag	**148**
Stone Tape	376
Straight-8	509
Straight Tach	509
Stranger to the Ground	365
Stumpy and His Friends	160
Suaviter	339
Substitute	349
Summer	161
Summit Route	425
Summit Route - variation finish	425
Sundance	183
Sun God	504
Sunny and Share	159
Sunny Boy	158
Sunny Pike	**156**
Sunny Sunday	159
Sunset Strip	268
Sunshine Arête	143
Supermodel	411
Supernatural	286
Svalinn	158
Swarm	513
Sweep	349
Swing to the Right	25
Switchblade	489
Sword of Damocles	99
Sylvester	273
Sylvester Straits	500

T

Entry	Page
Take Three	191
Tapestry	306
Tarkus	128
Teardrop Explodes	185
Tea Time Arête	114

Entry	Page
Ted Cheasby	434
Teenage Kicks	416
Telegraph Road	500
Ten Years After	522
Terminal Velocity	400
Terminator	209
Terminator 2	414
Terrace Crack	207
Thanatos/Electron	304
Thar She Blows	189
The Hand traverse Finish	308
Thespian	108
Thin Horizontal	190
Thirlmere Eliminate	432
Thomas	152
Thor	
Great Blake Rigg	169
Pillar Rock	315
Thor's Entrance	395
Three Kings, The	324
Thrice Claimed	190
Thumbscrew	363
Thunderbirds	216
Thunderclap	141
Thunder Slab	143
Tickle	147
Time and Motion Man	466
Times of Stress	477
Tipsy Crack	209
Tipton Slasher, The	495
Titanic Arête	532
Titus	220
Tomb, The	292
Tomorrow's Hero	184
Too Many Hands	267
Toots	185
Top Gear	460
Tophet Bastion	284
Tophet Grooves Direct	284
Tophet Ridge	286
Tophet Wall	286
Topsail	296
Tormentor, The	278
Tortoise, The	215
Torture Board, The	362
Totalitarian	440
Tottering Tortoise	399
Tracheotomy	92
Train Crazy Boy	532
Traverse of the Frogs	409
Trespasser Groove	231
Tricky Prick Ears	504
Trident Rout	122
Triermain Eliminate	434
Triffid	274
Trigger	200
Trilogy	68
Trim and Incline	298
Trinity	250
Trinity Slabs	154
Tritus	23
Tritus-Protus Connection	24
Trod 'A' Tween	420
Trod Lethara	420
Trod Methera	420
Trod Pimp	420
Trod Pip	420
Trod Tan	420
Trod Tethera	420
Trod Too Far	420
Trouble and Strife	143
Troutdale Pinnacle	386
Troutdale Pinnacle Direct	386
Troutdale Pinnacle Superdirect	386
True Cross	374
True North	372
Truss Buttress	477
Tumble	128
Tumbleweed Connection	404
Tunnel Vision	205
Tup	380
Tup's Purse	191
Twilight Zone	530
Two Pints and a Packet of Crisps	493

U

Entry	Page
Unfinished Arête	292
Unrecalled Activists	528
Upper Heron Crag	**408**
Upper Slab Route 1	214
Usain Bolt	495
Usurper	360

V

Entry	Page
Valhalla	
Great Blake Rigg	169
Hell's Wall	396

Entry	Page
Vandal	316
Veil, The	38
Venezuela	148
Vertigo	384
Via Media	434
Viennese Oyster	470
Vikings, The	284
Virgin Queen	512
Vlad the Impaler	456
Voyager	297
Voyager Direct	297
Voyage, The	404
V, The	484

W

Entry	Page
Wake Up Call	530
Waking the Witch	166
Walker's Gully	306
Wall and Corner	155
Wall and Crack Climb	260
Wall Climb	436
Wallowbarrow Crag	**150**
Wall Route	190
Walthwaite Gully	24
Warbird	450
War Hero	504
Warrior	36
Wasdale Crack, The	282
Waste Not, Want Not	42
Weathermen, The	163
Western Union	445
Western Wall	152
Westmorland Crags	277
Westmorland's Route	453
West Side Story	266
West Wall Climb	315
What Not	38
Wheels of Fire	396
Whinlatter Wall Direct	490
Whisky Galore	528
White Dwarf	432
White Ghyll	**32**
White Ghyll Chimney	34
White Ghyll Eliminate	36
White Ghyll Wall	38
White Noise	362
White Star Line	532
White Stone	**484**
White Wizard, The	240
Whit's End Direct	86
Why Study	176
Wicked Willie	522
Wide Open	526
Wild Bunch Left-Hand	226
Wildcat on the Swallowtail Line	468
Wilderness Edge	489
Wild Sheep	378
Wild West Show	267
Wild Winds	485
Wimpey Way	392
Witch	267
Woden's Cheek	393
Woden's Face	**392**
Woden's Face Direct	392
Woden's Needle	**395**
Woden's Wotsit	393
Wonderful Land	234
Woodhead's Climb	249
Woodhouse's Arête	132
Woolly Jumper	104
W, The	484

Y

Entry	Page
Yellow Fever	194
Yellow Peril	194
Yellow Slab, The	252
Yew Crag Knotts	**348**
Yew Crag Needle	349
Yew Tree Climb	436
Y-Front	473
Yggdrasil	169
Yodelling in the Canyon	526
Yorkshire Ripper	495
Younger than Yesterday	169

Z

Entry	Page
Zantom Phone	504
Zelda's Face	176
Zig Zag	
Castle Rock of Triermain	430
Raven Crag High Stile	334

ROCK+RUN SHOWROOM

✚ One of the largest ranges of Climbing & Mountaineering Footwear in the UK

✚ Expert guidance from our knowledgeable team

✚ Bespoke one-on-one appointments available

✚ Convenient South Lakes location

MORE INFO

 info@rockrun.co.uk
 015395 64540

 Unit 4, Shoreline Business Park
Sandside
Cumbria
LA7 7BF